LA227.2 Grant, Gerald.
G73   The perpetual dream : reform and
            experiment in the American college /
            Gerald Grant and David Riesman. --
            Chicago : University of Chicago
            Press, 1978.
               vi, 474 p. ; 24 cm.
               Bibliography: p. 419-459.
               Includes indexes.
               ISBN 0-226-30605-4

               1. Education, Higher--United
            States. I. Riesman, David, 1909-
            joint author. II. Title.

LA227.2.G73   378.73
                                77-11039

RPWOCW: B/NA A D0-111128 0629139B   05/23/79

The Perpetual Dream

The Perpetual Dream

Reform and
Experiment in the American College

Gerald Grant and David Riesman

The University of Chicago Press
Chicago and London

To Judith and Evelyn

The University of Chicago Press, Chicago 60637
The University of Chicago Press, Ltd., London

Library of Congress Cataloging in Publication Data

Grant, Gerald.
    The perpetual dream.

    Bibliography: p.
    Includes index.
    1. Education, Higher—United States. I. Riesman,
David, 1909–   joint author. II. Title.
LA227.2.G73   378.73   77–11039
ISBN 0–226–30605–4

Gerald Grant is Professor in the departments
of Sociology and Cultural Foundations of
Education at Syracuse University.

David Riesman is Henry Ford II Professor
of Social Sciences at Harvard University.

Contents

Reflections

Introduction

In this book we have attempted to assay as volatile a period of educational reform as America has ever experienced. We ourselves, like faculty and students elsewhere who have lived in its course, have sometimes been traumatized, sometimes exhilarated, sometimes disillusioned and depressed by the events that have partially reshaped our lives. These events are not yet understood, although scores if not hundreds of volumes have been written about them. Much of this literature has focused on the nature of political protest; there has been less said about what happened in an educational sense. And questions remain. Of many innovations, which seem worth preserving? What have we learned from a decade of experiment?

To understand what happened in the recent era, it is necessary to go back nearly fifty years in order to see how contemporary reforms are related to and distinguished from earlier anti-university experiments, such as those at St. John's and Black Mountain. In some ways, the thoughtful reappraisal of the undergraduate curriculum that has begun to take place on a number of leading campuses reminds us of the debates between John Dewey and Alexander Meiklejohn about the significance of the "Great Books" experiment at St. John's, which is the subject of Chapter 3. This book will not settle any of the great questions that now grip faculties any more than Dewey's debate did. But we hope our work will help both students and contemporary participants in the debate gain clarity about the choices they face, and that it will create a sober sense of the realities and dilemmas of reform without paralyzing either experiment or renewal.

There are many kinds of reform. Most writing about higher education assumes all change to be for the better, even when the "innovation" revives an ancient practice. American reformers are particularly reluctant to consider that things may turn out for the worse, as did the seventeenth-century pundit who concluded that the rogues who made a cathedral their garrison had reformed it "from the Church of God, to a den of thieves." We discuss a wide variety of reforms. Some of them, if not carried out by thieves masquerading as preachers, seem questionable to us. But, while we do not shrink from labeling a fraud for what it is, we have tried to avoid a debilitating or debunking spirit. Higher education's new diet may be lean, but it allows for variety and invention. In Chapter 10 we offer some proposals of our own.

But this book is not so much prescriptive as it is descriptive and analytical. In Chapter 2 we develop a typology of reform movements that attempts to place contemporary reforms in sociological and historical perspective. We highlight there what we have called the telic reforms—those attempts to change undergraduate education which embody a distinctive set of ends or purposes. Though these telic reforms have come into existence on a very small scale, their impact has been large: they have generated a productive dialogue about distinctive or competing purposes of undergraduate education. In Chapters 3–5, we discuss three models (in sociological terms, ideal-typical exemplars) of telic reform: St. John's College is illustrative of neoclassical revival, Kresge College represents the communal-expressives, and the College for Human Services is an example of the activist-radical impulse. But in writing about each college, we have tried to mirror its life in its full complexity and to be less concerned about justifying a typology.

But the typology is the basis of a major division in the book, between discussion of the telic reforms in Part I and the popular reforms in Part II. In the second part of the book, we are concerned with changes in the character of undergraduate education which are the result of increases in student autonomy, new patterns of organization, and attempts to respond to the demands of minorities and other previously disenfranchised groups. Chapter 6 attempts to explain the relation of these popular reforms to the campus political protests of the sixties and to see the ways in which student unrest actually brought innovation about. Our selection of cases to illustrate these complex interrelationships is more arbitrary than our choices for the models used in Part I, for there are so many—most of the newly founded colleges would be examples. Though we have done extensive fieldwork at quite a number of places, we present only a

few full-length portraits of institutions formed partially in response
to demands of popular reform. Florida's New College, one of the
wholly new private colleges now absorbed into the public system, is
the subject of Chapter 7. The University of California at Santa Cruz
is discussed in two chapters: Kresge, one of the subcolleges at Santa
Cruz, is portrayed as an example of the communal-expressive reform
movement in the first part of the book and the over-all development
of Santa Cruz as a genuine innovation in academic structure is de-
picted in Chapter 8. In the last chapter of Part II, we focus on developments in the state colleges of New Jersey as a means of examining
the ways in which the public sector has responded to popular demands for reform and to pressures to grant wider access.

Between us, we have visited more than four hundred colleges and
universities. Many of these were visits of only a day or two, often in
connection with other assignments. In fieldwork undertaken specifically for this volume, we have made fairly intensive visits to more
than thirty campuses. We have interviewed more than three hundred
faculty members, and in some cases have had two or three follow-up
conversations. Yet it would be wrong to characterize this work as a
random sample, or our follow-ups as panel interviewing. In our efforts to understand the patterns of reform in the American academic
system, we have relied on the more systematic survey work of others
to check our impressions and counter our biases. In the beginning,
we compiled lists of "experimental" colleges, curricular reforms, and
innovative practices, in order to sift serious efforts from claims by
promoters eager to attract attention and students—although the distinction between self-conscious promoter and consciously idealistic
zealot is not always easy to make. We have followed leads from colleagues, foundation officials, reports in such journals as *Change* and
the *Chronicle of Higher Education* or the daily press to discover colleges where something might be learned for our purposes. We cannot
say that we have been equally thorough in keeping up with the flood
of books and articles written about higher education, a minor growth
industry that is the principal scholarly focus of hundreds of researchers and faculty members. The Bibliography, although in part a reference for books and articles cited in the text, includes a number of
the more significant works that have helped to shape our thinking—
but a full bibliography of what has been written in the last decade
would be a volume quite as large as this one.

In preparing the ethnographies of the places finally chosen to illustrate our telic scheme, we have immersed ourselves in repeated fieldwork, sometimes visiting a college a half-dozen times or more in the
seven years we have been at work. And in a sense, the fieldwork does

not stop when the visit (which may last four days or four weeks) comes to an end. Our investigation continues by correspondence with those we have met, by visits with them at other locations, by telephone queries, and, as is explained more fully later, by the circulation of drafts to evoke criticisms and correction. Sociologists have been criticized for writing about education by counting heads and describing the arrangements of desks and chairs. But indeed it does matter in the atmosphere of a classroom whether the desks are, in ancient schoolroom fashion, fixed and in rows or arranged in a half-circle or a circle; whether the heads nod, whether people wander in late, whether they chat with each other, and so forth. Throughout, our effort has been to make use of such unobtrusive and quantifiable measures as are available but also to go beyond these and to describe the intentions of the actors in the context in which they acted. Sometimes our sensibility has not been up to the task, as is evident in what William Darkey, a former dean at St. John's College, wrote us in response to a draft of Chapter 3:

> An observer can't often glimpse and portray the sporadic, but not infrequent, excitement of fumbling for and discovering for one's self and for the first time important and obvious things. . . . Any account of the process is going to make it look as awkward as it is, and it will seem rather comical that adults should be engaged in it. The account will almost certainly lose the essence of what is going on—the way transcripts of lovers' conversations seem unbelievably silly, because they tend to miss what's really taking place.

Of course, almost any human activity looked at closely can lend itself readily to caricature, if not in the mind of the raconteur, then in the imagination of the reader. This is the more true, the more familiar the terrain. A social anthropologist writing about a nonliterate people may err in the direction of romanticism, even failing to see the demonic beneath the apparently peaceable and beautifully ritualized scene. The work of Erving Goffman has won a wide audience, not only because of his exceptional gifts of observation and his skill as a writer, but also because he seems to undress people we ourselves can recognize, people not so different from us. Many ethnomethodologists have created what they think of as science out of this kind of art, or artfulness. We who give accounts of academic institutions must be ever wary of unleashing a debunking spirit as we discover the gap between the idealism we Americans have had about education, and the day-to-day practice of it. A characteristic American cynicism is often the underside of our lofty aspirations.

All this needs to be said because the experimenting institutions that we have singled out have often made larger claims, and therefore can seem more ridiculous, than more pedestrian institutions which see their work in unexalted terms and where the problems are pedantry and banality and boredom. Such places, which are among the institutions Alexander Astin and Calvin Lee, in a book of that name some years ago, labeled "The Invisible Colleges," are rarely visited by observers of the national education scene. We did make an effort to visit precisely such institutions on occasion (Astin and Lee counted 494 of them), although not for extended periods of time, so as to gain a sense of the backdrop against which our experimenting models of telic and popular reforms stand out.

During the years that we have been at work on this volume, colleagues have humorously inquired whether any of these experimenting institutions would still be around when the book came out. The rapidity with which cycles of reform ebb and flow in America is one of the meanings we intend to signify with the title of this book. The campus has been a kind of dreamscape for utopian as well as practical reformers, some projecting their notions of an ideal community on the curriculum and extracurriculum, and others seeing the diversity of undergraduate experience as an epitome of the American dream that education can change one's life, at whatever age. These yearnings, so ingrained in a nation that believes deeply in a second (and often a third) chance for everyone, are never fulfilled but endlessly renewed. Colleges and universities have also been, like churches and sects, arenas for mobilizing political and cultural movements. The boundaries between university and society have always been highly permeable in America, and just as currents of reform have spread from the campus outward, other movements, such as the nascent T-group or encounter movement described in Chapter 4, have penetrated academe with astonishing rapidity.

Yet, this book will be read in the late 1970s about institutions we began to examine a decade ago, and whose faculties were themselves largely the product of that earlier period. What in the 1960s seemed to many idealists (both student and faculty), as worth trying often appears a decade or so later to be fruitless if not destructive. Readers of our accounts of New College in Sarasota, Kresge College of the University of California at Santa Cruz, and the several colleges dealt with more briefly in chapters 9 and 10, should recall the context in which these institutions began and temper their hindsight with compassion.

While many of the faculty involved were, as just suggested, the young protegés of the revolts of the 1960s, the leadership generally came from those who had been through some of the most traditional and classical educational institutions in the English-speaking world.

For example, some of the leading reformers at Santa Cruz were former Oxford dons. The first provost of Cowell College, Page Smith, had been a noted, but in professional terms not especially innovative, American historian at UCLA. The authors of this book are themselves products of traditional, part-classical education, much of which they found stifling, and they are well aware of the temptation, whether in education or child-rearing, to avoid the mistakes of one's parents or teachers by reversing the field and making a new set of mistakes! Thus many leaders of the reformist academic vanguard have considered that almost anything would be better than what they had themselves experienced as students and as young scholars.

Indeed, in reflecting on these older reformers who wanted to provide a better education for their students than they themselves had received, it occurs to us that their modesty betrayed them. They thought it possible that a tremendous industry like American education (and here we must include elementary and secondary schools as well as colleges and universities) could be changed by releasing constraints and abolishing traditions which had not, so they thought, been necessary in their own development and indeed had been actively harmful. Fearing to think themselves superior, they assumed that hundreds of thousands of college teachers—and the number involved is something like 400,000—were probably not so different from themselves. This great educational army was assumed to be as talented, as willing to work hard, and (despite or perhaps because of the pedantry to which they had been exposed) as well educated, as the elite vanguard. But the great mass of faculty were none of these things. Especially in the great expansion of the fifties and sixties, people had come into the academic life with very little sense of vocation, but often with the expectation of a quite obvious step upward in the economic system, as well as in the sociocultural system—with no calling for either teaching or scholarship, or any great interest in doing more than keeping their jobs. To have seen this clearly would have required from the reformers or originators an outlook toward human affairs which they themselves would have rejected as "elitist" and hence, in effect, as both un-American and immoral.

Un-American or not, there have been, in fact, reformers (more in the public-school sectors than in the colleges, though some also in the latter) who have taken the other tack and who, in a phrase not heard much at present, sought and still seek to develop "teacher-proof curricula." Contemptuously considering all teachers as beyond redemption, they have sought through programed instruction, or through the mass media, to reach students with materials, so to speak, untouched by teachers' hands. Much of the post-Sputnik science-education effort, led by such visionaries as Jerrold Zacharias, was of just this sort, and now again today, in the experiments with packaged modules, the so-called Keller Plan, and other devices, colleges are also beginning to move in this direction, either by bypassing the teacher completely, or by allowing him or her to remain available to those students who need help that the self-contained learning packages do not provide. While the founding innovators dealt with in this book have sometimes suffered from egalitarian sentimentality, the innovators who have sought to dispense with schools entirely or to diminish the mediating role of the teacher, seem to be afflicted with a cynical contempt, an unwillingness to see that even people who enter teaching mainly to make a living are not always beyond redemption, and that incremental changes might be made to improve their work.

Perhaps both groups do share one common failing, again characteristically American: namely, to overestimate what education itself can do. Their hope was either to change the general culture (as the activist radicals sought to do), or, a bit more modestly, to produce a new generation of self-motivated, deeply interested students, not only in the selective colleges but also in the exploding institutions of near-universal higher education, which came into being with the boom of the 1960s. Such faith in education as a panacea, of course, goes back long before that.

Some historians and sociologists writing today, both in the United States and in Europe, see education as anything but a panacea. Rather, it appears to be an effort to reproduce the status quo, almost a capitalist plot to provide the masses with false consciousness, consumer wants (including higher education), and the docility needed to sustain the organizations and factories of a hierarchical society. This is the view of such non-American critics as Alain Touraine, and of an ever-larger group of critics in this country as well. People holding such a view are functionalist in spite of themselves—they would reject the label of functional sociology with vehemence; but what these critics lack is a sense of the degree of muddle in the world, the confusion of purposes, the slippage of aim. They themselves are to a large degree the radical and quite undocile products of the education they attack. We will have occasion, in chapter 9 especially, to notice instances where the very effort to reduce inequality or to compensate for the previous deprivation of many black students, for example, has paradoxically reinforced the extant inequalities. Such a result was anything but purposeful; the benign intentions miscarried for reasons dealt with at length in this volume.

American higher education is in fact much too protean to be summed up in any neat formula. Any number of contradictory trends are going on at the same time. Given our methods, we were unable to sample all these trends, and our book therefore may mislead those who do not understand much about the majority of institutions, which have avoided both the sorts of extravagant claims often needed to get a major reform under way, and the disillusion apt to set in when high-flown attempts fail.

Yet we do not want our own sympathies to be misunderstood: American higher education needs more inventiveness, more imagination, more willingness to experiment and hence to fail, than is generally present. It devours enormous resources—not only of money, but of people's energies, including the income forgone by students and the time put in by them. Though it has proved almost impossible to measure the "productivity" of nonprofit institutions such as colleges, we suspect that we can get better measures of "value added" through college to the capacities of individuals, their sense of themselves and the world they will inhabit, their rational self-confidence —their own willingness to try something, and to endure frustration and failure. In pointing out where many experiments have gone awry, our aim is not to put a damper on experiments per se, but to urge that experiments have a sharper focus, with a longer purview of consequences and a more realistic sense of what is feasible.

Yet in another mood Americans can become almost overrealistic, overpractical. The line between excessive pragmatism (which would inhibit any bold plan) and extravagant unreality (which can only lead to disaster) is hard to draw in advance. Room must be left for the "miraculous" (which often means recognition of the significance of a particular person), even at the cost, in some instances, of catastrophe. One should also have an invisible net under the high-wire act of bold experiments to salvage both students and faculty who would otherwise be traumatized. What reformers need, perhaps, is a board of observers made up of reasonably knowledgeable and sympathetic but skeptical outsiders to watch for and warn against the potential harm to individual human beings who might become the casualties of unrealistic aims.

As self-appointed skeptical outsiders we have not always been warmly welcomed, but the occasions when we have not have been few. What has been true, and a pleasure to acknowledge here, is that this book is in a sense a collaboration with hundreds of teachers and students who have been helpful informants and critics (in some cases, nearly co-researchers!) through extensive correspondence over earlier drafts of this manuscript. For it has been central to our method to share these portraits with those who have sat for them, as a way both of protecting against the possibility of injury and of getting closer to the truth. At times we found ourselves catapulted into roles that were not part of our research plan. There is a sense in which the ethnographer is bound to become part of the community he is studying. As interested observers we sometimes became reluctant but always concerned participants—we should have known that we would inevitably be drawn into the dialogue itself.

The authors began to work together in 1969, and fieldwork for this volume was initiated in 1970, with grants first from the Ford Foundation, and later from the Carnegie Corporation, and the Hazen and Lilly Foundations. A grant from the Fund for the Improvement of Post-Secondary Education partially supported work on chapter 5. As in any good collaboration, the ultimate product is a joint effort, and we have interacted at every stage, criticizing and sometimes revising each other's work. But a division of labor was also essential. Gerald Grant conceived the typology of reform that provides the analytical structure for the book, and wrote the first draft of what has now been divided into the chapters on the telic and the popular reforms. In their present form, however, these chapters are very much an outcome of full coauthorship. Grant also wrote the chapters on St. John's, Kresge, the College for Human Services, Santa Cruz, and the concluding chapter on the future of undergraduate reform. David Riesman wrote the chapters on New College and the New Jersey colleges, Ramapo and Stockton. The chapter on Santa Cruz was originally written with Judith D. Grant, who also assisted in fieldwork at Kresge, St. John's, and the College for Human Services. Evelyn T. Riesman participated in fieldwork at New College and at the New Jersey colleges which are portrayed in Chapter 9.

We owe a special debt to those who read large portions of the manuscript or who gave critical attention to the analytical framework of the book developed in Chapters 2 and 6, or to our "modest proposal" in Chapter 10: Robert Birney, Peter Elbow, Robert J. Grant, Thomas Green, Robert Hassenger, Richard Hawkins, Emily Haynes, Wendy R. Kohli, Edward Kormondy, Marian Krizinofski, Barry O'Connell, Gerald Platt, Manfred Stanley, Martin Trow, Laurence Veysey, and Kenneth Wilson. Stephen Graubard, the editor of *Daedalus*, was especially helpful with reference to what are now Chapters 2 and 6, which originally appeared in condensed form in that journal.

Many of the tutors and officers of St. John's College responded at length to earlier drafts of Chapter 3, including Eva Brann, William A. Darkey, Harry Golding, Michael W. Ham, John Kieffer, Jacob

Klein, Robert A. Neidorf, J. Winfree Smith, Robert L. Spaeth, Ralph Swentzell, Richard D. Weigle, John White, and Gerald F. Zollars. Others who provided helpful responses were David L. Dresser, Thomas Ewens, Thomas Green, Robert Hutchins, Amy Apfel Kass, Clarence J. Kramer, Donald Meiklejohn, Robert E. Skeele, David Tresemer, and Celia Morris of *Change* magazine, where an excerpted version was published.

Earlier drafts of Chapter 4 were read by many at Kresge College and by the former chancellor of the University of California at Santa Cruz, Dean E. McHenry, and the vice-chancellor, Brewster Smith. Three students responded—David Goodwin, Don McCormick, and Alan Scrivener—as did a number of the faculty: Nancy Adler, May N. Diaz, Robert Edgar, William Everson, Robert Hine, Michael Kahn, David Kliger, Gary Miles, and Marcia Millmann. Joseph Gusfield, Rosabeth Moss Kanter, and Philip Slater also provided helpful criticism.

Audrey Cohen, the president of the College for Human Services, responded to each of our drafts of Chapter 5. Adele Brody, Barbara Buchanan, Laura Pires Houston, Stephen Sunderland, and Martin Trow were also careful readers.

Chapter 7, both in its earlier form as an article prepared for *Change* magazine, and as revised for this volume, benefited by the criticisms of Edith N. Anson, Furman C. Arthur, John H. Barcroft, Marshall Barry, Margaret Bates, George F. Baughman, Roger R. Benedetti, Douglas Berggren, Ronald Bergwerk, Neal Berte, Arthur Ross Borden, Jr., Joan Bragginton, Peter F. Buri, Victor Butterfield, Elizabeth Carney, Ronald Carson, Henry Chauncey, Arland F. Christ-Janer, Tom Clark, Paul B. Davis, Laszlo Deme, Benjamin DeMott, Justus Doenecke, Dallas W. Dort, E. David Dykstra, David Ebert, Millie P. Ellis, John Elmendorf, Mary Elmendorf, Nell P. Eurich, Clarence Faust, James Feeney, Nancy Ferraro, John French, Lawrence Fuchs, David S. Gorfein, Casey Green, Rodger W. Griffin, Jr., John Gustad, Gifford G. Hale, William Hamilton, Eugenia Hanfmann, Charles C. Harra, Edwin Harwood, Earl A. Helgeson, William Herman, Jerome Himelhoch, Philip H. Hiss, Marion C. Hoppin, Wesley A. Hotchkiss, William Jelin, Kermit K. Johnson, Max Kaplan, Mrs. William B. Kip, Robert H. Knox, Jr., Gilbert Kushner, Dorothy Lee, Kendall G. Lingle, M. J. Lunine, Michael Maccoby, John D. MacDonald, Cecil Mackey, Robert B. Mautz, George H. Mayer, Ray McClain, David McClelland, Charles McKay, Arthur McA. Miller, John Morrill, James G. Moseley, Jr., Emily Mumford, Thomas H. Murray, Samuel R. Neel, Jr., Jerrold Neugarten, Frank Newman, Carroll Newsome, Brian Norton, Robert J. Norwine, Allen Parkman, Henry Patterson, David Pini, Roger Pippin, Rollin B. Posey, Daniel Raff, Jack Rains, Pru Rains, Roger Renne, B. Gresham Riley, Marshall Robinson, Natalie Rosell, R. Danforth Ross, Robert Rubin, Robin Schmidt, Hendrick Serrie, David Smillie, William K. Smith, Lee Daniel Snyder, James J. Taylor, Thomas R. Todd, Jr., David Tresemer, Susan Tresemer, Marcello Truzzi, William W. Turnbull, Arthur Vidich, F. Champion Ward, Billie Wireman, E. T. York, Jr., David Young, Richard Zeckhauser, and Ricardo Zuñiga.

Our revisions of Chapter 8 benefited from conversation with a former student at Santa Cruz, Pat Cox, and with Ernest Lynton of the University of Massachusetts. Among the current and former faculty at Santa Cruz who read earlier drafts were Robert Bosler, Karl A. Lamb, Dean E. McHenry, Jacob B. Michaelsen, Page Smith, Byron Stookey, Laurence Veysey, Robert Werlin, Sheldon Wolin, and C. L. Barber.

We are grateful to readers of the many drafts (nine in all) of Chapter 9: Flavia Alaya, Ralph J. Bean, Norman Birnbaum, Henry Bischoff, Richard E. Bjork, Edward Booher, Henry S. Browne, John Robert Cassidy, Richard Chait, Henry Chauncey, William T. Daly, Emilia Doyaga, Paul H. Elovitz, Seymour J. Fader, Mary Fairbanks, Andrew Ford, Nathan Glazer, Pat Hecht, Robert E. Helsabeck, Harold Hodgkinson, Roger N. Johnson, Roger O. Johnson, Herman S. Kaufman, Allen Lacey, David Lester, Howard B. London, W. C. Lubenow, Ronald Marlowe, Elizabeth R. Marsh, William E. Murnion, Philip Nanzetta, Anthony Padovano, George T. Potter, Howard B. Radest, Bruce Robertson, Mark Sanford, Yole Sills, Andrea Simon, Ernest Simon, A. E. Tarallo, Woodward G. Thrombley, Wesley Tilley, Joseph Walsh, Frederick Waring, Jay H. Wholley, James W. Wickenden, and (too late for insertion in proper alphabetical order) Gordon K. Davies.

Finally, we owe deep thanks to Martha Fuller, who prepared both the Bibliography and the Index, and to Ruth Ford, Lynn McKay, Ella Rutledge, and Anne C. Woodlen, who typed endless drafts of the manuscript with extraordinary charity toward two authors who had many second thoughts.

Models of Telic Reform

The Telic Reforms

We might have begun our study of contemporary reform movements in a more philosophical way, inquiring first of all into what education might be, and then dividing it into its formal and informal parts, and higher and lower divisions. Broadly speaking, we know that both the family and the state have a role in education. We are also aware that much "higher education" takes place in settings other than traditional college campuses—in public libraries, over television, in ancillary programs of large corporations, through the military, and through many other channels of civic and cultural life. Reforms in these settings are undoubtedly important, too. But we began with the more restricted view of higher education as formally constituted, degree-granting institutions that play a role in the socialization and education of nearly half of all American youth at the postsecondary level.

Thus we restricted the scope of our inquiry to "merely" 3,000 formally constituted institutions of higher education and focused most of our efforts on what the experimenters themselves claimed to be reforms. Through a variety of methods, we began to investigate these claims and to attempt to understand the intentions of the reformers. Some of the reforms have a large resonance, representing attempts not only to change the university but to set forth new ideals. We call these telic reforms, reforms pointing toward a different conception of the ends of undergraduate education, to distinguish them from the more popular reforms of the last decade which have brought about a general loosening of the curriculum. The telic reforms approach the status of social movements or generic protests against contemporary American life. Of course, to some degree, the telic movements are in conflict with each other as well as in conflict with prevailing societal values. It was John Dewey who said it was the business of an intelligent theory to "ascertain the causes for the conflicts that exist and then, instead of taking one side or the other, to indicate a plan of operations proceeding from a level deeper and more inclusive than as represented by the practices and ideas of the contending parties." Here he has essentially stated our aim, although we have not constructed anything grand enough to be called either a sociological or an educational theory. Rather, in the more usual way of inductively oriented social scientists, we have looked at some cases, compared them, and arranged them in the typology of reform movements to be found in Appendix 1. In this chapter, we explain that typology and attempt to place the telic reform movements in historical perspective.

In Chapter 6, we discuss the popular reforms as partially a response to the meritocratic discontents that came to characterize student life in the most selective colleges and universities. By the early 1960s, the expansion of the American system of higher education had led to fierce competition for the admission to elite colleges and greatly intensified academic pressures for undergraduates who, once admitted, continued to compete for choice graduate-school opportunities. Students sought relief in a wide range of popular reforms that gave them a considerably greater degree of autonomy and resulted in dramatic changes in their relationships with teachers. Students were freer than before to pick and choose their way through the curriculum and to move at their own pace without penalty. The most popular of these reforms—student-designed majors, free-choice curricula, the abolition of fixed requirements—sought not to establish new institutional aims, but to slow the pace and expand the avenues of approach.* While these reforms began in the elite academic institutions, they spread to other colleges and universities. They were adopted in part out of misconceived notions that they would serve to quench campus revolts as well as out of genuinely educational motives on the part of a new generation of faculty who wished to change the processes of education in significant ways. The popular reforms modified the means of education within the constraints of the existing goals of the research-oriented university.

*We contrast the telic reforms with the popular as an end-means distinction, and occasionally slip into calling the popular reforms "nontelic." But the latter phrase misleads. Although the popular reformers were concerned with changes in the processes of education more than with changes in institutional goals, their reforms were not without educational purpose. For example, many felt that self-designed programs would result in more relevant or more meaningful educational experiences.

The telic reforms, on the other hand, embody a significantly different conception of the goals of undergraduate education.. To some degree, they represent an attack on the hegemony of the giant research-
oriented multiversities and their satellite university colleges. In one
sense, these telic reforms could be thought of as counterrevolution-
ary, that is, as counter to the rise of the research-oriented universities
that Christopher Jencks and David Riesman described in *The Academic Revolution*.[1] By "revolution," Jencks and Riesman meant the
crescent hegemony of the academic professions over previously influential parties: trustees and legislators, students, administrators,
religious denominations. That book, like others of its genre, noted
that the research universities were producing the faculties for collegiate institutions and took for granted the way in which competition
among the colleges led them to imitate the major university model.
But because of their resentment and later disaffection with the aims
of the academic vanguard, many faculty members trained under its
auspices have shown resistance to the model, and their ambivalence
as well as lack of resources limited the momentum with which it
could be imitated. Until the 1920s, the university college model that
was diffused by this imitative process (combined with elements from
its English, Scottish and German origins) was neither strong enough
at the center nor extensive enough at the periphery of American
higher education to incite rebellions that might establish contrasting models of higher education other than those affiliated with denominational groups.*

But in the 1930s, two of the telic movements—in our typology
the neoclassical and the aesthetic-expressive—arose in opposition to
the university college model, and they were followed later by what
we have called the communal-expressive and activist-radical. By telic
reforms, then, we mean to signify those reforms that emphasize ends
and purposes that are different from, if not hostile to, the goals of
the regnant research universities.

---

*It is arguable whether Catholic colleges ever constituted a contrasting model,
and in fact by 1960 they had for the most part moved toward secularism.
Vatican II served to fragment residual resistance among the lesser Catholic
colleges to the processes, already well underway, leading to the creation of a
system often only nominally Catholic, increasingly laicized, drawing students
from families who still wanted a protective social environment for their offspring but who were no longer likely to insist on a curriculum grounded in
Scholastic philosophy and the standard apologetics. Most colleges founded by
Protestants have long since given up any strong denominational ties, although
there are still a few in the hands of Fundamentalist sects committed to biblical
literalism and anti-modernist piety, and, like Protestant Fundamentalism in
general, they continue to show vitality at a time when the major more liberal
denominations are losing their hold.

One could have developed such a typology in abstraction, working out other possible or desirable ideal types. Our scheme does not seek to be exhaustive in this way but grows out of analysis and fieldwork at a wide range of institutions. We proceeded inductively, with the general aim of writing ethnographies or "natural histories" of a range of experiments. We did not write these accounts to fit an a priori scheme; rather the typology emerged as we came to understand the intentions of the founders of these experiments.

Although the institutions illustrating the ideal types are small, the chains of influence represented by these movements may be quite large. For example, from the Committee on the Liberal Arts at Chicago and the neoclassical experiment at St. John's that grew from it, one could trace direct influences to at least a score of colleges. The indirect influences have of course been even greater as vicarious news of these experiments has spread through alumni networks and through articles and books such as our own. (Americans—including many academics—who are tone deaf to philosophical discussions about education—will often attend to an account by someone who has been there, even if only as an occasional visitor.) In the last decade, when any sizable group of faculty has assembled to discuss fundamental curriculum reforms, the debate is likely to become oriented—consciously or unconsciously—toward the directional compass represented by the telic reforms. It even seems probable that a survey instrument could be developed, based upon this typology, that would show that most faculty would be oriented in their purposes, norms, and core values to one of the types of our scheme, despite their frequent confusion and ambivalence.

Essentially, the typology contrasts different models of undergraduate education, which can be translated into ideas about the purposes of such an experience, the values it should embody, and the forms of authority on which it ultimately rests. Each offers a distinctive vision of an educating community. Specific motives are associated with choosing one form or another, and these are accompanied by distinctive processes of education consonant with the ends desired. Students whose primary motivation is to be certified, licensed, and employed, for example, will not stay long at St. John's, where such aims not only have a low priority but are seen as vulgar.

I

St. John's College is the ideal-typical example of what we call the neoclassical college since it has sought to restore the classical curriculum with new intensity and purity. Like the other anti-university experiments, it was basically dominated by a moral imperative: a vision of human unity, of the good life in a Platonic mode. And like Plato's Socratic dialogues, the mode of discourse at St. John's is aporetic: "The argument either leads nowhere or it goes around in circles."* Beginning with the Socratic dialogues in the first year, and progressing through the 100-odd Great Books which have come to characterize the program, St. John's teaches that "one dogma and doctrine is not to be compromised: the assertion that learning is first and last for its own sake."[2] The idea of "dogma" in its Greek sense of "a formulated belief" is not foreign at St. John's, a community that believes education should not be instrumental to some other end, but should itself be an end. Thus the college should model the forms of life of liberally educated men, enabling students to join in this process and to experience it as its own reward. The object is to create a great conversation about the great questions. At root, these are connected with intellectual and moral virtue, and with all the Socratic paradoxes about whether and in what ways virtue is "teachable."

Scott Buchanan, the intellectual leader of the new St. John's, had come in 1937 from Robert Hutchins's college at Chicago, where he had taken part in an effort to discover a true curriculum of the liberal arts, which some saw as a return to the ideals of the nineteenth-century liberal-arts college. Buchanan was sympathetic to the disciplinarians' view that the faculties of mind were best sharpened by the classics, mathematics, and philosophy, but he aspired to a vision of the liberal arts that he felt the nineteenth-century colleges failed to realize.† He saw himself as a radical not a reactionary, and the transcendent ideals that Buchanan sought led him back to Plato. Buchanan was influenced by the general-education program that had been developed at Columbia College, which moved in this direction in terms of syllabus, but hardly at all in terms of so magisterial a moral inten-

---

*From Hannah Arendt, "Thinking and Moral Considerations: A Lecture," *Social Research*, 38, no. 3 (Autumn 1971), who makes a point in this essay that would find great favor at St. John's: "Could the activity of thinking as such, the habit of examining and reflecting upon whatever happens to come to pass, regardless of specific content and quite independent of results, could this activity be of such a nature that it 'conditions' men against evil doing?," p. 148.

†Buchanan was shaped both by his tutelage under Alexander Meiklejohn at Amherst and his graduate days at Oxford, but the Socratic model he created at St. John's differed consciously from the common curricular model of the nineteenth century; his was a grander vision than the "daily textbook assignments and remorseless recitations" that characterized that model as described, for example, in George W. Pierson, *Yale College: An Educational History, 1871–1921* (New Haven, *Yale University Press*, 1952), p. 69.

tion.[3] For him, the trivium and quadrivium were part of an underlying unity of knowledge: a monism to be attained by the Socratic dialogue. The end of knowledge was virtue: to know the good, and then, in fear and trembling, to live by it. The core values were a faith in the classical texts, the so-called Great Books, and a belief that virtue arose from submitting oneself to their tutelage and from grasping their continuing vitality and import.

If the ideal of the multiversity lies in the scientific method, in which the young teach the old by extending the frontiers of science, the ideal at St. John's is that the wisdom of the elders molds the young in a Socratic process. At St. John's the scale of pay is fixed by one's age; there are no professional ranks, and neither degrees nor teaching experiences elsewhere are taken into account.

The movements of opposition caricature not only each other, but perhaps inevitably the dominant university styles as well. The neo-classicals regarded and still regard the universities and the conventionally departmentalized colleges as vulgar and technocratic. They envisage the universities as sterile, exploiting knowledge for merely technical ends and preparing students not for the "calling" of life, but for superficial though profitable, vocationalism. They underestimated the diversity of what later came to be called the multiversity, and also its incremental inventiveness.[4]

Students were invited to come to St. John's College not for certification or entry into a meritocratic elite, but in order to become more civilized, in order to join an aristocratic great chain of being, stretching back through the medieval university to Plato's Academy. The graduates of St. John's College, an institution which in Scott Buchanan's words was designed to produce cultural misfits, are not rendered unemployable, but have in fact done well in law, teaching, business, and other fields. But though their St. John's virtues are not their undoing, St. John's is hardly the road toward "making it." On the contrary, to think of college as a launching pad for one's career would stamp one as unworthy of St. John's.

It is almost impossible to think of an enterprise like St. John's College existing under public auspices. For one thing, there is the crucial question of scale. A large institution would be wholly antithetical to the ideal of a community of scholars. So far as we know, only in the University of California system has anything like St. John's College been given houseroom without being swamped. A short-lived experiment was started at Berkeley by Professor Joseph Tussman, who, like Scott Buchanan, had come under the influence of Alexander Meiklejohn and his 1920s experiment at the University of Wisconsin.[5] A case could be made that the first college of the University of California at Santa Cruz, Cowell College, which began in 1965, also embodied some aspects of the St. John's model, although it soon abandoned whatever limited requirements it had possessed and lost much of its autonomy vis a vis the Boards of Studies —that is, the academic departments..

The neoclassical concept was obviously more at home in a small setting. Rather than let its community grow beyond four hundred students, St. John's founded a second campus in Santa Fe, New Mexico, in 1964. St. Mary's College of California, which has consciously patterned its curriculum on the St. John's model, is another imitator. Shimer College in Mt. Carroll, Illinois, a 1950s offshoot of Chicago now threatened with extinction, could also be viewed as a kind of analogue of St. John's with its nearly all-required program.

It is striking to realize that all the graduates of St. John's College since it began probably number less than the entering freshman class of one of the great state universities in any given year. Yet, despite its small scale, St. John's began a debate in the 1940s concerning the purposes of higher education that engaged the attention of John Dewey, Alexander Meiklejohn, Sidney Hook, Walter Lippmann, Jacques Maritain, Mark Van Doren, and many others; the cultural resonance continues to this day.

St. John's College resisted the university ideal as being too fractured into specialties, too tainted by careerism. But in one respect, St. John's had a great deal in common with the best Ivy League men's colleges—namely, the premium placed on the written tradition.

II

In the 1920s to learn the performing arts, one's best bet was probably at a conservatory or an art institute. A few liberal-arts colleges had, so to speak, musical appendages, such as Oberlin with its Conservatory. Some of the great state universities, such as Indiana, Illinois, Michigan in music, and Iowa in creative writing, were diverse enough and flexible enough to get away from traditional scholarly canons as to what is appropriate in a university setting.* In a way, they followed the land-grant model. Just as they had prepared people who wanted to teach home economics, they prepared people who

*Syracuse University, which in 1873 established the first degree-granting professional school of art, was an early exception to this pattern.

wanted to teach music or to enter "commercial" callings in the graphic arts as well as those who aspired to the fine arts.

But the creation of colleges whose main emphasis lay in the aesthetic dimension was mirrored by the founding of a kind of second generation of institutions devoted to the education of women. Vassar, Bryn Mawr, Smith, and Mount Holyoke had established that women could equal men in cognitive facility. Now Scripps, and later, to a lesser degree, Mills on the West Coast and Bennington and Sarah Lawrence on the East Coast, took advantage of the somewhat sheltered status of upper-class women to give freer rein to acknowledged creativity in the arts.

When David Riesman was a Harvard College undergraduate, Class of 1931, many of his closest friends were, or considered themselves, aesthetes. When Harvard was not merely muscular, they found it excessively verbal. Bennington College in 1932, the year of its founding, struck him as a dramatic and appealing contrast to all that had seemed donnish and pedestrian at Harvard College. Along with Sarah Lawrence and Black Mountain, it embodied what we have here termed the aesthetic-expressive ideal. That was not all there was to either Bennington or Sarah Lawrence, of course. Both, for example, gave employment to some of the Central European refugee scholars who were not aesthetes: for example, Erich Fromm and Peter Drucker, among others, had joined the Bennington faculty. Still, for many of the Bennington students, creative expression lay at the core of the enterprise.

In more recent decades, Bard College has also shared some of the aims of the colleges we term communal-expressive. Bard has in fact gone through several refoundings, including a ten-year period (1933–44) as an experimental college under the auspices of Teachers College at Columbia. Throughout its history Bard has sought to reject competition and academic pressure, to remove status distinctions between students and faculty, and to seek that elusive goal of "community" which often seems harder to obtain in small isolated anti-academic enclaves than in settings where faculty and students have extramural ties and emotional outlets that soften family quarrels. Black Mountain, particularly in its later days, under the poet-president Charles Olson, was dedicated to the development of creative expression.

To be sure, Black Mountain did not want to be a "one-sided art-music school," as the painter Joseph Albers put it, yet the college saw the academic disciplines as supplementing the arts, not the other way around.[6] The motivation of students was to develop artistic tal-

ent; the end of the community was to foster creativity and to experience beauty. The model was that of a bohemian artistic community;
and the process of education resembled a studio with its apprenticeship style of mutual creation and criticism, whether it be fiction or
sculpture. Black Mountain nurtured a cultural movement that supported and shaped the careers of John Cage, Merce Cunningham,
Buckminster Fuller, Paul Goodman, Robert Rauschenberg, Olson,
and Albers.

While St. John's College manages to survive only through the dedication of its tutors and the energy and magnanimity of its administrators and supporters, Black Mountain survives in an enormous cultural
legacy, even though the college itself, after many rescues from sudden death, perished in 1956. The Bauhaus, undone by Hitler, lives a
flourishing life in America; it has influenced the International Style
everywhere. Indeed, the native-born Americans among the Black
Mountain recruits have helped turn the United States into a mecca
for artists from all over the world. They form a major part of what
Harold Rosenberg has termed "the tradition of the new."

Correspondingly, although not fully institutionalized in the major
university centers,[7] work is now being done in the genres illuminated
by these artists; for example, at the Visual Arts Center at Harvard,
at the music departments at Princeton or Columbia, and, for a long
time now, in the workshops for writers at the University of Iowa.
Of course, radicals fear such inclusion as "cooptation," but it is more
properly seen as mutual infiltration, or, as Harold Lasswell put it in
a marvelous term, "restriction through partial incorporation."

Although the arts did not flourish on American campuses before
World War II, major gains were made in the 1960s. More than 80
campuses, three-fourths of them public institutions (UCLA is the
largest, awarding 232 fine-arts degrees in a recent year), now award
degrees in art. Among the private institutions which have sizable
programs are Brigham Young, Wellesley, Boston University, and
Northwestern, but no private institutions are among the first twenty
in numbers graduated and, with the exception of Stanford, no elite
private university awards more than twenty-five art degrees annually.[8]
And as more students are trained in the arts, pressure is created for
such programs to move downward as graduates seek jobs in the
lower schools. In 1976, the U. S. Office of Education initiated a
program to assimilate the arts into the regular public-school curriculum. The announcement claimed that it was the "first program
supported by Congress for arts education as an integral part of the
interdisciplinary teaching of academic subjects rather than an elec-

tive course of extra-curricular activity for children with artistic talents or interests."[9] Simultaneously, more money has been flowing into arts programs in public colleges and universities.

Viewed from the perspective of the discipleship that characterized both Black Mountain and the early Bennington, the new palaces of the arts rising in some of the public universities would be seen as corrupting in their giantism. Those early pioneers in education in the arts might also view the Carnegie Commission's recent anointing of the arts as somewhat of a curse.* One consequence of the imitation by the broader academic culture is that the colleges founded to give form to the aesthetic impulse have had perhaps an even harder time surviving than the other offbeat enterprises we are discussing here. For one thing, the polarization in terms of sex which relegated creative expression to the female domain has greatly moderated; with men encouraged to develop what would once have been thought "feminine" aspects of themselves, colleges specializing in aesthetic expressivity for women have had to reconsider their mandate. Bennington and Sarah Lawrence, along with most women's colleges, have gone coed; so has Immaculate Heart College, where recently there has been a great emphasis on the arts; Scripps has not had to join the near-panic rush toward coeducation because it is part of the Claremont group. Correspondingly, Bennington[10] and Sarah Lawrence, which have never been exclusively devoted to the arts, have lost their place in the vanguard, while, as we have noted, Black Mountain closed its doors in the mid-1950s. Of the four telic reforms, the aesthetic-expressive has been given short shrift in this volume. We do not devote a chapter to Black Mountain as we have to other illustrations of our typology, but refer the reader to Martin Duberman's brilliant chronicle of the life and death of that incredible experiment.[11]

III

In the nineteenth century, America was seen as the Promised Land by millions of natives and immigrants; but for myriads of small groups, the Covenant had long since been broken and the sense of

---

*Speaking for the commission, Clark Kerr said that in the future the "well-balanced campus" will need to add the creative arts to its endeavors as a fifth stream in addition to the professions, the humanities, the sciences, and the social sciences, "The Carnegie Commission Looks at the Arts," Carnegie Commission, 1973. Kerr also noted that the commission survey showed that students said their campuses did not provide sufficient opportunities for artistic expression.

mission that can be found in John Winthrop's "errand into the wilderness" had long since been betrayed. As higher education spread, and as the specifically religious impulse waned, it is understandable that a few institutions of higher education began to see themselves as the principal expression of the values of community, even though they also operated as peripheral members of a system valuing competition and cognitive rationality. Community was one theme at Black Mountain College, along with the emphasis on the arts; and like other utopian communities, Black Mountain suffered a series of schisms in its search for wholeness. Schisms, in fact, seem to be part of the "natural history" of communal-expressive ventures. Such institutions generally begin with a charismatic leader who is often not good at balancing either books or interests and is subsequently expelled.*

The full flowering of the communal-expressive movement in the several colleges that have been dominated by it occurred only with the growing influence of humanistic psychology. Much of the literature of humanistic psychology, including the journal of that name, focuses less on expressing its own particular ethos, than on differentiating itself from such major currents in psychology as behaviorism and traditional Freudian psychoanalysis. Its view of man tends to be Rousseauistic. Carl Rogers, Abraham Maslow, and a more distant and more intellectual mentor, Norman O. Brown, provided the movement with an ideology about the importance of the affective life: "Where ego was, there shall id be." The techniques used in these new ventures are often those of the T-group, the encounter group.[12]

The encounter movement is prominently linked to techniques developed in the National Training Labs in the 1950s and 1960s to help teachers, ministers, businessmen, and civil-rights workers become more sensitive to the feelings of others and more attuned to the factors affecting social interaction. Though Maslow and Rogers have had perhaps the widest influence on the growth of what we have called the communal-expressive movement in higher education, there are less obvious connections to the work of Kurt Lewin, Jacob Moreno, Elton Mayo, Douglas McGregor, and others concerned with creating environments supportive of human growth and change.

Paradoxically, the college that perhaps went furthest in grounding itself in these techniques, Johnston College, was founded in 1969 as

---

*Anyone who, like the authors of this essay, has met a number of these founding fathers is impressed on the one hand by their seemingly innocent plausibility, and on the other hand by the repeated gullibility of their devotees, including not only supposedly shrewd bankers and other donors but also faculty members and students of higher intellectual caliber than the evangelical leaders they follow.

an experimental college of the University of Redlands. The college departed from its parent institution with an evangelical fervor that would have been less at odds with the Baptist traditions of the early Redlands. Johnston College opened with a two-week retreat in the woods, in which faculty, students, and staff formed themselves into moderately intrusive encounter groups called Grok Groups in order to share their hopes and aims for the incipient college. The faculty included not only T-group leaders, but also observers of process, whose function it was to report on the affective life of all the constituencies of the college. Many were Rogerians, some of whom brought to their new secular religion the zeal of converts from earlier constraint. The founding chancellor of Johnston College, Pressley McCoy, had been associated with Protestant colleges and is a man of strongly evangelical bent. Indeed, a number of the original faculty of Johnston College had at some previous point either been in a seminary or had entered the priesthood or the ministry. Our impression is that many of the more experimental colleges, public and private, founded in recent years have been influenced by ex-priests and ex-ministers. Most of them, to be sure, are properly equipped with Ph.D.s, but for them affective education represents something like a return of the repressed or discarded religious impulse. In their own quests for identity, they tend to emphasize the negative identity of the new colleges as being at war with the overwhelming intellectuality and departmentalized rationalism of what they term the academic mainstream.*

In the war of negative identities against prevalent patterns at the University of Redlands, Johnston College lost the battle with its parent institution. Chancellor McCoy was ousted, and the struggling enterprise barely escaped termination. Now, five years later, the encounter-group emphasis is still present, but muted; it is no longer the sacred thread that binds the college together. Rather, Johnston College has come to resemble other new private colleges such as New College in Sarasota or Hampshire College in adopting the contract system which

---

*In the semi-autobiographical book, *The Quest for Identity*, Allen Wheelis describes the formation of himself as a psychoanalyst, as a refugee from a devout and constraining Fundamentalist Texas family; then he illustrates poignantly the way in which the new vocation has failed to satisfy the impulses which led to its adoption. See "The Vocational Hazards of Psychoanalysis," in *The Quest for Identity* (New York: Norton, 1958). Among some of the leaders of the counterculture one finds such formerly "hard" psychologists as Richard Alpert; in another vein, the former and still practicing classicist Norman O. Brown; and any number of previously rigid academic scholars who found a second career, or a new life, in trying to discard aspects of themselves now regarded as restricting or "unnatural."

allows students and faculty to negotiate what must be done to achieve a terminal degree, and to identify the way stations en route. There is still talk of community, of course, but it is no longer either euphoric or inflamed.

Some of the spirit that animated Johnston College at its founding was also present at the birth of Evergreen State College several years later, but it is considerably attenuated now. However, the communal-expressive impulse was widespread, even though it was often short-lived and seldom established as the dominant metaphor of an entire institution. Seeds of the so-called human potential movement found life at the College Within at Tufts University, the Inner College of the University of Connecticut, at an Esalen-like Center at the University of Oregon, Bensalem College at Fordham University, and a variety of "living-learning" experiments from Old Westbury to Fresno State. Rochdale College, though not actually a degree-granting institution, was set up in an apartment house near Toronto University where resident members were required to contribute labor and hire their own teachers and administrators. The College of the Person in Washington, D. C., advertised itself as a center for encounter, bodily awareness exercises, and Gestalt therapy "that will provide for emotional involvement and support, an opportunity to share feelings, perceptions, insights, love and concern."[13]

As the T-group of encounter style spread to many traditional classrooms in the late 1960s, the seminar table began to resemble the family dinner table.[14] Affective relations came to outweigh intellectual competition, although students as well as their teachers were often ambivalent about awarding academic credit for such explorations. The purest realization of the Communal-Expressive style that we have encountered is the subject of Chapter 4: Kresge College at the University of California at Santa Cruz, which opened in 1970. Kresge appealed to students as "a living learning community which concerns itself with the human as well as the intellectual needs of its members"; the catalogue statement continues: "One favorite Kresge metaphor was the organic image. Last year we thought of ourselves as an infant college, struggling to survive and grow and learn what a college should be. . . . Our eventual objective is to create a diversified system where each species is dependent upon every other for its welfare, and where all of us together make an integrated context which nourishes and sustains life."[15]

In its charter year, Kresge College declared that its aim was to "explore educational innovation through a human relations approach. . . . The excitement and creativity of a learning environment is the result of open, direct and explicit relationships."[16] This aim was to be

facilitated by organization into kin groups composed of a faculty
member and fifteen or so students who lived near one another, which
would meet as a seminar offshoot of a college-wide course, and
would often function as an encounter group. Although students attend classes in other boards and colleges at Santa Cruz as well, the
kin groups minimize the distinctions of rank and erase any boundary
between the curriculum and the life of the residence halls within
Kresge.

While the rest of Santa Cruz often views Kresge as a tribal family,
it is recognized that there are factions within. Thus, Kresge has faced
more slowly the problem of belief that came to an early head at
Johnston and the other experiments: the difficulty of eliciting consent from later generations who did not participate in the encounters
of the founding cadre and did not share its drama or charisma. By
1976, what had once been a college-wide experiment now retreated
as the "Corner of the College." By resisting diffusion, the founders,
who had been strengthened by the arrival of Philip Slater and Eliott
Aronson, hoped to maintain the intensity of the original experiment
on a smaller scale.

At the deepest level, the communal-expressive movement as illustrated by Johnston or by Kresge shows its religious side by a belief
in mystical oneness: the desire is to experience unity and to find
mutual growth in the support of a group, through openness to others.
(And to the Jungians among the founders of Kresge, as with Brother
Antoninus, now laicized and writing poetry as William Everson,
openness to introspective processes, to one's own subconscious, is a
crucial aspect of the Kresge experiment insofar as it enables students
to discover their calling by discovering their archetype). Because the
aspirations of the covenant are so exalted, the disappointment and
disillusion when it breaks down—when the company turns out not
to be composed of saints—can run bitter and deep. Mutual openness
can lead to exploitation and to what the political scientist, Jo Freeman, writing about women's groups, terms "the tyranny of structurelessness."[17]

While it would be all too easy to parody its saccharine excesses,
Kresge strikes us as an experiment of integrity that deserves the
careful attention of those who would hope that a better balance can
be struck between feeling and intellect,* and who believe that we

---

*We are aware that few things are more complex than the way the affective
and cognitive are linked and grounded in human experience. Thought is not
without feeling and feeling is entwined with perception and mental processes.
Though we speak in uneasy shorthand here, we are not misled into believing
that the distinction can be dealt with in brief compass.

have a great deal to learn about how to be more cooperative without sacrificing essential human diversity.

IV

If the communal-expressive colleges have identified principally with the counterculture, the colleges dominated by political activism in the 1960s have been at odds with the counterculture's softness, its emphasis on consensus. They sought change in the society, less consciously in themselves. In the early days of SDS, the two currents were fused, and often confused; members sought expressive comradeship as well as specific political mobilization and change.[18]

Even now, with the receding wave of protest, departments at many universities, eminent and nonelite alike, are dominated by faculty who were "radicalized" in the 1960s, often, of course, with leadership from the few charismatic elders. As Carnegie Commission surveys of faculty attitudes show, there are dramatic differences among fields, with sociology at one extreme and engineering or veterinary medicine at another. But if one asks not about enclaves within major institutions, but rather about colleges founded by or dominated by activist-radicals, then the list is short indeed.

Before World War I, in the absence of a strong socialist movement, no colleges devoted to working-class or socialist ideals were founded; rather, the YMCA and Catholic and Protestant groups founded a few colleges in the major cities to help give working-class children a start in life according to the traditional American belief in equality of opportunity. The Wobblies started no colleges. Indeed, in the area of the Northwest where the Wobblies have been something of a presence, Reed College began in 1911 as pehaps the purest expression of the university college ideal with no concessions whatever to the gentlemanly collegiate, the evangelical Christian, or the explicitly vocational.

In the period after World War I, several labor schools emerged, such as Brookwood, the Highlander Folk School, Commonwealth, and, as an urban radical institution, the Rand School of Social Science.[19] These schools sought to prepare union leaders rather than those who were likely to get out of the working-class through upward mobility. With the Rand School of Social Science, as in some measure with the New School for Social Research, the aim was more intellectual and less activist; for the faculty, these were scholarly institutions not intended to provide a fortress for direct political activism. In a way, Brookwood and Commonwealth were for the labor movement what Berea was intended to be for Appalachia: places which would help students from a deprived part of the society return to it with more training and a strong sense of mission.

The 1920s saw the founding of the college which was to become in the 1960s the most visible and highly charged base for political activism of any college in America. Antioch College (as it was later reconstituted by Arthur Morgan) represents an ideal-typical instance of the activist-radical college. Its commitment to extramural action began in the 1920s with its focus on the coop program by which Antioch students spent alternate terms on and off campus in work programs. These programs were not, as were those designed for non-affluent students at Northeastern or Cincinnati, designed to help them finance their education; in fact, their education at parental expense was in effect prolonged in order to help immerse them more fully in the dilemmas and contradictions of American life. Although the work program even to this day has not been fully integrated into the Antioch curriculum, the ideology of the program under the aegis of Arthur Morgan reflected an attempt to get away from bookishness, to provide mentors for students other than scholarly faculty, for whom, in fact, Arthur Morgan had an almost philistine lack of respect.[20]

Antioch was neither founded by radicals originally, nor was it in fact refounded by them during the era of Arthur Morgan. But it has been committed to social, political, and curricular change since that refounding, and in the 1960s it experienced with particular intensity the commitment of a large part of its faculty and student body to using the college for the political ends of the far left. Antioch expanded early, as a few other colleges did, to serve minority groups and had a small cadre committed to expressive-communitarian ideals that were now avowedly political. The college was never wholly "radicalized," but the largest single unit on the campus, although not formally a department, came to be the Marxist-oriented Institute for the Solution of Social Problems. Some departments became collectives in which student voting power outweighed that of the faculty, carrying further the pattern of community self-government that had prevailed at Antioch in an earlier day. The president, James Dixon, a physician who had founded with Marcus Raskin and Dick Gregory the short-lived New Party in the 1960s, encouraged these developments, often, it would appear, using students as leverage against a minority of more traditional faculty. Antioch's elaboration of an extensive network of more than a score of field centers around the country was seen by some as a financial drain on the home campus, further exacerbating confrontation tactics. One student vented his frustration at Antioch's brand of politics: "You can get anything you want on this campus if you place a rock through a pane of glass."[21]

At Goddard College there have been political battles less violent and visible than those at Antioch. The politics there has been more intramural, with fewer links to the national and international agenda of radicalism. And at Staten Island Community College, some faculty saw their mission as that of raising the consciousness of working-class students. But neither of these institutions became quite so polarized and polemical as Antioch; for comparisons, one would have to go to Tokyo or the Free University of West Berlin.

As the more civilized liberal-left consensus at Antioch eroded under radical pressures in the 1960s, everything came to be decided by votes, pressure tactics, strikes, and sit-ins. Violence reached a peak in the 1972–73 academic year. The campus was torn by a series of strikes (by cafeteria workers, minority students, radicals, fired faculty, and others) that went on for months. The grass grew knee-high on campus lawns; buildings were trashed; crime rates rose alarmingly. By June 1975, President James Dixon had been out-maneuvered by the College Council and was dismissed as president. Enrollment fell drastically after years of turmoil; one-fourth of the Yellow Springs faculty were given dismissal notices in one year.

William Birenbaum, who as president of the Staten Island Community College had launched programs for blacks, former drug addicts, veterans, and "community scholars" (chosen by a community group empowered to admit anyone deemed worthy, regardless of previous level of education), succeeded Dixon in 1976. In another of the fascinating connections we keep discovering among the telic reformers, Birenbaum had been influenced by Robert Hutchins during his student days at the University of Chicago (even though as head of the Hyde Park–Kenwood Community Council, Birenbaum later fought Hutchins over the university's seeming lack of concern for the black residents on its border).[22] After Chicago, Birenbaum went to Wayne State and the New School for Social Research, and eventually worked with the late Senator Robert Kennedy to found a new college in the Bedford-Stuyvesant ghetto. These commitments made him a natural choice for the modern Antioch, although even Birenbaum's formidable energies may be exhausted in attempting to coordinate Antioch's disillusioned yet still evolving network.

In fact, Antioch's complex metamorphoses have outrun our own ability to keep pace. Although we had prepared a chapter on Antioch for this volume, we later decided that the College for Human Services would be in some ways a better illustration of the activist-radical model. CHS, as nearly everyone refers to it, was founded on the lower West Side of New York in 1965 by an extraordinary woman, Audrey Cohen. The college grew from earlier efforts to find paraprofessional jobs for black women on welfare. Known then as the Women's Talent Corps, the college was unaccredited and offered no degrees. Now it seeks to award a master's degree in the human services to students still drawn mainly from the welfare rolls but also including recent Polish immigrants in addition to black and Spanish-speaking minorities. Graduates are urged to take up roles as change agents—not just to enter the helping professions but to transform them. They are to become client advocates skilled at breaking down bureaucratic resistance to "humane and caring" service. Students spend only two days a week at the college, with the other three devoted to internships in a wide variety of service agencies, from schools to mental-health clinics. Faculty act as advocates, too, seeking improved pay and responsibility for students as they make progress in class and on the job. The curriculum has gone far in recent years in the direction of so-called competence-based reforms, requiring students to demonstrate, in a series of "constructive actions," that they can perform as agents of change and improved service.

As at Antioch, students sometimes find it more tempting to try to change the college than the world outside, and the College for Human Services suffered a series of strikes in the early 1970s. But, perhaps because neither student nor faculty rebels had any tenure at CHS, and because Audrey Cohen did not hesitate to show some the door, the experiment not only survived but grew stronger. The curriculum, under development for more than a decade, demands a dedication approaching sainthood from its students. But it is also one of the most ingenious we have seen in terms of engaging students in a carefully articulated series of practical challenges.

Antioch and the College for Human Services illustrate different strains of the activist radical movement. Antioch, in its Marxist Institute for the Solution of Social Problems, was more grandly revolutionary for a brief time, but was not grounded in any stern tradition of radicalism. There has never been any very powerful endemic Socialist movement in America. Going back to Commonwealth and Brookwood, the activist-radical colleges have had only a sporadic life, although Antioch is an exception. The College for Human Services is closer to the impulses of Jane Addams and the early settlement-house leaders than it is to Marxist or more specifically radical political movements. Audrey Cohen is a practical reformer, though she uses the language of a revolutionary. The roots of this movement are manifold and difficult to trace. There are weak connections to

European Socialism, although more proximately, the labor-education movement and the civil-rights movements were important influences.

V

Our typology emphasizes the differences among the telic reforms. But the commonalities are also striking. Each of these experiments has a sense of mission. We suspect that many faculty who are attracted to them are not only dissatisfied with competitive life in the multiversity but yearn for a sense of identity and esprit. They want to join an institution that is capable of evoking the deep loyalties of the whole self and of engendering all-out efforts. They want to believe.* A visitor is immediately aware of the basic choices participants have exercised. Bridges have been cut; commitments have been made, and ideals are continually tested, including those of the visitor.

A spirit of vocation and intensity about teaching permeates these communities, partly as a result of the jettisoning of research and publication norms, but also from the growth of a new sense of mission. Of course, new ideals may fade for individuals if not institutions, and faculty who have sacrificed much in their own conversion often hide even from themselves the hurt they feel when their offerings are rejected by the intended acolytes. Yet there is some protection against such wounds since the expertise of the teacher is deemphasized. In all these radical experiments, teachers and students are seen as colearners: at St. John's students and tutors puzzle out the great texts together and at Black Mountain they joined others in creating paintings and poems. The egalitarian spirit[23] does not deny to teachers all authority, although the grounds of that authority do not lie in disciplinary expertise in the way that they do in the university colleges.

Nor is self-governance in itself necessarily egalitarian—certainly not at St. John's, where a small oligarchy on the Instruction Com-

---

*In a review of Duberman's *Black Mountain*, in the *Harvard Educational Review*, 43, no. 2 (May 1973), Laurence Veysey beautifully captures that spirit: "Many of us yearn in some part of our minds for a college setting utterly free from bureaucratic harassment, a place where nothing distracts from mutual learning and creation. The dream merges with that of community —an educational environment to be sure, but one where life and the classroom merge into each other, and where status dissolves in genuine human relationships" (p. 258). Veysey himself left the University of Wisconsin to teach at Santa Cruz.

mittee rules, nor at Kresge, where in the early years most important decisions were made by a few charismatic figures even while the community sought the ideal of participatory democracy. What does mark these colleges off from most modern universities is the devotion to community. Bonds of community are nourished by reinforcing participation in the full round of life, whether at the Friday night lecture at St. John's or the kin-group meeting at Kresge. At three of these institutions, there are no departments to compete for students. The important judgments have to do with whether students measure up to the ideals of the college, not whether they perform well according to the traditional standards developed by a departmentally organized faculty.*

Like the popular reforms, the telic experiments are bound together in their aversions to the multiversity model, but their arena is wider than that of the enemy—their hope is to create some notion of the good life whether in the Platonic or the Rogerian mode.

It is in this deepest sense that these institutions are "transdisciplinary," i.e., there is some notion of an end or a good to which academic disciplines are subordinate. Their sense of mission is reflected in the forms of teaching, too. At St. John's there is the belief that disciplines serve as falsifying lenses through which students preconceive and are likely to misconceive the "natural articulations of the intellectual world. . . . This college chooses to overcome these institutionalized prejudgments by substituting fundamental books for departments and elementary skills for disciplines."[24] The mixed-media event was born at Black Mountain, where poets, musicians, dancers, actors—and on occasion stray dogs—joined together to create productions. At Kresge, the disciplines were viewed as subordinate to the task of building community, and at CHS, subordinate to the aim of discovering the generic competencies of the "humane professional."

These transdisciplinary or interdisciplinary forms are quite distinct from conventional interpretations. If a discipline is the systematic study of a defined field by means of distinctive methods of analysis,[25] then interdisciplinary work has usually meant discussing some topic from a variety of these perspectives. But it would be better to describe that process as multidisciplinary when it means that the conversation is a sandwich with little interpenetration among the layers of sociology, philosophy, or economics. And like a sandwich, multi-

---

*Yet ironically, to the extent that such a judgment of the "whole" student reflects an ideology, it can be particularly damaging. To the degree that departmental verdicts are solely cognitive, they can be at least partially discounted, whereas ideological judgments are less easily turned aside, especially if they lead to one's exclusion from the group.

disciplinary occasions are usually short meals for transitory gatherings.

Interdisciplinary dialogue implies a more sustained conversation subsumed under a fundamental question or problem or set of such questions. It also means that there is an effort to understand the key metaphors and analytical frameworks of the other disciplines. Naturally, participants cannot be expected to master the depth and breadth of many disciplines; to do so clearly requires the power of genius. (More frequently, one finds a new subdiscipline created as the methods of one discipline are applied to another, as in psychohistory.) Interdisciplinary dialogue requires each participant to master at least one discipline and to be capable of understanding the technical apparatus of some others. Participants must become multilingual, acquiring a "reading" knowledge of several languages, more than Berlitz phrase books provide but less than educated citizens of the country would know. This knowledge grows and is tested in discourse with those trained in other disciplines who are equally committed to investigating the common questions.[26]

The telic reform communities provide a setting for such discourse, organizational structures that support and reward it, and transcendent questions that inspire it. The process is most evident at St. John's, where faculty members teach all subjects in a required program. Thus an anthropologist teaches mathematics, mathematicians lead students in biology experiments, and all read Plato. St. John's tutors frequently attend a class along with students a year before they are expected to teach it.

Of course, interdisciplinary dialogue may go stale. Sometimes it becomes fixed in amber because the community, while initially quite diverse in disciplinary make-up, becomes cut off from fresh infusions of disciplinary knowledge. Or later faculty recruits may be only naïve generalists with little or inadequate disciplinary training. Without faculty who are grounded in the disciplines there is little hope that the inquiry itself* can be disciplined. The difficulty arises if students in such a program never reach any depth themselves in any of the disciplines, particularly if their inadequacy is later projected as mild hostility toward all disciplines.

---

*Thomas Green makes the point that we only talk about disciplinary or interdisciplinary dialogue "when we focus attention upon what happens *in* the inquiry rather than on the purpose *of* the inquiry . . . But there are settings in which it doesn't make sense to talk about inquiry belonging to any discipline, and therefore it doesn't make sense to say that it is inter- or multidisciplinary either . . . one kind would be any situation in which I am called upon to decide what to do rather than to decide what is true." Letter to Gerald Grant, October 6, 1976, emphasis in the original.

We speak here of disciplines as guilds of scholars organized in the traditional branches of knowledge: philosophy, history, physics, and the like. But one can speak of discipline in a broad sense: the discipline of a group or a community, the state of order based upon submission to legitimate authority. We have tried to compare the telic reforms in this latter sense—and to contrast them with the multiversity ideal—under the column headed "Authority Grounded in" in Appendix 1. There we point to the grounds of authority that establish what John Dewey called "the moving spirit of the whole group."[27] In the multiversity, discipline in the narrow sense of the scholarly guilds is also the basis of discipline in the broad sense: authority in the research universities ultimately rests with those who possess consensually validated claims to specialized expertise.

In the telic reforms, disciplines in the narrow sense are subordinate to—and usually exist in uneasy tension with—the broad authority that establishes "the moving spirit of the whole group." That authority defines the relation between the student and the community into which he is being inducted. In what we have called the neo-classical model, the authority rests in the wisdom of the Socratic elders as interpreters of the texts of the liberal tradition. The young tutor who questions the selection of any particular reading or its relations to other aspects of the St. John's program is told to be patient: in time he will come to see the wisdom of the choice in the larger scheme of things. For the aesthetic-expressive model, the authority lies in submission to the sensibilities of the master artists. They determine what counts as art and what kind of community discipline will best sustain the tradition of artistic innovation.

In the communal-expressive case, the authority derives from the charisma of the founding prophet or guru, the one who can win the devotion of followers to a particular notion of a nurturing community. As Rosabeth Moss Kanter has written, community of this type is based in part on "the desire for strong relations within a collectivity, for intense emotional feeling among all members, for brotherhood and sharing."[28] The activist-radical model is grounded in an agenda of social or political reform, and the discipline lies in the experience of learning to effect change. The student at the College for Human Services must perform "constructive actions" that result in benefits to clients. The authority attaches to the one who creates a vision of a better society and who acts to bring about change in the desired direction. In the extreme case it is the author of the revolution; in democratic situations it is the one whose program of reform wins the most adherents or votes. Challenges to the authority of the activist-radical inevitably turn on the question of whether one is trying to understand the world or to change it, and at the College for Human Services the curriculum is based on the idea that one will understand it best by trying to change it.

We speak of the transcendent, and even this brief overview hints at the utopian strains that run through these reform movements, which will be more evident in the accounts in the chapters that follow. The utopian impulses are strong, representing a search for a more perfect union that, as we have noted, often leads to disunion and schism. Because the founders have made radical choices, not leaving many options open in the way that the contemporary university does, the alternative to opposition is withdrawal.

In addition to offering more options, the norms of the multiversity are more congruent with dominant societal values: individualistic achievement, pluralism, the production of useful knowledge. In a sense, with the exception of CHS, all the movements we have labeled telic reforms are impractical. They are the luxuries of a society that can afford to educate a leisure class, whether in the neoclassical Greek mode of St. John's or with the more Rousseauistic charms of Kresge. Or they might be justified on the grounds that it is prudent policy to pay for such diversions to keep youth off the streets at a time when a technologically oriented labor market cannot absorb all who seek employment. (St. John's and Black Mountain were in fact founded during the great depression decade, and the reformed Antioch and Kresge blossomed at a time when the labor market was flooded by an unprecedented expansion in the college-age population.) Neo-Marxists would in all likelihood condemn the experiments (excepting Antioch, perhaps) as keeping alive the illusion of change in a decadent capitalist society, as exemplars not of telic reforms but of repressive tolerance.

From a modern functionalist perspective, articulated most notably in the work of Talcott Parsons and Gerald Platt,[29] there is a question of whether these telic reform movements ought to be classified as within the domain of higher education at all. For Parsons and Platt, the primary societal function of the university is to guard cognitive culture and the interests that support it. Thus, scholarly research and graduate faculties, concerned "with the advancement, perpetuation and transmission of knowledge and with the development of cognitively significant competence," constitute the core of the academic system.[30] The primary function of graduate faculties is to maintain the standard of cognitive rationality; this function is blended in varying degrees with three others—undergraduate socialization, training in the professions, and the education of social critics or intellectuals as generalists.

The college experience should develop personalities that "can articulate with a differentiating, rationalizing, and changing society. Intelligence, universalistic standards of evaluation, autonomy, flexibility, and rationally oriented legitimate achievement are features of this extended socialization."[31] The principal aim of undergraduate education ought to be winning students to the values of a pluralistic, cognitively rational culture.

Certainly Parsons and Platt are right that technical skill and cognitive competence are crucially important qualities. And we would agree that internalization of rational standards is difficult, and that care must be exercised so that rationality will not be overwhelmed by emotions or ideology—the former can be seen as a danger in the early Kresge experiment and the latter as a tension at the College for Human Services. But in their concern to counter the excesses of the academic counterculture, Parsons and Platt have taken a position that in some respects limits our vision of what undergraduate education might encompass. They are concerned, for example, that "cultural objects which cannot be described in the pattern-form of a set of propositions should not be called knowledge."[32] Thus art criticism is knowledge but painting itself is not. This is an old distinction, but it comes to have practical importance in a college or university when we must decide whether a student who pots or paints is engaged in as valuable a learning activity as one who writes a critical monograph on pottery or painting. In making a pot, one learns to choose, learns an economy in the use of materials, learns something about the connection between feeling and cognition. Naturally, the position one takes on these matters also determines one's view of who are to be the gatekeepers of knowledge. Should the art historians or the artists themselves be members of teaching faculties? We think both.*

In this sense learning and the development of expressive gifts cannot be described in the "pattern-form of a set of propositions," but they have a proper place in the development of aesthetic sensibilities in undergraduate education. We are not served best by identify-

---

*Difficulties often arise when traditional departments oriented to the usual scholarly modes of assessment attempt to absorb or to coexist with creative artists. The University of California at San Diego achieved remarkable success by reversing the order, beginning with creators and adding the critics later. In Visual Arts under Paul Brock (who has since gone on to Fordham), they began with a core faculty of painters, sculptors, and film-makers, adding a distinguished faculty in art history and criticism later. The Music and Drama Departments were similarly successful, although we know of other cases when tensions were created when those labeled "critics" and those labeled "creative" were housed in the same department, each group ambivalent not only about the other, but about the parts of themselves represented in the other.

ing the values that justifiably dominate the graduate schools as the core values of all undergraduate education. The pluralism of higher education should not rest on so narrow a base. Higher education in America, and life in the multiversity itself, would not be as varied or enriching without the stimulus of the telic reforms, even though these experiments do violate the Parsonian ideals of appropriate university function.

The Neoclassical Revival

St. John's and the Great Books

St. John's College—actually two colleges on the same pattern, the original campus in Annapolis, Maryland, and the second in Santa Fe, New Mexico—stands in stark contrast to the others discussed in this volume. It is remarkable that its austere program not only survived but expanded in an era when most colleges yielded so fully to consumer preferences. For St. John's offers its students almost no choices about the form, content, or sequence of their studies. Each must complete a prescribed curriculum that includes four years of mathematics, laboratory sciences, philosophy, and languages. The program is even more of a radical challenge to faculty, who are expected to gain the competence to teach all parts of the curriculum, from physics to Greek. There is no formal distinction of rank among them; all are called tutors and salary is principally determined by age. We doubt whether St. John's could be started anew today, or whether funds could be obtained for such an uncompromising venture. A prospective founder might not even receive a courteous hearing from a major philanthropic organization.

Yet St. John's has existed for forty years essentially unchanged. An undistinguished liberal-arts college until 1937, it then "adopted a radically revolutionary program of required study of Great Books, language, science, and mathematics."[1] Walter Lippmann called it "the seedbed of the American Renaissance."[2] But it is too simple to say that it sought to restore the ideal of the early American liberal-arts colleges. Essentially, St. John's is not a reactionary college but a

radical neoclassical experiment whose roots lie in classical humanism
—above all, in Plato's Academy.*

Although St. John's founded a branch campus in Santa Fe in
1964, its growth has been slow and success has never been assured.
By many conventional standards, St. John's is a failure. Both campuses lose an alarming proportion of students. With few exceptions,
its faculty would not be regarded as distinguished scholars. When
measured by the usual indexes of research and publication, scholarly
production is abysmally low. Many students are discontented.

But St. John's remains peculiarly immune to such measures. "Your
objective criteria are a lot of nonsense," a St. John's tutor might
reply. "Our faculty should be rewarded for refusing to add to the
heaps of triviality that often pass as modern scholarship. Too many
of the gatekeepers of the modern disciplines are men of limited vision, unfit to judge us. Nor will we pander to students. Many will
leave; the way to wisdom is not easy, and few will persevere."

At once the most arrogant and humble of places, St. John's sees
education as despoiled by barbarians, dulled by the pursuit of narrow expertise, tainted by the careerism if not outright commercialism
of the faculty. It rejects the fractured educational philosophy of the
modern academy, bound together only by the thin ties of survey
courses and electives. Why, it asks, flatter the egos of adolescents
who do not yet have the wisdom to choose intelligently the stuff of a
good education?

But it assumes a humble posture internally. Both students and
faculty think of the authors of the Great Books as the only true
teachers at St. John's. The tutors are postulants attempting to gain
a deeper understanding of an intellectual tradition that can never be
fully mastered. And while St. John's will not suffer what it regards
as the folly that students know what is best, insofar as both students
and tutors seek to follow the question where it leads, both are equal.
At St. John's, there is the belief that he who helps most learns most.
And in fact, the best seniors at St. John's often tutor the new faculty
members in the mysteries of its curriculum. Unlike almost any other
institution of higher learning in America, the faculty member who
comes to St. John's is expected to abjure any right to special status

*St. John's had little in common, other than a required curriculum, with the
pedantic philological use of classical languages in the colonial American colleges which, in the minds of most of their countrymen, prepared timid souls
for the ministry, and an occasional pedant to carry on in a pedantic, not a
great tradition.

because of special knowledge or scholarly competence and to apprentice himself to the college's unique program.

Plato is the overwhelming presence in the place—his work shapes St. John's dialectical form, its ideal of governance, its vision of the good, its view of man. If the faculty were to choose a single voice to express their uncompromising aims and hopes, it would be that of the cofounder and first dean of the modern St. John's, Scott Buchanan, who wrote: "In our critical age, the reading of Plato by a large number of people could make the difference between a century of folly and a century of wisdom for the world."[3]

I

Scott Buchanan's melancholy spirit continues to brood over St. John's. Near the close of his life, he said that the mission of St. John's was "preparing people to be misfits . . . in the universe for the time being."[4] He wished for something greater than to have St. John's graduates merely adjust to the world. Extravagant judgments about him were common. Some saw him as a destructive needler or an irresponsible amateur. Others agreed with Mark Van Doren, a close friend, who said he was "more like his god Socrates than any man I knew." Scott Buchanan "is the one man in the world whom I simultaneously love and fear."[5] Jacob Klein, one of the most distinguished deans and tutors at St. John's in later years, remembers Buchanan as "An extraordinary man. I repeat, an *extra* ordinary man. He established the foundations. By the foundations, I mean way down here," he said, reaching over the side of his chair and stretching his fingertips to the floor with emphasis.[6]

But Buchanan—it was perhaps inevitable given the nature of his quest—was never satisfied with what had been created at St. John's. He was disappointed "when we got to be exclusively connected with the classics and the classical tradition." He saw the Great Books as a way to begin a discussion of what a truly liberating education might be like, but felt they should be used only as an experiment "until we find out what a college should really be."[7]

Stringfellow Barr was always more sanguine about St. John's than was Buchanan, and he once explained the difference: "The difference between Scott and me was that when I see a baby, I am enchanted with him; Scott is always feeling, 'Well, that's not the baby I had in mind. Babies ought to be better than that.' All human enterprises, including birth, seem to him a little disappointing."[8]

Alexander Meiklejohn, president of Amherst when Buchanan was an undergraduate there, enabled the latter, as he put it, clearly to see "the whole living Socratic method." As a senior, he was invited to join a faculty seminar that Meiklejohn led, and he began to see Meiklejohn's method of reform. Meiklejohn gradually engaged new members of the faculty in a dialogue about the educational progress, the curriculum, and the organization of the college, asking them "Why do we do this? Why do we do that?" At Amherst, Buchanan "majored in a funny way. I didn't concentrate. I had three majors when I got through, and a scattering of other studies. I had majored in mathematics and Greek and French—three years in each."[9] His program was not unlike the St. John's curriculum he was to invent twenty years later.

After graduation, Buchanan remained at Amherst, first as secretary of the Christian Association, and then for another year as an instructor in Greek, before entering Balliol College at Oxford as a Rhodes Scholar, in 1919. Buchanan went to Oxford to prepare to go to India. He intended to learn Sanskrit and thought he could study Indian culture there "because I had seen in the booklet about Oxford a picture and a little discourse on the Indian Centre. It had not said very much, but I just assumed that that was a place where such studies went on. It turned out that this was where they stored the records of the India Office, and it was always closed."[10] So for one term he read the classics, and for two years read Kant. Buchanan read Plato with A. D. Lindsay, a tutor who "would translate almost anything you wrote for him into a moral problem"—one of the characteristic ways in which Great Books are approached at St. John's.* His thesis was not accepted, and he came home to Amherst to care for his ill mother while teaching at Amherst High. He discovered he was not fitted for secondary teaching, and decided on graduate studies as the only way to carry on his gnawing interest in philosophy. He was admitted to Harvard's department on the recommendation of Alexander Meiklejohn, who received the following reply: "From what you tell me, Mr. Buchanan has done his original thinking, and he needs to be regularized." His thesis on the concept of possibility was nearly rejected, but Alfred North Whitehead came to his rescue. When asked for an opinion of Buchanan's paper,

---

*Not every book can be translated into a moral problem, of course, nor do all tutors wish to try to do so. St. John's is not in the business of teaching moral virtue, a teacher at Santa Fe wrote, "we're not at all sure what it is, and we're quite sure we don't know how to teach it." Letter from William Darkey, July 3, 1973.

Whitehead told the Harvard philosophers: "If you cannot understand this, so much the worse for you."[11]

After Harvard, and a brief term of teaching at City College in New York, Buchanan joined the People's Institute, an early "free university" without requirements, examinations, or course credits. Here immigrants and intellectuals came together to pursue subjects of common interest and set their own standards. Buchanan led seminars and chaired the large lectures held twice a week in the Great Hall at Cooper Union. He began to struggle with the problem which was to occupy him for the rest of his life and which became the principal *raison d'être* for the revolution at St. John's College: it was simply that knowledge was one but that men did not perceive that unity. In the dialogue that grew at the institute, Buchanan became increasingly troubled at the difficulty poets had in talking with mathematicians. How could men be brought to rediscover the complementarity of the trivium and the quadrivium—the commonalities of the underlying structures and symbols of thought? Buchanan refused to be fenced in to any one intellectual field: to him that was the great sin. "We are willing, and shamefully relieved, to admit that each has his specialty, his so-called field, and the other fellow has his, and we are ready to let the common human enterprise go by default."[12] The quest that was initiated by Buchanan has been a recurring theme at St. John's up to the present day. In a 1972 discussion of curricular revisions, the dean of the Santa Fe campus insisted, "We should never permit ourselves to begin our inquiry by asking, 'How can we teach this better?' The question should always be 'What is the relation of this part to the whole'?"[13]

Stringfellow Barr brought Buchanan to the University of Virginia in 1929 as a professor of philosophy. He had met Buchanan at Oxford, but disliked Buchanan's prickly questions, which were "always interfering with my notion of social intercourse." Barr said he was "the most remarkable man I have ever met," but he was reluctant to push Buchanan's appointment because he might put others off. Buchanan was hired and did put others off, but he was admired for his teaching.

While at Virginia, Buchanan sketched an early vision of the St. John's program in a radical proposal for a college within a college. The proposal, never enacted, envisioned that students would spend two years in a common program of reading the Great Books, followed by two years of individualized study under the supervision of a tutor. In 1936, the new young president of the University of Chicago, Robert Hutchins, provided Buchanan with an opportunity to carry his plans a step further when he asked him to serve on the

Committee on the Liberal Arts. Buchanan accepted, and left Virginia
for Chicago, bringing Barr reluctantly along. Hutchins had already
begun his acerb critique of American higher education and had designed the committee as the vehicle for major reforms at the University of Chicago, packing it with men like William Gorman, editor of
Hound and Horn. Hutchins liked an essay Gorman had written on
the liberal arts and wrote to him: "I read your piece on 'Nostalgia
for the Trivium.' Come to Chicago." Hutchins put Gorman to work
teaching in a Great Books course in the Law School along with
Malcolm Sharp, who had taught at Alexander Meiklejohn's Experimental College at the University of Wisconsin. Others invited to join
the committee as members or assistants included Richard McKeon,
brought from Columbia as dean of humanities, Mortimer Adler, Paul
Goodman (a student of McKeon's at Columbia), and two of Buchanan's Virginia graduate students, Catesby Taliaferro and Charles
Wallis. Buchanan, Barr, Taliaferro, Wallis, and Gorman (delayed
by a period of graduate study under the medievalist philosopher
Etienne Gilson) eventually went to teach at St. John's. Later Hutchins joined the board of visitors and governors, and Mortimer Adler
became a visiting lecturer.[14]

Buchanan and Barr had served a year on the committee when they
were approached by Richard Cleveland of the St. John's board, who
was seeking new leadership to lift the college out of a major crisis.
Cleveland sketched for them a brief history of St. John's. Heavily
in debt by 1936, the college suffered additional woes when it lost
accreditation: its president, Amos W. W. Woodcock, had insisted on
graduating a student to whom the faculty had declined to award a
degree. The board of trustees then fired Woodcock, and Cleveland
turned to Buchanan and Barr to see what could be done to give St.
John's new life.

The story is told at St. John's that Barr and Buchanan flipped a
coin and Barr became president, Buchanan dean. But as Barr tells it,
when Cleveland informed them that the board wanted them to come
to St. John's, Buchanan turned to Barr and said, "Well, that would
have to be you, because I don't answer my mail." Barr thought Buchanan should be president because he would be designing the program. Buchanan felt he could do that best as dean. Barr says he
accepted the presidency as a result of his experience of reading the
Great Books as a member of the Committee of the Liberal Arts. He
decided that if those books could stir him so profoundly, they could
do it "for the dumbest freshman in America."[15]

They arrived in the summer of 1937, and before classes opened
that fall they announced the "New Program, a four-year, all-required

curriculum, based on the study of some hundred Great Books from the Greeks to the present . . . No other American college is offering a curriculum similar to the New Program." Buchanan wrote that the New Program had been drawn to stem the decay that St. John's and other colleges had suffered as they followed the lead of Harvard some decades earlier in introducing the elective system. Buchanan saw undergraduate education as becoming "more and more special- ized and less and less related, until the American undergraduate wandered in a maze of scheduled 'offerings,' choosing those courses which were easiest or which were taught by men he liked, or which came at a convenient hour of the morning, or which seemed likely in some way to increase his chances of getting rich in later life."[16]

The old St. John's faculty met in special session in July 1937. Rumors abounded. Buchanan came before them and, with eloquence and passion, set forth his vision of a common liberal-arts curriculum. Any faculty member who wished to do so would be allowed to try his hand for a year, and most elected to remain, though with varying degrees of enthusiasm. Some were relieved that the college was not going to close. Some thought it astonishing that teachers of history or Greek would be expected to begin that fall to prepare themselves to teach freshman laboratory sciences. A few felt that if Buchanan was not suffering from delusions, he was at least encouraging a terrible superficiality by expecting faculty to range over the ancient classics and modern science and everything in between, including the *Summa Theologica*. At least one faculty member was scornful, and remarked, "A cake is never eaten as hot as it is baked."[17]

As dean, Buchanan initiated seminars that drew together faculty who were sympathetic to the New Program. In informal sessions held in his office on Saturdays, the faculty discussed the new curriculum and how best to teach it. As select tutors joined the New Program and old faculty converted or departed, St. John's was rapidly trans- formed into Buchanan's college, and it grew less bashful about pro- claiming its new beliefs. St. John's saw itself as a young David, kicking the shins of the conventional Goliaths. It shared the animus of other experimental colleges of that era—Antioch, Bennington, Black Mountain, and Sarah Lawrence—which differed widely among themselves but were agreed in their diagnosis of many of the faults of higher learning in America: textbook teaching, elaborate systems of prerequisites, shoddy specialization, and piecemeal knowledge en- couraged by the increasingly popular free elective system.

For a small college with a minuscule first class under the New Program (twenty students, of whom only eight finished), St. John's attracted unusually wide notice. In addition to the high praise of

Walter Lippmann,* and Mark Van Doren, the philosopher Jacques
Maritian returned to France after an American tour in 1939 to draw
attention to "the astonishing enterprise of Scott Buchanan and Stringfellow Barr at Annapolis . . . to completely revise a system of education and to rediscover the true conception of the liberal arts."[18]
There was inherent drama in the situation. With the college
foundering after the loss of accreditation, the Trustees had hired a
new president and dean who were turning the place inside out. But
this might not have attracted such attention had it not been that St.
John's also became a kind of national testing ground for the reform
movement led by Robert Maynard Hutchins: it would be the "pure"
experiment that Hutchins had been frustrated from achieving at
Chicago. Hutchins felt that the liberal arts should dominate the college years, which for him would be the last two years of high school
and the first two years of college. Specialized training would be reserved for the university and would not be allowed to encroach upon
the undergraduate years. St. John's did not adopt the whole of Hutchins's blueprint, but it broke ranks with the competition and began to
admit a few hardy high-school juniors who applied.† And the curriculum at St. John's reflected Hutchins's stinging rhetoric: it stood
in opposition to the "false democracy" that one kind of knowledge
is as good as another.
Milton Mayer, in a panegyric in *Harper's* in 1939, set the stage
for the debate that followed in the 1940s: "This is the education for
which President Robert M. Hutchins in Chicago has been touting
for ten years, and St. John's College today is the answer to the question, 'Yes, but will it work.' " Mayer's answer was an unqualified

---

*The Catholic *Brooklyn Tablet*, in an editorial of January 1939, made light
of Lippmann's "discovery" of St. John's: "The fact of the matter is that the
training which Mr. Lippmann so highly praises has been in vogue in every
Catholic college for centuries." But Mortimer Adler, in "Can Catholic Education Be Criticized," *Commonweal*, April 14, 1939, p. 682, responded that he
saw little to distinguish most graduates of Catholic colleges from those of
secular colleges. "They have not even read the outstanding authors in their
own philosophical tradition. They have not read Plato and Aristotle, St. Augustine and St. Thomas, except perhaps in excerpts and quotations . . . Catholic
colleges are much more textbook-ridden, much more beset by such pedagogical
evils as manuals and syllabi, than the secular colleges."
†In a letter of July 17, 1973, Richard Weigle, president of St. John's, put
the issue of early admission in more perspective. Actually, Barr decided to
admit high-school students after their sophomore year because the war had
decimated the student body and St. John's had turned down a government
training program the faculty found unacceptable. But the early admissions
effort failed because the students were "simply too young" to do the St. John's
program. However, the college continues to admit an occasional mature student who has not completed high school.

affirmation: he portrayed the old St. John's as a kind of mindless collegiate place, while the new, "by its very existence, threatens every college and university in America." He went on:

> St. Johnnies are not memorizing snatches from the books or learn-
> ing dates. They are being taught to bring to the reading they will
> do in later life, the arts of language, the processes of analyzing,
> criticizing terms and propositions, arguments and contradictions.
> They are sharpening the instrument—the only instrument—with
> which men are able to distinguish ends and means, significant and
> trivial, general and particular, and straight and crooked.[19]

St. John's impact on students or its tutors has never been carefully evaluated by outsiders (our own work is itself only a beginning in this direction). But in the 1940s, St. John's as it was thought to be became an important symbol in the debate between educational progressives and conservatives. St. John's was no longer seen as another reformist experimental college. Differences of substance and style now mattered more than criticism of the Goliaths shared by other, very different reformers. Indeed, the progressive reformers feared St. John's might be the advance wave of a new authoritarianism in American education. Mortimer Adler, who with Hutchins was closely associated with the birth of St. John's, created quite a stir with an article that, despite its relatively obscure publication in the *Daily Maroon*, the undergraduate newspaper at the University of Chicago, received wide attention. In "God and the Professors," Adler wrote:

> Democracy will not be fully achieved until modern culture is
> radically reformed. Science contributes nothing whatsoever to the
> understanding of democracy. Without the truths of philosophy
> and religion, democracy has no rational foundation. And America
> at present is at best a cult of local prejudice, a traditional persua-
> sion. Today it is challenged by other cults which seem to have
> more fight and no less right so far as American ability to defend
> democracy rationally is concerned. For all these reasons, I say we
> have more to fear from our professors than from Hitler. It is
> they who have made American education what it is both in content
> and method: in content, an indoctrination of positivism and natu-
> ralism; in method, an exhibition of anarchic individualism mas-
> querading as a democratic manner. Whether Hitler wins or not, the
> culture which is formed by such education cannot support what
> democracy we have against interior decay.[20]

Helen Merrill Lynd sketched the rise of new conservative pressures in education, noting the prominence of the "St. John's group" in the fundamentalist radio appeals of the Education for Freedom, Inc.[21] organization. Sidney Hook was critical of what he regarded as the doctrinaire style of St. John's in "Ballyhoo at St. John's."[22] But the high point of the debate was an exchange between John Dewey and Alexander Meiklejohn in *Fortune* magazine.[23]

Dewey argued that liberal education originally was restricted to an aristocratic class that was supported by the industry of slaves trained under an apprenticeship system. But in modern society, industry rested upon the continuous application of science. Therefore a truly liberal and liberating education would refuse to isolate vocational training, on any of its levels, "from a continuous education in social, moral, and scientific contexts within which wisely administered callings and professions must function." Dewey made a distinction between the Greek style of drawing upon written materials (i.e., "Great Books") to set forth alternative possibilities to stimulate thought, and the later medieval study in which written materials, controlled by the clerics who were the sole class possessing mastery of the linguistic tools and the moral authority to make them central in education, became the only link to higher culture:

> But the notion that language, linguistics, skills and studies can be used for the same ends and by the same methods under contemporary conditions as in the Greek, Alexandrian, or medieval times, is as absurd in principle as it would be injurious in practice, were it adopted. The attempt to re-establish linguistic skills and materials at the center of education, and to do it under the guise of "education for freedom" or even "liberal" education, is directly opposed to all that the democratic countries cherish as freedom. The idea that an adequate education of any kind can be obtained by means of a miscellaneous assortment of 100 books, more or less, is laughable when viewed practically. The five-foot bookshelf for adults to be read, reread, and digested at leisure throughout a lifetime, is one thing. Crowded into four years and dealt out in fixed doses, it is quite another thing.

Meiklejohn attacked Dewey for ignoring the experimental inquiry that was fostered in the laboratories at St. John's, asserting that the makers of the St. John's curriculum saw with unusual clarity that one needs to know what science is and does in order to understand the modern world. It was for this reason that the college required that every student devote half of his course of study to learning science or mathematics as a language upon which advanced scientific achievement depends. He also insisted the Great Books were no glib or dogmatic exercise:

Why should the study of the past, as carried on at St. John's College, lead to dogmatism? When, in the experimental college, we turn to ancient Athens to read what Homer, Euripides, Lucretius, and Plato have said about judgments of value, it did not mean in our opinion those writers had, for all time, fixed standards of value that we must accept as unchanged and unchangeable and, the same way when St. John's College turns to Homer and Plato to find the beginning for a study of the sciences and technology, it is not looking to those writers for the last words on those subjects, it is looking for the first words. . . . From the time of the Greeks, until the present, the knowledge and wisdom of men has been growing. . . . And the intention of the curriculum is that the student shall follow that growth in order that he may be better able to play his part in the intellectual and moral activity of his own time and country. As he follows a sequence of ideas, the [student] will be confronted, not with one static set of dogmatic beliefs, but with all the fundamental conflicts that run through our culture. He will find Pythagoras at war with Plato, Kant at war with Hume, Rousseau at war with Locke, Veblen at war with Adam Smith, and he must try to understand both sides of these controversies.

II

Buchanan believed, as Mark Van Doren remarked later, that he was embarked on "the first serious effort in contemporary America to build a single and rational curriculum suited to the needs of minds which have work to do, and which some day should be unwilling to forgive any system of education that has required of them less discipline than this. Education is honored when it is hard, and it is more honored when it is hard and good."[24]

Buchanan, too, identified the good with the hard, and, like a mid-nineteenth-century schoolmaster, he believed the boy should adjust to the curriculum, not the curriculum to the boy. The student was properly subordinate to the mature and wiser teacher, just as the good college was a place where the wisdom of older men, grounded in a great tradition, modified younger men.

Believing that the American college curriculum had become cluttered with "tidbit courses and ill-related subject matters," Buchanan sought "to find again the point at which the tradition of liberal education had been lost." Men in different universities had been engaged in this search for many years, and "by separate paths eventually converged upon the Great Books of the European intellectual tradition. These Great Books are the medium in which our liberal heritage has been rediscovered, in which it can be revived, in which it can be taught again in a liberal college." He defined these classics as books of lasting appeal, offering the largest number of possible interpretations, and raising the "persistent, unanswerable questions about the great themes in European thought" in a style that would excite and discipline the ordinary mind by its form alone. In seeking to order the Great Books, Buchanan believed that "the clearest historic pattern of the liberal arts for the modern mind is, curiously enough, to be found in the 13th Century." It was a modern trivium and quadrivium that would restore the central position of the speculative sciences that Buchanan sought.[25] But the curriculum that emerged was basically arranged chronologically, although the books are usually read without much attention to the historical context from which they emerged. They are read as commentaries on each other. Secondary sources, historical interpretations, psychological insights, or arguments about motivation—these are of little concern in the St. John's curriculum, and they are politely ignored when introduced in seminar discussion.

In praising the St. John's curriculum, Mark Van Doren said: "A proposal to plant the classics at the center of the college curriculum is simple in the sense that it can be stated in one breath. But it calls for so much intellectual labor and goodwill that most educators prefer to spend enormous sums of energy in doing easier things."[26] Undoubtedly, for those holdover faculty members who decided to join Buchanan's counterrevolution, the decision to abandon their previous fields and to become students of the Great Books required great intellectual labor. But insofar as Van Doren's statement implies that there was an open debate and fresh examination of how the list of Great Books should be drawn, it is inaccurate. The St. John's list is an elaboration of one John Erskine used in 1916 in an honors curriculum at Columbia, which the Committee on the Liberal Arts revised at Chicago. It was the Chicago list that was put into effect at St. John's in the fall of 1937 and for the most part remains unchanged today (see Appendix 2). Over the years, Yeats, Baudelaire, Freud, Einstein, and others have been added. Lucian, Quintilian, Bonaventura, Veblen, and Montesquieu have been dropped. But the basic format of studies has remained largely the same: seminars on the Great Books, formal lectures on Friday nights, intensive tutorials daily in mathematics and language, and laboratories. The twice-a-week laboratory sessions have undergone the most change, for Buchanan's idea of repeating "the crucial and canonical experiments in the history of science" never worked well. In the students' first two years, the laboratory now consists of biology, matter and measurement, and elementary chemistry. In the last two, mechanics, electricity, and magnetism are followed by some quantum physics, genetics, and neurobiology. St. John's is probably the only liberal-arts college in the United States, if not in the world, which insists that every student manage this and learn enough calculus to make it possible. The current St. John's curriculum, with authors classified under conventional subject headings (which is not the way they are taught), is listed in Appendix 3 as it appears in the 1977 catalog.

For transcript purposes, the program is translated into conventional credit hours. Stretching a point, a St. John's graduate can be said to have a dual major in language (28 credits) and mathematics (24). There are 27 science credits spread among physics, chemistry, and biology. Other credits are in philosophy (13), literature (8.5), history (2.5), political science (5), music (6), psychology (2), and economics (1). Such a distribution is arbitrary, of course. Does one count Aristotle's *Politics*, for example, as philosophy or political science? Under an earlier accounting of basically the same curriculum, the graduate was assigned 63 credits in law and 35 in philosophy. Students say that no matter how many credits are assigned to it, the whole curriculum is fundamentally philosophical. There is virtually no anthropology, art, modern economics, geology, or sociology. Social science, once treated with contempt, is still held in faint disrepute. History (2.5 credits) has never been regarded as particularly important, although the college claims to provide students with the critical skills that any historian needs to sift and evaluate evidence. Commonly criticized for failing to discuss the social context of the Great Books, tutors argue that "so-called historical backgrounds can never help to understand the central intention of works of tradition."[27]

Though St. John's grudgingly accepts the necessity of shredding the curriculum for transcript purposes, the college bends its efforts toward erasing such subject-matter distinctions within its teaching. Freshmen are not introduced to Plato simply as a philosopher to be understood in the historic development of that discipline. Plato and Aristotle are thinkers who cannot be fully appreciated apart from an understanding of the theorems of Euclid or the mind of Ptolemy. Buchanan sought to build a curriculum that would transcend the conventional boundaries of knowledge and would help students make unified sense out of the natural world (even the library's classification system was set aside for a time as books were arranged under the headings of the seven liberal arts—grammar, rhetoric, logic, arithmetic, geometry, astronomy, and music). Buchanan felt that modern science was arranged in lumps of quite disparate knowledge, amounting to no more than a "systematic sophistry." In 1953, at a conference on science and the liberal arts, he said, "I believe the sciences at present, mostly technological as they are, can smash any liberal program you set up, unless you face them belligerently and never give in." O. Meredith Wilson, then executive secretary of the Fund for the Advancement of Education, responded: "Isn't it more healthy for liberal education to approach this problem without initial dogmas? Isn't it better to discover somehow what there is that science can teach us, than to require that we teach 'science'? If you can find unity, find it; but to say impose it willy-nilly or die as liberal educators is to say: Well, we will impose reality on what is not real." Buchanan then replied: "I do not think the method of postulation says 'impose unity; you will find it or die in the attempt.' I think there are more people dying for not searching for it than the converse."[28]

St. John's tends to eschew any objective evaluation of its curriculum through usual tests and measurements. The original catalogue reverberates with the language of the mental disciplinarians of the 1800s who saw education as the disciplining of the mind. The liberal arts "are the arts of thinking" and "the arts of handling symbols," Buchanan wrote.[29] Languages are not taught in a conventional sense. The aim is an "understanding of the potentialities and the limitations of human speech." When the new program was instituted, students studied Greek, Latin, German, and French in consecutive years, learning none of them. Now Greek occupies the first two years and French the last two years; few become competent in Greek, while those who had high-school French generally do better in that subject. The math tutorial does not aim to train professional mathematicians, but to "acquaint students with mathematics as a mode of human understanding," and in music, "St. John's is not primarily interested in transmitting technical skills, but in acquainting the student with a mode of symbolic expression." Insofar as the Great Books themselves are concerned, a St. John's report concluded:

> The College makes no claim to training specialists, and recognizes that most undergraduates will not be able to read these books and talk about them with the skill and sophistication of trained scholars. Most students do, however, quickly overcome their initial fear and clumsiness when confronted by difficult books; they do improve steadily in their reading skill; they do understand much in these books astonishingly well. Even more important, in the seminar they begin to listen to reason and to submit with some pleasure to its disciplines.[30]

As one tutor, Eva Brann, has put it, the problem the curriculum poses is to learn how to ask a genuine question.[31] Since a genuine question arises out of one's peculiar effort to make sense of the world, how, then, does a student learn to do this by pondering questions others have asked? The best the curriculum can do is to require students to confront the classic dilemmas—others' problems rather than their own—and hope that in the process they acquire the problem-solving arts that will prepare them for a life of genuine questioning.

Assessing progress along such an arduous path is difficult, and at St. John's three kinds of evaluation are used: oral exams, an annual essay, and the don rag. The oral exam is an informal discussion between a student and his tutors of the texts that have been read that semester. The aim is not to discover what the student remembers but to assess the quality of his critical and interpretive opinions. The annual essay develops a student's thought on some aspect of the liberal arts. The enabling essay submitted by sophomores has a special significance. It is reviewed by the Instruction Committee, with the advice of all the student's tutors, and the discussion may go on into the early hours of the morning as each sophomore's record is considered by the faculty. The senior essay must be publicly defended in an hour-long oral examination. Tutors frequently complain that the students do not write enough and do not write well. In the essays that we sampled, students seem to have difficulty finding their own voice. The essays, like the seminars, tend to be an explication of a text. Students take themselves too seriously, said one tutor, and are overly concerned with demonstrating virtue, "sanctifying what they write." One occasionally finds a creative synthesis, such as a paper entitled "Mathematics and Music," which attempted to show that the processes at work to prove a mathematical proposition are the same as those that compel belief in a piece of music. More typical is a paper on Kant which alternates throughout a paragraph of quotation with three or four of explication.

So far as we know, the don rag at St. John's has no parallel in American higher education. At the end of each semester, all a student's tutors meet to discuss the student's progress or lack of it. One of the tutors chairs the session, and the student sits on one side of a table, facing his or her teachers. Then for twenty minutes or so, the tutors discuss the student's strengths and weaknesses, addressing their remarks to the chairman as though the student were not there. The student then is invited to respond, to offer his or her self-evaluation, and to query the tutors about their remarks. No marks are reported, although grades are privately recorded for use when students apply to graduate school. The nature of the session is one of diagnosis and advising. The don rag shocks some students into a creative re-examination of their modes of thinking and reading. But others say the process is superficial, since during don-rag week the average tutor may pass judgment on fifteen or sixteen students in the course of a day. Some fear they are type-cast as freshmen, that there is little sensitive appreciation of their development over time. It may be that the program is too talky and that tutors have an inadequate sample of written work for more careful and extended appraisals. Or perhaps tutors' initial judgments are correct and most students don't change as much as they think they do. We are inclined, however, to put more weight on the first interpretation.

In our visits to St. John's we sat in on only two don rags, and they were special or disciplinary sessions held for students threatened with suspension. Our request to return at semester's end to sample a wider range of don rags was declined by the Instruction Committee on the grounds that our presence might interfere with the process. But the don-rag reports that we were permitted to read gave us a picture of the proceedings. General judgments are made about a student's intelligence, describing him as able or mediocre or excellent, and the like. Tutors report on a student's "grasp of Greek" or ability to demonstrate in a math tutorial. But judgments of a student's moral fiber are more common. Words like "lazy" or "docile" are used: Mr. Jones's progress will depend on "his will to fight it out." Or, Miss Smith "began rather amorphously, and has come forward since and added force and passion to her participation; she has now deepened to sense the seriousness of the issues." Statements are frequently made about whether a student is working more or less than he or she did the previous semester.

This moral refrain points to the concern at St. John's with virtue (intellectual as well as moral) and the development of character. Although Buchanan aimed to produce misfits, the radicalism implicit in his agenda was devoutly nonpolitical or even antipolitical. The St. John's program is a mandate for living life as it should be lived, not a prescription for organizing society. It is no accident that freshmen begin their Greek tutorial with translations of Plato's *Meno*, the dialogue that treats the paradox that virtue is desirable yet we do not know if it can be taught. The St. John's curriculum confronts the student with the classically important dilemmas and seeks to create a dialogue about them in class and out: What is justice? How does one justify the ways of God to men? What has happened to man in the last four hundred years?

In this sense, the only evaluation that matters is one that is nearly impossible to have: What kind of lives do St. John's graduates lead? A tutor will often respond with a story when asked to provide evidence of the program's success. Jacob Klein told us about a meeting of alumni who were asked about the benefit of a St. John's education. One man stood up and said it had caused problems in his marriage. "You must understand that I am a chicken farmer and in order to make any money raising chickens you must cheat. My wife blames St. John's for the fact that I won't."

When he had been at St. John's nearly ten years, Buchanan wrote Hutchins: "I am still taking the moral and spiritual revolution seriously as in fact the only thing in the world worth living for. Fortunately it is the sort of thing that can restore our functions and redeem our lives and characters if we give ourselves to it."[32] But in 1946, Barr and Buchanan left St. John's after battling the Naval Academy, which they felt was threatening to take over the campus. Barr wanted to move the enterprise to Stockbridge, Massachusetts, but, after some indecision, neither the faculty nor the board concurred. Buchanan returned to speak at the commencement in 1947, having come to the view that the college ought to have a subject matter as well as liberal arts—"a nameable and a followable subject matter, a theme, and I thought law, in college, should be that."[33] He felt later that St. John's never went on with the necessary work of revising and changing the curriculum "in a very powerful way." He wanted to establish a "permanent revolutionary committee" that would continually feed changes into the undergraduate college. He also concluded later that the curriculum should have included Oriental as well as Western Great Books:

> We ought to have gone at the Oriental books simply and hard,
> and we'd have cracked them . . . The best way to learn these
> things is to teach them. Just bring them into class and assign them
> and go ahead. Don't stand on your competence. When we said
> we were incompetent to do this with the Oriental books, we did
> not mean scholarly competence. We meant in some deep way we
> did not have the imaginative and emotional concept for really
> understanding them.[34]

But St. John's stuck on the course that Buchanan had originally set for it, and paid little attention to his second thoughts. After a few tempestuous interim years, Richard D. Weigle was appointed president in 1949. Weigle taught history at Carleton College after earning his doctorate at Yale and had been in the Office of Far Eastern Affairs of the Department of State. As president, he brought financial stability to the college, admitted women in 1951, and in 1953 finally succeeded in winning for St. John's the accreditation it had been denied throughout the Barr–Buchanan years on the grounds of financial and administrative instability. And it was Weigle who established the branch campus in Santa Fe. Our effort to portray the intentions of the founders has not permitted us to adequately chronicle his twenty-eight year role as president.

III

Unlike the open adobe-style setting of the new campus in Santa Fe, set in a rim of the Sangre de Christo Mountains, one reaches the Annapolis campus of St. John's through the narrow streets of that old Maryland town. Just a block north of the State House, one finds the campus with its modern brick buildings mixed among the more attractive colonial structures on a gentle slope that stretches down to a tributary of the Severn River. We arrived for our first visit one November night in time for dinner, and found our way to the dining hall, where we joined the students who were queued up in the foyer. One of the civilized practices that survived into the 1970s at St. John's was that lines were not allowed to trail through the tables at dinnertime. Instead, as a table became available, diners were seated in groups of six or eight, and served by student waiters. Students were seated at random in the order in which they arrived, so that in a relatively short time everyone on the campus of about 375 knew everyone else in more than a superficial way. St. John's built its second campus to allow growth to take place without loss of this sense of community; it regards mass education as a contradiction in terms.

We were introduced first to the student on our right, a senior from Long Island who had given up an acting career and was now planning to become a minister. He had been suspended from the college at the end of his sophomore year for smoking marijuana. When he returned to the campus for an unauthorized visit, he was given a second year's suspension. This stirred other recollections at our table of the style of the stern but respected former dean, John Kieffer, who once expelled a female student for living with a man. Another student, hoping to trap him in a logical inconsistency, later asked what the dean would do if a student had had an affair with a girl in Hong Kong the previous summer, and the dean unhesitatingly replied, "I would expel you."

Women are now allowed to visit men's rooms—and sexual intimacy seems as common as at other colleges. St. John's may be the only campus where one can hear faculty seriously argue that students ought to be celibate, "for whoever knows anything about the life of learning will not entertain the frivolous notion that it ought to be a very natural or satisfied life, but will understand that it requires a certain tension of the soul and body and a certain reserve of deferred desire."[35] The college has given way but slowly to most modern demands and retains the cadences of an earlier time. Attendance is required. Classes begin with a call of the roll, and though the discussion may become heated, students usually address one another in the formal mode, using Mr., Mrs., or Miss. Elitism, generally the most damning accusation among contemporary students, has never passed out of fashion at St. John's. "We are in a sense justified in our elitism here," Nancy Polk wrote to her fellow students in 1973, "because we hope, through the cultivation of intellectual virtue, to improve our moral virtue as well."[36]

In both its statement of aims and its standards, St. John's is in fact elite. Applicants write an essay in which they must evaluate the quality of their previous education, discuss an important book, and describe the kind of life they would like to lead. A high proportion of those who apply (89 percent) are actually accepted; most students hesitate to apply after reading St. John's highly literate and uncompromising catalog. The college has always had difficulty filling its classes with students who meet its standards (it has maintained its insistence on three years of high-school math and two of foreign language).

Average scores on standardized tests of scholastic ability are high but not overpowering: about 650 on the verbal SAT and 620 on the math (about the same as the averages at Pomona or Carleton, but lower than those at Princeton or Bryn Mawr), with the scores in Santa Fe slightly higher in 1975.[37] Once admitted, students are shown their grades only on request, but there is a considerable amount of conversation and a fairly acute sense of who are the intellectual heavyweights. The intellectual pecking order is not posted daily, so to speak, as it was apparently in the elementary school in Jeffersonville, Vermont, that Scott Buchanan attended as a boy. (Buchanan's Jeffersonville classmates were seated according to their class standing, and you got your marks every day, "If you did something well, you moved up."[38])

Whether they move up or down, an exceptionally high number move out. St. John's attrition rate is severe with the heaviest withdrawals following the freshman and sophomore years. Among private colleges of similar selectivity, about one-quarter of a given freshman class eventually drop out or transfer to another college.[39] At St. John's, more than half of an entering class leaves before graduation. The increasingly difficult sequence in mathematics as well as the prescribed nature of the program drives many students out; others are eager to specialize in a discipline; some find the relentlessly bookish and serious nature of the place depressing.

The Program, as everyone refers to it, and informal assessments of how well classmates are doing in it, tend to take up most of the available time and social space at St. John's. Extracurricular activities are quite limited, and those that exist are often outgrowths of The Program. Discussions and criticisms of the curriculum are the most frequent topics in the *Collegian*, the student weekly. Occasionally, most of an issue will be given over to a committee report or a pages-long footnote to some aspect of The Program, such as a student's translation of the correspondence in 1832 between Karl Friedrich Gauss and Johan Bolyai on their discoveries in non-Euclidian geometry—complete with propositions, diagrams, and proofs.[40]

Students attend class fifteen to twenty hours a week, and three evenings are given over to formal parts of The Program. On Mondays and Thursdays, all students and faculty participate in a Great Books seminar that often continues past midnight in the coffee shop. There, with the intensity and animation characteristic of a crowd at a cockfight, the students reargue the themes of that night's reading of Nietzsche or St. Augustine, occasionally elbowing their way to a blackboard to demonstrate a point. On those two nights, every room in the college is in use as the entire community explores the texts that stand at the heart of the curriculum.

The formal lecture on Friday nights tends to take on the air of a social event. Most of the faculty and many spouses are there as well. The speaker may be Mortimer Adler on "The Common Sense of Politics," Edward Banfield on "The Unheavenly City," Leo Strauss on "The Problem of Faculties," Dieter Henrich on "The Basic Structure of Modern Philosophy," or the evening might be devoted to a concert by the Beaux Arts String Quartet, or a play by the Modern Theater Group. All rise as the dean escorts the speaker or performers to the rostrum. Once the program has begun, knitting needles are in evidence, but few pads and pencils, because of the St. John's belief "that a full notebook betokens an empty mind." Students are expected to train their memories so that questions may be asked later without the aid of notes. At the conclusion, after coffee and doughnuts, a signal is given for the question period to begin. One-third to one-half of those present generally assemble in a separate, smaller room, known, appropriately enough, as the Question-Period Room. The question periods may go on for three hours. Often, they take on the nature of an adversary proceeding, with the questioners seeking to find flaws or inconsistencies in the lecturer's argument and to exploit them if they can. It is sometimes difficult to understand the context in which the questions are asked unless one knows what students have been reading in their seminars in the previous weeks. Riesman, lecturing at St. John's on Freud twenty years ago, sought in vain to change what seemed to be a fairly uniform style of questioning (e.g., "To what extent is Freud in the tradition of Descartes?") by insisting that Freud's impact had less to do with his philosophy than with his invention of a method for rooting out and interpreting unconscious material. What was evident then has been reconfirmed on Grant's four recent visits: St. John's students find it extraordinarily difficult to suspend their own frames of reference to see what might be learned by attending to the frame of reference of the speaker. Mortimer Adler, a frequent lecturer at St. John's over the years, insists that students first say what they think he has said before they put their questions.

We attended a lecture given by Edward Sparrow, a tutor at St. John's, entitled, "Noun and Verb," which put forth a new metaphor of grammar in which he defined a grammatical sentence as a true sentence. The question period began with a woman tutor asking about the sentence "There was a sea fight yesterday." "Is that a sentence by your grammar?" "Yes," he replied, "if there was a sea fight yesterday." This then led to a discussion of probability and truthfulness, with a student who did not understand the mathematical concept of probability arguing with one who did. Then the dean joined the conversation, asking about the sea-fight sentence again, saying that it was being discussed as if it were a statement in the newspaper which could be established as true or false. He then asked, "What if it were the opening statement in a novel?" Sparrow replied that under his grammar the test would be its conceivability, and the dean responded sharply that then he would seem to be applying two tests and wasn't that inconsistent?—and so the questions went, in a brittle exchange, well past midnight.

At the end of the Friday-night question period—or at the end of the lecture for some students—Western civilization crumbles at St. John's, and students begin the orgies of loud music, drinking, pot-smoking, and dancing that characterize the weekend social life. There is very little quiet or intimate talk at such parties; in rejecting the intellectual mode the parties seem to be an almost strained demonstration that St. Johnnies can behave just like young people elsewhere.

Some forms of play are more stylish, however. Periodically, students dress formally for nineteenth-century waltzes in the Great Hall, capped by a champagne-and-strawberries June cotillion when the dancing goes on all night and quiche lorraine is served at dawn. Late in May, St. John's celebrates Reality Weekend, which begins with libations as torchbearers lead the Piraeus parade to the campus from the docks of Annapolis. In the vulgar version of the Battle of Salamis that follows, students in rowboats fight for possession of a greased watermelon that has been dropped in College Creek. A highlight of the weekend, following the Irregular Ellipsoid Hurling Contest (an egg throw), is the Epicycle race. In a dizzying contest, students demonstrate Ptolemy's theory of the epicycle by which he explained the sun's orbit about the earth. Students are linked by ropes. As the first student makes eight wide orbits about the "earth" student, a third "Venus" student makes five smaller revolutions about the first. The three students who complete this maneuver in the shortest time win.

But by Sunday afternoon of an ordinary weekend, the formidable demands of the program begin to reassert themselves, and one can almost feel the common mood change. One learns quickly if this is the week when the freshmen are beginning to struggle with the mathematics in the fifth book of Euclid's *Elements*, or if they are grappling with the first assignment in Thucydides, in which the best students will begin to ponder the implications for liberty in Pericles' funeral oration. Two of our dinner partners one Sunday evening were musicians: one a pianist, the other a cellist. They echoed the common complaint that The Program does violence to other serious pursuits; one simply cannot do music or any art that demands daily practice and do The Program, too. A tutor was to remark later that The Program was designed for angels—only they could do it entire. Until 1973, in fact, there had never been a summa granted at the new St. John's although one student came close enough in 1943 to provoke a debate among the faculty. When it was argued that no student deserved a summa, one tutor asked, what would we give to Hume? And Catesby Taliaferro answered, "A 'C' at best." George Comenetz argued that the student ought to be given a summa "because he's as good as we are," but John Kieffer disagreed: "A magna at best, then; a summa if he's better."[41]

Although The Program is taxing, there are more than a few students at St. John's who believe that it is the only curriculum worth mastering. One of our dinner companions, a sophomore from Baltimore, described The Program as a way of life for him—the only way. He almost visibly winced when we asked if he had any criticisms of The Program, replying: "If there's anything wrong here, it's wrong with me."

After dinner, another of our companions invited us to his room in the Chase-Stone dormitory. It was a single room, mildly disorderly, with a bed, desk, shapeless armchair, and some balls of red, blue, and yellow clay stuck to the ceiling. He explained that he had originally used these balls of clay to strengthen a broken arm. When one day he threw one up to the ceiling and it stuck, other students soon joined in the game. He offered us a bottle of Guinness Stout from a six-pack on the windowsill, and told us something about his story. He had originally applied to the Royal Academy in London, thinking he wanted to be an actor, but he was turned down. The curate of his church told him about St. John's, and he was impressed by reading the catalogue. He wanted to escape the horrible lecturing in high school, and he wanted to read the classics.

He felt that at their worst, the St. John's seminars degenerated into a kind of debate, in which the least able students got stomped on. But in the best seminars a real colleagueship of tutors and students was developed: "Last year, it was my seminar, as much as theirs.* He was referring to the junior seminar in which he read *Paradise Lost*, *Tom Jones*, and the Rationalist philosophers. He spoke proudly of the college's aims, but said that occasionally "I wonder if I really know anything, or if I'm simply a high-powered dilettante," a concern echoed in other interviews. He felt St. John's also tended to prejudice students against doing what was merely useful. He described a classmate who had been in an engineering curriculum before transferring to St. John's and who was really something of a genius with computers. He now felt that engineering was beneath him and that all that was important was to grapple with the "Great Questions." Such students may be typical of the audience St. John's is trying to reach. Until recently, in addition to attempts to recruit National Merit Scholars, literature was sent to 12,000 students who were identified by the American College Testing Program as having an interest in writing or expression, a concern about the intellectual atmosphere of the college to be attended, and a possible interest in the arts and humanities as a major field of study.

The only class in session that evening was an extracurricular seminar in the New Testament, led by J. Winfree Smith, Jr., a tutor since 1941, who had known both Barr and Buchanan as a student at the University of Virginia in the 1930s. Four males were huddled at one end of the large table that had been pushed together in the seminar room on the second floor of McDowell Hall as the class began. Three women straggled in over the next fifteen minutes. The blackboard

---

*St. John's alumni who read earlier drafts of this chapter almost always underscored this point. Neal Weiner, now teaching at Marlboro College, said that when he was a student at St. John's he felt it was up to him whether a class went well or not. He felt then as he does now as a teacher: if a class went well he was elated, if not he felt responsible.

showed evidence of a previous geometry lesson and a class in Greek earlier in the day. The group was reading St. John's Gospel in Greek, and translated about twelve lines in the hour and ten minutes before the class ended. It was a somber, almost dour class. There was a great deal of staring at the table, long silences, and a halting, apologetic style in the responses of the students, almost as if to dismiss their interpretations before giving voice to them. Most comments were addressed directly to the tutor, and the students waited quietly for his judgment or ruling on a particular translation. They began discussing the line, "Behold the Lamb of God who takes away the sin of the world." There was a fifteen-minute discussion of what "Lamb" meant in this context, at the end of which Smith offered three interpretations: the Passover Lamb, the use in the 53rd chapter of Isaiah, where a suffering servant is described as a lamb on whom the Lord has laid the iniquities of us all, and the sacrifice of lambs that was made daily in Jerusalem at this time. A boy suggested that a lamb might be a scapegoat. A girl in leotards, jeans, and sandals, sitting next to us, wondered whether "sin" was used in the singular because it referred to the common sin of mankind, and the tutor asked whether she meant by that a condition rather than an act. Three or four other students offered their translations of that particular line and discussed minor differences and emphases. In the next line, John the Baptist speaks of the "man who came before me," and the class discussed whether this referred to chronological order or rank. There was considerable discussion about whether the spirit "descending as a dove" was meant to be a bodily dove. The tutor said he felt the New Testament implied that the body, not just human nature, was raised in the Resurrection. A male student asked whether his particular flesh could be reassembled once it had decomposed molecularly, and a girl said perhaps what was meant was that genes contained information, or the code, and that it was the code that would in some sense determine the resurrection of the human form. A boy drew an analogy of the twenty-two parts of a radio that could be reassembled, saying that it was not the parts that were important, but the message or the program that was transmitted. Then there was an argument about whether the genetic code could account for a specific human form, when the body was created in interaction with the environment. After class, we chatted with Smith, who hurried out to participate in a rehearsal of the first part of *Henry IV*, which a number of the tutors were producing with students.*

*This class was more typical of a tutorial at St. John's than of a seminar, which tends to be more of an intellectual free-for-all. Yet a seminar might give fifteen minutes or even two hours to the discussion of a particular word.

The next morning, we met Clifford, a red-haired senior from Pennsylvania, at breakfast. It turned out that he was a laboratory assistant, and he invited us to visit the laboratory he would be working in that morning. He had a humorous perspective on life at St. John's and said that many of the labs were like crash courses. He joked that they blew a whistle and said, "Learn all you can about embryology in three weeks," and then blew the whistle again and said, "Now master comparative anatomy in four weeks and tell us why the scientists are wrong." The laboratory itself was led by John Sarkissian, a short, rotund, moustached man who had a light, easy way with the students, and they obviously liked him. Sarkissian had done his undergraduate work at the University of Chicago and the University of Illinois, earning an M.A. from the latter in 1948. He taught at the Pestalozzi-Froebel Teachers College in Chicago, Chicago City College, and the Universities of Indiana and Illinois before coming to St. John's as a tutor in 1963. The students were experimenting with a sonometer, a simple device in which three strings are stretched over two bridges. Sarkissian plucked the strings and asked questions about changes of pitch. At the end of an hour, they came to some conclusions about the way in which the gauge of the wire, the tension upon it, and the length formed by moving the bridges determined the sound. The students listened intently when asked whether two strings had the same pitch, and they disagreed among themselves. There were several examples of individual students holding out against the majority opinion. There was care in listening to determine when the middle, narrower-gauge string had the tension released upon it so that it would come closer to the pitch of the thicker string.

Our next class was a dull and dreary Greek tutorial in which the tutor went around the table calling on each student in turn to translate a few lines. Many had not prepared their recitations. The class then turned into a rather vapid discussion about how you know you know something.

We left the Greek class early to study the schedule posted in the dean's office, and we chose next to visit a senior math tutorial taught by Thomas K. Simpson in the next period. It turned out to be an excellent class. Simpson, a lively, ebullient man, wore a brown tweed jacket, wooly tan sweater, jeans, and mountain boots. Tall, thin, and energetic, he sat at the side rather than at the head of the table, bending way over, cocking his head, and looking up and down the table, depending upon which student was speaking. The students moved to the blackboard and explained their proofs in an entertaining but clear, intellectually exciting way. The discussion was brisk and students skillfully probed whoever was at the board. Simpson played an orchestrating role, helping the demonstrator get over a rough spot, or occasionally asking a question. One of the "students" in the class was Winfree Smith, who was auditing it in order to teach it the following year. Simpson had gone to Rensselaer Polytechnical Institute as an undergraduate, earning a degree in electrical engineering before the war. When he came home, he decided he had not been educated, and so he came to St. John's to start all over again as a freshman in 1946. He had taught for three years at the American University in Cairo, and had then earned a Master's of Arts in Teaching at Wesleyan, with the aim of teaching in high school, but ultimately he was called back to St. John's by Dean Jacob Klein.

IV

At St. John's Socrates is seen as the ideal teacher because he was the ideal student, assisting others in the act of discovery. Scott Buchanan sought tutors who delighted in the pursuit of the unanswerable questions and who had passed through "several stages of a Socratic dialectical education." Buchanan regarded most college teachers as mere experts who were angered by those who dared to question their authority and who desperately attempted to hold their ground with a flood of esoteric information when the challenge persisted. But he knew that some teachers developed that subtle combination of self-confidence and humility required to find out what a question meant. The good teacher finally discovers "the Socratic method of analyzing a question in terms of a subject matter and returning it to the questioner in a criticized and partially answerable form."[42]

At St. John's the tutor's task is to elicit opinions, not to offer them. The greatest virtue of a St. John's tutor is patience, Jacob Klein believes:

> If a tutor is not patient, he is bad. A student may talk nonsense, but that does not mean he will not come to see eventually that he is talking nonsense. The second thing is the quality of openness, of understanding. If a tutor is open, he will hear that grain of importance, of goodness, of brilliance, or of sense in the student's argument, and he will disregard all the rest and will concentrate on that valuable grain, and he will help others to see it.[43]

The overwhelming impression one receives on visiting classes is the restraint under which tutors operate—most noticeable, perhaps, in the evening seminars. Tutors usually begin with a single question: "Is there any method behind Liebniz's madness; some way to state generally what he is trying to do?" or "What does Herodotus mean by 'researches'?" It is not unusual for the tutor to remain silent, with only an occasional prod, for the remainder of the two hours. More often, the tutor struggles, "rather haphazardly, to extricate from the context of the conversation the point or points most worthy of consideration," by isolating assumptions and constructing a series of "verifying steps."[44] Of course, at St. John's, as elsewhere, patience does not always lead to enlightenment. Some students continue to talk nonsense while others become bored, angry, or discouraged. Nor are unanswerable questions necessarily delighting, and a curriculum that continues to confront students with these perplexities is not without its anxieties. Perpetual problems everywhere, they are perhaps exacerbated by St. John's persistent attention to developing critical rather than specialized skills, and its relative indifference to helping students master a body of knowledge.

The patient Socratic style[45] can also be a mask for inept teaching. Eva Brann, a Yale-trained archaeologist who taught at Stanford before coming to St. John's in 1957, is bored with those tutors "whose main contribution is to smoke a pipe and say, 'Why do you say that?' "[46] She sees the successful tutor as one who delights in the study of the Great Books and can talk intelligently about them without turning a class into a graduate seminar. Nor does she feel it is enough to be competent without being exciting. A tutor should be able to direct discussion of a point in Euclid in a way that conveys a sense of discovery. What matters is a certain fertility of mind in simple matters. In her view, the best tutors are deeply committed to the values of the program and are untroubled by the thought that they should be concerned with the more immediate, "relevant" problems of the world. St. John's College is no experiment, she says, unless Western civilization is an experiment.

Students teach each other at St. John's, and the common curriculum can provide the matrix for a complex and illuminating discussion. In a senior math class we visited in Santa Fe, for example, the students examined Einstein's essay on geometry and experience, borrowing analogies from the quite different mathematical languages of Newton, Euclid, and Lobachevsky. If a tutor is late or absent, the students may begin without him. While there are loafers at St. John's as elsewhere, there is probably less tolerance for slackness than at most institutions, and the obligation to contribute to the discussion is taken more seriously. Tutors will occasionally remark that a seminar has been poor because few good "teachers" emerged among the students or because the blend of personalities seemed ill-suited to the task. A "bad mix" can be disastrous because students who form a tutorial group see each other in all classes; hierarchies get fixed; roles are difficult to change.

If there is a general weakness, it is a tendency toward pickiness— an *explication de texte* that falls short of synthesis. In a senior tutorial we visited, for example, students analyzed Dylan Thomas's poem, "Refusal to Mourn the Death by Fire of a Child in London." It was an hour of very close textual criticism and an elaboration of some of the biblical images in the poem. But by the end of the hour, no holistic interpretation of the poem had been attempted, an omission that at first seemed intentional, since the tutor said they would focus on an over-all view of the poem the next day. We thought, how brilliant to let the initial confusion and the complexity of the poem sort itself out overnight, and we decided to return the next day. Though the poem was discussed again for about fifteen minutes, no over-all interpretation was attempted. Then the students turned to another poem.

These matters and others are sometimes discussed in archon groups. What Scott Buchanan once did to help new teachers in the Saturday seminars in his office has now been routinized in the form of archon meetings. An archon leads a group of tutors—say those who teach freshman lab—in weekly discussions of ways to improve their teaching or the content of what is taught. A new faculty member is paired in seminar with a senior tutor who can act as a helpful guide, and, when needed, as a restraining one. The emphasis at St. John's is decidedly on the classrooms. The expectation that tutors will audit other classes provides not only the opportunity to prepare for teaching them, but also a chance to observe and to discuss other styles of teaching.

At the point when a tutor is being considered for reappointment or tenure, the archon groups, the frequent auditing, and the team-taught seminar, provide a richness of observation and data about his teaching that few tenure committees possess. In addition, a committee is appointed to interview all of the seniors who have been taught by a tutor being considered for tenure. As a result of their shared intellectual experience, students and tutors have developed some common bench marks that enable them to talk about a teacher's capabilities in a discriminating way.

Research or publication carries no weight. In fact, many consider it a negative accomplishment, since one could not possibly teach such a demanding curriculum well if one were to "steal" time for writing and publishing. It is expected, for instance, that St. John's tutors will reread whatever book is to be discussed in seminar. And they seem to do so. Tutors may give an occasional Friday-night lecture, write an article about some aspect of the program for *The College* magazine, translate a Greek text that may be used in The Program, or spend a sabbatical revising a laboratory manual, but there is no expectation that they will do any of these things.

V

St. John's boasts that it dispenses with the trappings of academic rank in order to minimize unimportant distinctions and to emphasize the common task of teaching. To a significant degree, it succeeds in this aim, but important, if informal, hierarchies develop nevertheless. On the lowest echelon are the new and untenured tutors, who do not yet see that Euclid's Book Five has something very important to do with Descartes and Newton, and who are often at the mercy of senior students eager to show them up as sophists. Then there are the tenured, who are relatively secure and know their way around the program. But there is a clear distinction between those who are merely tenured and those who are eligible to serve as archons, to be the senior members of seminar teams, and to be part of the Instruction Committee that serves as the ruling oligarchy. Finally, there are the great tutors, living and dead, who seem legendary and are referred to as gods by students—Scott Buchanan, Richard Scofield, Jacob Klein, and others.

Every tutor who comes to St. John's makes a radical decision to abandon his or her discipline and to become an apprentice in an uncompromising program. Some, like Moses Hadas, may leave within a few months. Nicolas Nabokov came in 1941 and, with the composer Elliott Carter, devised a program of "great works of music" with works to be read over four years. Nabokov saw the St. John's curriculum as a more intelligent and pragmatic way to teach laymen something about music than the usual slipshod music-appreciation courses, but Scott Buchanan questioned whether Nabokov needed to spend so much time lecturing students on musical notation. Nabokov insisted that it was impossible to teach students anything about music until they knew its language. Yet he agreed to an experiment Buchanan proposed in which students were "goaded" into learning by exposing them to a Beethoven quartet with no preliminary explanation. The experiment was a comic fiasco, as Nabokov reported it, and he felt Buchanan never forgave him for calling Buchanan's bluff. Nabokov disliked the "hop hop" from one book to another, although he found the St. John's community "bright and even bril-

liant." Buchanan helped Nabokov find a job teaching history of music
courses at the Peabody Conservatory in Baltimore, and he left a few
years later, remarking: "At St. John's I always felt a bit of an im-
postor. But at the music school I taught the stuff I knew."[47]

Years later, in 1952, Peabody Conservatory returned the gift.
Douglas Allanbrook, a composer and teacher of music theory at
Peabody, came to St. John's and loved it, hopscotch and all. Most
tutors, like the classics scholar John Kieffer, learn to teach math and
science and to enjoy it. A few even gain excellence in a new field.
Robert Bart, who came from Harvard as an expert in comparative
literature, is now a recognized Newton scholar. It may be ten or
fifteen years before a tutor has taught all parts of the curriculum,
yet more than 80 percent of the faculty has taught Greek, though
few came prepared to teach it.

Unlike many contemporary experimental colleges, one does not do
"one's own thing" at St. John's (frequently defined as any subject
that interests the teacher) but does "their thing." And unlike more
volatile experiments, St. John's makes the commitment that the program will still be around in ten or fifteen years if the prospective
tutor is willing to make the commitment to master it. That commitment requires an act of humility, a subordination of one's own
agenda and a conformity to the preestablished aims of the program.
The St. John's tutor sees himself or herself as an interpreter of the
score, not a creator of new music.

But some who are willing to indenture themselves to the authority
of the Great Books find it chafing to submit to the personalities who
define the St. John's canon. Several of the ablest young tutors speak
resentfully of being molded to fit the program or being impaled on a
fixed curriculum that encourages little appreciation of the individual
talents they bring to it. They grow tired of hearing the Socratic shib-
boleth that the teacher has no wisdom, that the wisdom lies in the constant questioning. They must first approach the senior men with some
reverence, wait some years before suggesting even minor changes in
the lab manuals, and then couch criticism in the softest terms:

> For a long time you are told that there are these new mysteries,
> things you've never seen before. You may not like the way things
> are, but you cannot change your class. You must use the lab
> manuals as they have been written, even if you don't like them.
> You are told to do it two or three times and then you will come to
> discover the reasons why they are as they are, to appreciate them.

They also complain about a lack of spontaneity. Plato said anger
is irrational, unless occasioned by injustice; therefore, anger must be

repressed. "Too many of the faculty live in lucite cylinders," said one tutor. "They can see each other, but when they get too close they hit and back off."

Yet, despite complaints, each of these tutors finds that the inflexible structure makes possible a focus on teaching and intellectual growth that outweighs the disadvantages: "It's the last place where one can have a long-term sabbatical in the great tradition," one remarked. "I have been paid a generally comfortable salary to read the Great Books in an order that makes sense." And the Great Books do nourish and renew. For the best people, some of them on a second fifteen-year cycle of teaching The Program, there seems to be none of the dwarfing of the imagination that often occurs in insulated places.

The great sabbatical, accompanied by the suspicion that one is really uncivilized and ill-educated, may be the strongest motivation for tutors who are drawn to St. John's. Some say simply that they heard about the college too late to come as students. About half of the faculty hold the Ph.D. A number of them are scientists, who lost interest in seeking eminence in a specialized field; they sought to be reborn as humanists at St. John's, where they could also put their mathematical and scientific abilities to good use. Philosophers, linguists, theologians, and musicians are strongly represented. Of the fifty-one faculty members in Annapolis, nine earned their undergraduate degree at St. John's and thirteen others earned degrees at Chicago or Columbia, where integrated liberal-arts programs were strong influences. Eight earned degrees in education, and some of these as well as others, like Buchanan, taught in high school.[48] The salaries are modest, and the workload is heavy. "A tutor does not have to marry the College," said one, "but he soon realizes that she is a jealous mistress who claims him at least three nights a week." There are long seminars on Monday and Thursday nights, formal lectures on Friday nights, and frequently another night for a senior preceptorial* or a faculty meeting. The oral exams, don rags, enabling procedures, and archon groups take their toll, in addition to fourteen or fifteen hours of classroom teaching with responsibility for as many as fifty students.

We have noted the St. John's hostility to specialization. Yet tutors do not regard themselves as generalists so much as elementarists— probers of the fundamental questions that have plagued mankind. But over time, the St. John's faculty member comes to have as much

---

*The preceptorials have introduced an element of choice for juniors and seniors in recent years. Usually eighteen preceptorials are offered, lasting from mid-November to the end of January. In classes of no more than eight, upperclassmen meet to discuss a single book or scientific topic that interests them.

of a vested interest in the peculiar ordering of its curriculum as does the most specialized biochemist. Changes come on a small scale, and the list of Great Books is only slowly revised. Scott Buchanan argued that there should be a continuous, vigorous argument among the faculty to reassess the texts that the college's program is built upon. But the demands of doing what exists well leave little energy for inventing what ought to be. Some suggestions for major departures were made when the Santa Fe Campus was opened in 1964, but they were staunchly resisted. Only architecturally did the new college make a bow to the local landscape. Proposals to introduce anthropology, Spanish, or local art forms into the curriculum were quietly ignored, and veteran faculty from Annapolis were imported to oversee the replication of the original curriculum.* Sophomores in Annapolis and Santa Fe are likely to begin a discussion of Plotinus's *Fifth Ennead* on the same Monday night in November, and students often move from one campus to the other.

VI

The educational results that matter at St. John's are the paths that its alumni follow. The college claims to graduate men who, like the auxiliaries in Plato's *Republic*, have learned to live by principle, and it hopes they will achieve the wisdom to make them guardians. Yet the data that are available do not enable one to make judgments about the virtues of St. John's graduates. In the careers they choose, St. John's alumni do not appear to be greatly different from alumni elsewhere, yet one can see some of the imprint of the program in the emphasis on mathematics, law, philosophy, and teaching. A survey of alumni who had completed the program by 1961 showed that 60 percent had entered graduate or professional schools. In 1975, about 65 percent of Annapolis graduates and 60 percent of those at Santa Fe pursued full-time graduate study in the year after graduation; this is a high ratio, compared with the 53 percent who go on to further study at Princeton or the 46 percent at Amherst. But about 90 percent of the Princeton freshmen eventually graduate whereas about 50 percent drop out before graduation at St. John's. Of those oriented

---

*Only those who are prepared to make extraordinary efforts to be innovative in their teaching can afford to be critical of St. John's conservatism. The vested interest in the curriculum as it stands is understandable and, in terms of economy of time and effort, defensible. Nor should we imply that there is no change. As we have indicated earlier, books have been dropped and added, and other aspects of the curriculum have been modified.

to graduate school, the greatest numbers are found in law, mathematics, philosophy, education, and theology. Nearly one-fourth of all graduates chose careers in business and industry, 20 percent in teaching, 13 percent in government or law, 5 percent in the ministry and social work, 3 percent in medicine, 2 percent in library science. The college says nothing specific about producing misfits, but it does note in a 1964 self-evaluation that graduates experience "difficulty in choosing a field of study or a life career. It has not been unusual for a graduate to make two or even three false starts before finding himself."[49] Without having made a precise inquiry, we would guess that one has a better chance of having a discussion about Kant and Plato with one's waiter at an Annapolis restaurant than in almost any other city in the country.

Of course, St. John's would not make its case on vocational grounds. Quite the contrary, it admits that its graduates are at a disadvantage in a national job market where the greatest financial rewards go to the highly trained specialist. But they insist this is a short-term nonutility, and that the so-called thinking skills of the liberal arts will prove more truly useful in the long run.

One of the clearest effects of the St. John's program flows from its prescribed nature. While many students rebel and leave, others are thankful that they were not permitted to elect against mathematics or the Great Books. We are reminded of a girl who transferred to St. John's from the Philadelphia School of the Arts and who had always felt inept at any form of mathematics. She told us that she learned at St. John's that she was not so much inept as made to feel inept by insensitive earlier teaching. Forced to confront mathematics anew, she learned not only to master it, but to enjoy it, gaining in the process a new sense of confidence in her ability to learn new skills and reappraise old fears.

Of course it is difficult to generalize about such issues, and the research on the effects and impact of attending college in general is inconclusive.[50] Some of the most revealing insights about the impact of the St. John's program are found in the report of a self-study that was funded by the Ford Foundation in 1955. While there have been some changes in the past two decades, partly in response to alumni criticisms, the report remains one of the most informed commentaries about the program. As a part of the study, a seven-page questionnaire was sent to the nearly 600 alumni. About one-third replied, with responses proportionately distributed between graduates and nongraduates.

In general, alumni had a good opinion of St. John's, although the two-thirds of the sample who did not respond may have been less

sanguine. To the question "What are your present feelings and convictions about the St. John's program?," only 6 of 144 respondents
said they felt negative or hostile; 121 expressed approval. Seventy-
five percent firmly opposed the possibility of introducing electives.
One-third of those replying to the questionnaire "expressed complete
satisfaction with the present distribution of emphasis in the program."
Most often cited as an advantage of having attended St. John's (by
32 alumni) was "the ability to face, analyze, and solve problems
dealing with unfamiliar data."

But while the overwhelming majority of the alumni had good
feelings about the program in general, about half saw distinct disadvantages—most significantly, their lack at graduation of any specialized skills. The laboratory program (since revised but still a
source of complaint) came in for the harshest criticism. Of the 126
respondents, 105 said the laboratory experience was unsatisfactory.
A typical comment was, "I felt the victim of chaos, a lack of direction, and at times poor instruction. The efforts made to correlate
with the rest of the Program seemed silly." Another comment:
"I acquired at St. John's a certain revulsion to much of the natural
sciences that would be hard to overcome." Another said, "It is not
research, and it is perhaps a waste of everyone's time to ask students
to repeat routine experiments."

Sixty percent of those who answered the question about the language program felt that it was deficient in modern linguistics and
semantics. Half felt the language tutorials did not increase their
ability to read and understand poetry. They emphasized again and
again the need for more writing and for more modern forms of
mathematics. Twenty-three of 67 who used mathematics in their job
said that what they had learned at St. John's was not adequate. And
they found the college least successful in giving "direction to the
students' ambitions" and in "showing the relations between ideas
and the contemporary world."

The head of an educational foundation wrote that St. John's was
"Most successful in providing a perspective on our time and the basis
from which to judge and appreciate its values, assumptions and goals.
It is least successful in developing with precision those skills which
sharpen criticism and give form to invention and creative thought." A
researcher praised St. John's for "developing certain general attitudes,
such as a willingness to face the most difficult problems head-on and
the ability to resist facile, authoritative solutions. It is least successful in dealing with matters of fact and perhaps fails to realize sufficiently the importance of a broad factual sub-stratum in every field
of knowledge."

A librarian noted that St. John's was:

Most successful in bringing about the experience of "spontaneous learning" . . . This experience is the generator of a driving engine that can either bless or curse an individual for the rest of his life so long as his brain cells do not deteriorate. I am not thinking here so much about the content of the "spontaneous learning" experience as of the experience itself . . . It is this that many college graduates have never experienced, or if they did, it happened so few times that it left no impression on their intellectual and emotional memory . . . It was least successful in orienting the student to modern science and modern logics . . . It seems to me that a student could have done excellently in his work so far as the 1890's and from that time on be ridiculously naive about the state of these two fields of thought and investigation: indeed, he may be of the opinion that what has happened since 1890 is inferior to what happened before that approximate date. He may even think that modern math, sciences and logic are but a crude, superficial, awkward and illiterate interpretation of something that is old, noble and final. The student should be aware that just as his learning of the old can be a spontaneous experience, so can the discoveries and constructions of the new by our contemporaries—if he does not know that, then what is the value of "spontaneous learning"? Does it then become a refined pastime for the sons of gentlemen?

A number of comments by others as well emphasized the need for greater opportunity for the student to work on his own initiative and for more emphasis in the curriculum upon modern and contemporary thought. One comment conveyed something of St. John's prejudices even as it sought to overcome them:

There must be some time given to modern sociologists, statisticians, and political economists. These are a godless lot and mostly full of beans, but they do have something, and it takes more than an occasional lecture to evaluate them. In this one area, the Program is too parochial.

VII

In the hectic summer of 1937, Scott Buchanan wrote a prospectus of the New Program for the officials of the Rockefeller Foundation, who were impressed with his plans and offered to help underwrite them. But when he learned that the foundation wanted to monitor his experiment Buchanan refused the grant. He said that St. John's could not be assessed in conventional ways and that such an evaluation "would confuse and distort the sharp critical judgments we would need to make in maintaining our course."[51] That fear of being misunderstood continues to be a live concern at St. John's, and it sometimes exhibits itself in a prickly attitude toward visitors. Tutors are skeptical that others can appreciate what it is they are about and, like Buchanan, doubt the sensibilities of the assessors. We suspect that, in the early stages of our inquiry, St. John's latent hostility toward social scientists may have biased our own view in spite of our efforts to maintain an open attitude. The college takes a visitor's measure even more intently than the visitor takes its measure. St. John's departs so drastically from what passes as common sense in the world outside, and the tutors make such a sacrifice to stay there, that they understandably have their guard up against criticism. Like any sect that regards the supposed mainstream as not only powerful but also in some measure seductive, they find criticism the more perilous when it comes from apparent sympathizers. In fact, they are skeptical that there can truly be sympathetic outsiders. They remain heretical in asking of those who would seek to understand the college a willing suspension of disbelief.

St. John's is monastic in its disappointment with the world: its moral scrupulousness and high standards impress. Yet it is also oppressive in its dogmatism and its contempt for the world's "cheap and obvious standards."[52] It takes "little account of the contingencies of the single human soul."[53] There is but one measure, the platinum yardstick of The Program. Its etchings can be read only by those who are privy to its secrets, to whom they will tell how far the student has climbed out of Plato's cave. St. John's has been harsh in its condemnation of the sins of specialism elsewhere, but few of its own faculty seem troubled by the degree to which they have a vested interest in the particular set of books and exercises that make up the St. John's program.*

---

*We suspect that the really important lessons the college has to teach can be accomplished in two years, and that many students would profit from specialization and the responsibility of choice in the last half of their stay. Students need an opportunity to define and pursue a question in a more variegated context, not just to work with the pieces within the St. John's puzzle. The high dropout rate in the early years suggests that many students reach the same conclusion. Perhaps the college should offer a three-year B.A. for some of its own students, and a master's degree for those who have specialized elsewhere and wish to sit at St. John's high table for a year. It does award a Master of Arts to a tutor who has taught two years at St. John's, and the

As we have already indicated, some students emerge from completion of the arduous St. John's program with greatly increased self-confidence, others with troubling questions and doubts about the program and, more importantly, about themselves. Perhaps too many students learn at St. John's that they are failures—that they can never bridge the distance that separates them from the masters. But in an epoch such as our own, when the once aristocratic concept of genius has become democratized and everyone is urged to exalt his "creativity," St. John's provides a remedy—a joyfully administered cathartic in the hands of some tutors—for hubris. The willing subordination at St. John's of what Quentin Anderson has termed "the imperial self" is in this cultural context a valuable countersymbol.

St. John's is unique and remarkable. Its community is founded on a radical faith in the ability of liberal education to teach men and women to think for themselves and to become conscious of their social and moral obligations. It has embodied a vision and fostered a dialectic in the culture because it has been there to be criticized. It has kept alive an ideal of the liberal arts and a concern for the wholeness of intellectual experience in a pure form. It has been a kind of conscience of the liberal-arts colleges, a goad to all of higher education, and a declaration about how men should live.

college has designed a program on the Santa Fe campus that enables high-school teachers to earn a master's in three summers. In response to our judgment about the loss of opportunities for specialization, Dean Robert Neidorf replied: "We make no pretense to treat everything worth studying; we do endeavor to treat only things worth studying."

The Communal-Expressives

Kresge College at Santa Cruz

4

While its specific academic emphasis is "man and his environment," Santa Cruz's sixth liberal arts college will explore educational innovation through a human relations approach. Just as man's natural environment is the result of a delicate balance and interdependency, so the excitement and creativity of a learning environment is the result of open, direct and explicit relationships.

Catalog statement announcing the opening of Kresge College, 1970

Kresge has a certain image on campus, as the "touchy-feely" college— a college which few people take seriously. One Kresge faculty member related an incident to us about a meeting with her board of study, when she simply said the word "Kresge," and the entire room was filled with laughter. Another professor, recently faced with an overcrowded classroom at Stevenson College, found out that there was a larger room available at Kresge. But again, at the suggestion of a move to Kresge, his class broke out in spontaneous laughter.

City on a Hill Press, October 17, 1974

If Kresge College could have adopted the name of its patron saint rather than its benefactor, it would have been called Carl Rogers College. Rarely has a college derived as directly from the ideals of a contemporary movement as did Kresge, which drew its inspiration from the encounter or sensitivity-training movement associated with the work of Carl Rogers. To critics of that movement, the name Kresge would ironically describe the popular merchandising of traditional therapies, and they would ridicule the T-group movement as a dime-store crusade that promises happiness in a bag of jelly beans.

Often misunderstood, its high hopes vulnerable to parody, Kresge became an occasion of laughter on its own campus at the university of California at Santa Cruz. Yet it is easier to laugh at the excesses of the T-group movement than to understand the intentions of the founders of Kresge College and to discern the actual effects of an experiment designed in part to test whether men and women can live together more openly and cooperatively. Kresge, an institution temporarily transformed by the vapors that arose from a heady movement, is perhaps the most volatile of the experiments described in this volume. Kresge inhaled deeply and, viewed from traditional academic perspectives, "went under" for a time. But the experiment held sway over the whole college for only a few years and was much attenuated by the time this book went to press in 1977. The communal-expressives at Kresge retreated to occupy the "Corner of the College," which in later years claimed the loyalties of most of the devotees of the original experiment but only a minority of the total faculty.

The ethos of the early days continued to permeate the Kresge style, and the college continued to be perceived as one of the most distinctive on the campus. Although some laughed, Kresge was originally seen from within Santa Cruz as its own most avant-garde experiment, providing a defense against charges of incrementalism (reminding us of a comment made by a faculty member at Hampshire College in Massachusetts, who was eager to assure us that it was a "real experiment," not just "Amherst College with long hair"). Although Kresge has not been the only experiment at Santa Cruz, it is the only college there that qualifies as a genuine telic reform. Since most of the eight colleges at Santa Cruz must be classified as popular, or "means" reforms, the general development of the campus is treated in Chapter 8 of Part II of this book, and the reader is referred there for a wide-angled view of the setting in which Kresge was placed.

Kresge's founders had a vision of ends that was radically at odds with the norms of the contemporary multiversity, although they expressed an opposition of a profoundly different character than that which animated Scott Buchanan at St. John's. Yet, as we shall see in a moment, one of the Kresge founders had been influenced by Buchanan—still another illustration of the fascinating chains of influence among the telic reformers. Several others were closely associated with contemporary offshoots of humanistic psychology but what is remarkable is that three members of the leadership group were drawn not from the "soft" fields or the humanities but from the biological and physical sciences.

I

The founding provost of Kresge College, Robert Edgar, was a distinguished microbiologist at Cal Tech. He knew little about T-groups and related movements in humanistic psychology until Carl Rogers came to Cal Tech in 1967 to do a year-long series of workshops with faculty. Edgar sat in and soon became engrossed with new questions about teaching and the way he related to students. In fact, he felt he was not relating to students at all, but just standing at the blackboard and talking at them. And when he consciously tried to open up and relate more directly to students, he found they were afraid of him. As he thought about it, maybe he had been afraid of them, afraid of being attacked or put down; perhaps he had "poured it on" in order to silence them. (Few teachers achieve such remarkable insight or will admit to it if they do; difficulty may arise if, having reached the realization, one believes one can totally eliminate the fear.)

In an attempt to understand these anxieties Edgar spent the next two summers in personal growth exercises at the National Training Laboratories at Bethel, Maine. He began to study theories of organization and of work environments that encouraged human growth. He became convinced that one could create environments that supported growth, settings that helped persons to see larger possibilities and encouraged them to take risks. He saw analogies to science: most scientists were like scribblers in a monastery, endlessly repeating the same task. But creative science risked leaps into the unknown.

His immersion in these experiences affected work with his own graduate students. He began to attend to process in his teaching, to issues of transference, and to the affective content of language. As he grew less interested in the kind of science he had been engaged in, his own scientific production may have suffered. But he felt the students of that period were among the best he had ever had.

Edgar became absorbed in the question of the contexts for human growth, the choice, as Douglas McGregor posed it, between theory X view of the world and theory Y. Did men need to be goaded into work and high productivity through systems of reward and punishment? (McGregor's X organizations) Or could one create the grounds for growth and trust in settings in which persons would realize their fullest and most creative potential? (theory Y) Under the influence of Rogers, he approached these issues from a highly democratic, egalitarian stance, and he thought about applying his ideas by becoming master of one of the student houses at Cal Tech. Thus he was highly receptive when Dean McHenry approached him about the provostship of the sixth college at Santa Cruz. He told McHenry of the kind of radical experiment he hoped to launch, and in 1969 he came to Santa Cruz as professor of biology. In January 1970, he wrote a memo outlining his intentions:

> I believe people are creatively alive to the extent that they perceive themselves freely responsible for shaping their own destinies. This perception must be real in the sense that personal success *and* personal failure must both be possible outcomes of decisions and activities. Even benevolent intervention inhibits the growth of free and responsible behavior. To test this premise, I would like College Six to be, as much as possible, a participatory, consensual, democracy.
>
> To achieve this goal, I wish to leave as many decisions as possible to the newly forming college community. The community as a whole will create its own mechanisms for regulating collective activities. I would hope that these organizational structures would be creatively built to fill our felt needs and responsively change as our needs as a community change. By a participatory consensual democracy, I mean that all members of the community have the right to participate in decisions that will affect them and that no decision will be reached to which even one individual is opposed, whether he be provost or freshman. While this principle insures the honest valuing of the individual, it is likely to put enormous stresses on interpersonal relations and the achievement of meaningful decisions. This is where I hope the application of behavioral science skills can help the community develop open and effective communication and conflict resolution within a consensual decision-making framework. . . . Collective human activities are tremendously affected by the quality of interactions between people. I believe that placing a high priority on enhancing the quality of interpersonal interactions in the college will result in an exciting, productive and creative learning community. . . . Over the past twenty years, work in the field of applied behavioral sciences has led to the development of a variety of techniques and approaches to facilitate and improve interpersonal communication. Some but not all, of these techniques involve the use of small groups, sometimes called T-groups, sensitivity groups or encounter groups, to help people explore and extend their communication skills.
> These techniques have been developed and applied along two main lines. *Personal Growth* uses such techniques to create a climate in which individuals, through experimenting with their own behavior can learn more about themselves and develop improved ways of coping. The use of these techniques to facilitate task or goal oriented activities is often called *Organizational Development*

(OD). Following are some of the characteristics of the climate
that the OD approach attempts to achieve:

Honesty
Openness
Trust
Responsiveness
Responsibility
Empathy
Involvement

I think that in many college settings—classrooms, committees,
research groups—the achievement of such a climate requires and
should receive overt attention. Behavioral scientists skilled in these
approaches can greatly facilitate achieving these goals. I very
much want to see a concern for improving quality in interpersonal
relationships be a feature of College Six.[1]

In that original six-page memo, Edgar outlined an interdisciplinary
curriculum that would explore "urgent social and environmental
problems." The curriculum would place major emphasis on "courses
or experiences explicitly oriented toward the personal growth of the
individual." He intended to appoint two persons to help him plan
the college that year: one to plan the curriculum in the environmental sciences, the other to provide leadership in personal growth and
T-group process. He did not find the environmental scientist he
sought, but he knew he wanted Michael Kahn to shape Kresge's
focus on T-group process.

Edgar had met Kahn at Bethel, Maine, where he had participated
in Kahn's advanced personal growth workshop. Like Edgar, Kahn
had a traditional education. He earned his first degree at Harvard
in comparative literature. After acting eight years in the Hedgerow
Theatre Company, Kahn was encouraged by friends to join Scott
Buchanan's seminars at the World Government Foundation. He remembers that when Harris Wofford (who later became president of
the experimental college at Old Westbury, New York) had just returned with great excitement from a journey to India, Scott Buchanan
had said, "Now is the time to stop everything else and read Toynbee
for a year." Kahn once asked Buchanan what a man should do to be
saved, and Buchanan answered, "That is not the problem; the problem is, what do we read next?" Kahn decided to stay at the World
Government Foundation and spent the year with Buchanan, Wofford,
Stringfellow Barr, Steve Benedict, and others reading all twelve volumes of Toynbee.

That year was worth more than all his undergraduate education
at Harvard, Kahn told us sitting on a couch in his office, barefoot,

a deeply tanned guru confident his disciples would listen. His teaching was greatly influenced by Buchanan, although Buchanan's friends would find ludicrous the mere suggestion of an affinity with T-groups. Buchanan taught him to listen for deeper levels of communication. Reading Toynbee convinced him to read psychology, so he returned to Harvard for a Ph.D. There he met Timothy Leary, then a lecturer in the Department of Social Relations. "I adore him," he said. "He's one of the great martyrs of the culture." It was Leary who helped him to realize that "I can't spend my life fighting off your consciousness, wall you out, because to hold you off deprives me."

Kahn taught at Harvard, then at Yale and the University of Texas. Returning from a year's study of Zen in Japan, he agreed to help Edgar start Kresge College. Shortly before, he had visited John Boettiger, a faculty friend at Hampshire College in Amherst, Massachusetts; Kahn concluded that Kresge might usefully adapt the student contract method that had been developed at Hampshire.

Edgar and Kahn had become close friends as a result of Edgar's participation in Kahn's Bethel workshop. In Kahn's paper, "The Return of the Repressed,"[2] he described some of the ingredients: a series of body-movement exercises, finger painting, working with clay and psychodrama techniques, much of which he later rejected as too manipulative. He also began to see through "my own joy of being worshipped by the group," adding that occasionally he missed it, "because it's nice to be worshipped."

Wasn't democracy in such a group partially illusory, with the "nondirective" leader making it appear that his mandate arose spontaneously from the group? we interjected. He agreed that this tension certainly had become evident in later stages at Kresge, when extension of democratic process to newcomers threatened the visions of the founding cadre. But, at least initially, the founders were confident that flexible, organic growth could be achieved in harmony with their ideals.

Kahn and Edgar wanted Kresge to be a "straight-talk community" where, having explored its norms, one would "find them so attractive and rewarding one wouldn't want to go back to the old ones." An early memo on T-groups at Kresge expanded on this idea:

> Kresge was begun in the hope that it would be a *straight-talk* community. A straight-talk community means to us that the members talk straight and listen straight to each other. In such a community I may choose not to interact with you, but if and when I *do* choose to be with you, you have my assurance that I will try to be straight with you. When I talk to you I will tell you what I'm feeling, wanting, needing, fearing. I won't try to manipulate

you. When you talk to me I will try to listen straight to you and not lay a lot of things on you that you're not saying.

Since none of us on the training staff have ever yet lived in such a community (though we have desperately wanted to) we conclude that it doesn't just happen, but must be worked for, sweated for, suffered for. The original Kresge vision includes the belief that this dream of a straight-talk community was worth the sweat and tears. Thus we see our task of helping the community develop a way of teaching itself to pursue this dream. The best device we know for training ourselves to talk straight is the T-group . . . We believe the T-group is a major discovery in the history of applied behavioral science and we are trying to find out where it is and isn't useful in the development of Kresge.[3]

The memorandum defined "T-group" as a "sensitivity-training group" of persons who meet together for the purposes of exploring mutual feelings and interactions. Kahn stressed that the founders believed they were rooted in the right wing of the movement with its roots in the interpersonal skill training for business executives rather than in the radical wing which sometimes encouraged quick sex and aggression. The memo appealed for an eventual "withering away of the T-group," when the day comes that such techniques will be unnecessary "because the community will be living and working and interacting in such a way that whenever a feeling is appropriate it can be shared and whenever one is shared it can be accepted." The memo ended with a list of ten Barriers to Communication which were to be avoided if "human interaction" was not to turn "into a one-up game." These became known at Kresge as the Ten Combandments of T-grouping:

1. *Do not assume we know anyone's feelings except our own.* Each person is the world's sole expert on his own feelings. Thus telling another person what is going on in his head is mere speculation and is likely to lead to defensive behaviour on his part. . . . This is in marked contrast to the psychoanalytic ethic which maintains that the person is the last to know about his own feelings.

2. *Do not deal in opinions rather than feelings.* The statement of ideas and beliefs is very apt to cause a barrier in interpersonal interaction, whereas the statement of feelings is often the way around the barrier. My opinions are a matter of opinion; my feelings are a matter of incontrovertible, empirical fact. . . .

3. *On asking questions.* One of the most difficult roadblocks is question-asking. We all do it so much and we all have come to

think of it as an innocent and helpful way to carry on an interaction. It turns out that very often asking a question is a way to get the other person to reveal his feelings before you reveal yours. . . . This barrier is circumvented by each of us laying our own feelings on the line before we ask the other person to.

4. *Attend to the here and now.* It is more helpful to the interaction if we stay in the here and now. One of the easiest kinds of roadblocks to real communication is to talk about other times, other places, other people, as a way of avoiding the complexities of confronting the feeling happening at this time and this place.

5. *Don't be defensive.* We define *defensiveness* as refusing to listen to and accept another person's feelings about you. (Please note again how different this is than accepting his *opinions* about you.) When you tell me your feelings, I am often tempted to reply, "That's your problem," but that is not a meaningful statement. It is not anybody's *problem*, it is merely you honoring me by sharing your feelings with me. Your feelings are always useful information for me to have and my refusing to accept them is elementary one-upmanship.

6. *Don't be evaluative and judgmental.* We use the word *feedback* to describe one person sharing with another the effect that the other has upon him. This can raise all sorts of barriers unless it is given in terms which are nonevaluative, nonjudgmental, and in terms of one's own feelings.

7. *Avoid indirect confrontation.* Initiating direct confrontation is almost always valuable; indirect or bootlegged confrontation is self-protective and only serves to confuse. The most common form of this is taking a quick dig at somebody in passing while you are ostensibly occupied elsewhere.

8. *Refusing to risk self-exposure, disapproval, or rejection.* Risk-taking and self-exposure are worthwhile both to the individual and the group. They promote disarmament.

9. *Don't take aggressive advantage of another's self-exposure.* Risk-taking and self-exposure in others need support. I must never use another's self-exposure as a chance to one-up him. At such moments he is particularly vulnerable.

10. *Don't use "openness" as a weapon.* Freedom and truth and openness do not have absolute value and can be senselessly destructive if they are not employed in a context of sensitive responsibility for the other.

What these rules do, of course, is to completely shake the conventions of ordinary academic discourse: denying speculation, putting inquiry on the defensive, ruling out historical analogies, and disallowing irony or other forms of indirection. Their rejection of psychoanalysis was, of course, far too simplistic. Psychoanalysts use dream interpretation precisely because we often do not know our own feelings, because it is so hard to discover what they are; a capable analyst uses dreams as clues, not to force an interpretation, but to suggest one to see if it connects with the patient's conscious feeling. But what was striking was that these rules were nothing like a conversation with Kahn, a delightful man whose responses are laced with ironic asides, who enjoys inquiry and relishes debate. Why did these documents betray that reality? Was this an example of a utopian willing to live within the shell of the old sensibility when necessary, but only to protect the development of new forms of discourse within? That interpretation seems a touch too fanciful. Yet there was, particularly in the early days, a feeling that the burdens of the "old culture" must be thrown off to be born anew. The "commandments" concluded with an appeal to risk vulnerability, to live "unarmed":

> These barriers are very difficult to give up. They are not erected by accident. They are erected because the culture has taught us that it is dangerous to interact without their protection. The cultural lesson is that we must, whenever possible, be in the superior or victorious or one-up position, because the only alternative is to be one-down and humiliated. Therefore, so much of our interaction in the everyday world consists of protecting ourselves against being one-down. Joining a group intent on removing the roadblocks or barriers is frightening because when we stop trying to be constantly one-up we have in effect disarmed, and that is apt to make us feel vulnerable and exposed. To live with that vulnerability requires either considerable trust in the goodwill of our neighbors or else the discovery that the armament burden costs more than it's worth. We believe that sensitivity training is only successful when it provides each individual with a genuine choice about just how unarmed he wants to live in any given situation.

Kahn told us that Edgar stressed from the outset that Kresge was to be this kind of straight-talk college with a strong environmental focus. Although they later became estranged, Kahn felt at that time that Edgar was "touched by the magic fire." Kahn's voice rose in intensity and his arms raised in emphasis. "To me he was a poetic genius and I would follow him anywhere." Fresh from his immersion in Zen, Kahn wanted the religious metaphor to be central at Kresge, but when Edgar disagreed he accepted his vision. At that point Edgar told him he feared the religious metaphor and felt the "bishop" would be stronger than the "king." But they worked past this problem—"We are a marvelous team. We had tremendous energy. We had offices side by side down in the student apartments and we worked around the clock, 10 to 12 hours a day. We were just passionately involved."

Kahn wanted Kresge to be a community of "real trust, a caring community, a place where we took care of each other, looked out for each other, loved one another. I was willing to use any experience to help us get there: T-groups, micro-labs, workshops, psychodrama, anything." How would they know if it succeeded? "If you get high on LSD and walk into the dining room and sit down anywhere and people there would be your family and they would take care of you, and they would talk straight to you."

"Straight talk" became a job requirement. Kahn and Edgar spent much of their time in that first year hiring new faculty. "We asked them straight out would they be willing to play the straight-talk game and to go away for a weekend T-group experience. If they said no we didn't hire them."

Yet some who were ambivalent, and a few who were opposed, to these requirements slipped through. And more in later years. A faculty member who had left wrote to us later: "Faculty solidarity was felt to be essential to the success of the Kresge experiment. A number of faculty, including myself, and in several cases faculty wives, were subjected to pressure . . . to conform to the plans of the founders."[4]

Kahn often felt his intentions were misunderstood. He believed in academic standards, and the Scott Buchanan side of him was right-wing, so to speak. Straight talk was a way of establishing a special kind of community, but it was to be an intellectual community. "Bob Edgar and I both felt that every university we were ever in was anti-intellectual, that people were so jealous and competitive and insecure that they weren't able to really give themselves in intellectual exchange. If we were always in the game of comparing our consciousness with someone else or worrying that theirs is better, we couldn't have an ideal teaching and learning relationship. We wanted to build a pro-intellectual college where people cared about each other and where they weren't playing sick competitive games."

But at Santa Cruz faculty had to be hired by both a college and a department (called Boards of Study there), and frequently the departments sought those "who wanted to bring in highly competitive graduate students who were already mired deep in the traditional academic game." Kahn did not want Kresge to attract students who would waste their four years navel watching or grooving on the beach. Nor did he want "people who had castrated themselves and who were walking heads without bodies." Henry Hilgard, a faculty member who became an important influence in the founding of the college, was at first enraged by that image and accused Kahn of portraying intellectuals as castrati.

A student who directed us to Henry Hilgard said he was one of the most admired and approachable faculty members at Kresge, and one of those who "really ran things." Hilgard invited us into his office, a stunning room rising to a peak at least twenty-five feet high from which hung a huge bright weaving. He had gone to Harvard, received an M.D. at Stanford, and then decided he wanted to do research, which led him to Minnesota for a Ph.D. in biology. As a National Institutes of Health postdoctoral fellow, he came originally to Crown College, Santa Cruz's most traditional college, with a grant to do heart research.

Kresge was in the middle of its planning year when Hilgard heard about the embryo college from the vice-chancellor for the sciences, the physicist Matthew Sands, who later gave up that post to join the Kresge experiment himself. One Friday afternoon Edgar invited Hilgard to a planning retreat to begin that evening. Hilgard, angry at first to be invited so late (and saying as an aside that invitations are still a problem in a college committed to "spontaneity"), decided to cancel other plans. At the retreat, they cooked their own food, talked, and participated in some typical "touchy-feely exercises." Some of those who had come to try out the Kresge style were uncomfortable with this, but Hilgard liked it, adding in a matter-of-fact way that he was generally a self-confident person who did not fear revealing himself. He remembered how angry he had become at Kahn, challenging what he thought to be Kahn's view that "Santa Cruz was mostly a lot of academics doing a lot of bull-shit academic stuff and building their own careers, and at Kresge they wanted to build a caring community and shuck all that." He came to see that Kahn was not anti-intellectual in the way he first thought, but he wondered as he attended other planning sessions whether such a radical experiment would be viable even with Santa Cruz's latitude.

In the next quarter Hilgard became a participating faculty member in the "Creating Kresge College" course in which forty students had enrolled. They organized themselves in five family groups, later to be called kin groups. "This was so much better than my previous experience of advising students who came in on tip toes in fear and trembling to get you to sign their card." The kind of openness the

kin groups established was much healthier, and one got to know the
students in a totally different way, he felt.

We had met Carol Proudfoot outside Hilgard's office and were
eager to talk with her, as students and faculty had frequently mentioned her as a powerful influence in the founding of the college.
She said she would be willing to talk with us, but she did not seem
eager to do so and it took us several days to catch up with her. She
would make an appontment to meet us at a particular spot—say the
lawn near the sauna—and at the appointed time a student would
show up and say she couldn't be there, or a note on her door would
tell us to come another day. This all seemed like some kind of testing, and we even wondered whether this Sioux woman watched in
secret as we discovered the postponements. But when the meeting
did come it was relaxed, and there seemed to be good reasons for
the broken appointments. Dressed in a loose shirt and jeans, she
talked openly about her childhood on a Sioux reservation, and her
attendance at a Bureau of Indian Affairs residential school, which
she said gave her an early sense of what it meant to be oppressed.

After high school, she entered Rice, transferring later to the University of Texas at Austin, where she began to get involved in the
radical movement. She worked with the SDS in Ann Arbor, before
going to Harvard to do a Ph.D., taking courses in social psychology
and ethics. By 1968 she was worrying about the growing destructiveness of the radical movement. She felt a kind of corruption seep-
ing in, and she told David Dellinger that she felt it was harder and
harder for poets and artists to remain involved. A friend was killed
in the Newark riots. "Something inside me then flipped. I realized
I didn't want to be in this place . . ." She went to live with friends
in California, south of Mendocino. "I wanted to be alone. I spent
three months making a teepee. I paid attention to natural things. I
really burrowed down in the earth, got closer to the earth."

After that experience, she decided to go to a personal growth lab
where she met John and Joyce Weir. It had a great impact on her,
and the Weirs invited her to help them lead a special workshop at
Bethel for the international community. Warren Bennis was there,
she remembers, talking about the university of social change he was
seeking to invent. The following summer she went to an I-Ching lab,
connecting I-Ching with her Indian roots.

Not long after that Michael Kahn wrote to her, asking her to come
to Kresge to help lead the first orientation program. "It was heady,
powerful stuff. I liked Bob Edgar a lot." Later Edgar was troubled
and concerned that the college was developing in ways that were not

congruent with his own vision, yet he did not want to impose a hier-archial model, she thought. "I said it didn't have to be hierarchial, and talked about the early Christian communities, and about other ways of sharing sacred ground."

The following spring Edgar wrote asking if she wanted to come to Kresge as a poet in residence or counselor. "So I came down, and talked with him. We worked my fears. I felt something awful right about it, . . . yet I dreaded the idea of coming back to the university and getting caught up in the pace of bureaucratic bullshit . . . We . . . decided to throw the *I Ching* about whether I should come. . . . It talked about working with a wise ruler. It talked about providing nourishment to those who rule . . . It was really exciting to me. I felt that maybe it was time to share my powers, to grow with that, so I knew it was time to leave and this was the place to go."

Carol Proudfoot became counselor to the students and ceremonial leader. When it came time to move from the temporary quarters in the married student apartments to the newly built college on the slopes above, each of the kin groups stood in a circle around a bon-fire holding hands while they burned their unwanted possessions. When the fires died, they walked single file, holding hands, up through the woods to their new home. They were silent, their faces enrap-tured. Forcing students to choose what to throw away and what to keep for the journey was an important theme at Kresge. "We also make it difficult for students to figure out what college is all about," Carol said. "There's no required major here and we ask students what the hell they're in college for anyway." The stresses at Kresge created tensions of their own, and she worked closely with Michael Kahn, Matthew Sands, and others in developing peer counseling.

Matthew Sands came to Santa Cruz in 1969 as vice-chancellor of the sciences and was first associated with Merrill College, resigning that position to become a self-taught T-group leader at Kresge in 1970. Sands taught at M.I.T. after earning his doctorate there and coauthored a book on experimental electronics. At Cal Tech, he, like Edgar, had become "a fan of Carl Rogers and a believer in student-directed learning."

Sands visualized Kresge as three interrelated experiments: (1) in student-directed learning; (2) in a participatory style of governance; and (3) in the development of a more cooperative and less compe-titive life-style. Our first interview with Sands got off to a bad start when we asked him whether some students didn't label all hard work and striving as competitive activity, and therefore as bad, as a way to mask indolence. This angered him, and he said the students were generally right to see the world as selfishly competitive. But, wasn't there a lot of hard work to be done—creating Santa Cruz itself, for example? "Perhaps," he said, cooling a bit, but it was "mostly a big game and big shuck and people pretended to be solving problems but they were really out to line their pockets." Who were these indolent students, anyway? he asked. We described several, and he said he had known students like that at Cal Tech and M.I.T., too. We too had known students elsewhere who fashioned an undergraduate career by rewriting one paper, a four-year variation on a theme. But students could also use the T-group rhetoric as a long goof-off, we felt. He replied sardonically that there was no way he knew to prevent some students from goofing off. Some students in T-groups might develop leprosy. Had we seen any students with leprosy?

We were talking at cocktails at Sands's house on a sun deck that hung precariously over a high cliff. We felt the interview had gone badly, that Sands was stereotyping the big bad world that he had left; yet we had perhaps set him off with our own stereotype about masked indolence. At dinner, cooked by a student member of his kin group, we proceeded more cautiously. Driving back to the college, Sands surprised us by saying he was disappointed. He had hoped for an encounter but we hadn't quite engaged, had we?

Edgar, Kahn, Hilgard, Proudfoot, and Sands represent the founding core at Kresge. With the exception of Hilgard, they were directly influenced by the Rogerian wing of the encounter and T-group movement. They had experienced a change in their own consciousness, and Edgar, Sands, and Kahn had gone through a career transformation. They had sacrificed much and believed deeply in the educational potential of the movement. They bespoke the hope and innocence, very "American" in origin, of a nation that has forgotten Calvinism, fatalistic Catholicism, and other forms of caution in a country of an open frontier. They reflected an America in which many people believe that character is so malleable that it can really be altered by T-groups or by the National Training Laboratories (no doubt behavior can be altered somewhat and character a little), and that organizations can change to Douglas McGregor's theory Y without powerful precautions against the unscrupulous. Their own dramatic transformations had released such personal joy that their evangelism was nearly unbounded. And Kresge College gave them a magnificent opportunity to shape an institution around these newfound values. Though the founders conveyed their dream in the modern jargon of the T-group, it was a recurrent dream in America, reflecting a profound hopefulness about the redeeming power of educational communities. Their sense of mission seemed to be part of what David Cohen has called "a mad rush to repair the trauma of becoming modern."*

Among the others who came early and who played significant roles in shaping the ethos of the college was the former monk and poet Brother Antoninus, laicized as William Everson. While still a Dominican monk, he had met Kahn at an encounter session for theologians that Kahn had led at Esalen in 1968. A Jungian, Everson believes that college is a setting where one discovers one's vocation, a vocation which is "a calling and a surrender." Speaking slowly, stroking a long white beard and looking like Moses in denim and a sombrero, Everson told us the Kresge process enabled students to reach into the subconscious, "their still-point," and discover their true archetype in a Jungian sense. The crux of the college was to open students to that choice and commitment.

At the faculty wine party where we met Everson, we met David Kliger, a young chemist who had joined the college in the first full year. He had earned his first degree at Rutgers, received his doctorate at Cornell, and had spent two postgraduate years at Harvard before coming to Kresge. Kliger was committed to the ideals of the college. He was active in the central Community Affairs Committee, although he worried that the burdens Kresge imposed on the faculty might hinder his research. Marcia Millman was another early recruit. After Brandeis she had pursued graduate work at Yale but finding Yale uncongenial, had returned to Brandeis. After writing her thesis there on small group interactions, she became a faculty member who also led T-groups at Kresge. Philip Slater also became a consultant at Kresge and spent two terms on the faculty in 1976. Among early consultants from Esalen and the National Training Laboratories were Otis S. Farry, David R. Peters, Ted Kroeber, Sherman Kingsbury, and Margaret Rioch. They came to lead groups, plan rituals and orientation programs, and work with students and faculty on issues of governance.

Most of these consultants came from the more conservative group-dynamics wing of the T-group movement. But a few from Esalen

*In a perceptive essay, David Cohen writes of the way in which, early in the nineteenth century, "the school's mission came to be understood as both repairing loss and creating equality . . . schools, the reformers thought, would recreate social solidarity by remaking personal values, sentiments and ideas." American society was less stratified than the European and more deeply penetrated by democratic ideas, "as a result in seeking to preserve traditional values, they turned naturally to the rational design of new institutions and to the conscious construction of social morality." David Cohen, "Loss as a Theme in Social Policy," *Harvard Educational Review*, 46 no. 4 (November 1976):558–59.

favored the more dramatic Schutzian joy and marathon encounter approaches.[5] There has always been a tension in the movement between short-lived intimacy and expressiveness on the one hand, and long-term commitment to growth and change, on the other.

Edgar had a year in 1969–70 to read and think about the shape of Kresge College. At the end of that period, he wrote a memo expressing his uneasiness about the tensions between quick-won intimacy and more permanent community. Intimacy, he argued, was a "sense of closeness and experiencing one another which reduces, for a time at least, existential loneliness." But intimacy may be very temporary and limited compared to community, "which means going someplace together. It means sharing common goals and purposes, and common experiences . . . community is the ability of the people to collaborate, to share, to give something of themselves to one another toward a common objective."[6]

II

The year 1970–71 was known as the planning year, when Robert Edgar and Michael Kahn, joined mid-way in the year by Matthew Sands, initiated a year-long course called "Creating Kresge College." About twenty-five students registered in the first quarter, and nearly forty were enrolled by the end of the year. It was a year of experimenting with a variety of T-group and encounter styles, curricular planning, and student-faculty retreats. The fall quarter began with a retreat at a Boy Scout camp in the woods near Felton. Edgar remembers a number of nonverbal exercises, including one in which walks through the woods were taken with one person leading the other by the hand and silently pointing things out. Edgar joined a Native American woman. He stumbled and couldn't wait to get back on the road. But when it was her turn to lead she helped him experience the woods in a way he had never seen them before—as friendly and comforting; and he felt some of his fearfulness slip away. Students in the course helped to select the first-year faculty and worked with architects in an attempt to translate emerging thoughts about kin groups and T-group process into a workable and meaningful blueprint for living. The plan that resulted put groups of four to eight students into each apartment (there was no dining hall). Students in contiguous apartments were formed into kin groups. The most adventurous architectural expressions of the Kresge ethos were the octets—huge, loftlike living spaces, rising in a spiral on three levels and housing eight students. The first level was usually a kitchen-eating area, and the upper two levels were devoted to sleeping, working, and living. The octets contained no inner walls or partitions. There were no private spaces, with the exception of lockers lining the walls opposite two shower stalls in a basement room. As with other aspects of Kresge life, each student was forced to decide what balance to strike between his needs for privacy and demands for more communal sharing. Some later moved into regular apartments, others eventually built partitions, and a few preserved the unstructured space.

Faculty and students in the "Creating Kresge" course also worked on the themes of the community, designing orientation week and developing the philosophy of what was at first known as the "family unit" and later as the kin group. An early expression of the intentions of the orientation period follows:

> There will be a two-week orientation at the beginning of each year. Every member of the college, freshman to faculty, will be required to participate full time. The second week will be required for all freshmen and sophomores, and everyone else will be strongly encouraged to spend as much time with it as possible . . . The orientations will be an intense experience guided by a trained group of consultants. It will embody and encourage the general values and processes that wll be important at Kresge:
> 1. An open-mindedness to new ideas and approaches
> 2. An active responsible participation in your own lives and education to make them as personally meaningful as possible
> 3. A context of personal growth and creativity; and
> 4. A community spirit of sharing, of open communication and of understanding, trust and love.
>
> In addition, the orientation will be specifically intended to:
> 1. Develop the family group as the fundamental and most abiding social unit of the community
> 2. To create a total community consciousness for Kresge College; and
> 3. To open up personal sensitivity to the natural and social environment on the sensory and emotional, as well as the cognitive levels.[7]

Most students found the orientation week a positive, moving experience. Steven, a Floridian who entered Kresge after finishing a tour in the navy at San Diego, recalled it as both a frightening and powerful initiation. Orientation week began with Michael Kahn describing the dream he had for Kresge: "In this dream you didn't need to worry about being on top, people could be themselves and there wouldn't be a lot of competition and a lot of ego trips." The kin groups that met during orientation week seemed immediately beneficial to Steven, enabling him to talk to roommates about irritations and his needs for order. But at the heart of the orientation week were the exercises in the auditorium. One called for each person to physically contract into as tight and small a place as he could, and then to spread his body into as wide a space as he could manage. If the arms or legs of others were touched, they were to be explored if a participant felt like it. Another exercise directed participants to tense every muscle in the body and then relax every muscle. Yet another suggested seeking out a person in the room whom you thought ugly or irritating or who bothered you, and telling him or her why. This was followed by finding someone in the room who "turned you on" or whom you thought beautiful and telling that person why.

Steven, explaining that the exercises were optional, said he chose not to participate in the last. Mary Kay Orlandi, a new faculty member and a feminist who was not enamored of such T-group exercises, scoffed slightly at the idea of voluntariness. "I think the whole thing began with everyone lying down on the floor," she said. "Then you were told you could leave if you didn't want to participate, which would mean getting up and stepping over everyone else's bodies in order to get out."

One could, we suppose, view the orientation as a Rogerian version of jumping jacks or other warming-up exercises. They had the larger aim, of course, of binding people together in community and, in particular, of establishing kin groups, or "families," as they were called in an early planning document outlining the basic social organization at Kresge. In this original conception, each family would consist of fifteen to twenty members including the faculty advisor. The original hope was that student families would be living, working, cooking, and keeping house together:

> Thus, the family groups make an effort to establish living and working together cooperatively as the center of intensity for the entire college. We hope the close sharing relationships which can develop in such situations will be typical of the way students and faculty relate to one another. In this "home" situation where one is accepted and loved, personal problems can be worked out and one can, at times, retreat from the rigors of academic work. Academic planning and evaluation, however, will take place here, the family members being the most aware of the importance of the student's intellectual pursuits for his total existence.[8]

By July 1971, the families had been renamed kin groups. In a memorandum Robert Edgar stressed that kin groups would be voluntary and that they would be the basic "political units of the college, sending representatives to decision-making bodies." While "considerable energy would be expended to help them become close, caring interpersonal groups," academic planners decided that the kin groups would also function as the seminar units of the Kresge core course program.[9]

Kin groups were formed when 275 students and 18 faculty members arrived in the fall of 1971 for the second year of Kresge College. In the beginning, most students were randomly assigned to living units, and those in adjoining apartments had been formed into kin groups. Individual apartments were usually sex-segregated, but swaps were inevitably made as the term progressed. The groups varied in quality and intensity, and, while no account could be said to be typical, our evening with Matthew Sands's kin group can serve as an introduction.

We had gone along with Matt Sands when, two days earlier, he had knocked on the doors of the apartments of students in his kin group to see if in fact there would be a meeting that week. Some were unsure, others said yes, and no one had any objections when he asked if two guests could join them. When the night arrived, Sands and a student, Sarah, picked us up. Sarah told us Kresge had proved a joy to some and a pain to others. For her it was the "right space to be in." She was glad Kresge existed as an avenue of growth for some, even though it was no help to others. She believed with Don Juan in Carlos Castaneda's book that since every path leads nowhere you had better find a path you enjoy.

During the drive to college, Sands described a kin group that had taken a course in death. In addition to their readings and discussions they had visited a mortuary, watched an embalming, gone to a morgue, attended several funerals, talked to elderly people, and, as a final ritual,* had gone to the woods where they dug a grave

---

*The contemporary hunger for "ritual" and restoration of the warmth of the extended family or kin group has led many communal experiments in America to try to do instantly what it took centuries to develop in more traditional cultures. Susanne and Lloyd Rudolph have shown in their work on Indian family structure that extended families are functional in many ways though they also have claustrophobic or oppressive aspects. But the achievement of the right balance between the system and the people takes time. From the perspective of the Indian case, it would seem unbelievably visionary to think that one could establish similar relations by fiat—especially if one was also establishing egalitarian, democratic relations, because what makes the kin-group work in India

and one by one took turns climbing into it, being sprinkled by dirt, and having the others walk away and leave them alone in the grave for a few moments.

When we arrived at the college, about twelve students, two of them males, awaited us in the apartment. They greeted Matt Sands and Sarah, embracing each other, sometimes kissing. We were not introduced, but as people sat down, we introduced ourselves to those who sat nearby. A latecomer said the *Wizard of Oz* was on television in a few minutes. Wouldn't it be fun to watch it? Sands did not seem enthusiastic, saying he thought they were going to have a meeting, by which he presumably meant more of an encounter session. But the girl said she was dying to see it again and asked others if they would join her. Some members of the group began to stand up, and soon everyone followed her down to the commuter's lounge, where foam mattresses were pulled up in front of a color TV set. During a commercial break, someone explained that the *Wizard of Oz* was a favorite Kresge theme: Bob Edgar was the Cowardly Lion, Michael Kahn was the scarecrow, and Matt Sands was the Tin Man who didn't think he had a heart. At several points, students got up and sang and danced along with the action on the screen. At the end of the movie, two or three students rose to leave, and when Sands asked if they were going to stay for the meeting, they cheerily said no and went off. Several students dabbed wet eyes at the end of the movie, and Sands said that Dorothy had summed up the moral of Kresge College: you should follow your heart's true desire. You ought to look into yourself, discover your own feelings; it was the inward trip that mattered, not the journey to the Wizard. Sarah drew a different analogy, saying that the monkey monsters who came to attack Dorothy made her think of all the dilemmas at Kresge.

When we had drifted back to the apartment five students remained, and we sat in a circle on the floor. Margery, who had been silent earlier, began by saying that she was worried because she came from a "very together" family and felt she might never find another group to equal that. Her boyfriend had told her that she couldn't depend on her family, but had to depend on what was inside her, but she wasn't so sure. There was a silence while we all thought about this; then Sands reached over and held her hand, and said she could count on his support. After a pause, he added that in attending a summer workshop at Bethel he had discovered that you needed to

is hierarchy and authority, even though the authority may be more subtle and complex than it seems to the outsider. See Susanne H. and Lloyd I. Rudolph, "Rajput Adulthood," *Daedalus* (Spring 1976):145–67.

work hard to build those support structures, whether they were good families or good groups. Another girl in the group reached over and squeezed Margery's foot, saying she could count on her support, too. Sarah said she had been home recently and discovered "home wasn't home anymore." Either she had changed or her family had changed, or both. Anyway, she couldn't go back because whatever it was she idealized wasn't there anymore. One had to accept this and prepare for continual change throughout one's life.

After a long pause, Kathy said she wondered how people were feeling about the kin group. It was now toward the end of the second quarter, and they had not been meeting as regularly.* One or two members were not coming much at all. Margery said she was feeling the pressure of finals and wanted "a vacation from people a while." She added apologetically, "I'm really into studying and enjoying that but I hate to use that as a cop-out." Matt Sands probed in a light tone, "What are you trying to escape from? Are we getting to you?" She responded, "I guess I'm escaping from good feelings." After some further discussion about the temper of the group, Sands suggested, "Maybe we don't want to have a group anymore. Maybe it's come to an end." Kathy replied that she hoped they would not disband, that the group was terribly important for her. Sarah said she would be on leave next quarter but hoped the group would continue. Margery said that although she couldn't meet the group's payroll now, at exam time, she wanted it to go on. Kathy wondered if Margery was hurt that so few persons had come to help build a partition in her apartment though she had specifically asked for the group's help. Margery said she wasn't, that it had been a holiday weekend and when she woke up that Saturday she didn't much feel like making a wall herself.

They decided to meet again for a pot-luck supper with another kin group and to have a special session to discuss the group's future. Before breaking up, Kathy asked Sands whether he would give a course to the kin group next quarter on his specialty. "It was physics, wasn't it?" But she asked him not to give a regular physics course— she didn't think most people in the group would want that—but to pick a related topic that would be more interesting to members of the group. He seemed uneasy with her suggestion and responded that perhaps they would like to take his course in physical science.

---

*We are using what little poetic license is granted to sociologists to discuss this meeting at this point in our narrative although it actually occurred later. We had also attended a kin-group meeting during the 1971–72 year, but this meeting seems more typical to us, although it is actually drawn from our field notes of the 1973–74 academic year.

He noted that he had offered a nonphysics course for the kin group each quarter—perhaps it was more appropriate to continue with that.

After an embrace from Sands, in the Kresge fashion, we left the meeting, thinking how remarkable it was that this fifty-year-old physicist had established such easy, intimate, and seemingly honest relationships with eighteen- to twenty-year olds. He seldom asserted his authority; it was striking, for example, that he had gone along with the group decision to watch a TV movie. Perhaps, we mused, he tells students by his behavior that physics can't be making very great demands on his time or be terribly important if he can just as well watch a movie as go to a meeting. On the other hand, perhaps he wants to show students that one can be a physicist and still have time for television-watching with friends. Such willingness to "waste time" could also be a basis for gaining trust and providing access for students who might otherwise hesitate to approach an authority figure. Yet, was that a wince we noticed when Kathy treated his expertise in physics so offhandedly, something to be treated as a commodity to fit the needs of casual consumers? One could also raise the question of whether a physicist should be a T-group leader, both in terms of what he is being paid to do and what he is competent to do. That is, does he provide access to students in order for them to more fully benefit from his expertise as a physicist, or does he invite students to examine unconscious motives with a nonpsychologist? We had noticed that at this meeting the group did not proceed as a therapy group but as a support group, and Sands's role was not that of a therapist but of a sympathetic counselor who also happens to be a physicist.

Faculty kin-group leaders represented many disciplines, and each worked out his role differently, some of them embracing the T-group style while others were more hesitant. In the first full year, 225 students were formed into fourteen kin groups. Thirteen of the groups filed a report on their activities at the end of the year. Of these, five had disbanded, three continued for the year with sharply reduced participation, and five continued throughout the year at nearly full strength. The five most successful in terms of participation and longevity also had a strong academic focus, meeting once a week to discuss the readings in the Kresge core courses, though they usually did some T-grouping, but for the most part not in an intensive way. None of the groups became an active political unit; only two of them elected "representatives," and they expressed a distaste for governance and administrative issues. While the reports reflect the social aspect of the groups, and the importance of interpersonal support, such functions were apparently not sufficient to sustain kin groups that did not also have an academic focus.

We excerpt passages below from a year-end kin-group report written by a student participant. Kin Group 3 turned out to be a model of what the planners had in mind:

> We all got together during orientation. Kin group three was off and running. Our first few T-Groups were mostly reinforcements of our caring for each other and our desire to be honest and be involved with each other. A few social activities were held that first week. One was a picnic dinner at Henry Hilgard's and another was a breakfast at my apartment. The kin group seemed to generate much excitement about each other and about being at Kresge and what was in store for us the coming academic year.
>
> An agreement was made that we would continue T-grouping at least once every other week with a facilitator. We asked different facilitators each time, but we used Michael [Kahn] and Ted [Kroeber] most often. A good number of the kin group were in attendance at the T-groups, but most were mainly spectators instead of participants dealing with problems.
>
> Also included in kin group activities were academic discussions every other week based upon the readings for the core course. These didn't seem as together as they could have been, but some interesting discussions were held. Those of us taking Kresge I had written study plans and discussed them both with Bob [Edgar] and with the rest of the family.

The report goes on to detail fairly mundane matters such as "budget questions" and to recount a variety of pot-luck dinners, parties, and a "work day [when we] planted grass seed and redwood rounds and drank beer—it was fun." This easy and warm community seemed satisfying to most, although T-grouping was of concern to some:

> Towards the middle of fall quarter more people started dropping out of the T-grouping picture and a meeting was called to discuss T-grouping and the goals of the kin group as related to it. Sherman was asked to facilitate that meeting. Much complaint was voiced about how we weren't using T-groups honestly and that nothing really was accomplished during them because we were afraid to get angry with each other. Because our beginnings had been so calm and peaceful and caring, it seemed as if no one wanted to spoil the "good" relationship we all had with each other by expressing honest emotions. That meeting turned into a T-group

working problems between a couple of people and never really accomplished what we originally had gathered for.

At the end of the fall quarter we discussed our desires for the kin group's future and agreed that we wanted to work with each other in bonding our relationships. This same desire was echoed at the first few meetings winter quarter. Some in the group didn't want to T-group right away because they felt the need to re-establish trust with each other before T-grouping. Ted Kroeber was asked to be our permanent facilitator for the quarter and we met every Thursday night. One meeting we discussed goals for the family and for the college, and the role of the kin group in realizing those college goals. We saw a problem with time, and how at times we had to make decisions about what kind of time we had to put into the college. In many cases it was felt that spending the energy to keep the kin group together was the best way to keep the college together. Our goals as a kin group were to keep ourselves together and caring and in touch with each other's needs, and secondly to keep the college going. Ted suggested a series of nonverbal evenings to get us in touch with ourselves and each other, so we spent three consecutive Thursday nights doing so. The meeting after we discussed what had happened and how we felt about it. It was agreed that it had been a good time for all, and we felt very good about what had happened between us. About seventeen of us attended those evenings and that number remained fairly stable during the rest of the quarter.[10]

The evolution of Kin Group 4, titled "The History of the Alfred T. Jones and His Dog: Sasquatch Family, or the Saga of Kin-Group 4," tells of beach-party picnics, a pot-luck supper that turned into a tribal dance throughout the whole college, academic meetings to discuss readings for the core course, poetry readings, plans for a guerrilla theater, "tying up Kresge" with literally 1,000 yards of string, disenchantment with the "business and budget" matters of the college, and the group's search for "a unifying force." But eventually the group disbanded.

Our kin group started out as a group of enthusiastic people eagerly sharing an exciting new experience and willing to give of themselves to establish a close common bond. After dealing with a few crises and hasseling out some problems and decisions, meeting after meeting went by with very little happening. I personally felt very little incentive for looking for something undiscussed about myself to contribute just to provide some action. Most people settled interpersonal problems outside the group. We saw the goal of being a "supportive" group of people as a little outdated, and any other goals or projects we thought up probably wouldn't interest the group as a whole, or seemed artificially and arbitrarily imposed, and at any rate weren't implemented. The idea of using the group for continued personal growth failed—even though unanimously approved—due to the same unwillingness to open up, and the group eventually died.[11]

Of the fourteen groups, five failed that year. A common theme was a lack of purpose: "Goals seemed artificially and arbitrarily imposed" (Kin Group 1); "too great a diversity in members' needs (Group 7); "Meetings generally lacked content" (Group 9); "Conversations wandered from significant issues to gossip . . . there was very little sense of direction (Group 12); "no goals, biggest problem no direction . . ." (a kin group composed of dropouts from other kin groups). It was significant that none of these groups that failed had any sustained academic focus, and most of them did not meet as a seminar in the core course. There were also complaints that T-group pressures were resented by members in several of these groups, particularly in Group 7:

> I focus the group's problem on T-grouping, as this seems to me the group's main object of contention. Our leader, Michael Beeson [an assistant professor of mathematics who did graduate work at Stanford], was a firm believer in T-grouping, and he, along with several other enthusiastic members nobly tried to get us to T-group. However, there were some members just as strongly against it, some silent, and some who dropped out of the kin group early, because of group pressures.

One notices the attention in these reports paid to "energy level" as an important positive indicator and the corresponding fear of silence. The lack of perpetual feedback seemed threatening. How different from most traditional religious sects—particularly the Quakers, where silent contemplation is treasured. Faculty leaders of kin groups varied greatly in their commitment to T-grouping, one or two of them rejecting it or eschewing competence in that area. In this respect, too, the sharp contrast with traditional religions or tribal forms where the leader is carefully selected or tested, sometimes undergoing trial by fire, is striking.

Although kin groups were not consciously religious, their language of love and caring had religious overtones, and the overarching theme in all reports is the search for acceptance, belonging, love, and a "unifying force." The early dropouts from the kin groups were those who resented group pressures reinforced by the T-group rituals and those who had their needs for belonging satisfied in other contexts, such as commuters who had put down roots elsewhere.

Robert Edgar's hope that the kin groups would be the basic political units of a participatory democracy was difficult to fulfill, as
he admitted himself in a memo in the fall of 1971:

> Our communications system really stinks. As it presently exists
> if we had a good and rapid dispersal system through the kin
> groups it would help. We don't have that yet . . . the kin groups
> as a network do transmit knowledge mostly of values, how-
> ever . . .
> Structures that exist now in the community that I can see are 12
> kin groups that are very powerful with a lot of energy; a bunch of
> workshops that are very heterogeneous in vitality, size and per-
> manence; a rather tight administrative group with some peripheral
> people; various kinds of dyadic relationships and some wanderers
> and not much else. For example, not a faculty . . .
> Kin groups provide a format for [individuals] defining the goals
> as well as achieving them . . . The corporate goals are a com-
> pletely other matter. We have not yet developed suitable mecha-
> nisms for this. I'm sensitive to this being Provost. . . . We are very
> weak in this way.[12]

A direct attack on kin-group and T-group structure came later
that year from a group of faculty radicals who argued that "any
attempt to understand what is happening exclusively in terms of the
T-group perspective is doomed to fail." The radicals felt T-grouping
techniques could have an important role in creating community but
objected to the fact that "T-grouping forms the reference point for
much group activity throughout the college." The radicals feared
that T-grouping had established a "conceptual hegemony" in which
"community building is centered around emotional expression as the
most highly valued form of interaction." The radicals argued that
disputes could not be settled if one remained totally within the realm
of feeling which precluded rational analysis of a problem and did
not allow for differences in content. It was feared that "Continual
T-grouping can only sap more and more energy" and would lead to
fragmentation. The radicals wanted less emphasis on internal states
and more awareness "of oppressive structures in the real world."[13]
The faculty defenders of T-grouping, Michael Kahn and others,
responded that in fact very little T-grouping had taken place at
Kresge. In a sense, they were right, since for the most part what had
taken place in that year was short-term problem-solving in the kin
groups, only a few of which had sustained, highly directed T-groups.
Nor did they see T-grouping as a substitute for thought. It was being
used, they felt, as a "whipping boy . . . which has drawn the fire of

those people who find the exploration and the expression of feeling to be antithetical to their approach either to teaching or community building."[14]

Others discovered a basic problem with participatory democracy: though it is an error to assume that most people want to be full-time participants, one stays away only at the risk of being unrepresented when important decisions are made. Meeting time and required participation quickly escalate, especially in a new college that is establishing precedents and attempting to be open about feelings. By the end of the 1971–72 year, the first faculty member, Gary Miles, quit Kresge, saying "It's a question of how you want to spend your time. I personally like reading, talking about ideas and teaching, not necessarily getting involved in a lot of personal discussion . . . Every meeting begins with how do you feel about each other instead of the substance of the meeting."[15] Edgar also felt at this time that "nobody including ourselves realizes the difficulty of what we are trying to do. Building a community is just terribly difficult in terms of demands on your time and emotional demands as well."[16]

In meetings he attended Grant was struck with the emphasis on feelings. For example, a meeting of the Community Affairs Council called to select a faculty preceptor began with a free-floating discussion about possible candidates. After a number of random suggestions, and some confusion about who would be eligible and available for the preceptor job in the next year, Edgar suggested that they obtain a list of current faculty and go through it. One or two others seconded this suggestion, but no one, including some students and administrative staff, volunteered to carry it out; so after a minute or two, Edgar went himself to get the list. After his return, each faculty member's name was read. The comments were principally reports of feeling, of liking or disliking: "I liked him, but he's not in that place," or "Well, I don't think she would do it but I like her, put her down."

The council also discussed the selection of student proctors for the coming year and the replacement of a member of the administrative staff. Now there was a lengthy consideration of process and methods of selection. None of these matters seemed to be standardized at Kresge; each instance was an occasion for reconsidering who ought to participate in the decision at this particular moment in the life of the college. On the other hand, there was an obvious concern for fairness and for taking the feelings of all the subgroups in the college into account. The process itself was characteristic of Kresge and remarkably gentle. There was no point scoring. Everyone had an attentive hearing. The meeting took place on the redwood deck outside the sauna, and at one point a faculty member gave a student a back massage, two women held hands, heads rested on legs.

A discussion of housing policies for the coming year turned the group's attention to issues of substance and requests for data. In general, the information level of the group was low. There seemed to be little knowledge about housing decisions that had been taken at previous meetings, and few council members had read the account of housing allocation priorities that had been printed in the student newspaper a few days earlier.

The alternative to such lengthy discussions about process and the need to fill in information gaps for group members who "participate" erratically is of course to codify procedures by vesting appointive powers in the provost or adopting some representative system. But in a trade-off between efficiency and participation, Kresge has always chosen the latter, believing that it leads to more "ownership" of the decision-making process and higher "energy levels" and thus more real impact and good community feeling.

Sometimes the theory worked. By the spring of 1972, for example, the Kresge Food Coop was a student-run operation, annually purchasing $135,000 of food for nearly everyone at Kresge. But more often the efforts to maximize participation seemed fruitless. The college bursar concluded that it was apparent the experiment to make decisions through the kin groups was a failure: "Until the community forms some kind of decision-making process I need a group of people . . . to do research, to become knowledgeable about the college and university financial structure. . . . It will take months to learn the system. This is not a short project."[17] At the end of the year, Kresge had nominated no students for university-wide offices: "the dilemma is that Kresge has no process for making these nominations."[18] And the following fall the Community Affairs Committee sounded a common complaint: "We need people. We need more energy, particularly student energy from people who want to take an active role in shaping the community that they live in."[19]

By the year's end the announcements in one issue of the *Weekly Reader* gave a sense of the range of informal participation at Kresge: a student power workshop; a talk by political scientist Sheldon Wolin; workshops in card weaving, cosmology, dulcimer construction, and massage; a meeting of Kin Group 13; a picnic supper on the beach for Kin Groups 2 and 8 ("bring a pot-luck item and flashlights to see the invasion of crabs at midnight"); a personal growth lab on Tuesday from 4–6; a weekend camp-out, and a "Bitch-In" ("the college office staff wants to hear your bitches about ourselves, come lay it on Thursday 1–2:30").[20]

III

It is a partial distortion of the Kresge vision to single out formal participation in the academic program, since the experiment was integral, and the creation of the community itself was intended to constitute the form and much of the substance of the educational program. Even the kin groups were seen as having both social and academic functions, and the process of governance was even expected to provide data for social-science courses. The focus of the academic program as outlined in an early planning document was the "theme of man and his environment . . . construed in broad terms, to emphasize the study of man as much as all that which is around him and affected by him."[21]

It was this broad theme that was the basis of the Creating Kresge College course. In a statement of goals, Edgar urged that students "learn to take the initiative for their own education . . . in the context of real challenges and problems."* The freshmen who arrived in the fall of 1971 were strongly encouraged to take the Kresge core course, Man and the Environment, which constituted a third of the first-year program. It would be "a coherent sequence of lectures, experiences, exercises readings focusing around the theme 'Man and the Environment.' "[22] Its goal would be to examine "what insights the various academic disciplines can provide for understanding and living in the present world." The fall sequence would focus on "the community, the organization, the group and interpersonal relations" —which, in good part, meant Kresge College and its kin-group and community-program structure. The first quarter course was intended to fulfill breadth requirements in the social sciences, while winter and spring quarters would emphasize the humanities and the natural sciences.

Most of the eighteen faculty members participated in the core course in 1971–72. The major lectures were multimedia productions, with vignettes from plays, light and slide shows, music, and films. Two faculty members also discussed the week's reading on videotape, which were shown on closed-circuit television before kin-group meetings as a way to prime discussion. More than seventy work-

*Robert Edgar, "The Kresge Curriculum: A Proposal," mimeographed, July 20, 1971. It is interesting to note that the colleges that we have singled out as ideal types representing various telic reforms all share the aim of making students and faculty co-learners. Though St. John's, Antioch, Black Mountain, and Kresge vary greatly in other respects, each of them tried to put students and faculty on an equal footing and emphasized their common roles as learners in a joint enterprise.

shops were formed in the first weeks, ranging from jewelry making to "Getting the Shit Out of Santa Cruz," a study of the city's sewer system. Most of the workshops folded after a few weeks, but many continued throughout the year. A variety of activities at Kresge was connected with the course in one way or another, and in fact in early memoranda Man and the Environment was referred to not as the academic program or even the core course but as the "Community Program."

Plans for the winter term's natural-science sequence included an opening "Our Town" presentation in which faculty and students would discuss the pros and cons of building a nuclear power plant at Davenport. The scientists adopted a textbook on ecology, *The Subversive Science,* and decided to structure the lectures on themes of homeostasis (stability and instability in systems) and the boundaries between ecological systems and between organisms and their environment. Stanley Scher, a visiting professor of applied biology, gave the opening lectures on creation and birth, Matthew Sands on matter and energy, David Kliger on the universe of particles, Edgar on genetic structure, and Henry Hilgard on disease and the internal environment of man.[23]

The burdens of coordinating course planning with kin-group and other community activities began to wear heavily on many faculty members, and in the spring some began to withdraw from the course. A notable defector was Michael Kahn, who explained that the "time, energy and worry of being responsible for the Community Program is such that I cannot afford it more than any one consecutive year."[24]

Edgar later came to doubt that the core course had been successfully integrated, even in the first year when participation was high. Kresge had a variety of "interesting, groovy courses," but he was less sure whether it had created a distinctive curricular accent. Many of the courses and workshops offered that first year had an experiential cast, although some had a more directly political flavor: Yoga Meditations with Michael Beeson; Birth of a Poet; Yin, Yang: Prisons and Political Prisoners; Project Innovative Education; Pottery, Power Plant: Davenport; Community Camp Ground; Utopias and Intentional Communities; Calligraphy; Rock Climbing and Ski Touring; General Science; Dulcimer Construction; Woman's Rap; Meditation Workshop; Astrology; Self-Hypnosis; Sioux Tipi; Community Program Production; Natural Healing; Psychology Seminar; Writing a Movie; Organic Farm Power Conversion; Food Co-op; Classical Guitar; Arts and Crafts; Old People.

Even formal academic courses tended to be "experiential" and "expressive," and to seek an emotional connection with their subject matter. A seminar on Greek mythology jointly taught by a classics scholar and a member of the Department of Religious Studies ended with a ritual slaughter of a lamb on a hillside at dawn. The students spent the day talking, eating roasted lamb, and drinking wine.

Though it was less sensational, one could perceive a Kresge style in a course on the sociology of women. On the day that we visited, about fifty women and two men had assembled for the class. The instructor arrived about fifteen minutes late, a bit out of breath, dressed in slacks and an old sweater. We introduced ourselves and asked permission to sit in. The instructor, sitting crosslegged on a table in front of the class, explained that at the previous meeting they had discussed imagery in fairy tales. She handed out copies of the following week's assignment on sexism in the primary schools and read excerpts from it in a casual and entertaining way, priming the students' interest. It was a content analysis of children's readers and elementary-school storybooks, showing the stereotypical way in which young girls were represented as weak and dependent on boys, and were given no credit for inventiveness.

Then she suggested that the class break into small groups to discuss friendships at the latency period. She highlighted some recent research on friendship patterns of young girls vis-à-vis young boys. Girls 7 to 12 years old usually had a close friend with whom they shared everything and to whom they told everything. Boys were more likely to travel in packs. Was this so? What was their own experience?

The students, who had been sitting in rows, rearranged themselves, and we joined a group of five women. One woman opened the discussion by recalling a girlhood friend with whom she had played a fantasy game of burying their Barbie dolls, then digging them up; she wondered whether this represented an ambivalent attitude toward feminine roles. The woman to her right spoke at some length about the close relationship she had with her sister and the playhouse their father had built for them, which was a central element in their lives. Another member of the group discussed the hurt she felt in seeking friendships because her affections were seldom returned in kind. The fourth woman had no best friend, but was a tomboy who ran with the boys and acted as a spy in their war games. The fifth said she really had no close girl friend in her elementary-school years, but had developed such a relationship in high school. She talked about this with surprising intimacy, noting how her sexual feelings for her had developed, and how they had slept in each other's arms on one or two occasions, though their relationship had never become fully overt.

At this point, the instructor asked the groups to share themes that had emerged. She began the discussion herself saying that as she approached puberty she lost a friend whose breasts didn't develop as quickly as hers did. This set off a stream of comments and affirmations. The students discussed the experience of getting the first bra, of going away over the summer and returning home to find your friends had "bloomed" and you hadn't. One student discussed being "super-Peter Pannish" with her friend, staving off getting a bra as long as they could, holding on to girlhood. Some giggles and cries of recognition followed an account of the thrills of sneaking a look in the bureau drawers of her girl friend's older brother. Near the end, the instructor handed out three mimeographed sheets, asking everyone in the class to write about their experience at menarche, and to explain who told them about the "facts of life" and the context in which the discussion arose. There was a little resistance to this, some preferring to write their answers over the weekend, but the instructor asked them to complete the questionnaires before they left so that she could analyze the papers for their next session.

The teaching style is typical of Kresge. Small group process is employed to establish a more intimate setting of peer interaction. There is an attempt to connect exploration of a theme with personal experience, simultaneously encouraging expressions of feeling. The faculty member minimizes her role as an authority and presents herself as a facilitative member of the group who shares life material with them as a near equal.

Michael Kahn wrote about the Kresge ideal of teaching in a paper on the seminar. Traditional seminars tend to be of three types: "free-for-alls" in which the object is to score points and win the instructor's approval, frequently by use of "Socratease" to poke fun at your opponent's argument; "beauty contests" in which participants parade ideas past each other, seeking admiration; and "distinguished house tours" through a piece of intellectual architecture. The Kresge seminar ought to be a "barn-raising" in which a community gathers together to work on a mutual project. It should avoid argument and point scoring, since "argument produces insight less often than it produces ulcers and each time we can design a part of our lives to replace argument with collaborative exploration, we increase learning and, if only a little bit, decrease life stress."

The object is "to accept each other's vision," not to quarrel with it. It is important to do the assigned reading and to think critically about what one has read. A critical reading requires one to keep an eye open for the "cosmic question," the question that is "most fascinating or confusing or important to my life." The seminar could begin with each person reading his or her cosmic question. For the seminar itself, Kahn offered a set of guidelines, including advice for a problem every teacher encounters:

> What about the quiet person problem? Now there's a dilemma! On the one horn many of us tend to be uneasy about inviting a person in for fear they will feel coerced. On the other horn, experience indicates that many people who have been having trouble talking are considerably helped by having room specifically made for them. We might convert this dilemma to dialectic and try a synthesis something like this: Since my sharing *my feelings* is apt to reduce your experience of coercion, that might be one way to deal with the problem. The concerned person might share his/her feelings with the quiet person, e.g., "I'm worried that you haven't said anything. I'd really like to know what you've been thinking about if you feel like saying." Or, "I've been missing your participation today. I don't want to put you on the spot and still I want you to know that I'm anxious to hear from you if you feel like talking." Or, even, "I'm aware of your silence and am a little scared that I did something Tuesday that's turned you off."[25]

Here one senses the most benign and thoughtful statement of the Kresge ethos: the attention to feelings and emotional expression, the effort to be inclusive and mutually reinforcing, the insistence that no one be bored, and the shared responsibility of students and teachers.

The problems with such a view are not difficult to imagine: the emphasis on feeling and process can be an endless journey on the surface of ideas; intolerance for boredom may mean that there is little sympathy for the slow, intricate development of complex themes; the imperative to be inclusive and reinforcing may be at odds with the cultivation of excellence.

IV

In its third year Kresge nearly doubled in size, and its organizational forms and structures began to be severely tested. Faculty interest in the core course had dwindled to such an extent that it was decided to offer the course the first quarter and to continue only if enthusiasm developed. The multimedia theater presentations, known as the "community program," gave way to regular lectures, workshops were abandoned, and few kin groups participated. At the end of the quarter, the core course died after several faltering attempts by faculty to come to some agreement about the outlines of new common-core programs. A post mortem by a faculty committee later concluded that "faculty essentially made their own decision about what to teach."[26]

At the faculty retreat that fall, Edgar acknowledged that the kin-group structure was an inadequate means of governance. He proposed three major committees as the new decision-making bodies: Facilities and Resources, Academic Affairs, and Community Affairs. Any member of the college could serve on these committees simply by showing up when they met, and decisions would be made by those present at any given meeting. Membership fluctuated, with four or five regular members and ten to twenty who attended irregularly. Disagreements grew about committee jurisdiction. In the absence of bylaws, repeated arguments about appropriate process delayed decisions, and "committee members complained of being tired and discouraged by endless committee work." Since the provost frequently had to step in to resolve issues, some believed "that only a handful of people were making the decisions and a decentralized process for decision making did not in reality exist."[27]

The cynicism that began to develop about the ideology of loving and caring is reflected in this note from a student in the Kresge newsletter:

> Too often we tend to be of an overly trusting nature toward our fellow humans. The open door policy at Kresge has been a great help in so far as it makes it easier for us to visit each other and borrow things from our friends next door . . . The trouble is that in just our small group of apartments we have had about $400 of money and merchandise ripped off due to our gullibility.[28]

There were also complaints that "this college has too many dogs and not enough curbs." And other residents of the married student apartments that Kresge occupied that year before the completion of its new facilities accused Kresge students of being "the worst offenders in permitting dogs to run loose and in their blatant disregard for the university pet rules."[29] The massage and ritual affinity group announced that it had reconsidered the benefits of a purely spontaneous existence and concluded it was "important that meetings start on time; it is distracting to have people wandering in and out after we have begun, and we who arrive on time feel frustrated and ripped off when that happens—definitely not conducive to a close, warm group feeling."[30] Process consultants called in to help lead the annual community retreat (called "the Advance") concluded that, despite serious problems, "The work of the groups over the weekend was marked by seriousness of purpose, attention to the demands of the task of caring for each other and an absence of grimness or bickering."[31]

One student feared Kresge was dying of apathy. Noting the Kresge Coop had gone broke, she asked plaintively, "Why don't people come, why don't people care? My God, what's happening here?"[32]

Robert Edgar announced he would serve only one more year. Asked by a student interviewer if he was pleased with the way Kresge had developed, he replied: "No, but it's getting there, it's got a lot of life and energy, it's alive." In answer to a question about his goals, Edgar responded:

> I care about and wanted to promote in the Kresge community the intellectual life, creativity in people, preserve knowledge and wisdom and other qualities that are supposed to exist in the university . . . I wanted to create a community with an egalitarian mood. Students must have control and responsibility. Real intellectual activity needs a structureless society. A student is like the first explorers. Explorers had no guides, no structure. It is the same with a research scientist in his lab. I saw the idea of community interpersonal relationships as a way of creating an academic and scholarly community and not an end in itself. I was not setting up a commune.[33]

By this time, Edgar seemed to be dissociating himself from the more evangelistic anti-intellectual romanticism that characterized some aspects of the T-group movement at Kresge. He became even more pessimistic the following year, but his concern about irrational romanticism was not then linked with rejection of egalitarian ideals. While intellectual activity in the highest realms has a playful, artful dimension, in some ways it is odd to think of science as a structureless society, as does Edgar here. Science at Cal Tech could not have prospered without a supporting bureaucracy with its hierarchies of task and organization. Of course research scientists at the top of the meritocracy, a term that would characterize Edgar and his colleagues at Cal Tech, operate with enormous freedom within the peer group. A research scientist is free to chart his own course and to work odd hours in his own fashion; his activity is less structured. But would one expect a Kresge freshman to operate in a similar fashion? Should a college attempt to recreate the egalitarian climate of an elite laboratory?

V

The enrollment in the fourth year reached 590 students, and 282 of these lived in residence, the others being students who had moved off campus and were only loosely affiliated with Kresge. Of the resident students, about half had put Kresge down as the college of their first choice at Santa Cruz, some eager to participate in its kin-group experiment, others only dimly aware of it and attracted to Kresge because it was the newest college. The faculty agreed that perhaps 100 to 125 students identified with the core experiment, participated in kin groups, and worked on the "process" issues. This included most of the 40 students in the original Creating Kresge College group. By the end of the year it was decided to form a special "Corner of the College" to continue the original Kresge experiment and maintain its intensity. Kin-group membership was limited to resident students, and the faculty role in some groups was deemphasized by the appointment of student proctors, who frequently were training to be T-group leaders or counselors. The proctors maintained a "night watch" as the incidence of crime, and occasionally rape, rose on campus; they also were to be on the lookout for "troubled students."

Walls began to go up in many of the Kresge apartments, creating more private physical spaces. In December, the Community Affairs Committee suggested that the partitionless octets be changed to accommodate six persons instead of eight, although they saw this as a decision to be discussed by the whole community "in the context of college values."[34]

There was no attempt to regenerate the Kresge core program that fall. The faculty offered an amalgam of thirty-nine courses, many of them interdisciplinary. Several areas of concentration emerged: T-grouping and group process, environmental issues, women's studies. Early in the winter quarter, faculty met to reconsider curriculum issues, but "nothing was resolved. People once again were caught in the dilemma of whether to have a structured curriculum with specific teaching demands, or an organic growth of courses reflecting faculty interests out of which a coherent curriculum might develop in time."[35] Some of the faculty from the old core course formed a "Community Program Class" to reintroduce theater as a tool to build community and as a forum to discuss intellectual issues. It turned into a course that planned big parties and community celebrations (Mardi Gras, Casino Night), and a faculty review concluded it "has not worked out as hoped."[36]

Robert Edgar came away from the Winter Quarter discussion about the curriculum "filled with a deep sense of failure." In an open letter to the community, Edgar insisted that "Kresge must accept a major academic mission or the college will eventually degenerate into a student hostel and faculty drinking club." More than three-fourths of the faculty were present for the discussion, but only one person joined him in support of the notion that the college should have general education goals. He described Kresge's present practice as "offering uncoordinated college courses serving primarily the purposes of the individual faculty member," yet he emphasized that he was not looking for an abstract statement of educational goals:

> To me a curriculum is a system of educational opportunities, available to students, that appears in the catalog, that is fairly stable from year to year . . . that has a pattern that can be readily perceived and can be defended as legitimate, supporting and complementing the university-wide course offerings.[37]

Edgar suggested that Kresge's pattern ought to consist of clusters of courses on the environment, including natural-science courses for nonscientists, arts and crafts courses, one or two small college-based majors (probably including some sequence on group dynamics), and a group of interdisciplinary upper-division courses. This statement puts a different light on the thoughts he had expressed a year earlier about a "structureless" learning experience (by which he now seemed to mean a defined structure that permitted a great deal of freedom, not a total absence of structure), and it indicated a further distancing from the T-group or "touchy-feely" aspects of the college. Edgar asserted that the faculty was "depriving our students of a powerful learning experience," and added:

> The unwillingness of the faculty to explore what we might do if we accepted collective curricular goals is I believe irresponsible and will eventually lead to undesirable consequences . . . without a collegiate academic focus the substantial vitality that the college now has will become increasingly in conflict with and alienated from the academic pursuits of the university . . . [and] in the absence of an academic purpose the college will no longer be able to effectively argue for course support money, teaching assistants, or even faculty time.[38]

Although Edgar himself was filled with a sense of failure, there were indications that the community had grown strong enough to laugh at itself. Following the orientation that year, one student responded with this parody:

> This already legendary college carries with it heavy responsibility: we must be loving and free and intellectual giants and totally groovy at all times. We must work hard to keep the incredible Kresge image fresh and strong in the minds of all aware people. We must steel and discipline ourselves to concentrate to put much

of our energy into the Great Experiment. We must really try, we must free associate every morning upon rising, we must make eye contact with our brothers and sisters on the way to the head, we must water and admire our Cooper House plants every day, we must never be without our copy of *Gestalt Therapy Now* and the most recent *Organic Gardening*, we must keep our Indian print spreads clean and neat, brush our hair 100 strokes a day with a natural bristle brush, eat lots of granola, smile at all dogs and young children, etc., etc., etc., Yes, it's all very confusing.[39]

It may be that when values are more widely accepted, and more secure, the community can then tolerate, even encourage, a comic view of itself. And it may also be a reflection of the fact that Kresge had grown too large for everyone to share one church, and it is hard to laugh in church if it is the only church in town. Now there were several churches of competing faiths: a rising women's-studies group, a smaller radical politics core, and those of no sect who simply found Kresge a congenial place to live.

Some of the egalitarian structure of the early church gave way to more hierarchical structure in the governance process. It became clear to Edgar that a "walk-in" style of committee decision-making was not working, and he decided that "the committees needed to have chairpeople visible and acceptable to the rest of the campus if they were to assume real power in the college." The difficulty "of having an informed committee when its membership continued to fluctuate each week" also became evident: "The committees would become bogged down in explaining the details or history of some given issue which had been discussed previously and which now required that action or decision be taken."[40]

At the Winter Quarter Advance, which had become a yearly ritual of reassessment and reconsideration of decision-making structures, most students and faculty favored an end to the casual style of participation of the Community Affairs Committee. One member of the committee concluded the college "was caught in a paralysis of unclear or unstated policy—not knowing whether to go to a committee for help, wait for someone else to create direction, or to focus energy on projects ourselves."[41] A student who had felt that anybody who was present should be able to vote at committee meetings said he now believed such a policy "resulted in chaos." The committee had gone from "an inefficient group to a nearly hopeless one."[42] Over two days of discussion, with 50 to 250 persons participating, it was decided to limit the committee to 15 "committed" members who would serve at least one quarter under a chairperson appointed by the provost. The student members of the committee would self-select themselves (as it turned out, 38 students came to the next Community Affairs meeting, and 23 the following week, and they decided among themselves who the voting members would be for that quarter). Those who were not selected were to sit in a kibitzing gallery. Committee decisions would be binding on the entire college. Objectors could show up in the gallery the following week to voice complaints, and the committee could decide whether it wished to reconsider its decision. During the Advance, some students were concerned that such a system would not adequately represent the interests of the college, and discussion went on until five hold-out dissenters finally agreed to let the majority consensus stand. Less than 50 students remained to the end of that seven-hour meeting on the last day, causing one student to comment that "the most alienated and powerless people in the whole Kresge community are those folks who are easily bored."[43]

A frequent complaint was that "the goals of Kresge are damned hard to find and they have never been really decided upon, written up, and publicized." One student said that since nobody had polled student opinion on any issues, he didn't see "how any 'community' decision was really valid." He suspected an "unconscious elitism, snobbishness, and manipulation" and pointed out that both Michael Kahn and Henry Hilgard treated a critic harshly: "Instead of listening to a person telling of his real and valid concerns regarding the Kresge community, he was trashed . . ."[44]

But even that student concluded that "Klowntown is doing pretty well, all things considered." Provost Edgar felt reaffirmed by "our struggle for a meaningful functional egalitarian political system, our dedication to trying to hear everyone."[45] Hilgard "came back in touch with why I'm here—because I want matters of the heart to enter into my interactions with others . . . I find in Kresge an environment . . . where reason and warmth are compatible, where an attempt at appreciation goes before criticism."[46] Yet Hilgard felt he was "caught holding an egalitarian bag," which was not the reason he came to Kresge, although "I dig the ideal . . . I can't implement it without a lot of help."[47] The reaction of a freshman is worth quoting at length:

A surprising number of people have communicated to me that they were disappointed to some degree to see whatever it was at the Orientation dissipate or something during the year. The orientation was for me a very heavy and beautiful experience; it is the source for most of my personal emotional involvement with Kresge, and that's a lot. It was very educational. It taught me that I could trust a group of people who were, at the time, almost all strangers to me. It taught me that this community was supposed to be a caring community. It taught me that there were some very interesting people here at Kresge who were trying to create in their daily lives social forms which agreed with the ideal of the caring community—that, to me, is what "touchie-feelie" means. It confirmed my feeling that there were better ways for me to live than "playing it cool," that expressing feelings is a way of life that the people here respect.[48]

On a subsequent visit, we asked that freshman, a shy, bearded, intense young man named Peter, to elaborate on what social forms would be characteristic of a caring community. He was eager to discuss the college and to tell us about himself. Both parents had been artists. His mother was now a technical illustrator. He wasn't sure just what his father did, although he worked in management for an aircraft manufacturer. Peter had been in a program for gifted students in high school, where he had received high grades and had taken advanced placement courses that won him sophomore standing when he came to Kresge. Yet he looked upon high school as a horrible experience and came to detest grades and the grading system. "I was totally grade oriented. I had a tremendous need to get grades. I remember sitting in the chem exam and shaking even though I knew how to do the problems. For me personal growth would have to be getting away from that."

In a high-school psychology course, he read Carl Rogers, Fritz Perls, Paul Goodman, and what he called "existential therapists." He had experienced a good deal of hostility and some ridicule and rebuff at being "too sensitive." Yet he felt open hostility was preferable to what he called "empty tolerance." Kresge's ethos was very appealing to him, and the college was his first choice. On arrival he noticed quite a difference between the early founders and the new students. The "early settlers" were always hugging and touching each other and were committed to T-grouping. The later arrivals were less likely to do so. Yet he felt it was possible even for latecomers to express affection in ways that were impossible to use elsewhere. If he had to leave, he would miss that freedom:

> In another setting I'll have to feel my way more to test the ways in which it would be permissible to express my feelings. I would feel more reluctant to approach new people and strangers and try to involve myself with them. I gained involvement with several people more quickly and more widely than I would have anywhere else. I have a friend at Berkeley who's made only a tiny fraction of the contacts I've made here. That's very important in going away to college. There are people I can express things to.

In small group interaction here one thing I find really important is that if I project my feelings on others or put responsibility
on them, they will tell me what I'm doing. This consciousness is
the only way I can grow to learn. If I'm not told then I'll never
grow.

Of course, in order to profit from what he called these "interpersonal feedback loops," he had to learn not to swallow everything
that came from others whole, but to be able to see when others were
projecting on to him: "I had to develop autonomy about my own
feelings, to really be in touch with what I feel, to be able to judge
the feedback that comes from others." What of those who were not
so skilled, were they likely to be hurt if others unfairly projected
upon them? He didn't know of anyone who had been hurt, although
some people had left. This reminded us of Gregory Bateson's comment, "Those who aren't liked tend to slip away," and of the meeting we had attended where judgments about liking or trusting someone tended to outweigh comments about other kinds of competence.
Peter responded that some people at Kresge did take the position
that intuition and feeling were what mattered, adding perceptively
that if someone didn't get picked for a job they tended to conclude it
was more a reflection of whether he was liked than of his competence.

We had expected Peter to be enthusiastic. To get a more balanced
view of Kresge, we picked names at random from the student directory for interviews. One of the students chosen turned out to be a
well-scrubbed, neatly dressed woman named Dena who was working
part-time as a teacher's aide in a Santa Cruz elementary school. That
experience convinced her she didn't want to be a teacher, because of
all the "hassles teachers in public schools have to go through in order to teach the way they want to." She had transferred to Kresge
the previous fall after spending two years at a junior college in Los
Angeles, and she was majoring in sociology. She had recently decided she might want to work in the field of international relations,
and she was pleased to obtain a summer job as a mother's helper for
an American diplomat's family in Norway. Her own father is a minister and her mother a social worker, and she sees herself as a "minority member" at Kresge—never smoking marijuana, for example.

Yet Dena's feelings about Kresge are generally positive. She enjoyed orientation and felt the kin group helped her make friends and
gain acceptance easily. Although it took longer to make decisions,
the T-group process "helped the college to make decisions as a
group of concerned people rather than as a bunch of isolated individuals." She saw evidence of this in her own apartment, where people were not cleaning up the mess in the kitchen "and were getting

uptight about food and putting their names on their egg cartons."
They had a T-group about this, and "people got their feelings out"
and things went well for the next quarter. However, "things were
getting messy again," and it was time for another meeting.

"People are honest. They will tell you why they're mad. I've had
some good talks with people who didn't like my personality. I really
needed to hear it." Asked for an example of such feedback, she said
that on the way back from swimming recently her friend told her she
talked too fast and that she felt she just didn't want to listen to other
people. Such comments were frequent at Kresge. Grant replied he
might be irritated if every time he walked into a room a dozen people who didn't like the way he talked or comported himself told him
so. Perhaps it would be better to accept the fact that a certain proportion of people aren't going to like you? To hear it all the time
would be boring. Why be in an environment that legitimates such
intrusions? This struck her forcefully. Maybe she would find it irritating eventually, she admitted. Yet, she felt people at Kresge were
genuinely sensitive about giving criticism, and she needed to hear at
least some of the things she was hearing. She also heard good things:
"People at Kresge are happy-go-lucky. They are not in a hurry to
get things done. People are sensitive to your moods. If I was sitting
in the library and feeling lousy, people would come over and ask
what's the matter."

Dena said her father was eloquent; she always wanted to be like
him but wasn't. Perhaps that's why she talked so fast. She never felt
easy or sure of herself in groups, and in the past had been afraid to
speak up and had gone along with decisions she didn't believe in.
She is still somewhat reticent, and had been attacked in T-groups
for being too silent and unrevealing. But she has gotten to the point
where she's not afraid of being judged. "Now I'm more confident.
I think I can talk. I can tell people how I feel." And when someone in her group criticized her for being silent, she was able to say
she liked listening, and would speak when she felt like it. She was
now comfortable with her silences as well.

Academics were not a large part of her life. She had enjoyed a
group-dynamics course. They read Freud's *Totem and Taboo*, Philip
Slater's *Microcosm*, Melanie Klein, Margaret Rioch, and a book on
sensitivity training. She decided to major in sociology after a friend
invited her to a meeting of the department. She had thought of psychology but didn't want to take statistics. She was not very theoretically inclined and had not decided on any particular focus yet.

David, a senior, was quite different: very absorbed in scholarship.

We had interviewed him twice—once in 1972 when, as a member of the original Creating Kresge College group, he was heavily involved in college affairs, and again in 1974, when he had moved off campus.

David attended high school in Los Angeles, where his father is an insurance broker and his mother a librarian. He initially entered Santa Cruz's Stevenson College, where the faculty were good teachers but more distant than the Kresge faculty, he said. There was no "we-they" distinction among students and faculty at Kresge. He thought Henry Hilgard was Kresge's great success story, a faculty member who had been opposed to T-grouping but returned from the faculty retreat and changed his teaching, style, his way of relating to people—"all for the better."

As a Kresge sophomore, David took five courses a quarter (most students took three), published a paper in a British journal on *Finnegan's Wake*, learned several languages. Yet he took time out for a three-day massage workshop at Kresge and loved it.

He had served us tea when we first interviewed him, while roommates looked on from hammocks hanging overhead. We remarked that he was one of the few students at Kresge who had offered us food or drink, and he remembered this two years later, bringing a hot thermos of delicious coffee to share with us. He was now a senior living off campus, having decided that the lack of privacy at Kresge was at odds with his desire to pursue a scholarly career. He hoped to teach Hebrew literature and Jewish history and will go to Oxford for graduate studies.

Looking back at Kresge's development, he felt the faculty who were committed to sensitivity training and communal values tried to reenact in each orientation period what it took nearly a year for the original planning group to achieve. The founders were in the awkward position of trying simultaneously to impose new ideals and to make students feel they were choosing them. The founding group had also worked out an egalitarian, consensual model of governance that was much more difficult, if not impossible, to maintain when the college grew larger. He was sorry his choice of an intellectual career had forced his move off campus. While he now believed more in an intellectual meritocracy, there was no reason why Kresge must sacrifice academic standards on the altar of feeling. "You ought to be loving and caring and still do your reading."

We saw David a third time at the graduation ceremony in June, held in the main assembly at Kresge, rededicated that day as the Robert S. Edgar Town Hall. Members of the class that had created Kresge sat in a wide circle on the wooden floors, some wearing sandals and others in blue jeans, formal gowns, or jackets and ties. Their parents and friends sat ringed about them in chairs.

After Edgar's welcome and a poem read by Everson, Michael Kahn stepped forth in a crimson Harvard gown bearing a large sea-shell in his hands as though it were a holy vessel. Speaking softly of the need for ritual, he held the shell high, turning first to one side of the audience and then to the other, explaining that it was a "magic shell," a many-chambered nautilus. As the nautilus out-grew one chamber, it formed another, then another until finally it lived outside the shell. But it dragged the shell behind itself as a retreat in times of need, and Kahn hoped that the graduates would likewise consider Kresge as a shelter to which they could return.

Coming into the circle, Kahn explained that the nautilus was a creature that lived in the depths. Now holding the shell at eye level, he passed slowly before them. Anyone wishing to speak about some-thing "deep down" would hold the shell while they spoke.

First a mother took the shell and said how proud she was of her daughter on this day. Next a new member of the faculty, a dance teacher, rose to say he was glad to have come to Kresge—how right it felt, and how much pleasure his students had given him. A boy said, "This beautiful shell came from the deep to show its light. I hope the students of Kresge will do the same." A mother took the shell, couldn't speak at first, then said she wanted to touch it and speak of her pride in her son. Robert Edgar held the shell and intro-duced the new provost, May Diaz, an anthropologist from Berkeley. A student read from the *Wizard of Oz*: "Be what you is and not what you is not, for that is the way to happiness."

The shell passed many who remained motionless; then an Asian student reached for it and went to the center of the circle with four other students. They hugged and kissed each other and then sat down again. A girl in tangerine slacks held the shell, tried to speak, could not, cried, said thank you, cried again, and sat down. One or two others held the shell silently. A boy cried and said he was sad that he would not see his friends for a long time. Another student gave the Sioux signs of cherishing, respect, and gratitude.

A heavy girl wearing a patchwork denim skirt spoke somewhat giddily, saying she was "not much into academics" (long laughter from students). She had spent most of her time "on the boardwalk and at Brian's parties, and it just wowed her to think of graduating and she was *soooo* filled with love and gratitude that she had just one thing to say: Then she leaned her head back, let loose with an ear splitting scream, shaking her arms and body as though possessed and then sat down. After a pause, students applauded her, followed more hesitantly by parents, unsure as we were whether she was parodying the college or was an expression of it.

Another girl said quite soberly that she hoped Kresge students "would keep on caring for each other," and a girl in jeans added, "I just want to say in true T-group fashion I'm all warm, I'm all excited, I'm all sad and I love you guys all a real lot."

A few students spoke warmly of particular teachers, including the girl who said, "Bob Edgar, I want to tell you how grateful I am you were my teacher. I just want to say I love you." But there were not many comments about teaching or learning. It was a very Kresge-like moment, full of expression, of feeling, some of it treacly and forced, but most of it sincere and innocent. At the end, each graduate silently gave a rose to someone present who was especially important to them: a parent, a teacher, a friend.

No honors were distributed; there was no valedictory; no students were singled out for achievements. Pondering this on the way out, we recalled our interview with Gregory Bateson, the anthropologist who had lived and taught at Kresge for the past year. In his view, at Santa Cruz in general and Kresge particularly, students tended to be uninterested in striving for honors or in getting ahead. Not many in his large course on the ecology of mind were engaged with ideas. Perhaps ten "were sweating through some things that matter." Papers done in the course were generally deplorable. It was hard to get students to take seriously what was being said or for them to take themselves seriously when writing something. It was an amiable life at Kresge. It was pleasant. It was kindly. Students spoke a "horrible touchy-feely jargon," Bateson said, but in actual behavior they were unusually kind, but that didn't help you learn very much in Latin grammar or any other serious subject.

VI

The graduation of Kresge's first "full class" was a turning point and an occasion for retrospection, particularly for the founding cadre. Michael Kahn was in a somber mood when we talked with him one afternoon during graduation week, perhaps because our conversation was interrupted by a call about a troubled student, possibly suicidal. After making arrangements for the distraught student to spend the week at a hospital, Kahn remarked that one of the failed inter-

disciplinary hopes he and Edgar had for Kresge was to do a course
on schizophrenia, with Edgar treating the biological aspects and
Kahn the psychological.

Other hopes had been dashed, too. After the first year, it was more
and more difficult to hire the kind of faculty they wanted—those
who would be committed to "straight talk" and the heart of the
Kresge experiment. The departments controlled half the money to
do the recruiting, and Kresge could not bring in its own faculty
unilaterally.*

The college he and Edgar and a few students were planning in
1969–70 was "a beautiful little community," but soon after the first
full class came in 1970–71, "the dream began to crack." Kahn
blamed himself for failing to anticipate the attack that eventually
materialized:

> I plead guilty to an incredible naïveté about this generation. I
> really believed in this generation. I felt all you had to do with
> these Northern California middle-class kids was to provide them
> with a supportive environment with the barest sort of guidelines
> and they would get rid of the environment that led to My Lai,
> that led to napalming children in Vietnam, that led to Watergate.
> They would junk that and they would embrace the Kresge ex-
> periment, they would welcome it, they would make it their own.

In other words, if you created a supportive climate, people would
grow, would realize their potential, would be cooperative and creative? Yes, that's what he had thought—but he failed to stipulate:
"given no other pressures or opposition." He realized that he had
overlooked the possibility that the Kresge experiment embodied a
set of ideas that "would threaten a lot of people." And there were
others, including some radicals on the faculty, who would have opposed any existing authority structure in order to seize power. But
the T-group movement itself "enraged" some. Michael Kahn remembered a "powerful, open, interpersonal exploratory encounter" held in
his living room that first year—1970–71. Later, the students who had
participated attacked the encounter viciously, and Kahn felt they had
been turned against the experiment by faculty "who feared and ridiculed the movement, who themselves feared that kind of openness."

---

*As explained in more detail in Chapter 8, the Santa Cruz Colleges had
authority to develop their own majors but shared appointment powers with
departments. Half of each faculty member's salary was budgeted through his
or her college, and half through the department or Board of Studies (to use
the Santa Cruz terminology). Similarly, both college and department had an
equal voice in promotion and tenure decisions.

A few colleagues had spread a vicious rumor about him. It was the most difficult and traumatic year of his life. But the founders also had their share of successes. Although the original T-group emphasis had been moderated, particularly in the operation of kin groups, Kahn felt some excellent group leaders had been trained. A few had gone to graduate school to pursue interests in organizational theory. Matthew Sands was an example of a faculty member who had become "a fantastic group leader."

The ultimate "success" of the experiment, could not be known for years, but it seemed to him that many students were more open and more caring at least partly as a result of having come to Kresge, and that was not unimportant.

Matthew Sands felt the Kresge experiment had grown too fast and had lost most of its steam after the first year. Only a tenth of the original enthusiasm now remained. Perhaps nine or ten faculty members were committed to the dream, and more than twenty opposed it. The faculty radicals wanted the college to focus on external social change, not internal introspection; these were the Neo-Marxists who saw the "touchy-feely religion as the new opiate of the people." On the other side were the radical egalitarians who brought droves of students into every meeting that the faculty tried to have privately. So the faculty finally gave up meeting. Sands felt Edgar had been crushed by the radical opposition and had lost heart in the experiment at the end of the first full year. He was not sure why. It may have been because the opposition was so savage or because Edgar buckled under the enormity of the task.

Pointing in our direction, Sands also felt Edgar was "like you, and tended to believe that learning could only occur in courses." We didn't quarrel with his inference, but asked him to explain, to which he replied that Edgar did not have faith in experimental learning and, in Sands's view, was too concerned about a formal curriculum.

Looking at the outcomes of the Kresge experiment from a student perspective, Sands believed many students had experienced growth because they had discovered what was of importance to them. But one needed to keep in mind that Kresge students were also Santa Cruz students, and the college had a relatively small claim on them. They took courses elsewhere on campus as well. A great many, perhaps a majority, simply lived at Kresge. It was a roof over their heads. Of the 600 or so students now enrolled, 150 at most really attempted to participate in the dream that the place was all about.

Next we saw Henry Hilgard, whom we ran into at almost every meeting or event we attended at Kresge. Hilgard had been faculty preceptor (a job combining the responsibilities of a dean and house master) and a member of the Community Affairs Committee. He taught an introductory biology course to 550 students and another course in immunology. In the immunology course, each student was required to review two journal articles, which helped him to keep up with the research in his field. Hilgard also tried to spend one day a week in the lab doing his own research, and in the fall he would leave for a sabbatical at the National Cancer Institute in Lausanne, Switzerland.

The heavy load he has borne at Kresge has enabled Hilgard to do little publishing. Yet he doesn't feel he has atrophied intellectually. The Kresge experience has encouraged him to look at things more holistically than he might have previously. For example, it has affected the way he conceptualized a new text, *The Biology of People*, as well as his style of working with teaching assistants in his large course. Yet he makes plain that he is not a doctrinaire egalitarian and that the discussions about process and procedure sometimes seem endless at Kresge. But despite such irritations, he now can't imagine being happy any place else. He gets a headache just thinking about going through the interview process for a faculty job at a more traditional college. The deep friendships he has formed are very important to him.

> People are open, students are open. The kind of relationships one can have here are just qualitatively different—and the whole place supports that kind of thing. This is a community that has reduced the barriers to personal interaction. These are people I know and I feel connected with them. It's also a community that legitimates and encourages stroking. I get a lot of support from this community, and I need that support.

Hilgard was concerned, however, whether most students at Kresge were profiting intellectually. He suspected many were coasting. For a minority, perhaps 20 percent, the nongraded curriculum at Santa Cruz is beneficial. But he fears too many just flounder and "Some just get into the state of 'I want, I want, I want' and never really get out and do any academic work."

Robert Edgar seemed calm, as if relieved now to be passing the reins to a new provost. The tension had gone from him, and he seemed glad of the opportunity to reflect on what had happened at Kresge. In that first year the major accents were laid down: working on problems in small human groups, a consensual style of decision-making, the kin-group structure, the core curriculum. The curriculum had been disappointing: it had not evoked the sustained loyalty of the faculty. He had never shared the hopes of some that the political and psychological processes of the college itself could sustain a curriculum, that community behavior could operate as a data pool from which faculty could draw on in teaching their discipline and thus in building the college.

We asked how an egalitarian and inclusive community like Kresge, which placed such value on social harmony, faced the stress of meritocratic decisions, such as rehiring faculty. Edgar replied that they really hadn't crossed that bridge, although they had discussed the idea of having a committee of outsiders come and do that. In a way, he realized, that "was a cop-out, yet one could consensually decide to have some categories of decision-making that were nonconsensual." The initial choice of faculty was a special case, "a very gamey exercise, and people only presented a special part of themselves." You mean they lie? we asked, and he laughed, "Well, I didn't say that."

Examining other aspects of the college, particularly its encounter- and kin-group process, Edgar felt some students had been hurt and others helped. Some had been helped to grow and to change and to take risks in a supportive environment, including the risk of leaving college altogether. He supposed some were hurt—perhaps those for whom the T-group had become a kind of dependency or stasis.

There were times in his role as provost when he himself was hurt. It bothered him, for example, to make decisions on the basis of incomplete data; you couldn't just say you didn't understand something and simply work on it; real time was unlike laboratory time. There had also been pain in his relationship with Michael Kahn, which he described as a struggle over the issue of whether Kresge "should simply be a T-group college or a more complex ecological interrelation of spaces and places." Edgar clearly opted for the latter view, whereas he believed that Kahn would have wished that those who were uninterested in a "straight-talk" experiment would go elsewhere. "We gradually stopped talking to one another although we are still very fond of each other."

What he was happiest about, like Hilgard, was the friends he had made. They mattered more than anything else. And the college had given him and his friends a rare opportunity to create something.

What had he learned? He responded with a story. He had recently gone to a scientific meeting of a kind he hadn't attended for some years to prepare himself for the research he would do on leave next year at Cambridge University. It was a meeting to discuss genetic research on nematodes. The high-status microbiologists had dominated the meeting and had pretty much kept out others like agricul-

tural biologists who had been working on the way nematodes created
havoc with some kinds of crops. Edgar had been asked to summarize
the proceedings, and he did discuss the papers that were given and
their interrelationships. But then he brought up the issue of the exclusion of the agriculturally oriented biologists. Was that the best
way for science to proceed? he asked. Should scientists discourage
collaboration among the various subfields of biology? He was both
surprised and delighted by the willingness of his colleagues to discuss this issue once it had been raised. But the point he wished to
make was that this was something he would never have done prior
to his Kresge experience: "I would have been blind to the process
at work in forming a new group."

He hoped Kresge students would make an impact in this way on
the groups they would join and the organizations in which they
would work. Perhaps the course or trajectory of these groups would
be "altered a bit" by the student experience at Kresge. Edgar had
no expectations of great shifts or societal change, but he did see
some increments, "some willingness to be more open to change and
to look at affective issues and processes."

He was committed to the idea of diversity within the college as
well as without. His measure of success would be to ask an outside
observer to question participants about the meaning of the Kresge
experiment. If the observer found each had a different view, he
would conclude that the experiment was successful. He feared the
college might be growing too somnolent, settling down, behaving too
much like a regularly oiled machine. Edgar's basic impulse, the root
of his feeling about the need for a participatory style of governance,
is to keep reminding people: These are your decisions; this organization can be what you want it to be. These are your choices; make
your inputs, create your own world.

VII

The appointment of May Diaz, a Berkeley anthropologist, as the new
provost of Kresge was resented initially because it was mandated by
the chancellor of Santa Cruz, Dean McHenry. Feelings ran deep.
The selection process revealed the growing diversity within Kresge
and forced the recognition that the college was not a big happy kin
group but a complex organization composed of several subcultures.
In addition to the T-groupers, there was now a women's caucus, a
group of radical faculty, and a sizable number of diverse faculty
who were increasingly willing to voice their discontent about the

declining but still dominating T-group ethos. Philip Slater, a sociologist who was asked to evaluate Kresge's program, noted:

> Much commitment on the part of faculty at Kresge has been lost by a failure to appreciate contributions to the life of the college that fall outside a rather narrow and monolithic definition of the dream . . . What peripheral people say is that they want differences allowed: that they respect Kresge but don't want to worship it—that Kresge is a glorious phenomenon they would like to share in, but it isn't quite their thing and they don't know how to contribute since their skills are made to seem irrelevant or unimportant. They say they are made to feel that if they don't live up to certain norms they are attacking Kresge. They feel that one must be totally supportive of the core people in order not to be defined as against them.[49]

The T-group enthusiasts felt most strongly about Elliott Aronson, a social psychologist with a touch of Michael Kahn's charisma. In the end, Aronson decided to come as a faculty member, joining Kahn and other faculty interested in continuing the T-group experiment on a more intense but less expansive scale in the Corner of the College. The kin groups continued, but it was felt that the Corner of the College would give students who wished it an opportunity to make a commitment to a more intensive "living-learning" experiment. Most faculty had withdrawn from regular participation in kin groups.

The new provost, May Diaz, described herself as an anthropologist "who enjoys listening to many voices and putting a lot of loose ends together." She said plainly that the touchy-feely image was one that the college was beginning to fight:

> There has been a response in terms of a stereotype and it's made much more difficult for Kresge to do what it intended to do. One of the goals of Kresge is to create a viable, positive, stimulating learning environment, and one aspect of that is to create communication and trust, a sense of solidarity, a sense of community among the people involved in that. I think there are a number of forms for doing that. I'm probably more of an eclectic than some of the original founders.[50]

As provost, she was perceived as a fair-minded and straightforward administrator who played no favorites. Her first effort was to push discussion of a new five-year academic plan for the college. Interdisciplinary clusters were proposed in woman's studies, natural sciences, political economy, and community development, but by spring no firm college major had emerged. Two new courses were approved for the women's-studies program: Women in Therapy and Women in American Music. New faculty positions in dance and electronic music were also approved. Some enthusiasm developed for a major program in communications that would include both T-groupers interested in "interpersonal communications" and those working in more traditional scholarly fields such as sociolinguistics and cybernetic theory.

Although the Kresge experiment was partially transformed under the new provost's leadership, much of the core ethos remained, particularly in the processes of governance. The Advance, Kresge's perennial self-examination, revealed anew the tensions in the college. There was more willingness to acknowledge the diversity that now existed, but a reluctance to give up T-group process as the principal means for coping with it.

Characteristically, the solution to the perceived ills of the college came in the form of suggestions for more intimate, closer contacts. The remedy proposed for declining student participation was to "encourage personal, verbal contact." One response to faculty dissatisfactions was to urge that "kin groups adopt a faculty member." The primary self-definition of the college was that "we encourage and support close connection of faculty to students."[51]

Yet strong concerns were also expressed about the need for "personal protection" against too much involvement, "so people don't have to fight the norms of the college to keep their health and sanity." Or, "short-term payoff is interrelating; long-term payoff is unclear."

Of course, if the way to solve problems is to establish close, intimate connections, and if intimacy demands an intense commitment, many problems will go unsolved because the personal cost of working on any particular problem is too great. But the crucial issue is much broader; it is the confusion at Kresge between what is private and what is public.* Friendships or increased intimacy—private relationships—are frequently proposed as the means of solving public issues. Yet the realms of the private and the public are governed by different principles. We are not rational or "fair" in our friendships. A loving relationship is not governed by rational self-interest. We can decide on whim or emotional need to like or not like someone; there is no need to explain the basis for friendship. In friendship we tend to suspend critical attitudes in favor of understanding and acceptance. And it is the need for acceptance or group support, grounded in mutual feelings, that is at the center of the Kresge ex-

*We are indebted to our colleague Thomas F. Green for insights into this distinction.

periment. But in the realm of public relationships, there is a need to be concerned about different principles: equity, fairness, rational criteria of judgment, and commonly agreed-upon procedures to adjust competing claims. Other than the Advance itself, Kresge never created a satisfactory forum for the discussion of these public issues. Participants in the Advance groped for a definition of the Kresge community:

> We came up with two descriptions of the community. One is all 650 students, which make up the static and formal community, and then the more dynamic and changing "blob" of all those attending college functions and participating in the decision-making process—and the question of which community we were trying to make decisions for was raised.[52]

The problem is as old as Aristotle: how do members of a community establish a framework or constitution within which they will pursue common purposes. As Aristotle noted, most constitutions provide for an oligarchic element (committees) and a democratic element (the general public or its representatives). Thus the manner of elections to committees becomes a crucial matter, and one that was never very satisfactorily resolved at Kresge, as indicated by the description of its committee structure as a self-selected "dynamic blob" of shifting participants.

There was a deep and unresolved conflict in the community between the ideal of solving problems in private "trusting" groups, on the one hand, and the need for open and public process, on the other. The result was a kind of torment of secrecy, which spilled out in comments about "feelings of coercion by inner groups," "a tangible lack of trust," "the mystique behind the committee structure," and the absence of a "mechanism for more believable representation in decision-making." Yet the underlying belief that problems could be solved in close, caring relationships was such a strong element of the Kresge ethos that it was perhaps inevitable that the community would refuse to adopt a public and more impersonal means of recognizing group conflicts. Those who were thus denied a voice in the community or were opposed to the emphasis on T-grouping tended to withdraw. This may explain the continued concern about lack of participation or "low energy."

The Advance itself was the principal legitimate, college-wide forum for the expression of dissent. But typically it became a forum for building oceanic feelings of trust in which disagreement became less and less legitimate as the hours wore on. Advances that started with 150 or 200 members of the community tended to end with 50 to 75 members making the decisions after others drifted away. Process consultants would attempt to build feelings of trust and solidarity. Philip Slater, in the 1975 Advance, suggested that Kresge was characterized by "pluralistic ignorance" in which "a lot of people share norms but don't know that they share them." But it could be doubted whether this was true. The minutes reveal sharp disagreements on a number of norms, but an absence of means for dealing with differences at the group level. The basic problem was the failure to recognize that the principles that can govern family or "kin-group" life cannot be expected to form the basis of a wider polity. But the desire for inclusion, for acceptance and social harmony, was so intense at Kresge that it should not be surprising that the community refused to adopt the means for dealing with divisions of opinion that were often based on differences of perception or knowledge. Traditionally, constitutions have been ways of formalizing the settlement of disputes with those whom you need not like but with whom you wish to live in peace. Since Kresge demanded obeisance to the ideal of liking and acceptance, it was often difficult for it to live in peace. Its saving grace was that it was not monolithic but one college amid eight others at Santa Cruz, and one in which students need live only part of their lives.

VIII

In revising this chapter in 1976, we turned first to a sheaf of letters in response to circulation of an earlier draft. Copies had been sent to everyone named in it, including some whose names have been deleted at their request. The responses (sixteen letters in reply to a mailing of thirty-three copies) were thoughtful, vivid, sometimes quite angry. Two ran more than ten pages. Philip Slater was perhaps the most perturbed. He felt that we* were so overwhelmed by bias as to be incapable of understanding what Kresge was about:

> It's obvious that your instinctive reaction to the college is one of creeping flesh, and although you try hard at times to be "objective" in the usual sense of that term, the loathing leaks through . . . Attacking Kresge is easy. Innovations are easy to hit . . . There's just as much wrong with play-it-safe academia. There's life and energy and experimentation at Kresge, but all people seem to see

---

*Though we have used the editorial "we" throughout this book, this chapter on Kresge College was written by Gerald Grant. Slater's letter, as well as the others cited here, was addressed to him.

is assault on ancient tradition. It's easy to ridicule Kresge, but most academics are too thoroughly brainwashed to be able to attack Harvard or Berkeley with the same enthusiasm. I guess I still haven't learned not to be upset when those who make themselves vulnerable and take risks get trashed by those too armored and afraid to do either.

In a way, the criticism is a confirmation of the portrait, since "risk" here is defined in stereotypic Kresge terms. There is no risk in writing something; risk exists only in "open, direct and explicit relationships." Slater explained that he left the university years ago (he taught at Brandeis and Harvard) "because I think most academics are too stupid to carry on an interesting intellectual exchange." He views Kresge as "the only significant academic innovation of my adult lifetime" and the "only university in the country that I would consider spending time in—the only one offering any real intellectual stimulation or a humane environment." Slater, an early consultant, in fact joined the experiment full-time in the spring of 1976 to work in the Corner of the College community. He felt the "Corner" was gaining ground, although less than one-fifth of the students were associated with it. Perhaps his most serious complaint was that "in general you treat experimentation and change as failure and decay, as if the first year was supposed to be the final form of things." Slater also felt that our account underestimated the quality of Kresge students and gave too little emphasis to the more traditional academic accomplishments of some of the founders.

Most of those we described as part of the founding group responded (Edgar, Kahn, Everson, and Kliger but not Sands, Hilgard, or Proudfoot). After a second reading, Kahn offered a précis of our account that was also in part a deft caricature, concluding that all of it was true, but that there were "other truths" he would like to see included. Foremost among these was a keener sense of how life-denying traditional universities are: "The governance is fascistic, self-serving and secretive; the teaching is spotty, ranging from inspired to terrible and the social structure is dreadful." What he and his colleagues had discovered at Kresge was not that the experiment was a failure and that therefore everyone should retreat to the safety zone of tradition, but that Kresge had wrestled with dilemmas worth struggling with. For him the critical issue was to see the Kresge experiment not as a choice between a "nice environment" or "learning" but to see the values as orthogonal and positively correlated. If one could not eliminate competition, one could at least reduce it to a comfortable level so that an "intellectually cooperative atmosphere" could replace the "criterion of success as victory."[53] In a final post mortem, he emphasized they had made "some staggering miscalculations about where the kids were . . . We came on much too strong . . . Instead of starting small and modest with people clamoring for the experiment and letting others join as they would, we tried to get *everyone* in the college involved instantly."

Kahn was not flattered by our portrait of him. "Am I really such a pretentious, humorless ass as the character who bears my name? I don't know whether to think I have just had a painfully accurate glimpse in a mirror or whether you have painted a not-altogether veridical picture. I suspect both." Edgar found aspects of our biographical approach offensive, although we had told him in the first interview that our way of understanding the evolution of an institution was to explain the intentions of the founders in the context of their biographies. He did not ask us to delete his name as did another faculty member, a T-group enthusiast who felt we invaded her privacy, and had not properly obtained the consent of "research subjects," a vulgar term we feel is inappropriate to describe observation in natural settings. We had not only obtained consent beforehand, and distributed to Edgar and others examples of previously published work in this vein, but we circulated drafts widely in order to give respondents an opportunity to raise objections. What better way to obtain consent than to show someone what you have written about them prior to publication? We deleted the faculty member's name as requested, and we cut away that which Edgar cited as offensive (not that we do so in every instance; some warts that readers want converted to dimples remain). Where there is a pattern to responses, and where more than one person cites a contrary interpretation or singles out a false note, we regard revision as virtually mandatory.

It would have been hard for many at Kresge to believe that a vice-chancellor who previously had thought Edgar most inept wrote that our account "increases my respect for him in communicating his own sharp awareness of the problems." Naturally, we are as interested in how others view the principals as in how they view themselves, and here we had some reassurance from the former Dominican monk who joined the Kresge experiment in the early days. William Everson felt we had captured the essence of the Kresge experiment and the personalities of the protagonists. In particular, he singled out Edgar as gaining stature in our rendering and "Kahn, the hardest one to get down, emerges convincingly." Everson felt that we had portrayed "a sense of valiant enterprise against great odds, the omnipresence of failure, a failure momentarily overcome then succumbed to. A pathos and a nostalgia for the realization of a great dream, and the inevitable loss of that dream."

David, the student whose graduation we attended in 1974, came back the following summer after a year at Oxford and wrote that Kresge was at least a partial success, and "much closer to the ideal community" than some of the despairing remarks of the founders might indicate. On a three-week visit, he was impressed by the "cohesiveness of the college," and by the willingness of faculty and students "to talk honestly to one another, and to meet one another." David argued that Kresge students had more diverse and interesting life-styles than others at Santa Cruz: "There is an enormous feeling at Kresge that people there are, for all this world's problems, *enjoying themselves*, and creating an exciting and vibrant community, even if it is not nearly as experimental and loving as the founders had wanted."

Some respondents criticized the draft for giving too much emphasis to the early years and not enough attention to changes as the college expanded and diversified. We must agree, and we attribute this fault to the pacing of our fieldwork. Another common theme of the letters was that we did not stress enough the fact that Kresge students and faculty were not captives but free to roam for courses and friendships in other departments and colleges at Santa Cruz. We did say this, of course, but for Edgar not strongly enough. He wrote that Kresge was not a "real College" but "something *in addition* to a conventional program and must compete with it for resources, energy and interest." Kresge might be better compared now to the Harvard houses in that it "represents to most people a recreational part of their existence," Edgar believed. But unlike Kresge, the Harvard houses have no authority to hire faculty, no role in their promotion, no authority to launch a college major, and no sense of themselves as colleges. Edgar's comments reflect disappointed hopes, not earlier intentions.

Finally, Edgar found our analysis of the "confusion between the public and private domains annoying" because he regarded the dilemma as in principle unresolvable. What was important was to remain open to change:

> Because above all else, I wanted to found a college that would be an alive, organic organization that could grow and change to meet the needs and aspirations of the people who were willing to work in it and benefit from it, more importantly learn from it. To me, more than any other place I have been, Kresge has these attributes.

Edgar, and nearly every one of the founders of Kresge, came to the college fresh from the flush of conversion experiences that had released in them new energies, that had legitimated new styles of life and allowed for the expression of what had hitherto been repressed. Organic growth was for them inexplicably bound up with the ecstasies of the T-group and a participatory style of human encounter through which they had come to feel born again. It was difficult for them to recognize that what they experienced as dramatic renewal, others sometimes felt as constraining and, on occasion, manipulative.

The Activist-Radical Impulse

The College for Human Services

The quarters of the College for Human Services are properly unprepossessing. As befits honest reformers, the place is frugal, a bit drab and hand-me-down. Most of its two hundred students are mothers who have been on welfare, although there has been a slight increase in the number of men who have come to the college in recent years. Better than 90 percent of the students are black, Spanish-American, or Polish-American.* Two mornings a week they come out of a subway at Varick and Houston Streets in lower Manhattan and enter a sooty building. On the eleventh floor they turn down a hall lined with offices that have been converted to classrooms. Some rooms have bright rugs, but there are few luxuries. A library of several thousand volumes is at one end of the hall; nearby is a student lounge with a few chairs and tables, but the students do little lounging because the two days they spend at the college are filled with classes and conferences from 8:30 A.M. to 5:00 P.M. The other three days of the week they are employed as interns† in schools, hospitals, social-work agencies, museums, and in a variety of other training positions that comprise what the college calls the human services.

When it opened in 1965 the college was called the Woman's Talent Corps, and no degree was given. By 1970, it had won accreditation

---

*As this book goes to press the proportions have changed somewhat. In 1977, about 60 percent of the students were black, 25 percent Spanish-American, 12 percent Polish-American (most of them recent immigrants who originally worked in a Polish Slavic center in Brooklyn), and the remainder other whites and Orientals.

†Because "intern" fails to convey the change-oriented perspective of the college, CHS itself never uses the word.

from New York State and the power to grant the two-year associate in arts degree. At that time, it sought to establish career ladders for low-income black women beginning as paraprofessionals. The students' median age was 37, and most scored below ninth-grade level on tests of verbal and mathematical ability. But although it was successful in getting women off welfare and employed in paraprofessional positions, the college was forced to conclude that its hoped-for career ladders were largely illusory. These ladders had too many steps and bumped into very low ceilings. Yet, in fact, some "paraprofessional" graduates were hard to distinguish from the professionals with whom they worked—apart from the size of their paychecks.

The college increasingly took on an activist and change-oriented mission designed not just to find routes up for its graduates but to change both the pathways and the professions. Paradoxically, though it pursued this mission in its later stages in the context of developing a performance- or competence-based curriculum that it hoped would be the basis of major reforms in the "human service professions," its language of competence was not technical. The curriculum was arranged as a series of "constructive actions," and each student was asked to "act as a change agent, planning, researching and promoting progress to improve human service delivery." Thus, though the college undertook the mission of consciously shaping the values of its students and of identifying them with a program of societal change, in some ways, as we shall see, the aims of the founders asked too much of students who, in many cases, simply wanted a decent job at decent pay.

Although the College of Human Services stands in this volume as an illustration of what we have identified in our typology as the activist-radical reform movement, it will become clear that this is but one of the many strands of reform the college has planned and encouraged. The other strands include devising new roles for faculty, granting access to the most deprived groups of students, and seeking to reform some professions by making assessment depend on the judgment of the client as much as that of fellow professionals.

I

The college was created by Audrey Cohen, a determined visionary and radical woman. She is shrewd, tough—although suave where necessary—and a fighter. She still bristles at the mention of a 1969 *New Republic* article by Joseph Featherstone that described the Talent Corps (as it was then called) as a college that "was started by a handful of reformist middle-class ladies with the idea of training poor women for jobs as assistants to professionals."[1] As an egalitarian, she resented being identified with the upper-middle class, yet she lives off Park Avenue, sends her daughters to the Chapin School, and earns a college president's salary. Though she is reminiscent of the settlement-house reformers of the nineteenth century and their notion of *noblesse oblige*, Audrey Cohen has more ambitious aims involving the reform of the professions and of higher education. Yet the parallel is not altogether unfair. In her emphasis on service and practical competence and her criticism of traditional universities, she has much in common with Jane Addams and Lillian Wald.

Audrey Cohen was born in Pittsburgh and graduated in 1953 from the University of Pittsburgh with a degree in political science. She taught high school for three years, was active in the civil-rights movement in Washington, D.C., and pursued graduate studies at George Washington University. It was in Washington in 1958 that she founded Part-Time Research Associates, utilizing the talents of married women to do research tasks for a variety of clients. She employed more than two hundred women, and the experience proved to be an early illustration that performance does not necessarily correlate with credentials. When her husband changed jobs, she moved to New York, and in 1964 founded the Women's Talent Corps, turning her energies away from the employment of suburban housewives to the placement of black women in burgeoning federal programs.

The Women's Talent Corps received a grant from the Federal Office of Economic Opportunity in 1966 not only to train these women but to create permanent jobs for them in the human-service sector. At that time, the college did not talk so much about transforming the professions as it did about reducing the antagonism between professionals and the poor neighborhoods they were supposed to serve, although the seeds of its later emphasis on the primary role of social change could be read even in its early history.[2] Of the 120 women accepted for the initial program, 113 completed a thirty-week training cycle and were subsequently employed.* The college

---

*Even if one looks at CHS only as a job training program for welfare recipients, its achievement is extraordinary. During the period 1967–72, two-thirds of the students were on welfare when they enrolled, and their median income was $3,120. About 80 percent completed the first-year program, and 92 percent of these were offered permanent employment. In 1972, the average salary of graduates was about $7,000. Completion rates over a two-year period are not as high, since first-year graduates who are offered jobs often cannot afford to return for a second year. In early 1977, with the prospects for the college's authorization to award the bachelor's or master's degree not encour-

was especially proud that it had established a foothold for "new careers" in several agencies. In the schools, the title "educational assistant" was created to denote pedagogical responsibilities in contrast with jobs for nonteaching community aides. At the time, the college was convinced it had achieved a breakthrough in helping to create new positions such as case aide, lay therapist, and community liaison assistant, and felt these would be first rungs on a ladder, not dead-end, nose-wiping jobs.

The core faculty were described in a 1968 report as "hardheaded do-gooders"—women who had had enough experience with incompetence among professionals as volunteers and mothers not to be awed by credentials or jargon. Most of the twenty faculty were white, perhaps one-third were Jewish. There were two blacks and one Puerto Rican among them, including the vice-president, Laura Pires Houston, a Cape Verdean who had graduated from Smith College and earned an M.A. in social work at Columbia. Laura Houston played a critical role in CHS's early development and continued in a consultant capacity to advise the college in important ways when she later returned to Columbia to complete her doctorate. Most of the white women had backgrounds in education or social work (only three had degrees in the field), and there were two lawyers and a few former journalists among them. Several were married to ministers or had studied theology. There were no men in the major administrative posts, and when we visited CHS in 1970 we observed that lines of authority seemed more loose and relaxed than would be typical of most male-dominated organizations.

Doris Younger, who became chairman of the faculty, graduated from the University of Pennsylvania and the Yale Divinity School (where she met her husband, a Baptist minister) and trained women as school reading aides before joining the college. The codirectors of field training were known as the two Barbaras: Barbara McHam had gone on to do graduate work in educational psychology after Bennington, and had worked as an admissions counselor at Friends Seminary and as a counselor at the Women's House of Detention. Barbara Buchanan earned her first degree at Wells, did graduate work at Union Theological and Teachers College, and had worked with her husband, an Episcopal minister, who served in two New York City parishes. Janith Jordan, academic director, had taught in

aging, there are reports of greatly increased attrition rates. For detailed information, see Sylvia Hack, "A Statistical Report on the College for Human Services, 1967–72," June 1973, p. 27.

a Detroit high school after finishing a master's in education at Michigan State.

Several of this first generation of faculty eventually went on to help launch other experiments. Barbara Buchanan joined the new College of Public and Community Services at the University of Massachusetts in Boston. William Statsky, who headed the college's early legal-assistant program, to be described more fully later, became a member of the founding faculty of the Antioch School of Law.

One of the first males to assume an administrative post was Kalu Kalu, a Biafran who had studied economics at Yale and Berkeley. Stephen Sunderland came from City University in 1972 as dean of research and planning, assuming most of Laura Houston's responsibilities. Sunderland had studied political science at Indiana after Hunter College, and earned his doctorate in organizational behavior at Case Western Reserve, where he also taught briefly. Earlier, he had been director of the higher-education program for the National Training Labs and headed the student academic-freedom project at the National Student Association. Among other later arrivals who became part of the core faculty was Roy Okada, a Hawaiian who earned a doctorate in English at the University of Wisconsin and who is now director of education. Ruth Messinger, a Radcliffe graduate, studied social work at Columbia and helped run an experimental school on the Upper West Side. Tom Webber, a former Peace Corps volunteer whose father was a minister in the East Harlem Protestant Parish, had graduated from Harvard, worked in a storefront tutoring program in the Bronx, and entered a doctoral program at Teacher's College designed to produce change agents. Adele Brody graduated from St. John's University Law School in the 1940s, married, practiced conventional law, then took a job with the Urban League in the late 1960s. Later, influenced by Frank Riessman, she became interested in the new careers movement, which eventually led her to the college. Pearl Daniels is a black woman who came to the college as a student in her mid-thirties, having dropped out of Textile High years earlier. She became an outstanding student at CHS and is now director of admissions and counseling.

In those first years, the college also laid the foundation for a new faculty role, "coordinating teachers" who divided their time to include supervising students on the job and, more importantly, acting as advocates for students in establishing career ladders. A student assigned to a legal-services office, for example, might begin with responsibilities no weightier than filing or answering the telephone. As the student learns more in class and on the job, the faculty member negotiates increased responsibilities, such as legal research or initial client interviews. Eventually, in successful cases, the student should receive increased pay and a redefinition of job. Coordinating teachers also sought to identify potential "teachers" as supervisors for the students at the agencies where they worked. The college expected the agency to help teach and make the job a learning experience.

Since the students are supported by federal training grants (now under CETA funds[3] through the City of New York), the college gains leverage with the agency by making students available as "free" labor. In the second year of training, the agency assumes half the cost. Of course, though the college was founded in the days of Lindsay optimism, it is now operating in an era of Beame budgets. Yet CHS believes that the need for preparing "human service workers" continues to be acute, projecting a demand for millions of additional jobs in order to provide adequate education, health care, and recreational services.[4]

The college added a second year to its training program in 1967. In 1968, it applied for a college charter with authority to grant the degree of Associate in Arts. The Department of Higher Education of the State Department of Education rejected the application on the grounds that most of its students had not graduated from high school, its faculty did not possess advanced degrees nor sufficient college teaching experience, and it did not have an adequate library or endowment. The reviewing officers praised the "social effectiveness of this dedicated and imaginative group of women," but concluded that the Talent Corps lacked the essential characteristics of a degree-granting institution.

Although such a decision is usually regarded as final, Audrey Cohen chose to ignore the door that had been shut in her face. Noting that technically the decision was not binding on the final authority, the Board of Regents, she began a campaign for approval at that level. She asked for a review of the college's program by Alvin Eurich's Academy for Educational Development, which subsequently recommended its approval as a degree-granting institution. She also hired a lawyer to contest the endowment requirement. Some concessions were made to demands for specialist faculty within the college's interdisciplinary structure. Not least, the college initiated a broad campaign to generate political and educational support.

On the matter of admissions standards, the college argued that job performance did not correlate with previous credentials and that students should be admitted without regard to previous formal education if they could pass basic reading and math tests. In response to criticism that the college did not adequately evaluate student performance, the Educational Testing Service was asked to advise whether tests had been developed that could be adapted to the college's program. When the ETS experts could furnish none, the college cited this as evidence of the need for CHS to develop new measures of student performance.

Internally, however, some faculty and students opposed seeking degree status, fearing that bending to bureaucratic requirements would mean sacrificing freedom to experiment. Yet other students were equally strong in their desire to obtain the "piece of paper" that opened doors in a diploma-conscious society. When it was suggested that the charter campaign would be an ideal project for the final unit of the first-year curriculum on social change, faculty members took sides. Some argued that the best way to learn about social change was to participate in an effort to win college status for themselves. Others opposed the campaign on the grounds that it upset curriculum plans and coerced students. In the end a compromise was reached in which students could choose among several action projects. Many participated in the charter effort, organizing letter-writing campaigns, seeking support for the college in agencies where they worked, collecting petitions, and so forth. In May 1970, the Board of Regents provisionally approved a college charter for a period of five years.

Although buoyed by the successful charter campaign, satisfaction was blunted by the increasing realization that the college's early enthusiasm about establishing new routes to professional careers was naïve. Mounting evidence showed that many of their students were held to terminal paraprofessional positions or assigned "aide" jobs normally filled by nonhigh-school graduates. Administrators in some state hospitals originally favored creating new paraprofessional positions in recreational therapy but could not get these approved by the head of the Department of Mental Hygiene or by the Civil Service. At the end of two years' training, graduates were hired as ward attendants, a position for which not even a high-school diploma was required, and which had little to do with the positions for which students were trained. New York City schools agreed to a six-step ladder for educational assistants, but relatively few such positions were approved, and few city schools offered possibilities for graduates to climb more than one or two rungs on this ladder. The college concluded that "the gains apparently won last year through negotiation with the Board of Education have to a considerable extent proved illusory."[5] The city's Housing and Development agency "set up a model career ladder on paper, but when it came to two years of study and likelihood of an AA degree, Talent Corps graduates did not fit into the ladders . . ."[6]

The right to award the A.A. degree, granted by the Regents in 1970, would help some graduates overcome hurdles to advancement on the job. But a parallel change in consciousness about the nature of the training the college wanted to give was also occurring. Less emphasis was put on the concept of training paraprofessionals as helpers who could move upward in traditional channels and more was given to the idea that the helping professions themselves needed major reform to emphasize "humane service." When the college opened, it sought to produce students who would "lighten the work-load and increase the effectiveness of the professional to whom they were assigned as an assistant."[7] A year later, the college emphasized the "belief of the Talent Corps that the para-professional, under supervision, is capable of performing a wide variety of tasks, many of which are professional in nature."[8]

The college increasingly emphasized that it "seeks to be both a teaching institution and an action institution . . . to stimulate its students to bring about institutional change without depriving them of the opportunity for a job." The College for Human Services would uphold its "primary mission" of promoting integration and "opening up the system" to minorities, and it would be

> . . . equally concerned with changing human service institutions so that they become more responsive to human needs. The more the College works in this area, the clearer it becomes that the shortcomings of the present system affect the public at large, and that basic changes are needed in the way service is delivered to everyone. . . . To this end, it will seek to create a new kind of credential, a two-year professional degree based on a definition which emphasizes humane performance rather than simply academic knowledge.[9]

The college recognized the burdens it placed on students in setting forth the model of "the participation of workers as agents of change in the work they perform—in its design, delivery and control." It was a model that some students rejected. In an interview in 1972, one student let down her hair: "A lot of this change stuff is a lot of crap. You just go out there and try to change them [the bureaucracies] and you'll be changing yourself right out of a job." As we have seen, the college was usually two or three strides ahead of some students, who simply wanted a good, paying job with a title. While some were willing to try to make some leaps forward, others were fearful. On a visit with student interns at St. Luke's Hospital, we found that one had withdrawn after the first year because the demands of the college were so great. A second-year student described her difficulty in making even small changes, such as addressing a patient "Senora" Lopez when other staff called out, "Lopez, Mary." Yet she had also helped to establish a career ladder by which paraprofessionals could move from clerical to minor administrative positions. The hospital supervisor compared CHS students favorably to other paraprofessionals: he felt they were more eager to learn, more open to criticism, and less inhibited in talking to doctors and other professional staff about the problems of patients.

The new emphasis that Audrey Cohen was putting on reforming the professions in the context of seeking authority for a full professional certificate (and eventually a master's degree) created major tensions in the college. When CHS added a second year to its original thirty-week program, it hired more black and Spanish-speaking male faculty, some of whom opposed the move to a new credential, believing the college should concentrate on the more limited goal of "opening the system" to minorities. Students petitioned for three days of classes, saying two days were insufficient to improve their deficiencies in English and math.[10] Members of the Student Council accused Audrey Cohen of being a politician who had duped outside agencies into thinking she was an innovative educator. "We do not want the College for Human Services to grant us a master's degree in two years when many of us feel we need remedial work," the students wrote. "We feel Mrs. Cohen has hit upon a great idea . . . that new routes in education should be carved out and performance should be as important as academic achievement. But she has made a joke of her own ideas. Our training is shabby, our academic classes are poor and once again we feel we have been taken advantage of."[11]

When Audrey Cohen fired the black director of the second-year program in 1972, charges of racism were raised, a boycott ensued, and some faculty resigned, as did the black chairman of the board of trustees, Preston Wilcox (though he was not entirely in sympathy with the faculty, whom he described as being of "questionable talent").[12] Audrey Cohen's resignation was demanded, and the faculty strike committee (which by no means represented all minority faculty) urged her replacement by a black or Puerto Rican president. Unlike many white liberals who caved in under such demands, Audrey Cohen replied by answering their specific charges, pointed out the acceptance of the college's program by many agencies, and hired a lawyer to defend her in the grievance hearings that were being pursued by the dismissed director. When she was upheld, she then proceeded to fire more than a dozen members of the faculty. She pointedly informed dissident faculty that the demand for her resignation had been based on considerations of color, not performance.[13] We cannot recount here the details of the two strikes that occurred during this two-year period, but their results were significant. The college began to pay more attention to basic skill training and to more seriously pursue a master's degree program. While continuing to recruit poor minority students, it also set out to raise the entrance requirements. Although a diploma was not required, students increasingly had the equivalent of a high-school education and some had a year or more in community colleges. Starting salaries for new faculty rose from $8,500 to $13,500.

The new emphasis on basic skills was also influenced by the college's experience with the Legal Service Assistant program (LSA), which was a joint venture with Columbia University Law School. The LSA was one of the most carefully investigated programs undertaken by the college. Students in the legal-aid program spent one-third of their time in the interdisciplinary core curriculum at the college, one-third in courses in legal skills and analysis at Columbia, with special emphasis on so-called poverty law (welfare family law, landlord-tenant actions), and one-third on the job as practicing legal aides.[14] In the report or study made of this program, Columbia was critical of the college's general-education program and noted that students' main problem on the job was related to their limited facility in written English. Yet the report also noted that there was little correlation between grades earned and student job performance, an observation that pleased the college.

Classes were initially held one day a week at Columbia University, and lectures and research assignments were given. But students varied greatly in their ability to do the academic work, and heavy job demands led to erratic attendance and failure to complete assignments. The coordinator arranged to have the class at the college in the second year and also met small groups of students in the neighborhood law offices. Of the twenty-three students initially accepted in the program, eighteen completed the first year, of whom sixteen were offered jobs; eleven of these continued to hold their jobs for the second year, of whom nine received special merit increases in the offices where they worked.[15]

A second study made by Statsky, then a member of the CHS faculty, revealed three broad levels on which the legal aides were working: six of the sixteen hired for the second year earned considerable independence, frequently handling routine cases to the point of courtroom appearances, when an attorney took over. Five performed limited legal tasks under close supervision, and five others worked as clerical aides and messengers (one operated a switchboard). Statsky's report also noted that poor work habits and "an unsatisfactory concept of time" constituted a major problem for five of the sixteen aides and a minor problem for four others.[16]

Statsky's study showed that some minority students with only grade-school skills at entrance could rise in two years of an intensive program to perform "professional" roles. On the other hand, it revealed the inherent difficulties of overcoming basic skill deficiencies and patterns of lateness and frequent absences, and of designing an academic program to fit such a diverse group. Only about one of every four students reached a "professional" level (i.e., six of the twenty-three who began the program). Further questions emerged: should the college give a professional school a veto over its program? If it refused to operate joint programs, where could it obtain specialized training?

The college decided to terminate the Legal Service program and to put its effort into developing new performance standards for a generic professional of human service. In effect, it ruled out the more specialized professions such as law or medicine and concentrated on social work, guidance and counseling, education, and other areas where there is no clearly defined or highly structured knowledge base underlying practice.

In a typically prescient essay,[17] Nathan Glazer has noted that the schools that train social workers, teachers, city planners, or ministers have been dubbed "professional schools" by courtesy, since they do not rest on the same base of special or technical knowledge as the classic professions of law and medicine. These schools have courted status by replacing practitioners with scholars and researchers. Schools of education train teachers, but they are increasingly staffed by psychologists, sociologists, historians, philosophers, and relatively few master teachers or practitioners. Sociologists and psychologists may be more interested in their specialties than in the quality of service practitioners deliver.

The most useful training for the "minor professions" of education and social work takes place on the job, although both have clear and important links to the academic disciplines. The problem the College for Human Services confronted was how to shape a curriculum that would draw on the disciplines in a way that would permit performance- or competence-based evaluation on the job. The college believed from the beginning that "all work with people involves basic similarities and depends on a common store of concepts and techniques."[18]

But if professional standing in the minor professions was not tied to specialized knowledge in the traditional sense, what, then, was the basis for judging the competence of the humane professional? For the next several years, the college attempted to answer the question stated most cogently by Laura Houston: "What does 'professional' really mean in terms of service, of results?"[19]

The traditional professions answer that (a) initial entry is controlled by certification through professional schools, and (b) only other professionals who possess the specialized knowledge and the privileged access to information about clients can judge the competence of practitioners. The College for Human Services and other critics of the professions have argued that certification procedures in professional schools are inadequate because they rely on grades and formal requirements though research studies have shown that (except perhaps in the field of engineering research) grades rarely relate to occupational success.[20] Initial entry, they claim, has sometimes been unfairly restricted to protect a profit monopoly as much as to protect standards. They argue that lax supervision of some self-interested professionals has resulted in inadequate protection for clients as well as increased isolation from standards of humane service. But in some aspects, the college's idea of the professional as client advocate is in direct conflict with the traditional ethic, which prohibits professionals from urging clients to embark on a particular course of action or to make what might be unnecessary purchases of services. It is clear that this attempt to be "objective" and "noncommercial" may be read by disadvantaged clients as coldness or indifference. Thus the defense attorney who puts on a fist-pounding show in the courtroom may lose the case, incurring the wrath of both judge and professional peers, but nonetheless be admired by the defendant, who believes he put up a good fight. (Such a lawyer, however, would fail the performance test if he lost most of his cases!)[21]

The college has attempted to devise an assessment system that includes clients as well as professionals, faculty, and student peers. In the fall of 1971, after the decision had been made to pursue a professional certificate, the faculty organized itself into five committees: education, day care, drug therapy, social work, and health professions. Each of these committees included some persons from the agencies where students had been placed. Each group attempted to define a standard of professional competence in that field, drawn from their own experience in supervision and observation, on the

basis of job descriptions, association statements, licensing requirements, and performance.

When we visited the college again in the spring of 1972, the faculty expressed frustration that they were not getting at generic "competencies." At a meeting of the top college staff Audrey Cohen asked
for advice, and Grant suggested that the college curriculum could
be the means of developing their understanding of the competencies
they sought to define. Students and faculty could together interview
and observe professionals at work. They could evolve methods for
distinguishing between "humane" and not so "humane" performance,
for example. After several days of joint observation, students and
faculty might independently record their impressions of how models
for each profession might be characterized. Such an exercise might
be a first step toward developing a vocabulary to describe professional competence, values, and skills. In the process, students could
learn the skills of interviewing, observation, note-taking, and so
forth. Yet Grant realized he was suggesting something closer to a
doctoral research program than to first-level professional training.
Audrey Cohen called in the research director to hear this scheme,
and the group immediately began to discuss whether and how it
might be practicable to move forward in this fashion.*

In its effort to define the professional competence of "humane" human service workers, the college turned in 1973 to empirical research. In 1973, David McClelland, the Harvard social psychologist,
and his private research firm, the McBer Company, were retained as
research consultants. McClelland had recently published an article,
"Testing for Competence Rather than for Intelligence," which appealed to the college in part because it argued that generic subsets
of personal attributes that underlie competence could be defined.[22]
The study done for CHS by the McBer Company was an important
step toward building a new competence-based curriculum. Their research did not involve direct observation but relied on analysis of
critical incidents or events described by exemplary human service
workers. Sixty-two such workers were selected by the college on the

---

*While this suggestion was not pursued in this form, as becomes clear in
the text, it is worth citing to demonstrate how quickly any idea from any
source was examined and plucked for whatever yield it might have. The incident also illustrates how the line between observer and observed, rarely un-
broken in any research, was frequently crossed at the college. In fact, a researcher who refused to interact beyond minimal professional courtesies would
not be tolerated at the College for Human Services.

basis of its own observations in various agencies. While not imputing any "superior knowledge of professional performance" to the college, McBer argued that the "college alone can define its mission" and that it was appropriate for them to define it in terms of producing practitioners resembling the sixty-two regarded as exemplary by the college.

The results of the research are interesting, although one can doubt whether the process really defines competencies of human service workers. Each of the sixty-two human service workers selected by the college was asked to describe the job during the previous years. The instructions required them to write page-long accounts of ten critical incidents or "samples of your life and work."

The incidents cited as successes seem typical of what many professionals would regard as good practice: a teacher devised a contract with a third grade boy to get him to stop practicing Kung Fu in class; a worker reduced tension levels in an interracial teen center; a subordinate initiated dinner with an "impossible boss," clearing the air and creating a good relationship.

Finally, the incidents were analyzed from the point of view of "competencies" unique to human services work. These were competencies aggregated as a result of "the intuitions of creative readers of the incidents." Thus, for example, the "competence" of "persisting in spite of discouragement and roadblocks" was the outcome of an aggregate of the following events cited in the critical incidents:

> . . . insisting on payments to a family with five children whose benefits were cut off because their father had died; staying with a suicidal person; reacting to direct and public criticism from immediate superior; overcoming the board's unwillingness to invest in a program for the foreign born; recognizing the gradualism inherent in changing a system by very sustained and patient effort; working in an impossible multi-agency system to help an intolerable and overwhelming family situation in housing; facing overwhelming defeat.

As a result of this analysis, David McClelland derived the following seven competencies:

1. Strong faith that human needs can and must be met:
   a. That every client can change and grow
   b. That attitude change is possible and it itself is worthwhile
   c. That you can get the system to adjust to the needs of the individual at least some of the time
2. Ability to identify correctly the human problem:
   a. By being a good listener and observer

    b. By being able to get other people to talk openly and freely
3. Ability to arrive at realistic, achievable goals in collaboration with clients
4. Imaginativeness in thinking of solutions to problems
    a. Through use of own human relations skills
    b. Through knowledge of resources and regulations
5. Persistence in pursuing solutions, often against hostile authorities
6. Ability to remain task-oriented under stress, hostility
7. Skills in getting interested parties to work together to arrive at common goals.[23]

Though many questions may be raised about the validity of the McBer Company's methods and the value of the findings, and though the report was never adopted as such, it became the basis of continued discussion among the faculty and was an important step toward the college's goal of basing its program on new definitions of competence and on new professional models.

When the faculty met in the spring of 1974 to work on the concrete details of the new curriculum for the class that would enter in the summer, the fruits of the long months of searching for new definitions and new directions finally began to be realized. After weeks of work, a light dawned.*

Two years later, faculty still speak of the euphoria of the "breakthrough." In retrospect, as in most quite complex matters, it seems simple. The group were talking about two different kinds of competencies. On the one hand, students were asked to do something: "to design and implement a learning-helping environment" or "to conduct human service research." On the other hand they were concerned with aspects of performances: consciousness of one's own values, or understanding the larger system within which an action was embedded. Thus the competencies were a statement of actions or functions, as well as of values or dimensions. Both aspects—the accomplishment itself as well as an awareness of its value—constituted a professional performance. In a sense, the curriculum was as old as the sixteenth-century Jesuit ideal, *actione contemplativus*, acting with

---

*This feeling of exhilaration is characteristic of groups involved in developing so-called competence-based programs. It seems to happen at the moment of producing a "grid" of some sort—in this case a performance grid. There no doubt is genuine insight and achievement as well as a feeling of relief that a consensus has been reached. Such typologies, however, often strike the outsider as too pat and too full of jargon.

purpose and contemplative awareness. Like the Jesuits, the College also emphasized the need to judge human action in its fullness:

> It is clear that the dimensions can only serve their purpose as a guide to learning and assessment if they encompass every significant aspect of performance. Any breakdown of performance into its supposed elements is, of course, artificial. Knowledge, skills, attitudes, the components into which learning is most commonly analyzed, are totally inappropriate for performance-based education because they disregard the active interplay of insight, experience, judgment, purpose, etc., that comprises a living performance. Instead of dealing in such rigid categories, the College has tried to develop the dimensions as a filter which makes it possible to focus on the various aspects of performance without forgetting their relationship to the whole.[24]

This "whole" to be assessed by the college was called a "constructive action." The curriculum as the student would encounter it subsumes his learning and experience into a series of constructive actions demonstrating different facets of competence. The performance grid summarizing this development, which has remained the basic Bible of the new curriculum, is shown in Appendix 4. Appendix 5 details sample facets of the curriculum related to the first four competencies.

A "grid," no matter how neat it is or how much euphoria it induces in the faculty, is not sufficient to establish a new profession, however. Now several steps were taken. The first was to use the new curriculum to seek authority from New York State to grant a degree certifying its students as Masters of Human Services. A profession also needs wider recognition from funding sources, policymaking groups, educational institutions, and other professions. In June 1974, at a conference at Columbia University, the college brought together a broad potential support group and made a simple announcement of a new profession of the human services.

There were about 60 guests at the conference, including government and foundation officials, representatives from agencies where CHS students worked, a sprinkling of representatives from academic institutions, a few feminists, representatives from the teachers union and the Public Education Association. A number of social-work professionals were also present, including a member of the Council of Social Work, a traditional New York agency concerned about maintaining high standards.

Once the guests (including Grant) had settled into their chairs, Audrey Cohen explained that they were going to play the "change game." A ten-page document explained the game, which was based on the following premise:

> A new profession is being created to deal with the massive service delivery problems evidenced in schools, hospitals, counseling centers, prisons, and other agencies that presently deliver services to people. The new profession is predicated on a new standard of service delivery, new accountability to the clients, and new approach to the education of professionals.[25]

Each person was assigned to a small group with a role to play answering possible objections from clients, traditional professionals, union officials, potential employers, or students in this new college. The catch was that the participants were not allowed to agree with criticisms but were told to think of positive responses to them. It was their task to "champion the new profession and to find the specific ways and means to make its acceptance a reality." Prior to the conference, the college faculty played the role of devil's advocate, listing all the objections each of these groups might have to the college or the new profession. The difficulty was not in finding the objections but in countering them. The "game" itself was a bold and ingenious stroke, a "constructive action" on the part of the college that maximized helpful responses and minimized the possibility of the conference turning into a "stop-the-college" event. A few participants resented what they regarded as manipulation and said so. But most joined the game, amused if not convinced.

In a group on the students' perspective, a black woman alumnus of the college now teaching children better dental care said one of the best arguments for the college was that it gave students like her a second chance when no other institution would. Thomas Corcoran, an officer of the Fund for the Improvement of Postsecondary Education, said that although the college's rhetoric was not far different from what other colleges promised, its faculty provided more supervision and advocacy on the job. Others pointed out that while students took a risk, since the college was not authorized to grant a master's degree, it had compiled a good record in placing students, and had made good on its advocacy claims by securing paychecks for students in training.

The college moderator was not entirely successful in keeping the members of the group from joining the critics. A New York school principal wondered whether the college wasn't authorizing a new bureaucracy in the guise of attacking the old. He disagreed with those who argued that the college's two-year degree would "give it an edge on the market," because he doubted it would gain acceptance against five-year master's candidates in the keen competition for jobs among students in education and the social services today.

Harold Lewis, dean of social work at Hunter College, said the college might be able to build on the "street experiences" of its students in an intense two-year program. But he did not know of another master's program in the country that would accept students who did not have a B.A. He also asserted that there were no valid measures to assess the competencies the college was talking about. During the remainder of the day, the college heard expressions of support from many participants, but was warned that strong opposition would come from groups that had established the standard of a five-year master's. At the close of the conference, Lewis spoke for the Council of Social Work, saying that it was opposed to the formation of this new profession until the college specified with more rigor and more detail what it was they were really doing that was any different.

Such opposition was not unexpected, and following the conference the college did what it asks its students to do: it attempted to work around and minimize the effects of "negative field forces," while maximizing the positive elements for change. The most prestigious supporters at the conference were asked to form a task force to establish the new profession and win wider recognition of it. Others were politely ignored.

In August 1974, the college explained its new curriculum and the research on which it was based in a two-volume proposal seeking the authority to grant the master's degree. The proposal[26] highlighted three fundamental propositions the program had been designed to test:

1. That disadvantaged persons may be exceptionally qualified to serve others with intelligence, purpose and humanity.
2. That a performance-based program can prepare professionals in two rather than the usual five or six years.
3. That a new profession, human services, can serve clients better by responding to needs rather than within boundaries defined by traditional professions.*

A year later, the New York State Department of Education rejected the college's application, principally on the grounds that it

---

*In language characteristic of the reformer's zeal, the proposal states: "in other words it is now possible to establish a new profession of Human Services which brings together every aspect of direct service to the individual" (p. 5). CHS's hopes would indeed be dystopian (and possibly dangerous for the clients themselves) if the college turned out all-purpose human-service activists who failed to realize the legitimacy of other, more traditional "helping" professionals.

could not authorize a master's degree that was not built upon a bachelor's program.[27]

This time, the college responded in some of the same ways as it had in 1968, seeking other avenues of support and trying to demonstrate that its students would have the equivalent of a bachelor's degree. But it also tried another tactic. Since the model could not be sold in New York, why not export it? Audrey Cohen obtained a grant to disseminate the college's model and began consulting at several colleges in California, Massachusetts, and Pennsylvania. Lincoln University expressed considerable interest. In 1976, its faculty, with the support of Jerome Ziegler, then Commissioner of Higher Education in Pennsylvania, approved a program that was based on the CHS model, although its exit requirements included a core academic program as well as standardized tests. In 1977, CHS won a temporary license to confer the master's degree at a branch it established in Florida. The college has since resubmitted its application for degree-granting authority in New York.

II

In the summer of 1975, we attended an admission session conducted by the college counselor and admissions director. One of the early arrivals was Jose Morales, who had been born in Puerto Rico and had made heels in a New York shoe factory for 23 years. In March, when the factory closed, his children urged him to return to school despite his age of 41, and a friend who worked with his wife as a teacher's aide had told him about the College for Human Services. Like the other seven applicants who arrived for a group interview that morning, he had survived an earlier screening. Nervousness showed in the strained conversation among strangers—in this particular session six Polish-speaking applicants and one black participated along with Morales.* Half were women. After waiting fifteen minutes past the appointment hour, the door was locked to later arrivals.

Jan Powell, a college counselor, and Pearl Daniels, the admissions director, explained the history of the college, noting that CHS now

---

*This session was atypical in its ethnic representation; it happened to come at a point when the college was recruiting students for placements in the Polish-Slavic center in Brooklyn. But similar sessions are held for all applicants. Student names are disguised in these accounts; faculty identities have not been except in those cases where confidentiality was requested.

had no power to grant the master's degree and that the agencies in which students would be placed were not legally bound to hire them. Thus the students could finish the program without either a degree or a job. Pearl Daniels warned them of the demands and rigor of the program, of the impact it would make on their lives and those of their families. The women would need two babysitters—one as backup for the other. Divorce and separation rate of the students was high. They would receive a weekly stipend of $99.75 and free dental care in the first year. In the second year, part of the cost would be paid by the agencies and regarded as taxable salary; thus in effect they would suffer a pay cut. She urged them to try to save part of their stipend in the first year, despite the difficulty. She knew many were coming off welfare and would want to do a little catch-up spending, "but if you're going to buy a color TV, buy a small one."

During the two-hour conversation that followed, students were invited to introduce themselves, to say why they wanted to come to the college, and to inquire about any aspect of the program. One student asked if she could switch jobs. A Muslim wanted to know if he would have time to pray. A woman asked if she had an obligation to pay the stipend back to the college if she could not finish the program. In the second hour, the applicants were more at ease, laughing, occasionally disagreeing.

Pearl Daniels and Jan Powell responded candidly to questions (yes, you could switch, but it was not encouraged; it might be difficult to observe Muslim prayer practices within the college's hectic schedule; no, it was not necessary to pay back any part of the stipend). But most of the interviewers' attention was focused on the interaction of the participants. Throughout the morning they evaluated candidates on eight criteria: (1) general appearance (dress, grooming, manners); (2) communication ability (listens to others, waits for them to finish, effectively expresses own ideas and opinions); (3) relevancy of comments to group discussion (comprehension, appropriateness, understanding of what is taking place in group); (4) attitudes toward peers (interest in peer comments, openness to other points of view); (5) attitude toward group leaders (interaction, attention, quality of relationship, any hostility toward authority?); (6) expressed social concerns (awareness of problems and solutions, knowledgeability, values, recognition of need for change); (7) demonstrated potential for helping others (listening, evidence of warmth and empathy); (8) academic motivation (willingness to try, readiness to see learning as a positive way to change society, others, and self). Daniels and Powell made clear that the college sought insight into the attitudes and motivation of potential students. Selection was made with a view toward the goals of the program, in this case, a profile of the highly motivated "humane" worker who listens, has empathy, sees need for change, and has the determination to get results.

At the end of the session, students spent the afternoon taking the college's own examinations while the interviewers compared their ratings. The first student they discussed was a Polish male, Jerzy Kielow, 21, single, a high-school graduate living with his mother, who spoke some Spanish in addition to Polish. Jan Powell felt he was isolated and withdrawn; he had sat apart, did not join in, hadn't bothered to turn around when she went to the board behind him to draw a diagram explaining the curriculum. Before the interview began he approached her about including his girl friend in the interview. When he was told no, he was unable to accept such a refusal, and he came back to plead this case. The interviewers noted that his oral presentation did not match the expectations they had on the basis of the polished application essay he had written; they wondered whether he had written it and made a note to look carefully at the examination he was taking that afternoon. He raised no questions and did not seem to remember Jan Powell, who had met him and other Polish applicants at a neighborhood center several weeks ago. Grant wondered whether Kielow's stilted and insecure presentation reflected a kind of culture shock he must have felt at encountering such an egalitarian setting, where college admissions officers gave applicants permission to address them by their first names and strangers were asked to speak quite personally about their motives. Pearl Daniels considered this but replied that to be successful at the college, a student would have to be able to interact successfully in a group. His application was laid aside as doubtful, pending review of his exam.

The admissions officer warmed to a 45-year-old Polish woman who had three children, had worked in a hospital in Poland, but had spent most of her life mothering and now wanted to do something for herself. They liked this "budding feminist" and gave her high marks for comments she made about the need for Poles in her neighborhood to make overtures to the nearby Puerto Rican community. The Black Muslim was a high-school dropout, now 26. As a child, he had bagged heroin for his parents, shot it up himself at age 14, and kicked the habit at 22 when he converted to his new religion. Jan Powell felt hostility toward his insistence on making time for Muslim prayers five times a day and wondered whether someone who wore Muslim garb as a "badge" could "fold other

people in," or be open to their point of view. Yet she was impressed
by his honesty and his care for five foster children whom he and his
Muslim wife have taken in. He was put in the category of "probably
admit" pending exam results. Jose Morales was appealing to both
interviewers. They felt that this man who helped Spanish-speaking
people fill out the forms in the welfare office so they could avoid the
sharks' fees, who listened, and was enthusiastic, was "our kind of
student." They admitted him at once, along with the older Polish
woman.

The examination which students were taking was homegrown. No
nationally standardized tests are given: the college does not find
these useful for its own diagnostic purposes, and many of its applicants resent such tests (we find the college's practice more justifiable
at entrance than at exit, as we shall discuss in more detail later in
this chapter). CHS follows the principle that even unsuccessful applicants should learn something from taking a test. Hence the first
reading comprehension question is a short article from the *New York
Daily News* explaining a simple test for diagnosing sickle-cell anemia,
a hereditary disease found almost exclusively among blacks. There
are also excerpts from Ralph Ellison's *Invisible Man* and an editorial by W.E.B. DuBois hailing the black soldier of World War I:
"Out of this war will rise an American Negro, with the right to vote
and the right to work and the right to live without insult."

The college's ideology seeps into the model answer sheet used to
grade exams. For example, on a 25-word vocabulary test, the model
answer for "professional" is given as "someone who has competence
and commitment to serve." The word "service" is defined as "really
helping." One of the questions following the W.E.B. DuBois editorial
asks whether students would make the same arguments about the
black soldier in the Vietnam War, and the answer sheet reads: "No.
He was fighting other people of color. If there is a right side, it is
more the Communists. There are no immediate benefits for the returning black G.I. except a small G.I. Bill." But questions cast in
this way constituted less than 20 points on a 385-point scale. It
would be misleading to interpret the whole test as ideological and
designed to screen out those with "incorrect" political views. In fact,
the college's bias is more like that of a religious group seeking postulants who hear its call for service and social change, those who
would be good candidates for the college's "ideology of citizen
empowerment."

The exam also includes questions about the college, based upon
the materials distributed to students in advance and the explanations

given to the students in the admissions session. It concludes with a short math quiz.

Jerzy Kielow's scores confirmed the interviewers' suspicions that he may have had help writing his application. His comprehension and math scores were so low as to eliminate him. Jose Morales scored 315 (250 is "passing") with an excellent comprehension but weak math skills. Of the eight, five were accepted, two rejected, one provisionally admitted. Two of those admitted had a year of college, three were high-school graduates, and Morales had completed the 11th grade.

The admissions process, like the college itself, is compassionate but tough. It not only admits a student but, acting as a proxy for various agencies, in effect is hiring him.* The reputation of the college rests on the performance of its students, and while CHS takes chances, it can not risk many disasters on the job. Yet CHS has been secure enough, for example, to turn down a major "training contract" from a state agency that wanted the college to cut its curriculum to order and give up its hopes for a master's level program.

A typical negotiating strategy was illustrated on the day Ruth Messinger and Bonnie Hall went to the Manhattan Development Center to secure placements for fourteen students. They met with the heads of several mental-health facilities associated with the center. Some of these were residential facilities for severely mentally retarded children, others community halfway houses or mental-health therapy centers. Dr. Alphonse Sorhaindo was perhaps the most favorably disposed of the group toward the College for Human Services and was eager to have its students as internes.

But others around the table were more skeptical. After polite probing of the curriculum, they feared that shrinking budgets would force them to dismiss the CHS students at the end of the program. But at this point Ruth Messinger intervened to explain that Audrey Cohen had negotiated in Albany with the associate commissioner of the State Department of Mental Hygiene. He had agreed that they would find funds and "job lines" for fifty-five CHS students at the completion of the two-year program. Ruth Messinger showed them a copy of that letter and promised that the college would hold the commissioner—not them—responsible for the jobs. This was typical of the college's strategy of negotiating job quotas at the highest level so

---

*This, of course, makes dismissal more difficult, since to fail a student is essentially to "fire" him. But the college tries not to shirk that responsibility. Though it grants wide access, it does not guarantee exit.

that local agencies were relieved of the burden of justifying new budget positions whenever possible. Although such high-level endorsement is crucial, the college must still win its way into individual agencies and obtain the director's signature to a seven-page contract, the heart of which reads:

> The College and the Agency agree to this relationship in order to: a) develop appropriate new educational routes into the human service profession; b) plan and implement training leading to professional employment; c) jointly employ a system of performance-based assessment criteria which will insure professional competence; d) initiate and implement procedures for acquiring the academic degrees and certification that will assure Program Graduates appropriate professional status; and e) provide skilled workers who, both during the course of the program and thereafter, will improve, supplement and expand human service delivery and demonstrate new and effective professional roles.

The contract then spells out the agency's responsibilities and declares in detail what the college will do: that it will help to devise the educational component of training on the job, and make a determination of what portion of time will be spent in work and/or study.* At the negotiating session we are describing here, one of the directors of the Manhattan Development Center voiced his poor opinion of the CHS students who worked at his agency in 1971: they "shouldn't have been working with patients at all." He wanted assurances that subsequent students would be adequately supervised, explaining that his staff was already stretched too thin. Ruth Messinger said that they had made some mistakes and that they were now recruiting abler students. Incompetent students would not be retained. Coordinating teachers, she admitted, had been under increasing pressure and had carried an excessive workload. By morning's end, the director, who had been consistently doubtful, agreed to take four students personally under his wing. While we cannot tell what motivated the director partially to overcome his doubts, it was our impression that the persistent and nondefensive style in which Ruth Messinger and Bonnie Hall had responded to his criticisms had proved disarming.

"Become an effective learner and potential professional," is the simple declaration students hear as they begin classes at CHS. For

---

*The full two-year program is organized in three broad phases, and the number of hours devoted to a formal educational component, as compared with the number of hours on the job, varies. The amount of compensation given by the agency and the amount paid by the college out of its CETA funds are adjusted proportionately.

most of them, the idea that one can learn more or less effectively is a novel one. Perhaps an even greater discovery is the variety of attitudes their classmates have about the likelihood of positive growth and change. This, of course, is the "value dimension" of the first competency, as set forth in Appendix 4. The purpose of learning is to "Demonstrate your readiness to work toward realizing your personal and professional goals and helping the College fulfill its mission by joining the College as . . . a potential professional."

From one viewpoint, the first competency is a course on CHS and its unique language of "crystals," "performance grids," and "constructive actions." Students are being asked if, on the basis of more detailed knowledge of what the place is about, they are ready to make a contract to pursue the college's goals. Particularly for students in a high-risk category (which at CHS may mean recent parole on a felony charge), this is a moment of commitment, when they must decide if they "really want to get off the corner."

By the end of the four-week period devoted to the first competency, students must write a proposal describing their personal goals over the next two years and outlining the steps by which they will reach them. In the process, they must demonstrate an understanding of how others will help them reach these goals (the self-and-others dimension), that they understand how the college's aims contrast with those of traditional professional education (the systems dimension), and how they can "determine and rank long and short range goals and develop alternative strategies to meet them" (the problem-solving skills dimension). Students keep a log or diary during this first competency unit, which includes an exercise in assessing the values of the CHS teachers they are encountering in class. Students also read autobiographies showing contrasting values and learning styles.

Grant had met Jose Morales in June and it was November when he caught up with him again. Morales had completed the first competency on becoming a learner, and the second on establishing a professional relationship at the worksite; now he was in the midst of the third: "working with others in groups, helping to establish clear goals." Grant and he went to lunch together, and in spite of his high original expectations Morales did not seem discouraged. The only reservation he expressed was that perhaps the screening should be tougher—fewer students should be taken with deficiencies in basic skills and with family problems. Yet it seemed remarkable to him that there were no drunks and nobody high on drugs in the college, compared with what he knew of other colleges in the city. He winced when it was suggested that perhaps classes should be tracked in skill areas—"tracking" was virtually a forbidden word—

but on reflection he thought this was needed. Of course, if the college had been tougher, he might not have been accepted. His math was poor and he didn't know how to write a paragraph. In fact it wasn't until the second day of his skills class that he knew what a paragraph was. Now he could write one.

Morales said he was no professional yet, "not by a long shot," but he was learning. In fact, when he was admitted he thought a mistake had been made. He didn't think he was ready or prepared to be a professional. "It was like telling me I was going to be chief surgeon at Mt. Sinai. What the hell am I going to do with a scalpel in my hand? I might cut myself." But after the first competency (which he called "the orientation period"), he realized it was possible "to take your own experiences in life, your own true feeling, and if you want to make a contribution to the community you can."

He was inclined now to think one could change things. That was something that he had learned. He discovered values he didn't know he had—for example, the way his religion affected his outlook. Also, "how do you say it? . . . fatalistic . . . I was willing to just let things be, but coming here I learned you can really change things." His wife tells him he has changed, that he doesn't explode at the children so much. He's more likely to listen instead of brushing them away. But things weren't going that well on the job. He was not sure he was cut out to be a teacher (his job placement was as a teacher's aide in an alternative high school). Maybe he would do better at counseling. But one could talk about the problems—that was also a virtue of the college.

Over several years, Grant visited more than a score of classes at the college. Some were stimulating, some not so successful, and others minor disasters. What distinguished them was the attention to student field experiences; the common, cumulative curriculum tied to a series of student "constructive actions"; the subjugation of disciplinary divisions of knowledge to the functional categories of the competency goals, and the deemphasis of reading or analysis of texts. Nothing is labeled psychology or sociology or economics. Many CHS students, to be sure, would not know how to answer if asked whether they were learning any sociology. They do, of course, though not in a formal, structured sense. Adele Brody, a lawyer by training, teaches what in many sociology departments would be called a course on formal organizations. But the students do not read S. M. Lipset, Peter Blau, or any of the standard sources in this field. Adele Brody distributes copies of agency budgets and teaches students how to read them to find out who makes decisions, or how informal structures may block a decision that originates in formal channels.

A Polish student in her late twenties could not describe what she had learned by using formal sociological categories. She had had a smattering of sociology at Staten Island Community College, and contrasted it with CHS, where "we are dealing with more realistic problems of people, of the agencies of the city." What did she mean by that? She replied:

> To be effective in the situation. To analyze the client's problems —to know what is realistic, what is not. How to deal with a particular client, know yourself, know your emotions. Once you're in the agency, how to feel it out. Know who to go to see to get something done.

The practical, applied emphasis is evident in many classes. When a student asked Kalu Kalu, "How do we know how much a dollar is really worth?" he turned the question back on the students and guided them in constructing an index comparing today's prices of basic products with those of ten years ago. Yet if they were asked to define a cost-price index, many of these students would not be able to give the textbook answer.

The reading lists in the formal curriculum guides are impressive. Under Competency V (Counseling), for example, 71 books are listed, from Samuel Butler to Thomas Szasz, and including Freud, Erikson, Haim Ginott, Camus, Robert Coles, Arthur Janov, Jung, Marx, Maslow, Nietzsche, Wilhelm Reich, Carl Rogers, Shakespeare, Skinner, and Tennessee Williams. Even many doctoral students would not be at ease with the range of literature listed! This is no modest list of 100 great books; it is closer to 1,000 (if one adds all the competencies).

In actuality, traditional reading of this sort has a low priority. The students' acquaintance with books is painfully thin. Faculty members acknowledge this by assigning only short xeroxed articles or chapters—seldom books. Frequently key passages are read in class, an open acknowledgement that not many have read the assignment. There are few written assignments or "bookish" demands. The college stresses action. Students have hectic schedules, and the faculty are overburdened themselves. In one class a faculty member announced a standard written assignment to be completed over the weekend. A student outburst followed—fists banged, there were loud groans and shouts of "We can't do it. No way!" She backed down. After class she admitted that they had not exactly demonstrated "professional behavior" and she resolved not to be intimidated a second time.

Many students are not skilled at analyzing texts. In one class, a student explained the book *Parent Effectiveness Training* as being about "reverse psychology . . . you know, it's like when your kid wants to go to the store to get some bubble gum and you don't want him to go, you use reverse psychology on him." Another student, who had outstanding on-the-job ratings, when asked what readings had been helpful, could not think of any. Finally she thought of Rousseau, but when pressed she couldn't "remember what his philosophy is."

Yet a class in group dynamics, in which students were analyzing the makeup of their own group, was a model that most teachers would envy. Similarly, Tom Webber's class was lackluster and withdrawn when he attempted to get students to discuss an article by Ronald Hyman on teaching methods. But when he left the text, and asked students what they would do in a tutoring center for 42 high-school students on a day when 10 volunteer college tutors did not show up, the discussion covered all the strategies that one would find among a group of student teachers at Hunter or Berkeley.

However, an observer recoils from the notion that students who have such cursory acquaintance with the books that ask some of the most profound and disturbing questions about the human condition are certified as human service workers. But should one compare these students with some ideal, or with what the average nurse or primary-school teacher knows of Rousseau? Furthermore, will reading Rousseau or Shakespeare improve their performance? Are not most liberal arts, and even many more "technical," courses taught to students in social work and teaching arbitrary; don't they at least have only weak correlations with performance? Doesn't the foregoing disjunction between discussing Rousseau and discussing what to do in a tutoring center simply confirm the Aristotelian distinction between theoretical and practical wisdom? To know something is not to do something well. One cannot justify Rousseau or Shakespeare in relation to short-term rewards.

Any attempt to justify the importance of gaining wisdom through reading only amounts to a vulgarization and an admission of defeat. Can music be justified to someone who has never heard a bar? Books can be valued only after they are experienced, and the traditional sources must be included in any professional curriculum on the grounds that our notion of a humane life is impoverished without them. Yet we know that professional education in America is often impoverished even when it is accompanied by a smattering of the liberal arts.[28]

What of more specialized or technical knowledge? A teacher of mathematics obviously needs to know mathematics. A pharmacologist must understand certain branches of chemistry and biology. The college's position is that most specialized knowledge can be learned on the job. With no laboratories, the scientific knowledge imparted crucially depends on the resources devoted to students on the job, and here opportunities vary enormously.

Gladys King, a 45-year-old black student who interns as a counselor in an alternative high school in the Williamsburg section of Brooklyn, faces the problem many of the more able CHS students confront. In the competition for jobs, will they be better off with training for a specific position? She wants to be a counselor-teacher and has decided to take those specific courses in a community college in the evening. Did she choose that avenue of training because she needed specific credentials or because she lacked knowledge to do the work she wanted to do?

> I really do need more academic preparation to feel educated as a whole person. Maybe it's an inadequate feeling on my part. I will probably end up doing the same work I am doing now [by which she meant counseling], but I would like to be a counselor-teacher. I need science courses, not more counseling courses. Also math courses. These are the courses I need to feel like a well-rounded person. To me a well-rounded person means an adequate person. So I can function better in my job. If I am asked to assist the math teacher or assist the science teacher, I would like to know that I am prepared for that.

Gladys King's dilemma points up some of the limitations and problems of the CHS program. She is a fascinating, strong-willed woman typical of many of the older blacks at the college. She was born in Georgia, never finished high school, but earned an equivalency certificate after she came to New York. Before coming to CHS she worked as a playground supervisor, then became assistant to the director of a local community-action program. She had earlier taken a six-week program through the University Without Walls, which was designed to teach participants about federal programs to help church and community groups finance nonprofit housing. Having paid tuition out of her own pocket, she was dismayed to get no college credit for this program; nor would Pace College give her credit when she applied to a business administration program there. She deeply believes in CHS and its performance-based style, but she needs the additional insurance that would come from more tradi-

tional courses. CHS for her seems to be merely another chapter in
the frustration of putting a high degree of effort into programs that
bring questionable monetary rewards. She suspects the college gives
adequate preparation for social work and counseling, but for teaching, some science and math seem necessary.

Another area of technical knowledge that the college does not
teach well would be called "tests and measurements" in a traditional
catalog. The prejudice (which may be a fair prejudgment in some
instances) that most of these tests are bad or ill-used is imparted to
the students but they are taught little that will allow them to be
sophisticated critics or users of such tests. The college's ideology also
infects discussions of modern social science. For example, in one
class the *Coleman Report* was lumped with other "social theories
that blame the victim for not learning." Although the *Coleman Report* does provide evidence that home environment affects achievement test scores more than do differences in school quality (measured by traditional indicators such as cost per pupil), Coleman also
argues that learning opportunities for poor children could be improved through economic integration (schools that have a good mix
of lower-, middle-, and upper-class families). In some classrooms at
CHS, students are more willing to discuss the complexities than are
fervent faculty. One teacher presented as unchallengeable the notion
that in school it was "white middle-class prejudices that turn black
kids off," whereas an older black woman later challenged a classmate: "What makes you think black kids can't learn to read from
Dick and Jane readers? I learned to read from Dick and Jane books."
The school's change-oriented ideology also infects the way material
is presented. A film on the community organizer Saul Alinsky, presents him as a model to be emulated without question, and much of
the discussion about him sounds like a testimonial.

While the fault lies somewhat in ideological bias, it is also a reflection of the faculty's limited knowledge. There are no sociologists
at CHS who are likely to have read the full *Coleman Report* and
secondary analyses of it. The faculty's disciplinary training in social
sciences is not strong. It does shine in other areas: interviewing skills,
group dynamics, a detailed knowledge of how human resources agencies in New York work, and explanations of new laws affecting client
rights in many sectors. A deputy director of a mental-health agency
was surprised that CHS students who had been on the job only a
few months were familiar with court decisions affecting the mentally
ill which professionals on his staff had not read. Moreover, the students saw in the decisions implications relevant to improving the
treatment of patients in his facility.

The college also employs an excellent staff to teach basic writing skills to students who enter with severe handicaps in this area. Whenever possible, writing is taught in the context of reports or memos likely to be required on the job. During the first year students spend two hours a week in writing clinics. Some make extraordinary progress, but others do not, and poor writing ability is one of the most frequent criticisms one hears from supervisors of CHS students.

The best teaching grows out of the "constructive action" projects students must develop on the job. This kind of teaching—the college's trademark—is focused on clarifying and generalizing what is learned in the field and what needs to be learned in order to complete the individual projects. Faculty sometimes grow weary, however, of students who do little or no reading and tend to dismiss a theoretical point or criticize a position without really understanding it. Such students must be convinced that a theory is useful even if it does not have a specific, immediate application to a client with a problem. It may be useful for understanding the role of the supervisor or the organizational setting in which one is working.

Of course, much can be taught that does relate to the immediate, practical problem. The case method that has been so effective in teaching education, social work, counseling, is utilized at CHS for the study of real, rather than hypothetical material.*

The most difficult and challenging task students face comes on the heels of the four-week competency unit on "becoming an effective learner." During this time, something of an orientation period as we have said, students are at the college five days a week. With the second competency ("establish a professional relationship at the worksite with coworkers and citizens"), they begin to spend three days each week on the job. In more than a few agencies which have agreed to employ CHS students, a multitude of problems develops as they are actually integrated into the work setting. Some supervisors are openly skeptical that these students—many without high school diplomas and just off welfare—are in fact potential professionals. At Morrisania Hospital in the Bronx, ten positions in social work had been negotiated. But when the students showed up, they were not accepted, though ultimately they were allowed to remain in a variety of other human service capacities. In a public school to which they

---

*Obviously, there are kinds of skills—such as interviewing and negotiating—that cannot be learned out of a case-study textbook, no matter how wide or interesting is the range of cases presented. We are indebted to Zelda Gamson's acute perceptions of some of the issues raised by the use of the case-study method.

had been assigned, teachers would not allow two CHS students into the teachers' lounge. And even where there is no hostility, students must overcome the common perception that CHS is a community college preparing paraprofessionals. When students who are treated by the college as professionals are placed in paraprofessional or sub-professional positions, it is difficult if not impossible for them to make the jump to professional status. The self-doubts of the students themselves (sometimes grounded in realistic self-appraisals of deficiencies in knowledge in specialized fields), the natural tendency to seek good relationships with coworkers (difficult if you are seen by paraprofessionals as a ratebuster on the way up), and the gatekeepers who are protecting the existing positions with the tariff of the five-year master's compound the problems.

One hears about these battles in visits to field sites: the efforts to gain access to client records, or to professional staff seminars or other equivalents of the executive washroom. The outcomes of these struggles vary, of course, and even where the host agency is hospitable, students may be relegated to paraprofessional positions at the end of their training because of budget restrictions or lack of formal degree requirements.

The quality of the student placement is the linchpin on which the whole program turns. One model site is the Museum of Natural History, where a Spanish-speaking student works as a teaching aide in the Mexican wing. Here the college had tapped the resources of a Ph.D.-level museum staff who worked closely with the intern, tutoring him, guiding his reading in Mayan culture, and teaching him museum procedures. Similarly, at the Keener Clinic, a residential facility for retarded children, students rotated through internships in physical therapy, behavior-modification techniques, and classroom training. They also participated in a weekly seminar under the direction of a Columbia doctoral student in psychology. In other placements, the college has not been as successful. At the Polish-Slavic Center in Brooklyn, for example, efforts to turn students into switchboard operators and envelope stuffers had to be warded off.

In its attempt to push the pendulum of reform in the direction of more humane service to clients, the college's rhetoric sometimes sounds like quotations from Chairman Mao,* and the appeals to

*For example: "We cannot doubt that the Human Service Society will become a reality. A massive change in the use of human power is coming in this century, and we must prepare for it now. It will be a change as great as that which took individual workers out of their ground floor shops and into the assembly lines. The industrial age swept a whole society away in its path. The Human Service Society will mean an equally sweeping change, but the motive

the students to act as change agents may strike some ears as the slogans of *agents provocateurs*. But the day-to-day realities of the college, in contrast to the clarion calls in proposals to funding agencies, reflect a sober awareness that change usually comes a step at a time. A random sampling of student constructive action projects reveals the following quite modest proposals:

To organize a school library.

To publicize the community programs in the Henry Street Settlement House neighborhood.

To open a "general store" in a high school selling pens, papers, books to raise money for school teams and give students a sense of identity.

To plan a program for the training of child-care workers.

To teach coworkers a simple vocabulary to converse by hand signals with deaf children.

To make patients at Morrisania Hospital more aware of their rights.

The proposal to organize a school library competently described twelve tasks the student would perform, such as ordering and cataloging books, establishing a circulation flow, and so forth. The student who wanted to plan a child-care program needed a good deal of help. His folder included a confused miscellany of pamphlets—one on child care from birth to eighteen, another on alcoholism and drugs. The student showed little awareness that he would need to draw upon the skills of teachers, developmental psychologists, nutritionists, and others to plan such a program. The Morrisania Hospital proposal was more typical; it involved discovering and publicizing a variety of patient rights and benefits.

Just as the proposals are not as radical as the rhetoric, faculty do not insist in practice upon rigid application of the rule that the client is always right. Jose Morales, for instance, eventually became discouraged in his teaching at an alternative high school. Among other things, students seldom showed up for class, or arrived forty or fifty minutes late. Why didn't he try making a contract with them? it was suggested. If he agrees to come, they should, too. He had tried that, but students sat on all committees and hired and fired the teachers, who had no power to enforce such contracts. With the support of his coordinating teacher, he resigned the job and transferred to an-

force will be a concern for the quality of individual human life." "Two-Year Professional Program Leading to the Degree of Master of Human Services," mimeographed, August 1974, I: xi.

other agency. Though he eventually did go back to the school at the request of other students and faculty, the experience had left him with serious doubts as to whether he should pursue the profession.

The student working at the Museum of Natural History argued with the coordinating teacher who insisted that he take the initiative in approaching families and groups of children to teach them about the exhibits in the Mexican wing. She also suggested that the student include a display on how Mayans ground corn on every tour. When the student responded that he didn't want to buttonhole visitors who didn't have a certain threshold of interest, the teacher wondered whether he wasn't being "elitist" by making the visitors responsible for asking for or signaling their need for service. But she did not argue her bias overbearingly or insist she was right.

On some occasions the students have learned their lessons so well that they have come close to losing their jobs. A Spanish-speaking student working in the emergency ward of the Morrisania Hospital pressed for treatment for a patient who had been turned away by the doctor in charge. When he refused, she appealed to higher authority. Subsequently, he sought her dismissal.

Clearly, the kind of assessment one receives often depends on who does the assessing. The doctor we have just mentioned "failed" the student, but the patients and other lay professionals in the hospital took her side. The college has tried to reflect this reality by establishing an assessment procedure in which clients, peers, supervisors, and faculty all participate, but in which the teacher makes the final decision. Assessment of constructive action proposals, written work, and on-the-job performance occur throughout the year, and the major evaluation comes with the student year-end review. One year, the CHS counseling staff and the agency supervisors were asked to fill out assessment forms responding to the dimensions of competence as listed on the performance grid. Were students able to identify goals, understand systems, and so forth? Nearly 90 percent of the agency supervisors returned the forms—a remarkably high proportion. Faculty and counselors then discussed each student's case, in an attempt to make an over-all assessment. The process was both stimulating and frustrating. Different parties put different interpretations on the criteria. Judgments about the same student diverged. How to combine them? To secure and evaluate clients' assessments was difficult (the college even attempted to interview preschool children about a teacher's performance in one instance). The sheer amount of paper generated was overwhelming. The college now occupied the eleventh floor for their classes; the feeling began to grow that they would have to rent the twelfth just to store the assessment forms!* The data included not just the rating sheets but the student's entire portfolio, which one faculty member described as being like a 400-page novel (he thought he could read four or five portfolios in a morning, but found he could hardly get through one in that time).

In the spring of 1976 attempts were made to "standardize" and simplify the assessment process; but now another basic problem arose. Should students be assessed only on *performance* of a constructive action? What if the proposal fails utterly but the student learns a great deal from the experience? Does the faculty have absolute or relative notions of what constitutes a good performance? Is it fair to a student to "fail" him or her at the year-end review? Must such a student repeat the entire year? After listening to a faculty committee discuss these matters, an observer was impressed with the committee's willingness to discuss so candidly the difficulties of what they were attempting, and to raise questions that challenged some of the core ideas of the program.

In contrast to the elusive measures reflected on the forms, faculty members use unambiguous indicators of performance when they talk informally about students they are supervising: Do they get to work regularly and on time? (actually one of the most difficult and crucial matters). Do they participate in class and complete assignments? Can they write? Do they dress, look, and act like professionals? Are they serious and motivated? Perhaps it is a mistake to cast the language of assessment in the same language as the teaching goals of the program.

Sometimes real differences of opinion arose between faculty and agency supervisors. A supervisor at a social-work agency told me that she considered three of the four CHS students assigned to her as unlikely candidates for professional status. They had serious deficiencies in reading, writing, and analytical skills. When the faculty member suggested that their greater empathy and understanding of clients should compensate for their deficiencies, the supervisor replied quite firmly that "just having lived is not enough." She insisted that sophisticated diagnostic skills were required to analyze the difficulties of problem families and write the reports demanded by the city agencies. Do they need to write all those reports? the faculty

---

*The forms do not only pertain to students. The college faculty follows its own preaching on assessment. Students complete elaborate faculty evaluation forms at the end of every competency (8–10 weeks). Faculty observe each others' classes and spend a day observing each other in their supervisory roles in the field. CHS has one of the most thoroughgoing faculty assessment systems we have seen.

member inquired, asking her to give an example of what she meant by "diagnostic skills." The supervisor replied that if they did not write the reports well, it would be a burden on the agency. As to diagnostic skills, she felt that three of the CHS students were below bachelor's-degree expectations and certainly not up to the master's-degree-level social worker who would be expected to "know enough about therapy to try to evoke the neurotic patterns that parents were afflicted with that led them to child abuse or whatever."

At another agency, the Keener Clinic, supervisors felt that CHS students might be at the bachelor's level, but not the master's, on two grounds. Their basic writing and math skills were low, and, secondly, they lacked specialized knowledge. For example, CHS students would not know enough about psychological testing to administer and interpret a battery of tests. Could such skills be taught on the job? Yes, but more time would be required on the agency's part, and students would need stronger basic skills.

III

There are a multitude of contexts in which one could analyze the significance of the reforms attempted by the College for Human Services. One could challenge its most basic premise of the need for a "human service" society on the grounds that it makes more sense to strengthen the family through direct grant programs than to enlarge the army of paid professionals who perform familylike functions.* But complex modern societies cannot do without bureaucracies, and few persons would disagree with the aim of making them more responsive to human needs. Although CHS has rejected the term "paraprofessional" to describe its graduates because the term has meant a restriction of opportunities, there is a sense in which it has indeed hastened the development of a needed paraprofessional resource. "Para———" can mean "near" or "alongside" as well as "subsidiary to." The college fosters a leavening of the professions, some of which have severely and arbitrarily restricted entry. CHS seeks to supply in the human services the analogue of the physician associate in medical practice. The difficulties of establishing these roles and new performance measures within the framework of the

---

*This brings to mind the comment of a CHS student at Morrisania Hospital who said, "We aren't paraprofessionals; you should turn the word around: professional parents."

various professions that the college includes within the mantle of "human services" are, of course, enormous. The achievements of the College for Human Services, begun by amateurs in rented quarters on short-cycle budgets, are remarkable.

The program took ten years to develop. Not a long time as historians would measure it, but much longer than most contemporary American educational innovators are willing to wait: they expect to have committee meetings this month and a revolution next semester. Some faculty members have come and gone, but a core has remained for most of the decade. Audrey Cohen's tenure really began in 1964, and has run twelve years. The average term for college presidents is now less than five years, and deanships turn over quickly, yet most significant innovations in American education have not been successfully developed and institutionalized in less than a decade.

While questions remain as to the adequacy of the faculty's training in the disciplines, few departmentally organized faculties could have sustained such a complex developmental process. Conventional disciplinary ambitions had to be abandoned by a faculty willing to devote itself for a decade to the task of testing the emerging ideas about a performance-based curriculum. It might have been possible to maintain the esprit of the CHS faculty within a larger university, particularly if it were organized as a subcollege or semi-autonomous unit to protect its very different reward systems and forms of organization, but it could only have been done with great difficulty.

What does account for the high morale? Salaries are low, fringe benefits minimal, the work week long, the academic year a calendar year. CHS began as a volunteer college built with the talents of gifted women who worked full time for part-time salaries. Faculty were attracted by the ideals of the college, its sense of social mission, and its visible human accomplishments as students moved off welfare and began to rise in responsible jobs.

CHS also exemplifies the wisdom of thinking big but starting small. Its fundamental aim—to establish a performance-based and job-related curriculum designed to deliver improved service to clients —involved complex networks of funding sources, dozens of city agencies, supplementary task forces, and research consultants. But because the scale was small—never more than two hundred students and about twenty faculty—the program was manageable. The faculty could meet as a committee of the whole, with the maximum opportunity for communication. Each new wrinkle of the common curriculum was tested and appraised by all. Collegial learning was maximized. Visitors and consultants were plied with practical questions about the next step in the curriculum development process. The faculty had a keen sense of its own history and seemed to enjoy talking over earlier stages in the developmental process.

Though idealistic reformers, they were resilient in the face of not infrequent setbacks—"hard-headed do-gooders," if you will. When students slipped, faculty were not crushed—nor did they allow themselves to become devastated as again and again they saw the gap between hopes and outcome. The practical, job-related realities of the program helped to protect them from the rigidities of their own rhetoric.

Underlying all the talk about competent performance was a true religious sense of dedication. Most faculty members recoiled at sloppy, uncaring performance. Their desire to restore idealism to service was a blend of the Puritanism and the Evangelism of the reformer. Written materials sound like epistles to shore up lonely missionaries. CHS asks for a commitment to its "way," to the belief that in service and in giving one will be reborn.

Since a researcher is asked to make a commitment as well, this chapter has been a difficult one to write. A series of discussions about the ground rules for the research came to a head when Dean Stephen Sunderland suggested that he viewed the relationship as a potential conversion experience:

> I see you as part of a strategy that the College wishes to use to spread the word about the College's good works . . . and as a potential convert to the form of education and assessment that we see as necessary for a different kind of professional, social, and intellectual world.*

Sunderland was continually on guard, questioning "enterprises such as yours [the research] in terms of their usefulness to meeting the change goals" of the college. On one occasion, he ushered Grant out of a tense meeting called by dissatisfied students, and it was with some difficulty that Grant established his right to interview

---

*Letter from Sunderland to Grant, February 18, 1976. The stages of the research relationship moved in tandem with the development of the college over a six-year period. At first Grant was treated like an expert; later he was challenged as to whether and in what sense he was a "humane professional." After some discussion Grant was ultimately given assurances that he deemed minimally necessary for responsible research. This included access to records, random interviews in the field, and the right of the college to review the manuscript prior to publication (something we have provided for routinely), but without any veto powers.

sources in city agencies without the benefit of "chaperones" from the college.

As we look back on the first decade it is clear that CHS can point to major accomplishments, but it continues to face unresolved tensions. It has established itself, surmounted internal crises and strikes, invented a new curriculum, survived harrowing cutbacks in funds for the human services in New York, extended political support networks locally and nationally; and it has drawn together a faculty dedicated to its vision of social change. Yet in the decade to come, the college will face critical problems. It must find a way to sustain the esprit of students whose jobs do not match the college's hopes, to refine the knowledge base that underlies its performance-based program, and to rationalize its proposed new degree structure to skeptical external audiences.*

Although nearly one-third of the CHS students have now had some college and fewer have been on welfare, most still face a radical transition as they leave homebound roles to meet the demands of both college and a new job—a total work week of 50 hours or more. It is doubtful that many could survive that transition without the structure that the CHS core curriculum provides or the support on the job that CHS faculty furnish as both advocates and supervisors. The practical, step-by-step nature of the CHS "performance grid" has holding power for many of these students. Yet the curriculum of constructive actions also creates role conflicts of major proportions. They are asked to become change agents, not just to hold their own as they learn the ropes, but to transform the professions by creating one that as yet is undefined. To have been chosen by CHS was a major boost in confidence for most students, and for many the curriculum is a transforming experience. But they experience difficulty in adjusting the college's hopes to the realities of the marketplace. While most students have been successful in gaining permanent employment upon completion of the program, few attain jobs at the professional level. Some are placed in aide jobs that are usually held by those with only high-school diplomas.

Obviously, CHS students enter the job market at a disadvantage without a degree, and there is no guarantee that New York will grant

---

*As we have mentioned, CHS's reapplication for the authority to award the master's degree in New York State has not been acted upon as this book goes to press.

the college's second appeal for the master's. Theoretically, it should be possible for mature adults with some college experience to earn a master's degree in an intensive two-year apprentice-style program. In practice, however, there are some serious objections that the college will need to meet:

1. The college will have to offer different degrees for different levels of competence, and distinctions will be difficult to make. Student placements, of course, vary greatly according to the level of the student's work, and the opportunities for learning on the job are also uneven—a problem that has been exacerbated by cutbacks in agency supervisory personnel.

2. Is the assessment system valid? The program specifies that students must "function" as counselors or teachers, but there is disagreement about what constitutes an adequate level of functioning. The problem is compounded by the conflating of personality and characterological values in a number of competency statements. For example, as part of the counseling competency, students are told to "Demonstrate in counseling practice that you are flexible, tough, willing to risk yourself, resilient in the face of difficulty, optimistic and able to remain focused in confused or emotional situations."

To some degree, all programs preparing teachers or social workers share similar difficulties. No program can avoid subjective measures, nor would it be desirable to do so. But at CHS the subjective nature of the assessments is not offset by any nationally standardized measures or achievement tests. In adapting the CHS program, Lincoln University in Pennsylvania required that students pass national undergraduate record exams at the level achieved by its college seniors, take mathematics proficiency exams, and complete a series of standard courses in psychology, sociology, statistics, and other subjects in addition to demonstrating the eight competencies listed on the performance grid.[29]

3. Can a generic degree in the human services make its way into a declining market against the competition of students prepared in specific fields? CHS students may not be able to land jobs in competition with students who have traditional preparation in psychology, education, social work, and other fields. It remains to be seen how well CHS students can make their way outside the specific placements the college has negotiated for them as part of the training process. However, if they can become armed with an accredited master's degree, it seems likely that some will be able to create new positions, as the college and its graduates have done in the past.

Much will depend on the climate of client assessment that the college—along with others—is able to create.*

4. Can the college distinguish variations in performance tied to degree levels? No one who has interviewed CHS students over the course of their two-year program would doubt that most who stay for the full course make extraordinary progress. However, they begin from different baselines and progress at different rates. Some do reach levels that seem equivalent to those of master's students elsewhere—the degree seldom indicates high proficiency in America. Others are prepared for more useful and interesting work than they would qualify for in other settings, but are not much beyond the paraprofessional level. And some are in-between, closer to the bachelor's degree. CHS has lengthened its program from 30 weeks a year to 50, and has raised its entrance levels so that more students now enter with at least some college. It has also attempted to distinguish between bachelor's and master's degrees (but has dropped the A.A.).

The college has not been sentimental in its judgments to date. Of 113 students who enrolled in the first "master's program" class in 1974, 76 were certified as having completed the first year, of whom 63 were hired for a second year by the agency in which they had been placed. Of these, 58 were admitted to a second year at CHS, and 51 of these won permanent positions in the agencies in 1976. But in its report to Albany seeking degree-granting powers, the faculty recommended only 12 of these students for the master's degree, and 5 for the bachelor's; 10 students were classified as needing more time to complete all the "constructive actions" before a judgment could be made. Whether any college could continue with such low completion rates is doubtful, however.

The invention of the CHS performance grid was a genuine breakthrough for the faculty, but the task of "filling in the boxes" or showing the connections between theory and practice is an ambitious one. CHS has a small faculty, and although it now has a few Ph.D.s where formerly it had none, the disciplinary training of the faculty has little depth. Like teachers in the normal schools of an earlier day, or law schools before they began hiring Ph.D.s, CHS faculty are practitioners, not scholars. Most do not regard the disciplines as

---

*CHS has developed a manual for client assessment that includes a checklist for clients. It encourages them to ask whether the professional understood and accepted the real reason why they sought service, whether the professional put them off or made any assumptions they felt were inaccurate. See Stephen Sunderland, "Citizen Empowerment Manual," mimeographed, 1976, p. 3.

irrelevant, but they are skeptical that any particular knowledge base underlies performance in the human services. Their refusal to equate a list of courses with competence is admirable. The CHS performance grid becomes a filter through which the faculty can search the disciplines for useful knowledge. That search is infused with an evangelical commitment to social change—which sometimes leads to a debunking of what is not fully understood: the result is the development of a curriculum that, though at points truncated and even anti-intellectual, is nonetheless dynamic. The unresolved issue for the college is the question of how deeply the faculty itself needs to be grounded in the disciplines in order to make an intelligent search and to distinguish values from ideology.* Not every faculty member needs a standard Ph.D.—far from it. But the faculty could benefit from a better mix of scholars and practitioners than it now has. Since CHS has achieved some recognition for the genuine advances it has made, it may be more willing and financially able to seek better trained faculty; however, whether or not it expands its faculty the tension will remain. The tension between knowledge and action is endemic to the activist-radical mode, and Audrey Cohen would probably sympathize with Arthur Morgan of Antioch, who said toward the end of his distinguished career that he wished he had been more ruthless in eliminating faculty who "came here to teach my subject" and did not share his vision of the college as a "revolution" and "a way of life."[30] Yet, as at Antioch, there are some faculty at CHS who are both grounded in the disciplines *and* committed to social change.

---

*By ideology we mean here not a conscious deception or lie, but what Karl Mannheim called the "cant mentality," that fails to uncover the incongruities in thought in "response to certain vital-emotional interests." See Karl Mannheim, *Ideology and Utopia,* (New York: Harcourt, Brace & World, 1955), p. 195. To be aware of the danger of ideology in this sense is to recall Max Weber's assertion that "The primary task of a useful teacher is to teach his students to recognize 'inconvenient' facts—I mean facts that are inconvenient for their party opinions." H. H. Gerth and C. Wright Mills, eds., *From Max Weber* (New York: Oxford University Press, 1946), p. 146.

The Search for Options

Less Pressure, More Options

Meritocratic Discontents and Popular Reforms

6

In contrast with our discussion in Part I of the telic reforms, our effort in this chapter is to suggest the major lines of the popular reforms that have brought widespread changes in curriculum and extracurriculum during the last dozen years. These do not involve a radical reorientation of institutional goals but affect the relations between students and faculty, the processes of education, and the context in which it takes place. We do not want to imply that the contemporary educational landscape is unrecognizable to all but youthful eyes. One can still get a classical education in any good college or university if one looks for it, and catalogs show that much of the traditional remains. Yet only a very few institutions have stood unequivocally unaltered during the period of change that overtook both American society and its educational institutions in the 1960s and thereafter. While both individual students and institutions have been unevenly affected by these changes, there is no doubt that almost everywhere requirements have been relaxed, the paths toward a degree have been made more multiple and open, and the gold standard of academic currency (in some cases more nominal than real) has been diluted by grade inflation.*

---

*The mammoth studies of curricular changes and of the attitudes and preferences of undergraduates, graduate students, and faculty made by the Carnegie Commission on Higher Education in 1969, whose results were made available by the commission in a series of volumes, were repeated in a series of surveys undertaken by the Carnegie Council on Policy Studies in Higher Education in 1975–76. We are indebted to Clark Kerr, Verne Stadtman, and Arthur Levine of the Carnegie Council, and also to Professors Robert Blackburn and Martin Trow for discussions of this work, some of which now appears in published form: Blackburn at al., *Changing Practices in Undergrad-*

For indeed, the climate of higher education has changed commensurately with the climate of the country. So rapid have the changes been that the 1950s have become an (often unwarranted) epoch for nostalgia hunters. Those were the years in which the civil-rights movement was in its "black and white together" stage, before the movement began in the predominantly white colleges for the massive recruitment of nonwhite students, before their subsequent organization and demands (by no means universal among blacks but felt as such by many whites) for black-studies programs, special admissions and financial aid policies, and various degrees of separatism in and out of the classroom. Those were the years in which John Kennedy could seem an appealing symbol to ever so many young people, and the Peace Corps likewise. It was a period in which higher education was to receive massive infusions of state and federal support, which in a decade would permit the doubling of enrollments and the tripling of faculty. It was a period in which the proportion of people who graduated from high school and went on to college greatly increased and seemingly would increase indefinitely until the point of near-universal higher education was reached. As the "war babies" of the post-World War II era entered adolescence, the expansive imagery was sustained. Not only demographically but psychologically the country seemed to be focusing on its youth—the symbol of future hopes, its affluence, and its continuing growth.

But this was also the era in which the conflict in Vietnam, noticed by only a few from 1954 until 1965, exploded on the campuses with the threat of the draft and the excitements of teach-ins (the first of which took place at the University of Michigan in 1965). Beginning in the more selective colleges, frustrated college students, often veterans of the civil-rights movement, started to oppose the war. Finding that a nearly intractable enterprise, they began to turn on the universities as readier targets. For it seemed that they too were part of the war machine—in ranking students to qualify them for draft deferments, in providing ROTC training or allowing recruiting for the services or the CIA (actually the agency which on its analytic side was most skeptical of the war), or in aiding the war effort through various sorts of research that began to be seen as complicitous.

uate Education, and Trow, Aspects of American Higher Education, 1969–1975, reports for the Carnegie Council for Policy Studies in Higher Education, 1976. These studies lend quantitative support to what in an earlier draft of this chapter we had ourselves concluded and published originally in much abbreviated form: Gerald Grant and David Riesman, "An Ecology of Academic Reform," Daedalus, 104, no. 1 (1975):166–91.

Only a very small proportion of faculty and students ever spent their time in protest meetings, rallies, and demonstrations even on the more agitated campuses. Yet a small proportion of a large base can still be a sizable—and threatening—number, and since many activist students were also among the more talented and dramaturgical, their activities had a stunning impact. While much of the public at large was repulsed, the institutions themselves in most cases proved pliable. Students got onto boards of trustees (or invaded their meetings), drafted reports proposing educational reforms (Ira Magaziner's at Brown University was one of the most notable), and campaigned ceaselessly in fiery columns in the student papers for alterations in the established ways of conducting academic business.

The changes brought about in this manner are those we are terming "popular reforms." They included changes in curriculum, which not only introduced black and other ethnic studies and later women's studies, but also provided opportunities for credit for off-campus work. The now forgotten "Princeton Plan" gave students time off to campaign for liberal candidates in the elections of 1970—at least such was the premise. After the Cambodian invasions and the killings at Kent State and Jackson State, many colleges came to a halt and in effect granted academic amnesty to students whether or not they had completed a term's work. Requirements evaporated, either piecemeal or through large-scale demolition. Open admissions, always a reality in many state universities and colleges, became a political issue when it implied recruiting of, and providing academic enrichment for, minorities who possessed what would hitherto have been deemed inadequate high-school preparation. Parietal regulations disappeared with such astonishing speed that it is a surprise to come upon a college that still forbids co-residential living and thus defends what students would regard as hypocrisy.

While these changes were taking place inside existing institutions, a number of people were engaged in founding new colleges and universities, public and private. The literature of faculty and student protest furnished the ammunition for demolishing older academic conventions. After all, many faculty members, administrators, even legislators, had children of college age who were themselves involved in protests, and the war between the generations brought with it some older converts.

Though the majority of new or vastly expanded colleges and universities probably were not creations of the reforming impulse, a great many were, and they took pains to spread the gospel. As they attracted students and faculty, more traditional institutions sought to keep pace, for, in comparison with other countries, Americans have always feared obsolescence and have had fewer brakes on change than more hierarchical societies.

Among the new institutions founded during the sixties, some had no traditional departments and emphasized interdisciplinary programs or contract-based individuated learning. Evergreen State College in Olympia, Washington; New Jersey's Stockton State and Ramapo Colleges (Chapter 9); the College of Old Westbury in the State University of New York system (both in its early days under Harris Wofford and later under John Maguire); Hampshire College; the University of Wisconsin, Green Bay—were all nondepartmental in original structure. Johnston College of the University of Redlands, Sterling University in Ottawa, Kansas, and many others emphasized nontraditional learning for what Patricia Cross has termed the "new students." Adults and especially older women returning to or finishing college were given the opportunity to participate in individuated programs at places like Empire State College of the State University of New York or Minnesota Metropolitan University. Yet these new colleges and new programs did not drive out the old. Colleges still teach chemistry, English (which more and more means American) literature, art history, political science, even philosophy; they teach economics to an enormous number of students, a few of whom select it as their major, and many more in business administration or in other fields, including "pre-law," who recognize its importance. Psychology, sociology, and, increasingly, anthropology are popular among students who believe that these subjects will teach them about themselves, and, as many perhaps mistakenly hope, will lead to careers in the human services area directly after the baccalaureate, or after some graduate work.

What has happened in fact is that the college curriculum has been expanded. At some colleges, for example, black and other ethnic studies have been added as the result of student and often faculty and administration pressures; often these are organized in new departments, though they may draw on the knowledge base and faculty of existing departments. Women's studies, both within established departments such as history, sociology, psychology, economics, and as separate departments and majors, have spread with extraordinary speed, and are served by a whole new outpouring of texts and scholarly journals. Environmental studies (around which the University of Wisconsin at Green Bay and the College of the Atlantic initially organized their entire curricula) have been seen as a way to respond to interest in the environment; and law schools have added courses in environmental law, medical schools in environment-related subjects, and schools of education, adopting a different focus, have added departments of "learning environments." The interest in the environment has been seen by natural scientists as a way of attracting students with "relevant" subject matter.

It is clear that to an uneven extent the major or field of concentration has lost, however, a good deal of its earlier rigidity. In fields like mathematics and chemistry sequences remain. But in less technical departments, students can fulfill academic requirements in a greater variety of ways than before: with courses in related departments; with so-called experiential off-campus learning; or with self-paced courses, in which, according to the Carnegie Council survey, 30 percent of the nation's students have participated. The pass/no credit option, favored by a majority of the students in 1969, is now favored by only a third, but the surveys report that nearly half have made use of it. Still the major stands as the focus of the average student's academic experience, in part because of the increasing vocational pressures felt by undergraduates in recent years. What has dramatically changed is the place of any kind of general education or core curriculum; in all but a few institutions, the hold of the curriculum as a set of more or less systematic pathways toward a baccalaureate degree has become attenuated. Grade inflation and the loosening of requirements have weakened the role of faculty members and departments as gatekeepers of the degree (and whatever honors may be bestowed along with it). In the language of the student movement, students have "gained control over the decisions which affect their own lives"; in the language of the market, the student consumer has become king.

I

Political protests on American campuses in the late sixties swirled around two issues: civil-rights questions were prominent in the Columbia University protests of 1968 and spawned the free-speech movement at Berkeley, which was led by a number of students who had taken part in the Mississippi Freedom Summer Project of 1964; and in the meantime the Vietnam War had become perhaps the major political issue not only on selective college campuses but at state universities large enough to have a sizable minority of activist students.

Studies by Kenneth Keniston, Richard Flacks, Brewster Smith et al., Richard Braungart, and many others, as well as more systematic surveys by the American Council on Education, have illustrated that "protest-prone" campuses could be defined at the outset by the presence of a "critical mass" of able, affluent (often Jewish) students from college-educated, business and professional families. Often well versed already in the politics of protest, they saw the campus as a locale for recruitment and mobilization for what began as mainly off-campus activism: stopping troop trains in Oakland, California, for example, or seeking to organize impoverished urban black (and occasionally white) enclaves. When the university itself became an object of attack, it was often for its supposed complicity in the evils of the general society: through research believed to aid the war effort, through investment policies regarded as reactionary (e.g., holding stock of companies investing in South Africa), or through ROTC or on-campus recruiting for corporations seen as shapers of militarism, makers of napalm or fragmentation bombs, and biochemical weapons, or for the CIA.

Some of the altered governance structures set up on many campuses came about through protests against such alleged university complicity or against disciplinary action taken after occupation of buildings, invasion of faculty or trustee meetings (or holding members of either group as prisoners), or trashing and even bombing and burning of academic and occasionally faculty buildings and homes. Where attempts to gain amnesty were not successful, students demanded reciprocity at least. Administrators and faculty were to be called to account before tribunals similar to those set up to discipline students—and on some campuses the customary student judicial court operated like a Jacobin tribunal capable of censuring faculty and administration. As we shall see, only later did these structures of codetermination begin to affect curricular options.

However, it was very early in the Berkeley Free Speech Movement that its leaders discovered the propagandistic value of an attack on the "multiversity," Clark Kerr's neutral term which picked up pejorative meaning as it came to be seen as an additional device for the mobilization of students and delegitimizing of institutional authority. What began as a tactic soon acquired a life of its own, and a movement of the pedagogic left began, with faculty as well as student adherents. Often it merged with the political left—as both later did in some measure with the counterculture, which, in traditional terms, was nonpolitical or even anti-political but which, when applied to the university, sought to substitute the values of camaraderie, personal authenticity, and sometimes hedonism for those of competition and formal campus authority.

It should be emphasized, contrary to common labeling and misunderstanding, that the protests were almost never simply *student* protests; a number of faculty were involved as either the gurus or as younger leaders and instigators.[1] It should not be forgotten in this connection that the anti-Vietnam War protests escalated with the teach-in, which began as a serious effort by concerned and knowledgeable faculty to educate their colleagues and students about Southeast Asia and the tragedies of the war. Only later did the teach-in lose its role as elucidator and frequently become a kind of revivalist rally, satisfied with denouncing the United States as racist, imperialist,and genocidal without making any particular effort to learn more about the sources of the Vietnam War, the complexities of the politics of both Vietnams, or the practical methods of expanding the anti-war base through avoiding destructively provocative demonstrations and exporting the teach-in format to other communities.

The anti-war protests had large political consequences. It is conceivable that they may even have prolonged the war. Many of those who had supported Eugene McCarthy and had helped engender the resignation of President Johnson sought to "punish" Hubert Humphrey in 1968 and may have contributed the small margin by which Richard Nixon defeated him.[2] Similarly, the popular perception of the student protests as attacks on the flag or the presidency led to a backlash that helped ensure the overwhelming reelection of President Nixon in 1972.[3]

Even today, contrary to general belief, there are still political protests to be found, but they have lost the attention of the media, since they now often occur at the less selective and visible campuses. Though the Vetnam War has of course been defused as an issue, efforts to restore the ROTC or challenges to civil rights can still spark protests. Racial flare-ups in dining halls or dormitories, unfair treatment of black students on campus or by local police, harassment of faculty or administrators, threatened cuts in financial aid to disadvantaged students are still potentially explosive issues.

But the political legacy persists in other ways as well. The generation of students who came to political maturity in college and graduate school in the 1960s is becoming more influential in academic life as faculty members or administrators, and in professional life, whether in the academic guilds or in efforts to reshape the distribution of medical and legal services. Civic activities as well, ranging from the moderation of Common Cause to the efforts to block commercial or governmental activities thought to be harmful to the environment, reflect the leadership training provided by the protests of the sixties. And, just as the anti-war protests may well have prolonged the war, so the student-faculty movements have left a legacy of right-wing reaction that continues to tighten the noose on the support now available from state and federal sources for higher education (though this is hardly the only cause of the erosion of support). As many had warned at the time, entering the political arena brought the universities many more political enemies than friends.

Even though some of the anti-university slogans were appropriated (such as the famous Berkeley pun on IBM that students were not to be stapled or otherwise mutilated), the political left and the pedagogic left continued to overlap. Many faculty have since separated themselves from the legacy of protest, however. For example, some leading social scientists who were early movers and shakers in the anti-war and civil-rights movements began to insist on the maintenance of scholarly standards, even to the point of opposing formal involvement of students in admissions policies, faculty appointment and retention policies, and curricular alteration. Thus, some of them became targets of student hostility themselves when they refused to cater to student pedagogical and countercultural attitudes. (Even the radical sociologist, Alvin Gouldner suffered from such attacks recently at the University of Amsterdam, and earlier, in this country, Herbert Marcuse, Barrington Moore, Jr., and other well-known radicals found themselves, in the parlance of the day, "up against the wall" when they would not, for example, countenance student illiteracy or provide amnesty for academic nonperformance or failure.) The old left was book-nourished and cared about ideas; so did an off-campus anarchist like Paul Goodman, whose talks and writings had been an early influence on both the student politicals and counterculturists but who, in such later writings as *Notes of a Neolithic Conservative*, made clear his distance from prevailing anti-intellectual modes.

Yet these are the notable exceptions; on the whole, it was in the interest of both the political and pedagogic "change-prone" students and faculty, whether they saw themselves as reformers or as revolutionaries or as some mixture of both, to mute the differences of their ultimate objectives whenever they were turning their attacks on academic institutions. And while the educational consequences were secondary to the political ones, their actions did have consequences.

Everything about a college or university came under scrutiny. Never was there so much discussion of educational policy in terms of admissions standards, the curriculum, and who was to control it; the significance of grading and of alternative modes of evaluation or nonevaluation; the independence of students from traditional parietal restraints on campus and any monitoring of their activities off-campus; and, of long-lasting importance, the nature of teacher-student and, to a lesser degree, student-student interactions.

In the 1960s, many quite different protest groups created experimental colleges and programs, such as the famous experimental college of San Francisco State led by Russell Nixon, or the Berkeley student-sponsored program that created massive controversy by inviting Eldridge Cleaver to give a course at a time when he was most incendiary. Many less well-known institutions followed in the wake of these visible ones and created off-campus institutions where one could find courses in Frantz Fanon, astrology, the legal rights of American Indians, women's studies, Eastern religions, and could register for encounter-group sessions as well. Students as well as faculty taught in these programs: graduate students, where these existed, off-campus radicals like Cleaver, and assorted mystics, beats, and hustlers. In general colleges and universities responded to these offshoots through the process Harold Lasswell has termed "restriction through partial incorporation"; regulations were set up concerning how much academic credit students could get for off-campus activities of various sorts, and faculty brought into their own courses some of the content and more of the style—what might be called the rap-session style—of the experimental colleges.

Most such programs proved fleeting, often depending (particularly in the private experimental colleges) on the zeal and stamina of one or two charismatic figures. Sometimes, too, there was an irreparable conflict of goals, as when Stanford's experimental programs were divided between those who sought to focus on the nonwhite population of East Palo Alto (renamed Nairobi) and those with more individualistic interests. Institutions that started inner colleges, such as the College Within at Tufts, were likely to be dependent upon a single fervent leader, such as Seymour Simches at Tufts; the College survives even to this day, but in attenuated form as the vocational interests of students and the structures of the traditional academic disciplines have begun to reassert themselves. Yet one can find legacies of these earlier movements in many universities. The term "student" during this period came to include the really quite remarkable number of young, and now not so young, people who were hooked on the life-style of the university and its circumambient community, even or perhaps especially when they had been among the most perfervid critics of the "multiversity" and/or of the town or city which was its uneasy and sometimes combatively reactive host. Our chapter on New College in Sarasota describes the "students" who stayed on in Sarasota after becoming alienated from both college and town. Here, as elsewhere, the distinction between students and nonstudents, many of whom became overstaying "guests" in the dormitories and the cafeteria line, was another one of those distinctions regarded as undemocratic and hierarchical by both the political and the pedagogic left. One result was greatly to increase the number of auxiliaries—borrowed, one often felt, from Central Casting—who could be relied upon for a demonstration even in the 1970s, when many students, weary of demonstrations or anxious about their studies and their postbaccalaureate futures, could no longer be readily mobilized to join in the festive or political euphoria that had characterized a demonstration or building takeover.

Now such demonstrations seldom reach the media; administrators handle them in a conciliatory way, almost universally avoiding the police "bust" for which radical students used to plot and pray. But as the campuses appear quiet and the students, particularly the less studious ones, have even sometimes returned to the old-fashioned collegiate style, there is a temptation to underestimate the more permanent impact of the pedagogic left.

We state at the outset our tentative conclusion: that the most widespread and significant impact of the educational upheaval of the sixties was to bring about a considerably greater degree of autonomy for students. They were free to plan their courses of study in a way they had never done before. The most important change was the virtual or complete abolition of fixed requirements in many departments and of mandatory distribution requirements, whether of breadth or depth, including class attendance and the time, mode, and kinds of credits needed to secure a baccalaureate degree.* Virtually everywhere, the physical education requirement was abandoned, though in some institutions, intramural sports including such innovative physical activities as ballet, Asian martial arts, or yoga, flourished as never before. For a student, in the antique phrase, to be rusticated on grounds of conduct was almost unheard of. The University of Virginia has, despite opposition, maintained a severe honor code. But in many places even widespread cheating on examinations and plagiarism on term papers would not, save in the service academies, and now the situation is in doubt even there, get a student into trouble.

---

*There remain a few traditional, usually small, liberal-arts colleges run by Protestant denominations (although virtually none that are Catholic) where class attendance is still required, where the very small size of the faculty can be used to limit options, and where curricular coherence has remained relatively "unliberated." (It should be pointed out, however, that size alone is not the determining factor here; New College of Sarasota, which is discussed in Chapter 7, is a small college of a very different character.)

In the more arduous areas of language, science, and mathematics, intradepartmental requirements for majors, especially in such a field as chemistry, remain quite firm and even rigid; but the collapse of general education and of breadth or distribution requirements freed nonmajors from these demanding courses.

Where students were permitted and even encouraged to "do their own thing," faculty were of course free to do theirs. Younger faculty members, especially, who had entered academic life in the seemingly golden years of the fifties and sixties, felt liberated enough to concentrate on their specialties, and to limit their workloads by offering courses that attracted only a few students. Thus despite the drop in enrollment on many campuses the size of catalogues virtually doubled, and the number of courses with less than five students in them also proliferated. Shortened terms, and more modularized schedules of instruction, led in many cases to a 4–1–4 calendar, so that faculty could schedule courses in such hobbies as Chinese gourmet cooking, harpsichord making, and indeed astrology, while still maintaining departmental standing through their specialized, discipline-based offerings.

Altogether, the result was a far greater degree of autonomy for the students. They were free to plan their course of study, or not to plan it. They could devise their own majors, delay such a decision, teach courses themselves for credit (a marvelous way of learning when seriously done), and follow their inclinations at their own pace into various forms of "experiential" and off-campus learning. With the end of the draft, the "stop-out" again became a possibility for male students, and upper middle-class women liberated enough to be on their own often followed suit. Even in the selective residential institutions, the notion of a curriculum built around four consecutive years began to seem almost archaic. Despite the recession, adept students found they could get lower-level blue-collar or service jobs even if they did not have a financial "need" to work. Parents and faculty members alike, if consulted at all, were inclined to favor rather than frown upon such periods—which in an era of horrendous inflation brought them a welcome moratorium as well.

It is true, of course, that students often gain more freedom than they actually use. Consider the experimental New Plan of Worcester Polytechnic Institute, which permits students to negotiate their own admissions and proceed at their own pace, without great penalties for delay or failure, through what had once been a no-nonsense, almost entirely fixed, set of engineering and science requirements. Knowing that they were in a seller's market students in institutions

such as Worcester have tended to follow traditional paths through
the curriculum recommended by "unreconstructed" faculty, rather
than either succumbing to the pitfalls or risking the opportunities of
freedom. It should be noted in this connection that central to these
reforms is what we might term the sanitized transcript, which erases
all incompletes, tentatives, and failing grades, and records only successes. However, the pass/no credit option has in the last few years
become increasingly less satisfying, or is used by diligent students
to provide leeway for even harder work, for example, on essential
pre-med courses.* The Buckley Amendment, which permits students
to see their own files and what has been written about them, only
carried further the institutionalization of the sanitized transcript.
Such reforms have their origins in the often convenient conclusion
on the part of faculty members that colleges should not serve as
screening or accrediting agencies, that the ranking of students was
basically anti-egalitarian, and that litigation, or at any rate (to use a
term which says much about the era) "hassles" over grades and
recommendations were to be avoided. These latter fears were rendered the more realistic since, as already indicated, students were
absorbed into policymaking roles previously reserved for faculty,
often—as they could make brutally clear to intransigent faculty—
holding the fate of the latter in their hands by their formal voice on
departmental or institution-wide committees on promotion and tenure.

These changes had a decisive effect on the climate of the campus,
the trajectories of students, and the grandeurs and miseries of teaching. They were often upsetting and even cruelly demeaning to
teachers who had entered on their calling or vocation in an earlier
day and who were not, like some of their age-mates, glad to abandon
the responsibilities of adulthood in order to seek to become adolescents again.

As with many empirically based typologies, it is far from easy to
draw a line between the telic reforms described in Part I of our book
and the nationwide sweep of what we have termed in Part II as the
movement toward an overoptioned life. One way of looking at the
latter group of changes is to see them as bringing to the smaller
institutions, such as regional state or local private colleges, some of
the benefits as well as some of the drawbacks of the multiversity.

---

*The Carnegie Council studies show that, in 1969, 50 percent of under-
graduates agreed strongly or with reservations that undergraduate education
would be improved if grades were abolished; in 1975, 32 percent did. (Faculty
percentages over the same period dropped from 34 percent to 19 percent.) See
Trow, *Aspects of American Higher Education, 1969–1975*, Table 3, p. 14.

In educational units within the multiversity, as in the deregulated liberal-arts colleges, the options sought and retained by students vary greatly, as does the holding power of institutions against the inevitable lessening of loyalty on the part of both students and faculty.

II

We must now go back to the beginning of the student-faculty movements of the mid-sixties and ask why there was such widespread resonance among both graduate and undergraduate students to the rhetoric attacking what were in fact the comparatively loose requirements of American colleges and universities. Was there something in the experience of this particular generation of students that had made it possible for some of the most privileged young people in the world to believe themselves oppressed? We believe that, precisely in the institutions in which protest began, we can trace a sequence of events that is not likely to recur. On the one hand, the post-World War II baby boom, added to the growth in the number of high-school graduates and of those attending college, caused the number of undergraduates to double within a decade—an unprecedented demographic bulge which also, of course, brought about a corresponding tripling of faculty. At the same time, academic pressures in the best high schools intensified with the post-Sputnik preoccupations of adults. Many flagship state universities became *de facto* more selective (though in many states they were required by law to admit all high-school graduates), and the heightened expectations of both faculty and students brought increased pressures. The degree of difficulty varied, of course; the multiversity was uneven in the extent to which programs were overenrolled and the faculty could insist on greater selectivity; a number of institutions—including many private colleges with relatively open doors to any who could pay tuition—remained relatively unaffected.

On the whole, however, faculty who were themselves better trained took the better preparation and increased diligence of their students for granted: harder, more complex, and better work did not bring more "reward" in terms of a rise in grades during the early and middle 1960s. In his brilliant social-science fantasy Michael Young coined the term "meritocracy" for this phenomenon and described as a scenario for a distant future, a reaction against competitive anxieties and pressures, especially on the part of those successful at surmounting them.[4] These resentments contributed, in ways still not wholly understood, to the political protests and to the success of the politically minded activists in enlarging their constituencies.

We have already noted that the Berkeley radicals of the Free Speech Movement quickly discovered the effectiveness of attacking the alleged overbureaucratization of universities as well as their alliances with and subservience to a corrupt society, but similar charges were heard as well at good small liberal-arts colleges. However, when social scientists surveyed demonstrators at Berkeley, Harvard, Columbia, and elsewhere, and compared them with those who were not demonstrating, they were sometimes surprised to discover that the protesters were often those least dissatisfied with their education, with the most access to faculty, and generally with good academic records. Thus, for example, Robert Somer's 1964 survey of 285 Berkeley students revealed that most were satisfied with the quality of education.[5] (A majority said they were satisfied with "courses, examinations, professors, etc." and agreed that Berkeley tries to "provide top quality educational experience for students here.") Marshall Meyer came to similar conclusions about Harvard students in a survey done during the demonstrations after the occupation of University Hall in the spring of 1969.[6]

What students appeared to be complaining about could in a way be traced to the very quality of the education they recognized they had been receiving: yes, they were receiving excellent education; on the large campuses their faculty, though often unavailable individually, at least to the shy and nonassertive, were first-rate. But in order to do reasonably well in the increased competition, the students were forced to keep up a pace which the men could not interrupt for fear of the draft, and which the women, except in the upper and professional strata, were hard put to justify to parents who saw their futures in terms of the sexist limitations of the past. We wish the surveys had asked questions not only about the quality but about the competitive anxieties engendered by the new intensity of education, about whether or not the students would have preferred to move at a more relaxed pace.

Amply supplied with students, many faculty laid on longer and more demanding reading lists (at times, a kind of advertising to one's peers, leading one of us in the 1950s to refer to reading lists as the status equivalent of large tailfin automobiles); in some selective colleges and universities, one could get the impression that every course competed for a student's full time. This does not mean, of course, that students read all the assigned books and articles, but rather that, like many faculty themselves, they constantly felt "behind," forced to balance competing curricular and noncurricular interests in a way which would get them through what they came to call the "system" with the kind of grades that would satisfy their own superegos, their parents, and prospective postbaccalaureate schools or, less commonly, employers.

A minority of students, participating in the civil-rights movements, had already sought to find and identify themselves with an oppressed class. If one looks today at the photographs of the Free Speech Movement leaders at Berkeley in 1964, one sees clean-shaven young men and well-dressed young people of both sexes; only later did students adopt what one of our colleagues has termed "proletarian drag." And especially after white students were made to feel unwelcome in an increasingly nationalist black milieu, a small number of students on selective campuses picked up a quasi-Marxist lingo and spoke of themselves as an oppressed class; one UCLA white student in a widely circulated polemic, spoke of the "student as nigger." Another type of Marxist lingo saw the students as being forcefully drilled to take their places in what C. Wright Mills had called the "command posts" of a rotten society. Of course, in attacking the universities for this supposed mission, they were also in a way criticizing themselves as the presumptive beneficiaries.

Just these attitudes, in the early years of student rebellion, more often antagonized than enlisted students of working-class origin and their parents, who felt that these affluent, seemingly insouciant students were seeking to tear down the very values of upward social mobility and success which represented the height of aspiration for the less privileged. It did not help matters that the males among the privileged were in general able to avoid the draft. For a time, they were in college or graduate school, where they generally stood well in their classes, and when they were no longer sheltered in college they could get teaching and other service jobs (including places in the Peace Corps) which with rare exceptions kept them out of Vietnam. Ground combat was fought almost exclusively by the children of the working class, rarely by the children of the slums who could not pass the army qualification test. The moral dilemmas and occasional perils of potential exile which the Vietnam War brought to privileged youth heightened their sense of guilt and their periodic efforts to establish solidarity with the poor and the working class. But these very efforts, as already suggested, often proved self-defeating as they took up what they assumed was black and/or working-class argot, appeared to have ample time for demonstrations, and otherwise showed their insensitivity to the very different pragmatic problems and moral attitudes of noncollege-bound youth or of those who were attending less sophisticated institutions.

To understand the pressures under which students in the more selective institutions were working, it is necessary to look back into recent but often forgotten history. Until the 1930s, a few well-known colleges had something of a national appeal, but at the undergraduate level, the contemporary sense of a national prestige ranking emerged only after World War II.[7] Since most colleges depended largely on local applicants and were not in excessive demand, neither children nor their parents were anxious about college entry. For example, although Harvard College began nationwide talent searches around 1937, a student of average ability[8] and moderate wealth or enterprise could easily get in until the rush of veterans began after World War II. Once the freshman year with its shock of complexity had been surmounted, students could find ways through the curriculum that would enable them to graduate with the appropriate and in no way discreditable gentleman's C. What distinguished Harvard College even in the pre-World War II era, however (and such schools as Reed, Swarthmore, and Bryn Mawr as well), was the difficulty of doing truly outstanding work at the behest of the minority of outstanding men (and, mostly they were men) on the faculties who were capable of recognizing and responding to excellence.*

Colleges did not have an opportunity to become selective on a large scale until the late 1950s. The pressures began to be felt at ever earlier levels in the schools, as records were built up for college entry; and these pressures were intensified by the growing competition for places in medical schools, good law schools, and other top-flight postbaccalaureate institutions.

Except for a short time in the immediate post-war period, there has never been a time, however, when a student who could pay tuition and the cost of subsistence could not find entry in some college somewhere. Only a small minority of colleges has ever been seriously selective. Thus, the phenomenon of multiple applications and the

---

*Paradoxically, in certain departments it may well be easier to graduate from Harvard today with a summa cum laude than it was in the 1920s or 1930s, thanks both to the increased level of student ability and to grade inflation, especially as it relates to the awarding of honors. However, it has also become increasingly discreditable to graduate in that small minority of those who do not even gain the minimal "cum laude in general studies," and the pressure to gain highest honors has been greatly enhanced by the demographic factors we have been describing and by the increasing competetiveness of entry to the best graduate and professional schools.

race to get into the "best" places actually occurs among a numerically small minority, but of course it is a highly influential one. And
at the graduate level, apart from medical schools and some specialized programs, such as those in clinical psychology and currently
agriculture and veterinary medicine, almost anyone with a baccalaureate degree and tuition can get further education somewhere. The
law schools, for example, are capable of almost indefinite expansion;
and there are always many more new doctoral programs than candidates to fill them. Some anxious students and their families tend
not to be aware of these facts and to believe that they have been
"selected," when, in fact, they have merely been admitted to an open-
door institution—one which, however, manages to conceal the degree of its actual readiness of access.

There are still great differences among regions and among high
schools in the extent to which college attendance, let alone attendance at a selective college, is taken for granted. In California, for
example, little social stigma is attached to attending one of the local
community colleges, many of which are new, architecturally stunning, and staffed with some excellent faculty—though often it is
assumed that students will transfer to finish the baccalaureate at a
state college or at the University of California. Only about 5 percent
of California's students leave the state for higher education elsewhere. By contrast, in New Jersey, as we shall see in Chapter 9, the
state system has lacked prestige, and even now, when it has been
considerably strengthened, there is strong pressure on upper- and
upper-middle class students to enter a selective private college or to
submit to the high-tuition and other tariff barriers at the distinguished
state universities (such as Michigan, Vermont, Wisconsin-Madison,
Virginia, Harpur College of the State University of New York at
Binghamton, Chapel Hill, the explicitly selective University of California, and others). Massachusetts, although it has an abundance of
well-known private colleges and universities, is in somewhat the same
position as New Jersey—and its selective state university at Amherst
will allow only a 3 percent ratio of out-of-state students. Thus, national aggregate statistics conceal great intra- and interstate differences in the proportion of those who go on to college—and the day
of what Martin Trow has referred to as near-universal college attendance seems an unlikely prospect if one is thinking of post-high-
school college entrance and not of possibilities for lifelong adult
education of some sort.

However, with increasing family mobility in a country in which
mobility has always been high, a considerable pool of prospective
college entrants developed after World War II whose attendance

was not channeled by religious ties, local or state pride, or vestiges
of family tradition (Jewish students from reasonably well-to-do families have been free of such considerations, as the country became
more national, more mobile, more secular). Meanwhile, the break-
down in provincial ties meant that more and more colleges had to
enlarge their orbits of recruiting and strengthen their ability to compete by developing a faculty and student body of high quality. Thus,
to take an example from the public sector, the University of Michigan and Michigan State University did not divide up the state geo-
graphically or attempt to prevent duplications, though MSU sustained
its land-grant tradition in addition to seeking to become a university
of world-wide status. Both universities recruited from each other's
immediate geographic vicinity, and outside the state as well. The
University of Michigan, like Wisconsin in an earlier era and Colorado and Virginia now, draws large numbers of out-of-state students
willing to pay high tuition (a bonus which is increasingly insufficient
to satisfy chauvinist legislatures), while Michigan State University
has particularly sought National Merit Scholars, using its own resources to help finance what is said to be the second largest, if not
the largest, group of such scholars in the country. (Similarly, Berkeley earlier, and UCLA later, built dormitories, among other reasons so as to be able to recruit students from the very backyards of
their rivals.)

Dormitory building, in fact, symbolized some of the new pressures
for expansion. Institutions such as Boston College, a once-urban
Jesuit college set up to boost the upward mobility of the lower-
middle-class Irish of Boston and to winnow out a few Jesuit scho-
lastics for the order, moved to the suburbs and built dormitories,
in part to be able to compete for the bright Catholic elite with Notre
Dame and The College of Holy Cross or Georgetown. Later on, as
the University of Massachusetts, in 1964–65, inaugurated a Boston
campus, and as Boston State College became attractive for its liberal
arts as well as its vocational programs, the many metropolitan schools
founded by various religious and secular groups faced the situation
of private colleges elsewhere, except for the most highly selective
and some of the more fundamentalist ones, as they attempted to
compete with excellent neighboring public institutions with relatively
low tuition. Drawing less from Boston and more from the rest of the
country, the Arts and Sciences departments of Boston College became much more competitive; and one could say that dormitory
building everywhere could be seen as a symbol of heightened meritocratic pressures.

In the past, the desire to provide college educations for the able and ambitious children of the "poor but honest" classes had led not only to the founding of twenty-seven quite diverse Jesuit institutions, but also to the creation of numerous urban Catholic colleges for men or women by other religious orders and a few dioceses, mainly east of the Mississippi. Similarly, the Methodists created a string of urban institutions stretching from Boston University in the East to the University of Southern California in the West; other Protestant denominations, including such "Churches of the Disinherited" as the Seventh Day Adventists did likewise; in addition, the YMCA, which built Sir George Williams University in Montreal, developed the schools out of which Roosevelt and Northeastern broke away. The enhanced egalitarianism that resulted from the large increase in the numbers attending colleges made college attendance itself less a privilege, and the competition among an enlarged pool of contestants for the numerically small number of truly selective colleges became fierce. In 1956, when the first National Merit Scholarships were awarded, high schools—in a kind of sponsored mobility[9]—allowed 58,000 students who ranked in the top 5 percent of their classes to take the qualifying test. But egalitarian fairness led to the demand that all be able to compete, and by 1964, the number tested had grown to 800,000, and provision had been made for more winners.[10]

But in fact the expansion increased the pool of strivers and losers. This last point can be put in another perspective by looking at the use of test scores at a specific institution. When Harvard began to use the SAT to select a talented few in the late 1930s, there was virtually no penalty for not doing well. Students of average ability from affluent or alumni families were not required to take the exam, and there were many other bases for admission to Harvard and other socially or intellectually attractive colleges. But as the tests became required screening devices at nearly all colleges which aspired to distinction, the primary function of the SAT became that of identifying the failures, not the successes. Not just failure to win a scholarship, but failure to gain admission to one's chosen college became the penalty of not doing outstandingly well.*

*We do not believe that the prestige of the more distinguished colleges is largely factitious; there are real advantages beyond imagery and prestige. However, it should also be emphasized that these colleges differ considerably from each other in the degree to which they provide self-confidence for the losers, once they arrive. Harvard in this respect may polarize outcomes somewhat more than otherwise comparable Ivy League institutions do. (One unpublished study by David Winter, professor of psychology at Wesleyan, indicates that Radcliffe women even today lose self-confidence more quickly in comparison

The number of colleges joining the College Entrance Examination Board rose from 79 in 1948 to 707 in 1966.[11] Simultaneously with the growth of television and an increasingly national culture, these developments reflected the "nationalization" of a number of the more selective colleges. Winning a National Merit Scholarship or being a runner-up gave the student psychological justification for leaving home and peer group and brought many invitations to do so. All these potential customers had available to them college guides listing test scores for hundreds of colleges, and in large cities matching agencies developed which could bring students and colleges together. Football players might be wooed for the sake of alumni and legislative support; but collecting National Merit Scholars became important in attracting faculty and visibility among intellectuals.[12]

If the demographic bulge pressured children through their parents' heightened concern about qualifying for a "good" college, the Russian launching of Sputnik in 1957 gave both schools and colleges leverage over local and national budgets and provided an ideology to justify honors programs, accelerated curricula, and an intensified attack on academic laxity. National committees of scholars took an interest in secondary education and pioneered in developing new, more abstract, and more challenging high-school programs in mathematics and some of the natural sciences. In suburban communities, educated parents supported these programs, while major universities encouraged the high schools through Advanced Placement, which in effect allowed high schools to offer college-level courses for college credit. Efforts occurred also to make Americans less monolingual, with high schools offering courses in Russian, Chinese, and (later) Swahili as well as in the more traditional languages.* The Sputnik impulse thus spread beyond the sciences, although, of course, there were geographic variations in its impact. With the increased pressure for college entry, students in suburban high schools and in the private schools began to compile dossiers of impressive activities and offices. Activities that had been in some measure ends in themselves thus had another purpose. For example, students applying to some colleges quickly learned that they should show social concern by being involved in tutoring or environmental cleanup programs; it

with equally capable students at the leading women's colleges. Based on an unpublished memorandum and personal communication from David Winter, Spring 1976).

*This last impulse seems, to our regret, to have spent itself, and America may in fact be reprovincializing itself as, in colleges, high schools, and at the graduate level also, language requirements are dropped—not that standards of literacy in spoken and written English are being correspondingly improved.

was important to indicate not only cognitive ability on the College Boards and in class standing, but to show one's popularity by election as student-government president, and to demonstrate well-rounded-ness of one's gifts by writing poetry or playing the French horn. And while many students dropped such activities as soon as they arrived at college, in some cases the pressure for postbaccalaureate entry, especially to law or medical schools, often forced college students to continue such activities, including participation in sports, which thus became contaminated by careerism. Resentment about the inau-thenticity of these games had a role in fostering the drive for auton-omy in the curriculum and the extracurriculum and the struggle to prevent self-alienation which gave support to the counterculture in the 1960s.

A majority of *all* male students entering four-year colleges in the 1960s proclaimed their intention of continuing in some form of post-baccalaureate education; and in the selective colleges the overwhelm-ing majority of both sexes had this intention. The increase in the proportion of those attending college had become so great that in the 1960s a college degree was no more distinctive proportionately than a high-school diploma had been in 1920.[13]

Correspondingly, a number of relatively unselective state and pri-vate colleges were salted with a "critical mass" of undergraduates who could no longer be dismissed as oddballs and DAR's (damned average raisers) but competed for grades and faculty recognition that would win them places in postbaccalaureate programs.[14] No less im-portant was the fact, as we have already indicated, that faculty mem-bers themselves had increasingly been trained in competitive, high-pressure graduate schools, bringing expectations of high-level work to the students in less selective institutions,[15] and the increased abil-ity and diligence they found made it possible for many students to seek to respond, though often with paradoxical results. A study by Kenneth M. Wilson demonstrates these tendencies in an extreme form, showing that for a selective group of colleges, as better stu-dents were admitted, grades remained constant: in other words, abler students were doing more and better work for relatively less "re-ward" in terms of grades—in effect, grade deflation.[16] Although Wil-son's sample was restricted to a small group of women's colleges, we suspect the galling phenomenon of reducing "pay" while intensifying both the work and the competition was widespread among selective institutions before the onset of campus protests.

Michael Young, in *The Rise of the Meritocracy*, notes that it is high-status women who first of all turn against achievement and success and concern themselves with the losers.[17] In this country in recent years, women have not been comfortable in winning over other women, even where men were not directly involved. For example, at Mount Holyoke College 30 percent of the entering freshmen said in 1964 that they disliked competitive situations; by 1970, the proportion had grown to 43 percent.[18] At Vassar, the shift in the same period was from 30 percent to 49 percent. Some wings of the women's-liberation movements, movements which as a whole opened many new careers and enlarged expectations for college-educated women, sometimes turned fiercely against any woman who became a "movement star," no matter how useful she was to their political agenda.[19]

Not only for supposedly nurturing and noncombative women, but also for men, misgivings concerning success have been a minor theme in American life ever since colonial times. The Calvinist sense of success as a sign of grace was never iron-clad insurance against doubt; for a number of writers and critics all through the nineteenth-century, their own success and that of their expanding country were not unequivocal blessings.[20]

This latent motif became much more prominent, when, for the first time, the 1960s brought to the more selective colleges "critical masses" of students from families where the father and often the mother had attended college. It was problematic that these students would do better than their parents simply by getting the same amount of education. Their responses to this constellation varied. Some engaged in, and presently even more are engaging in, defensive credentialing, securing not one but two degrees, and working even harder for grades than their parents may have done. Others joined the contrameritocracy, preferring not to compete, debunking success, and in some cases concluding that the system of competition itself was evil and should be destroyed.[21]

In the enhanced competition of the middle sixties, many able students preferred not to test their own adequacy; they had come as valedictorian stars from good high schools only to find themselves in competition with hundreds of others who seemed even more assured and articulate (although in fact often hiding their own anxieties). To throw all this over for the heady camaraderie of the countercultural movement or by a pretended indifference to the curriculum could allow them to maintain secret narcissistic fantasies of greatness along with a public posture of righteous indignation about unfair and demeaning competition.

It is significant that the attitudes made visible by an academic elite gradually filtered downward, and in time they came to influence the outlook of more provincial faculty and students as well. In a 1968 survey by Daniel Yankelovich, one-third of *all* college students expressed doubts about being successful, and half had doubts about the value of making money.[22] Thirty-one percent of the respondents said that they no longer believed that hard work paid off, a figure which rose to 43 percent a year later, and to 61 percent by 1971. The cynicism that had enveloped those at the high end of the academic ladder was clearly working its way downward.

It was the more selective and affluent colleges which suddenly expanded their efforts to recruit a highly visible presence of black (and to a lesser degree, other nonwhite) students. Often they sought out precisely those supposed "authentic ghetto blacks" whose education, motivation, and sophistication had been most handicapped. In addition to the handicaps of inadequate academic preparation and an unrealistic understanding of what selective colleges were like—no members of their families had attended such colleges—these students experienced great difficulties in adjusting to the social discrepancies between themselves and the majority of visible white students. (The more poorly prepared white students, high-risk applicants on whom the most academically elite institutions were always ready to take some gambles, were neither so physically visible nor so well-organized as the blacks appeared to be. Well-prepared blacks from outstanding preparatory schools, feeling guilt similar to that of liberal upper-middle-class whites but under even more severe pressure for communal solidarity, often sought to lead their black "brothers and sisters" in contrameritocratic activities that might make them more comfortable and make the adjustments, and the possibility of graduation from college, less hazardous.) The more selective colleges were in fact competing for a very limited number of black high school graduates who had the required combination of family resources and test scores that would make them eligible for admission.[23] Moreover, only a few white administrators or faculty knew how to go about looking for highly motivated and psychologically secure black students, and often left matters to black student recruiters or administrators of black programs, understandably eager to meet "quotas" and willing to fudge the usual standards. Deans and admissions committees vied with each other in telling success stories about rough "black diamonds" they had discovered in unlikely ghetto high schools, ignoring the statistical realities and inevitable traumas that a more thorough assessment would have revealed.

There has been abundant evidence of a lack of realism among isolated black high-school youth. Some do not realize, for example, that one cannot enter a good law school without a college degree. In recent years, black graduates of selective colleges have sometimes reported that it would have been less humiliating for them to attend a traditional black college, at least for the first two "decompression" years, transferring later to a state college, before going on to graduate or professional work at a major black or white university. Some whites, particularly those on athletic scholarships at selective colleges, have also suffered such humiliations, but underprepared whites have never been the target of such an ambitious dragnet as was launched for blacks in recent years. Black parents wanting "the best" for their children, as well as the students themselves, have been tempted (as have many whites) to turn down Oberlin for Harvard, or the College of Wooster for Oberlin, or Cleveland State University for any of these. Thus at every level black students have, with notable exceptions, tended to be overmatched by average white students in a kind of upward suction process based on the sudden competition which was so greatly intensified after the assassination of Martin Luther King, Jr. (One of us remembers a black high-school counselor in an inner-city Detroit high school who commented that, after having been ignored for most of his professional life, he was besieged by recruiters from white colleges, as if every black were a potential 7'9" basketball star coveted for a new kind of well-intentioned slave market.)[24]

For blacks hastily recruited at test-score levels often several hundred points below that of the average for whites, and with only a remote knowledge of the world they were about to enter, it was a further affront to be asked by liberal white students, faculty, and administrators about their plans to return to "their people" or to serve as professionals in the ghetto. No other "immigrant" group has been subject to such an imposition in the first generation. And, of course, there was pressure from within their own race as well: terms such as "bourgeois" or "middle-class" became synonyms for "Uncle Tom." Though the gates of privilege had been swung open in one sense, help in essential skills was often hard to come by.

When liberal whites faced blacks on the athletic field, the game spirit of competition generally prevailed. But when the competition was for academic preference, beating blacks could become less a source of pride than of shame and guilt, as the white students recognized the handicaps under which many blacks operated both psychologically and academically. The white students in the selective colleges suddenly discovered at first hand the differences in achievement, based not on race but on social and cultural class, and the double standards of admission under which their black classmates had been selected—differences of which they had previously been only vaguely aware. They began to be afraid that they might be racists if they considered academic or cognitive judgments as important measures of individual quality; and so, as a by-product, the "merit" in meritocracy came under aggressive questioning.[25]

If one played down meritocratic tests in admitting students to college, in order to compensate for past injustice, then it was no longer possible to do what many state universities with *de facto* open admissions have done in the past: namely to send poorly prepared students home again at Thanksgiving or Christmas with the feeling that they had had their chance. Instead, like the high schools, colleges began to pass unqualified students along, either through putting courses on a pass/no credit basis, or by finding what the British call "soft options." Many white liberal faculty consciously applied a double standard in grading black students, an easier solution than providing tutoring which was often doomed to failure because of the implicit humiliation involved.[26] Many liberal and radical white students began to turn away from the competition which produced such unequal results despite the opportunity for equal entry.

Much to the dismay of scholarly black faculty and hard-working black students, many whites turned against any measures of comparative success when they began to interpret success as deriving only, rather than in large measure, from cumulated advantages. Those who came from backgrounds often more disadvantaged than those of many blacks remained isolated and invisible—only much later, and at other social levels, to coalesce in the revival of the "new ethnicity" among urban poor whites. Under the quite commonly mistaken assumption that black students in predominantly white colleges would feel more at home in "relevant" black-studies programs, many such courses were hastily organized, and faculty were recruited to staff and teach in them who were supposed to be "models" of success for black students. For some of the latter, it was humiliating to have "models" who were sometimes poorly prepared.[27]

We should make it clear that student interest in a particular subject does not make it unworthy of inclusion in the curriculum. What matters is the seriousness with which the work is done and the quality of the students and researchers who are involved. It is tragic when, whether by design or social pressure, black-studies programs are confined to blacks. It is also regrettable that, for the most part, women's-studies courses have been confined to women, although men often need the "role model" of a bright woman faculty member more than do the women themselves. The curriculum can be enriched for all by such additions—we are not speaking of the budget!

—just as it has been enriched steadily since the trivium and quadrivium were abandoned as the only solid academic fare.

Nor do we intend to imply by this discussion that the effort to recruit more blacks was a mistake, or that one can eliminate all pain and humiliation in any revolution—even a quiet one—for the increase in proportion of blacks attending college was a change of that magnitude. We are not sure that the process could have gone otherwise. Our intention here has been to show the special burden that blacks (and some whites) have borne, particularly in the most privileged and liberal sectors of academe, in the hope that cycles of misplaced sympathy, unintended condescension, and white liberal guilt will not repeat themselves.

Though the movements on the pedagogical left had somewhat different sources than those that formed political protests, the currents of educational reform were fed by the rising tide of political activism on campus. It is not surprising that a generation caught in the squeeze we have described as more work for less reward would resonate to an appeal for gaining more control over the pace and shape of their own education. By the early 1970s a profound change had occurred. Some of the shift may be explained by the usual cycles of contraction and expansion, looseness and fixity, that are discussed in Chapter 10. But the rapidity and extensiveness of the shift—to be documented in a moment—cannot be explained solely as a historical swing of the pendulum toward the loosening of authority and the struggle for freedom in the curriculum that we have lumped under the title of popular reforms.

It seems likely that faculty on many campuses were motivated for a variety of reasons to grant students new powers and a near-total freedom of choice. Required core programs had begun to be seen as burdens (and occasionally as somewhat intellectually inferior) by many faculty who were feeling the same competitive pressures as students. The elimination of core requirements would enable them to plan more courses that would reflect their needs as researchers instead of submitting to a fixed program. It also enabled others to abandon courses that tied them to the obligations of keeping up with a particular field. Political protests—particularly on those leading campuses that were for a time under siege—no doubt also affected faculty dispositions. In the later stages of the protest, when, as we have noted, the activists sought to enlarge their constituencies by appealing to students with educational grievances, demands for educational reform became more numerous. Leaders on the pedagogical left skillfully exploited the tensions generated by the war protests, and they presented a specific set of demands, in contrast with the global aims of the war protesters, about which something could realistically be done. The faculty could not stop the war or end the university's "complicity" in a society political radicals charged was corrupt, but they could change the curriculum and give students a share in running the campus. Few faculty believed that these concessions would bring an end to protest (although many believed the reforms would at least mollify some of the protesters), but acquiescence gave them the feeling of taking *some* action in response to an amorphous movement that had been oppressively unmanageable. Thus the pedagogical left, like the political left, was not just a student movement. A sizable percentage of the faculty were convinced of the need for relaxations in the curriculum that would permit more experiment and innovation. And many believed that student-directed education was the best kind of education. The changes in recruitment and admissions policies discussed in the previous section, which had resulted in an expanded enrollment of relatively underprepared minority students, were further evidence of the need for "soft options" and fewer hurdles in the curriculum.

A 1972 survey of academic deans in 115 selective colleges and univertisies showed that three-fourths of these institutions permitted students to plan their course of study and define their major (21 percent of the institutions had students do so frequently; 52 percent said this was occasional practice). Eighty-three percent of the colleges grant credit for individual work or study away from the campus; 22 percent allow such work to count for up to one-quarter of the credits required for a degree; 9 percent give credit for such study even when it is pursued in the absence of faculty supervision. Three-fifths of these selective colleges allow students to initiate new courses. More significantly, 28 percent permit undergraduates to conduct their own courses for credit. Many academic deans who participated in the 1972 survey expected these developments to go still further: 54 percent said they planned further liberalization in policies for granting academic credit, while only 3 percent anticipated a tightening of regulations. Administrators at the University of California, Santa Cruz, where virtually all grading is on a pass/no record basis, have speculated that any effort to return to formal grading, in order to satisfy some students concerned with postbaccalaureate placement, would bring about a massive student protest.

The fluidity of enrollment that has resulted from the newfound student freedom has, of course, led to new administrative difficulties and uncertainties. Even where provisions for preregistration remain,

students are frequent "no-shows," just as their cult of spontaneity
makes them poor at responding to letters and awkward in arranging
formal meetings with faculty. A college or university is not like an
Eastern Airlines shuttle, where a new plane can be added for one
or two passengers who have not made a reservation! Thus, student
freedom often leads to queuing, or occasionally to waiting up all
night to sign up for a course which is suddenly popular and overenrolled. Even the students' desires for small classes and intimacy
often prove self-defeating under such conditions of untrammeled and
unchanneled freedom. A hundred students may show up to register
for a seminar limited to ten; or, at Harvard, it is not unusual for
three times the number who can be accepted to show up for an
honors concentration. What Thomas Schelling has termed "the ecology of micro-motives" operates here, with each student supposing
that he or she can gain the necessary entreé to the overenrolled
course or program and being quite unwilling to see the many costs
of the necessary waiting and frustration.[28] As students crowd, lem-
minglike, into the already overenrolled fields on the ground that the
one the other students are choosing must be "the best," we see that
curricular freedom has created an inevitable traffic jam.

Only at an unusually well-endowed institution can esoteric or
traditional subjects be protected in the face of underenrollment.
Here professors can afford to make high demands on students, and
those who are compelling and dynamic are able to maintain their
own constituencies—not only because they may be gatekeepers to
medical school but because there are students available who want
to test their adequacy in courses in which they know they will get
a "real" grade. Teaching—like preaching—is affected by fashion and
styles, and only the handful of institutions which have striven to
maintain the telic reforms rather than bow to the currently popular
ones have been able to withstand the influences of the marketplace.

Some curricular changes had to be introduced to take account of
altered admissions standards even before the falling off in college enrollments forced many once-selective colleges to dip further down into
the pool of applicants. The deflation of quality in terms of test scores
(although accompanied by an inflation of grades) went even beyond
the national decline of scores which many reports from Educational
Testing Service have delineated. Some eminent colleges have been
making clear that, like Bowdoin, they no longer use test scores in
admissions or use them only in part. Indeed, comparison of recent
editions of one of the best-known college guides, James Cass and
Max Birnbaum's *Comparative Guide to American Colleges*, indi-

cates a shift in the last several years from an emphasis on test scores to an emphasis on student free choice. The introduction to the 1972 edition states: "We are witnessing a retreat, today, from the excessive emphasis on academic grades and test scores that marked the 1960s . . . Therefore, assessments in the Selectivity Index have been treated with special care." This and other recent editions also note that students have been consulted in making judgments about colleges, a new development. Plainly, the customer has begun to be courted in a way that was not true for the selective colleges in the early 1960s.

Some of the major curricular changes have been handled extramurally. Credit for work done or supposed experience gained in extramural activities had spread widely through academia by the time of a Carnegie survey in 1970.[29] (Indeed, during the period of activism, many students had managed to get through their institutions while primarily majoring in a cocurriculum of their own devising in political tactics and organizational reform.)

Also added to the curriculum were not only new subjects based on scientific developments and on student pressures, but also new opportunities for work in the performing arts (a necessity in the men's colleges which went coed) as well as credit in liberal arts colleges for activities once considered vocational, such as preparation for schoolteaching, or, within sociology departments, for field work in social agencies or probation departments. Still, if one compares catalogues of today with those of a dozen years ago, in general one sees the same departments along with the new additions, and, notably and advantageously, some movement away from a too exclusive emphasis on the Western World.

It would require a close examination of textbooks as well as course titles to see what actual changes have resulted from student free choice in those subjects, such as the softer social sciences or literature, where faculty are more easily influenced by student tastes. Samuel McCracken, formerly of Reed College, has described some of the emergent styles in the teaching of English.[30] In our own field of sociology, the old-fashioned textbook competes against readers and anthologies with hip titles and flashy photographic displays, allowing the teacher to pick and choose at whim or to negotiate with students, i.e., with the more articulate students, what the class will agree to read.*

---

*That such developments are by no means confined to the United States is wonderfully illustrated by Alvin Gouldner's "Letter from Amsterdam," written as a farewell to a university where he had taught for some years and

It should be clear that these changes, though offensive to traditionalist faculty, are not invariably changes for the worse. Everything depends on context, and on the degree to which college helps combat the students' intellectual and moral deficiencies or simply adapts to these. Much pedantry has vanished, although it is clear that more remains than meets the eye when one visits experimental colleges and finds faculty *faute de mieux* falling back on what they had themselves learned in graduate school, unable to live up to their own desires to "make it new."

The same can be said of changes in the style of teaching. Formal lectures still exist, ever so many of them, and while many students disapprove of them ideologically, they vote with their feet in favor of them if the lecturer is sufficiently attractive. Often they listen with a depressing passivity, leaning forward only to take notes on something that is likely to be on the exam. They do not act as if they were in the presence of a human being thinking or, indeed, as if any thinking were required on their part. Thus, they continue schoolboy habits, though more and more—in the arenas of curriculum, admissions, and even tenure—they exert the power of adults.

At the same time that students were gaining more control over their curricular pathways through the abolition of requirements and the adoption of pass/no credit modes of grading, the minority of campus activists were also securing more direct, formal control over academic policy. Thus, a 1970 Carnegie survey of 1,230 colleges and universities found that 58 percent had given students more control over academic policy, with the proportion higher in the more selective colleges. This same survey showed that while two-year colleges reported small increases in dismissals for academic reasons, 8 percent of colleges awarding master's degrees and 20 percent of those awarding the doctorate reported decreases in academic dismissals. In many public and private institutions, students sit on boards of trustees (even where faculty do not), take a hand in admissions decisions, and have a voice in the retention and promotion of faculty.

Yet, from a variety of sources, such as the survey by Harold Hodgkinson to which reference has already been made, as well as our own visits to facuty-student assemblies and discussions with student representatives, it would seem that many students have become

where he suffered constantly from having to negotiate with students, i.e., with their radical and often insolent leadership, as to what they would agree to read. The "Letter from Amsterdam," dated at the end of term in 1975, has not been published but has been widely circulated, and in correspondence Gouldner has given us permission to refer to it.

dissatisfied with the formal powers they have won. Sometimes they feel they are mere tokens. At other times, such as when they participate on search committees, student performance has varied from creativity and helpfulness to the exercise of a semi-veto by mobilizing students against candidates to such a degree that they fearfully withdraw their names. If the student representatives, however chosen (by election, by lot, rotation, etc.), feel that their efforts are nugatory and often attend meetings infrequently, the student body at large almost never believes that any particular group can speak on its behalf. We have seen in Chapter 4 how at Kresge College such an abdication led to an effort to bring everybody in on everything; similar developments have occurred at small private colleges such as Hampshire and Goddard, and at tiny Marlboro College's (200+ students) traditional "Town Meeting." If campus questions are to be settled by group pressure and even violence, as happened in the late 1960s and early seventies at Antioch College, then as in many Western democracies, the formal or electoral or representative processes tend to fall into disrepair.[31]

Student guides to courses are not new, and, as in the case of the very large course guide at the University of Illinois, they can be extremely cruel. Course guides, and a fortiori guides to the microclimates of subdepartments, can be extremely valuable both for faculty and students. (One of the most impressive is the 1974 edition of the Barnard Columbia Course Guide.) But for the most part, since the classroom is territory which a school principal can enter but a college administrator cannot, judgments of quality of teaching tend to be notably inaccurate and time-bound.

Contrary to legend, teaching has for the most part been taken into account in appointment and promotion at most universities, including those devoted to major research. Ordinarily, good teachers are considered an enhancement of a department's appeal, especially to prospective graduate students. Indeed, in the selective institutions, the students are so able that faculty are often ashamed of doing a bad job as teachers; it is at the middle-level institutions where they may shirk their teaching as much as they dare, trying to flatter students by giving them time off, or more reward for less work —a sharp reversal of the meritocratic pressures of the mid-1960s. The focus on teaching has been intensified by pressure from legislators as well as from students, thus combining the Philistinism of the traditional right, which saw no point in esoteric research, with the radicalism of the political-pedagogic left, which saw research as at worst complicitous, at best careerist.

One of the ironies of the current situation is that the mandate to increase teaching in terms of hours, a requirement often imposed by regents or legislators, and the dependence of faculty on student judgment, make for less innovative teaching: as we have sometimes put it, "teach or perish" can lead to more sudden death than the longer lead time given to "publish or perish." A course which is experimental runs the risk, by that very fact, of being a total flop. A reputation as a "poor teacher," like a harsh write-up in a student course guide, cannot be easily overcome—yet a teacher-scholar who has not published has little chance for a new start somewhere else. In contrast, those working in science have the opportunity to publish negative results, that is, experiments which have not panned out. In all scholarly fields, there can be second chances: earlier mistakes can be redeemed. However, total neglect can be devastating in the absence of support provided by referees and colleagues.

To be sure, the feedback provided through student evaluations may liberate as well as intimidate faculty, and some institutions have provided in-house support for faculty development, for example, the opportunity for criticism from an office of institutional research which is not directly connected with the channels of promotion. (Where such opportunities exist, faculty rarely make use of them. They still apparently believe that, since they were once students, they *should* know how to teach, and should not need help in becoming less awkward teachers.)

In the 1960s efforts to become pals with students were sometimes expressive of the same idealism that we have discussed in connection with Kresge College in Chapter 4. But often, what began in idealism ended in panic when, by the middle 1970s, many faculty were haunted by the nightmare that their department or course would be abolished altogether for want of customers. In other cases department heads struggled with the specter of courses which were over-applied for, and which reflected shifting vocational trends in roller-coaster enrollments.

Changes in student traffic have perhaps been most marked in the least attended but fastest growing segment of higher education—the community colleges. Both from aggregate data and examination of the catalogues of a number of community colleges from all over the country we have concluded that the present employment market has changed the nature of what was once thought of as the "revolving door" of American higher education. Whereas at one time two-thirds of the students in community colleges enrolled in transfer programs, now over half appear to be in vocational programs. Such programs, incidentally, are more expensive for the institution, requiring a higher faculty/student ratio, more skillful and scarce faculty who can teach crafts that can be lucratively practiced, and often expensive equipment as well. Where once Burton Clark saw the function of the "open door [community] college" as that of "cooling out" people from higher education who in fact did not succeed in completing a baccalaureate degree, the danger may now be that the vocational programs are putting a ceiling on student aspirations. While the state of the economy in general justifies a cautionary realism, it does not justify using aggregate data to curb the hopes and discourage even the slim chances for "meaningful work" of those students who wish to pursue their education further. Some students do persist; others are willing to accept placement in low-status but perhaps relatively high-paying positions, such as dental hygienist or licensed practical nurse, auto mechanic, or welder.[32]

The community colleges have an extraordinary flexibility, and since many were begun only in the middle 1960s, they have been able to recruit faculty to meet changing conditions and are not stuck, like some traditional colleges, with five classicists who must share one student every second year. Some community colleges declare openly that they are prepared to offer a course desired by any seven people within commuting range (including commuting range by faculty) who are prepared to pay the minimum fees. The leaders are often extremely impressive men, like Peter Masiko of Miami-Dade Community College, whose two branches enroll over 30,000 students and whose buildings dwarf those of most major universities. And the faculty in community colleges seems more content than in any other segment of higher education. Many who originally taught in high schools are now teaching thirteenth and fourteenth grade at lower teaching loads, higher salaries, and improved status without having had to secure the doctorate (except for certain top positions where the doctorate in education is desired); in fact the doctorate may be a handicap: an indication of a "trained incapacity" for effective teaching.

Grade inflation is an inevitable outgrowth of the loosening of restraints and the rise of anti-meritocratic sentiments we have discussed. Thorstein Veblen, who did his best to discourage undergraduates, gave them all Cs, believing grades had no place in a true institution of higher learning—he rejected everything collegiate as a survival of knightly tourneys and other barbaric sports. But often the current mode of discrediting credentialism and showing disrespect for academic convention is not to give everyone a C but to give everyone an A—seldom acknowledged as a rip-off on those faculty who still give grades in Swiss francs. Yet that is but one strand of a complex phenomenon. In some cases, faculty now award grades for relative growth rather than according to an absolute standard. In other cases, particularly in those selective institutions that feel a responsibility to pass the underqualified blacks they admitted, grade inflation begins with the development of a double standard and then expands as white faculty feel guilty about grading white students more severely even when the latter do not complain about reverse discrimination.

A report on grading practices at major universities, including Berkeley, gives a graphic picture. Whereas a C was an acceptable grade at the beginning of the 1960s, it was a *de facto* failing grade by the end of the decade, with the average of all grades approaching B. Some institutions instituted grades above A (e.g., 4.5 on a numerical scale) since they were already coming close to the ceiling in available grades.[33] The experience of Syracuse University similarly illustrates the dramatic reversal of the cycle of more work for less reward. In the enrollment boom of the period 1958–64, Syracuse became more selective in its admissions policies, raising the mean SAT scores achieved by its entering freshmen by nearly 100 points. But "A" grades during this period remained constant as reflected in the number graduating with honors—about 10 percent—clearly a reduction in rewards. Selectivity reached a peak in 1965, and declined slightly thereafter as the inflationary period began. Grades rose slowly in the late 1960s so that 16 percent of the 1971 graduates earned As, 23.5 percent of the 1972 class, and 27 percent of the 1973 class. The trend continued until 1976, when Syracuse "devalued" by raising the grade-point average required for honors.

Those academicians who tried to maintain standards—a word which on the lips of many became virtually equivalent to racism—were sometimes undercut by their junior colleagues or teaching assistants, who had been students themselves in the late 1960s and were socialized into the new culture of dissent.[34] Furthermore, much of the teaching was done by graduate students for whom the acceptable spread of grades was between A and B. One Harvard teaching fellow, writing to David Riesman, asked in effect how he could grade undergraduates more severely than graduate students, who were seldom given a grade less than B.

Today, many private colleges simply cannot afford to fail students because their budgets are so precarious, and in a public institution a faculty member who fails a "disproportionate" number of students may be called to account by the chairman who feels that the department may lose out as students seek other, less threatening fields.

With even greater speed than that with which students were gaining control over the curriculum, they were eliminating the last vestiges of parietal restraints on their conduct in nonacademic arenas. It was really quite extraordinary to watch the wildfire spread of conviction on the part of college authorities, even in the more provincial and religiously dominated schools, that students were now adult enough to, as the phrase goes, "take control of their own lives." Indeed, this freedom became a persuasive part of college literature aimed at students even while efforts were made to reassure parents that nothing could go seriously amiss.

In the earlier era, students and faculty had both been satisfied with policies which kept up appearances, allowing students to sleep with each other while advising them to do so discreetly. Student pregnancies tended to get hushed up, although there were some notorious instances of the residual double standard, by which women might be expelled and men merely chastised. But for the students of the 1960s, what became almost uniformly regarded as "natural" relations of the sexes (unchaperoned relations rarely found by ethnographers among people supposedly closer to nature) became the battle cry everywhere; and it was difficult for faculty, who in any case disliked being bothered with noncurricular matters, to apply more stringent rules to undergraduates than did permissive parents themselves. They simply could not find the language with which to defend a supervision which many students from permissive homes and sophisticated high schools had been free of since the early teens.[35] Thus, efforts to establish wing-by-wing or floor-by-floor sex separation gave way under persistent student argument by the more vocal activists to "liberated" corridors and bathrooms, even though on a few campuses today, thanks in part to the women's-liberation movements, there has been an effort to restore the option of single-sex enclaves for women. These, however, have sometimes tended to become lesbian in orientation and hence unappetizing for the more sheltered students who at least on entrance would prefer some degree of protection from the constant sexual pressures.

There is a widespread mythology about the function of the socalled incest taboo where men and women students live side by side in the same corridor or even bedroom suites. The only study with which the authors are familiar, an analysis of a co-residential dormitory at a great state university, indicates that in some corridors, thanks to enforcement by the women, such a taboo does prevail and the men go elsewhere to forage, while in nearby corridors, there is no such taboo and the men have all the conveniences.[36]

Of course, long before students were demanding an end to hypocrisy and indeed were making single-sex education itself "unnatural," scholarly faculty members had been eager to shed the seminarylike obligation to socialize the young—a drive that lingered late into this century even in major institutions. But the very demographic boom which created the competitive pressures against which students reacted in ways already suggested, also helped make scholarship increasingly the source of faculty authority; and the obligations of scholarship seemed generally incompatible with responsibilities for the moral socialization of increasingly precocious undergraduates. Thus responsibilities for student life came more and more in the great state universities to be delegated to deans of students and residence-hall student assistants who could protect the faculty from unseemly knowledge of some of the more unappetizing consequences of their abdication.

The growing authority of the academic disciplines fragmented any consensus as to the kind of life which should prevail outside the curriculum: faculty selected for profound understanding of rocks or microbes or even Hittite texts did not feel qualified to deal with the ever-changing, and, beneath appearances, diverse needs of undergraduates. As Oscar and Mary Handlin wrote in a work prepared for the Carnegie Commission, the expansion of the professoriate during the boom years of the fifties and sixties attracted many for motives that were less than noble, and "deficiencies in faculty were now less easily contained or concealed informally." As our chapter on Kresge College suggests, and much the same might be said of New College in Sarasota, many faculty were ready to abdicate parental responsibilities not only because the demands of their disciplines left no time for fathering, but also because they did not want to be fathers, because they hoped to become children again, or at least teenagers. The ability of older faculty to "pass," at least to the outside eye of the visitor through dress and demeanor, often astonished us. We needed a scorecard to tell faculty and students apart,[37] as we did in the early days at New College, one of the first entirely new campuses formed partially in response to changes in the undergraduate climate.

III

In the United States, an election which is won by a 55 percent majority is looked upon as a landslide. At the very height of the popular reforms in the late 1960s, many faculty and students went along with what seemed to be overwhelming national currents either out of disorientation or expediency; they were at best reluctant converts. There were also a number of faculty who insisted on maintaining the goal of disinterested scholarship, often at considerable risk. Some went into voluntary exile, as in the case of one anthropologist, an unreconstructed liberal, who refused to condone black terrorism (including bombings) and went to Canada, as did a noted Cornell political scientist for somewhat analogous reasons. After the paroxysms of the post-Cambodian demonstrations, the almost physical smell of fear began to disappear from the protest-prone campuses with their continuous reminders in "trashed" windows and charred buildings of the persuasive power of mobs, whatever their ideological coloring. A less visible legacy of the protests was the truncated academic careers of undergraduates and graduate students who had been granted amnesty for work not done, but whose records were sometimes insufficient when they wanted to pursue postbaccalaureate study.

The brave and vocal and the silently coerced began to reassert themselves, as we have seen in noting the changed attitudes toward pass/no credit grading and the as yet relatively unsuccessful efforts to combat grade inflation. As employment prospects darkened both for undergraduates and graduate students, license to "do your own thing" lost much of its allure—as the history, in Chapter 4, of Kresge College indicates. Indeed, the University of California at Santa Cruz as a whole has suffered from the shift of student perspectives, as we shall see in Chapter 8. Hence, in many institutions, faculty thought the moment opportune to recapture lost ground and to regain curricular authority—but with the counterculture now incorporated into the styles of life of many adults as well as teenagers, almost nowhere was the effort made to interfere with the noncurricular freedoms (and accompanying peer tyrannies) students had been granted.

In the vast majority of institutions, any effort to restore requirements and establish some core curricular coherence could not succeed, so desperately did private institutions need students who could pay tuition, while public institutions needed students for the sake of funding formulas. But in that small number of highly selective university colleges that are heavily overapplied, it became possible for faculty to consider the curtailment of *laissez faire* and to discuss ways of achieving greater curricular coherence.

In 1971, Princeton's retiring president, Robert Goheen, appointed Marvin Bressler, professor of Sociology, as chairman of what came

to be known as the "Bressler Commission": a distinguished group
of senior faculty who were to reexamine the curriculum with an eye
to deciding what was most worth knowing and what should therefore
be required. There was interminable debate: "How can one expect
that students should know computer science if they have not read
Plato?" Or, "Even if they have done both computer science and
Plato, how can we, as mere provincial Westerners, exclude requirements for knowledge of Asian or African history and culture?" The
upshot was a civilized and reflective *Report* and a stalemate in terms
of faculty action. Several years later, a Yale faculty committee,
chaired by the political scientist Robert Dahl, went through the same
exercise—and with the same outcome. As we go to press, Harvard
College's Task Force on a Core Curriculum, chaired by the political
scientist James Q. Wilson and supported by the dean of faculty,
Henry Rosovsky, has reported nearly two years of work to the Faculty of Arts and Sciences and has been met by a barrage of criticism.
Natural scientists and especially mathematicians, who generally see
and only want to see the most gifted students (who in fact generally
make good use of opportunities to work in nonscience areas under
their own initiative) believe there is no need for any requirements;
many faculty in the humanities insist that their particular turf must
be included in contrast to a *Report* which emphasizes modes of
thought and cognitive styles rather than specific epochs and disciplines. And while many students privately would like more guidance
through a catalogue containing 2,000 courses, the articulate students,
as represented in the *Crimson*, the student daily, join those faculty
who are opposed to any requirements whatsoever. Even in the Ivy
League university-colleges, the students are now so diverse in preparation and background, as well as in willingness to enter fields in
which they are not assured of doing well, that it is not only hard for
faculties to decide on what is most worth knowing, but perhaps even
harder to compel faculty members to teach captive audiences and to
act as curricular policemen.

It is true that certain of these unwelcome chores could be forced
back upon the high schools if these major institutions were willing
to insist, for example, that all applicants know calculus and a foreign language and possess the ability to read and write English. But
such a plan would militate especially against the desire of just these
colleges—and their feeling of responsibility—for the recruitment of
minority students, very few of whom have such preparation. The desired diversity (which frequently does not operate in the self-segrega-
tion of residential life or of many classrooms) is too important a

responsibility to surrender and would in fact invite a renewal of protests if the effort were made.

Thus, we conclude that the popular reforms of the sixties are here to stay, even though enthusiasm for them has greatly ebbed. It would take the zeal of the St. John's faculty to create a newly coherent curriculum out of the shards left over from the 1960s, in the form of residual distribution requirements and attenuated general-education programs. And, as we have seen, St. John's is hardly a luminous magnet for large numbers of students. To be sure, as we shall see in the following chapter, neither is New College, which symbolizes a decade of almost continuous experiment with a variety of popular reforms. What remains is the patternless multiversity where such coherence as exists is intradepartmental, and where as a result of the popular reforms, the minority of students who want to create their own individuated program find neither help nor hindrance in doing so.

New College

7 When New College in Sarasota became part of the Sarasota branch of the University of South Florida in the fall of 1975, a stormy decade of independent existence ended. New College must stand in this volume as a prototype of the many experimental institutions founded in the 1960s which were not rooted in a particular telic reform. The New College experience is a case study of how wildly a college can fluctuate in its aspirations when it begins with a wish to be nontraditional but lacks a clear definition of ultimate purpose.

I

As we shall see, the founders of New College* had a plurality of aims, many of them rudimentary. The community of Sarasota, Florida, was in a sense a highly unlikely setting for an experimental

---

*The name itself, with its implications of innovation, was an accident. When the trustees sought a charter, they had to have a name, and they simply indicated "new college" pro tem. Later, in keeping with some of the early spirit of the place, they sought to associate it with New College at Oxford, and in fact that college's Warden was involved in some of the early publicity. That the name New College stuck probably did help turn recruitment by the college toward the innovative side, though that was not among its original ambitions. Indeed, though there are a number of places called "New College" in the country—including a program for freshmen at Hofstra University; New College, a subcollege of the University of Alabama; and New College of Sonoma State University, which is now the Hutchins School of Liberal Studies—it is New College in Sarasota, rather than the other institutions similarly designated, which is known to guidance counselors in the East and Midwest.

college. The expatriates who constitute a large part of Sarasota's population are, of course, mainly postparental and of modest income, imports largely from the Middle West who give the impression of being somewhat more conservative than their cousins who chose to go off to Southern California. Then there are the right-wing zealots—both indigenous and imported—some exceedingly well-to-do, but others more typical Sun Belt Goldwater types. Sarasota is the home of "Let Freedom Ring," a right-wing telephone advertisement, and of a number of members of the John Birch Society as well. But the town has also attracted a substantial number of more cosmopolitan individuals who enjoy the small resident colony of artists and the well-known Asolo Theatre (which provides opportunities for a master of fine arts program tied into Florida State University's School of Theatre). Though initially part-time winter visitors for the most part, they often ended up making Sarasota their home—it was a winter haven less gaudy than the Florida east coast and one where seclusion away from the center of town was possible.

Such were the individuals who supplied much of the initial leadership that created and sustained New College. Thus, Dallas Dort, for much of its history chairman of the New College board of trustees and for a time acting president, is a well-to-do son of a Michigan auto magnate; after Princeton, he was one of the activists of the New Deal, who, after government service in World War II, came to Sarasota, then relatively undeveloped, bought a large and desolate acreage, cleared it, and termed himself a rancher: he is cultivated, liberal by Sarasota standards, and comfortable in the company of academic people. The former northerner who actually started New College is Philip Hiss, a graduate of Choate (a relative of Alger Hiss), a partially self-taught designer-architect who in the post-Sputnik years became chairman of the Sarasota School Board.

These new residents found education in Florida in a disgraceful state. Most of the winter residents and those settlers new to the state were probably unaware of the fact that, like many southern states, Florida was spending more per capita on higher education than many northern states and was trying hard both to upgrade and to expand its system. But the progress was slow, and educational standards were in general a blow to civic pride, even for those whose children or grandchildren went to prep schools or elite colleges and universities elsewhere.

During the 1950s a number of concerned citizens began to talk about founding a college in Sarasota. Perhaps the main energizer was Philip Hiss. His was the post-Sputnik, Council for Basic Education spirit of the period: his concern was that education in general and education in Florida in particular was too slack, too indolent, lacking in either aesthetic or intellectual distinction. He had become chairman of the Sarasota School Board at a time when much hope was pinned on better training of teachers and more rigid standards in the public schools, and it was he who took much of the initiative in bringing together the congeries of people and organizations that created New College and who served as its first board chairman.

Another source of energy and support was John McNeil Whitney, a local Congregationalist minister, who established contact with the Board for Homeland Ministries of the United Church of Christ (Congregationalist), which was also concerned about the state of liberal-arts education in the South. The board offered to contribute $600,000 over a ten-year period for an independent college which would be tenuously affiliated but in no way controlled by the church —provided other money could be raised to make such an enterprise viable.

While Hiss and Whitney and their elite allies were seeking ideas and support for New College, the chamber of commerce commissioned a market survey which concluded that there was need for a college in the greater Sarasota area, which included the town of Bradenton and surrounding Manatee County to the north. Like any other service industry, the college that the chamber projected was expected to bring money into Sarasota through spending by students, staff, and visitors. It would be a resource for local children (and, indeed, for adults) as well as a monument to civic pride. Thus a tension existed from the beginning between the college envisioned by the Sarasota businessmen and many local residents and the college conceived by the founders.

The college that Philip Hiss had in mind was to be a small and highly selective one: a national college recruiting students and faculty from all over the country. He began with no particular model in mind, thus without what we have called a telic aim; rather, he wanted to do better, more strenuously, and more rapidly, what the top-flight small liberal-arts colleges were also attempting. He went in search of educational ideas, and in 1960 he hunted up Riesman in Cambridge. He wanted to know, for example, whether the projected calendar, eventually adopted, for a three-year curriculum based on an eleven-month program, would be feasible; the traditional college calendar, a hangover from an agricultural era (and an expression of the desire of many professors for a long summer recess) seemed to him inexcusably wasteful and dilatory. It is not surprising that in some of its early publicity, though not in the communications of Hiss himself, who was allergic to any kind of bombast, the prospective college was referred to as "the Harvard of the South." Another aim of Hiss, an amateur architect himself, was architectural distinction to match intellectual "class"; he interviewed some of the country's leading architects, and, as we shall see, fastened on I. M. Pei as the architect-planner of the new college.*

Given Philip Hiss's ideals, it would have been difficult to find a less suitable president for the new college than George Baughman, who seems originally to have come to the attention of the trustees through Alvin Eurich, an official for the Fund for the Advancement of Education, a Ford Foundation offshoot, and former vice-president of New York University. Baughman appealed to some of the Sarasota trustees as a Florida native; educated as a lawyer at the University of Florida and former vice-president there, he had become financial vice-president of New York University. He also had connections through his activity in the United Church. Baughman was not shy in contributing to his own reputation as a fund raiser (his fellow administrators at NYU declare, however, that it was inflated); and it seemed plausible that a Florida native would know how to raise money locally as well as nationally. He aimed for a college of around 1,200 students—far larger than what Philip Hiss had envisaged and twice as large as the highest number ever actually recruited (the college now has between 300 and 400 students). Such a college, Baughman asserted, would be large enough to field athletic teams, an anathema to Hiss; and Baughman was prepared to tell Sarasotans not only that the new college would serve their children, but that it would serve them by providing adult education, as well as by enriching the local community in the ways the chamber of commerce had intended. He seemed ready to declaim whatever might appeal to the particular audience he was addressing; hence he told some, in congruence with Hiss, that it would be a college of national eminence.

It was Hiss, however, who was mainly responsible for the selection of the academic dean—again someone originally recommended by Alvin Eurich, who, with his wife Nell, took an interest in the col-

---

*As a hedge against the possible failure of the college, and with the notion that on the Bay Shore side of Route 41 on the Charles Ringling Estate which the college had acquired a wholly new campus would be built, the Pei buildings were designed in such a way that they could, if necessary, be used ultimately for a conference center; thus each dormitory room was a separate suite with its own bath—an arrangement which intensified the solipsism of students. We have made use of a valuable history which includes discussion of problems of land acquisition and schisms among the trustees brought about by this and other issues; see Ronald Bergwerk, "The Greening of Sarasota: A Study of Prehistoric New College," an Independent Study Project done under the sociologist Marcello Truzzi in 1973.

lege from the outset. John Gustad had taught psychology at the University of Maryland and was then dean of Alfred University and looked upon as a spokesman for pedagogic innovation. Gustad apparently gained the impression that Baughman would be primarily the external fund raiser, while he himself would be in charge of developing a curriculum and recruiting a faculty—a common enough misconception of an effective and realistic division of labor. Faculty frequently dream that they can recruit what Thorstein Veblen would have termed a "captain of erudition," who will raise money, protect them from the local community, and in no way bother them. Few men willing to be college presidents, it turns out, are that modest; few, unless they have the arrogant insouciance of a Robert Hutchins, have the charisma or éclat to get away with telling the locals that they are yokels and should keep quiet! Philip Hiss himself was anything but a yokel; he wanted a hand in the curricular development of the college and was not prepared, like the businessmen who succeeded him on the board of trustees, to defer to academic authority, interfering perodically only to complain, as we shall see, that the countercultural behavior of the students made even more arduous the difficult task of raising in Sarasota the comparatively large sums needed for debt service on the buildings and for the high proportion of costs not covered by tuition.

It was not difficult for this triumvirate of Hiss, Gustad, and Baughman to agree on what might be called the "negative identity" of New College: it would be an institution with no "frills"; while Baughman wanted sports he recognized that he could not field teams for intercollegiate athletics and was willing to dispense with fraternities and avoid other concessions to what Hiss and Gustad rejected as "collegiate." But this limited consensus did not extend to the content of the curriculum or the styles and concerns of the faculty, and in the absence of clear telic principle, it was not surprising that, by the time Gustad started to recruit, he was already drawing a mixed bag: some faculty shared the post-Sputnik image of a traditional college which would lead students through to postbaccalaureate education; others were attracted by an image of a school without departments, with an emphasis on Independent Study (a term then much in use but not yet sufficiently tested to demonstrate how little independence and how little study often resulted)—and then there were some faculty who simply liked the idea of no longer shoveling snow.

Neither Hiss nor Gustad had any particular program for the arts at New College, nor for establishing relationships with already extant institutions such as the nearby Ringling School of Art or the Asolo Theatre, which was not wholly monopolized either by its local patrons or by the University of South Florida. Although a few adjunct faculty were recruited who had retired to Sarasota, New College never did establish, except in the field of music, ties with the enclaves of artists and academicians who had become Sarasota residents.

Baughman had declared that a school with New College's ambitions should not open until it had $10,000,000 in hand, but when some $6,000,000 had been collected or pledged (about one-third of which turned out later to be either uncollectable or in the form of heavily mortgaged, overpriced real estate), Baughman decided to take the gamble and open nonetheless. In his haste he was like many American college promoters whose enterprises later foundered. And many faculty and others have judged him harshly for beginning with too little, too soon. No doubt, Baughman promised too much to too many, but we are not convinced that it was an error to start when he did. Perhaps more important was the mistaken assumption that Sarasota was in fact an appropriate locale for a national college. Opening in 1964, New College was on the map before Hampshire, Kirkland, and many other competitors, with comparable imagery, greater resources, and fewer geographical disadvantages, were ready to compete for students.

New College's opening involved another gamble, unique so far as we know in the annals of recent private college founding: the intention was to "buy" National Merit Scholars as one would athletes, paying where necessary virtually their full tuition and expenses, and, on the average, two-thirds of total cost. (Indeed, it was not until 1970, as the *Institutional Self-Study* produced that year for purposes of accreditation revealed, that New College students were paying two-thirds of tuition and fees well over $3,000.) In the charter class of 100 extremely bright and talented students, the preeminent figure was Robert Norwine, the first director of admissions, who had been dean of admissions at Wesleyan and had helped that affluent and ambitious institution to recruit outstanding students in the 1950s. His driving, no-nonsense and businesslike qualities and his unequivocally meritocratic reliance on test scores had not rendered him popular with Wesleyan faculty; and at New College, even from the outset, he was not widely admired.*

---

*In time Norwine left the admissions office to become director of development, where he was not especially successful (New College went through a number of directors of development). He returned temporarily to admissions, then became vice-president, only to be dismissed by Arland Christ-Janer, who in 1973 came from the presidency of the College Board to be the last president of the college. Norwine became active in the development of Florida real estate, and his later history both at the college and in Sarasota has in our

Norwine did not work alone; he found a southerner, Mildred Ellis, who is still on hand, already at work recruiting students in Florida and neighboring states; and she was joined by Earl Helgeson, a graduate of Yale Law School, who had worked at that school in admissions, and later temporarily succeeded Norwine. But what Norwine brought with him no one else on the staff possessed—namely, knowledge of the guidance-counselor circuit in the North, and judgment as to where to look for students initially and where not to look for them. At first he avoided the mid-Atlantic belt from which the export trade in innovation has generally come—that is, the upper-middle-class suburban (often Jewish) students who might be diffident about coming to an unknown college in Sarasota. Rather, he recruited in midwestern, southern, and western cities and towns and schools, as well as in the less sophisticated areas of the East. What he wanted and got were National Merit Scholar winners and finalists: students who not only had extremely high test scores, but who had often been successful as valedictorians, newspaper editors, etc. Many came from families that had had no tradition of Ivy League connections. A number of the most interesting students were Catholic graduates of parochial schools who preferred not to attend Notre Dame or Holy Cross or schools in the Ivy League.*

It should be clear that these students were attracted by the subsidy and by the blank Rorschach card named New College, but not by its *lack* of accreditation and uncertain future. The hidden contradictions between the mandates of "excellence" and "innovation" had not yet been sorted out; what the students read into the card was the promise of freedom, made in a pocket-sized catalogue (the first we had seen) which did not specify a list of courses to be taught and assured them of the opportunity of moving at their own pace, in Independent Study. (It should be recalled that the college was geared to a three-year baccalaureate norm, a plan which was projected to cut the subsidy and costs to students in expense and earnings foregone by 25 percent.) A number of students in the first group had turned down Reed, Oberlin, or Harvard to come to New College, in many cases without ever having visited there.

Meanwhile, of course, John Gustad had been recruiting the faculty. He persuaded Aaron Sayvetz, who had been with him at Alfred and had been before that one of the influential leaders in the Natural

judgment colored the estimate by his former associates at New College of his contribution in getting the college started.

*The *Institutional Self-Study* indicates that the average subsidy of the first year was $2,100, and that the men—contrary to the more common constellation at that time—had slightly higher verbal test scores than the women.

Sciences Program of The College of the University of Chicago, to join him. He sought out and recruited the late Fillmore Sanford, a Virginia-born psychologist who was then with the American Psychological Association, and, as another senior professor, Harvard-trained Arthur Borden, who was made dean of humanities—he is still a figure in the college and in Sarasota art circles. William Smith is a fine teacher of mathematics who—after a one-year absence at Hobart—returned to New College the following year and remains a much admired person there.* One of the few early recruits to remain was Douglas Berggren, a philosopher who had done his undergraduate work at Carleton (where he later taught), had studied at Oxford, and received a doctorate in philosophy at Yale. While there were to be no departments but three major divisions—Natural Science, Humanities, Social Science—the faculty were given conventional titles according to their discipline, and possessed the usual academic ranks.

Gustad's curricular program, which was presented at a conference on experimental colleges held under the auspices of Florida State University, would not seem particularly daring or evangelical today.[1] Since only very gifted students would be recruited, grades and credits were to be dispensed with; however, assessments would be provided by a college examiner who, in the style of The College of the University of Chicago, would supervise comprehensive examinations at the end of the first year (and would also serve as an institutional researcher to report back to the faculty on student academic progress and emotional attitudes and stress). Entering students would be required to take work in all three major areas, as well as to study a foreign language. Like many later reformers, Gustad deprecated survey courses in favor of courses stressing modes of thought or analysis. The second year was to be given over to specialization, principally by means of Independent Study, while, in the third and final years students would do a research project and, in addition, integrate what they had learned in a Senior Seminar.† The spartan

---

*Since the foregoing was written, William Smith has reluctantly left New College of the University of South Florida because of the uncertain financial future and the fear of not having any retirement income.

†This hope for a culminating Senior Seminar, an all-encompassing synthesis, is something which turns up again and again in the plans for experimental colleges in this period. While there is much to be said for spreading general education throughout a three- or four-year undergraduate program, as well as for allowing students to do highly specialized work as freshmen, the notion that newly recruited inexperienced faculty can create the wished-for but unachieved unity of all science and learning seems only slightly less fantastic than the expectation that students can create it on their own. It is hardly surprising that the New College Senior Seminar never really came off. (It should be added in

image which New College wanted to present was emphasized by the three-year baccalaureate, which would incidentally provide faculty with a respite not only in August but also during the interim terms set aside for Independent Study. Of course, the three-year degree was not a new idea: Charles W. Eliot had campaigned for it at Harvard; Hutchins' college at Chicago and Shimer College had developed accelerated programs, as Simon's Rock Early College did later; and in many institutions it had been possible for a long time for able and highly motivated students to graduate in three years. But the calendar was another indication that New College's aim was to be strictly academic: to do better what the more traditional liberal-arts colleges were accomplishing, as it was believed, in slovenly and unimaginative fashion.

At the time New College was founded, Independent Study had not yet been given a major trial at the undergraduate level—nor had graduate students, for whom such work is *de rigueur* in writing a dissertation, traditionally received the supervision and support they required. Many of the superior students whom New College recruited for its opening class had felt cramped in their often provincial high schools, where they had usually managed to secure top grades and to get by with little work. But even now, no generally applicable method is available by which to measure the personal qualities required for successful Independent Study—the stamina of the long-distance runner or track star which enables students to endure frustration; the absence of narcissism which makes it possible to plow ahead with work that is not utterly dazzling; the ability to pace oneself when the hated monitoring of school and family is removed. One shrewd observer who visited New College after it had been in operation several years made the sarcastic comment that no one should be allowed to do Independent Study who had College Board scores above 650 (New College was later classified by Alexander Astin as one of the ten most selective colleges in the country in terms of the test scores of its students, many of them well over 700). The point of the comment was that overachievers who had had to work in high school and who did not have exalted expectations for their performances were more likely to be successful there. It is true that many students in their senior years at good liberal-arts colleges do an independent thesis, as every single senior does at Princeton, but such efforts are structured by the requirements of a specific depart-

fairness that Gustad and the faculty who had conceived the idea had, for the most part, left.)

ment and supervised by faculty who set both timetables and limits. Some New College faculty, often as anarchic as some of the students themselves, were not prepared to act in the role of monitoring mentors,[2] while those who were more traditional, such as Robert Knox, a professor of literature (with degrees from Harvard), were attractive to those students who sought structure and anathema to others who on personal and ideological grounds fought every sign of it.

The promotional literature, which boasted of the "first-class minds" (now the phrase is "the best and the brightest") which made up the student body, began to be believed by the faculty, as well as by many of the students. Those who failed to achieve independence or "creativity" at New College felt that they did not really belong there.*

Even before the draft made students want to maintain the shelter of college for as long as possible, it became clear that the three-year degree was not going to work out as planned. Faculty and some students complained that the eleven-month sequence was too arduous. Independent Study, contrary to all expectations, demanded a great deal of faculty time and effort.

For one thing, to meet the often esoteric interests of students in a small and isolated college, those faculty members who were responsive—and this has been true of the majority of faculty—had to extend themselves in order to cover the fields in which their students wanted to work. Often they had to bone up themselves on a new subject only peripherally related to their specialties, in order to act as mentors on a one-to-one basis. And the closeness that developed in a college that threw faculty and students in upon each other, neither group finding much diversion in Sarasota, meant that academic and personal concerns easily became intertwined; a seminar or tutorial might start in an office and end up at the faculty member's home or in a convenient beer joint many hours later.

With the return to a regular academic calendar, the well-paid faculty did not reduce its salaries, despite the precariousness of col-

---

*Several years after the college opened, a sociologist on the faculty declared in an interview in the student paper, that New College was recruiting "students who read too easily and tend to think that because they have read Riesman or Weber, they have mastered the field . . ." One alumnus told us that his most heartening experience at New College had been when former Provost John Barcroft (now with the National Endowment for the Humanities) had remarked that by no means all the students had first-class minds and that the very idea of such a mind was a myth. Barcroft had a capacity many faculty lacked for realizing the extent to which, in the most selective colleges, students often frighten each other.

lege finances. The students attracted to New College often preferred a *Wanderjahr* at home or abroad before completing their degrees, and the emphasis later put on off-campus terms facilitated this pattern. Even so, the three-year degree remained as an option, and now that the draft is no longer an issue, it is pursued by as many as one-third of the student body.

The college's already sufficient problems at its opening were aggravated by the unanticipated chaos of the residential arrangements. Since the Pei dormitory cluster was unfinished when the first students arrived, a resort hotel on one of the nearby keys was made available, with a bus to transport students on the six-mile jaunt between this residence and the Ringling Estate whose buildings served for classrooms, a small library, dining hall, and lounge. The student "guests" were not the most sedate, and since class attendance was not required (and as has already been mentioned, grades were not given), they did not always regard the journey to the campus as worthwhile. In this connection, it must be recalled that in 1964, parietal regulations were still in effect, even at selective private colleges catering to the children of the well-to-do, many of whom had already lived away from home at boarding school or abroad. But because many of the first group of New College students were not the products of permissive homes or progressive private secondary schools and had not had previous exposure to the temptations of living away from home, the results were predictable. It was not surprising that the social freedom of a resort hotel led to the sort of social and sexual laissez-faire which (although concealed) was not absent from colleges even in a more conventional era and which is so open and commonplace today. Moreover, an articulate minority of this early group resisted all constraints, parietal or curricular, and in this they had support from some of the faculty Gustad had recruited. There was an implicit contract, they felt, implied in the literature about Independent Study.

A newly established institution needs what Burton Clark in his book *The Distinctive College* refers to as a saga, usually created by a charismatic president, the momentum of whose ideas may carry the institution along even without continual administrative drive. This was all the more true of those colleges begun in the 1960s on the assumption that "innovation" was per se desirable, thus attracting faculty and students who could interpret the term in contradictory ways—some telic in their desire for curricular and communal wholeness, others "popular" in their willingness to legitimate what anyone could argue was an innovation. We have been convinced by our examination of a number of such institutions that, sheer survival apart, they become viable only if they are led by a president and top administration who are ceaselessly vigilant to a point many faculty would regard as tyrannical. For freedom to flourish, it is they who must provide the obdurate structure; they who must be relentless in insisting on quality control of faculty performance and student work; they who must bear the obloquy of appearing square and even stuffy, not only intramurally but also to the radical-chic elements in the private foundations and government agencies who were eager in the sixties, and even now, in an altered climate, often rather bravely remain eager, to take responsibility for sponsoring experiments, which, by their very nature, may fail. Implicit in what has been said is a job description of the president as someone who is capable simultaneously of containing internal conflict and sustaining external support.

George Baughman had come to Sarasota to begin building the college in 1961; John Gustad, to recruit faculty and plan curriculum, two years later. Not only did they not agree with each other, nor with Philip Hiss, but Baughman proved wholly unable to win internal support even while he was having difficulty sustaining his drive for additional external resources. Indeed, the contrast between the strenuous adventure and excellence that Philip Hiss had dreamed of —and which was more illustrated than enhanced by the temporary visit of Arnold Toynbee as visiting professor—and the college Sarasotans discovered they had acquired was a sharp one indeed: what stood out were insolent beatniks (to use an old-fashioned term), many of them pallid night people more often seen in Sarasota's dives than on its beaches or in its circumambient flotilla of boats.

II

Not unexpectedly, the countercultural styles of a number of Santa Cruz students did not endear them to the local retirement and resort community either; but then the University of California did not depend on the town of Santa Cruz for support. In contrast, the ill will that developed early between town and gown in Sarasota, although based principally on symbolic gestures such as dress, drink, and— later—drugs, rather than on political activism,* was felt by President

---

*As we shall see, a young economist considerably later set up Project REAL, which engaged students in work with migrant laborers and also in tutoring in Booker School, an all-black school that, when integration was ordered, found its autonomy defended by the New College tutors. Early in the

Baughman and many trustees to be damaging to local fund-raising efforts.

Correspondingly, the students found the Sarasota to which they had access to be both empty and forbidding. Many Sarasota residents drive pastel-colored luxury cars with agonizing slowness. Most faculty were so absorbed in the affairs of the college that they rarely established connections with resident artists and writers or with the local colony of retired college presidents and other academicians, let alone with members of the Elks, the chamber of commerce, churches, or other local groups who might have been sources of at least moderate support. (Only music was a continuously shared affair between the college and the community.) Indeed, one of the ironies of New College has been the combination of distaste for Sarasota and the frequent unwillingness on the part of students to leave the home away from home they have discovered. Former students continue to frequent the college as nonpaying guests; a few have made contacts, as a number of students also have done, with the Ringling School of Art.* Similarly, a number of faculty members who shared the common distaste for Sarasota have stayed on since the merger with the University of South Florida, despite the threats many made at the time that, even if there were no "good" jobs available elsewhere, they would leave for other parts. Some discovered that they or members of their families had more attachments in Sarasota than they fully appreciated—of course, this is a common experience of potentially mobile Americans. (Others, however, would leave if they could find jobs, not so much out of antagonism to New

1960s, several students, mainly from Irish Catholic homes, became ardent pacifists. But on the whole, the activism of New College was principally intramural; it became visible in endless debates as to what the college was entitled to require of its students and what role students should play in all decisions, including evaluations of academic progress. The recent relative improvement in the relations between the college and its milieu has come about partly because what seemed to be shocking and unmannerly modes of behavior in 1964 have since become far more universal. The children and grandchildren of Sarasota's residents often return from other colleges flaunting similar styles and making similar speeches.

*Considerably later, some New College students recognized the elderly as a deprived group, and sought to establish relations with them. Jerrold Neugarten, who was elected a trustee while a student at Harvard Law School, was one of those who arranged for students to teach adult-education classes. And a program called "Dial-A-Student" has given lonely Sarasotans the opportunity to invite students to visit or read to them, a contact that is sometimes reciprocated when residents are invited back to campus for a meal or discussion. But none of these developments, though creating a small climate of support for the college, has even now worked wholly to overcome the suspicions generated in the early days.

College or even Sarasota, as out of a feeling of being trapped by the merger into an uncertain financial situation—in some cases after they had left jobs at more secure institutions; the New College trustees and former presidents are blamed for leaving them marooned —and some have turned to union activism in their bitterness.)

But although both students and faculty were beginning to feel the pressures of an increasingly threatened and uncomfortable community, the most serious conflicts were developing within the college itself. Even before the college opened, there were strains between Gustad and Baughman. Hiss, who had recruited Gustad, resigned as chairman of the board; by his own lights, as he complained in correspondence and conversation with us, he felt his efforts were unappreciated and his educational ideas unwelcome, and that he had become a liability to the college as a clearly identified liberal in a conservative milieu. Gustad offered to resign as well on the ground that he had been Hiss's appointee, and Baughman refused to offer his help and support. In part, the issue was a symbolic one, a way to force a showdown with the president. In January 1965, the faculty moved a vote of no confidence in Baughman; with one or two exceptions everyone signed it, including Gustad.

A meeting of the board followed at which the three divisional heads and some faculty were asked to appear. Most testified that Baughman was ineffective—even as a money raiser—and complained about his interference in academic matters. But the board became convinced that, given time, he could raise the necessary money. Some of the most influential local trustees, such as the leading newspaper editor, David Lindsay, had reputations for conservatism, and there later developed the stereotype that the northern trustees were liberal and the Sarasotans conservative, although in fact the divisions on the board were not along regional lines. When Nell Eurich joined the board later in that first year and became chairman of its Educational Personnel and Policies Committee, she quickly achieved a dominant voice on the pro-innovation side, winning support from many of the local trustees. At any rate, many on the board saw Gustad as insubordinate, and hence, whatever their doubts about Baughman, which increased as they became better acquainted with his flamboyance, they felt it necessary to support the top man. Moreover, he had allies not only locally and in the state, but among some of the more moderate, academically oriented faculty who had misgivings about Gustad and his more fervent supporters. A few students, alienated by the rebellious and anarchic quality of many of their peers, were also sympathetic. One of them, a student who eventually left, wrote in the student paper, the *Catalyst*, that student conduct offended his religious and ethical sensibilities, that he wanted more structure, and that, while perhaps this was an indication of his own weakness, he could not help it. Some students sympathized with the president's need to develop local sources of support, although few were drawn to him personally.

The news that the provost and academic dean had been relieved of his duties hit students as well as faculty with dramatic force. Rumors spread. The story that Dean Sayvetz of the Natural Sciences Division was leaving broke shortly thereafter in the local papers, and he did leave. Fillmore Sanford, head of the Social Sciences Division, announced that he was leaving, and made no move to recruit others, so that his successor arrived to find not a single social scientist still on hand. A charismatic anthropologist (along with Gustad) found a position at Ohio State University. Indeed, at this point he and a few other faculty members withdrew all effort, in effect punishing the students for the faculty's quarrel with the institution. Other faculty, however, although no less unhappy with the president's actions, felt it was self-indulgent of their colleagues to behave in this way. Their sense of duty was helpful both to the majority of students who were opposed to the president and to a minority who all along had felt out of place vis-à-vis the rebellious and anarchic style of their more vocal fellow students.

The majority of students stayed, some with a feeling of disloyalty made all the more intense by the fact that they could not afford, without New College's subsidy, the kind of tuition charged at any comparable college. Two of the three division heads left, as did the majority of faculty, at the very time when initial efforts were being made to recruit additional faculty in order to teach returning students in upper-level courses. New College was seeking to cover the entire liberal-arts spectrum with a kind of Noah's Ark semidepartmentalism: two philosophers, two mathematicians, two people in history, two in the arts, etc.—in fact a lavish faculty/student ratio had been maintained from the beginning and was cited in all college publicity as one of the institution's chief virtues. Several adjunct faculty were recruited from the area (including George Mayer, currently the provost, who came in the second year and four years later shifted to the University of South Florida while continuing to teach part-time at New College—a dual role that was to have important implications later on). Such strokes of good fortune aside, it would have taken both an extensive knowledge of academia and many connections with leading centers of graduate training to recruit new faculty from the expanding but at that time readily employable crop of new Ph.D.s at a time of year when most had already made their arrangements for the coming academic season. The task was made no easier when some of those who were departing at least hinted that anyone who came to take their places was a scab.

Some of the trustees may have thought that support from Sarasota and Bradenton mattered more than what might be said in the executive offices of the American Psychological Association in Washington, D.C., or around the lunch table at the Quadrangle Club at the University of Chicago. But for an institution with the national ambitions of New College, this was true only in the very short run. The uproar among students and the virtual depletion of leading faculty made the trustees realize that they had not solved matters when they allowed the president to fire Gustad. Some of the local trustees had already come to distrust Baughman's evangelical promotion of the college. The mobilization of out-of-town trustees also tended to undermine his support. If the college was to be saved at this point of near total disarray, it would be necessary quickly to find a new president, while continuing to recruit both faculty and students, and to persuade as many as possible to stay on. Mrs. Nell Eurich, an original sponsor although she became a trustee only later, took her children out of school in Aspen, Colorado, and came to Sarasota as acting chief academic officer to try to save the dream. In talking with faculty, she persuaded several to stay, though she was unable to prevent the alienation of others; she had greater success with the students.

Along with her husband, Alvin Eurich, she was widely acquainted in academic circles and with the foundations; and she brought to New College energetic devotion to its ideals, resilience, and *sangfroid*. The chaos she found on arrival bordered on hysteria. On our first visit a year later, we talked with a young woman, a "convinced" Quaker, who had applied only to New College and to Radcliffe, and who, when the split came, was urged by one of her teachers to transfer to The College of the University of Chicago; he made arrangements to get her in there. But she and her friends stayed on in part because Nell Eurich convinced them that if they left, New College would collapse; they did not want that. The young woman said that it took more courage for new students to come after the split than for those who were already enrolled to stay on.

It was heartening to morale when Nell Eurich found a president in John Elmendorf, then a vice-president at Brown. A New Haven-born graduate of the University of North Carolina, and deeply influenced by the model of Frank Graham there, Elmendorf had taken his doctorate in linguistics, and with his wife, Mary, a North Carolinian, also a graduate of Chapel Hill, had taught at Putney School and had worked for the American Friends Service Committee in Europe. Later, while his wife ran the CARE program in Mexico, Elmendorf had become vice-president of Mexico City College (now the University of the Americas), a shoestring private college he managed to help keep afloat with funds both indigenous and North American. Elmendorf commuted from Providence to New College to talk to students and persuade them to stay, and to interview possible faculty recruits.

John and Mary Elmendorf, active Quakers and internationalists, former schoolteachers, with two teen-age children of their own, liked and enjoyed young people and quickly established an easy camaraderie with New College students. In the early years of their incumbency, both knew every student by name and, beyond that, the details of their lives and concerns. Mary Elmendorf took a hand in helping place students in off-campus internships as assistants to Peace Corps volunteers in Latin America and in the Caribbean, an interest developed during the family's days in Mexico.*

Robert Knox, Jr., who has already been mentioned, was one of the second year's recruits. So was Jerome Himmelhoch, who also had his A.B. and Ph.D. from Harvard, had been a Rhodes Scholar, and who came from Goddard to teach sociology. Berggren had recruited another Yale-trained philosopher, a former student of his, Gresham Riley, who later, as provost, helped pilot New College through the intricate dilemmas of merger.

Meanwhile, Robert Norwine recruited a second group of students much like the first, and eventually two-thirds of them graduated— many to win Fulbrights and Woodrow Wilson Fellowships and to solidify the picture of New College as a training ground for "excellence."

For some years, although Baughman had been forced out, he refused to leave the home provided for the president by the college,

---

*As the wife of a vice-president of a university like Brown and in a city like Providence, Mary Elmendorf's activism was no problem for the Brown faculty. But at New College and in Sarasota she felt cramped, while faculty often felt she knew too much and interfered too much. Toward the end of her stay, she took a doctorate in anthropology through the Graduate School of the Union of Experimenting Colleges and Universities (of which her husband had for a time been one of the officers), writing a thesis befitting her quietly ardent feminism on the role of Mayan women in developmental change in Mexico. After her husband was fired as president in 1972, she taught for several terms at Hampshire College—an example of the kind of networks and exchanges we have repeatedly noticed; later, both Elmendorfs went round the world with Chapman College's World Campus Afloat.

and maintained the honorific title of president of the New College Foundation in a vain hope that he would continue to raise money for the institution. But though Gustad was the one who had left, it was his rather than Baughman's image of the college which survived, as it entered a new phase in its history.

III

By the middle 1960s, "excellence" and "innovation" no longer could be used interchangeably—in fact in many minds they were the antithesis of each other.

"Excellence" meant maintaining the Humanities core, as Douglas Berggren sought to do, and in that division more joint teaching went on than in others. It also meant the weekly research colloquium of the Natural Science Division. Of all the academic areas at New College this one was most committed to inducting students quickly into research, taking them to professional meetings, and working with them on publishable papers. To other members of the faculty, "innovation" meant rejecting those aspects of the college which were a prelude to graduate school. It meant an emphasis on the affective life, on spontaneity, on being willing to wait while students discovered their interests, or took leaves of absence to explore the so-called real world. John Elmendorf tended to side with this latter interpretation. He was sympathetic, for example, to a particularly dramaturgical student whose high principle led him to refuse to read anything that was assigned but whose erudition brought him to read almost anything else and gave him a reputation for originality that (as is often the case with scholars) was not entirely deserved. Though he was not given a degree, he was appointed to teach cinema as holder of the Student Chair at the college, and eventually he got his degree at the end of the first decade. Elmendorf also supported William Hamilton, a theologian who has been one of the leaders in the "Death of God" discussion (and who had come down from the Colgate Divinity School at the University of Rochester), when he offered a course simply entitled "Monday Nights," in order, as he put it, to be able to discuss with students whatever he felt like on that particular Monday, and when he let students make their own self-evaluations. Both the course title and the self-evaluations went down without alteration on the students' transcripts. Hamilton's behavior horrified what came to be known as the Tory Caucus, and when Elmendorf asked him to assume the role of provost, he felt that he was really not sufficiently welcome, and, with a good deal of regret, he left—later to turn up for a year (another illustration of these Johnny Appleseeds of academia) at Empire State College.

Many of those like Hamilton who identified with Elmendorf and the more experimentally minded faculty and students were in fact dedicated scholar-teachers, but the polarization that had occurred among faculty tended to conceal the fact. However, there was a group on the faculty, whom one might see as a mix of communal-expressive individuals and political activists, who saw the so-called Tories as pedants, uptight over sex and slackness, but uninvolved in either local or national political crusades or in encounter-type relationships with students. Mary Elmendorf tended to side with this latter group; politically active herself (she later campaigned for Eugene McCarthy, and, later still, for George McGovern), and, as already indicated, close to students, she made many faculty uncomfortable—a situation not unknown among active spouses, especially in the smaller academic milieux. But John Elmendorf, ever jovial, relaxed and of Friendly persuasion, did not reject even his avowed enemies among the "Tories" but valued the pluralism of the college and sought to hold it within reasonable balance.

But what he could not ever hold in balance was the budgetary situation. Elmendorf has declared that on arrival he found the college near bankruptcy; we are inclined to believe him, although Baughman denies Elmendorf's contention. (The question is perhaps inherently ambiguous because of problems of evaluating the Florida real estate donated to the college in part for tax purposes; the discrepancies are sometimes testimony to the adage that it is more blessed to give than to receive!) There is no doubt that, from his very first days onward, Elmendorf had to hit the foundation and philanthropic trails in a mood of chronic desperation. Though he made dire proclamations, his outer sanguinity probably made it easier for faculty and students, not in any case prepared to listen to such declarations, to deny the grim financial realities. During the academic year 1967–68, he had a conversation with Robert Mautz, then chancellor of the State University System of Florida, about the possibility of merger with the University of South Florida or perhaps with some other branch of the state university system, along the lines now finally undertaken. But a grant of $200,000 from a Ford Foundation affiliate staved off for a time his pursuit of what those faculty members who heard of the conversation regarded as an all too inevitable solution.

A string of development officers followed. Robert Norwine, who had worked on admissions, had the job for a while. And in the last

years of the college's independent life there were bitter recrimina-
tions against him, as well as against Elmendorf and the board of
trustees for not having done a better job of keeping afloat a college
regarded by faculty and students as truly unique.

Like other small private colleges and a few public ones, New
College suffered from cash-flow problems. It could not predict what
the yield would be of those who had been accepted for admission,
and hence how much money from tuition and dormitory fees would
be coming in; nor was it possible to anticipate the decisions of students, for example, to take off at the last moment in the spring term,
with catastrophic effects on tuition and dormitory and cafeteria fees.
Recourse to the banks was a frequent but expensive remedy, and the
periodic deficits were covered by a devoted Sarasotan on the board
who finally concluded that the college was a bottomless pit, and that
he could not go on indefinitely filling up the hole.

When Elmendorf was making his pitch to foundations or attending the periodic conferences of those concerned with educational
reform or the Carnegie Commission on Higher Education when it
met in Miami in 1970, he defended New College as a place which
prepared faculty for work in other experimental colleges. At one
time, in fact, he sought unsuccessfully to get rid of tenure and to
substitute rotation on a five-year basis with this end in view. Along
with Johnston College, New College was one of the first to adopt
the contract system by which students had to declare what their aims
were, both in general and in a particular term or year, and to secure
faculty approval to pursue them. The great emphasis on off-campus
study followed the lead of Antioch College but gave somewhat
greater care to linking the academic with the field experience. Some
of the students whom Mary Elmendorf placed in Spanish-speaking
America, for example, eventually went on to do graduate work in
Latin American Studies. It was clear that Elmendorf did not place
a very high priority on teaching, declaring that New College "has
set as its operational mode the thesis that a college is first of all a
learning establishment, not a *teaching* establishment, where judgments will be made on the levels of learning achievement, rather
than on the degree to which students have succeeded in responding
to 'teaching.' (We *do* have a faculty, and they *do* 'teach,' but this is
viewed institutionally, as a necessary evil, rather than prima facie
need.)"[3] Some faculty took this statement as it was presumably intended, to mean that students were to learn how to learn, with the
faculty serving as facilitators; other faculty took this statement and
Elmendorf's general outlook as legitimating their own dislike for
teaching without leading them to assume the alternative and no less

difficult role of mentor; but more conservative faculty read the statement to suggest that faculty were dispensable and that students might
do much better off campus than on.*

IV

Beginning in 1966, we made more or less biannual visits of four or
five days each to New College. We sat in on classes, talked formally
and informally with students, faculty, administrators, and trustees.
Always, there was some salient issue, at once pedagogic and political, concerning which the campus was agitated and divided. Should
the contract system, for example, remain an option, or should it be
made compulsory? (Eventually, the latter decision was taken, at the
insistence of more scholarly faculty, who felt it would be a worthwhile means of quality control.) Should students have unlimited
time to complete their degrees, as David Gorfein, the aggressive and
tough-minded experimental psychologist, vehemently urged, no doubt
buttressed by the fact that the Natural Sciences Division to which
he had moved from the Social Science Division maintained reasonable consensus on what completion might mean? To some, Gorfein's
highly specialized work in physiological psychology—and his refusal
to work with colleagues in teaching science to nonspecialists—seemed
inappropriate for a college devoted to liberal education.

But in all divisions, there were mentors of comparable seriousness. And what was impressive to us from the outset was the number of students who, in the face of all the distractions, the endless
battles, the time-consuming efforts at "full participation," had connected with a mentor and a subject matter with an intensity rarely
found elsewhere. A letter to Riesman from Charles K. McKay, a
New College graduate now in a Ph.D. program in philosophy at
Cornell is typical:

---

*Early in the 1970s, Elmendorf secured a small Carnegie grant to see
whether some modus vivendi could be established between the college and
the communes which had sprung up all around the country; the Harvard-
trained social psychologist David Tresemer and his wife Susan, along with
several other young people, visited communes to see whether communards
were willing to establish some sort of exchange with New College, perhaps
with a faculty member and some students coming out to live in the commune
or some of the commune members spending a season at New College. It
turned out that the communards wanted skills, which New College was not
prepared to provide, and not credentials—thus the hope that New College
might become a halfway house of this sort fell through.

I was a little amazed that I got into New College. As I was only eleventh out of my high school class of 283, the counselor assured me that I would not get in, as did my parents. The image, at least in Dayton, Ohio, was of an incredibly selective place, which would accept nothing less than genius.

God, did we read! And did we absorb! I sometimes felt that New College, at least in 1968, was a speed-reading class that had somehow developed hysteria! Of course, what to do with it once you had it . . . nobody asked you to write papers much, or develop research projects, or that sort of thing.

The great contribution of New College, for me, and for those who took it at its word—not all did, even from the beginning— was the promise that one could live as an intellectual, that the mind and the accumulation of culture could have a very direct relevance to one's own life, however outwardly meagre, that one was not a slave of culture, but free to criticize it and to choose another.[4]

Another letter, from David Smillie, professor of psychology, gave one faculty point of view:

"Innovation" has covered a concern to provide young people with an experience which will make them feel whole and human and happy. Particularly during the late sixties and early seventies . . . there was a desperate sense of things falling apart. I was interested then, and am still interested, in the students' involvement with R. D. Laing as social philosopher, since I think that this interest expressed their own feeling of having been betrayed by society and by their parents. As "innovators" we faculty were their parent surrogates attempting to provide a Laingian therapy. "Kingsley Hall" was an ideal name for the living-learning arrangement worked out by Pat Patterson [and William Herman and other students with him].

David Smillie went on to say that the faculty who shared this concern with wholeness had deep intellectual interests of their own, which they sought to share with students as "a kind of therapy for the malaise in which we found ourselves. The methods utilized were a removal of external constraints, the attempt to establish close working relationships with the student, the introduction of existential themes (of one kind or another) into the course content."

Lacking a "critical mass" in their own specialized fields, often as scholarly but less publication-minded than many of their colleagues, the relatively isolated faculty were eager for student disciples, and some students were extraordinarily ready to respond. At its best,

New College developed an intellectual as well as an academic intensity that in fact became its dominant outlook. It was a seedbed for the nonconformist subculture that Burton Clark and Martin Trow saw as an influential if not characteristic stance at many other colleges.

And yet the danger was that faculty were often stretched beyond their fields of competence in order to respond to students who had no one else around to turn to. Thus, a political scientist whose specialty is Africa, Margaret Bates, supervised a senior essay on the life and times of Huey Long. In such situations, haunted by their scientific superegos, faculty members often worried that they were not providing their students with adequate instruction, and at times of course they sent them elsewhere for an off-campus term. (However, more indolent teachers took advantage of the situation; we recall one who told us he was comforted by no longer having to keep up with his field since he did not have to prepare students in a major or field of concentration. In fact, for some, sending a student on to a doctoral program represented failure rather than success, an unwarranted concession to prevailing academic norms.)

The Natural Sciences Division was, as we have said, the refuge of students who wanted a more structured milieu without necessarily establishing the kind of intense relationships David Smillie described. And here the atmosphere was strictly professional. On our visit in 1974, we talked with a young biologist who was about to take half a dozen students to a professional meeting in San Diego where there would be no other undergraduates. In biology especially, as Oliver Fulton and Martin Trow have noted in a Carnegie Commission survey, faculty in good liberal-arts colleges publish as regularly as those in research universities.[5] To be sure, some of these "science jocks" were regarded by fellow students as unduly submissive to the constraints of their fields of inquiry, even or especially when they had become partner-apprentices to faculty. However, many of these students who, after all, had chosen to come to a liberal-arts college rather than to attend Cal Tech or Rice or M.I.T., having easily finished their required studies in three years, had then used the available fourth year for that "Eriksonian" moratorium which preoccupied other students (and many ex-student hangers-on) during their entire Sarasota sojourn.

When we looked somewhat at random through a series of contracts and transcripts, the high quality and seriousness we had observed in random class visits were confirmed. Also confirmed was our impression of many students who were lost, who combined indolence with grandiosity, avoiding putting to the test their "first-class minds." Whereas at its best, the contract system invites a student to think about his or her total trajectory in college and after, this imperative is likely to manifest itself only under rigorous faculty questioning and discussion; clearly, some faculty concluded that, with their malleable, uncommitted and identity-seeking students, they would be lucky to work out together a serious program for a single term. To illustrate: we noted one contract in which a student simply declared that her goal was to prepare for a thesis, to pursue an idea (unstated) in economics, and to secure "a conative experience with art." She named faculty members with whom she would work on a tutorial basis and stated that she was going to take a course on Death and Dying. A more grandiose plan was that of a student who declared that he wanted to pursue "structural sociology . . . to theorize possible solutions to present city and urban problems . . ." In addition, in the time allowed for noncurricular activities, he would go scuba diving ten hours a week and participate in student government as well. His contract would be complete when he and his mentor agreed that he had performed adequately in two courses plus a tutorial in urban architecture.

It is not surprising that similar variability occurred in faculty evaluations entered on the transcripts: some faculty would simply state that the student had met his or her own expectations, while others would write detailed comments, shared, of course, with the student, about the accomplishments and limitations of the student's work and approach. The burden placed on the Student Academic Status Committee—and on the registrar—was a heavy one, since there were many delinquent records, sometimes as a result of a failure on the part of the faculty themselves to turn in evaluations.

Many students, however, failed to ever make any meaningful connection. The traditional props and supports on which students have generally depended—tests, trots, cram sessions, an active athletic program—did not exist. If one should miss a class or two and then fall behind and not do the reading, it not only would seem hopeless to catch up, but the prevailing ideology might make the effort seem inconsequential. While the eager students received enthusiastic response, as we have mentioned, there was little systematic effort by the Student Academic Status Committee to keep track of or to press the recusant ones. Students drifted away either psychologically or physically, without anyone seeming to care or notice; and the counselors, who over the years struggled valiantly to cope with student alienation, always had far more traffic than they could handle, as did those faculty such as David Smillie who, in addition to their regular burdens, assumed somethng of a counseling role.*

A few faculty members sought to involve students in political activities or other off-campus enterprises. Marshall Barry, an assistant professor of economics, started Project REAL which, among other things, put students in touch with Florida migrant workers—not an activity designed to win a popularity contest among some of the Sarasota donors and trustees. Students also did tutoring at Booker School, a black elementary school in Sarasota and, when integration came, sought to support the school in its efforts to remain autonomous rather than to accept merger. As already noted, Mary Elmendorf was an active campaigner for Eugene McCarthy (and later for George McGovern), and she brought a few students along with her. Indeed, the Elmendorfs provided moral support to radical pacifists who were early opponents of the Vietnam War up to the point at which the students—a rare occurrence—resorted to violence. Three students went to Selma at the time of the civil-rights demonstrations there, and there was continuous agitation to recruit more black students to New College (out of idealism as well as exoticism). Some later went to work for Ralph Nader, others took part in various environmentalist crusades.

Nevertheless, the college lacked the political subcultures that often drew students at other experimental colleges out of individual and into collective and often instrumentally active alienation.

The women's movements at the college, however, were an exception. The one serious sit-in which occurred was organized by a women's-liberation group which took over President Elmendorf's office—a group that came to be referred to as the South Hall 21. They had rallied around Robin Morgan, the feminist poet and writer, who had been elected to the Student Chair, a faculty position financed from student funds and filled by the students themselves. Their "nonnegotiable demands" included the hiring of a woman gynecologist for the college health service, provisions for free contraceptives, and abortion referrals—the latter illegal at that time under Florida law. At first, these students refused to talk with President Elmendorf, the reasonable Quaker, who characteristically remained unruffled, and, reflecting on the incident years later, not only

---

*When in the second year of the college, David French, the college examiner, was injured in an auto accident, he left Sarasota, and no one took his place either as examiner or as an institutional researcher. The very elaborate self-study of 1970 which was prepared for accreditation purposes was no substitute.

retained no animosity vis-à-vis the sit-in group, but also concluded that the affair had not damaged the college. However, the local papers, whose editor and publisher has been an active member of the board, gave full play to the episode, which amused neither the board nor more conservative Sarasotans. Nor were most board members entertained when the sit-in was followed by the temporary incursion into their meeting of a men's group who termed themselves the "Flaming Faggots." Many women students disapproved of the sit-in, even though concern with the women's movements has remained high at New College as at other comparable institutions; many students did recognize the precarious dependence of the college on Sarasota beneficiaries and saw no point in guerilla theater.

Even though in the years since its founding New College had gradually begun to draw more students from sophisticated and affluent suburbs, for entering women students it was sometimes an intimidating atmosphere. As at other places where adults abdicated (and as we have seen in Chapter 6 there were very few places where they did not), women from conservative backgrounds would sometimes find themselves ill-prepared for the stimulating and provocative sexual environment in which they found themselves. A few promptly left because they felt too square, while others conformed to the tyranny of the supposedly enlightened. Due to attrition and leaves of absence, there were often more new students than returning ones, and the freshmen were often taunted by accusations that they were less independent or wild than their legendary predecessors.

In Kingsley Hall, a section of the dormitories, several older students, with the aid of a resident faculty member, sought to create a less destructive and more therapeutic milieu. Although the unit was temporary, vanishing as the students who had started it graduated, it helped point the way toward providing for new students a less traumatic and more organized orientation to the college.*

As was the case elsewhere in larger university centers, it seems possible that the women's-liberation movements gained strength from the discovery that, for many male students, "women's liberation" meant near-compulsory subordination to male sexual invitations. The feeling of having been exploited under the guise of liberation led in turn to heightened solidarity among some of the more politically

---

*Dr. Eugenia Hanfmann, director of counseling services at Brandeis, interviewed a number of New College students in 1970 and reported her findings to the Committee on Student Life, arguing that the college needed a greatly enlarged adult presence in the often lonely and anxious life of students who appeared more independent than they were. Her report was released in mimeograph at Brandeis University in 1971.

self-conscious women. For example, when Riesman spoke shortly
after the sit-in to a regular meeting of a women's-studies group,
there was a fair amount of talk of world revolution: since women
were a majority of the world's population, it was fitting that those
at New College should join forces with the politicization of women
in that diverse congeries of nation-states loosely termed the third
world. Any woman at New College who was not preparing for this
global revolution was deficient in her duty—one timid student asked
whether her decision to go to medical school could be justified by
the fact that she was preparing to serve a deprived inner-city clientele, a rationalization greeted with some skepticism.

But such students constituted a very small group, and, on returning in 1974, Riesman led a discussion with a much larger number of
students of both sexes who, though not politically active, were concerned like students everywhere with their own futures. In other
selective liberal-arts colleges, many students were also concerned
with the future of the planet, but the level of that concern was frequently shallow or even faddish, though idealistic, as among the sub-
culture of vegetarians and organic food devotees, the environmentalists who never think of the problem of trade-offs as between jobs
and amenities, and a large number who, while making use of every
technological convenience (from transistor radios to hi-fi equipment
to travel by sport car or jet plane) have a general animus against
science and technology as inherently evil. In contrast, the small number of New College students with planetary anxieties possessed exceptional technical and political knowledge of nuclear arms-control
issues—long a concern of Riesman's, but one not shared by most
students during the excitement over the Vietnam War. Some had
pondered Robert Heilbroner's *An Essay on the Human Prospect*,
and similar works, and asked how an individual should live in the
face of impending catastrophe. When Riesman declared that their
enormous involvement in student self-governance was, if not a generous gift of precious time, then at least a questionable expenditure
of effort at a time when there were many more significant benefits to
be derived from a residential college, they were willing to listen, if
not always to agree.

V

If a number of students were on this occasion pondering the long-
run future with an effort at somber realism, they were on the whole
inclined to view the impending merger with the University of South

Florida with resignation. They wanted to be sure that "New College" would be writ large on their diplomas, with "of the University of South Florida" in as small print as possible. And many regretted what they anticipated would be the dilution of an institution to which, as we have seen, they were attached by an ambivalent loyalty. At least the merger offered the returning students the benefit of the out-of-state but still very low tuition of the state university system.*

While some faculty had announced their intention to leave and did in fact leave, the majority remained. Many of the faculty, however, viewed the impending merger not only with less resignation than the students, but also, it may be, with less realism. Like faculty elsewhere, they had perhaps been misled by the boom period of the sixties when there was a surplus of applicants, not appreciating the extent to which underenrollment at the college in the last several years had contributed to its insolvency. In 1970, Elmendorf had rescued the college with a four-to-one Ford Foundation matching grant of $1 million which he used as leverage to get trustees and others to contribute as the matching accounts became due or overdue.†

Elmendorf had been summarily dismissed by the trustees in May 1972, though he was granted severance pay and an option to buy the home near the Sarasota keys where so many students and faculty had been informally entertained. Dallas Dort, who had remained as chairman of the board in the face of a recent heart attack, after having taken over from Louis LaMotte, a retired General Motors executive who had stepped in when Hiss resigned, moved into the vacuum as interim president. Meanwhile an elaborate, characteristi-

---

*We have not been able to visit New College since the merger, but have sought to keep in touch by extensive correspondence and telephone. According to faculty reports, the students are even more serious than in 1974—some are even willing to consider entrepreneurial careers which would have been almost inconceivable earlier. Such "activism" as remains flares up in conflicts with the University of South Florida authorities, for example, over the endemic issue on many campuses of armed security police. (In the past, students have suffered greatly from vandalism, theft, and rape, but still have insisted on preferring the doctrines of Rousseau to those of Hobbes.) There have also been struggles over meal plans and dormitory fees, etc.

†It is understandable that the faculty, looking at the wealth of Sarasota, would forget that many of these in-migrants were alumni of northern colleges with other ties and loyalties (including trusteeships) elsewhere. Moreover, many had already established responsibilities to other Sarasota philanthropies, such as the Asolo Theatre and the various musical activities. For many trustees, New College was often only an additional and part-time responsibility and an institution that, as has already been suggested, was not turning out as they had initially expected.

cally tripartite—students, faculty, trustees—search for a new president began.

We happened to be visiting the college when Frank Newman, then at Stanford and principal organizer and author of the well-known "Newman Report" (now president of the University of Rhode Island), was visiting as a potential candidate. He was highly regarded by many of the faculty and students who met him. His whole record as well as what he said at New College made clear, though he did not possess the Ph.D., that he was basically an educator and would regard money raising as one of his functions but not to the exclusion of educational policy. Nevertheless, we gained the impression that some faculty concluded that Frank Newman would make an excellent "outside" representative, and that they could successfully keep him from bothering the faculty—a conception reminiscent of the error that had been made vis-à-vis George Baughman when the college began.

At the invitation of Victor Butterfield, the retired president of Wesleyan University, who had briefly stepped in as acting president when John Elmendorf had a heart attack in 1968 (one which followed an invasion of a trustees' meeting by a former student), and Nell Eurich, leading members of the Educational Personnel and Policies Committee, Riesman's aid was recruited in the presidential search, while in turn many of those considered, whether suggested by Riesman or not, consulted him about whether New College might be viable and what he felt were its prospects. A number of these candidates reported that, far from being courted by an institution that was, to put it mildly, precarious in terms of funds and the size of its applicant pool, they were instead treated (as had happened in some small measure to Frank Newman also) to quite savage grilling. Were they anti-feminist? Were they sufficiently sympathetic to the natural sciences? Would they allow students to continue to serve on joint faculty-student committees concerning academic progress? The questioning often took place in an atmosphere more of accusation than of inquiry.* New College was in a position where it offered to a prospective president not only a looming deficit and a shortfall in enrollments, but a heavily tenured and yet deeply divided faculty, some of whom went privately to the trustees to complain about the

---

*While some college faculties underestimate themselves—a "who, little us?" phenomenon—and do not go after potential faculty or presidents who might in fact be interested, the New College Search Committees suffered from no such inhibitions, inviting many people who would not for long consider such a mass of liabilities and either declined to allow themselves to be considered or merely took advantage of a free trip to Sarasota.

surly behavior toward prospective candidates of some of their colleagues and a number of students.

We have observed similar behavior toward candidates for administrative positions at other institutions. Part of the story is characteristic student and faculty snobbery toward administrators or toward any faculty member who would consider, more than in a disdainfully amateur way, becoming an administrator. The ambivalent searchers generally ignore the actual psychic toll and isolation of the job of the president (and, often more seriously still, of his or her spouse) even in the most established institutions. Furthermore, the persuasion of uniqueness at New College of which we have already spoken gave faculty and students an exaggerated view of what they had to offer a prospective administrator—although it must be added that, just as paranoids have real enemies or soon create them, so do academic narcissists frequently express a measure of the truth. After a year-long search, demoralizing to all concerned, the college recruited Arland Christ-Janer, then the president of the College Entrance Examination Board and, before that, president of Boston University. The faculty expected him not only to keep the college afloat, but to meet humanly understandable demands for cost-of-living increases, even though for a small private college, beset with cash-flow problems and run always at a deficit, New College salaries were quite generous—at or beyond state university system levels, for example, when fringe benefits were included. When Christ-Janer decided that, in view of the refusal of the trustees to continue to bail the college out, there was no possible solution except to make an arrangement with the University of South Florida, a number of individuals said to him that, since the college had always operated at a deficit, they did not see why it could not go on doing so.

Several weeks prior to Riesman's visit in October 1974, he had been in Tallahassee discussing the prospects of merger with state university system officials. That system was itself in a state of severe budgetary crisis, and it looked as if any prospect which would require an additional legislative appropriation for New College in the spring 1975 legislative session had little chance. Florida, as we noted at the outset of this chapter, was attempting to "catch up" in public as in private higher education, yet it was experiencing severe economic straights. The demographic boom had faded, and a dramatic drop in the construction and citrus industries as well as expanded demands from competing state services such as health care, environmental protection, etc., were putting enormous burdens on a state without an income tax. Neither the University of Florida nor Florida

State University was happy at what seemed like a coup in the "up-start" ambitions of the University of South Florida.* There was the additional obvious fear that if the regents and the legislature "bailed out" New College, except for the University of Miami (whose medi-cal school gets state support), hardly a private college in the state would not similarly seek public shelter. Indeed, while the negotia-tions were proceeding with New College, they were simultaneously being carried on as well with Eckerd College (formerly Florida Pres-byterian College), whose financial situation was far superior to that of New College, and which was in a position to make demands on the St. Petersburg campus of the University of South Florida.

There had of course been precedents in which private colleges and universities of substantial scale had become branches of state systems. The State University of New York at Buffalo, the Univer-sity of Missouri at Kansas City, and the University of Pittsburgh, had become "state-related," as had previously black Lincoln Uni-versity in Pennsylvania. (There are of course also cases where mu-nicipal universities, such as Cincinnati, Akron, and Louisville, have come under state auspices, a mutation that seems likely to take place with the City University of New York.) But none of these instances resembled what enemies saw as the mini-Penn Central parade of bankrupt private Florida colleges which would seek state-system linkages if New College secured one. The only comparable example Riesman could come up with when questioned in Tallahassee and in Sarasota was the absorption of Western College by Miami Univer-sity, in Oxford, Ohio, but the reports of the difficulties the Western College experimental division of Miami was having in recruiting any susbstantial number of students and therefore in sustaining its inde-pendent faculty were not heartening.

Riesman found himself in a situation more often experienced than reported by ethnographers where, with considerable sense of moral ambiguity and doubts as to the correctness of his judgment, he sought to persuade both officials in Tallahassee and faculty and students at New College that the merger offered not only a hope of last resort but actually a useful national model. In speaking with the chancellor as well as with critical officials at Florida State University, Riesman pointed out that New College might continue to recruit to Florida

*The University of South Florida faculty either paid no attention to the plans for merger or were inclined to oppose them as another arbitrary action of the administration of Cecil Mackey, who has since resigned to become pres-ident of Texas Tech University. That Mackey was prepared to work with New College because of his own pedagogical (and political) liberalism was incon-ceivable to both his own faculty and that of New College.

some outstanding undergraduates as well as to retain some who might otherwise leave the state for private liberal-arts colleges still afloat elsewhere. And he argued against the "domino theory" that New College would be an entering wedge for the subsidy of all of private higher education, making the obvious point that the legislature could always draw the line at whatever point it wished to, whether it did so on the basis of the relative uniqueness of New College (which, even if not quite as unique as many faculty and students believed, had attained national visibility) or simply by pointing to the worsening financial prospects of the state system. With what seems to have been considerable enterprise, Marshall M. Criser, chairman of the board of regents, supported the merger. The retiring chancellor, Robert B. Mautz, went along, while the chancellor-designate, E. T. York, Jr., who would take office in January 1975, promised support. (The State Commissioner of Education, an elected official, Ralph Turlington, had visited New College, and efforts had been made to persuade him also to support the plan, but he ended up as an opponent.) Important in the final legislative action was the work of Robert Johnston, a Republican in a Democratic state, who not only represented Sarasota in the legislature, but intelligently lobbied for the merger. He won the support of a number of his education-minded colleagues.

Nevertheless, if the trustees at New College had not guaranteed that they would, on completion of the merger, form New College Foundation, Inc., which would provide approximately $750,000 for each of the next two years to help support the additional costs the merger would involve, no such action would have been conceivable. The brilliant and energetic but almost universally disliked president of the University of South Florida, Cecil Mackey, could not have carried his own institution with him on behalf of the merger even though the University of South Florida was engaged in developing branch campuses in Fort Myers, and in St. Petersburg, and was planning as well to found one in the Sarasota-Bradenton area—all to be upper-division and graduate campuses on what had become the Florida State model. Without the additional money from the reorganized New College trustees, he could not have supported the higher faculty/student ratio at New College nor maintained New College faculty and staff who would not be absorbed and whose areas of expertise would not mesh with the needs of the new branch campus.*

---

*Arland Christ-Janer, who under the new arrangement would obviously have no job at New College, had announced his acceptance of the presidency of

Some faculty believed that Christ-Janer had come to New College with the mandate of gracefully terminating it and with merger arrangements already in mind. Our perhaps mistaken judgment has been that he was as shocked by the budgetary situation as anyone. He was also criticized for not keeping faculty and students fully informed as negotiations proceeded. But, in fact, although he did have a liaison committee, he was only periodically on campus, and was fiendishly busy working with legislators and state officials as well as with Cecil Mackey; some faculty, in a comparison not meant to be flattering, likened him to Henry Kissinger. The actual burden of working out details and of keeping the morale of New College faculty and students bearable was left in the hands of Gresham Riley, the young Yale-trained philosopher from Mississippi who had taken his first degree at Southern Baptist Baylor University, and who, despite his unconcealed "squareness," appeared to have an exceptional gift for rapport with the most dissident representatives of the New College counterculture.

Some faculty sought counsel with the notion of holding up the merger plans through litigation, arguing that their rights to tenure would take priority in bankruptcy proceedings, and that the college properties were being sold to the state system at too low an evaluation. Others attacked the merger because it seemed to them that a New College no longer wholly autonomous would be a desecration of original ideals. Our own perhaps unjust reaction was to regard such faculty as kamikazes, prepared to destroy the only chance of their less-mobile colleagues for any kind of security, and unprepared to work diligently with counterparts at USF to see what advantages there might be in merger on straight pedagogic grounds. Perhaps there would be benefits, for example, in widening the orbit of faculty to whom New College students might have access and also in broadening the student body to include a more heterogeneous commuter population. Riesman urged New College admissions officers, in a decimated office puzzled as to how to proceed, to work with financial-aid and other officers at USF; Nancy E. Ferraro, recorder (in effect, registrar), did see the importance of making such connec-

Stephens College, a women's college in Columbia, Missouri. A search began for someone to head the New College Foundation, which was to assume the unenviable task of asking New College trustees and other donors to continue to support an institution they could no longer consider truly "theirs"—an obligation barely met for the first two years. As we go to press, an anonymous trustee who gave $500,000 has helped to induce enough pledges from other trustees to provide almost $900,000 as a commitment for the 1976–77 academic year and to provide virtual assurance for the 1977–78 year as well.

tions, as did Furman C. Arthur, the dedicated director of public relations. But most faculty simply waited to see what would happen —an understandable reaction among those who had purposefully chosen a small undergraduate college. They saw the dramatically growing "multiversity" which now seemed to be encroaching on them as a mixed blessing indeed!

Prior to the crucial legislative session in the spring of 1975, the commissioner of education, Ralph Turlington, who had previously left matters in the hands of the chancellor and the board of regents of the State University System, expressed questions as to whether the merger should be renegotiated. There were legal technicalities to be faced also, since the Sarasota branch campus was supposed to be only for upper-division students, particularly, as elsewhere in the Florida State System, for transfers from community colleges.*

Yet, when the legislative session came, the necessary enabling legislation emerged through the abbreviated chaos of a Florida legislative session. The lawyer retained by some faculty apparently counseled against litigation, and, to the astonishment of many, ourselves included, the merger did go through. Gresham Riley, who had devotedly stayed on as provost although he had concluded several years earlier that he had been at New College long enough, felt that he could in all good conscience leave at the end of the 1974–75 academic year, having in fact borne chief responsibility for the internal arrangements and having served for many faculty, although by no means all, as one administrator they could trust. The good fortune of George Mayer's willingness to serve as provost (he had maintained his residence in Sarasota when he transferred his main allegiance to USF), and the friendship and confidence of many New College faculty which he enjoyed, have certainly proved crucial. But few New College students or faculty seem to have sought wider contacts as the University of South Florida started to establish its own programs on the spacious but underutilized Sarasota campus. New College undergraduates who would never have allowed a word of male chauvinism or of racism to be uttered tended to retain the scorn they had expressed in 1974 toward the "Philistine," upwardly mobile, older commuter students who were now coming to what had been their campus. They seemed to see these students through the lens of the movie *Easy Rider*. We had argued with them in the fall

---

*In fact, in the past, transfers from more conventional colleges and universities had often made excellent use of New College's freedoms, having a wider perspective than freshmen and a greater appreciation for the intensity of commitment New College at its best made possible.

of 1974 to be wary of stereotypes. True, like most stereotypes, it was not entirely false: USF's students are mostly "first-generation-in-college," but the different cadres now inhabiting the New College campus actually have more in common than they would have had even a few years earlier.

Among New College faculty, the stereotypes of their new colleagues seemed even less justified, for in a number of fields (such as anthropology) USF clearly has a breadth and distinction that New College lacks. But then, New College faculty had always in the main insulated themselves; they had not sought contacts with the often extremely dedicated and pedagogically innovative faculty of Eckerd College nor, as indicated earlier, even with the colony of artists and writers who were their Sarasota neighbors. Such isolation is for some a reflection of their dedication to teaching in a situation which places immense demands on faculty—demands which tend to be cumulative, as students come to expect more and more. Others, disappointed in their personal lives or their hopes for an advancing academic career, have devoted themselves with intensity to a life of scholarship (as the young historian and energetic teacher, Justus Doenecke, has done) or have succumbed (like some Santa Cruz faculty) to the *dolce far niente* climate.

With independence gone and uniqueness jeopardized, New College faculty live on with no clear sense of mission. They are victims of the budgetary and demographic crunch of the 1970s, just as they had once symbolized the "do your own thing" movements of the sixties.

To Seem Small As It Grows Large

The Cluster Colleges at Santa Cruz

8

When it was aborning, few campuses seemed to offer as much promise or to draw as much praise as the University of California at Santa Cruz. Yet a decade later it was demoralized. In the founding era, Chancellor Dean McHenry opened a new college every year at Santa Cruz. But by the time his successor, Mark Christensen, came down from Berkeley in 1974, the boom was over and faculty were beginning to feel the pinch of retrenchment. Enrollment at what was once the most favored campus in the California system was falling off sharply. A once-buoyant faculty was feeling middle-aged, and some feared that the great white whale of the counterculture was rotting high on the beach at Santa Cruz. In 1976, eighteen months after assuming the chancellorship, Christensen was forced out.

Yet we hope to show in this account that such a portrait, while true enough in outline, overstates the gloom.* Despite its recent reverses, Santa Cruz was, and in most ways continues to be, one of the most genuine successes of the last decade. One learns this not from its dispirited faculty but from the students who have been drawn to this stunningly beautiful campus. It is a mellow, Mediterranean landscape, and students delight in its distinctive colleges clustered like Italian hill towns among the redwoods.

Particularly in its early years, when it won wide notice as the first university in the nation to adopt pass/fail grading† across the board,

*This chapter was originally written with Judith Dunn Grant, who also assisted in the fieldwork in four visits to Santa Cruz.

†As reported in Table 3, a 1974 alumni survey showed that 67 percent of Santa Cruz graduates cited pass/fail grading as one of the most important aspects of their undergraduate experience. The only factor outranking the grading-evaluation system was "student friendships."

Santa Cruz was something of a refuge for bright, upper-middle-class students who wished to escape the usual forms of academic competition and find a way to live less pressured lives. While many pursue conventional academic careers, Santa Cruz has a peculiar power to woo a premed out of the chemistry lab and into the redwoods to study organic dyes. A high proportion of its students are undecided about careers, and some of them turn in their book bags for potters' wheels or join communes in the hills.[1]

Some of the faculty also come to deescalate. They are more likely than faculty on other UC campuses to be in conflict about their level of ambition and to seek relief from the pace they had known in the elite institutions where they did their graduate work (and where a good number of them had also taught). Santa Cruz is a satisfying place for many, although more than a few are troubled, ambivalent, or guilt-ridden. A decade after its founding, there may be more disappointment among both faculty and administrators over visions thwarted than joy about what has been achieved. Yet we think many goals have been realized, perhaps because no particular dream has triumphed.

I

Though downward escalation is the theme that perhaps characterizes Santa Cruz more than any other, it was not the image that was dominant in the eyes of its founders. Clark Kerr's vision for Santa Cruz developed when he was chancellor at Berkeley, where he tried but failed to create a collegiate environment. He did reshape the Berkeley campus physically—not just by planting one tree, but by planting an entire eucalyptus grove. But he found it impossible to affect the environment of undergraduate education, to establish college communities, and to bring a sense of Swarthmore to Berkeley. And he could not win the faculty, organized as they were in departments and professional schools, to this vision.

When Kerr left the Berkeley chancellorship to become president of the entire University of California in 1958, he asked his graduate school roommate, Dean McHenry, then a political scientist at UCLA, to be his assistant for academic planning. As Berkeley roommates, they had argued about who had had the better undergraduate education: Kerr at Swarthmore with its intense feeling of intellectual community, or McHenry at UCLA with its research faculty and library. In developing the plan for the Santa Cruz campus in the early 1960s, Kerr told McHenry "to find some way to make it seem small as it grows large," to bring the advantages of UCLA and Swarthmore together. Thus the cluster-college plan at Santa Cruz evolved.[2]

To develop an intimate scale of university education on the collegiate model each college could have a distinctive architectural and curricular personality. Each would offer its members a sense of community, but would differ in emphasis, aim, style, and curriculum.* Kerr, who had just vacationed in a seacoast village in the south of France, conceived the college as walled and humanly proportioned cities, offering a density and warmth of human society inside, yet within an easy walk to the forest solitude. The buildings, to be no more than two-thirds the height of the redwoods, were to be built among the trees beyond the hillside meadows above Monterey Bay.

Kerr set the broad goals for the new campus and named Dean McHenry as the chancellor who was to realize them. McHenry was in some ways an unlikely choice for Santa Cruz. A solid, but not distinguished, political scientist at UCLA he rose from assistant professor to head the social-science division. He had no reputation for innovative teaching, and some feared he might be wedded to the departmentalism that Santa Cruz sought to curb. McHenry seemed hearty and genial, with a farm boy's openness, which was misleading; for underneath he was shrewd and disciplined. He pained some faculty because he appeared easily impressed by academic big shots and too eager to hire status-winners. But McHenry was also deeply and earnestly idealistic. During the Depression he and Clark Kerr had worked in a government program to promote a barter economy among the self-help cooperatives that had been formed in California. He campaigned for the Socialist Upton Sinclair, the Democratic nominee for governor in 1934, and joined the Utopian Society. Decades later he would teach a course on utopias at Santa Cruz.

While not inspiring or charismatic, McHenry may have been the ideal mentor for Santa Cruz. He was tough enough not to need to be liked. He was unafraid of appointing strong leaders as college provosts. Behind the scenes, he maintained the creative tensions between colleges and departments, allowing neither to gain hegemony over the developing campus. He believed in utopian experiment, but possessed the practical skills and political instincts that gave the university credibility not only with the legislators and the public, but also with the diverse individuals who were Santa Cruz's pioneers.

*Kerr's vision for Santa Cruz went beyond the more traditional cluster-college model that had evolved at the Claremont colleges, but he noted in an interview that Claremont had created an image and a demonstration of the worth of the model which made it immeasurably easier for the legislature in California to regard it as feasible.

Among these was Byron Stookey, the first head of academic planning. He had first come to Santa Cruz in 1963, when he accompanied David Riesman, who had been asked by Kerr to visit several University of California campuses. Stookey, then thirty, had returned to Harvard after military service as an administrator and part-time teacher. Almost painfully shy, he, too, seemed an improbable choice. But the students who later wrote an affectionate history of Cowell College were drawn to this "tremendously sensitive individual" who was "neither outgoing nor glib" but "an idealist with conviction and faith." And they were captivated by his ideas.[3]

Stookey hoped it would be possible "to establish an institution which, though massive and public, offers live and powerful education. And in the process to test the feasibility of creating warmth and richness in a cool, planned environment."[4]

He was not so naïve as to believe Santa Cruz was the first university to organize itself into colleges. What was new at Santa Cruz was the political leverage that was built into the experiment so that it could be "tried wholeheartedly in a public university." Two years after he took over the planning post at Santa Cruz, Stookey wrote of his hopes for the campus in an essay in the *Harvard Educational Review*. Influenced by his experiences as a lecturer in general education and as associate director of the freshman seminar program at Harvard, where he had relatively little influence, Stookey argued that a "full-blown collegial system" would be in constant jeopardy if the power to hire and promote, to establish degree requirements, to allocate budgets and office space, rested solely with the departmentally organized faculty. At Santa Cruz, matters would be otherwise.

At first, there would be no academic departments: "better that the student should discover the validities and limits of fields for himself than that we should plant hedgerows from the start and then spend time, in remedial programs of 'General Education,' trying to overcome them." Provosts would have a major role in recruitment and promotion of faculty. Minimum requirements could be established later by the disciplines, but "every college is free to develop its own forms of general education and teaching."

> Virtually every member of the faculty will be a member of a college. Most of his undergraduate teaching will be carried on there, his office or study may be located there, he will participate there in the determination of educational policy and his salary, typically, will come in part from the budget of the college . . . when it is time for him to be considered for tenure or promotion, both the dean of his division and the Provost of his college will have their say.

Stookey's design encouraged a creative disorder. Following the core courses in the freshman and sophomore years, students would plan their own majors and would be allowed to do independent study and through other means to chart their own courses, relying on comprehensive exams as a quality check. The student would provide "continuity from course to course and from year to year; it is in his experience that our requirements and efforts must cohere . . ." And if Santa Cruz were to be a human institution, it "must give place to passion, irrationality, vision and eccentricity."

Men of Stookey's quality, touched with charisma, were often found among the first provosts at Santa Cruz (no woman was named provost until May Diaz was appointed at Kresge in 1974). And although it seemed to happen in an offhand way, the selection of the first provost was crucial. Page Smith, a UCLA historian who became the provost of Cowell, stopped by one day to see McHenry on the way to Northern California where his daughter was attending summer camp. They talked and went out on the porch. Then McHenry asked Smith to have his picture taken in a UCSC sweatshirt. Shortly after, McHenry wrote Page Smith, asking him to be the provost of Santa Cruz's first college, Cowell. Smith says the invitation came as a surprise, although McHenry had written to him earlier, complimenting Smith on his book on John Adams (which won the Bancroft Prize) and suggesting that he drop in if he ever came by Santa Cruz. And McHenry knew Smith's reputation as a stimulating teacher at UCLA who put his lectures on film and then went around personally to talk with students.

We most vividly remember Page Smith at a dinner party in his home deep in the country hills. He greeted us in slippers and a red velvet dinner jacket and led us through a side gate where we were startled by his South American Arcana chickens which flapped down from overhanging pine branches. A donnish Gary Cooper, Smith brushed the hair off his forehead and peered at us quizzically, as though he had a comic expectation of the world. We enjoyed the evening in the living room filled with rare painted eggs and his wife's paintings and tapestries.

But it was earlier in the faculty lounge at Cowell, when he was not distracted by being host, that he talked most openly about his five years as provost. The relaxed conversation became a dialogue about teaching in the context of his biography. He had been most influenced by his Dartmouth mentor, Eugen Rosenstock-Huessy, who saw the academic world as spiritually and intellectually desiccated. "Thus, I had no illusions about academe." After Smith graduated, in the 1930s, Rosenstock-Huessy encouraged him to volunteer for the Civilian Conservation Corps, which he considered an analogue for William James's moral equivalent to war. Smith embraced the CCC, working first in Maryland and later in Tunbridge, Vermont, before he was drafted, fought, and was wounded. After the war, he applied to Harvard to do work in history; he was turned down in that field but he was admitted in literature because that was his undergraduate major. Once at Harvard, however, he went to David Owen in the history department and said he was 28, had children, and didn't want to study Icelandic and Middle High German. Couldn't he come over into history? Owen consented, but warned him that he would find that the Harvard department did not deal with Rosenstock-Huessy's sweeping ideas but concerned itself with turning out professional historians.

He was offered a post at UCLA after finishing his doctorate, and he enjoyed teaching and devoted himself to it. He published an article about the "debilitating effects" of grades and at a planning conference suggested that one of the new University of California campuses should be built on the collegiate model. Yet he knew the costs of teaching, and when offered the provostship of a college committed to teaching he had some reluctance. For six or seven years at UCLA he had a "funny kind of compulsion" to require his students to turn in a paper every Friday, and he spent the weekend reading seventy papers for Monday's classes. During that period he had been hospitalized twice with bleeding ulcers and had suffered a long, trying bout with hepatitis. But after coming to Cowell, despite the pressures of the provostship, he felt marvelously healthy. Of course, having power at the top mattered, but his new assignment had also brought an emotional shift, a shift of consciousness. At Cowell, he wanted to create for everyone an educational experience that was delightful and pleasing rather than a strain and worry.

For Smith, the traditional academic world was the last stronghold of the Puritan ethic in which learning was necessarily difficult and painful. Once he had subscribed to it. But now Smith believed that the freedom and exuberance of play was essential to learning. Yet, in the early days at Cowell, flashes of the Puritan ethic returned to him. "I would see a student out there in the plaza looking at the sunset, and the thought would cross my mind, why isn't he in the library?" He remembers that when he once told a student to put his shirt on, the student retorted sharply, "Why should I have to put on my shirt because you've got a hangup about the body?" The student had just the right rejoinder, he said. He would no longer do such a thing; nor, of course, would he ever interfere with a student who was enjoying the sunset. Rather, we should have a life in community that encourages us to enjoy the sunset together. It was this transformation in his own thinking that led him to write *As a City on the Hill*, a description of that kind of ideal community.

Remembering the student and his shirt, he began to talk about the sexual revolution. We noted that perhaps it was not as widespread as portrayed in the media, thinking of a newspaper clipping we had seen while walking down the hall in Stevenson the night before, which reported that one of Kinsey's researchers found that premarital sexual intercourse had not increased greatly. He replied, "Yes, I believed those statistics for a few years too, but I don't anymore. I now believe it's a revolution as deep and as wide as is possible. The attitude change, the styles of living, the styles of growing up together." Yes, we replied, even if the incidence of premarital sex had not changed as much as asserted, the feelings of guilt certainly have diminished.

"At first," he said, "I thought we could create something close to the ideal environment for education, in which people would enjoy it." Part of the delight that Smith was after was expressed in the Cowell culture breaks. All classes were cancelled for two or three days, and the entire faculty and student body would join together in a poetry or music festival. But once a delightful educational environment with less stress, small classes, and no grades was achieved, true reform lay much deeper, Smith felt.

What were the deeper problems? Smith replied that one of the reasons he had invited Norman O. Brown to teach at Cowell was his Phi Beta Kappa address stipulating that mystery had a key place in the life of the mind. For example, nobody could give a convincing account of the reasons for the uproar on the campus over Cambodia. Smith believed that events happened in spontaneous and incomprehensible ways, and he spurned academicians who forced them into neat causal paradigms. Smith regarded the conventional disciplines as dead weights and spoke in emotional tones of an academy that misspent its time compiling dusty bins of monographs. The great scholars were the nineteenth-century narrative historians. Students, furthermore, don't want to hear people lecture about narrow academic notions.

This gave us a chance to ask him about his course on the chicken, which we had heard criticized and ridiculed by some faculty at Santa Cruz. One said it showed Page Smith had "gone off the deep end." "Ah yes," he brightened, he would not only tell us about it but escort us to his class. On the way to the seminar room Smith told us that the course had been born in discussions with a Cowell biologist, Charles Daniel, who raises chickens as he does. "The academic world interacts only with its own ideas and seldom looks at anything concrete," Smith explained. "The chicken is a fine mundane object. We are inexperienced in looking, so the students begin the course by simply looking at chickens." Later the course examined the place of chickens in the folklore and mythology of many cultures and considered the ravages of technology that practices in the chicken industry exemplified.

About twenty students were sitting in a circle in the seminar room. A girl said her faculty advisor at Crown College would not sign her card. "He thought this course was just terrible and shouldn't be allowed at any university." Smith responded that if the same course were called the "Age of Jackson," no questions would be raised.

On the way over we had mentioned Clifford Geertz's article on the Balinese cockfight in *Daedalus*, and Smith shared it with his students and then asked for other references. A boy held up a book from an agricultural experiment station describing sizes, qualities, and types of eggs. Another student had found over one hundred references to chickens in childrens' literature and in Bartlett's *Quotations*. Daniel then introduced that day's speaker, Bhuwan L. Joshi, who, after earning his doctorate at Berkeley and doing some traditional research in psychology, had gone through a personal transformation and was now writing about the politics of Nepal. On this day the class was spellbound as he read from the Vedas and discussed the idea of the yolk of the egg as a symbolic sun. The class exemplified Rosentock-Huessey's aphorism that "you can only go as far forward as you can go back," as well as Page Smith's belief that "if the student were to be brought back to the sources of things and ideas, then the need for the professorial would diminish."

Another early participant in the Santa Cruz experiment was Alan Chadwick, who looked to the source of things in a different sense. Chadwick was seen as an eccentric nut by some and as a great mystic by his student disciples. He described himself as a "philosophical gardener" who had been invited by Paul Lee and other faculty to nurture growth at Santa Cruz. Although he was never listed in the catalogue or given an appointment, in the early years one-third to one-half of the students "studied" under this autocratic, barking perfectionist, who planted seeds by the phases of the moon. The garden project symbolized something that ran quite deep at Santa Cruz. Under Chadwick, students literally transformed the campus as they planted flowers along college pathways, grew vegetables, and cultivated the hillside above Cowell College where free bouquets were placed on stands each morning.

We had lunch with Chadwick one day in his garden. Several students sat reverently at the board table when they were not silently serving leek soup, homemade barley and raisin bread, and a salad of unwashed carrots. Chadwick talked about the analogy between tending a garden and tending people. "You don't have to tell a plant what to do. It tells you. It reveals its needs." Most of the young people dining so quietly with us had dropped out of Santa Cruz to work full time in the garden. One girl said that, for her, college became a choice between reading a book and talking with a friend in need. She always chose the friend, and felt a student should choose the book. Chadwick became irritated as we questioned other young gardeners. He announced, "Perhaps I should tell our visitors that one of the things we try to do without here is words." Chadwick had become disenchanted with the students after nearly seven years at Santa Cruz. They had grown careless and lazy. Students smashed his teapot and misused his things. They ran over flowerpots with their automobiles. The campus had grown too fast and was too hurried.

But the garden project and its offshoots made an imprint on the campus. In 1972 it claimed a $30,000 annual operating budget. Work in the garden sometimes earned academic credit. One student developed a program with a psychology professor to apply horticultural principles to the raising of children. Some students and dropouts worked 24 acres of university-owned land to produce food to help feed 300 people a day at the student-run Whole Earth Restaurant. There the Brandenberg Concerto may be playing as diners linger over yogurt, bean sprouts, and vegetable soup at picnic tables on a sunny redwood balcony.

Like Alan Chadwick, Jasper Rose is an Englishman and shares a Tolstoyan distaste for the technocratic world. Both are dramatic. Chadwick was a Shakespearean actor, and Rose, who wears his King's College gown when lecturing, organized Shakespearean readings. But where Chadwick is Lear, Rose has a touch of Falstaff. He believed in Chadwick's garden project and the small world of craft and community. First as senior preceptor of Cowell, then as provost succeeding Smith, Rose worked to establish arts and crafts as a college major.

Rose greeted us effervescently, clapping our hands between his and leading us into his office with its red walls, an Oriental rug, roll-top desk, and quaint hanging lamp—he refuses to use fluores-

cent lighting. Later we toured his wife's painting class and various
arts-and-crafts facilities. When we visited the print shop, a student
offered us some cheddar cheese, and we stood there, eating and talking. Like the Oxford reformer, William Morris, Rose sees arts and
crafts, through which people live to enjoy, share pains, and support
each other, as the way out of the vast technocratic ugliness and
sterility of society. We ought to live on a small enough scale so we
could walk through the rain to visit each other. We should learn to
be more materially independent, to grow our own food, make our
clothes and pots, and create our physical environment. Rose wanted
to retain "some of the amateur because it involves the emotions
rather than the professional point of view—a genuine love of doing
the thing rather than earning your bread and butter. The retention
of the sense that the individual education is what matters is the
starkest opposition of the training of the masses."

Rose believes that undergraduates spend too much time in formal
work. "At Oxford and Cambridge there is very little of this. The
student has lots of time to do other things. But in the American
university you feel the students are fed a diet and have to lay a
paper egg." We are demonized by time. Crafts teach one "to slow
down and woo a topic." In the crafts program there are two days
of drawing and painting, two days of ceramics, and one day of art
history. "If you are doing pottery, it is better to do it for a day."

Many Cowell students take arts-and-crafts courses, and about
twenty are majoring in them. Probably few will devote their lives to
the skills they are learning here, but we agreed that the curriculum
should look beyond the marketplace and that people learn more than
skills in such a program. Rose said, "Ah yes, in making things one
learns first of all patience. One also learns standards of judgment.
You also learn to cooperate with others, to respect materials . . .
You find styrofoam cups left all around here, but you don't find clay
pots left all around because clay pots have a life and value in the
next generation." That was what civilization was about—creating
things that were worth keeping and learning to appreciate those
things (though somehow, we thought to ourselves, it didn't keep
students from running over Chadwick's flower pots).

Rose hoped Santa Cruz would be less concerned with status as
time went on. It was turning out numbers and doing a pretty good
job of educating a lot of people. But too many young faculty were
slaving to become great men. "Perhaps more of them ought to ask
themselves whether their piece of work was better than a really good
dinner." The basic problem of the place was ecological. "There were
too many eggs and too many baskets. We want to have small col-

leges, but we also must be successful in big science. . . . Things are conceived on the wrong scale. It would be something just to create a good collegial life itself. You can only do so much." Technology ran afoul of its own ambition. The heating pipes at Cowell didn't work. Could he be serious that society could get along without a lot of high technical skill? To some extent, yes. We should expose children (i.e., put them out in the cold to die after birth) rather than develop elaborate abortion techniques. We should be willing to "sign off" at sixty and not go on to create problems. But surely he must recognize that it had taken a lot of technical skill to build the university where we now stood? Yes, he admitted, but we could have done a lot better. It was too big and had grown too fast. People needed to create things on a small scale and simply enjoy the afternoon. Perhaps Cowell itself was a failure. In terms of the job that needed to be done, only a small beachhead had been established. He wondered at times whether it was wiser to persist or to leave the battlefield and regroup. After our talk we were walking across the Cowell courtyard when Jasper Rose stooped to collect some leaflets and paper cups that fluttered in the light wind. We helped as students sunning on the benches watched.

II

Cowell opened in 1965, and a new and quite different college followed every year. Stevenson (1966) was originally headed by the sociologist Charles Page and became known as the social-science college. Crown (1967) attracted the largest number of hard scientists and was headed by biologist Kenneth V. Thimann. It was seen as straight and square. Philip Bell, a Quaker from Haverford and an economist with an interest in Africa, was the founding provost of Merrill (1968), which started out with a third-world image. At College V (1969) Provost James Hall launched an aesthetics major, and students joined extracurricular guilds in printmaking, photography, pottery, silk screening, lithography, jazz, and chamber music. We have devoted another chapter to the extraordinary experiment led by Robert Edgar at the sixth college, Kresge (1970), which organized itself in kin groups and attempted to form a "caring community" heavily influenced by the humanistic psychology of Carl Rogers and Abraham Maslow. Oakes College (1971) focused on ethnic minorities, and College VIII (1972) on environmental planning.

A look at the role of the provost of Cowell College highlights the challenges of the founding era. While the provost of each subsequent college had an independent mandate and developed a distinctive environment, what happened at Cowell had strong effects on the future of all. Cowell set the internal tone and the external image of the whole campus. Most importantly, Page Smith picked the initial faculty before the departments developed, before he had to share the power of appointment with them. Indeed, the early Cowell faculty formed the core of the later departments, and established much campus-wide policy. An early meeting of the Cowell faculty, which was then the total faculty on the campus, decided to abolish grades entirely and offer all courses on a pass/fail basis.*

Students who wrote a history of Cowell portrayed Page Smith as an experimenter who "collected a group of educational dissenters."[5] But they did not look like dissenters—at least in a 1965 photograph of the forty-one faculty who came the first year, only five were women, and the men have short hair and are wearing ties, tweed coats, and white shirts. Most came from elite graduate schools: Harvard, Berkeley, Stanford, and Yale account for the origins of twenty-four. Some were quite traditional scholars who simply found Santa Cruz an attractive and congenial place to write and teach. But many, perhaps most, dissented from the norms that operated in the graduate schools from which they came. We interviewed thirty-one faculty members, some of whom we saw two or three times over the course of our visits. In the vignettes that follow we try to describe the impulses drawing them to Santa Cruz, and the joys and misgivings some of them subsequently felt.

The Cowell faculty was generally young, which perhaps gave balding, gentle, fatherly Bert Kaplan his particular appeal. He was among the first faculty recruited, and his courses, difficult to place in any particular field, were highly popular. Kaplan earned his first degree at Brooklyn College and his doctorate at Harvard. He published two books before coming to Santa Cruz: one on the Hutterites and another on mental illness. He had started a program in humanistic psychology and had been chairman of the department at Rice.

He asked us to his cluttered office at Cowell. The lights were off and he drew blinds to darken the room. Talking in a slow halting near-whisper, he caught us off guard with his candor. Later, when we asked about his work, he said he no longer wanted to publish. In addition to his books, he had, until recently, regularly published two or three journal articles a year. He had attended all the professional meetings and had generally accepted five or six lecture engagements

---

*Now "pass/forget," i.e., failures, are simply not recorded. In the science department, students have the option of a letter grade.

at other universities. He does not go to meetings now, and has published virtually nothing in three or four years. He declines book reviews. But he does write every morning at his desk and feels he is learning more and would publish better stuff now. He doesn't feel impelled to write now, perhaps because he enjoys saying everything he has to say directly to his students. We suggested that he might be asking new questions, and that after a time he might want to publish in new fields. No, he responded softly, he didn't think he would. He would rather say it all to his students than address fellow psychologists with whom he could no longer identify. He teaches the Socratic dialogues and smiled as he described offering courses in religion and literature "with a thin gloss of psychology." He gives no exams; his students keep journals and do projects. He invited us to an evening class where the students would sing psalms.

Kaplan felt inchoateness was the essence of early Santa Cruz: It began with a rudimentary set of conditions. "Through time, we'll find out what happened," he said. In the beginning one planned and organized, trying to actualize Byron Stookey's conception of seductive education. Later, it was not necessary to push and plan. A new college unfolded every year and a thousand flowers bloomed. Of the blooming flowers, which were most fragrant to him? "Let's go take a look," he responded, leading us into the sunshine and the Cowell courtyard where students lounged and talked. We looked down across the athletic fields and out across the bay as we walked to Alan Chadwick's blooming garden project, then out the back gate to Merrill College with its lovely blue roofs and students lunching in the sunshine. Was he struck by the slower tempo at Santa Cruz? Yes, indeed. At Rice, everyone moves on schedule in orderly platoons. Here, fluidity is characteristic. Nobody knows what anyone is doing or what is going to happen. We parted for our next appointment.

Eugene Switkes met us at his office in the natural-sciences building nestled among the redwoods near the library. He was then twenty-eight, with sideburns to the earlobes, a leather vest, button-down shirt, and hiking boots. An Oberlin undergraduate, he went on to Harvard in chemistry and to Cambridge for a post-doctorate. There he debated dropping out of academic life and opening a business in New Hampshire. He had also considered a position at the University of Rochester and an advanced fellowship program at the University of Michigan. Santa Cruz was attractive to him because he wanted to teach and to be involved with undergraduates, but he did not want to abandon serious research as he thought he might do at colleges like Oberlin and Reed. Yet he was unsure what really mattered for promotion and tenure at Santa Cruz. He saw the danger of sacrificing the professional quality possible in departmental disciplines for "sexy" interdepartmental courses in the colleges that had little content. "If we do that, the place will go flat quickly," he said. He thought Santa Cruz needed three kinds of people: (1) outstanding researchers dedicated to research; (2) great teachers, no longer doing much research but asking fundamental questions about how to teach science to undergraduates in an anti-intellectual and anti-scientific culture; and (3) mixtures of the two, whose reasonably good research would inspire undergraduates to go into science.

We told Switkes about Bert Kaplan's literal answer to our question about the most fragrant flowers in Santa Cruz. Switkes thought there was much concern with literal answers. People were intensely seeking something or intensely doing nothing. He told us about two students who came to him to discover what organic plants they could use to make dyes. He sent them to the Berkeley library, regarding the Santa Cruz library as inadequate, and they found three excellent books: *Stain Technique of the Vine* by W. H. Emig; *The Chemistry and Physics of Organic Pigments* by Lyde S. Pratt; and *Dyestuffs and Coal Tar Products* by Thomas Becall and others. He also assigned *Eye and Brain: The Psychology of Seeing* by R. L. Gregory. In the lab they looked at the physics of color, i.e., what happens on a molecular level when something is red. They measured spectra. He met with them about three hours a week for tutorials to discuss their findings and readings. He introduced them to a faculty botanist who helped identify the actual plants from which they could extract the dyes. They considered the lower degree of toxicity of natural dyes and the danger of stripping the forest of certain ferns. The botanist is writing a small research paper growing out of this mutual interest. Switkes found the work relevant to his own studies of how the nervous system processes visual information: why we see something as red or why when we mix two colors we get another. He had submitted one paper to a chemistry journal. Although these studies are an outgrowth of work he had done before coming to Santa Cruz, he has now developed more theoretical and conceptual interests. He taught a course on visual perception to nonscientists that was more speculative than such a course would be if he were teaching scientists, in which case he would emphasize quantitative matters, problem-solving, and methodology.

He also teaches the introductory chemistry course required for biology majors and premeds. It is a standard course with textbooks, lectures, and exams, and 190 students are registered. He recently gave a course on his specialty to about sixteen juniors. Some did good work, but he found the atmosphere unlike Harvard or Oberlin. "There is somewhat less tenacity. Students won't give up, but they will come in and ask for help earlier than I think they should. Maybe we on the faculty encourage it. Maybe it's grown in the culture here in California." He became very involved with some of his students. "I have become much less detached than I ought to be in some ways." Yet despite the intimacy, students often thought their written evaluations did not reflect a precise sense of who they were.

Switkes felt that the superstructure and politics at Santa Cruz sometimes inhibited innovation. There was a chancellor, a college, divisions, and boards—and progress was very slow. He feared the cumbersome process would repel the brilliant interdisciplinary scientist he was trying to lure from Berkeley. The politics in the appointments system in the University of California made Santa Cruz an uncertain place. At Harvard members of a department would threaten to resign in order to get their man. Here, he felt, they would be too insecure.

Word that Sheldon Wolin was leaving Santa Cruz for Princeton had spread the day we met him in the Cowell faculty lounge. A respected political scientist who appears regularly in the *New York Review of Books*, as well as in the professional journals, Wolin has taught at Harvard, Oxford, Northwestern, Oberlin, and Berkeley, where he held tenure. Students find him a stimulating and demanding teacher who responds to their written work. He seemed relaxed, in blue sweater and khakis, and pleased by our report of the students' view of him. It was true he was going to Princeton. "I've discovered my real roots are in the East." But geography was perhaps secondary to other dissatisfactions he felt at Santa Cruz.

He left Berkeley because he grew uncomfortable with the ideological splintering of the late 1960s. He had been attracted by the chance to launch a new graduate program at Santa Cruz and by the idea of undergraduate teaching in the colleges. Now he realized he seriously miscalculated both his desire to teach undergraduates and the totality of the demands he would face. Unrelieved association with undergraduates was intellectually stultifying. Students made heavy demands on him: to provide extra class sessions, to read other papers they had written, and to talk about their problems. "It doesn't take many conversations like that to fill up a day, or week for that matter." Santa Cruz students were often insistent—unlike students at Oberlin where, although undergraduate education is taken seriously, there are clear limits of student imposition on faculty time "so that you can get some work done." Here, a student who had to wait five minutes beyond his appointment time knocked petulantly on Wolin's door and asked to see Wolin's written evaluation of him. "You cannot resist the demands. You run out of gas. It's very difficult." He paused and added, "Perhaps if I had a different orientation, I could relax and enjoy it and it would be a fine life. I really do feel very, very desperately, in terms of the things that brought me into academic life, I haven't learned a thing here."

Yet Wolin felt that, despite students' demands and their glib sophistication, there was a certain blandness, a shying away from sharp intellectual exchange or precision among students and faculty as well. Classes were low-keyed, often agreeably boring. In his teaching, Wolin tried to make students aware of conflicting assumptions, "to make them want to almost hit each other. But it doesn't even get close to that here. It tends to be light, fuzzy, and billowy. Things are so nonabrasive. Only the scientists tend to have any of that toughness here."

We sensed what he described and asked whether it might not also be valuable that people are allowed, even encouraged, to become less cruel and more gentle. He nodded that he saw that but went on to think about the effect of ambiguous standards, which he felt had constrained the intellectual growth of young faculty who had to do an extraordinary amount of administration, committee work, and hiring before their own dissertations were finished. Anti-professional, anti-disciplinary themes were very influential in their own work. "It's a sterile period of teaching for many who are doing a kind of anti-sociology and anti-politics course of one kind or another."

Wolin perceived a crisis in the morale of younger faculty because of the lack of criteria on evaluation or promotion. The promotions committee changed every year, provosts came and went; different boards (departments) had different norms, the rules of the game were changing, and people pushed their favorites in different ways. A faculty member could not be sure if devoting his time to his college would pay off. Santa Cruz had not yet found anything to take the place of the old, clearer standards. The colleges lacked rigorous measures of competent teaching. Yardsticks seemed arbitrary and capricious, although in his experience the promotion committees have been uniformly talented.

Yet, in order to have a graduate program, the old standards were essential. Good students are attracted by faculty who have published and have some reputation. Wolin's proposal for a more ambitious graduate program had been turned down. The promises for graduate program support on which he was depending evaporated with tighter budgets. Graduate programs, particularly in the social sciences, were generally weak, he thought. But, given the extraordinary demands on faculty at Santa Cruz, he felt it was unrealistic to enforce the old publication standards. We talked about something even more difficult: how to make a judgment about the intellectual vitality of a colleague. Are there ideas he or she is investigating? Wolin said that frequently, when younger faculty came up for promotion, they had published nothing and did not even have any interests that would lead to publication.

Wolin was pessimistic about the future of Santa Cruz. There was a leadership vacuum that made it impossible to clarify goals. Whereas at Berkeley direction came from the graduate and professional schools, in the amalgamated, federalized Santa Cruz system there was a diffusion of purpose. While many felt that the colleges were weak, Wolin felt the boards were weak. There was silence at the top. "It is very difficult to find people on this campus who can say what this place is supposed to be or where it is going. It is not really an experimental institution. There is freedom. You can do things. You can teach what you want. Once you have said that, you have said it all."

A young social scientist whom Wolin had described as confronting a crisis in his career had come from one of the leading graduate schools in 1965 and was an assistant professor facing an up or out decision when we interviewed him in 1972. He had been attracted by the beauty, warmth, openness, and attention to undergraduate teaching at Santa Cruz. "But I had a lot of naïve notions about what that meant." Why naïve? "Well, there was some openness, but there was never a commitment to radical restructuring." He feared Santa Cruz was becoming "another big bogus university concerned with status and bringing in the big shots so their prestige will rub off on others." He chose to concentrate on teaching and undertook a heavy administrative burden, helping to develop two new college majors and spending hours advising students. During the last two years he had been heavily involved working with students in the graduate program on history of consciousness. "I felt that the lively and intimate learning relationships that existed between students and faculty came closer to fulfilling what I had hoped for at Santa Cruz." Several years ago his chairman had said, "Hey, write a book review or something I can wave around, would you." He felt some pressure, but was sure he would be promoted to associate. "Then all of a sudden Brewster Smith, vice-chancellor for the social sciences, showed up and he was your boss. Smith asked some very pointed questions about my interests and what the publishing payoff of those interests was going to be." So he turned out some book reviews, an essay, and a chapter of a textbook.

He no longer found teaching so exciting. "Now I don't feel that I'm learning in the classroom. I'm going through the motions, telling students stuff I already know." After he and a young sociologist had planned a course on the modern sociological classics, they threw the whole reading list out, an hour before the first class, deciding they didn't want to teach that way. They divided the class into field research collectives.

He added as we left that he was quite uncertain about receiving tenure. "Even if I do, I fear I would be a second-class citizen here." Two years later he wrote to us from a public commuter college in the East. He found the work stimulating but "so damn much harder than in Santa Cruz." It was at times "unbearably frustrating and discouraging" working with new job-oriented students, yet more in tune with his personality "than the slow simple life of Santa Cruz . . . I sometimes wonder what made me choose Santa Cruz originally or why I stayed there so long."

There are also faculty members like Karl Lamb, Laurence Veysey, and Frank Barron, who continue to publish and find Santa Cruz more attractive than traditional research-oriented universities. Lamb, a Yale undergraduate who completed his graduate work at Brasenose College, Oxford, writes about politics, and conservative movements in particular. He finds the good students at Santa Cruz better than those he taught at Michigan, and delights in the fact that he can teach a course on writing (listed as "Daily Fiction" in the catalog, requiring 300-word themes each day) at Cowell, whereas when he was at Michigan he could offer only departmentally approved courses in political science. In the beginning, Lamb found the Cowell core course in Western civilization a source of great conversation among the faculty. Everyone in humanities and social sciences taught a section, and Lamb recalled Bernard Haley, the distinguished economist, coming into the dining hall one morning to report he had stayed up until 3:00 A.M. reading Plato for his section. Yet the dual structure of boards (departments) and colleges can be cumbersome, and he regrets losing some excellent faculty prospects because of the time it took to coordinate recruiting and interviewing. But Lamb is not dissatisfied, "And I'm never going back to shoveling snow in Ann Arbor."

Neither did Laurence Veysey care for the winters in Wisconsin, where he had taught after finishing at Berkeley. Veysey came in the second year to join the Stevenson faculty, and he has enjoyed teaching in its interdisciplinary major in social thought, which is quite selective and demanding. Veysey, a historian (*The Emergence of the American University; The Communal Experience*) thinks his department did the right thing in deciding not to admit any graduate students for the next several years. There were few promising applicants, and Santa Cruz could not match the depth in doctoral studies that was found at Davis or Berkeley. Could Santa Cruz be a university without graduate students, we asked? He felt that the campus did not need graduate students in every department. In areas of strength, say astronomy, it would inevitably attract graduate students, but it ought not to compete in every area; it might be better to develop a particular alternative, such as the history of consciousness program. Personally, he was happy at Santa Cruz, and he took frequent leaves to do research and publish. His principal worry was that the faculty was becoming too chummy, that tough judgments on tenure were not being made. There seemed to be a growing provincialism, "people who talk about getting parking meters on their street rather than about their work and ideas."

Frank Barron, a psychologist at College V who had taught at Berkeley before coming to Santa Cruz, was more emphatic than either Lamb or Veysey about the burdens of the dual structure of boards and colleges, feeling it doubled the work of other universities. But he felt his freedom in teaching more than made up for it. One of his favorite courses is the psychology of consciousness, in which his students took psychological tests as if they were the main character in a literary work like Truman Capote's *In Cold Blood*.

Barron's specialty is the creative process (*Creativity and Personal Freedom: Artists in the Making*), and he helped to develop the major in aesthetics at College V. He gave a standardized test in an introductory course and found students did well, exceeding the scores of students at the University of Illinois, for example, although they were not competing for grades. Belief in astrology is strong; half the students in Barron's personality class raised their hands when he asked how many believed in the astrological signs, and virtually all answered positively when he asked about extrasensory perception. His research shows that many students have a strikingly low sense of well-being. He is not sure why. He agreed with Wolin that many students demand that teachers set things up for them and serve their needs. He was on leave this semester and could be less helpful to students. When he did come on campus students seldom sought him out, as though he was worthless if he was powerless to help them.

Such avoidance could destroy one's self-respect. One needed a strong sense of self-confidence to make demands on students. Some faculty at Santa Cruz had it; some did not.

Faculty may be exhausted, but many Santa Cruz students are exhilarated. There has been an extraordinary shift in the relations between students and faculty, a radical reduction in the traditional role distance and forms of deference. The students we interviewed were enthusiastic about the faculty, who were perceived as exciting teachers responsive to student needs. Santa Cruz students, unlike those at most colleges, are apt to be pleased with the advising system. Faculty in general are likely to be regarded as friends, or at least they seem as approachable as friends. When we asked students in our interviews to cite three persons at Santa Cruz whom they might consult if they had a critical decision to make, they were about twice as likely to cite a faculty member as a fellow student.*

In a 1974 survey, three-fifths of Santa Cruz's alumni said faculty contact was one of the most important factors in their undergraduate experience.[6] And 59 percent of the Santa Cruz faculty (as compared with 29 percent of the Berkeley faculty) reported in 1972 that they interacted frequently with students in informal settings.[7]

When pressed for criticisms students say that some classes are poorly prepared and lacking in structure. A few students also characterize the faculty as conformist liberals too eager to be relevant. The pass/fail grading system also presented problems for some applicants to graduate schools: about 20 percent reported difficulties. Medical-school applicants were most likely to complain, (although 82 percent of those who applied were admitted).[8] Most alumni, however, did not find that pass/fail had put them at any disadvantage when applying to graduate schools, and they argued for retention of Santa Cruz's grading system by an 8–1 margin. Another frequently expressed concern was the homogeneity of the student body. In fact, however, minority representation has increased in recent years, and Santa Cruz now draws more transfers from the Midwest and the East.

Generally, faculty and students agree on the relative emphasis on educational and other goals. We can compare student and faculty views across all the campuses of the University of California as reported in a 1972 survey by Richard E. Peterson. Peterson's goals

---

*In answer to the question, "If you had a critical decision to make, name three people at Santa Cruz you might consult," students cited thirty-one faculty members and seventeen students.

inventory shows that Santa Cruz faculty and students give the highest ratings of any California campus to individual personal development, humanism-altruism, cultural-aesthetic awareness, and innovation. They give the lowest rank of any campus to research and vocational preparation. Santa Cruz is the only campus where concern for innovation and experimentation is given a higher rating by faculty than research. When asked what the goal emphasis should ideally be, the faculty thought that the emphasis on research was about right, but that still more importance should be attached to innovation. The students agreed with them.[9]

Although its popularity declined by the early 1970s, Santa Cruz had been the most desirable campus in the California system, and it was flooded with applicants of high ability. In the early years, three-fourths of the entering freshmen ranked in the top tenth of their high-school graduating class.* They were affluent (55 percent came from families with annual incomes exceeding $20,000, compared with a nationwide figure of 39 percent). A high proportion had parents who were professionals, and about twice as many Santa Cruz parents had graduate degrees as did those of entering freshmen elsewhere.

By these objective measures, the first cadres of Santa Cruz students look like "winners" and appear similar to students at other elite colleges. But, psychologically, they are quite different. Apparently, they do not wish to "win," and they do not expect to. Although their entrance scores put them at the top of the heap when compared with national norms, they expect to be less successful, on the whole, than freshmen elsewhere (only 16 percent of freshmen at elite Santa Cruz expect to be "More successful than most," compared with an average of 19 percent nationwide). They also have lower expectations for finding a job they prefer than the average freshman (40 percent at Santa Cruz "estimate chances are very good that I will find a job in a preferred field" as compared with a national norm of 57 percent). Santa Cruz students expect to lose the race with their less able peers —or, perhaps more accurately, most do not want to race at all.[10]

Santa Cruz freshmen are twice as likely as others to cite "avoiding pressure" as a "very important" factor affecting their choice of career. Rapid advancement, high earnings, and prestige matter rela-

---

*By the mid-seventies, Scholastic Aptitude Test scores had dropped an average 60 points or more. Verbal scores for males dropped from a median of 627 in the late 1960s to 558 in 1975; math scores in the same period declined from 648 to 588. They dropped nationally, of course, but not by margins as wide as these. In the beginning, Santa Cruz was closer to Princeton; by 1975, to the State University of New York at Stony Brook.

tively little to Santa Cruz freshmen, whereas "working with ideas" and "independence" are important elements in their decision. Considering what objectives in life are "essential or very important," Santa Cruz freshmen are less likely than other freshmen to answer "to be an authority in my field," "to raise a family," or "to be well off financially." They are more likely to want to "achieve in performing art," "influence social values," and "be involved in environmental cleanup."

Business and engineering were the two most frequent occupations of their fathers, but Santa Cruz students overwhelmingly reject these careers. In political orientation, they are far left or liberal. Our own questionnaire shows that, whereas students generally come from cities and suburbs, they wish to live in small towns or rural areas.

In the course of our visits to Santa Cruz, we talked with more than forty students, but the portraits that follow are drawn from interviews with fourteen who completed our questionnaire in 1972, prior to a follow-up session that lasted about two hours.

One of the first students we interviewed was a junior named Samual, who had graduated from a suburban California high school.* In the freshman directory he appeared clean-shaven, but the young man who greeted us had a beard and shoulder-length hair. He invited us into his neat room with a large mobile and wicker bird-cage chair hanging from the ceiling. When we admired a poster of the Grand Canyon, Samual said that he had loved looking at it so much that he had gone there over his spring break. He pointed out a particular ledge where he had hiked. He had begun in literature, then branched into a double major with politics, finally deciding to major in politics entirely. He planned to teach and hoped to enter Berkeley or Chicago for graduate study in political science.

He generally liked Santa Cruz, although he wrote on the questionnaire that "Teachers aren't demanding enough on a specific day-to-day level, it's too easy to slide." He expanded in our interview: "Sometimes I get a real down about this being a place where you can mellow out and take it easy for four years. Go surfing; go out in the meadow and do nothing; just glide along. In some ways 'mellowing out' may be descriptive of a significant majority here." Santa Cruz seemed to him a safe plateau with no demands to climb higher.

For the most part his courses were stimulating. He took Oriental art, a large lecture course that he felt many students took as padding. He found the lectures of Mary Holmes, an art historian, excit-

*Following the practice of earlier chapters, the identity of students has been disguised.

ing. Two papers of two pages each were required: one a discussion of some jade pieces, the other an analysis of three characteristic styles of painting. We looked at these papers. The instructor had made a few comments—one noted the worthlessness of xeroxed reproductions of the paintings he had analyzed—and a "P-plus" on the cover of each.

The second of his three fall courses was Astronomy I, a lecture course with a section in which they did small problem sets. Although Santa Cruz students tended to avoid science courses, seldom taking more than the required three, Samual enjoyed them, and this was his fourth. He had skimmed the standard textbook by George Abell, *Exploration of the Universe*. Neither the art nor the astronomy course was rigorous, and he saved his energy for Sheldon Wolin's Philosophy and Politics, which was required for majors like himself.

Samual found Wolin a first-rate scholar and a stimulating teacher, with time to talk with students. There were about twenty students in that class. The course began with a detailed look at Hobbes's *Leviathan* and the questions of authority, representation, and justice. In addition, the reading included Camus's *The Fall*, Seymour Hirsch's *My Lai IV*, and Hannah Arendt's *Between Past and Future*. A slow reader, Samual covered about half the required reading, but felt that most students might have read two-thirds. He believed that the pass/forget system would not hurt his chances of getting into graduate school, and he expected to receive good recommendations. He knew a girl with similar evaluations who had recently entered Harvard Law School.

Our next student came from Andover. Roger had graduated at the top of his class at Andover, but he was less self-confident than Samual, deciding on Santa Cruz after being turned down by Princeton and Harvard. He suspected that they had typed him as an unimaginative grind. Roger worried that he was not intrinsically interested in any topic, but took his enjoyment from any subject in which he got a good grade. At Santa Cruz he began to question his motivation. Although it was his fifth choice, he liked the university; coming here was a great relief. Freshman year without grades and pressure was like "air coming out of a big balloon." Still, he feared letting go and seemed to be talking about himself when describing other students there. They were friendly, but unwilling to make commitments; they wanted a good time and always had the feeling "maybe something will come up." They were unable to overcome the middle-class values they said they abhorred. He felt the average student did less than half the assigned reading, and he feared he wasted his own time. Prep-school friends in Ivy League colleges seemed to work harder and learn more. Recently, he had found little satisfaction in his courses. He could not concentrate. Perhaps he should drop out and work full-time on the construction job he enjoyed the summer before.

Roger wanted a Ph.D. in politics and liked the idea of a professor's life, but he doubted whether he could keep up with the research. Perhaps he should settle for being a high-school teacher. Teachers here should teach you how to organize and analyze things, he insisted; most students wanted more structure. Roger had a high opinion of most Santa Cruz faculty, who were "sometimes not provocative or incisive," but "receptive and interesting." Some college courses, as compared with departmental courses, were a farce, but standards as to what qualified for credit were tightening.

We talked with other students who had struggled with Roger's conflicts and who had found new directions. Matthew had persevered unhappily in mathematics for two years until dropping it in his junior year to be a potter. When we talked with him he was blissfully cramming every studio course into his schedule that he could. He thought the freedom from traditional structures and pressures which elated him discomfited many because it confronted them with the difficult lifetime choices. Some don't choose, but simply drift. Students were friendly and easy-going and "you can depend on them in times of need," but "they don't work hard enough for themselves. They're not pushed to work and they don't."

Peggy's father, a small-town Catholic lawyer, thought she would make a good legal secretary. But she had discovered the excitement of intellectual life in a history seminar she took at a local junior college during high school and had been drawn to Santa Cruz where she could explore the world civilization program at Cowell without the pressures and competition she feared at Berkeley.

Peggy was greatly influenced by Jasper Rose. "I think of him in heroic terms," she said reverently. She decided to major in medieval history, and although her postgraduate plans were unsettled, her parents would support her for one year after graduation. She might like to teach college history, but "teaching seems a very difficult and extreme responsibility." She was uncertain if she wanted to be an authority, but "I may get enough nerve later."

She would like to teach like Jasper Rose, who "doesn't tell people but shows them the way." Rose's course on William Morris, the pre-Raphaelites, and the Industrial Revolution was "magnificent." In addition to the term paper there were two principal requirements: to teach yourself a craft and to produce something. She had taught herself egg tempura and calligraphy. Calligraphy might become her life's work—"it's one of the few things in the world one can be 'perfect' at." Everyone brought four mass-produced objects to the final examination and was asked to judge which was the most beautiful, the ugliest, the most useful, and the most useless. Rose wanted the students to notice, value, and do some things well. Work should be enjoyable and evoke a commitment of one's whole self. Such insights had led Peggy to be less goal- and achievement-oriented. Although she came to Santa Cruz seeking wide exposure to ideas, she no longer pursued that aim. In fact, why was our questionnaire so goal-oriented? "Nobody is interested in that kind of thing anymore."

She was torn between theorizing and enjoyment of community. She and some friends had formed a co-op which built a kitchen in one of the Cowell houses. She was attracted to a former student's plan to start a self-sufficient "college farm" with crops, cows, and vineyards. There students would work and study all year in a real community. On the other hand, one of her most satisfying courses was a student-directed seminar on human freedom in which each of six students pursued a different theorist: Marx, Hannah Arendt, St. Augustine, and Piaget, among others. They met twice a week, chairing the meeting in rotation. The faculty members who formally sponsored the course seldom came.

Even in a portrait gallery as limited as this one, one can see wide variations as well as some commonalities in these generally affluent, intellectually able students who are seeking less competitive forms of life. Though reluctant to take on workloads demanded by many traditional careers, they are hesitant to abandon the material comforts and status their parents have achieved. They share with many of the faculty an ambivalence about the value and costs of the achievement ethic. Santa Cruz encouraged such students to let go, to explore, and to enjoy. It provided a moratorium on grade-grubbing and encouraged them to pursue their undergraduate education as more than a way-station to graduate school—but for some, also less.

Most of the courses that were given at Santa Cruz would be found in regular departments elsewhere, such as history or economics, and many students did prepare for the professions through entry to traditional graduate schools. But at Santa Cruz the study of biochemistry might bring one to independent work with a biochemist on natural dyes for tie-dying. One could obtain a degree as a potter or as a T-group leader. Many programs in the arts did not expect professional levels of performance.[11]

Yet even traditional academic subjects were affected by the Santa Cruz ambience. Page Smith's idea that there should be large mea-

sures of play and delightful exploration in the curriculum took many
shapes, but the most memorable one was invented the first year at
Cowell: the Culture Break. It faded in later years, but it established
a curricular accent that is beautifully captured in a student's description:

> The Culture Break is the most distinctive form of celebration at
> Cowell. In it the fancies, tastes, talents, and imaginations of the
> community are exploited for the benefit of all . . .
> The first break was going to be a surprise. Mary Holmes in her
> full and colorful regalia would ride atop a horse led by Jasper
> Rose, who, along with her, would be tossing flowers hither and
> thither. They would ride into the fieldhouse on a Monday morning
> and proclaim to all the eager faces (awaiting the lecture) to arise!
> arise! and cast off their books . . .
> When the break was formally inaugurated, there were no classes
> for the next two days . . . the faculty presented scenes from *King
> Lear* in the morning, and after lunch there was a debate on
> whether "King Lear's Madness is Heaven's Sense." That evening
> there were buses to Cabrillo College to see *Antigone*. The next
> morning the Stratford, Ontario, film production of *Oedipus Rex*
> was shown. In the afternoon there was a concert, and in the
> evening the debate: "Resolved, that the Greek Way and Zeus'
> Eagles are Preferable to the Safeway and Lyndon's Beagles or
> Resolved, that the Effluence of Greek Sobriety is Preferable to the
> Affluence of the Great Society.[12]

The Culture Break became an institution at Cowell, a time when
the whole community came together to ponder and to play. It was
usually organized around an essential question, embellished with
drama, song, light-hearted outdoor games, pageants, and discussions.
Significantly, the Culture Break was a spontaneous outgrowth of the
Cowell general-education program, its two-year core course in world
civilization. No doubt a community needs to have an intellectual
culture in common before it can rise to the level of pun and the play
of paradox.

There was a vital sense of the colleges as centers of intellectual
community in the early years at Santa Cruz. Most Cowell faculty
members took part in the required two year core-course sequence,
and a physicist, for example, learned about the Han empire along
with the students in his section. Humanities requirements were satisfied by first-year emphasis on history, literature, and philosophy.
Page Smith opened the second year of the course with a lecture on
the American Revolution. He demonstrated loading a musket, fired
it, then passed a bottle of madeira and a box of snuff as the Cowell

Madrigals sang Revolutionary songs. The first quarter of the fifteen-credit course was devoted to American history, and the remaining quarters to the cultures of China, Japan, India, and the Middle East.

Students had themes and short assignments in their seminar sections, but the principal requirement was a comprehensive examination at the end of the first year. The disastrous results were a turning point for the college. A committee of eight seminar leaders, the two lecturers, and the provost graded the 500 students enrolled and failed 114. It is rare to fail more than 2 or 3 percent of the students in an elite college. The experience may have been crucial in setting the limits on "play" and determining that pass/fail was not an empty phrase at Santa Cruz. It is not unusual for an experimental college to establish an image in the first year that anything goes, with the result that serious students often do not subsequently apply. Mindful of this the Cowell faculty upheld their standards. When 63 students retook the exam in July, 42 failed again.

Most of the core courses developed by the Santa Cruz colleges during the founding stage collapsed a few years later. Cowell's was one of the most long-lived. Its world-civilization sequence continued as a core course until it had virtually disappeared by 1974. Stevenson's core course began in 1966 as a year-long requirement for all entering freshmen, but by the mid-seventies it was reduced to one quarter. Crown offered a package of courses under the general theme "Science, Culture, and Man" from which freshmen were encouraged, but not required, to select a seminar. Merrill, the "third-world" college, was the first to emphasize that it had no required courses. The College V core course combined a studio experience in "making art" with a later critical experience in reading, writing, and discussion about art with a scholar. It was the cornerstone of College V's belief that "art, in some appropriate way, can and should be a part of everyone's life." But after a lively run of several years, this course, too, disappeared. Kresge's core course on "Man and His Environment" had an intense life for two years before it disbanded.

Why such lack of longevity? In part Santa Cruz shared in the general revolt against requirements that developed in the late 1960s as both faculty and students sought to do their own thing, and doing things in common became more difficult. A 1972 faculty survey showed that half the Santa Cruz faculty were opposed to required courses.[13] And, as faculties grew more egalitarian, junior members were less willing to subordinate themselves to the leadership that was required to coordinate core-course efforts. Faculty willingness to set aside private agenda in order to work on core enterprises was more likely to occur in the early years of the college's founding when community feelings ran high and identities were forged. As the college expanded, this spirit dissipated.

Another crucial factor in the development of the colleges has been the turnover of the provosts. By 1974, sixteen provosts had been appointed for the first six colleges, with an average tenure of about four years. Only four provosts served more than five years, and these were the founding provosts in the colleges that developed the most ambitious core programs. Three of these four served in the only colleges to develop a college major, that is, to offer a complete upper-division concentration as an alternative to a major in a discipline or department.

Turnover among provosts tends to increase during the years subsequent to the founding stage, when a provost has maximum power and funds to appoint new faculty and establish programs. The position has less appeal in subsequent years when the provost is stuck with the faculty thus acquired. In an analysis of the collegiate structure, Robert Adams and Jacob Michaelson argued that attention to core courses and college programs had suffered because faculty felt (1) general-education issues lay outside their special field of competence; (2) they were not highly rewarded for developing such competence; and (3) if they did so, the skills and knowledge they developed were not very applicable or salable to a shrinking academic market.[14] As economists, Adams and Michaelson suggested altering the reward structure. Under their plan, the colleges would not merely share responsibility for promotion and tenure with the departments, as is currently the case, but would have primary control over promotion for faculty who agreed to teach at least two-fifths of the time in the college.

Many faculty, particularly those associated with the early core-course efforts, assert that the collegiate plan is a "failure" at Santa Cruz and that the boards or departments have won out. Page Smith says that he was the only provost who really had a free hand, since he was able to hire the first faculty and initiate programs at Cowell before the departments were formed. But a few years later, when the boards had grown entrenched, Smith felt outmaneuvered and saw the faculty gradually reforming along disciplinary lines.

In 1974, after a junior faculty member (whose devotion to collegiate ideals Smith admired) was denied tenure, Smith resigned, saying that a university that had no place for such a teacher had no place for him. Others who had devoted themselves to college programs at the expense of scholarship were denied tenure as well, but, on the whole, promotion practices at Santa Cruz have been much softer than those at Berkeley or UCLA.

Those faculty who believe Santa Cruz has gone the way of most departmentalized universities point out that by the mid-seventies about 80 percent of all courses were offered under departmental authority and only 20 percent remained under college sponsorship. Yet formal sponsorship of courses may not be the most relevant indicator. We asked students to list all courses they had taken in the past year and to specify the three courses they had found "most stimulating" since entering Santa Cruz. Analysis showed that 40 percent of the courses taken were taught by faculty within the student's own college—even though they might have been listed under a departmental rubric. Further, slightly more than half the courses in the "most stimulating" category were offered by "within-my-own-college" faculty. Although students may not be following a formally designed "college major," many appear to be constructing their majors from courses given within their own college faculty. Hence the collegiate ideal seems realized in the sense that it provides an intimate setting for intellectual interaction between students and faculty that is distinctively different from that of Berkeley or UCLA. Our data confirm what is evident to anyone who visits classes at Santa Cruz. There are virtually no "classroom" buildings. The locale for most teaching is actually in the college setting, where classrooms, faculty offices, and student apartments are located.

While the core-course sequences have petered out in most colleges, college majors have persevered in Cowell (world civilization), Stevenson (modern society and social thought), and College V (aesthetic studies). Moreover, if our sample survey is correct, many students apparently design a major on the basis of the intellectual interests of the faculty in their own college, although they are formally enrolled in a department.

Most students perceive the colleges at Santa Cruz as distinctively different from one another, and very few wish to transfer to another college within Santa Cruz—although a significant number do move off campus as upperclassmen.* In a survey that drew responses from 1,143 alumni who graduated in the first seven classes (1967–73) at Santa Cruz, Mark Messer found that 71 percent rated affiliation with a college as a significant aspect of their undergraduate experience. Only 25 percent said that it was insignificant, and 36 percent said that such affiliation was very significant.[15]

In general, Santa Cruz alumni have a high opinion of their undergraduate experience and of the quality of teaching. Less than 9 per-

---

*In our survey, 86 percent said "colleges within Santa Cruz are very 'different' from one another," and less than 10 percent wished to transfer to another college on campus.

cent of the alumni said that they would not choose Santa Cruz again (of course an alumni survey excludes the dropouts who left prior to graduation).

When alumni responses are analyzed by college, significant differences in enthusiasms appear. For example, 56 percent of Stevenson and Cowell alumni, but only 30 percent of College V alumni, rated atmosphere in the college as one of the four most important factors.[16]

Table 1	Santa Cruz Alumni Ratings: Percent Mentioning "Atmosphere in the College" as One of the Four Most Important Factors in Their Educational Experience
Cowell	56
Stevenson	56
Crown	48
Merrill	44
College V	30

SOURCE: Messer Survey.
NOTE: Transfer students were excluded.

Messer's survey also supports the view that each college developed a distinctive curricular "personality" and had significantly different effects on student growth. The data in Table 2 shows, for example, that Merrill College's emphasis on "third-world" and crosscultural study is indicated by the disproportionate number of its alumni who claim substantial progress in "awareness of differing cultures, philosophies, and ways of life." College V alumni were twice as likely to report aesthetic growth and significantly more likely to claim that they developed new areas of learning.

Of course, alumni perceptions may be influenced by the claims of the college itself—perhaps the respondents believed the college's advertisements. But the question was not cast in the college context. It asked, "In thinking over *your experience at UCSC*, to what extent do you feel that you made progress or were benefited in each of the following respects while you were an undergraduate?" When the results were analyzed by college, the reported effects emerged.

Table 3 shows that "Atmosphere in the college" is considered nearly as important by alumni as "major program." Since college majors were not offered in all colleges nor intended for most students, it is surprising that as many as 28 percent considered them important.

A strong tradition of excellent teaching was established at Cowell. Nearly two-thirds of its alumni judged its required courses to be very

Table 2	**Santa Cruz Alumni Ratings: Percent Mentioning That They Experienced "Very Much" Growth in Each of the Following Categories**					
	Cowell	Ste-venson	Crown	Merrill	Five	Total Sample
Development of a world view and personal philosophy of life	33	40	32	43	39	36
Broadened literary acquaintance and appreciation	42	24	19	24	21	28
Development of an interest in new fields of learning	32	34	29	36	46	33
Development of general thinking skills	32	31	32	24	9	30
Social Development— Experience and skills in relating to others	36	40	35	30	36	36
Awareness of different cultures, philosophies, and ways of life	30	31	21	39	24	29
Aesthetic sensitivity: appreciation and enjoy-ment of art, music, drama, etc.	33	24	32	24	49	29
Competence in a particular field of learning	19	25	25	25	21	22
Writing and speaking: clear, correct, and effec-tive communication	19	17	11	20	9	16
Development of career plans and skills	11	14	16	12	15	13
Appreciation of religious, moral, and ethical standards	11	15	12	20	15	14
Development of a centered identity and sense of self-confidence	21	23	18	23	19	21
Bases for improved economic status	5	8	5	3	3	5

SOURCE: Messer Survey.
NOTE: Transfer students excluded.

Table 3   **Santa Cruz Alumni Ratings: Percent Mentioning**
That the Following Factors Were Most Important at
the Time They Were Students

Student friendships	72
Pass/fail grading and evaluation of academic work	67
Faculty contact	58
Major program	52
"Atmosphere in the college"	49
Individual study	44
College major	28
Thesis or comprehensive exam	19
Faculty advisors in major	10
Campus-wide required courses	1

SOURCE: Messer Survey.

valuable, whereas seldom did more than one-third of the alumni of
other colleges report that level of excellence. As the colleges aged,
the intensity of the collegiate ethos seemed on the whole to decline;
yet at Cowell it remains fairly high. Stability and quality of administrative leadership also seem relevant. Merrill, the college with the
greatest provost turnover, had the lowest combined ratings on the
quality of college offerings, as shown in Table 4. Undoubtedly,
Cowell's high ratings on several measures reflect not only the charisma of Page Smith, but the college's founding role with the initial
enthusiasms that implies. But Crown, the third college, also ranks
high. Though in many ways Crown is traditional, "square," and
scholarly, the widely admired leadership of the distinguished biologist Kenneth V. Thimann, who served as its provost for the first
seven years, undoubtedly made a difference. While Crown offered
no required core course and established no college major, it became

Table 4   **Santa Cruz Alumni Ratings: Percent Rating the**
Value of Required College Courses

	Very Valuable	Moderately Valuable	Very and Moderate Combined
Cowell	64	24	88
Stevenson	26	48	74
Crown	34	47	81
Merrill	23	44	67
College V	12	33	45

SOURCE: Messer Survey.

known as the home of the most distinguished scientists on the campus and attracted many students who wished to emulate them.

The data gathered by Messer in Table 5 show that although college *esprit* wanes over time, the relative importance of affiliation with a particular college remains at least "moderately significant" for nearly two-thirds of the 1973 graduates in all except College V.

Table 5   Santa Cruz Alumni Ratings: Percent, by College and Year Graduated, Stating That Affiliation with Their College Was "Very Significant"

	Cowell	Stevenson	Crown	Merrill	College V
1969	62				
1970	44	42			
1971	76	58	37		
1972	57	41	43	29	
1973	55	41	39	44	14

SOURCE: Messer Survey.

The ebbing of the college spirit helps to explain the paradox that, while most students have high praise for Santa Cruz, many college-oriented faculty say that it has "failed." This is also confirmed by a steady increase recorded in an academic or disciplinary index for the years 1967–73 and a corresponding decrease in a collegiate index. Messer constructed an index of academic orientation composed of students who (1) graduated with honors; (2) said that their academic major or departmental course was one of four most important factors affecting their undergraduate experience; (3) responded near the top of a seven-point scale on how much academic work mattered to them; and (4) claimed significant growth on general thinking skills.

Students who scored high on the collegiate index were those who (1) said affiliation with a college was a "very significant" part of their over-all undergraduate experience; (2) believed that a college major, a particular college course, or the atmosphere in the college was one of the four most important factors in their undergraduate experiences; and (3) lived on campus in college quarters during their senior year.

One could quarrel with an index that relegates the value of the college plan at Santa Cruz to largely nonacademic factors. Supporters of the collegiate pattern could claim that development of general thinking skills was as much or more an outcome of the college experience as what departments did. Similarly, life in a college could stimulate a student's willingness to try for honors, and the general honors inflation of the late 1960s and early 1970s could artificially influence the academic index in the years reported here. Nonetheless, even with these qualifications in mind, the trends in Table 6 are significant.

Table 6   **Santa Cruz Alumni Ratings: Percent Scoring High on Academic and Collegiate Indexes by College and Year Graduated**

	Percent Scoring High on Academic Index	Percent Scoring High on Collegiate Index
Total sample	31	22
College:		
Cowell	31	40
Stevenson	30	17
Crown	33	22
Merrill	26	17
V	31	13
Year graduated:		
1967–68	27	21
1969	29	24
1970	28	24
1971	34	28
1972	29	21
1973	34	19

SOURCE: Messer Survey.
NOTE: See text for explanation of how collegiate and academic indexes were constructed. Excludes percent scoring medium or low.

III

An astute reader of an earlier draft of this chapter argued that we had been charmed down the primrose path by Jasper Rose and Page Smith, who had actually left Cowell in something of a shambles. He put a hard edge on some of the soft judgments we have made, asserting that Santa Cruz faculty had attracted excellent students with a rare opportunity to make a mark but had "blown it." In his view the graduate program was a "total disaster," tenure decisions had been undistinguished, and Santa Cruz was undergoing a delayed identity crisis now that an educational "fashion" had played itself out. We had made the case for an institution deeply oriented toward students, and had given a fair assessment of their responses. But he

did not believe we had adequately examined another important issue—namely, whether these conditions best served the students' own
long-term interests:

> Can one say that Santa Cruz did this . . . or that the wide diversity
> of educational "experiences" really contributed towards this end?
> My own view is that it left a significant number of students with a
> feeling and reality of powerlessness, that it served to give them
> some resources for withdrawing from the world but very few for
> becoming engaged in it.[17]

Our critic may be right that we took too uncritical a view of Smith
and Rose (and our portrait is purposely lopsided in its emphasis on
Cowell, the first college), but the large question he raises is unanswerable in the short term. We try to consider it in other places in
this book, particularly in Chapters 2 and 10, but the only satisfying
answer is to look at the lives of graduates.

As to the realizations of Santa Cruz's aims, particularly its concern
about establishing a scholarly reputation, we are inclined to think he
asks too much. But his response is a vivid manifestation of the paradox
that, while students are generally pleased with Santa Cruz, faculty
are much more likely to regard it as a failure. Such an observation
is quite consistent with our feeling that Santa Cruz can be seen as a
remarkable success when we recall the intentions of its founders:
(1) to establish a climate of curricular innovation; (2) to develop distinctive collegiate environments; (3) to facilitate renewed emphasis
on teaching; (4) to work toward an enriched student-faculty interaction on a campus that would continue to seem small as it grew large.

In its curricular pluralism, its establishment of colleges with dramatically different architectures and personalities, the enthusiasm of
its students about the quality of teaching and of faculty interaction,
Santa Cruz seems to have actualized its ideals to an extraordinary
degree.

Viewed from the perspective of the relative power of students and
faculty, these reforms greatly strengthened the students' hands. The
traditional powers of a faculty organized in disciplines were significantly weakened, and the demands that students could make of faculty were considerably strengthened. Santa Cruz's founders achieved
what they set out to do: they created a university campus that was
more responsive to students and, through the establishment of college communities, placed more emphasis on the quality of teaching.

What may be most important about Santa Cruz is that it represents a significant innovation in the organizational structure of the
university. By giving faculty dual appointments in both a college and

a department—and by giving each unit a say in hiring, promotion, and tenure—Santa Cruz moderated the pressures toward an orientation exclusively to research and visible scholarly production that exist in a traditional elite university. However, while the intensity was diminished, the norms of research productivity were not virtually eliminated or set aside as they were in many of the experimental efforts of the late 1960s. Peterson's scales seem right in showing that Santa Cruz was the lowest ranked of any of the eight University of California campuses in terms of its research orientation. But when Santa Cruz is compared to sixteen California state colleges (including those in the process of converting to university status like San Francisco), it clearly outranks them. That is, the research norms at Santa Cruz are more intense than those at the best state colleges, yet "softer" than those at any of the university campuses.

In a 1970 Carnegie Commission classification of institutions of higher education based on number of Ph.D.'s awarded, federal support for scientific research, and number of professional programs, Santa Cruz was classified as a liberal-arts college, whereas the university campuses at Berkeley, Davis, Los Angeles, and San Diego were classified as research universities (a category that included the fifty universities leading in terms of federal support). Irvine, Riverside, and Santa Barbara fell in the "doctoral granting universities" category (institutions that awarded forty or more Ph.D.'s in 1970 and received more than $3 million in federal support). Most of the state colleges, now called state universities, were classified as "comprehensive universities and colleges," which meant they had "extremely limited doctoral programs" and offered at least two professional or occupational programs in addition to liberal arts. Santa Cruz was classified among the elite liberal-arts colleges such as Amherst, Carleton, Claremont, Reed, and Swarthmore.[18] This designation was partly a reflection of its youth; it seems likely that Santa Cruz will eventually be classified with doctoral granting universities (although in 1975 it had only 326 graduate students compared with an earlier "low-range" projection of at least 850). Yet the ambiguity does exist and that is the point. Santa Cruz is not Berkeley, but it is not Swarthmore either. It shares some of Berkeley's research orientation and much of Swarthmore's collegiate focus. But a student at Swarthmore would not have the range of collegiate options enjoyed at Santa Cruz nor the access to as distinguished a faculty in the sciences.

While students applaud the shifts in norms at Santa Cruz, many faculty understandably find the ambiguity distressful. Santa Cruz confronts its faculty with a number of fundamental choices about the kind of teachers and scholars they wish to be. Does a new faculty member wish to join the faculty at Kresge, and become a member of a student kin group there, or to go to Crown, where the faculty drink sherry and tea in the common room? Regardless of which college he or she is in, how will he invest his effort, how much time will he spend with students; how much in developing college programs, how much in developing a reputation in his department?

At most traditional universities the norms and reward systems are generally clear: Faculty who can win research grants and publish win promotions.[19] At Santa Cruz, a faculty member like Sheldon Wolin, who wishes to publish frequently, finds the student demands and community expectations in Santa Cruz's collegial environment to be exhausting. Young faculty who devote themselves entirely to the collegial ideal, as they might at teaching-oriented institutions, find that they put their bid for tenure at risk. Some older faculty with tenure who abandon research in favor of devotion to the collegiate ideal are quite happy. Others feel keenly the loss of the esteem of their colleagues or are guilt-ridden because the model they offer is not one that most younger faculty and students can emulate without risk. But some do enjoy a middle ground: they enjoy teaching in a collegiate environment that has such a wide latitude for experimentation, yet they continue to be productive researchers and scholars. But it is not easy to strike the balance between Swarthmore and Berkeley and to satisfy the needs of students, the expectations of colleagues, and the demands of one's own ego in the Santa Cruz setting.

Whereas some faculty thrived on this tension, others left—most of them voluntarily in the years of expanding opportunities in higher education. As faculty markets grew more restricted in the 1970s, there were movements to reduce the ambiguity in norms at Santa Cruz. One faculty proposal urged that the departments be made responsible for introductory courses while the college programs become the primary focus of upper-division studies.[20]

A major self-study recommended strengthening the hand of colleges in recruitment and promotion, devoting new energies to general-education programs, and adopting a get-tough attitude toward some of the soft options and spongy courses. Significantly, the report argued that Santa Cruz should not try to compete with Berkeley, and should accept a more limited role in graduate education.[21]

Another proposal, by John Marcum, the provost of Merrill College, argued that Santa Cruz was "settling into the familiar mold of a departmental campus" and that the faculty was suffering from "cognitive dissonance" over the college-department structure. Marcum proposed that either the academic program should be put fully in the hands of the departments (relegating provosts to the role of deans of students on the Harvard House pattern), or the colleges should be made the principal centers of academic programs (with the provosts having powers analogous to academic deans).[22]

The strength of the departments or "boards" at Santa Cruz was frequently overestimated. One study of sixty faculty who had come up for promotion in the early 1970s showed that thirteen of them were rejected. In six cases there was a disagreement between the department and the college as to whether a faculty member should be promoted. In all six cases, the college's view prevailed.[23] What some faculty may be complaining about is that the colleges don't disagree often enough.

In 1975 a movement to strengthen the colleges—called "reaggregation"—gained some prominence on the campus. Reaggregation was to permit a voluntary movement of faculty from college to college so that they could regroup according to mutual intellectual and academic interests and promote both new research programs and new undergraduate majors. Of 320 faculty at Santa Cruz, 170 responded to questionnaires about possibilities for realignments. In the first round, however, only ten faculty members chose reaggregation and won approval.[24] Resistance came both from those, like the natural scientists, who did not want to upset existing relationships with disciplinary colleagues, and from untenured faculty who had invested heavily in developing programs at a particular college and feared they would "lose credit" by moving. In short, the existing dual structure of departmental and college ties at Santa Cruz seems to have gathered considerable momentum of its own. We suspect that for some time faculty at Santa Cruz will go on complaining about the tensions of the dual structure, arguing about it, and making proposals to change it. We certainly hope they will, since we believe that there is no better evidence that Santa Cruz is living up to its original promise. We can think of few campuses where there is more genuine attention to educational issues, of no university that has achieved a more vibrant pluralism in the forms of intellectual, social, and aesthetic experience for undergraduates.

The Public/Private Dichotomy

Two New Experimental Public Colleges in New Jersey

9

Most of the reforms we designate as "telic" have been carried out in the past in private colleges which have remained small by choice —colleges able to select rather than merely admit their students; in which leaders could seek to infuse their institutions with a radically new spirit, based on a cohesive faith and a willingness on the part of administrators and faculty to work "impossible" hours in order to bring it to life. Moreover, such colleges have had private boards of governors or trustees (often alumni), involved by choice and willing to be educated by a charismatic president and to follow his vision.* Such colleges of an earlier era are familiar to us: Black Mountain, Goddard, Berea, Bennington, and many others. These have had an influence on the telic reforms of today, and even on "traditional" education as well.

Although almost no public institution, whether a comprehensive college, regional university, or a flagship (and often also land-grant) state university, has remained small by choice, efforts at innovation have been made in colleges or subcolleges within such institutions. As we have seen in Part I, an attempt at telic reform was made at

*A dramatic exception can be seen in the case of Alexander Meiklejohn at Amherst College, who could not carry his board with him in his radical reforms in the middle 1920s. That he was able later to build a "telic" experiment as a subcollege of the University of Wisconsin highlights the shift of the locus of experiment from private to public institutions and reminds us that not all boards of trustees of private institutions have been prepared to institute drastic reforms and not all state legislatures are anti-intellectual know-nothings.

one of the Santa Cruz colleges of the University of California system: Kreske provided a setting small enough in scale to seek a unified vision. Mammoth Michigan State University has created several subcolleges, as did its offshoot, Oakland University, when it became independent of MSU. The small Residential College at the University of Michigan embraced many of the popular reforms of the sixties: a high degree of personalism in student-faculty relations; efforts at participatory democracy; nondepartmentalized courses. The newest state University in Michigan is an amalgamation that calls itself the Grand Valley State Colleges; it is comprised of one unit, the College of Arts and Sciences, which has a regular program typical of a comprehensive regional institution, and several smaller experimental spinoffs—Thomas Jefferson College, William James College, and College IV. The University of Minnesota has also developed an experimental college, as has the University of Alabama, with the hope that the experimental modes of its New College would infiltrate the rest of the campus. Attempts to create cluster colleges or "living-learning" units have been made at the University of Massachusetts in Amherst and at the State University of New York in Buffalo. The University of Massachusetts in Boston created a nonresidential College of Public and Community Service (College III) comparable to the private College for Human Services, which aims both to improve access for previously disadvantaged students of all ages and to improve social services in a metropolitan area (College IV has recently been added as still another innovative venture).

Sweeping curricular changes, however, other than the loosening of requirements discussed in Chapter 6, have proved virtually impossible to achieve in major institutions, public or private. The effort at Brown University to pioneer "modes of inquiry" courses for entering students failed because of the intrinsic difficulty of the enterprise, departmental resistance, and the lack of student interest. The Bressler Commission at Princeton sought to establish faculty agreement on what their undergraduates should learn, but no consensus could be reached. A committee of eminent professors at Yale, chaired by Professor Robert Dahl, made a similar attempt to modify the undergraduate curriculum. But at both Princeton and Yale, the departments have held fast. Changes, however, do occur incrementally within departments with the growth of knowledge and with experiments in interdisciplinary teaching which are not paraded as "innovations," but indeed begin, as Thomas Kuhn describes scientific revolutions,[1] in an unheralded way.

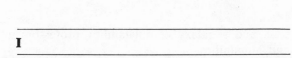

I

In the West, as in the South and most of the Middle West, public higher education had a head start over the private institutions. Flagship campuses enroll students from the entire social spectrum of their state, even though a relatively small number of students will prefer top-flight private universities such as Duke, Rice; Cal Tech, Stanford, and Chicago, or less selective private colleges, for denominational reasons or out of preference for smallness. But in the East, private education, as it came to be known after the middle of the nineteenth century, had such prestige that even when public universities gained a measure of distinction and, because of fiscal limitations, an unavoidable selectivity, most residents still looked first to the leading private institutions and attended the state University only *faute de mieux*.

Once concerned state officials and elites in the mid-Atlantic and northeastern states had decided to develop their systems of public higher education, they naturally looked to California as the pacesetter. Its three-tier system, with the selective multicampus University of California[2]—especially its graduate and professional schools, at the top, its less selective state colleges offering wide variation in quality and inventiveness, and the "open-door" community colleges —was very much in the minds of the planners in New York, for example, who created out of a congeries of diverse institutions the State University of New York.

Indeed, when Nelson Rockefeller became governor of New York, he was prepared to throw the resources of the state behind an effort to overtake California. There were already some nuclei of excellence. Harpur College, which had begun in the immediate post–World War II period to recruit some of the brightest students in the state, became the nucleus of the new State University at Binghamton. The once-private State University of Buffalo, a full-fledged institution of uneven quality but high aspirations, was taken over, and under Rockefeller's aegis, a bond issue of $600 million was floated to build a new campus. Martin Meyerson, who had been acting chancellor at Berkeley, was brought in as president. What had been a teachers college and then a comprehensive college with some graduate programs became the State University of New York at Albany, again with massive infusions of money and a wholly new campus. And in 1957, the fourth university campus was started at Stony Brook on Long Island with instant distinction in the natural sciences and medicine, and a galaxy of outstanding professors in the social sciences and humanities.

But New York was not satisfied to institute massive public-works projects along traditional lines. It would show what it could do in the way of experiment as well: the College at Old Westbury attempted innovation in access, in program, and in governance. Empire State College inaugurated efforts to reach adults who could not come to the campus either as residents or commuters, through packaged modules and home-office mentors patterned after the Open University in the United Kingdom. Going beyond the old-fashioned model of the correspondence school, Empire State College set up learning centers in the major cities of the state, not excluding New York, which permitted students at periodic intervals to sit down with mentors to plan a program toward a degree that validated previous formal and informal learning and served a student body that was almost totally made up of adults.

A variety of efforts were made in other mid-Atlantic and New England states as well to expand access to public education and at the same time to make evident that, even with vastly increasing enrollments, the public sector is still capable of creating enclaves of innovation: that state systems need not be rigid or (in the commonly understood pejorative sense) "bureaucratic." A powerful motivating factor has been the fact that these states are the locale of nationally oriented universities and university colleges which have been inaccessible to many residents without the aptitudes, family backing, and the necessary financial support or self-confidence to seek and to gain admittance. Like many midwestern and southern states, these states also harbor a large number of nonselective private colleges which rarely offer enough financial aid to overcome the public/private tuition differential. Moreover, there has been an overriding populist belief that, rather than subsidize students to attend private institutions, the state should have its own system geared to both quality and equality.

Certainly in no state was the need for improvement in public higher education more evident than in New Jersey. For years, it had exported proportionately more students than any other state, a balance of payments that exists even today. It has traditionally been the happy hunting ground for recruiters from all over. Many of the students it exports, however, have attended unselective colleges in neighboring states.[3] Northern New Jersey, thanks to its commuters from the New York Metropolitan Area and a rich industrial base in pharmaceuticals, oil refining, and manufacturing, is an area of some

wealth and prosperity. The southern tip of the state, however, re-
sembles Appalachia in its poverty, although in ethnic makeup it is
approximately half-Catholic, with clusters of low-income blacks in
Camden, Trenton, and Atlantic City. Attracted toward New York
on the one side and Philadelphia on the other, and with Newark's
comparative lack of recognition as any sort of cultural capital, New
Jersey has had no superabundance of state pride. It has a national
university, Princeton, which has chosen to stay small and which, of
course, can admit only a very small fraction of New Jersey college-
going residents. There is a cluster of private colleges and universities, mainly denominational in origin. In their various ecumenical
leagues some have made valiant efforts to recruit the less advantaged;
none is truly distinguished.

Seeing a vacuum in this situation, an energetic academic entrepreneur, Peter Sammartino, developed the multicampus Fairleigh
Dickinson University after World War II with close to 20,000 students, locating campuses in growing centers of suburban population
(as well as in England and the Caribbean), and laying on programs
in business management and other vocational areas in response to
what seemed to be increasing student demands. But the university
could provide only limited financial aid.

At the end of World War II, New Jersey possessed a network of
six state colleges, as well as the Newark College of Engineering, now
renamed the New Jersey Institute of Technology, which had both
city and state support. All were principally devoted to preparing
elementary-school teachers; Montclair State College had a somewhat
higher status, drawing on the wealthier New Jersey suburbs and preparing teachers for the secondary schools. Rutgers College was
founded as a private institution in colonial times; its companion,
Douglass College, was founded in 1918. Though Rutgers was finally
designated as the State University in 1956, the two colleges remained
highly selective in terms of test scores, as did the later addition—
Cook College—which included the land-grant parts of the New
Brunswick campus. The reach of Rutgers was expanded by the addition of the Law School, once independent, the Business School, a
liberal-arts branch campus (all located in Newark), and a medical
school, which later became part of the separate New Jersey College
of Medicine. The Rutgers network also embraced the Camden College of Arts and Sciences, a commuter college set up for women
sixty years ago, and a branch of University College (with evening
and adult-education programs), in Paterson.

The state colleges were under the control of the State Department
of Education in Trenton, headed by Commissioner Frederick Rau-

binger, whose orientation was toward the public schools and the state colleges which trained many of their teachers. When it became apparent in the post-Sputnik era, however, that the state needed multipurpose colleges with wider missions than teacher training, a concerned group of citizens took it upon themselves to form a committee and study the matter. With Henry Chauncey the moving spirit behind this effort, Governor Hughes appointed President Robert Goheen of Princeton University to be chairman of a Citizen's Committee, which also included innovative-minded Edward Booher, president of McGraw-Hill, Helen Stevenson Meyner (now a congresswoman), as well as a number of other civic leaders. This group increased its number to 100 and in December 1965 delivered the report of its study. Entitled *A Call to Action*, the report became part of a campaign to create a new Department of Higher Education.

In a way, what occurred was a form of covert class warfare between more or less patrician graduates of private institutions of higher education and the New Jersey Educational Association, which fostered unionization of the state colleges and also represented the schoolteachers. Some faculty and administrators at Montclair State, Trenton State, and other colleges shared these aspirations for improvement and upgrading. Thus, the six teacher-training institutions were to be transformed and reorganized in New Jersey's effort to catch up with the rest of the country and to offer more diversified opportunities to its own residents.[4]

At first no new colleges had been on the agenda. But pressure for a new college in the northern area soon came from Bergen County, with its expanding suburbs and exurbs, the largest county in the state with no four-year public college. In the midst of much political dealing, it became obvious that this would be considered only if the influential politicians from the southern part of the state, headed by the former State Senator "Hap" Farley from Atlantic County, could also acquire a college in one of the southern shore counties.

By this time, Raubinger had resigned to take a position elsewhere. Somewhat later, Ralph Dungan, who had been an associate of President Kennedy and was President Johnson's ambassador to Chile, was recruited as the first chancellor of the newly constituted Board of Higher Education, which included some of the founding group as well as representatives of diverse political, regional, and ethnic factions within the state.

If the legislative aim had been to provide additional accommodation for the less affluent students, older people, and those often working part- or full-time, this could have been accomplished by further expansion of the existing public institutions* and by locating a new college in Monmouth County, which was rapidly becoming a bedroom community for New York. Actually, however, the New Jersey State Colleges, except for Jersey City State, were tempted to move away from inner-city locations, and in several cases to shed their former names (dropping the nomenclature of the old-style institutions following the example of the two new colleges). Thus Newark State in Union became Kean College of New Jersey; Paterson State moved to North Haledon and became William Paterson College of New Jersey. To be sure, an urban focus would seem an imperative need, but this need is not necessarily met by an urban location.

In 1968 a bond issue authorized the establishment of the two new colleges. The Higher Education Act of 1966 permitted each of these state colleges to have its own local board to be appointed by the governor on the recommendation of the Board of Higher Education, and delegated to these boards the selection of presidents and many of the details of site and curricular planning.

In the initial planning the two colleges were called Northern New Jersey State College and Southern New Jersey State College.[5] It was clear that Richard E. Bjork would become president of one of them. Bjork was a forceful and energetic person who had been dean of Plattsburgh State College, part of the SUNY system, and an administrator at Rochester Institute of Technology. He had grown up in Astoria, Oregon, had gone to Yale on a scholarship, and had taken a doctorate in political science at Michigan State University under Edward Weidner. He had originally been interviewed by Ralph Dungan, chairman of the Department of Higher Education, in an effort to find a president for Trenton State College; while the Trenton State trustees vacillated, Bjork decided to take another job. Dungan, however, who had been impressed by his managerial abilities, then decided to bring him to the state as vice-chancellor of the state system and also for a year as acting president of Glassboro State College.

When George Potter was chosen as president of the northern college, Bjork at about the same time was made president of the southern one. It is interesting to consider the possible difference it

---

*Livingston College, an experimenting college of Rutgers University, opened on the New Brunswick campus in 1969 under Dean Ernest Lynton. It instituted overlapping, and in practice conflicting, popular reforms: powerful commitment to a multiracial institution; a "do your own thing" curriculum which would, save at the graduate university-wide level, not be heavily departmentalized; and a commitment to participatory democracy. Livingston suffered many of the vicissitudes of Old Westbury, antagonized an increasingly conservative legislature, exhausted its faculty with multiple tasks.

might have made had those original geographical names remained. When Bjork attended his first meeting with the board of trustees, which was made up mainly of New Jersey business people, including a newspaper publisher, and a woman active in civic affairs in Vineland County, he fought fiercely against such a regional label, for his aim was to create a college which would draw students from the entire state and which, by having a distinctive name, would establish the fact that it was to be different from the old-style state college. He was delighted when a high-school student from Lawrence County resurrected the name of Richard Stockton, a signer of the Declaration of Independence, and a resident of Princeton, whose mansion, Morven, is now the Governor's Mansion; Bjork fought to call the new college Richard Stockton State College—and succeeded.

After a site had finally been found for the northern college, the board of trustees met with President Potter to discuss what it should be called, and there was mutual determination to choose a name that would not even include the term "state college." The name chosen was Ramapo College of New Jersey, since the estate that had been purchased was on Ramapo Valley Road, which leads toward the Ramapo Mountains.

Neither the Board of Higher Education nor the officials in the Department of Higher Education headed by Ralph Dungan seemed to have had any particular vision for the two new colleges, except for the over-all mandate that they not be restricted to the education of teachers. Beyond that, Ralph Dungan and his associate, Mary Fairbanks, hoped that the two new colleges would set a model for the others already in existence. Dungan, however, despite his respect for his former associate, President Bjork, became inevitably preoccupied with the intricate problems of Rutgers, and those at Ramapo and Stockton felt that there was little concern at Trenton for their unique sense of mission. They did get extra start-up funds, concessions based in part on size, but neither Potter nor Bjork believed there were adequate funding formulas for the new colleges, which have remained at less than optimal size economically and have suffered as inflation has lowered the value of the original bond issues. Nevertheless, both presidents went ahead with their ambitious plans, feeling their own boards of trustees would support them in their desire to create institutions of distinction. Both wanted interesting and innovative programs, such as were being attempted in many new colleges over the country. Just as in the design of the buildings, they sought to get the best architects, using the ideas and materials of the times, so also they sought the best faculty available (most of them young) whose ideas and training made them lean toward new forms of teaching and toward freedom in planning their programs.

Although both colleges began by attracting students statewide and, especially at Ramapo, from all social classes, the hope of the presidents and many initial faculty of gaining national visibility seems, in retrospect, to have been unrealistic. In a state which had one of the lowest per capita expenditures on higher education in the nation (along with Massachusetts), and with the large demands made by the expansion of public higher education throughout the state, financial resources were simply not forthcoming. But if aspirations had not been so high to begin with, the institutions would not have become as notable and interesting as they are today.*

II

Though George Potter came from Oxford, he was no typical don. He had started off at Loughborough College, then had gone to Oxford and become involved in the Workers Education Movement, which was dedicated to the expectation that, although its students would remain workers, they were entitled to the same kind of cultivated literacy as the best of university-educated Englishmen. The Great Books movement in the last century had been linked to the British Worker Education Movement; indeed one of the first lists of books used by John Erskine in his famous Columbia program had been partly adopted from the WEA. Scott Buchanan was himself part of a similar kind of workers' movement at the Peoples Institute in Lower Manhattan and was aware of the links to the British program.

But it was not Potter's work in the United Kingdom, which he had left to come to the University of Alberta, so much as his tenure as vice-president and role in the development of the Grand Valley State Colleges in Michigan, which qualified him for the Ramapo presi-

---

*The two colleges have achieved different sorts of visibility outside the state. Since Ramapo is within commuting range of New York City, where 30 percent of its faculty reside, and since George Potter writes and speaks tirelessly about the college and its experimental aims, and does so effectively, Ramapo figures in educational circles as one of the more innovative colleges in its area. President Bjork of Stockton is active in the American Association of State Colleges and Universities (that group of some 300 comprehensive colleges and regional state universities which Alden Dunham termed "the Colleges of the Forgotten Americans"), and is well known in the league of state college presidents for his forcefulness and his unusually wide knowledge of trends in contemporary higher education.

dency. Thus, Potter appealed to the trustees as someone possessing the academic and intellectual distinction of Oxford—with evident decency and a comfortably "non-U" British accent—combined with impressive experience as a North American administrator.

Potter's first problem was to decide, along with the trustees, where the college should be located. Some members of the board had in mind a college that would reflect their cultural concerns and be an asset to the wealthy Bergen County communities. However, Ralph Dungan and some members of the Board of Higher Education wanted it to have a minority and urban orientation. Except for small pockets adjoining the Hudson River, however, Bergen County's population is not urban; its zoning and its expensive real estate imply the relative absence of inner-city problems. While Potter could appreciate these concerns and, as we shall see, sought to respond to them by special efforts to recruit disadvantaged minority students, he was particularly interested in locating the college in an accessible and attractive place, with surrounding open space and beauty that would add something to the intellectual life and high academic quality he dreamed of. There were definite conflicts among the members of the board of trustees on this matter. Though Mrs. Florence Thomases, one of the trustees and currently chairman of the board, an upper-middle-class, well-to-do resident of Englewood, with great concern for the fate of nonwhite students, insisted that the college be located in Hackensack, the mayor did not in fact want to surrender potential taxable properties to an academic institution; nor did he believe that his decaying downtown could be uplifted by the parking and other problems that would be created by the building of a new state college. Actually, Hackensack, while having a large working-class population, has a small black population. On the other hand, many blacks feared that a college in Hackensack might draw only blacks from neighboring towns and would thus in fact be segregated.*

Sites were looked at on the Meadowlands, near Paramus, and at other places mainly marked by throughways and hence cut off from ready access—but such sites would have required ground fill and endless delays in starting construction. So, too, a number of places

---

*A similar issue arose when it was decided to expand and hence relocate the State University of New York at Buffalo. When Martin Meyerson became president, he was attracted by the notion of a waterfront location which would be accessible to Buffalo's minorities. This would have required reversal of plans underway to build a new campus in suburban Amherst. A number of blacks said to Meyerson that they preferred a "real college" in the suburbs to one in the ghetto; after all, they were familiar enough with the ghetto. As already noted, the university ended up in Amherst.

(such as Upper Saddle River) were looked at on the northern edge
of New Jersey at the New York State border, near where the college now sits. Much of this is estate country, and some residents
strongly objected, pointing out that the roads were too narrow, the
facilities too limited. But the well-to-do exurbanites where Ramapo
finally was located realized that a housing project would be even less
welcome. Thus the struggle over zoning turned out to be minimal
—they knew that if they got the college the housing project would
probably have to be located elsewhere: the college might even turn
out to be an asset.

Potter and the board recruited the distinguished firm of architectural planners, Sasaki, Dawson and DeMay of Watertown, Massachusetts, who associated themselves with a New Jersey firm and
hunted all over northern New Jersey for locations. Meanwhile, Potter took an office in Hackensack, realizing the immense importance
of actually opening the college at a new site by the fall of 1971.
Hence, beginning in 1969, even though a definite site had not yet
been chosen, plans went ahead on the design of buildings on the
so-called fast-track model, allowing the construction to proceed
rapidly. While matters were at an impasse as to a variety of not
wholly satisfactory sites, each involving problems of land assembly,
clearance, and potential litigation, the owner of an estate died who
had already been negotiating with the college to sell part of his tract;
and eventually, after many further delays caused by haggling over
price with the Trenton authorities and over zoning with the local
authorities, this estate, with a mansion suitable for the administration building, and an old attractive house for the president across
the road from the college, was finally acquired. Though a concession
was made to Mrs. Thomases that a center would be created in Hackensack with commuter buses running back and forth, funds never
became available and the Hackensack center or extension did not
materialize.

If Potter had been a more anxious person, a touch of madness
might well have set in during this period. A myriad of complexities
had to be handled through a number of agencies in Trenton. But
once the site was acquired, the building plans were ready. The architects did the miraculous, and the buildings were up and ready to
receive an expected 800 students (1,200 actually enrolled), a year
after construction started, that is, for the opening of the fall term
in 1971.

From the south, one can approach Ramapo College from Route 17,
which is one of those depressingly American four-lane roads, un-

evenly lined by neon-lit restaurants, gas stations, speculatively held
vacant lots, and auto dealers; or via Interstate 202 which passes the
college's property to the west; or via the New York State Thruway,
since Mahwah is just by the border at the very northern tip of New
Jersey. On one side, the college is only a short distance from a large
Ford automobile assembly plant at Mahwah, to which the working-
class population commutes from all over New York and New Jersey.
On the other side, the Ramapo Valley Road leads out toward the
Ramapo Mountains and the estate country, rolling and beautiful.
Set in woods and for the most part out of sight of the Valley Road,
the college's buildings have met with little objection from the residents of the area; in its own particular way it "belongs" on Ramapo
Valley Road, not on Route 17. The rambling mansion on the estate
is unchanged except for some remodeling inside to make offices for
the administration. The elegant York Room is left as it was, and is
used for informal lectures, discussions, and social events. The ultra-
modern rectangular steel and glass buildings in back seem almost
camouflaged by the mirrored reflection of the woods and sky in the
huge surfaces of one-way glass. In themselves, the buildings are not
so interesting, but in the setting with the trees and garden with walks
and sculpture, the entire effect is stunning. There is much that is
designed to be functional: the whole campus is "barrier free";[6] the
interiors of the buildings are functional in that the walls are movable
and room sizes and shapes can be changed around for various needs.
However, one discerning faculty member commented that the buildings are like the college itself: they seem more functional and appropriate than they are in practice: no windows can be opened; the
outside rooms are too bright; the inside rooms are too dark; and
though supposed to be soundproof, the buildings are noisy; there is
not enough space, no place for "workshops," and no "people pockets" (a phrase employed in describing the plans for the University
of Wisconsin-Green Bay). Space problems, of course, are related to
the square-foot-per-student assessment based on the state government formula which, for a college with these aspirations, is not
adequate.

In fact, Ramapo is still cramped for space, even though its student
enrollment has declined slightly from a plateau of some 3,500 FTE
(full time equivalent) students (head count of 5,000); President
Potter believes that economies of scale can only be reached at an
enrollment of 5,000 FTE. Ramapo's original plan had been to give
each of the "schools" into which it is divided its separate quarters,
within which faculty and students in the school could create a "shop,"

a kind of working space. Ramapo houses 1,000 students on campus, but not as many as it or they would like; a few reside in the nearby motels, or rent houses or rooms in towns in the area. Moreover, the hope Potter originally had of building faculty housing has never materialized.* In the *Self-Study Report* completed in 1975 (under the leadership of Fredrick Waring, director of institutional research) in preparation for the accreditation visit of the Middle States Association, the School of Environmental Studies, for example, declares that it lacks any permanent quarters which could serve as places for faculty and students to form the kinds of ties implicit in the Ramapo plan of school "citizenry." Similarly, the School of Contemporary Arts has lacked sufficient space for theater and studio work, though the new library building will free space now occupied which can be used for these purposes.

In spite of these drawbacks, the general effect of the campus is attractive and spacious. This attractiveness, as well as the style of the faculty, have helped make it possible for the college to bring a number of exurbanite residents of the region to many of its cultural, artistic, and academic programs. Adults are enrolled both in the regular academic courses and in the Saturday College, an adult-education program that has drawn in people from the surrounding area. A group called "Friends of Ramapo" has been developed to support cultural and artistic activities at the college; its members are invited to concert series, poetry readings, and dramatic productions. And they are also to be found at some events in the "Master Lecture Series," which are presumably organized around a particular topic by one of the schools but in actual fact are usually prepared by a single faculty member; the programs often have an appeal, to use old-fashioned terminology, to highbrows, or middlebrows, or both within the college community. Some of these lectures are reminiscent of the offerings at the New School for Social Research in New York in their range and relative sophistication. In the first year, the programs were devoted to a study of the mass media, for which the metropolitan area supplied a ready availability of talent; in the spring

---

*At the time of our first visit, only a single faculty member, to our knowledge, had bought a home in the vicinity of the college. Besides the one-third of the faculty who continue to reside in New York City (some of them are in the arts, where Manhattan is "where it's at"), another one-fifth or so reside elsewhere in New York, as far up the river as Hastings. Only about 20 percent reside in Bergen County itself, where real estate is generally big and expensive. To create any kind of faculty community—in the sense in which Kresge College sought to create a community—is therefore out of the question.

of 1977, to give another perhaps quite atypical* illustration, the series was to be devoted to "Being and Consciousness," with lectures jointly coordinated by faculty members from Teacher Education, Metropolitan and Community Studies, and American Studies.

When Potter described the plan of organization of the college to his board, some members were astonished, even shocked. They had expected a traditional academic program. Instead, Potter sought a curriculum which would be "interdisciplinary and nondepartmental." His wish for a nondepartmentalized college reflected, not the constraints experienced by the contemporary American graduate student, but rather his British background (he does not have the Ph.D. which in the United Kingdom even now matters much less than in the United States). He cared about individuated instruction in the liberal arts. And he wanted to give students a wide latitude in choosing among the schools into which the college would be divided. It does not seem too far-fetched to compare this approach to the spirit of the dons who rule the Oxbridge Colleges, at least in the humanities, even to this day, where the don or tutor is responsible to students on an individual, collegiate basis, rather than as a member of a university-wide academic department.

Thus, the college was to be divided into schools (somewhat on the model of the University of Sussex), each of which would include faculty from more than a single disciplinary background, though they would retain their disciplinary titles and (as in any case the collective-bargaining contract would have required) the standard academic ranks. Typically, the range of disciplines represented within any particular school is very wide. The original School of Human Environment included faculty trained in the natural sciences, the social sciences, and also the humanities; growing rapidly beyond the 600 or so students thought manageable in terms of Ramapo's concept of

*Perhaps more typical is the Master Lecture Series for the fall of 1976 on the subject "Politics of Higher Education: Access and Economics." The lecturers included such guests as William Birenbaum, Florence Howe, Elizabeth McCormack (the innovative former president of Manhattanville College), Franklyn Jenifer, a black professor of biology at Livingston College, chairman of the Rutgers University Senate, and a man deeply concerned with equal opportunity. Indeed, Fred Wilkes, formerly director of field and community services and assistant to President Potter at the very start of Ramapo, much concerned with the Educational Opportunity Fund program and now its state executive director, was another guest, as were Stanley Aronowitz, Leon Botstein, and George Potter. Ramapo belongs among the experimenting colleges which continue to take an interest in higher education, though at most institutions this is no longer a common subject for discourse as it had earlier been in the era of protest.

school citizenship, it has since been subdivided several times. The School of American Studies embraces not only people trained in American history and literature, but also economists, philosophers, political scientists, and sociologists. Another kind of mixture brought together both young people holding their first teaching job and practitioners, such as a labor organizer from the School of Social Relations, or a polymer chemist from industry now in the School of Theoretical and Applied Sciences.

Since its opening in the fall of 1971, Ramapo has modified its structure as a cluster of liberal-arts schools in a number of ways. Today there is a greater emphasis on disciplinary majors or tracks. This is partly a reflection of the growth and size of the college, and hence, unevenly, of the schools; partly it reflects, too, a willingness, within limits, to create undergraduate preprofessional curricula. A student entering Ramapo is asked to choose one of the seven inter-disciplinary schools, in which he must complete 32 (out of a total of 120) credits in all-college requirements, including a sequence of tu-torials, Scope and Methods (which is a major or track, within a school), and a Senior Seminar. A major may itself be interdiscipli-nary, as in the case of Intercultural Studies, or Metropolitan Studies. A concentration in Science in Cultural Perspective, for example, might include History and Philosophy of Science, the Sociology of Medicine, and problems of ethics and values in the application of science. (Such a student can also take a Master Lecture Course for two credits, which often offers interdisciplinary subjects, for example, "Science and Society: New Perspectives.")[7] Options for what Ram-apo calls co-majors also exist. Thus, if a student in the School of American Studies wants to major in folklore with a co-major in music, such a program can be arranged.

Most students, however, enter Ramapo hoping to pursue a plan of study which will satisfy them and, if need be, their parents, as to its value in terms of an entry-level job.[8] A larger number of students seek a program in business administration than in any other field, but until just now the faculty has resisted the temptation to establish a business degree. Instead, students have been required to take their major in one of the schools and then do their business co-major within the Division of Professional Institutes; in accounting, market-ing, data processing, business law, or similar offerings. In fact, in 1976–77, 850 students have been following this track. Many of the Ramapo faculty share the widespread academic belief that business subjects cannot be taught in a "liberal-arts way"—which at Ramapo, in rhetoric if not in reality, means an interdisciplinary way. (We shall say more about this conflict at the end of the chapter.) Business is also looked down upon as unduly preprofessional, but in fact many Ramapo students pursue such majors. They can receive a B.S. in chemistry (eight credits are required) in the School of Theoretical and Applied Science; they can get a B.S. in instrumentation science in the School of Theoretical and Applied Science; they can pursue economics or history in four schools; sociology and political science in five. In the School of Contemporary Arts, students doing the fine-arts major can concentrate in visual arts, theater, or music, with 46 credits in one of the three, and 14 divided between the other two areas. For students hoping to work as musicians and artists, teachers, or perhaps in advertising, these would be "preprofessional" options. Indeed, there is a Division of Teacher Education and Physical Education which provides enough credit hours and prescribed work, including internships, in teacher education to allow certification— once, of course, the staple of the New Jersey State Colleges, and now a waning asset. In the School of Metropolitan and Community Studies, there are opportunities offered for internships in various agencies which could be seen as preprofessional opportunities. Plainly, the schools differ in the degree to which they are geared to prepare the students for postbaccalaureate employment. The School of Theoretical and Applied Science, considered one of the best schools of science in the state college system, takes with great seriousness not only the career problems of faculty, but also those of students, with the result that many faculty in other schools look down on it as a trade school.

Perhaps the most uncompromisingly liberal-arts oriented of any of the schools has been the School of Intercultural Studies, whose first director was Flavia Alaya.* This school attempts to relate students not only to contemporary Western cultures and literatures but to the past as well: for example it has courses on prehistoric Greek archaeology, on the life of Renaissance Europe, on the Islamic worlds. In the contemporary fields there are, for example, courses on "The Art and Thought of Jean-Paul Sartre" and "The Novel within the Novel," in which *Don Quixote*, *Tristram Shandy*, and *Swann's Way* are found on the reading list, and in which the practical problems of the writing of novels are treated within the novels themselves. It is not surprising that such courses do not have the heaviest registration but they provide a haven for faculty and attract some of the most capable students. The course on the novel attracted 13 students last year.

*Dr. Alaya won a Guggenheim Fellowship for studies in comparative literature in 1974–75—the only person, so far as we know, from any of the New Jersey state colleges to receive this distinguished award.

However, the school declares in the catalogue that career opportunities are open in many areas of government, business, and the human services "which increasingly demand the cultural sensitivity and global awareness fostered by the School."[9]

In the original design, there were to be "tutorials" for freshmen, who, with a relatively small number of transfers, were at the outset the only students. In the present design, tutors meet with each student individually for discussion and advising on academic and non-academic problems and then join the tutor's group of 15 to 20 students once a week for general discussion. In a student's first year it is the tutorial that aids him in his orientation to the college, and in program and career planning. The second- and third-year tutorials are devoted to some topic or topics mutually selected by student and tutor which may involve reading and research with seminar-type discussions. These vary enormously, according to the professor's devotion and the care taken in planning a structured sequence—but such variability, of course, is found throughout academia. In one freshman tutorial we visited in the spring of the first year much time had been spent in deciding what to discuss—a common enough situation with faculty who hesitate to exercise authority—and the students had settled finally on a book on adolescence by George Goethals and Dennis Klos;[10] students were permitted to draw on personal experience as a way of responding to the text. The class was engrossing for some, a waste of time for others—in any case, a taxing enterprise which, because of its unstructured nature, demands greater vigilance and greater talent than are common in academic life. Partly for this reason, perhaps, it has been recently decided that tutorials in the junior and senior years should be dropped. Part of the work of the tutorial, now supplemented by the Learning Center, is to give students special assistance where their deficiencies are most serious— and this demanding task, too, is performed with great unevenness. Although the college ranks with Montclair State in having the highest median test scores of any college in the state system,* the students span nearly the entire range from above 600 to below 400 on the SATs, and there is an equally wide divergence of affective motivations and abilities.

---

*Stockton has perhaps one-quarter of its student body with SAT scores of 550 or above—scores higher than those to be found in most private colleges. But both Stockton and Ramapo have students who go down on the SAT scale as low as 300. It is interesting that the great majority of the low-scoring students are white—in 1975–76 at Stockton, 18 percent of students had SAT scores of 400 and under.

Indeed, some students arrive at their senior year through "social promotion"—as they do at many high schools—without knowing how to read a text or write a coherent essay.* However, since the tutorial program was not originally designed to teach basic skills, nor is this now its principal function, the Learning Center has been set up as the explicit locale where students can acquire the basic literacy, capacity for self-expression, and other skills which most of the faculty would have attained well before reaching the tenth grade. Few if any of the faculty are prepared for the sheer labor and one-to-one mutual frustrations they are likely to encounter if they take seriously the obligation of seeing to it that students become able to read a complicated text, write a coherent essay, and acquire minimal quantitative ability.[11]

Interdisciplinary courses are very important at Ramapo. They exist throughout the structure, and are usually team-taught: in the freshman program, in Scope and Methods, and in the Senior Seminars, which are supposed to crown a student's work and which ideally are given by two faculty members to a group of fifteen students. Some faculty have found team teaching to be very rewarding; they learn from each other and find that they can be more creative than when teaching alone. The team-teaching approach has sometimes presented difficulties, however. The faculty have not been prepared to work in colleagueship, and if they are young and inexperienced and have not themselves arrived at any interdisciplinary focus, they can rarely take the time and effort—with their heavy teaching loads and many committee meetings—for the joint preparation that a genuinely interdisciplinary Senior Seminar would require. Of the 37 seminars offered in the fall of 1976, only 13 were team-taught. Though the titles sound very interesting, a number seem too avant-garde, too ambitious, or too specialized perhaps for the majority of Ramapo students. Students can choose their seminars, but they cannot always get into one of their choice. A small group of fifteen students will usually consist of some who are not really interested in the subject, but are simply there as captives. Even if a course is not team-taught, the interdisciplinary model remains, though in the opinion of some faculty members, such courses may not in fact be as creative and interesting as they are reputed to be. Their success depends on who is teaching, how firmly the person is established in a particular field,

---

*Leo McLaughlin was asked recently to become director of the tutorial program and to see what could be done to improve it—a step noted with approval by the report of the Middle States Association evaluation team in October 1975.

and how well he is able to go beyond it. Interdisciplinary teaching can be used by poorly trained people to cover up weakness. Indeed, "interdisciplinary" has been criticized by some as simply a catchword, often meaningless.

In some places, though perhaps not at Ramapo, faculty in team-taught interdisciplinary courses are often tempted to talk to each other, leaving the students far behind, especially those without adequate vocabulary or historical knowledge. Another problem, of course, is the expense of assigning two or three faculty members to a somewhat rarefied interdisciplinary course that attracts only a small number of students.

George Potter, his assistants, and other planners appear to have begun with the assumption that Ramapo would indeed draw a diverse student body, and that if they recruited a lively, diverse faculty and then encouraged them to form themselves into schools, appropriate matching of students and faculty in such a setting would occur. One of the conclusions we have drawn from looking at colleges which have sought to be pedagogically innovative is that it is just such colleges that are most in need of ceaselessly vigilant leadership: laissez-faire is not suitable for them. In this case, for example, to recruit psychologists or anthropologists, political scientists or historians, on the basis of a particular school's internal planning has undoubted advantages; it puts together potentially interesting mixes. But there is the serious drawback of only limited over-all coordination, when what is needed is a great deal, in order to see for instance that, within a particular discipline, various subdisciplines are represented, or to see that faculty are teaching above all basic and necessary subjects, and that students are provided with a sense of the college-wide opportunities in their particular discipline. Yet, having said this, we must also recognize that the spirited faculty recruited to Ramapo, like faculty elsewhere, would almost certainly have resisted tight over-all direction and quality control of scholarship and practice. Such tasks of leadership, of course, are made no easier by faculty unionization or by the budgetary controls and financial exigencies that are a particular peril to new colleges just getting under way. Nevertheless, there is a need at Ramapo for tightening up, both in terms of school policies and student trajectories, which the president, academic vice-president, and many faculty are beginning to recognize.

The schools, while providing a structure and an enclave for students and faculty, also can create problems of too much independence and even isolation. In fact, they facilitate the development of intraschool networks of pedagogically or politically homogeneous groups with orientations in a particular and sometimes too narrow sense. For example, a group of psychologists who labeled themselves as humanistic, in opposition to what they saw as the behavioristic or mechanistic tendencies prevailing in psychology at other institutions, formed a nucleus within the School of Metropolitan and Community Studies and attracted a much larger number of students than did even the urban and community-studies courses themselves. Yet, when some of their psychology majors decided to apply to graduate school in, for example, clinical psychology, they realized that they had in effect been isolated in a corner of an enormous field and lacked the kind of grasp of the discipline that would win them admission to highly competitive APA-approved programs. In other words, students limited by offerings in their own school and not well advised by faculty about courses in their discipline in other schools, found themselves in serious trouble. Thus it was that in 1973 distribution requirements in psychology were initiated. Similarly, what is now the School of Social Relations began within the School of Human Environment as a politically radical enclave concerned, as the Academic Information Bulletin for 1975–76 puts it, with "an interdisciplinary approach to a critical analysis of modern societies . . . : what are the prevailing social divisions within these societies based on class, race, and sex, . . . how do these divisions grow out of and reinforce existing ideological, political and economic structure, . . . and how do individual and group consciousness develop and under what conditions are they transformed? Throughout this analysis the goal is, in part, to find concrete strategies and alternatives for social change."

Many Ramapo faculty members themselves, not to speak of the local community, regarded such concerns as radical. The fear of allowing the School of Social Relations to become something of an ideological hothouse had led the president and vice-president to be hesitant about its creation in the first place. When it was finally agreed that the would-be School of Social Relations would have to meet college-wide criteria of scholarship within three years, and would also have to approach a minimum of 300 "citizens," the desired "critical mass," a wide variety of students showed up and provided the School with a claim for full establishment. The radical critiques of society, of "the system," promulgated by members of the school, held an appeal for some of the black students who found themselves in a predominantly white suburban setting; these radical critiques were congruent with the prevailing cynicism in the society at large, which hunts for villains in a quasi-capitalist order (as Joseph Schumpeter many years ago predicted) when that order begins to lose legitimacy even—and especially—among its beneficiaries.[12]

With both President Potter and Vice-President Cassidy objecting to the creation of the School for Social Relations, the board of trustees first voted by divided majority to support the view of the administrators. But after a group of faculty and students had called for another vote and had themselves shared in the stormy meeting, there were enough strong advocates who favored the creation of the school to get the board to reverse itself. Earlier, when the matter had come up before the faculty of the college as a whole, only one individual had openly opposed the setting up of the school, which he regarded as unscholarly and as catering to short-sighted desires for "relevance." Though other faculty were also unhappy at the situation, the decentralized structure made it possible for them to disregard this new school and confine their concerns to their own professional and political arenas. This sort of situation is not only to be found at Ramapo, of course. Such programs may get by, and in the end students whose principal need is for more disciplined, basic studies may actually be shortchanged (however highly motivated), for they rarely acquire the critical and scholarly background that many radical faculty themselves possess.

Potter never lost sight of his aim of recruiting faculty of the highest possible caliber. With Robert Cassidy he made an effort to take advantage of the pool of available faculty and graduate students in the New York Metropolitan area as well as to recruit nationally. In the present faculty roster, there are by rough count twenty faculty members (not including four from Teachers College) either with terminal degrees or master's degrees from Columbia University; twelve from different branches of the City University of New York, mainly CCNY; three from Fordham; one from SUNY Stony Brook; five from Brooklyn Polytechnic Institute; one from Yeshiva. Others came from within New Jersey itself: Rutgers is much the largest source, with fourteen by our count holding terminal or master's degrees from that institution; two from Fairleigh Dickinson University; two from Seton Hall; one from Princeton. (Only in the Learning Skills Center have any recruits come from other New Jersey state colleges, with one from Jersey City State, and another from Montclair State.) A number come from Pennsylvania. From outside the local orbit, faculty come from Chapel Hill, Alabama, and Tulane; Berkeley and Irvine; the Big Ten; and a number from the University of Chicago. Thus, in terms of degrees held, a very large number come from major research institutions at the graduate level and many also from outstanding liberal-arts colleges from the Ivy League to Stanford at the undergraduate level. It should be added that some of the localism in the hiring of the first recruits reflects the fact that although 800 students were expected when the college opened in the fall of 1971, 1,200 showed up, making it necessary for part-time faculty to be assembled from nearby institutions. National recruiting was also, in effect, limited by budgetary restrictions—one example among a great many of the way in which the aspirations of the two new colleges were hamstrung by civil-service regulations—a situation which handicaps many public institutions.

The scarcity and expense of housing in the Ramapo area itself (only one-fifth of the faculty live in Bergen County) and the inability of the college to provide any faculty housing forced many to commute from where they had been living, in New York City and in other areas of New York and northern New Jersey, or to find places more or less throughout the suburban areas. In spite of all the talk about urban problems that goes on at Ramapo, and in spite of the original concern that almost led to locating the college in Hackensack, virtually no faculty live in these small urban centers or in troubled cities such as Newark.

Long-distance automobile commuting has left its toll on faculty and on students. Whatever their original enthusiasm, some have settled into' a routine of coming to the college to give their courses and tutorials on, let us say, a Monday, Wednesday, Thursday schedule, or a Tuesday, Wednesday, Friday schedule—the idea that Wednesday would be a day for faculty to get together still holds, more or less, but many Senior Seminars are also scheduled for that day. There are very few people to be found on weekdays after hours, except in the dormitories. To be sure, the "Saturday College," does help fill up the empty space on weekends.

At first the Ramapo and Stockton faculties alike resented having to be represented for collective-bargaining purposes by the New Jersey Education Association, which in their minds was associated with low academic status. And they realized, in our judgment correctly, that the provisions then applying to the retention of faculty after a three-year probationary period, which actually meant notification of those not to be retained at least six months before the end of that period, would not serve to promote people for their scholarship, for the quality of their teaching (which takes time to develop and evaluate), and for service both to the college itself and to outside constituencies. Nor did such a provision allow for flexibility in responding to diverse and changing student interests at which both colleges aimed. The éclat with which both colleges began brought applications from individuals who had recently received their doctorates or hoped soon to receive them—individuals who, though the current academic depression was beginning to be felt, would still not have been desperate enough ordinarily to seek positions at most other state colleges in the Northeast.

While in the early 1960s many state colleges and regional universities harbored the hope of developing graduate programs, it was clear from the outset that this was neither a realistic possibility nor a stated aim of Stockton and Ramapo: these colleges were to be oriented entirely to the teaching of undergraduates, and the quality of that teaching would be the primary factor in recruitment and retention, with scholarship a significant evidence of continued intellectual life, just as the exhibits of painters or the compositions and performances of musicians would be.

While in general faculty at Ramapo have depended for recognition and reward on their schools, work in the Senior Seminars, which are sometimes interschool courses, can also be a source of recognition. So can work in the Learning Skills Center, a college-wide enterprise. However, there is always the danger that faculty members oriented toward teaching can quickly lose their ties to the worlds of scholarship, the arts, or public affairs as they immerse themselves in the policies of their particular schools or of the college as a whole. When President Potter became aware of this, he named an executive director of research and development, as of January 1977, with threefold responsibilities: to help faculty members develop grant and research proposals; to encourage other scholarly activities—such as the Faculty Colloquia already in existence—which would bring together faculty members from various disciplines to exchange ideas for new interdisciplinary, perhaps team-taught, courses; and also to stimulate the writing of articles that might be published in the *Ramapo Papers*.

It is convenient for faculty and administrators at Ramapo to put the blame on "Trenton" when the college fails to fulfill the ambitions cherished by many of its founders and initial cadres. Still, there is no doubt that additional resources would help by making it easier to "carry" unproductive faculty already on tenure while searching for mature additions both in terms of teaching and scholarship. And indeed, George Potter and Richard Bjork have both worked with the authorities in Trenton in an effort to establish for their colleges a funding formula that is more generous than the standard "body count" used for the state college system generally.* As we shall see, by recruiting a young faculty, the new state colleges were at first served by system-wide formulae based on average salaries, but in a period of stasis or retrenchment any still-more-generous arrangement would have been regarded as inequitable by the other state colleges and could hardly have been supported by Dungan.

Given the relative autonomy of the various schools, it is perhaps not surprising that Ramapo, for approximately the same number of students as Stockton, has more than twice the percentage of tenured faculty. There are seventeen tenured faculty who have neither the doctorate nor other appropriate terminal degree such as Master of Fine Arts, M.B.A. or J.D. Possession of a degree is surely no sign— though we do not believe it a negative sign—of capacity as a teacher-scholar. Such strictures do not apply generally to the practicing artist. However, it seems to be a general rule, subject of course to exceptions, that a person who has started toward the doctorate but has not completed the dissertation, is a poor bet, even for a teaching-oriented college. The failure to complete a dissertation is in fact often evidence of a lack of interest in or appreciation for scholarship: a warning signal that the person may become both stale and dated as a teacher after an initial burst of energy and enthusiasm.

However, the great majority of faculty attracted to Ramapo did possess, or soon achieved, terminal degrees. A number had attained scholarly distinction. Some of these scholarly faculty found teaching the diverse student body drawn to Ramapo to be unrewarding and difficult, while others found it stimulating and exciting to awaken in hitherto ill-educated students an interest in literature, history, the arts, and the sciences. Such faculty have declared that they would not be happy teaching in any other kind of milieu.

But there were others, especially among the younger faculty drawn to Ramapo, who had been graduate students when the protest movements of the 1960s began. Not only in the "softer" fields, but even in the natural sciences, a number concluded that they had surrendered too much of their own affective and personal lives to fit into

---

*Efforts to develop new formulas, which could be accepted as equitable on a statewide basis, have repeatedly been presented at Trenton by George Potter —formulas which would take account, for example, of the fact that economics of scale in terms of essential administrative overhead would not appear until the new colleges reached an FTE count of 5,000 or so. Not only have these proposals been ignored or rejected, but the new state policies of funding on a credit-hour basis rather than on an FTE student basis have in fact cut into the resources of the new colleges and in our judgment, have harmed their educational aims as well.

what they termed the "rat race" of the research- and graduate-oriented university. Their wish was not to publish scholarly articles which now seemed merely destructive of the Canadian forests, but rather to devote themselves to teaching students—preferably, in fact, nonelite students. But the difficulty is that to wish to teach such students does not render one capable of doing so. Indeed, if there is any misapprehension against which our book might help to warn future academic experimenters, it is the notion that someone who rejects conventional discipline-bound education, which is largely tied to the classroom, the library or the laboratory, will necessarily be capable either of inventing an alternative or of adopting one already structured by someone else. In the former case, he may lack the very great talent required; in the latter, he is likely to find that the same rebelliousness that has led to rejection of the conventional programs from which he has fled is brought into play against the supposed or actual constraints of the new alternative.

These issues were intensified by egalitarian sentiment. In the early days of experimentation, some Ramapo faculty acted as if they believed that it would be elitist to take account of the differences between the "bottom third" now being recruited into college and what they themselves, products of very different backgrounds and advanced education, had become: that a difference, let us say, of 200 points on the SAT raised questions merely of cultural bias, even racism, and class distinction. Some of the faculty of this persuasion liked the idea of tutorials, and occasionally in the early years at both Ramapo and Stockton (where the term used is "preceptorials") they experimented with rap sessions and encounter groups (as at Kresge College)—though now these are far less in evidence. The first wave of recruits also liked the notion of creating programs of the various schools together with the students rather than presenting a set of preconceived slots into which students would have to fit themselves. And yet there are at Ramapo faculty members who told us, even in the first year, that although they approved intellectually of the tutorials, they were uncomfortable with them; while it was undoubtedly a weakness of theirs, they preferred lecturing even though it ran against their ethos and, in some measure, against that of the institution. (Lectures, however, were also seen as ways of drawing the whole college together; the Master Lecture Series provided, and continues to provide, "relevant" topics for discussion that reach beyond the framework of particular schools; they can be taken for credit, but as we have seen are also open to the public.)

The insistence on the interdisciplinary (one of the more common features of the popular reforms of the 1960s) at Ramapo involved not only courses but the structures of the schools themselves. With great variance among them, the schools are in a sense small colleges, often relating diverse fields in new and interesting ways. A school's faculty is, thus, likely to be made up of people who do not know the intramural languages of all their colleagues. Since the schools have a large share in the appointment of their own faculty members, subject to a college-wide review and the over-all decision of the academic vice-president, questions of quality control, on which we have already touched, inevitably arise.[13] It may be that a philosopher is not evaluating another philosopher but, let us say, a sociologist; or a medieval historian is evaluating a psychologist; but again, such disparities would operate quite differently among the various schools. And there are also differences among the schools in the degree to which participation in tenure decisions has in practice become democratized—or in the extent to which not only nontenured faculty but also undergraduates participate. Such participation can readily precipitate a situation, widespread today in academic life, where the nontenured must court popularity among students and are subject not only to the judgment of their seniors but also to that of their own age cohort. In turn, this can lead to efforts to keep out of the tenure ladder altogether the most able people, in terms of either their ability as teachers or as scholars or their involvement in other extramural professional activities.

Interdisciplinary courses (often simply called that to sound interesting), when truly multidisciplinary and involving a knowledge by each participant of the intellectual and linguistic patterns of the other fields, and when team-taught, can present other sorts of problems, such as a faculty member's fear of exposing himself or herself to the judgment of another, particularly if both are competing for tenure.[14] Actually, such a situation is rare at Ramapo because of the early grant of tenure which marks a sharp contrast with Stockton. In other words, early tenure may have great advantages when it gives people security in the experiments of team teaching, or when people want to try something else which is pedagogically innovative and hence stands a good chance of failure. But on the whole, early tenure tends to freeze a college in the face of shifting student interests, thus limiting the setting of new priorities, while at the same time running the risks in terms of quality control to which we have already referred.

As already indicated, despite the relative autonomy of the schools the vice-president for academic affairs and the president have sought to review all recommendations for promotion to tenure; on occasion, individual members of the board of trustees have also been involved, as well as the board collectively. As yet, no tenure quotas or ceilings have been established; indeed, as indicated, the administration has thought it wise to support for tenure those who have devoted themselves to the development of the several schools even if their qualifications as scholars and the length of their experience as undergraduate teachers are not outstanding. However, some faculty feel that tenure has often been granted too easily to those who have put together an interdisciplinary course or have served on a personnel or other committee, when their youth or lack of a doctorate would ordinarily have been a negative factor. Because so many faculty are of the same age group, there is fierce competition. Older faculty are disturbed by the lack of reliance on traditional criteria. Although Ramapo has not reached the 90 percent tenure rate of Jersey City State College and other long-established state institutions, 58 percent of its 170 faculty members are on tenure.

For a reading as to how its young college was doing, at the request of the State Department of Higher Education at Trenton, outside consultants were called in to make assessments. A number of distinguished scholars were among them, including Norman Birnbaum of Amherst College for the newly established School of Social Relations, Lynton U. Caldwell of Indiana for the School of Environmental Studies, Nathan Glazer of Harvard for the School of Metropolitan and Community Studies, and Charles Overberger, vice-president of the University of Michigan, for the School of Theoretical and Applied Science. On the whole, their reports express admiration for the enthusiasm of faculty, though some questions are raised as to how long such enthusiasm can last in the absence of scholarly renewal. However, these program reviews are by necessity too cursory to give a picture of what teaching is like for the wide range of students at Ramapo or how well the students are being prepared for the postbaccalaureate training to which a number aspire. Furthermore, these program reviews had no direct bearing on individual tenure decisions.[15]

Any liberal-arts college that seeks to do more than simply provide credentials or to give students a program entirely consisting of electives is likely to find that the aims of faculty and those of entering students are not wholly congruent. Scholarly faculty want to move middlebrow students toward avant-garde culture. Radical faculty want to move them from, for example, the often traditional Catholicism of their parents or, in the case of black students, where the generation gap between southern-born parents and their children can be very wide, from the residues of the Protestant ethic toward either a black nationalist or a nonwhite ideological perspective. However, as the American Council on Education survey of entering students at Ramapo indicates, the Ramapo student body, although diverse in social origins, is far less diverse in social attitudes than might be anticipated. Not only does the college continue to enroll a considerable number of upper-middle-class students, but even among its students from working-class or lower-middle-class backgrounds whose parents have not had any experience in college, the attitudes expressed are strikingly similar to those of liberal students at selective colleges. To illustrate: 90 percent believe that the government is not adequately controlling pollution; a similar proportion believe that women should have job equality, and 80 percent believe that the wealthy should pay more taxes and that the government provides insufficient protection for consumers. As would be true at many colleges, 70 percent believe that marijuana should be legal. A similar proportion believe that students should help evaluate faculty (an issue on which the Carnegie Commission surveys showed students exhibited greater caution in 1975 than in 1969). The students who identify themselves as conservatives and far-right have never exceeded 10 percent.*

However, this does not mean that most of the students at Ramapo are avant garde in their aesthetic and intellectual tastes. Yet there are enough recruits for some of the highly sophisticated course offerings which the catalogue sets forth, and some faculty in those courses are willing to devote themselves to helping students meet rather stringent academic demands. For example, in the School of Intercultural Studies, there are a number of offerings in foreign literatures, such as Russian and German; and the college catalogue suggests that it is possible to study Chinese, Sanskrit, or Swahili in Independent Study.[16] Indeed, a few faculty have gone far beyond the call of duty in teaching such languages.

The new regulation that students are to pay by the credit hour rather than on a term basis is likely, in our judgment, to be educationally harmful. It may mean that students will question whether, for example, a Senior Seminar on "Theater of the Absurd," on "Radical Ideologies and Conflict," or the many credit hours one would need to learn a new language are worth the expenditure.

---

*The American Council on Education data for Ramapo entering freshmen (supplied by Frederick Waring, director of institutional research) indicates that the women are on the whole a bit more liberal than the men, although over the last three or four years slightly more men than women—somewhere between 6 and 8 percent—have identified with the far left.

Faculty who are reputed to be stringent graders or are said to assign an excessive amount of work may also find themselves with smaller registrations. Although the regulation has not been in effect long enough to measure its results, it is clear that both the new and the established state colleges will lose money as students decide not to take courses for credit beyond the required minimum.

On the whole, the Ramapo faculty does not make large demands, having sometimes concluded rather too quickly that their students are beyond redemption. Such evaluations can obviously misjudge the level of student ability and interest. But if some faculty err by underestimating the ability of their students or their own ability to motivate them, others tend, as we have seen, to idealize the students and to overestimate what all but a handful can do. They may assume, for example, that a group of music students will naturally respond to rock or rhythm-and-blues and be fascinated by the gadgetry of avant-garde electronic music. The faculty who appear to gain the greatest satisfaction from teaching are those who take the time to find out where students are open to new perspectives and to work patiently from there, not giving up in the face of frequent frustration.

Thus the School of Contemporary Arts has attracted more students than anticipated, and more than one might expect in a college which, like most, is seen as a route toward career insurance and upward mobility. In some instances, graduates of the school get jobs teaching art in high schools, but the proportion who do so is small, and many are enrolled in its courses who are students of other schools. It is clear that others, however, including older students returning as much for culture as career, have readily concluded that they might as well choose liberal-arts programs since in an uncertain economy, a substantial minority of college graduates is not likely to obtain "college-level" jobs even through directly vocational tracks.

Although the ambience of Ramapo remains that of a liberal-arts college, students can pursue vocational programs more or less directly within and among the schools. There is a social-work major within the School of Metropolitan and Community Studies; one can pursue a business major along with a co-major in one of the schools;[17] and in the School of Theoretical and Applied Science there are majors which lead either toward professional schools or toward immediate postbaccalaureate employment. The brighter, well-prepared students are those who tend to enroll in the "impractical" liberal-arts courses, and they are, as elsewhere, students whom faculty find it rewarding to teach. Nevertheless, many faculty who have come with somewhat idealized images of highly motivated and eager

students have been disappointed and disillusioned, since there is
great diversity in the student body, and the majority are ill-prepared.
One unremittingly dedicated scholar on the Ramapo faculty described a number of his colleagues as, in a not uncommon phrase,
those who came to "do good" and stayed to do well. They had come
to Ramapo because it was new and advertised itself as being different from others in the state-system league—and indeed, in spite of
pressures from within and without, it does remain different—but not
as different as some of its advocates would claim.

All the New Jersey state colleges have had Educational Opportunity
Fund programs, principally under black directors who have sought
to recruit and help define as disadvantaged, primarily nonwhite undergraduates, and have put together financial-aid packages for them
by a combination of state and federal funding and, wherever possible in these rather isolated settings, on-campus jobs. At the outset,
Ramapo's black director of community services (presently head of
the Educational Opportunity Fund program for the entire state system) complained, as did his counterparts at Stockton and other
institutions, about the danger to black students of the softness and
gullibility of white liberal faculty who allow them to get away with
minimal or shoddy work. At Ramapo, failures were not recorded
and grading was in any case confused. Remedial courses were
planned and offered from the outset, with partial credit offered to
remove the stigma customarily associated with them. But because
it was almost impossible to fail at Ramapo during the first year, it
proved difficult to persuade those who needed remedial help actually
to enter the necessary program, when they could get by with a ninth-
grade reading level and with no substantial quantitative skills.
    As often happens, it is the scholarly black faculty who are the
most vociferous opponents of laxity. At Stockton, it was a black
faculty member who recognized that the underprepared black students needed a disciplined curriculum: such faculty have often had
to fight a two-front war against the ideologically defended and/or
hustler black faculty and students on the one side, and the liberal
or radical white faculty on the other, who condescend to black
students, regarding their often cavalier and inattentive manner as
the very models of authenticity and spontaneity.
    Perhaps benefiting to some extent from its on-campus housing,
Ramapo has managed to maintain something like an 8 to 10 percent nonwhite enrollment. (Stockton, much further away than Ramapo from centers of black and Spanish-American population, yet
seeking black students statewide, recruited around 6 percent until

the academic year, 1975–76, when its nonwhite enrollment dropped to around 4 percent.) There has been a determined effort at Ramapo to advertise the college's interest in black cultural and political concerns. For example, James Farmer was one of the first lecturers in the Master Lecture Series. Nikki Giovanni, the well-known black poet then teaching at Rutgers's Livingston College, also came up to speak—and Ramapo itself has a black economist, a black botanist, and a black musician on its faculty. Indeed, when we were on campus in the early spring of 1972, a number of black students as well as many white students and faculty turned out excitedly to greet Sister Elizabeth McAllister who had been associated with Philip Berrigan in his anti-Vietnam War activities. (This black turnout was something of a surprise to us, since on many campuses, even when blacks began to turn against the Vietnam War toward the end of the 1960s, the war was mainly a preoccupation of the whites.)

The students at Ramapo are a varied lot—from the 1,000 housed on campus (some of whom have part-time jobs) to those who are commuters and also are usually working part-time. According to the ACE data, half are Catholic; the number of Jewish students is under 10 percent, and, as already noted, the number of nonwhite students is about 8 percent.[18] But in terms of family background, the students are in some respects atypical for a largely commuter state college. Approximately half the parents have had some college experience, although not necessarily a college degree. Nearly half the families have income above the national median—a reflection of the general wealth of Bergen County. Many students who live off campus and have jobs schedule classes to fit their nonworking hours. Among the "first-generation-in-college" group, there seems to be surprisingly little tension with parents over the cultural attitudes which have filtered down from the avant-garde. Apparently, these students rarely discuss with their parents issues that arise in their classes; they use their homes as places to sleep, eat, and rest, but not for exchanges with parents from whom they may already have broken away during high school. Many students have broken away also from the traditional religion of their parents. One would expect this in the contemporary world of American Catholicism in which, as Andrew Greeley has noted, there is a split between the hierarchy and the once-obedient laity. Thus, neither home nor traditional religion offers much counterweight to faculty subcultures. When Ramapo began, newly recruited faculty were themselves often unsure, for example, as to how they should address their students—whether they should be on a first-name basis with them. Now the schools

have to some degree developed diverse life-styles. In the Schools of
Theoretical and Applied Science and of American Studies, the faculty are rather square; they take attendance, take grades seriously,
procedures which provide some students with a feeling of security.
Faculty members may not be models of careers for many, but they
can provide models of possible styles of life and outlook.

On the whole, Ramapo students appear to illustrate the findings
of the polling studies by Daniel Yankelovich discussed in Chapter
6, namely that the attitudes of the upper-middle-class, anti-war, and
often anti-American, and countercultural students in the selective
colleges in the 1960s have been, so to speak, percolating down.
Furthermore, the working-class students in these settings are not
involuntary captives. Their consciousness may be raised to the degree that they will look down on the jobs they are likely to get,
without reaching the level of revolutionary discontent for which
some of the faculty may be aiming.[19]

From the beginning there has been a minority of politically active
students at Ramapo. In the first year of the college, we met with a
group of students who were about to drive to Trenton to protest
the planned increase in what was then, in comparison with public
institutions in other states, a rather modest level of tuition—especially in the light of the inability of a succession of governors and
legislators to pass a state income tax which would help support
higher education and other public services (the income tax finally
squeaked through in 1976).* The student paper, *Horizons*, like student papers in so many colleges, has been in the hands of the student
left and supportive of faculty against even the mild administration of
President George Potter (whom the paper on the whole treats rather
benignly). The authorities in Trenton, of course, are seen as starving
the college while depriving students of necessary services. Another
focus for student activists was the field study of Mahwah undertaken
by a group in the School of Metropolitan and Community Studies; and
another group in Environmental Studies developed a field project on
the Ramapo Valley which culminated in a regional conference and

---

*Actually a number of these students appeared to be sufficiently well-to-
do to afford the tuition at a private college, such as nearby Bloomfield College, which was as a matter of fact at the point of bankruptcy, or Fairleigh
Dickinson University, whose founder-president, Peter Sammartino, told us
that he saw Ramapo as a threat to his hopes for expansion. On inquiry, a
number of students said that they preferred to have their own cars and even
to travel rather than to spend large sums of money on tuition at a private
institution that would not necessarily be any better than Ramapo and would
not be as exciting as Ramapo was, particularly in its early years.

a book. Still others made efforts to get involved with helping the
Ramapo Mountain people, a strange and hostile group isolated there
for a hundred years or more.

Perhaps we should mention here another kind of percolating down
which is not political but a reflection of the influence of the literary
and artistic avant-garde: *Trillium*, which students publish with some
faculty advice and the help of Denis Murphy (associate professor in
the School of American Studies), is a magazine of poetry, prose,
lithography, and art, most of it very creative, varied, often far-out
and worthy of the best college students anywhere.

The trajectory of a particular student, and the discovery of a
connection between his interest and faculty concerns, is often a
matter of chance, in spite of efforts to keep the tutorial program alive
and to improve that aspect of college life so often disgracefully neglected—the capable and disinterested advising of students by faculty
who know the whole institution and who are blinded neither by mis-
judgments of the student nor by their own interests, ideologies, or
prejudices. With the exception of those special cases where faculty
and students are working together on some project, or where a student is particularly dedicated, there is in general a serious lack of
communication between students and faculty at Ramapo, a complaint which highly educated and cultivated faculty quite commonly
voice today; it stems from their students' lack of cultural sophistication, their limited historical consciousness, and their general unwillingness to believe that they need to work or do anything to overcome
this gap.

As we write, growth at Ramapo appears to have come to an end;
in fact, enrollment has fallen a little in 1975–76 and in the first term
of 1977. But experiment continues. The insistence that schools must
be interdisciplinary remains a dominant motif. Moreover, there is
some evidence that Ramapo has been determined to hold on to its
initial efforts to stress the liberal arts as against the vocational. The
fight to establish a School of Business Administration already mentioned (dramatized by a petition which was signed by 2,000 students), which had earlier been approved by faculty vote and by the
Department of Higher Education, has turned, polemically at least,
on the question of whether such a school could be truly "interdisciplinary." Though the Division of Professional Institutes includes
persons trained in economics and statistics, opponents of allowing
the business program to become a school note that no philosophers
or sociologists are included—instead they are scattered through three
or four of the extant schools, none of which is prepared to release

faculty lines in a frozen budget in order to allow a School of Business Administration to acquire the requisite mixture. The proponents point out that the word "interdisciplinary" has a different meaning in some schools than in others: being interdisciplinary in the School of Contemporary Arts, for example, means in practice that a student who does painting will also work in music and dance—not that the school has the wide range of disciplines to be found in such larger units as American Studies or in such diverse ones as Intercultural Studies. However, a memorandum of April 13, 1977, states that it has been decided that the "Division of Business Administration" is to be formed and is to be treated on the same terms as a school; that a co-major in another school will still be required; but that a degree will be given in "Business Administration." In other words, while the faculty have held out against giving business the equivalence of a school, they have made some interim concessions to the largest enrolled field in the college.

The assumption that prevails at Ramapo, at least on the level of ideology, is that the average student learns what it means to be interdisciplinary as a result of school citizenship. Not to be a citizen of a school which meets one's interests, as has been the situation of the business co-majors, is a hardship, because such students must find their tutors, tutorials, and Senior Seminars and a varying number of their courses in the schools to which they belong. However, they may have a co-major in another school or division. There is also great variety in the Senior Seminars and in the Scope and Methods courses (offered for sophomores by every school). These often cover a single discipline, such as political science—itself, a rather large universe. It is possible, in fact, to pursue a bachelor of arts program in political science in five different schools, or in philosophy in four. But the bachelor of science program in biology, chemistry, or mathematics exists only in the School of Theoretical and Applied Science. However, the all-college Scope and Methods and Senior Seminar requirements can be met in different ways, depending on the school in which one registers.

As with other experimenting colleges, Ramapo began with an emphasis on participatory democracy. And, as has also happened elsewhere, the strenuous demands for the innovative teaching of a nonhomogeneous student body competed with the demands for innovative participative processes, and attendance at unit meetings and at the College Assembly has waned.[20] Furthermore, faculty-student governance has had to compete with the system-wide collective bargaining which is both the outgrowth of and the further impetus toward centralization. Because of the original antipathy of

Ramapo faculty members to the NEA affiliate (the New Jersey Education Association), this union was rapidly replaced, as at Stockton, by overwhelming support for the more militant AFT union which won out as the collective-bargaining representative for the state colleges. Union activists at Ramapo must spend time at Trenton and with their fellow activists at the other state colleges. Grievance machinery—followed, when a claimant is unsuccessful, by a spate of litigation—tends to replace both confidentiality and collegiality. Not only the energies of the faculty are drawn into these processes, but those of the administration; Vice-president Cassidy must prepare himself for lengthy hearings—an expenditure of precious time not then available for academic planning or for implementing the valuable exchanges of faculty with other experimenting institutions which he is eager to get started. In our experience, most administrators of unionized campuses come to see themselves as forced into a legalistic framework in which not only the letters they write but the conversations they hold may become subjects of grievance proceedings, which may then be followed perhaps by external resort to compulsory arbitration or the courts. However, we have met a few rather combative college and university presidents who prefer dealing with a union to coping with the "organized anarchy" of a faculty senate and its individualistic members.[21] In such a climate, it is not unusual for faculty members to be satisfied with a modest academic effort, to be "job-holders" rather than tireless innovators—and in the end it is the students who suffer.[22]

At Ramapo, faculty malaise is no greater than that found nationwide in similar colleges and universities. But Ramapo suffers more than many others. Perhaps because its aspirations are more exalted, the gap seems larger between the innovative image the college presents and the daily reality of seeking to staff the tutorials, enhance the momentum of the Learning Skills Center, and through the faculty colloquia, the *Ramapo Papers*, and other collective efforts, to maintain a cooperative momentum.

III

When Richard Bjork became president of Stockton State College in September 1969, the board of trustees which had been appointed by former Democratic Governor Hughes with recommendations from the Board of Higher Education, was already established. There had been agitation for a college for Southern New Jersey for some time. The referendum of 1968 had given the mandate for both Ramapo and Stockton, and had stipulated that the southern college be in Atlantic, Cumberland, or Cape May counties. Bjork and his small group of planners visited twenty-six sites in the three-county area. There was virtually no pressure on them for an Atlantic City location: as a resort, Atlantic City had long since lost "class"; instead it has gained a high unemployment rate. It is nearly half nonwhite; those whites who could afford to had left the city for the suburbs. Mrs. Magda Leuchter, the civic-minded wife of the editorial chairman of the *Vineland Times-Journal*, currently the chairperson of the Stockton board of trustees, would have liked to see the college located in Vineland, but she exerted no great pressure to this end and Bjork had a relatively free hand.

He chose a site near Pomona as close to the northern border of Atlantic County as could be found: twelve miles northwest of Atlantic City in the Pine Barrens, a sparsely settled area. However, both the Atlantic City Expressway leading to Philadelphia and the Garden State Parkway, leading north and south, pass near the college, as does a highway on which are scattered bars, shops, and the motels where Stockton would put up the faculty and staff it was seeking to recruit. The site was a large estate, formerly used for hunting, with a small lake, woods, and slightly undulating sandy land. It provided ample space with immediate availability for building and expansion; Bjork promised to keep some of the land intact, while offering space to facilities such as a hospital, with which the college could develop a mutually beneficial relationship.

When President Bjork came to Atlantic City, he bought a home near there, and moved quickly to establish ties to the local business and professional people. He was named director and is now the chairman of the board of The Mainland Bank in Linwood; he knows the local political leaders, the real-estate people, the black and white ministers and priests. When faculty were recruited, he asked realtors to show them housing within a thirty-mile radius of the college, for he very much wanted to avoid the building up of a faculty colony—and indeed, the faculty live over a widely dispersed area, some commuting from as far as Philadelphia. Bjork urged faculty members to integrate themselves into their local communities, to speak before the chambers of commerce, and to become good citizens and advertise the college. Furthermore, just as he, along with many activist environmentalists, wanted to preserve the ecology of the Pine Barrens, so he was anxious also not to invade its indigenous populace with a faculty housing cluster.

The Pine Barrens have a unique and sparse population, a throwback to an earlier period of history, as well as a mixed group of subsistence farmers, part-time clamdiggers and fishermen, and commuters to plants in Vineland and elsewhere. Southern New Jersey is not only poor; it has a sizable Fundamentalist population, many of whom supported the Reverend Carl McIntyre's Shelton College in Cape May which the state education authorities closed down, an action that precipitated the charge that the state was opening a Red and godless college (Stockton) while destroying a Christian one. Nevertheless, like the rest of New Jersey, the South is also 50 percent Catholic, with many Italians, Irish, and Polish residents, as well as a considerable number of Jews, a number of them resident in Margate, south of Atlantic City, or in areas to the west, and some of them still engaged in the declining commercial life of the coastal resorts.

For its first half-year, while the college buildings were being completed, Stockton was temporarily located at a rather seedy hotel on the Boardwalk in Atlantic City. The Mayflower Hotel provided some makeshift classrooms as well as dormitory space, but it seemed to us hardly an optimal place to begin. When later in the spring we visited the nearly deserted hotel, it was evident that it offered none of the opulence of a resort, but in contrast with the sparkling new campus it presented an air of underrepair and undermaintenance characteristic of many potentially renewable urban structures. In addition to the unattractiveness of the building, there were real hazards. Students reported (with some exaggeration) that hard drugs and prostitutes were omnipresent. Yet a few members of the Stockton faculty have still held on to what has been termed "the coming over on the Mayflower syndrome," the feeling of great camaraderie that developed in those early days under difficult conditions.

Fortunately, this makeshift arrangement did not last long, and in January the move to the new campus took place. In the two-story hallways—large open spaces in which students and faculty could periodically congregate—workmen were still putting up temporary symbols to designate the different programs and offices, since the original design had intentionally not set aside space for specific curricular activities. In fact, one element that gave Stockton an initial air of innovation was the building plan, which was based on the use of prefabricated materials. For the architect, Bjork recruited Richard Geddes, dean of the School of Architecture at Princeton, whose Stockton State College buildings went up at a per-square-foot cost one-quarter as high as Geddes' handsome new West Building erected at about the same time at the Institute for Advanced Study at Princeton. Stockton, like Ramapo, has a great deal of glass, but some of its buildings are quite massive with cement-block walls and interest-

ing geometric shapes. The internal structure in some buildings is
aesthetic with the steel beams showing—suggestive of a factory and
actually quite stunning in its own way. The design is modular in the
sense that new buildings and additions, all interconnected, have been
easily added with campus growth.

Richard Bjork was a close observer of national trends in higher education; he gave a course in this field in the college's first year. And
before Stockton opened, he visited a large number of the better-
known innovative institutions across the country: the newly opened
Old Westbury, the still-being-planned SUNY College at Purchase,
as well as Hampshire College, Evergreen State College, Santa Cruz,
Irvine, and others. Irvine impressed him especially, with its interdisciplinary focus on management sciences and the behavioral sciences.
Indeed, Irvine had been able to establish several nondepartmental
structures which maintained quality control of its faculty and had
not succumbed to the pitfall of recruiting people who called themselves interdisciplinary but were in fact anti-disciplinary.
    Bjork, however, did not plan the curriculum or recruit the initial
faculty for the college, though he did interview most of the recruits.
He left this task to his vice-president for academic affairs, Wesley
Tilley, a humanist who had been at the University of Chicago during
the Hutchins era and had had experience as a dean at Milliken University in Illinois and elsewhere. Deeply committed to the liberal
arts, Tilley proposed a curriculum in which a program of General
Studies would be spread throughout the four years of a student's
career; he hoped the thrust of such a program would not be topical
(a course in Women's Studies does in fact now exist at Stockton) but
would rather be cast in terms of modes of inquiry and analysis. Each
student was to be free to create his or her own program of studies,
provided it was approved by a "preceptor" (analogous to the Ramapo tutor) and a supervising committee. On entry, each student was
to be assigned a preceptor "to help guide him or her through life at
the college."[23] Thus students are grouped into preceptorials—unlike
the tutorials at Ramapo, these provide no academic credit; they vary
greatly in style and substance. Originally, five preceptorials were
grouped together in a "collegium," which was given a limited
amount of money for group dining or other activities particularly
concerned with governance. But when it turned out that the collegia
were not to be the basis of student governance, but that student
volunteers were instead to be chosen for the College Council by lot,
this basis of organization disappeared and they have vanished.

Ordinarily, students would major in an interdepartmental "faculty," such as Arts and Humanities, Natural Sciences and Mathematics, or Social and Behavioral Sciences. It should be noted that these broad groupings, since they include fields generally linked together, are less eclectic than some of the schools at Ramapo, which include people from all three areas. A student could also take a degree in Liberal Studies, as an alternative to General Studies, which meant six to eight courses of a specialized sort in a field remote from his or her major program within a particular faculty. The definition of "remote" was left to the preceptor, and subject to review by the General Studies director. The hope was that a student could, for example, combine history and mathematics, or literature, music, and economics, thus in effect having two or three majors. The first director of General Studies, Kenneth Tompkins, also directed "Experimental Studies," a part of the Faculty of Experimental Studies; this included a program in teacher development, a reflection, perhaps, of the hope that the college would have an impact on the teaching profession. (Gordon Davies was Director of Academic Advising.)

By commuting to Atlantic City in the year before the college opened, Tilley was able to have a hand in naming the academic deans, and, with their assistance, the first faculty were recruited. Bjork accepted the complicated structure Tilley designed. Experimental Studies, however, seemed to him too radical and too amorphous; and its faculty included some who went further than most in their desire to be peers of the students—engaging in rap sessions, holding classes in their homes (sometimes a hardship for the minority of students without cars), and even smoking pot with them. (All the faculty were on a first-name basis with students, and in the initial years it took courage for three or four of the younger teachers to insist on wearing a coat and tie or to refuse to "light up" with students.) During the second year, Bjork decided to disband Experimental Studies—Tompkins eventually became professor of literature, and one other faculty member, Woodworth G. Thrombley, stayed on and is now vice-president for academic affairs. The rest of the group, including Davies, were either released by Bjork or themselves concluded it was best to leave.

Except for Experimental Studies, Bjork found the nondepartmental and free-wheeling ideas of Tilley an asset. He wanted Stockton to draw students from the entire state, and an image of novelty and innovation was attractive. Though on the whole the Stockton board of trustees (except for Mrs. Leuchter) has been conservative, it has been supportive of Bjork's management. The nondepartmental organization meant that faculty could erect fewer defenses against the president's wish for maximum flexibility, which would make possible a turnover of faculty to meet changing student interests. There are still no departments, but there are "programs," which have departmental names (Biology, Literature, Language, Mathematics, Philosophy and Religion). There are "program coordinators," often assistant professors, without the power of the typical departmental chairman in a departmentalized institution. And there is a very large and increasing group of programs geared to changing vocational opportunities: Business Studies; Health Sciences (offering, for example, a Bachelor of Science in Nursing for nonbaccalaureate nurses, Public Health, Speech Pathology and Audiology, and Medical Communications Science); also Information and Systems Science; Transportation Systems; Social Work. It is inconceivable that Stockton students wanting a degree in business management or marketing or accounting would find the obstacles students had met at Ramapo. The Business Program now attracts more students than any other.

Stockton established at the outset programs to take advantage of the area's unusual environmental setting: the nearby Pine Barrens are a unique formation found nowhere else on earth, and the ocean and swamplands are not far away. The Program in Environmental Studies in the Faculty of Natural Sciences and Mathematics has been one of the most popular, appealing to the growing interest in the environment among students and to vocational possibilities in nearby fisheries, state agencies, and organizations for park and water management. There was from the outset an imaginative math course designed to overcome "math anxiety" through games that would interest students in numbers and reduce their fears. A program in Criminal Justice, aiming to prepare probation officers and correction workers, has also existed from the outset. And there are courses designed to help students find employment in the nearby facility operated by the Federal Aviation Authority. There are opportunities for internships and Independent Study as well.

What will lead to a job is, of course, not always clear. A faculty member in the Program in Environmental Studies noted that graduates were not always finding places in areas directly related to their undergraduate major and concluded that a broader program, with a greater stress on basic work in the natural sciences, would give students a wider horizon and would allow more specific technical training to occur on the job. If short-run student interests had made Stockton wholly geared to market pressures—as it might have without Thrombley and his cohorts—students would have ended up doing only "their own thing" at an economically precarious time when

they could find themselves both without a job and without the con-
cededly mixed blessings of a liberal-arts education. As Bjork admitted in a local news story,[24] some continuities are inevitable. And
since the college began planning prior to the economic recession, it is
not surprising that there remains a large arts and humanities faculty.

From the outset Stockton drew a faculty with "good" degrees; the
college had advertised in *Academe*, a publication of the AAUP, and
in professional journals. Potential faculty had been told that Stockton was to be different from the usual college, more responsive to
students and to society. The faculty—mostly young—have degrees
from the Ivy League, the Big Ten, and the University of California.
Some were teaching at small liberal-arts colleges, and had received
undergraduate degrees at prestigious institutions. Rutgers and other
nearby state universities have on the whole been drawn upon primarily in the more directly preprofessional areas.[25]

In the first year fewer teachers were recruited in the social sciences than in the humanities. Among them were some who offered
"relevant" and "pop" courses. One sociologist wrote a column for the
student paper, *Argo*; another went around with a tape recorder to
get students talking about their problems with identity and personal
adjustment. None of these faculty members remains at Stockton.

By no means all the recruits in the first wave of faculty were attracted by the idea of innovation per se, although some enjoyed the
prospect of helping inaugurate a new college. Most who have stayed
on are not seeking to relive their youth by overidentification with
adolescents, but rather are concerned with doing as interesting a job
of teaching, either singly or in team efforts, as opportunity and
funding—and workloads as defined by collective bargaining—permit. Vice-president Thrombley supports them in a certain freedom,
which in some of the heavily departmentalized universities might be
more difficult to attain without robbing faculty members of their
disciplinary base.

Bjork, however, looks at these matters not from the point of view
of those doing the teaching, but rather as an outsider. A former
faculty member spoke of Bjork's commitment to public service:
"He sees himself as a public servant working in only one of many
state agencies. This attitude prompts him to get the college ever
more heavily involved in public service/continuing education activities, and it is also the side that appealed so much to the original
board of trustees." Bjork is reminiscent of other men in public life
who are highly intelligent, hard-working, authoritative, and dedicated. They waste no words. They take the dedication of their sub-

ordinates for granted, not fully appreciating that they themselves
are, after all, in the spotlight and that, at least from the point of
view of insecure faculty members, deans, and vice presidents, they
are relatively unassailable.

There is a certain irony in how quickly the faculty assumed a
fairly well-entrenched suspicion of and hostility toward President
Bjork—an attitude which goes somewhat beyond the widely prevalent faculty attitude toward administrators: one faculty member
put it in terms of a conflict between "a radical president in an increasingly conservative faculty." What was meant by this was that
Bjork had taken literally the wish of many faculty who came to academic maturity in the 1960s to become "student-centered"—interdisciplinary, flexible in their responsiveness to students. But now the
faculty have waked up to the fact that the absence of departments
means the absence of a hierarchy to operate as a buffer between
themselves and the president. The faculty realize that the president
is instantly accessible to students, including those who would want
to complain about faculty inaccessibility; and, while the president
is accessible to the faculty as well, they have found him combative,
sharp in response to criticism, and often opaque concerning future plans. Indeed, the president's dismantling of the Experimental
Studies Program, which he announced during the course of its second year, came as something of a surprise to then Vice-President
Tilley and to those in the program, since Bjork had not made his
views clear at the outset. (He had let a hundred flowers bloom and
was now, after the Chinese fashion, pulling out what he considered
to be weeds.)

The students did not at once realize that the president was trying
to make them his allies. When in the first year Tilley had terminated
three faculty members under pressure from Bjork, students joined
faculty in demonstrations and protests. This minority of student
activists was led by some transfers from Livingston College who saw
the three faculty members as oppressed; many faculty thought that
in the first whirligig year no one should be let go, since there had
been insufficient time to prove oneself. Bjork, however, thought that
he was protecting student interests in these terminations, since the
faculty in question had not worked out well for the typical Stockton
student. Nor did the active students at first recognize that the faculty's
desire to switch from their involuntary representation by the New
Jersey Education Association to the more militant American Federa-
tion of Teachers was not necessarily in the students' interest. A Student Union was formed, which supported a short strike by faculty

in 1973. A little later, however, when the faculty again voted to strike, joining a statewide move, there was no student support.

Most presidents of liberal-arts colleges come originally from the faculty and regard their former colleagues, in terms of personal relations at any rate, as perhaps their most important constituency, to be befriended and protected against pressures or to be coaxed into yielding when that appears the only feasible course. To be sure, in times of retrenchment, and often at other times as well, faculty do not always reciprocate, and presidents feel betrayed, just as faculty feel betrayed by what they see as presidential expediency.

Bjork did not come into administration as a former professor, although he has done some teaching and at present gives a course called "Bureaucracy and Public Policy." Rather, he had begun as a dean of students, a position in which one often sees the casualties created by sarcastic or even sadistic faculty, and in which one can often acquire, as many student counselors do, an anti-faculty perspective. Indeed, on his side, Bjork showed no interest in the faculty personally; and faculty felt their relation to him was simply that of employee to employer. Moreover, the faculty did not appreciate Bjork's ties to the local business and banking interests. Nor did they appreciate his time-consuming efforts in Trenton, where he worked with the chancellor's office, with the legislature, and as one of the leaders of the state-college presidents in centralized collective bargaining. When the move to the finished campus came in the middle of the first year, Bjork took the hunting lodge by the lake as his office, a choice of location which was seen as a purposeful attempt to put distance between himself and his faculty. (The lodge was burned during the spring demonstration; the police believe it was arson, but that has not been proven.)

Bjork, having instructed Tilley to find an "interesting" faculty— not "set in their ways"—was determined not to allow them to develop rigidities. While he had in the first year relented in the struggle over three faculty members, letting only one go (thus leaving Tilley exposed to faculty attack), the other two were terminated in the following year. Indeed, faculty have been terminated or have departed with great regularity: Stockton has a 28 percent tenure rate and has set a 50 percent tenure quota, which the union claims is illegitimate. Clearly, Bjork's rule by fiat has been destructive of faculty morale. Senior tenured faculty, beyond the wrench of seeing friends and colleagues leave, find it difficult to plan for the programs in which they serve when they have little to say in who will be kept on, when the future of the program coordinators is uncertain, and when the flow of student traffic is irregular and undependable. The union movement has gathered strength, and the grievance procedures in the collective-bargaining contract have become the first line of defense, with, as elsewhere in academic life, litigation as a further resort. No successor to Bjork is likely to be able to fend off increasing union strength.

For the really dedicated faculty, interested in going beyond the call of duty, for example, in team teaching or in the General Studies Program, the coming of the union has meant an increasingly close negotiation of workloads, and hence the beginnings of a system for restricting the level of effort, at least in terms of hours, which faculty members can put in without additional compensation. However, recently the college has sought to work out with the union a method of recompensing faculty who are willing to carry workloads beyond the norm.

Stockton had begun with very few senior faculty. But special circumstances had brought a few who were able to make use of legitimate exceptions to the rules for the three-year probationary period before the granting of tenure and the eight years of experience required for promotion to full professorship. Some had reasons for wanting to leave positions they had; others were attracted and intrigued by the new college and had enough interest and dedication to new ideas in teaching to take a chance, even without tenure.

But even if President Bjork had been able to recruit more senior faculty at the outset, he did not want to. Since New Jersey funding is granted on the basis of average faculty salaries, deploying younger faculty at lower rates of compensation could save money to use for other purposes—for example, for the effort to recruit students statewide. What is more, in the "Preliminary Report of the Task Force on Ten-Year Staffing Plan," presented on January 24, 1977, by a faculty-staff-administration committee, it was pointed out that the bulge of young faculty recruited in the first years of the college would lead to a 75 percent tenure rate within the next decade unless severe restrictions were adopted. The report recommended that Stockton reduce the number of teachers on the tenure track by recruiting one-fifth in the instructor category and another 5 to 10 percent as temporary visiting faculty. Such a plan would permit renewal and redistribution of faculty, while at the same time restricting severely the granting of tenure to somewhere between one-half and two-thirds of those eligible. The report made the further recommendations that the state statutes be modified so that the probationary period which had been raised to five years be again raised to seven years, "allowing more time for natural attrition and evaluation." Furthermore, it was suggested that those who were considered to deserve tenure but who, due to the unavailability of tenure positions, could not be granted it, be permitted to stay on until a tenure slot should become vacant (although this provision would require a statutory change and would no doubt conflict with AAUP stipulations). However, in the fall of 1976, Bjork added to the already growing mistrust by going before the New Jersey Assembly Education Committee to attack the institution of tenure on the ground that it was not necessary for the protection of academic freedom, and that there was no reason to provide for a select few a status beyond that already granted by collective-bargaining agreements, civil-service regulations, "and court decisions which accord individuals property rights in their positions."[26] From the outset, President Bjork has taken the position of the student as client or consumer: in his view, faculty members should be no more immune to the consequences of criticism for poor performance than any other supplier of goods and services. Bjork is prepared, if there is to be collective bargaining, to make tenure a negotiable issue along with salaries and workloads.

If Bjork bore down hard on the faculty to get them to be responsive to changing student demands, he was, as has already been suggested, no more protective of the academic deans. His view concerning both his deans and faculty has been that it is easier to fire people than to persuade them to change. He has not wanted to have collegial relationships with his "employees," but has remained aloof, thus feeling free to use his power to hire and fire. In this situation he has been able also to terminate courses and rearrange interdisciplinary programs with considerable flexibility, according to what he felt to be student demands. For example, in 1976–77 he merged the Faculty of Management Sciences with the Faculty of Health Sciences to create a new unit, Professional Studies, which implied a strictly vocational purpose that would have a wide appeal.

Administrators and deans at Stockton State College do not hold membership in the union and thus have limited job security. In five years, seventeen deans have left. Many administrators also have left. There were, however, a few exceptions to this fast turnover: one was an assistant to the president whom Bjork respected and took into his confidence, Richard Chait. When Stockton was being planned, Bjork had met Chait, a new Ph.D. in Educational Studies from the University of Wisconsin, at the annual meetings of the American Association for Higher Education. Chait was taken on with the understanding that, after a stipulated number of years, he would move on.

Chait felt secure enough in his position to argue with Bjork privately. But he also felt that many young faculty were unrealistic in their understanding of their students and of what was expected of them as teachers in a state college. Yet Chait also sympathized with faculty and knew a few of them well, but was not able to know most of them. He also sympathized with Bjork and knew how to get along with him. He was neither an "enemy" nor a "yes-man," for which Bjork respected him. Since he was close to Bjork, he was regarded by faculty who did not know him well as the president's eyes and ears on campus, and they either feared or sought him out for this. They could not understand how a young radical coming from Madison, who had taught American black history in the Extension Division, could be so square. He obviously played an important role in keeping the place together in those difficult years. But after the agreed-on length of time, Chait did move on, and Bjork, in his cool manner, made no effort to prevent this.

The Evaluation Team Report of the Middle States Association (made in 1975) gently suggested that a different, less "managerial," style might now be useful in the president's office, and cautioned the college about what appeared to them to be "an excessive use of words such as 'flexibility'." The report implied that the term might be useful as an image but was dangerous as a slogan, and that faculty was certainly likely to react to it in the latter way.[27] Bjork is himself prepared to be evaluated—as a state civil servant, by the board of trustees, and by the Board of Higher Education and the chancellor who will be selected to replace Ralph Dungan.

But it has become clear that Bjork is unlikely to change his ways. From his point of view, many faculty members are seeking to retain the "innovative" status quo created by Wesley Tilley and the first group of recruits. Those who hold this now traditional point of view, Bjork would say, are inattentive to the altered economic and cultural climate of the mid-seventies, and its effect on state-system funding and on student career aspirations. From the faculty members' point of view, "flexibility" means heightened insecurity. Some of the often imaginative General Studies courses may be pushed aside, for example, by marketing courses in the growing Program of Business Studies in the Faculty of Professional Studies.* Or, if the Faculty of

---

*We should make clear our position on the recurring arguments between what is called "vocational" or "applied," in contrast to supposedly pure scholarship for its own sake. No one is more vocational than a professor of English literature who is preparing his or her students to become professors of English literature. Everything depends on how a subject is taught; with greater or less difficulty, all subjects can be taught in a liberal or emancipating way;

Arts and Humanities wins the right, now being sought in Trenton, to grant the Bachelor of Fine Arts degree, other courses will be pushed aside to make more room for studio or music courses.

Even if Bjork did seek to change his ways and to become more conciliatory, the faculty would not be likely to respond; the wall of distrust is now too high. Though all the state colleges voted to oust the NJEA and to install in its place an AFT union, the Stockton faculty's overwhelming (95 to 1) vote in favor of AFT can be taken in part as a vote of no-confidence in the president. The latter is quite prepared to deal with the union, both locally and, as we have seen earlier, in statewide collective bargaining. As in many state and a few private institutions throughout the country, a "managerial" outlook has evoked an "employee" response.*

Shortly after Democratic Governor Byrne came into office in 1974, President Bjork and a very few others among the state college presidents were willing to take the risk of a strike the union was calling on both salary and procedural issues, for they believed that the union was not strong enough to sustain the strike either in the legislature, which was desperately short of funds for all New Jersey public services, or with the public at large, including students who might insist that the striking faculty were letting them down. But, to the dismay of these presidents, the governor gave in to the union on many issues—it was reported at the time that the union had threatened that it was prepared to resort to violence to gain its ends, but it seems doubtful that the governor was intimidated; rather, having been elected himself with union support, and indifferent to the academic concerns of the state-college presidents, it is likely that the union's approval was important to him.

Some faculty are inclined to see the president's wish in the matter of housing to scatter them about the countryside as analogous to

---

all can be taught in dreary and routine fashion. But what has been said has to be qualified by the realization that, if one is working with the traditional materials of the liberal arts, particularly with something like the Great Books program, the books may be evocative for students even if the faculty member is not. To teach what are called vocational subjects in a similarly evocative way takes greater inventiveness, but certainly a course in management or labor relations in the Program of Business Studies can be as multidisciplinary as any of the team-taught Stockton or Ramapo courses.

*Unionization of some sort would in any case have been inevitable at both Stockton and Ramapo. The Public Employees Relations Commission ruled early in the career of the two colleges that both would be part of an already unionized state-college unit whose bargains, except for local grievances, are system-wide. Strikes are also generally system-wide, as with the most recent one, which occurred in early 1974 shortly after Governor Byrne came into their being scattered in locations on the campus: their view of the president's motto is "divide and rule." There is still a sense of turmoil with the nonretention and sudden resignation of faculty members and people in administration. Moreover, because there are continuous student evaluations of teaching by "finely tuned teaching scores," as one person put it, the college has become less innovative in its course offerings: a course taught for the first time receives a lower student evaluation, as a rule, than other courses. The faculty are learning that innovation rarely pays.

Very likely the competition at Stockton would be like what was described to us as a "sharks' pool" at Ramapo if other conditions were the same. But at Stockton the struggle is not so much among the faculty; rather, their antagonism is directed against Bjork. They don't know from year to year what his standards are or what the reasons will be for retention or nonretention. Thus they cannot compete with each other, not knowing what they are competing for. Older faculty are often unhappy that they cannot protect younger faculty they would like to bring along, even though they do not themselves suffer such anxieties.

The basic premise of Bjork's attitude toward students is that they should be treated in the way that many claim they want to be treated —as adults. That is, the college is not going to act *in loco parentis*. Students must be on their own. They must find their own health care in the areas where they live; in the first few years there was not even any on-campus counseling service (an issue about which Bjork now seems to have relented). For, as he made clear, the purpose of a state college was to provide an education; and there were other state and local agencies which could serve other needs. If students get into trouble with the police, they should not expect the college to come to their aid. However, he has not been able on this matter either to hold firmly to his reluctance to provide help for students with

office. In general, as many observers have noted, unionization serves to further centralization, taking power away not only from local college administrations but also from traditional faculty senates. In the democratized committee and governance structures of today, the union meeting may be the only place where faculty can get together and legitimately say "no" to students who want to enter the meeting. Students may lose out to the degree that unionization brings with it promotion based on credentials and seniority rather than on all too human subjective judgments of excellence in teaching and scholarship. For a discussion and critique of the growing power of public-employee unions, see Jack D. Douglas, "Urban Politics and Public Employee Unions," in Lawrence Chickering, ed., *Public Employee Unions* (San Francisco: Institute for Contemporary Studies, 1976).

noncurricular problems. In practice, the faculty, and many administrators as well, do not live up to his insistence on student independence when students are in serious difficulty. Indeed, although students in general were making loud demands for total independence at the time the college began, Stockton students were not always happy with Bjork's policy, nor did they warm to him personally.

The campus provides very little in the way of casual meeting places other than the cafeteria. A private dining room can be made by partitioning off part of the cafeteria which students and faculty can use for meetings. The cafeteria and the recreation rooms for pool and Ping-pong seem to be the main centers of social life. Since most of the students are commuters, they do not contribute much to the social life of the college. There are 250 housing units on campus which house 1,000 students; and these, in accordance with Bjork's philosophy, are entirely under student control.* One faculty member described the housing scene as a "jungle." She went on to say that students continually tried to find lodgings or motels around the area which would allow them more privacy and quiet. And because Stockton is located near resort areas, students can often find inexpensive housing in the off-season. However, the on-campus housing situation seems more acceptable to the students themselves than to the older generation. Actually, the design of the housing units is attractive. They are separate garden-style housekeeping apartments located on the north shore of the lake and surrounded by trees. Each unit houses four, either a family with children or four students of the same sex; there are two bedrooms, living room, kitchen, and bath. There is some attempt to create a community here, with parties, brunches, and fireside chats. Four plain-clothesmen live in the housing area all of the time.

Before Stockton opened, Bjork had commissioned Heller Associates to do a market survey to see who the prospective students might be and what interests and opportunities would draw them to a new, largely commuter college. The survey revealed that the college would be attractive to South New Jersey students coming from homes with

*We ourselves consider the abdication of adults from student residential life as an instance of nonbenign neglect, though it often is the result of student insistence. Except in a rare college such as Earlham, student residential life today is fine for the street-wise but often traumatic for the less hip and self-protective. A number of students, we have been informed, have left Stockton housing because of the destructiveness and inconsiderateness students so commonly exhibit toward each other under the amiable labels of tolerance and noninterference.

considerably lower median incomes than those at Ramapo, and with fewer college-educated parents. With the plan to house one-quarter of the present student body on campus, statewide recruiting would be feasible and would add to the number of black students and the currently rather small percentage of students from above-average income brackets by increasing the number from the northern counties. Not many Atlantic City blacks took advantage of the college, even though bus service had been arranged from the city to the campus, a service that was later abandoned, in fact, for lack of student support.

The survey also indicated that the aims of the prospective students would be more explicitly vocational than those of the students attracted in the first years to Ramapo. The data on current entering freshmen indicates that this has remained so. In the entering class for the fall of 1976, according to the American Council on Education-UCLA research program, 58 percent of the students live more than fifty miles from the college, and for two-thirds of the applicants, Stockton was their first choice. One-third were attracted by the low tuition and only 10 percent by the wish to live at home, while close to one-quarter were drawn by the particular educational programs Stockton offers. A smaller percentage than at Ramapo hope to go on for the doctorate (11.6 percent), though 35 percent of the entering freshmen, most of them directly out of high school, hope to attain a master's degree. In terms of religious preference, these entering students are fairly representative of the area: 42 percent are Roman Catholic (as against the national average for four-year colleges of 31 percent), 5 percent are Jewish (where the national average is a little over 3 percent, although among the 22 percent who avow no religious preference there are in many colleges, but probably not at Stockton, students of Jewish background who have abandoned Judaism).

In terms of test scores, 10 percent of Stockton students have verbal SAT scores of 550 and over—and nearly 30 percent have scores under 400. More than one-third of the students have math SAT scores of 550 and over, and a little over one-fifth are at 400 and below. The drop in verbal scores recorded since the college opened has been large and mirrors a trend which has been seen nationally. The number scoring at 600 and over on the verbal SAT has declined from nearly 10 percent in 1972–73 to 3.5 percent in the class that entered in the fall of 1976; the number who have had verbal scores under 300 has increased from 1 percent to 4.5 percent in those five years.*

*We are indebted to President Bjork for supplying us with the raw ACE data and useful summaries of trends as well as other evaluations and docu-

Stockton has been from the outset aggressive in recruiting, with the result that it is currently the only one of the state colleges whose enrollment grew in the academic year 1976–77. Among other devices, Stockton has been bringing in busloads of students from high schools to see the campus. Rivals have criticized Bjork for these tactics, which have everywhere, of course, become more widespread as enrollments, particularly of white post-high school males, have unevenly declined. But while enrollment is essential under state FTE (full-time equivalent) funding formulas, the long-run impact on Stockton of the drop in average test scores may prove of even greater damage, not only in terms of faculty morale but in terms of Stockton's statewide reputation for intellectual and artistic quality. This is a trade-off with which the administrators of all but a few overapplied private and public institutions struggle. Bjork has taken a populist, if no longer quite so popular, line in opting for the open door.

A minority of the entering students at Stockton, as we have noted, came to the college with the intention of going on to graduate or professional school. They were at least nominally prepared to take the faculty as models, and they accepted them as gatekeepers. The students were sorted into preceptorials as mentioned earlier, which were supposed to be small enclaves suitable for advising and orientation. But, somewhat like the tutorials at Ramapo, they worked very unevenly, and the *Self-Study* devoted much of its effort to examining them, proposing that they should focus on content rather than exclusively on process. Students found their real homes not here but in their departmental programs.

Though, like some of the faculty, some of the students had been drawn to Stockton by its air of novelty, others were attracted by the avowedly preprofessional programs. On the whole the caliber of students has been disappointing to many faculty. For the commuting students, most of whom work part-time, Stockton is the available college which they hope will take them where they want to go; they do not tend to be all that attentive to the faculty's intellectual norms.[28] Correspondingly, the faculty have had to decide whether to concentrate on the minority of extremely able students who not only declare postbaccalaureate ambitions but have a reasonably good chance of going on to graduate school, or on the academically mediocre ones who form the great majority. And then there is the "bottom third," who need remedial skills if they are to cope with

---

ments prepared in the summer of 1976 by a number of administrative offices in the college. One of the characteristics of Stockton from the outset has been the continuous accumulation of data relevant to long-range planning, despite the lack of an Office of Institutional Research such as Ramapo possesses.

the Stockton programs at all. When the first full class graduated in 1975, some of these students had a very hard time on the job market: they still lacked basic skills, either in writing or in quantitative subjects—and the best jobs naturally went to those who had both. What is more, in the academic year 1975–76, 40 percent of the students either stopped out, dropped out, or did not return. Though an attrition rate of 50 percent or more is common in state colleges over the four-year span, the Stockton rate has been unusually high and is a source of great concern.

We do not have data on reasons for the attrition, but it is clear from the SAT scores of Stockton students that their low ability makes it hard for them to stick it out. Also, the fact that they almost all have jobs, leaving very little time for college work, is perhaps the most important cause of academic distress. Though there has been some tightening up all along the line at Stockton, and although most students are now choosing the A-F grading system over the still extant H-S-N (High, Satisfactory, No Credit), most of the students who leave prefer fading away to flunking out. Some may of course return; others may have concluded that, considering income forgone or delayed entry into full-time employment, the costs of continuing with higher education outweigh the benefits.[29]

In addition to the Skills Acquisition and Development Center, which makes an admirable effort to use students in tutoring others (an arrangement which presumably strengthens the skills of both), a much stronger emphasis has been put on Basic Skills, a new program which, unlike the comparable program at Ramapo, does not provide students with automatic credit. Kenneth Tompkins, the program coordinator of Basic Skills (or BASK) has struggled to keep it in the hands of faculty, against the wishes of Bjork, who wanted it taught by specially trained professionals. Tompkins and the other senior men associated with BASK hope this program will gain strength and visibility at the college. Since it is a new program, it is too early to say what its impact will be, either in reducing attrition or in persuading students that they lack and need basic skills in expression and in quantitative work.

As in other four-year institutions, the problem of how to handle what no one likes to call remedial work can be serious, especially with transfer students who are likely to demand two years' full faith and credit for their work in a community college, though it may bear no relation to the program they are entering at Stockton. Stockton's insistence that such work be reappraised either by examination or otherwise means that some students require five years to get the Stockton baccalaureate degree. On the other hand, it has been pointed out to us that, as at other four-year institutions, transfer students often bring with them a more mature sense of purpose than do those entering as freshmen. We recall in the first year of the college meeting a number of veterans who had transferred from Camden Community College or Brookdale Community College and who, on a campus dominated by freshmen, provided a leavening of experience —even a certain "collegiate" flavor—as, over faculty opposition, they requested more facilities for competitive sports and even talked about starting a fraternity.

If one compares the catalogue for 1976–77 with that for the preceding year, one can see that General Studies, though still offering an enormous variety of courses, occupies a somewhat less prominent place in the most recent announcement. Students are understandably less inclined to be experimental. And, as there are no full-time appointments in General Studies, the faculty teaching these courses recognize that, if they lack tenure, their strongest support is likely to come from within their programs and not from teaching General Studies courses or encouraging students to develop an individuated curriculum outside of a particular major.

However, the General Studies Program still has a great variety of courses, which focus not only on methods of inquiry, but on group behavior, skills in communication, the arts, and specific, sometimes quite esoteric, topics. Some courses in General Studies aim at general integration and synthesis; some are designed, as the catalogue puts it, to "help students develop their own creativity, understanding of self, in spiritual and intellectual awareness, taught typically in an experiential mode."[30] Some courses in General Studies are off-beat and quite avant-garde: for example "French Cinema: The New Wave Movement," or a jointly taught course, "The Ascent of Man," taught by a physicist, a biologist-anthropologist, and a philosopher. A political scientist teaches a course called "Humanistic Politics: Freud and Marx." These are all courses that one could easily match at Ramapo.

For some of the earlier faculty recruits to Stockton who are still deeply involved with General Studies, antagonism toward the pre-professional thrust of the college remains—sometimes even when the profession in question is their own. In some cases they had in fact arrived at Stockton with negative feelings concerning their own graduate training. And yet at the same time, they have been rarely as pedagogically (let alone politically) revolutionary as they often appeared to be: it is important to them to show that they can be successful at the old games even though they tend to disparage them. Thus, they are often self-consciously proud of students who have

gone on to do distinguished work in a graduate program at a major
university, or happy with the relatively small minority who have succeeded in entering a competitive medical or law school.

None of this ambivalence is meant to imply that students at Stockton who came to the college wanting to enter a serious and scholarly program have trouble finding one; there are many such arenas.
The natural sciences at Stockton, as at Ramapo, provide a good deal
of challenge for those who want to be stretched by serious and demanding teaching. Mathematics and the natural sciences at colleges
such as Stockton have an advantage in addition to their pedagogic
seriousness and presumed vocational suitability: they can offer safe
harbors against cultural as well as vocational winds. There is reasonable consensus about what is good work, and students are not left
at sea as to where they stand.

Stockton, like Ramapo, has made serious efforts to bring together
what C. P. Snow terms the "two cultures" in various kinds of joint
efforts. We referred just now to a General Studies course which aims
at such an enterprise. Given the difficulty, even in the best liberal-
arts colleges, in getting students in the nonscience areas to penetrate
the increasing complexities of science, the effort of Ramapo and
Stockton in this domain is unusual.

Inevitably, any efforts at innovative and especially collective teaching, whether within or across the lines of traditional academic disciplines, require far more effort and are more risky than regular
course presentations.[31] Like the General Studies courses, the preceptorials too have suffered, for the preceptors are diverse not only
in degrees of seriousness, but also in powers of drawing students
who are not compelled to attend preceptorials—in the past students
came only to get their registration cards signed and saw their preceptors only once or twice a year. Stockton's very thoughtful *Self-
Study* shows its awareness of these problems, which, of course, are
not unique.

We have already noted that there was at the outset a certain tension between some faculty and a number of students concerning the
role of athletics. President Bjork's view that students were to be left
entirely to their own devices did not remove the fear (shared by
avant-garde faculty and students), when a group of students founded
club sports and wanted to play other clubs, that Stockton might degenerate into a jock college. There is now at least one fraternity, and
there are a great many club sports; the fear of "athletic overempha-
sis" appears to have vanished.[32]

Students are involved in a number of other activities and projects,
among them *Stockpot*, a literary journal edited by a small group of

students with the advice of Stephen Dunn, an assistant professor of creative writing. It is very impressive. (The Spring 1976 issue includes contributions, articles, and photographs, from students and faculty. There is a poem by a student, Sandy Beach, entitled "Saturday Night at the Movies," which won honorable mention in the 1976 competition of the *Hiram Poetry Review*; she has also published elsewhere.) And any issue of the *Stockton Chronicle* will indicate that there is an active program of concerts and lectures, although not as elaborate as the program at Ramapo. A day-care center on campus and other projects have gotten part of their support from student activity fees. As student tuition and various fees have virtually doubled in the last five years to $879, an effort is being made to give students needing financial aid preference for on-campus work experiences, and there is an attempt to have financial aid keep pace with rising costs.[33]

Governance at Stockton reflects the prevalent student feeling that no one group should presume to take authority and that everyone should have an equal chance to participate. Stockton began with the creation of a College Council which was to represent all constituencies—administrators, faculty, staff, and students—and in which some students and faculty would also be elected at large. Others, as already mentioned, were selected by lot from a group who had volunteered. Meetings were open, and we ourselves attended one of them, chaired by a voluble Southerner who enjoyed the ritual of motions and amendments even when adhering to them seemed needlessly to delay what obviously were often desultory and poorly attended proceedings. It was soon recognized that whatever was resolved at meetings was not necessarily to be conclusive: every decision had to go through the president's office for approval or veto.

By the second year of Stockton (1972–73), the belief prevailed —as reported by Harold Hodgkinson, an outside evaluator—that Stockton was not democratically run. To aid his study of the campus senates as experiments in democracy, Hodgkinson had distributed the Institutional Functioning Inventory, an instrument prepared by the Educational Testing Service, on a random basis, to faculty, students, and administrators. He reports his findings not only about authoritarian governance, but also about generally low faculty morale, though there was agreement among faculty and administrators that the institution was conceived as a student-centered program.[34] In fact, the *Stockton Self-Study* (done two years later by Professors William Daly and Robert Helsabeck) just referred to, suggests that there is now a greater realism on campus; individuals know where the president stands, and no pretense is made that decision-making in the ultimate sense, apart from efforts to solicit opinions from all constituencies, is either decentralized or democratized.

IV

Our efforts to understand Stockton and Ramapo began in the same year they opened, the academic year of 1971–72, when we visited each campus for nearly a week, and in addition, met informally with their top officials and some of their faculty; we also had two opportunities for discussion with officials of the State Department of Higher Education. Moreover, we sought to gain some understanding of the other state institutions in the New Jersey system by informal conversations with members of the Board of Higher Education, by brief visits to Trenton State College and to Livingston College at Rutgers, as well as by conversation and correspondence with faculty members at other New Jersey state colleges. In view of the brevity of these visits and the great changes which have overtaken both institutions in the interim, we at first concluded that we were in no position to write anything concerning the two colleges, since it proved impossible to accept repeated invitations for re-visits. And when five years later we decided that we did want illustrations in this volume of what we have termed popular reforms as they operated in new state colleges, we concluded it was important to concentrate on institutions which were located in the seaboard states which had been laggard in public higher education. Our task became clear: to seek to understand the changes that had occurred at Stockton State College and at Ramapo, as well as what had stayed the same, when, with somewhat comparable financial resources, a relatively free hand for their administrators, and a wish to "make it new" both in curricular and in physical terms, they attempted to develop exciting new institutions which would put themselves, and indeed New Jersey, on the map of innovative higher education. (In this connection, it is beside the point that Richard Bjork at Stockton soon abandoned the label of "innovative," or "experimental," which he felt put him in dubious company and would not sell in South Jersey; for as we have seen, almost in spite of himself, such adjectives do fit the kind of college he has created.)

The work we then undertook over a two-year period consisted of circulating a total of eight drafts of this chapter to faculty, administrators, and others who are knowledgeable concerning the two colleges. Their extraordinary willingness to respond to repeated calls for information and correction has given us the confidence that what appears here, though there are surely still errors of fact and many open issues of interpretation, is not too wide of the mark. Naturally, we have kept in touch vicariously with both institutions in the interim since our visits, by reading student papers, official documents, newspaper accounts, *ad hoc* committee reports, and accreditation reports—for example, the Middle States Association Accreditation team gave Ramapo high marks for vitality although suggesting that more structure might now be requisite. Naturally, when we could, we talked with visitors from both institutions, including top officials, faculty, and former faculty and administrators. As in all our work, we sought to take account of the biases of our informants; even so, paradoxes remain, and we are inclined to think that no reader of this chapter at either institution will be quite satisfied with our account. One thing is clear from a series of letters, telephone conversations, marginal annotations to successive drafts, and visits: understandable public-relations concerns aside, many individuals at both colleges are themselves curious about their own institution and about its sibling-competitor. Despite frustration and often bitterness and even animosity, faculty members and administrators continue to fight for their divergent pedagogic ideals.

This is significant, since at both institutions, as at all those we have described in this volume, except perhaps the two St. John's Colleges, there has been a common tendency (as with other new institutions that sought to be experimental), for faculty to become exhausted; or as they describe themselves, burned out. We think that this phenomenon reflects not only the long hours put in to get a new institution started but also the tensions and anxieties of people who have passionate pedagogic convictions, and often strong political opinions concerning the governance of the institution or the management of the society at large. At Ramapo, what seems to us (though not to the leaders themselves) a laissez-faire style of management has meant that one's colleague group can change one's situation, as it were, overnight; since a new interdisciplinary course may be added at any time to compete with one's own, there is a ceaseless effort at pedagogic one-upmanship. At Stockton, managed from the top with no illusions about participation, the anxieties rest on the question as to how President Bjork will interpret the student "vote" and shift his priorities for expansion in some areas, shrinkage in others. In any case, the exhaustion we have noted was in part the result of the rapidity with which both institutions grew. Before a program could be established, it might double in size, requiring additional new faculty who had not shared in the original planning; or the program might quite suddenly disappear altogether.

We have said that Richard Bjork denies that Stockton is an experimental or, in the new lingo, "experimenting" college. Yet it is also clear that there is innovation and cultural ferment at both colleges; and neither has become what many Ramapo and some Stockton faculty feared they might: that is, a "trade school." In fact, what is striking at both institutions is the role of the arts. Ramapo had not been prepared for this, having no real theater and/or studio space until just now. A faculty member at Stockton confirms this unexpected situation, too, and writes: "A great surprise here is the continued popularity of the arts. It has replaced 'sensitivity' in the area of self-exploration for ever so many. . . . This is a dimension of American and South Jersey life which the President never foresaw . . ."

If one turns to the differences between the two institutions, certainly their location is a theme we have continually emphasized. President Bjork may not have foreseen that in South Jersey there would be students, to be sure a minority in comparison with those in programs leading to careers in business and industry, who wanted to express themselves in the arts. But he did make use of Stockton's location to build a focus in environmental science which has brought some imaginative faculty, attentive to students, with whom a warm sense of colleagueship could be maintained. Above all, Richard Bjork fitted what the more conservative elements of South Jersey saw as the proper role of a college president, that is, the business-like, no-nonsense manager who puts students on their mettle without pampering them, while monitoring faculty and seeing to it that they did their jobs in ways that would keep attracting student traffic. Bjork possesses some of the strengths of industrial managers: forcefulness, the ability to make decisions and to judge markets, and at the same time the ability to delegate and to be flexible when opposition is sufficiently forceful. His faculty, more depressed by his coldness than impressed by his accomplishments, rarely appreciate what he has accomplished in increasing enrollments in the poorest part of the state and in securing from Trenton a level of funding considerably higher than the state college average. Yet even at Trenton Bjork did not maintain the good relations he had at the outset with his first backer, Ralph Dungan; and as new members of Stockton's board of trustees are added, not all of them South Jersey residents, it may well be that the president's honeymoon with his board, which has lasted since the college began, is coming to an end. Furthermore, the fact that Bjork is accessible to students and is concerned to lay on a program with wide appeal does not mean that he has formed close personal ties with students any more than he has in general with faculty or with independent-minded administrators. And while Bjork may consider himself a public servant of the State of New Jersey, faculty of the sort attracted to Stockton do not regard themselves in that light.

If by an exercise of counterfactual imagination we could conceive of Bjork as president of Ramapo, and Potter of Stockton, we can immediately see that neither would have worked out at the other institution. Bjork would have struck the original Ramapo Board as rude and tactless, willful and certainly lacking in any desire to placate faculty, some of whom have maintained independent access to board members. More conciliatory, rarely combative, George Potter could on most issues carry his board with him through persuasion —a tactic less successful with many of his faculty. Yet even there, he has continuously sought to create good relations with faculty; and the latter, whatever their insecurities, are not afraid that students will get to him first and turn him against any particular faculty member, even though he is accessible to both groups in the academic community. Warm and cordial of manner, genuinely concerned with ideas and eager to keep Ramapo a haven for ideas and for creative work in the arts, Potter is the very opposite of the managerial president. Although his North American administrative experience has been entirely in public higher education, he possesses what many might think of as a small-private-college manner, suitable to the aspirations of many Bergen County residents who, whatever their initial misgivings, now belong to the Friends of Ramapo and give support to the college. Even at the cost of losing students that the college could ill afford to lose, he was prepared to limit the extent to which Ramapo would become an undergraduate school of business—and if there was snobbery in this judgment, a snobbery almost endemic to liberal-arts colleges, it was also in its way an act of courage: an effort to hold high the banner of the liberal arts in a state college system which, once geared to turning out schoolteachers, could quickly become geared to turning out, so the fear ran, narrow technocrats and semi-literate accountants.

Certainly, as this chapter has indicated, differences between Ramapo and Stockton reflect the dramatically different presidential styles. President Potter, far from discarding the label of "innovation," has emphasized the freedom of students to plan their own courses of study. A number have in this way discovered, with the help of faculty, interests they did not know they had when they entered; had Ramapo allowed itself to become a "trade school," such students would not have had such horizons opened to them. On the surface, at any rate, Stockton strikes the visitor as a tight ship; Ramapo appears as a more relaxed place, where a receptive president and vice-president respond as best they can to the wishes and demands of vocal students and faculty.

For a certain portion of its student body, for example, older highly motivated women returning to college either for vocational or "cultural" reasons, or well-to-do students who find Ramapo the "best buy," far superior to many of the less selective private colleges in the area, the relative freedom of passage through the college which Ramapo still offers may be optimal for some, and certainly not harmful for others—those who have had time to think about what they want to do, or what would be interesting to do, and who, if they make a mistake, have the family backing for second and even third chances to secure the necessary credentials. But for most New Jersey state college students even at Ramapo, working part-time and commuting, this kind of program is an "elitist" education which can be disorienting—as indeed it is for some noncosmopolitan students in elite colleges also, as we have seen in Chapter 8.

Alden Dunham, author of *The Colleges of the Forgotten Americans: A Profile of State Colleges and Universities*,[35] might be inclined to argue that Ramapo and Stockton would have been better off with a number of faculty possessing the degree of Doctor of Arts, a degree pioneered by Carnegie-Mellon and a number of other institutions. It is a degree which is not aimed at "an original contribution to scholarship" (the often euphemistic label for the Ph.D. dissertation), but which, though no less scholarly, focuses on problems of pedagogy rather than exclusively on problems of the content of the various disciplines. Yet, according to Richard Chait (former assistant to President Bjork), among the hundreds of applicants for positions at Stockton, not one had secured the Doctor of Arts degree—which, to be sure, had only recently been instituted. It has been Dunham's hope that those preparing for a Doctor of Arts would in the course of their training learn something about problems of teaching in state colleges, and about postsecondary education generally, and hence, be less likely to feel disillusioned as well as often secretly inadequate on their first teaching jobs. Furthermore, those graduate students who have opted for the Doctor of Arts degree would seem less likely to believe that they had let their mentors down if they did not carry forward their work.[36]

Many faculty, both at Ramapo and Stockton, struggle with the question as to how to reach and teach students who are in college only on a semi-voluntary basis, not only working part-time but commuting and spending what leisure time they have often with noncollege peers. Students have arrived in college through social promotion, and it is a kind of handicraft labor with seldom visible results to undertake the basic skill training left out of their elementary and secondary school preparation. It is not clear that the Doctor of Arts programs now in existence know how to prepare faculty to undertake basic skill training at something called a college, let alone to enjoy it and feel good and legitimate about it.[37] Certainly, egalitarian rhetoric, and the shift of label from "higher education" to "postsecondary education" are not enough to help faculty members faced with the kinds of students now coming to colleges like Stockton and Ramapo. Such students are already turned off by "academics" (as they refer to their studies), obviously eager for a credential—yet perhaps not so obviously prepared to believe that a college education should in some fashion be different from simply the thirteenth, fourteenth, fifteenth, and sixteenth years of schooling.

A faculty member at Stockton writes concerning his own puzzlement: "How do you teach these kinds of students, what do you teach them? It seems to me that you must avoid the incipient paternalism in assuming that they are not good enough for the recent French novel. You must also avoid giving undergraduate courses in 'what you wanted but never got in graduate school.' Stockton has not found the way. The bizarre, avant-garde courses have not increased absolutely and declined relatively to the curriculum as a whole. They are there and will be." He then goes on to say that what is lacking is any intellectual drive among faculty to thresh such questions out, so that they might be checked in their vagaries or misinterpretations —if not by their students, at least by a sympathetic group of colleagues. He comments that there is "simply no money available to let people work together on these [collegially taught] kinds of courses." He continues that there is no shared tradition, such as the University of Chicago or, we might add, St. John's, would provide for the faculty.

In fact, one of the complaints most frequently voiced by faculty at both institutions concerns their isolation from each other. One Ramapo faculty member wrote us that when he had a scholarly paper on which he wanted criticisms from colleagues, he could find no one at Ramapo to show it to. The college was too small for expertise in many areas, and he had to turn to a friend at Fairleigh Dickinson University. In this respect, Stockton faculty are even worse off, for they are isolated from any metropolitan community as well as from each other, both in their scattered homes and in their scattered offices. They are, like the majority of students, commuters; but what both colleges have been attempting is the kind of education provided more commonly in residential settings, whether public as in the case of Santa Cruz, or private as in the instance of New College. In talking orally with faculty and staff after their accrediting team visit, Emilia Doyaga, academic vice-president (now acting president) of the SUNY College at Old Westbury, made many suggestions to the Stockton faculty as to what would be useful in the way of planning and structure—suggestions which would only be feasible if the faculty had some kind of collegial organization which, in cooperation with the president, could engage in long-range planning both for the college over-all and for individual units. As we have already noted, the report of the Accrediting Team strongly implies that Stockton now needs another kind of leadership, more collegial and less "managerial." Yet the fact is that both presidents, Richard Bjork and George Potter, are the senior presidents in the state college system, though neither college has succeeded in setting a standard for the rest of that system. The other state colleges, with enrollments averaging about three times those of Ramapo and Stockton, have had their own internal agendas for incremental reform—to whatever degree that might be possible in a situation of continuing fiscal crisis and heavily tenured faculty, and within the controls imposed by state-wide collective bargaining and system-wide regulations. Neither Ramapo nor Stockton has reached the hoped-for size of 5,000 FTE students, or is likely to within the foreseeable future, despite intense efforts by both presidents to publicize the achievements of their institutions inside and outside New Jersey. Indeed, if one looks at both colleges from a national perspective, one is struck by their similarities: their maintenance of an interdisciplinary, relatively undepartmentalized structure; their insistence—with full presidential support in the case of Ramapo, and reluctant acquiescence in the case of Stockton—on providing a liberal-arts education, as well as immediate vocational opportunities, for a mass commuter student body. Both colleges have become cultural centers in their respective areas. While not matching the achievements of the SUNY System, both have faculties which in quality and dedication would seem equal or superior to most state colleges in the Northeast.

Reflections

A Modest Proposal

Reflections on the Future of Undergraduate Reform

Like the Church of Rome after Luther, the modern secular cathedrals we call universities remain strong and retain their hegemony on the academic landscape. Even the most distinctive reformers who wrote new creeds—those we have referred to as telic reforms—won relatively few adherents and met only mixed success. Yet, like the Protestant reformers, they sometimes succeeded by partial incorporation as the modern university expanded to take on the aims of the aesthetic expressives or made room for some of the T-group heretics. The multiversity adds new functions with relative ease. It is a pluralist cathedral where different sects may worship at the side altars as long as most of the offerings support the central tenets of the utilitarian and research-oriented faiths.

Yet occasionally a visionary from one of the side altars will seize the main pulpit—as did Scott Buchanan and Robert Hutchins—to lecture the vulgar utilitarians and then march off to found a rival church. The telic reformers carried on a kind of institutionalized dialogue about what the purposes of undergraduate education ought to be. They created models of undergraduate experience radically at odds with a vision of the college as either a vocational training facility or an anteroom to the graduate schools.

The dialogue about purposes, which we discuss in Chapter 2, differs markedly from the rise of the popular reforms described in Chapter 6. Like the telic reforms, the popular reforms were often cast in the rhetoric of an assault on the graduate-school mentality that dominated the multiversity. And in fact, they were an attack on departmentalism and on the required sequences of courses established by the graduate schools. Yet in another sense, the popular reforms of the last decade were an extension of the elective system that was the foundation of the modern graduate school. In this chapter we want to place our reflections on some of the popular reforms in the context of earlier cycles of prescription and freedom in the curriculum, and offer a proposal for achieving a greater measure of intellectual community for undergraduates that will take into account the realities of the modern university.* The chapter ends with some considerations of the constraints that will affect the future course of undergraduate reform.

I

The shape of the undergraduate curriculum has been determined in all eras by three variables: depth, breadth, and fixity. Charles W. Eliot attacked the fixed structure of the nineteenth-century liberal-arts curriculum at Harvard with a verbal arsenal not unlike that of latter-day reformers. Early in his forty-year reign as president of Harvard, Eliot reflected on the success of his elective reform as illustrated by his son Charles's undergraduate career. Charles had enrolled at Harvard in 1878, when the old fixed requirements remained in place only for the freshman year, which President Eliot saw as largely a continuation of his son's "uncongenial school studies." At the end of his freshman year, Eliot recorded, his son expressed "thanksgiving that his 'classical education' was at last ended." Eliot regarded the new free-choice curriculum as an elysium and reported that young Charles found all his electives to his liking. Electives were identified with liberty, better teaching, and the rise of desirable specialization. They were also an important means by which students

---

*Our discussion in this chapter, as throughout most of the book, is primarily concerned with four-year colleges and universities. Our account neglects the fastest growing sector of higher education in the United States, the two-year community colleges, enrolling about 4 million of an estimated 11.3 million full- and part-time students in 1976. By extension, of course, the two-year colleges are affected by what happens in the universities, since nearly half their students do transfer to four-year colleges. But this percentage has been declining from about two-thirds who transferred in the mid-1960s to 52 percent by the end of the decade and probably less than half today. The largest share of the two-year college enrollment is comprised of so-called terminal students who enter the job market after completing training programs, and adults who are pursuing avocational courses on a part-time basis. See Engin Holmstrom, "Transfers from Junior to Senior Colleges," American Council on Education, 1972. Enrollment figures for 1976 based on fall survey by the National Center for Educational Statistics, reported in the *Chronicle of Higher Education*, November 22, 1976, p. 3.

could exercise a blunt judgment about faculty quality by voting with their feet.[1]

Eliot was a leader of the free elective system that transformed provincial colleges into universities that were an American amalgam influenced by the German model. Research scholars could not work at their specializations if they were tied to the teaching requirements of the fixed classical curriculum. As the graduate schools became a permanent and then a dominating feature of American higher education, they established their own requirements and a new bureaucracy of departments to police the lower precincts.* They fostered and enhanced the system of competition that led to the syndrome of more work and less reward that we described in Chapter 6.

In the last decade, as in the 1860s and 1870s, the swing to elective free choice has been a means of dismantling the old system of requirements and of accommodating a more diverse student body. Though a few colleges tried bravely to maintain core curricula, the large-scale Study of Education at Stanford, which resulted in a multivolume report in 1968–69, led not to greater integration of the curriculum but to greater formlessness and an increase in the variety of options that students could choose as paths toward a Stanford degree (including many that took place off campus). Similarly, Daniel Bell's magnificent study in 1966 of general-education programs, which focused on Columbia College but cast long side-glances at Chicago and Harvard, led, as the late Lionel Trilling has pointed out, to no coherent faculty discourse: Trilling recalls Bell's "brilliant report" as a "sad and significant event in the culture of our time . . . From my long experience of the College, I can recall no meetings on an educational topic that were so poorly attended and so lacking in vivacity as those in which the report was considered. If I remember correctly, these meetings led to no action whatever, not even to the resolve to look further into the matter."[2] The College of the University of Chicago, although no longer relatively autonomous from the graduate divisions, maintained its core curriculum as did its offshoot, Shimer College, in Mount Carroll, Illinois. We have already seen that St. John's was wholly uncompromising. Some of the smaller denominational schools also maintained core require-

---

*Of course, the "policemen" who went out from these graduate departments to do the policing in liberal-arts colleges often imposed more requirements than their former mentors would insist upon. Students were not told, for example, that many sociology departments would prefer to have a graduate student who had taken his first degree in history or economics, advice that Joseph Zelan gives in "Undergraduates in Sociology," in Martin Trow, ed., *Teachers and Students* (New York: McGraw-Hill, 1975), p. 198.

ments, although it soon became difficult to distinguish the wished-for but rare interdisciplinary teacher from the undisciplined or even anti-disciplinary.

The explosion of knowledge in fact made interdisciplinary programs much more difficult to attain, and indeed the more advanced the field, the more difficult the establishment of its relations with neighboring fields, as was notably the case in mathematical economics or in experimental psychology. Though the great state universities, such as Minnesota, had also sought to maintain general-education requirements, they were considered by the faculty to be intellectually second-rate, as adult education still tends to be regarded; and at Harvard, General Education, never as coherent as at Columbia or Chicago, became the rubric under which not only traditional required courses but also some fairly experimental ones, like some of the Freshman Seminars or courses in the residential Houses, were offered—often scholarly courses, but not part of a rationale that carried credibility with faculty or students. Similarly, the Bressler Committee set up at Princeton in 1971 tried to determine if it would be possible to arrive at a core curriculum adapted to the contemporary world, one in which computer sciences would count as well as Plato. The faculty could not agree: no department or segment of it could admit that its subject was not absolutely essential to every educated person, while the students themselves lent no support to the reimposition of requirements.*

The abolition of requirements of all sorts was pushed to the furthest extreme in the experimentally inclined elite colleges. Our own sense of the salience of increased options as the principal innovation of many experiments is confirmed in several studies. Of thirteen "new innovative institutions" listed in a Carnegie Commission Report in 1973, only three required any core subject matter, and virtually all emphasized individualized, self-paced, and student-planned curricula. The report reads like a litany: "Evergreen is a student-oriented college that holds the individual responsible for his own learning . . . Hampshire offers a study plan to students who can be responsible for

---

*Cogent, compelling, and realistic advising is, in the absence of a curriculum, the only way in which students can be given guidance which is responsive to their needs rather than to their wants—including the want of students in many selective colleges to present only their John Barrymore profile to the world and not test themselves in areas where they might prove inadequate. The difference that cogent advising by a freshman preceptor could make at Princeton is illustrated by the report of the psychologist, Roy Heath, *The Reasonable Adventurer* (Pittsburgh, University of Pittsburgh Press, 1964).

their own learning . . . At Livingston options and opportunities for independent study are available in all fields . . . Thomas Jefferson College advocates the concept of 'ad hocracy' in educational programming . . . At Purchase [of the State University of New York] . . . there are no college-wide graduation requirements."[3]

Perhaps the best example of the high-water mark of these curricular reforms is Hampshire College. When it opened in 1970, it attracted eleven applicants for every place. Hampshire had no departments, no grades, student-designed examinations, and free choice of courses. Students invented courses, taught some, designed their own majors, and followed their own bents. It was a college in which the central paradigm was to keep the options open. What attracted students was the realization that they would not be pushed into fixed modes or courses of study and would be freed of competition for grades as they would not be at most university colleges. Similarly, faculty were attracted by the freedom to teach outside the bounds of departmental structures. (Some also sought relief from the publish-or-perish competition in the graduate-oriented universities.) Yet there were many paradoxes in the pursuit of these goals for faculty as well as students.

During the first week of classes at Hampshire, complaints were raised about the one required course in human development, and a year later that had been virtually abolished. At the end of a lengthy meeting in which students adopted a governing charter, it was decided that student representation on policymaking committees would not be elective. Instead, every student would be presumed eligible (unless she or he struck his name from the college register), and names would be chosen at random by a computer.

In annual visits of a week or more in the first four years of Hampshire's growth, we were struck by faculty gripes about endless meetings and student complaints about isolation and lack of community. Faculty always seem to complain about meetings, and this did not seem out of the ordinary to us at first. But we were forced to note the persistence and urgency of the complaints, and to wonder why faculty felt it so necessary to attend. The causes were complex, arising partly out of the feeling of newness at Hampshire and their desire to be part of it, partly out of fear that in the absence of the usual scholarly visibility it was necessary to achieve visibility in the community, and partly because the egalitarian nature of the governance system required more participation of students and junior faculty in committees. But there was something else, we began to realize,

the need to protect the hidden dreams. These faculty had been drawn
to Hampshire because they shared common dislike—sometimes ha-
tred—of the dominant multiversity. They were united in their opposition but not their aspirations. They had no common vision other
than freedom of options for all. But they had private visions of what
a college ought to be, and they hoped their dream could be brought
into reality. Moreover, in their wish that others might share their
enthusiasm, they felt it necessary to point out the loveliness of their
vision at every opportunity, or at least to be ever watchful that this
dream not be killed. The destruction of the dream could happen at
any meeting in so fluid a situation.*

Nor were faculty willing to settle for a partial dream, a limited
turf or program. They, too, wanted all the options open, the possibility of total success. A fixed program would mean limiting some
possibilities of existence, putting boundaries on one's freedom to
grow or develop in new ways.

Faculty who were drawn to programs like those at Hampshire felt
confident of their teaching abilities, and usually they had been highly
regarded teachers on more research-oriented campuses. Yet in an
environment like Hampshire, the expectations of good teaching
quickly escalated. Without the assured availability of students, faculty found themselves engaged in an exhausting competition that
many came to regard as more draining (and often more wounding)
than the publish-and-perish pressures they had sought to escape. In
the early years at Hampshire, faculty were each allotted three-minute
spots on a videotape to publicize their courses. These were available
for viewing in the library during registration, and students picked
their courses from the ads. For most faculty, the process was fun the
first time.

Students, too, we learned in interviews, were not free of competitive anxieties just because they were free of grades. They wanted to
know how they compared with students elsewhere, and frequently
asked us how they stacked up against the competition. And, in a
curricular system in which each student designed his or her major,
students commonly felt they had not been as creative or brilliant as
their peers. And there was no way of knowing, because there were
no common standards of comparison. One learned to mask his com-

---

*Could it be that those colleges are most healthy in which faculty feel most
free to skip meetings, i.e., where trust is high and fear of being dealt out is
low? This might be stated as Grant-Riesman's Law: Institutional morale is
inversely correlated with mean attendance at *governance* meetings!

petitive anxiety, to affect nonchalance, but it was a rare interview in which their discomfort did not surface. "Everyone has the elite attitude that the work they are doing is better than the work you are doing," said a freshman from a Connecticut prep school. "Even when they bring it up and pretend it is not important, you know it isn't true."

Each student proceeds in relative isolation on his or her own track with little sense of the progress or destination of others. Every journey seems exotic, but there is little chance to compare travel notes about experiences across the same terrain. For some, the journey is exhilarating, yet there is a mild shock when one discovers that one is not so unique, that one's plans or responses made in isolation are quite "average." One day, after a rainy week, a young woman raced to the roof to take a picture of the beautiful sunset, only to find that dozens of others were already there snapping the same postcard view. The temporary dismay dissolved into laughter, with students perhaps unconsciously acknowledging that the search for uniqueness can be a kind of self-induced hell that prolongs rather than restrains adolescent feelings of grandiosity.

Although students everywhere are likely to complain about the lack of community, at Hampshire student concern about loneliness and isolation was unusually intense.[4] Many described the college in images of a friendly place without friendship, "almost like a commune, yet with people being isolated." Another student told us poignantly, "Everyone is dying for close relationships, but also afraid of them." Students pointed to the perpetual messes in their kitchen suites, the difficulties of organizing any long-term commitments. The irony, of course, is that, in a system in which one keeps all the options open, one option is closed: the joy of a particular choice, which is the ground of friendship, vocation, and community.[5] In order to have a relation, students must have resources to share and common interests around which friendship and even love can form. Like a number of other colleges that offered students unlimited curricular pathways, Hampshire had an air of transiency. Many students seemed poised for flight. Of course, such attitudes are not limited to elite institutions; we are reminded of a Kansas City community college that recently adopted the grade of "V," meaning that the "student has vanished without explanation."[6]

Another form of security was abolished that is a keystone of traditional colleges and universities: tenure, a lifetime commitment by the institution to a particular faculty member. The premise was that options should be kept open for new faculty. Yet the outcome was otherwise. At Hampshire, the rate of nonreappointment under its contract system, particularly in the early years, was lower than at many traditional colleges.

The results were especially clear at Evergreen State College in Olympia, Washington, which also had few requirements and operated on a faculty contract system; no faculty member among the first 100 contracts to come up for review was denied reappointment. It was easier to reappoint a mediocre or even incompetent faculty member for another three years than to make the more agonizing decision for nonrenewal that tenure forces upon colleagues.* The administrative turnover at Evergreen was high,† however, and a policy of rotational deanships was inaugurated. But at the end of four years, Evergreen pulled back, acknowledging that deans were not a fungible species and that, while the rotational policy gave everyone the chance to serve, the result was what one of Evergreen's most respected faculty members called a "self-lobotomy of institutional memory." Just as free-choice curricula reduce the authority of faculty by forcing them to sell their wares to student customers through competition with other faculty, the authority of the deans is lessened as well. After several years of such competition, many faculty feel sucked dry and used up.‡ They also begin to think tenure is not such a bad idea, not only because it reduces insecurity, but because it underscores an important formal difference in membership rights between faculty and students. Tenure also restores the privilege to choose one's colleagues and to be chosen.

In a situation in which faculty are selling their wares to students but are not empowered to require students to study anything, they are stripped of traditional authority and increasingly are seen as

---

*From the beginning, Evergreen made an effort to help faculty develop. The test was not, "Is this the best person we can get?," but "Is this person interested in trying to become a better teacher?" The renewal policy was based on "growth through mutual evaluation and self-evaluation," which perversely had the effect of making any denial of a contract the most devastating charge a faculty member could make against a colleague.

†It might be asked why deans left when nobody fired them. We suspect most deans found little satisfaction in a system where they could make little imprint on the faculty or the institution other than keeping the options open.

‡In writing to Grant about an earlier draft of this chapter, Hampshire's vice-president, Robert C. Birney, acknowledged that a college that relied on "the power to inspire rather than the power to require" put special burdens on the faculty (burdens he felt were justified in light of what Hampshire achieved). Whatever our interviews may have shown at an earlier stage (Riesman visited Hampshire in its planning stage and Grant made four visits in the years 1970–74), Birney was convinced that "many of our good people have got their second wind, and I think now feel that they know how to make this

"resource persons" rather than as teachers. In the competition for customers, some become chummy and hesitate to make demands. Yet in interviews, students express admiration for those faculty who do make stiff demands and refuse to court favor, secretly despising those who are soft on students and on each other. Even at experimental campuses like Hampshire and Evergreen, however, not all teachers see themselves as waiters giving kindly advice about the student menu. Some faculty can be quite demanding in negotiating and enforcing individualized "contracts" with students. But the system encourages shopping around, and even the unusual faculty member who can exercise personal authority in this way pays a price in time and fatigue.

Evergreen, Hampshire, and other colleges like them are illustrative of the far swing of the pendulum. But as we noted in Chapter 6, many traditional colleges and universities have also moved in the direction of reform, reducing fixed requirements and increasing student autonomy. Surveyors at the University of Michigan who examined changes nationwide between 1967 and 1974 found that on the average general-education requirements had dropped from 43 percent of a student's course load to 33 percent. There was a marked move away from required courses and a sharp decline in such basic requirements as math and foreign languages. Only half the institutions required foreign-language courses (as compared with 72 percent in 1967), and just 20 percent stipulated any courses in mathematics, compared with 33 percent earlier.[7]

Yet more interesting were the changes in subject choices revealed by transcripts in ten institutions. In all but two of the institutions, students turned away from general-education courses, and in five of them the drop was in the range of 12 to 33 percent. Students used their increased elective power not to substitute other broad-gauged requirements but to concentrate more heavily in one area. This confirms the conclusions drawn from our interviews: that students who were given complete freedom often followed a program that was a variation of a single theme. They did not roam or take large risks, but played from strength. Often the resulting "concentration" was very skewed, with many courses in particular areas of interest, such

system work" (letter of January 19, 1977). Evergreen also searched for a second wind in 1976, admitting that its faculty suffered from " 'flameout'—a state of high anxiety and low morale, brought on by overwork, ambiguity of roles and standards, uncertainty about the future, and lack of effective support by colleagues." Report of the "Long Range Curriculum Disappearing Task Force," mimeographed, June 1976, p. 3.

as population control, or heavy emphasis in one corner of a discipline, such as courses on Maslow, Rogers, and other humanistic psychologists with very little awareness of the broader map of cognitive,
experimental, and social psychology.* Although the Michigan survey
did not attempt to analyze the shift in history courses, our work
suggests that many students neglect the historical perspective when
they have autonomy to plan their own programs, a risk that is more
serious than in Eliot's day, when the high-school curriculum was
heavily saturated with history. The question of how much autonomy
students should be allowed has always been debated among experimenters and traditionalists. If one believes that history or an understanding of the language of mathematics is essential to modern
literacy, one is unlikely to leave this learning to chance. The experimenters emphasize the value of choice, of self-motivated learning,
of freedom to learn from one's mistakes. Traditionalists cite the
values of coherence, logical sequence, the obligation of a teacher to
insist that a student build a firm foundation before expressing his
individuality in the architecture of the upper stories.

As the leader of the elective reforms in the nineteenth century,
Eliot came to see free choice as a student's right, and he not only
stood against the idea of a "broad general foundation" but saw such
architectural metaphors as misleading. He opposed even the modest
distribution requirements that Cornell introduced at the turn of the
century and admitted he was "fundamentally a complete skeptic as
to the necessity of any subject whatever as an element in the educa-
cation of a gentleman and a scholar." As the historian, Hugh Hawkins, has pointed out, when authorities at Yale argued that electives
should be postponed because freshmen and sophomores were too
young to make intelligent choices, Eliot responded that although
there might be temptations for a young student in a heady environment, the "wise decision is to withdraw [the youth] betimes from a
discipline which he is outgrowing, and put him under a discipline
which he is to grow up to." For Eliot, "at eighteen the American
boy has passed the age when a compulsory external discipline is
useful."[8] An important difference between Eliot and later neoclassi-

---

*In a large university, concentrating more heavily in a single area also can
be a way of softening demands. Since there is a duplication among courses,
students can get by on half a dozen books in as many courses, since people
in the same field seldom share syllabi. At the same time we recognize that
programs that are variations on a theme can be quite challenging and exhilarating for a serious student who becomes deeply immersed in a field; much
depends on the quality of advising and the floor from which a student begins
to specialize.

cists like Scott Buchanan who prescribed all-required programs was their view that the college years began as early as fourteen. Thus, choice about specialization could safely begin at eighteen or nineteen, when it was laid on a foundation of studies that permitted wise choices.*

In our discussion of the paradoxes of reform as illustrated by Hampshire, Evergreen, and the other "free universities" of the last decade, we have been unfair to the totality of these experiments. Many students used options wisely to create stimulating programs, and while the reduced authority of faculty created strains it also gave many students increased access. We have observed that in no way did these colleges represent a "controlled experiment." If half of the Hampshire students had been randomly sent to traditional colleges, we might find that the benefits at Hampshire outweighed the risks for some or most of them.† But in pointing to these paradoxes, we are being mindful of some of the natural limits of these reforms.

When Grant visited Evergreen during its first year, the faculty scoffed at his suggestion that rotational deanships took too Panglossian a view of the distribution of administrative talent. They similarly rejected the idea that there should be any constraints on student choice. Four years later, in 1976, some faculty had come to regard a quotation on the title page of the catalog as faintly ridiculous: "You are your own creator; you appear in the splendor of your own," although it could be taken for a hip translation of Charles Eliot. That spring, the faculty accepted a proposal to institute a permanent structure of deans. At a faculty meeting Grant attended, a young poet recalled the early days at Evergreen when twenty of his colleagues had set themselves up in a corner of the library solely to encourage students to come and write individual contracts. He described the group as the "crazy wing," evoking laughter when he added, "If you don't think it was crazy, you weren't there." The principal item on the agenda was a consideration of plans to provide more continuity in the Evergreen curriculum. It was introduced with

---

*Now, however, we have the paradox that the "college years" do begin at fourteen—but in just the opposite direction from what Scott Buchanan or Robert Hutchins would have wished. That is, the high schools now offer many of the freedoms of the colleges, not requiring math and science sequences, and abolishing language requirements since most colleges no longer insist upon them. Many high schools have also virtually abandoned history, substituting "social studies" instead.

†For many students, Hampshire or Evergreen represented the best choices. We are reminded of the comment made by a colleague's son, who transferred from Harvard to Hampshire and back again, that one could appreciate neither place without having been in the other.

the comment that a few counterrevolutionaries on the faculty were now ready to go back, at least partially, to a system that provided an equivalent to departments.

The increase of elective options has often occurred at a time of enrollment stagnation or decline (as was the case in the mid-nineteenth century), although this was not the case in the last decade. But it was a factor in the sense that relative growth or loss was affected by what one's competitors offered. And the early success of institutions like Hampshire encouraged others to follow suit, and a bandwagon developed that over time diffused any competitive advantage. The Evergreen faculty, in fact, was told by its admissions officer that what may once have looked appealing to students now was a distinct disadvantage because there was no assurance that a successful program could be repeated. Applicants could not see clear pathways to jobs in the multiplicity of study options at Evergreen. A faculty survey showed that, while Evergreen wanted to maintain an experimental posture, most faculty wanted more emphasis on "academic continuity," increased attention to basic skills, and "more precise qualifications for obtaining individual contracts."[9]

Evergreen seems to us to be something of a bellwether; there is evidence that the disenchantment with the overoptioned life has spread rapidly not only among the avowedly experimental colleges but in traditional settings as well. One cannot help but remark on the cyclical nature of these reforms, even if one cannot agree on underlying causes. The wheel began to turn toward the end of Eliot's reign at Harvard when the dean he appointed in 1902 characterized the elective system as "the theory that all studies are born free and equal but that the new studies are freer and more equal than the old."[10]

Eliot's successor, A. Lawrence Lowell, rose to the presidency of Harvard on a platform directly opposed to Eliot's reforms. Lowell was concerned about "intellectual and social cohesion." In a report written a year before he was named president in 1909, Lowell indicted the elective system: It assured no systematic education and was destructive of a sense of community because there was no "spirit of emulation" since men were "out of sight of one another." Lowell's report recommended institution of a system of concentration and distribution of courses to insure that students had mastery in one field and breadth in each of the others "in which an educated man ought not to be wholly ignorant." It was adopted by the faculty with only limited opposition.[11]

Lowell's concern for community was connected with his fear that intellectual standards had declined under the free elective system.

He wanted to restore a sense of competitive excellence that he felt
was uniquely possible in a community in which a man could measure
his achievement by a common standard.

Without belaboring the analogy, it seems to us that the academic
world is ripe for a new generation of Lowells. Certainly his sentiments are on the rise. Many faculty are as tired as students of "doing
their own thing." There is a search for new sources of marrow in a
splintered curriculum, new sources of cohesion and community to
counter the sense of solipsism. The escape from the competitive
pressures has led to grade inflation and an erosion of public confidence; now some faculties are seeking ways to restore a sense of
"honors" without compromising open access.[12]

Actually, the reaction sparked by Lowell's sentiments against Eliot's
radical free-choice curriculum (Harvard students were permitted to
pick any sixteen courses at will) brought only limited change in
Harvard's departmentalism. In the long run, Lowell's concentration
and distribution requirements fostered the growth of departmental
structures. There was no turning back to the departmentless college
community of the pre-Eliot era. Although Hutchins at Chicago, Meiklejohn at Wisconsin, and Buchanan at St. John's made war on the
departments in the 1930s, departments continued to grow. Gradually, they became the key power centers in the major universities, and
by the 1950s research professorships, elaborate systems of requirements and prerequisites, and systems of distribution requirements
that were more akin to a political division of the spoils than to discussions of educational philosophy were prevalent.*

The rapid progress of departments may be illustrated by developments at Berkeley and Yale. In 1902, Berkeley required fifteen units
of work in a single department. At Yale, in 1906, the major was
defined as three year-long courses, or eighteen units. In the period
1948–51, there were some countermoves against specialization at
Berkeley, but these were defeated by the departments. By 1958, the

---

*The historian Laurence Veysey asks what explains the rapid rise of the de-
partments to such dominance in American universities: "What would a university have been like which rewarded brilliance of achievement" without departmental labels? Veysey asserts that the usual explanation—departments were
a natural outgrowth of the growth of knowledge—is not adequate. He suggests
that the departmental structures simply reflect the American penchant for
business-like organization and efficient span of control. See Veysey, "Stability
and Experiment in the American Undergraduate Curriculum," in Carl Kaysen,
ed., *Content and Context* (New York: McGraw-Hill, 1973), p. 32. We suspect
that both factors were at work: the departments were an outgrowth of both
the growth in knowledge and the growth in size of institutions.

collegiate "general" degree (i.e., a nondepartmental major) was eliminated by Berkeley, and students were virtually forced to align with departments, which by then required a minimum of thirty hours and abolished the upper limits on the number of courses a student could take in any one area. In 1955, specialization at Yale began in the sophomore year, and thirty-six units (or the equivalent of twelve courses) were required for the major. As the departments controlled more and more of the student traffic and added courses and prerequisites, little of the curriculum was left "unaffiliated." Some departments grew so large and added so many subspecialties that they became miniuniversities—e.g., political-science departments with historians, philosophers, political sociologists; economics departments with economic historians, developmental economists, specialists in energy and resource allocation, and the like. Thus the departments, through a combination of major and distribution requirements, created an undergraduate program that in its heavy prescription was reminiscent in some respects of the nineteenth-century liberal-arts college (although it was softened by a wider sampling of elective subjects).

Eliot's reforms crushed the old college and, along with Hopkins, Clark, and Cornell, facilitated the specialization out of which the departments and major graduate schools were built. The popular reforms of the last decade did not crush the departments so much as they offered new pathways around them. The general loosening also ushered in a variety of changes in organizational patterns, notably at Santa Cruz and also at the University of Wisconsin–Green Bay. In a few institutions—Evergreen and Hampshire and, to some degree, Stockton and Ramapo—departmental structures were, if not destroyed, greatly subordinated. Yet the departments generally remain dominant, perhaps even strengthened by some of the failures and obvious mediocrities of the overoptioned curriculum. Departments reflect an organization of academic disciplines that performs essential functions of discovery, dissemination, and quality control. The department is a powerful social unit as well, fostering links of colleagueship that are at once national and local. No adequate substitute for these functions came out of the last generation of reforms.

II

Thus one can argue that the departmental organization should be preserved, particularly at the graduate level, while sympathizing with Lowell's sentiments about the need for other forms of intellectual community at the undergraduate level. In fact, one could argue that while the departments form a satisfactory community for groups of specialists and graduate students who choose to associate with them, they are not the best form of community for general undergraduate education. What, then, ought to be the basis of intellectual and social community for undergraduates? This is the heart of the debate that is being renewed with a gathering momentum. We offer here a modest proposal.

We do not think there is any one best form that serves the needs of all undergraduates, whether it is the monism of St. John's or the do-as-you-please style at Hampshire. Nor do we think it likely that university faculties will agree on any unified version of liberal education. What is needed (and possible) is a set of options that are larger and more satisfying than the isotope-like trajectories of individualized curricula on the one hand, or departmental-vocational specialization on the other. Coherence and community do not require uniformity. More glue may be needed in the undergraduate curriculum, but it can come from several pots. We favor a pluralism of core programs or subcolleges of which the early Santa Cruz represents an appealing ideal. Such programs or subcolleges need not dominate the undergraduate curriculum, either in number of courses or in number of years. But to serve as the basis of community, they should be integrating experiences, as was, for example, the early Cowell College at Santa Cruz or Meiklejohn's two-year Experimental College at the University of Wisconsin.

As soon as one mentions Meiklejohn's college, one is reminded that it failed, as did its attempted renaissance under Joseph Tussman at Berkeley thirty years later. At Santa Cruz itself, many of the core programs have degenerated. A 1970 survey turned up forty-four subcolleges that had been founded in the 1960s or earlier, most of them containing no more than 600 students.[13] We would estimate that by 1977 more than half these experiments had failed or were in serious trouble. Among the casualties were Bensalem College at Fordham, Monteith at Wayne State, Johnston College of the University of Redlands, and the subcolleges at Old Westbury. On the positive side of the ledger, the Santa Cruz colleges have survived more than a decade despite demoralization. The Residential College at the University of Michigan, and Justin Morrill, Lyman Briggs, and James Madison at Michigan State have had varied careers, but continue. The subcollege pattern has been successfully expanded at Grand Valley State College in Michigan, Western Washington State College, and the Claremont Colleges. At Oakland University, Allport College (emphasizing the behavioral sciences) and New Charter

College (offering a four-year general-education program in place of distribution requirements) continue in a second decade. At the University of the Pacific, the first subcollege was founded in 1962 and two others have been added since; one of them, Elbert Covell, offers all instruction in Spanish. Research on the institutions that have survived indicates that the cluster college pattern provides significant benefits to students in enriched faculty-student interaction resulting in higher satisfaction and increased learning.[14]

The cluster college is no panacea. Although creating smaller social units is a virtue in itself in the anomic multiversities, it is not sufficient. More than changes in scale or organization are needed in order to create conditions for collaborative interdisciplinary inquiry as a foundation of revitalized intellectual communities for undergraduates. A heightened sense of common purpose and common experiences are uniquely possible in such communities. And these experiences are as important in renewing the vocation of faculty members as they are in fostering the growth of students. Cluster colleges may be one organizational form through which these aims are realized; we shall discuss others as well.

Some of the cluster colleges failed because they were social units without intellectual substance. But why have interdisciplinary programs and subcolleges that articulate a sense of purpose and developed a common curriculum (like Meiklejohn's) also failed? Some ran against the tide of the rebellion against all requirements that we outlined in Chapter 6. But there are other reasons that continue to apply in an era when faculty seem ready to reassert authority and students are willing (or at least less unwilling) to accept it.

Aside from endemic clashes of personality,* the most pervasive difficulty has been the cost to faculty who join such efforts within research-oriented institutions at the risk of being stamped as pariahs "sent down" to work in the prep school. They fear loss of visibility in their discipline, hence the loss of both mobility and tenure. Should they have tenure and choose to stay put, they may lose peer status and pay by bucking the dominant reward system. They may be pained when they can no longer keep up with the literature of their

*Quite apart from loss of status or rewards, some of these experiments fail because of unanticipated clashes of personality. Like marriages, they involve very subtle matchings, which are especially hard to assess from a distance. Faculty members are often inept in choosing their true colleagues, often assuming, as we have seen, that people who have the same enemies will turn out to be friends. College faculty have often gotten where they are by presenting their good profiles, disguising their incompetence. In a more tightly knit collegial situation they become very anxious unless they are with people they can trust, and with whose personalities they feel compatible and complementary.

original discipline and may feel lost when they attend its national or regional meetings. It is not rare for young, enthusiastic faculty members to be bitter and burned out a few years after the exciting dawn of such experimental ventures. Is their only choice to migrate to a St. John's or a small liberal-arts college, perhaps church-related, that retains some semblance of a core curriculum? It ought not to be.

What proposal could take account of these realities yet have some chance of enactment in the major universities? Let us assume one essential condition for the growth of such enterprises: deep commitment to their success at the presidential level, assuring support sufficient to countervail the by-now natural hegemony of the departments over undergraduate programs. Without firm evidence of such leadership, those faculty members whose participation is most desired are unlikely to risk large expenditures of energy at a time when governance reform has enlarged the circle of those who exercise veto powers. Secondarily, we make the assumption that research, scholarship, and judgments about tenure cannot, and should not be set aside in a research-oriented institution. Thus one must first attract and recruit to such programs not the young and untried, but those grayer heads who are secure in their disciplines, who have achieved some reputation as scholars, and who are men and women of breadth of learning. They may be growing just a bit out of touch with more technical aspects of research in their field and may be themselves in search of integrative paradigms. But these are not anti-disciplinary reformers who would innoculate students against any specialization. They would see themselves as conversant with research in their field even though they do not themselves engage in it any more. At a mature point in their careers they would be inclined to consider the virtues of general education as their interests are drawn again to questions of epistemology and philosophy of history and science.

Such scholars might typically devote the last ten to fifteen years of their careers to such enterprises, including years of semiretirement when they might be on half-pay. These teachers emeriti, in groups of four to eight, would be the founders, organizers, and master teachers of the kind of common programs we envision, serving from 75–250 students, depending upon the intensity and length of the experiment. They would take a leading role in advising, in meeting with students, and in assuring continuity in the program. They would be full-time teachers, though they would be augmented by two other categories of faculty who could work half-time and spend a shorter length of time in the program, perhaps only two or three years.

One group ought to consist of advanced graduate students who would serve as teaching fellows. They should be selected from among those who have demonstrated some excellence as teachers as well as some scholarly promise. Exposure to distinguished emeriti faculty who would be committed to helping these young Ph.D. candidates become better teachers would be a major attraction. But bonuses in pay and other privileges should also be attached to these appointments. They should be regarded as plums for those graduate students with the greatest academic promise, and should be seen as an essential part of their preparation as teachers. The intellectual experience would give valuable added dimension to most doctoral programs, yet it would not undermine disciplinary scholarship and would provide a less threatening context for the discussion of one's qualities as a teacher. With all the talk about evaluation of teaching and new reward systems, we know no better procedure than to offer the young teacher an opportunity to observe good teaching, to be observed in teaching, and to have an opportunity to work with perceptive mentors who are neither competitors nor judges of his or her own scholarship. Such an experience might constitute half of a graduate student's load in a two-year period midway in his or her studies.*

A third category of teachers could be drawn from those mid-career faculty, typically in their thirties, who have recently been awarded tenure. In the life of many such researchers, early projects are drawing to a close. Often conceived under the pressure of getting a dissertation done, such projects are then drawn out into a string of publications, perhaps worthy but not close to one's heart. These able, well-trained scholars believe in their disciplines. Yet they are also in search of new perspectives on their field and new directions for their work. The temptation for some is to abandon their disciplines, or to begin a long slide into mediocre and lifeless performance within their departments while pursuing an avocation. They are ripe for renewal. They could be invited into the interdisciplinary program on a full- or part-time basis for a period of two or three years, at which time they would return to their departments. The work in the interdisciplinary program ought to precede a sabbatical, an opportunity for re-immersion in full-time scholarly pursuits along whatever new tracks had been opened up. Mid-career faculty would also enrich the program

---

*We are aware that we ask a great deal here of graduate students who are in fast-moving fields, who may be coping with the demands of parenthood in two-career families, or who have been conditioned to regard teaching as a handicap in competition with those pursuing full-time research. In some cases, therefore, the appointment might better come as a postdoctoral fellowship. Of course the restricted employment market combined with contemporary emphasis on excellence in teaching ought to act as an inducement somewhat counterbalancing these other pressures.

with perspectives from recent research and make connections between old texts and new without being allowed to turn the program into an inflated version of a survey course.

An obvious advantage of this arrangement is that it allows for a natural structure of leadership among the faculty of such programs, which too often in our experience have foundered on rejection of all hierarchies. The young, idealistic, but often insecure faculty who have begun such experiments in the past have often been unwilling to accept one of their own as master teacher. Yet such leadership—and willingness to respond to it—is essential.[15]

Such an arrangement also maximizes opportunities for peer learning among both faculty and students. Successful programs of this type offer faculty the most desirable reward: the opportunity to learn from each other. An equivalent of the archon group at St. John's or the faculty book seminar at Evergreen is a vital aspect of such programs. It is an occasion, usually weekly, where the faculty gathers apart from students to discuss a text or a paper. It is the context for the development of a new collegial group, and it must have a rigorously intellectual focus that excludes organizational matters.

Particularly in an age when wider access to the university has resulted in admission of great numbers of students from the bottom third of the ability distribution, there is a need to encourage forms of peer teaching. Opportunities for student colleagueship are enhanced when students interact in small groups as they pursue common goals. We do not underestimate the effort required to produce this happy result; the simple presence of common goals does not guarantee cooperation or protect against the possibility of destructive competition. Yet the abhorrence of requirements and competition was so great in the last decade as to virtually deny the possibility of the kind of student colleagueship we envision here. Self-designed programs isolated students from one another, and programs of "independent study" were often concordats of mutual neglect. In such a Brownian motion, students may collide but they seldom cooperate. The benefits of colleagueship are great for able students as well as for the least prepared, although the larger numerical mix tends to favor the former. We are not suggesting that the primary aim of new core programs should be to reach the bottom third, or that the programs can replace other special tutoring and counseling services such students may need. We digress in anticipation of the criticism that core programs are inimical to the needs of those students.[16]

Yet core programs are unlikely to survive if they abandon rigorous standards of evaluation out of misplaced sympathy. Experimental core curricula or subcollege programs often lose the confidence of the faculty as a whole because they are seen as offering a soft option in which nobody fails. Even where faculty and students are believed to be serious, critics in the regular departments harbor the suspicion that the subcollege programs are too talky and suffer from the cult of intimacy, sheltering students against tougher prerequisites in statistics or in the physics lab.

Such criticism can be deflected by incorporating at least one requirement that is undeniably tough and immune to criticism that the program is slipshod. It should be a requirement that encourages students to work to the hilt, to stretch themselves. Careful means of assessment must be developed, so that excellent performance may be convincingly discriminated from that which is ordinary or below par. The idea of performance, of some sort of public assessment, can be important. The defense of a thesis on a small scale, the publishing of papers in mimeograph form can boost confidence and serve as a learning experience as well. Alverno College in Milwaukee has developed an ingenious series of exercises in its core program in the liberal arts.[17] Some, adapted from assessment procedures developed by American Telephone & Telegraph, require students to develop communication skills by demonstrating their ability to advance an argument in small groups. These exercises are videotaped, and each student graduates with a reel showing her progress on tape over four years. Swarthmore imports external assessors from other colleges to examine their honors candidates. In a marine biology program at Florida State University, some skeptical senior faculty who served on juries examining students were won over to the quality of the program. Assessments through such means as foreign-service exams or the employment of examiners from business or professional life may be useful. Where possible, faculty from regular departments should be employed as assessors in order to interest them in the program and to assure them of its quality.

Undeniably, the best of these programs have been plagued with a common obstacle: the difficulty of attracting students. Some founders are inclined to believe that they have lost students because the programs are too demanding or too out of touch with do-your-own-thing impulses. But from the student point of view, when they were not seen as havens for freaks, the programs were often perceived not just as traditional liberal education, but as anti-vocational, anti-science, or both. There is more than a grain of truth in such perceptions. The most vigorous proponents of core curricula have been humanistic defenders of liberal culture whose spirits rage against both the utilitarian and the scientific ethos. Rarely have the founders of such programs emulated those at St. John's in asking the humanists to enter the laboratory or to teach mathematics (which we have forgotten was part of the original quadrivium) as well as Plato. Many students do not see such general-education programs as relevant to their career aims, and they are quite content to enter freshman programs that prepare them to be nurses or engineers and to skip Plato. It is neither likely nor perhaps desirable that replications of the St. John's program will be attempted in the modern university. But core programs can be initiated without mandating a faculty of Renaissance men, though it is crucial that scientists and faculty from the professional schools be included in planning and teaching. Such participation need not corrupt the core curricula nor turn them into bastard offspring of vocational and liberal education. There are many faculty in the professional schools who would be eager to teach at least some of the time in a genuinely liberal core program. In fact, one model of such a program might combine full-time study in the freshman year with a second-year split between the core program and vocational or preprofessional studies. In the second year (which could be the senior year with perhaps greater benefit), the core program would draw together future nurses, accountants, lawyers, industrial chemists, and teachers to discuss the history and meaning of professionalism and its ethical problems.

Other steps could be taken to assure a student market. The most obvious would be to offer a sufficient range of programs to allow and require each student to choose one that appeals—each core program being the equivalent of six to ten regular courses. Another approach would establish a core program as a prerequisite to receiving an honors degree, for example. Some professional schools or departments which receive a large number of applications might give preference to those who complete certain core programs. But none of these devices is as important as assuring that high-quality faculty from the humanities, the sciences, and the professional schools are attracted to core programs in sufficient numbers.

At least three objections may be raised to the scenario we have drawn. First, it may seem that we decry the overoptioned curriculum only to substitute another set of options called core programs or subcolleges. Are core programs simply overgrown courses? It could be argued that there are no essential differences between them and programs in which a unique "core" is constructed and designed by each student. This is to confuse atoms with molecules. A student who encounters a series of atomlike courses may put together his own molecule. But the experience of sniffing oxygen and hydrogen separately is very different from taking a plunge into the water. At their best, core programs are interdisciplinary experiences that draw out the bondlike connections among subject matters to create intellectual substance of a different order. This experience should not be left to chance.

Another criticism commonly raised against core programs is that they impose an elitist view. They are castigated as the New Pietism, as attempts to teach a fixed set of moral dogmas under the guise of curriculum. Alain Touraine puts a Neo-Marxist twist on this argument, asserting that the "predominant concern [of general education movements] was the consolidation of the ruling class."[18] But we are arguing not for a preferred set of attitudes or intellectual manners but for a more coherent pluralism. Touraine and others underestimate the degree of diversity that existed among the proponents of general education even in an earlier era; the varied experiments in the 1930s and 1940s at St. John's, Sarah Lawrence, Bennington, and Harvard are a vivid illustration.

Finally, some will object that ours is merely a pragmatic prescription for creating more core programs with too little attention to assessing their social value or desirability. We do think there is societal value in core programs; this has been endlessly discussed and is implicit in much of what we say in this chapter and in the book as a whole. What has not been discussed, as Daniel Bell has pointed out, are the practical staffing difficulties the colleges and universities will have to face. He warns us:

> . . . it is much easier, and more the academic habit, to deal with ideological questions than with organizational difficulties, and many of the problems of the general education courses, which are actually rooted in institutional dilemmas, have been masked by argument about intellectual content.[19]

We do not intend to sketch out model programs in any detail, although we have pointed to a number of them. Nor do we think it would matter much if we did. Faculties do not take programs off the shelf and install them, although they may selectively borrow from any number of experiments, fitting them to the needs of the local landscape and clientele. This is as it should be. For the teacher, the process of inventing and refining such programs is a critical aspect of renewal.

Variety in such programs is desirable. Yet we would predict that some kinds of questions are likely to recur: What is the nature of "community" in the modern world? What is justice? How does one balance equality and opportunity, order and freedom? How does a technological civilization serve man without ensnaring him? What are the limits of growth? What knowledge is most worth having? How can I know myself?

The greatest benefit of such programs is that they seem by nature to lead to the development of historical perspective, an imperative that cannot be said to occur other than peripherally if at all in much of the contemporary curriculum. We have asked how these programs may fit into the scheme of the multiversity, where most of the students are now and where more will be in the future. This educational conglomerate cannot be divested of its many functions,[20] which require of the modern president something approaching genius in the skills of political leadership. If the university is to be more than a skillfully coordinated department store—recognizing, however, that such a store was a great invention—it must somewhere demonstrate that its connections are deeper than the aisles through which consumer preferences are expressed. Core programs are a test of whether many parts can be joined in coherent wholes. If we cannot find a way for such dialogue as a central aspect of creating intellectual communities for undergraduates, how may we do it as a society? Our modest proposal should not be interpreted as either a longing for some overarching curricular unity (for we clearly believe that such a cultural syllabus is neither possible nor desirable), or as an interdict against all specialism (which would impoverish our lives as it stripped the gears on which modern society functions). We are urging that some core programs be established as one important axis of undergraduate experience. They should occupy one-third or less of an undergraduate's program, leaving time for an adequate grounding in a discipline or professional training as well as room to stretch one's appreciation of the arts and music. At the same time, we realize that such programs are not a panacea. Teachers of the quality we have in mind are not in large supply; the workability of our proposals must be tested. It is critically important to allow for experiments, to subsidize and encourage a multiplicity of creative efforts.

III

In what has just been said, there is the danger that our preferences have skewed our prophecies. We may be overestimating the readiness for reforms that would bring more coherence and a keener sense of intellectual community into the lives of undergraduates. We are also aware of the constraints that an era of declining resources, new demands for accountability, and rising union leadership will bring in the next decade, at a time when many of those in academic life seem spent and all too willing to relinquish collegial initiatives.

While the pattern of unionism varies, and while its differential impact is difficult to judge, we fear that collective bargaining will make experimentation with new sorts of courses and new modes of teaching less likely, by creating an adversary situation between faculty and those defined as "management," i.e., the top administration who are less able to support innovative teaching than would otherwise be the case. We are familiar with the arguments of unionists that only powerful agencies can counter the impulses of populist legislators who deride research and who see the long summer vacations of faculty members, for example, as mere opportunism. Thus, it is argued, the unions through political leverage can maintain faculty-student ratios and create the floor from which imagination can rise. Maybe so. But we believe a faculty member who wrote us from a recently unionized and respected university may be more prescient than the new shop stewards of academe are prepared to admit. The writer noted that he had been a "union man" throughout his school days, having joined both the teamsters and the pipefitters, and had a generally positive attitude toward unions. But he decided collective bargaining "would not do anything to improve our situation," explaining:

> My judgment is that collective bargaining will contribute to the further bureaucratization and administrative reductionism of public higher education. I can't see it going any other way. I am very sad about this development—almost to the point of looking around for some other place in society to locate the kind of teaching and scholarship to which I'm personally committed. I know that sounds very end-of-the-worldish, but I have been convinced that institutions can become moribund, even very important ones like those associated with higher education.[21]

Unions are one response to a public that has a less generous attitude toward higher education than it did in the post-Sputnik decade. But campus protests and rising costs are not the only factors affecting the popular mood, and hence the climate for innovation and reform. The public has grown antagonistic to higher education on other grounds as well: they have come to believe that faculty members, like teachers in the public schools, are not producing sufficiently educated men and women and that the very reforms which the students have won have resulted in producing graduates who are often shockingly illiterate and quantitatively inept. The demand for "accountability" that began in the schools has spread to the public colleges and universities. The legislature, hard pressed on all sides by mounting social expectations and diminishing or static revenues, is not so sure that higher education is per se "a good thing"; it wants to make sure that faculty are doing their jobs, though definitions and expectations are in practice hard to come by.

Legislators want measures of "productivity" of the sort that no nonprofit institution can provide where there is no "bottom line." One form this reaction takes is to compel faculty to spend a certain number of "contact hours" with students. It is a measure often evaded, and the result is that the legislature and the public feel cheated. But where it is adhered to, it may inhibit good teaching by insisting on more than can be accomplished creatively. Another formula used to measure output is the number of degrees awarded in relation to the number of faculty and the size of the budget. But with grade inflation and an increasing scramble for jobs, the mere possession of a degree is no longer taken as a mark of productivity. In such a milieu the spread of the movement for competence-based education may be seen as a reform, one of whose aims is to monitor faculty rather than to allow them total autonomy in deciding who is to qualify for the coveted credential. At lower levels of schooling, tests come to be used as a basis for judging teachers. At the college level, liberal-arts faculty violently resent what they consider to be trivial measures that ignore the fact that their long-run impact on students can only be measured (if at all) over a lifetime.

If the new "legislative oversight" has been one source of malaise among faculty, limited mobility may have depressed morale even more sharply. Many faculty who entered academic life in the expansionist era of the 1960s now feel trapped. Often, they have had to accept positions at institutions of a lower level of academic distinction than the ones where they were themselves trained, and without the previous hope that they could move if they achieved scholarly distinction, or were recognized as outstanding teachers.

In spite of all that has been said, it seems conceivable that this very lack of mobility might encourage faculty to make an effort at mutuality and at incremental, if not revolutionary change. Similarly, students could conclude that, since a baccalaureate degree no longer guarantees upward mobility and an improved standard of living—union membership would be a better predictor of income than a degree—they might as well give up the search for defensive credentials and turn to the liberal arts as a way of making life worth living, whatever their occupational future.*

In considering the speed with which the reforms pioneered in small experimental colleges spread in the 1960s to major, once-traditional universities, it should be recalled that there was a short period when Hampshire received a proportionately higher number of applications than any college in the Northeast, and when students turned down Radcliffe, Yale, or even Wesleyan to attend. Just as the experimental colleges which were fugitive on many campuses led faculty to conclude that they would not be outoptioned by the pedagogic left, so the small pioneers like New College in Sarasota, Hampshire, and, in the public domain, Santa Cruz, had an influence out of all proportion to their numbers.[22] In the past, academic reforms seem to have begun either in the kinds of offbeat, mostly private colleges discussed at the outset of this essay or in the major research-oriented universities, and to have spread as graduates of these institutions went to teach in places beyond the vanguard orbits. Today, the chains of influence are less hierarchical.

In thinking, then, about the possibilities for a new wave of educational reform in which some major pacesetter institutions might consider changes of a telic sort, we must remember that it does not take many institutions in this country to start a trend. But we must also recognize that the very fact that the movements of pedagogic reform succeeded the wave of political activism, or were in some measure coterminous with the latter, has left many faculties polarized. Even more are plagued with an overwhelming sense of weariness at the endless committee meetings to which they have been committed by governance reforms and the legacies of earlier battles. Thus, moral and intellectual energies may not generally be available for reconsideration of ultimate educational questions. The management of decline is not an art that comes easily to the American booster spirit. A good climate for innovation depends on new resources which can be counted on, rather than on the short-term injections provided by the federal government or a few foundations whose willingness to back seemingly *outré* academic adventures is a significant justification for the role of private philanthropy. And that role

---

*We are, of course, not suggesting that the liberal arts are poor vocational preparation; our discussion of St. John's College suggests the opposite. We believe that the confidence students or prospective employers may get as to the students' seriousness and their ability to learn new and difficult subjects will depend on the quality and intensity of their work as undergraduates.

is threatened by populist attacks on the major foundations precisely because they have had the courage to back unpopular ventures in such areas as race relations and, as in the case of federal agencies themselves, to support research which can be made to sound not only esoteric but ludicrous when exploited by demagogues. But if we had to make an over-all judgment, it would be that the country is so diverse and the places from which leadership can come are likewise so manifold, that qualitative growth is not likely to vanish.

When it comes to the telic reforms represented by the aesthetic-expressive colleges, it seems fair to say that their influence is already at work in most major and many less exalted institutions. The once "feminine" values of sensibility and aesthetic development are very much alive in music, though they have less vitality in the plastic arts and in architecture. Even ballet has been legitimated, for men as well as women, in and out of class. The donnish gamesmanship of the stag college no longer charms and sustains its devotees. In an incremental way, the mandate of the aesthetic-expressive colleges is being followed both in preprofessional and liberal-arts programs.

When it comes to the other two variants of our typology, our account has already suggested both our hopes and our misgivings. While we would very much like to see greater generosity and mutuality in a college setting, we do not see this as a polar opposite of cognitive rationality. Nor do we share the faith of its adherents that the encounter group is the optimal way to approach the development of humane sensibilities. We do, however, share the conviction that the search for more cooperative styles is worthwhile insofar as it does not sacrifice essential freedoms. No college has in fact been able to accomplish this in formal institutional terms, though we are somewhat in awe of the hope and ambition expressed by the founders of Kresge College.

The activist-radical model, whether at the College for Human Services or at Antioch, has always been a volatile mixture. The danger lies in the corruption of idealism into ideology, or the degeneration of strategies of change to perpetual confrontation or violence. The strength lies in praxis, in reflective engagement, particularly if tied to a curriculum of inquiry rather than to one of indoctrination. The College for Human Services, in fashioning a dual role for faculty as both classroom teacher and supervisor-advocate on the job, strove to achieve that ideal, although zealous faculty did not always respect it. At Antioch the radicals grouped together in the Institute for the Solution of Social Problems, not the study of them, and fantasies of omnipotence gained a powerful hold. Such fantasies of omnipotence were a danger on many campuses in the late 1960s; fantasies of total powerlessness are more likely to be the danger now. Fantasies of powerlessness are inappropriate when we think about what kinds of human quality can be cultivated in a college setting which can support the rationality necessary for modern society and also foster the more nurturing and expressive values suggested by the telic reforms.

1 An Ecology of Academic Reform

Reform Type	Student's Primary Motivations	Institutionally Valued Ends	Model
Multiversity	certification employability licensure	knowledge; expertise; community service	bureaucratic at low end of prestige ladder; stratified collegial at top

<table>
<tr><td rowspan="4">The Four Telic Reform Movements</td><td>Neo-classical (St. John's)</td><td>to be civilized; to enter intellectual aristocracy</td><td>intellectual and moral virtue; to know the good</td><td>community of scholars</td></tr>
<tr><td>Aesthetic-expressive (Black Mountain)</td><td>to release and develop creativity</td><td>to foster creativity</td><td>Bohemian artistic community</td></tr>
<tr><td>Communal-expressive (Kresge)</td><td>to attain acceptance; to express feelings; to obtain group support</td><td>to achieve social harmony</td><td>tribal family</td></tr>
<tr><td>Activist-radical (College for Human Services)</td><td>to participate in social change; to act against injustice</td><td>to generate radical critique; to train "change agents"</td><td>college as instrument of political or social reform</td></tr>
</table>

Norms; Core Values	Process; Style of Education	Historical Roots	Authority Grounded in
cognitive rationality; meritocratic	scientific method	German university built on Scottish and English collegiate models	judgments of expert peers
faith in classical texts; Platonic idealism; aristocratic	Socratic; modeling the elders	Plato's Academy	texts; wisdom of elders
creative expression— aesthetic	studio- apprenticeship; informal seminar	Bauhaus bohemias; Paris; Bloomsbury; Manhattan	aesthetic sensibility of masters
affective loving support; egalitarian- humanistic	encounter, T-group ritual; interpersonal feedback	National Training Laboratory; Utopian Communities	charisma of prophet or guru
political power and influence; egalitarian- populist	engagement; field study; activist scholarship	labor education; civil-rights movements; early settlement houses	authors of reform movement

2   The St. John's Curriculum

	Literature	Philosophy and Theology	History and Social Science	Mathematics and Natural Science	Music
First Year	Homer Aeschylus Sophocles Euripides Aristophanes	Plato Aristotle Lucretius Marcus Aurelius	Herodotus Thucydides Plutarch	Euclid* Nicomachus* Ptolemy* Lavoisier* Dalton*	
Second Year	Virgil Dante Chaucer Rabelais Shakespeare Donne* Marvell* Cervantes	Aristotle Epictetus Plotinus *The Bible* Augustine Anselm Thomas Aquinas Luther Calvin Montaigne Bacon Maimonides	Plutarch Tacitus Dante Machiavelli	Ptolemy* Apollonius* Galen Copernicus* Kepler Harvey* Descartes* Darwin* Mendel* Lamarck* Pascal* Viète*	Palestrina* Bach* Mozart* Beethoven* Schubert* Verdi Stravinsky* Haydn*
Third Year	Milton Swift Racine* Fielding Melville La Fontaine* Jane Austen	Descartes Pascal Hobbes Spinoza Locke Berkeley Leibniz Hume Kant	Locke Rousseau Adam Smith *U.S.* *Constitution* Hamilton, Madison, Jay	Galileo* Kepler* Newton* Leibniz Huygens* Dedekind*	Mozart

Fourth Year	Molière*
	Goethe
	Tolstoy
	Dostoevski
	Baudelaire*
	Rimbaud*
	Valéry*
	Yeats*
	Kafka
	Mann
	Lewis Carroll
	Mark Twain
		Hegel
		Kierkegaard
		Nietzsche.
		William James
		Jung
		Heidegger
		Thoreau
			Hegel
			Marx
			Documents
			  from Ameri-
			  can Political
			  History
			Tocqueville
				Faraday*
				Lobachevski*
				Maxwell*
				J. J. Thom-
				  son*
				Bohr*
				Millikan*
				Schrödinger*
				Darwin*
				Freud
				Einstein*
					Wagner

NOTE: Books studied in the tutorials or laboratory are indicated with an asterisk.

Freshman Year

Homer:	*Iliad, Odyssey*
Aeschylus:	*Agamemnon, Choephoroe, Eumenides, Prometheus Bound*
Sophocles:	*Oedipus Rex, Oedipus at Colonus, Antigone*
Thucydides:	*Peloponnesian War*
Euripides:	*Hippolytus, Medea, Bacchae*
Herodotus:	*History**
Aristophanes:	*Clouds, Birds*
Plato:	*Ion, Meno, Gorgias, Republic, Apology, Crito, Phaedo, Symposium, Parmenides, Theaetetus, Sophist, Timaeus, Phaedrus*
Aristotle:	*Poetics, Physics, * Metaphysics, * Ethics, * On Generation and Corruption, * The Politics*
Euclid:	*Elements**
Lucretius:	*On the Nature of Things*
Plutarch:	*Pericles, Alcibiades*
Marcus Aurelius:	*Meditations**
Nicomachus:	*Arithmetic**
Lavoisier:	*Elements of Chemistry**
Essays by:	*Archimedes, Torricelli, Pascal, Fahrenheit, Black, Avogadro, Dalton, Wollaston, Gay-Lussac, Cannizzaro, Mach, Bridgman, Couper, Morveau, Proust, Berthollet, Richter, T. Thomson, Whewell, Berzelius, Dulong, Mendeleev*

Sophomore Year

	*The Bible**
Aristotle:	*De Anima, On Interpretation,* Posterior Analytics,* Categories,* Parts of Animals,* Generation of Animals**
Apollonius:	*Conics**
Virgil:	*Aeneid*
Plutarch:	*Caesar, Antony, Brutus, Cato the Younger, Pompey, Cicero*
Epictetus:	*Discourses, Manual*
Tacitus:	*Annals*
Ptolemy:	*Almagest**
Galen:	*On the Natural Faculties*
Plotinus:	*The Enneads**
Diophantus:	*Arithmetic**
Augustine:	*Confessions, City of God**
St. Anselm:	*Proslogium*
Maimonides:	*Eight Chapters on Ethics*
Aquinas:	*Summa Theologica,* Summa Contra Gentiles**
Dante:	*Divine Comedy*
Chaucer:	*Canterbury Tales**
Machiavelli:	*The Prince, Discourses**
Copernicus:	*On the Revolution of the Spheres**
Luther:	*The Freedom of a Christian, Secular Authority*

Rabelais:	*Gargantua and Pantagruel**
Calvin:	*Institutes**
Palestrina:	*Missa Papae Marcelli*
Montaigne:	*Essays**
Viète:	*Introduction to the Analytical Art*
Bacon:	*Novum Organum**
Shakespeare:	*Richard II, Henry IV, Henry V, The Tempest, As You Like It, Hamlet, Othello, Macbeth, King Lear, Coriolanus, Sonnets**
Kepler:	*Epitome IV*
Harvey:	*Motion of the Heart and Blood*
Descartes:	*Geometry**
Pascal:	*Generation of Conic Sections*
Bach:	*St. Matthew Passion, Inventions*
Haydn:	*Quartets**
Lamarck:	*Philosophical Zoology*
Mozart:	*Operas**
Beethoven:	*Sonatas**
Schubert:	*Songs**
Darwin:	*Origin of Species*
Verdi:	*Otello*
Mendel:	*Experiments in Plant Hybridization*
Stravinsky:	*Symphony of Psalms*
Des Prez:	*Mass*
Poems by:	*Marvell, Donne, and other 17th-century poets*
Essays by:	*Bernard, Weismann, John Maynard Smith, Dreisch, Boven, Teilhard de Chardin*

Junior Year

Cervantes:	*Don Quixote*
Galileo:	*Two New Sciences*
Hobbes:	*Leviathan*
Descartes:	*Discourse on Method, Meditations, Rules for the Direction of the Mind*
Milton:	*Paradise Lost, Samson Agonistes*
La Rochefoucauld:	*Maximes**
La Fontaine:	*Fables**
Pascal:	*Pensées**
Huygens:	*Treatise on Light,* On the Movement of Bodies by Impact*
Spinoza:	*Theologico-Political Treatise*
Locke:	*Second Treatise of Government*
Racine:	*Phèdre*
Newton:	*Principia**
Leibniz:	*Monadology, Discourse on Metaphysics, Principles of Nature and Grace Founded on Reason, Essay on Dynamics*
Swift:	*Gulliver's Travels*
Berkeley:	*Principles of Human Knowledge*
Fielding:	*Tom Jones*
Hume:	*Treatise of Human Nature,* Dialogues Concerning Natural Religion, Enquiry Concerning Human Understanding*
Rousseau:	*Social Contract*

Adam Smith:	*Wealth of Nations*
Kant:	*Critique of Pure Reason,* Fundamental Principles of Metaphysics of Morals*
Mozart:	*Don Giovanni*
Jane Austen:	*Pride and Prejudice*
Hamilton, Jay, and Madison:	*The Federalist*
Melville:	*Billy Budd, Benito Cereno, Moby Dick*
Dedekind:	*Essay on the Theory of Numbers*
Essays by:	*Boscovich, Thomas Young*

Senior Year

Shakespeare:	*Antony and Cleopatra*
Molière:	*The Misanthrope, Tartuffe*
Goethe:	*Faust*
Hegel:	*Introduction to the History of Philosophy, Preface to the Phenomenology, Logic (from the Encyclopedia), Philosophy of History,* Philosophy of Right,* Philosophy of Spirit**
Lobachevsky:	*Theory of Parallels**
Tocqueville:	*Democracy in America**
Lincoln:	*Speeches**
Kierkegaard:	*Philosophical Fragments, Fear and Trembling*
Wagner:	*Tristan and Isolde*
Thoreau:	*Walden*
Marx:	*Communist Manifesto, Capital,* Political and Economic Manuscripts of 1844**
Dostoevski:	*Brothers Karamazov, The Possessed*
Tolstoy:	*War and Peace*
Lewis Carroll:	*Alice in Wonderland*
Mark Twain:	*Huckleberry Finn*
William James:	*Psychology, Briefer Course*
Nietzsche:	*Birth of Tragedy, Thus Spake Zarathustra,* Beyond Good and Evil**
Freud:	*General Introduction to Psychoanalysis, Civilization and Its Discontents, Beyond the Pleasure Principle*
Valéry:	*Poems**
Jung:	*Two Essays in Analytic Psychology**
Mann:	*Death in Venice*
Kafka:	*The Trial*
Heidegger:	*What is Philosophy?*
Heisenberg:	*The Physical Principles of the Quantum Theory* Supreme Court Opinions**
Millikan:	*The Electron**
Wittgenstein:	*Philosophical Investigations*
Keynes:	*General Theory of Employment, Interest and Money*
Poems by:	*Yeats, T. S. Eliot, Wallace Stevens, Baudelaire, Rimbaud and others*
Essays by:	*Faraday, Lorenz, J. J. Thomson, Whitehead, Minkowski, Rutherford, Einstein, Davisson, Bohr, Schrödinger, Maxwell*

SOURCE: St. John's Catalogue, 1976–77.
NOTE: Books read in part are indicated with an asterisk.

4

The Performance Grid: College for Human Services

	D I M E N S I O N S	A. Purpose Describe appropriate and realistic purposes and demonstrate reasonable success in achieving them.

COMPETENCIES

I. Become an effective learner and potential professional, accepting the responsibility for identifying your learning goals and finding appropriate resources for achieving them.

II. Establish professional relationships at the worksite . . . with co-workers and citizens.

III. Work with others in groups . . . helping to establish clear goals and achieve optimum results

IV. Function as a Teacher . . . helping people to define and achieve appropriate learning goals.

V. Function as a Counselor . . . helping people to resolve problems in a manner that promotes their growth and independence.

VI. Function as Community Liaison . . . working with the people and resources of the community to meet community needs.

VII. Function as a Supervisor . . . taking the responsibility for teaching, encouraging, and enabling other workers to make the best use of their abilities on behalf of citizens.

VIII. Act as a change agent, planning, researching, and promoting programs . . . to improve Human Service delivery.

B. Values	C. Self & Others	D. Systems	E. Skills
Demonstrate a clear understanding of your values and persistence in working for them.	Demonstrate an understanding of yourself and others in relation to your purposes.	Demonstrate an understanding of systems in relation to your purposes.	Demonstrate an ability to make good use of necessary and appropriate skills in the achievement of your purposes.

The FACETS of
competent performance:
the intersection of
competencies and dimensions
(see Appendix 5 for examples)

Facets of the Curriculum: College for Human Services

	A. Purpose	B. Values
I. Learning	FACET 3: Demonstrate your readiness to work toward realizing your personal and professional goals and helping the College fulfill its mission by joining the College as a learner and potential professional.	FACET 3: Describe your views on the potential of all people for positive growth and change and explain how your views affect your performance. (Allport, Erikson, Maslow)
II. Relationships	FACET 4: Demonstrate reasonable success in achieving specific, planned relationships with one or more clients or pupils and one or more supervisors.	FACET 3: Explore your beliefs about the essential nature of human beings in relation to those of others and explain how your beliefs affect your work. (Hobbes, Skinner, Freud, Allport, Erikson, Maslow, Rogers)
III. Groups	FACET 3: Demonstrate reasonable success in helping a group achieve its common purpose while working toward your individual purpose.	FACET 3: Describe your views on the issue of decision making in groups and explain how your views affect your performance. (Locke, Mill, Ibsen)
IV. Teaching	FACET 3: Describe what you plan to do to help individual learners achieve goals you have agreed on together and explain how you will determine that the goals have been realized.	FACET 5: Demonstrate in your performance as a teacher that you are open, honest, caring, and confident of the ability of learners to take increased responsibility for their learning.

C. Self & Others	D. Systems	E. Skills
FACET 4: Demonstrate in practice an understanding of preparation as the initial stage of professional practice. (Schwartz, Moustakas, Allport)	**FACET 1:** Demonstrate your understanding of the components of the new Human Service profession—new service delivery, assessment, education—in relation to the traditional professions. (Dumpson, Gartner, Rosner, NASW Guidelines)	**FACET 1:** Demonstrate that you are able to use problem solving skills to determine and rank long and short range goals and develop alternate strategies for reaching them.
FACET 3: Understand and apply in practice various aspects of the helping relationship—identifying the client, making a beginning, establishing trust, sharing expectations, fostering self-direction. (Perlman, Schwartz, Rogers, Rosenthal, Combs)	**FACET 3:** Demonstrate in practice an understanding of your responsibilities as a student-practitioner in your agency: service goals, work responsibilities, standards, regulations, agency styles.	**FACET 2:** Use assessment skills to record and analyze critical incidents related to your establishing professional relationships at the worksite.
FACET 3: Demonstrate in practice an understanding of alternative approaches to working in groups and their applicability to specific situations. (Maslow, Lewin, Coyle, Bales, Thelen, Bennis)	**FACET 4:** Demonstrate in practice an understanding of groups as cultural units (Kluckhohn, Barnouw, Goode)	**FACET 3:** Demonstrate the ability to use interpersonal skills as appropriate to one's role as group member or leader. (Miles, Schwartz)
FACET 5: Show that you understand and can use various theoretical approaches to learning both as a teacher and as a learner. (Piaget, Skinner, Bruner)	**FACET 4:** Show an understanding of the issue of equal educational opportunity, explain the issue in relation to your values, and describe how it affects your work as a teacher. (Clark, Katz, Harvard Educational Review)	**FACET 4:** Use research skills to find appropriate learning resources and to investigate your agency as a system for promoting learning.

Notes

Chapter 2

1. Christopher Jencks and David Riesman, *The Academic Revolution* (New York: Doubleday, 1968; paperback, Chicago: University of Chicago Press, 1977).

2. Eva Brann, "What are the Beliefs and Teachings of St. John's College," *The Collegian*, St. John's College (May 1975), p. 10.

3. The best account of the Columbia program and a superbly cogent examination of the larger issues with which our essay deals is Daniel Bell, *The Reforming of General Education: The Columbia College Experience and Its National Setting* (New York: Columbia University Press, 1966).

4. For an evocative discussion of the sorts of innovation that go on in departments without ever being so labeled, and of the pedantry and pretentiousness that are also there, see Martin Trow, "The Public and Private Lives of Higher Education," paper read at the Second National Forum on New Planning and Management Practices in Post-Secondary Education, Education Commission of the States (Chicago, November 16, 1973); revised version in *Daedalus*, 104, no. 1 (Winter 1975), 113–27.

5. For an account of the short, unhappy life of what came to be called Tussman College, see his book, *Experiment at Berkeley* (New York: Oxford University Press, 1969).

6. This quotation and our account of Black Mountain are drawn from Martin Duberman's magnificent history, *Black Mountain: An Exploration in Community* (New York: Dutton, 1972).

7. Bernard Beckerman, Dean of the School of Arts at Columbia, describes the checkered career of the arts on Morningside Heights, which have flourished and wilted since the early years of the century but "have never been firmly rooted as part of undergraduate education." See his lecture, "Arts Education for Undergraduates," *Seminar Reports* (New York: Columbia Seminar on General and Continuing Education in the

Humanities, May 15, 1974), 1, no. 8: 1–3. Beckerman touches on the problem of the difficulties in the university setting of subordinating creative to scholarly standards, a theme developed by James Ackerman in "The Arts in Higher Education," *Content and Context: Essays on College Education*, ed. Carl Kaysen (New York: McGraw-Hill, 1973), pp. 219–66. Oliver Fulton and Martin Trow also provide survey evidence to show that assessment of creative work causes a strain in the leading universities. See "Research Activity in American Higher Education," *Sociology of Education*, 47, no. 1 (Winter, 1974): 69.

8. For statistics and historical profiles on the growth of the arts on American campuses see the following works: James Cass and Max Birnbaum, eds., *Comparative Guide to American Colleges* (New York: Harper & Row, 1972), pp. 813–15; Laurence Veysey, "The Humanities, 1860–1920," in Alexandra M. Oleson, ed., *The Organization of Knowledge in American Society, 1860–1920*, forthcoming; Jack Morrison *The Rise of the Arts on the American Campus* (New York: McGraw-Hill, 1973).

9. New York Times, "U.S. Starts Arts Program in the Schools," August 4, 1976, p. 35.

10. Bennington's long tradition of political and cultural nonconformity and its impact on students is reported in two volumes by Theodore Newcomb: *Personality and Social Change: Attitude Formation in a Student Community* (New York: Dryden, 1943); and Newcomb et al., *Persistence and Change: Bennington College and Its Students after Twenty-Five Years* (New York: John Wiley, 1967); see also David Riesman's review of *Persistence and Change* in *American Journal of Sociology*, 73, no. 5 (March 1968): 628–30.

11. Duberman, *Black Mountain: An Exploration in Community* (New York: Dutton, 1972; Doubleday Anchor paper edition, 1973).

12. For a discussion of the rubrics of the movement, see Lawrence N. Solomon and Betty Berzon, eds., *New Perspectives on Encounter Groups* (San Francisco: Jossey-Bass, 1972), and Kurt W. Back, *Beyond Words* (Baltimore: Penguin, 1973).

13. For brief reports on the College of the Person and similar experiments, see John Coyne and Tom Hebert, *This Way Out: A Guide to Alternatives to Traditional College Education in the United States, Europe and the Third World* (New York: E. P. Dutton, 1972). For an account of experiments at the University of Oregon, see Joseph Fashing and Steven E. Deutsch, *Academics in Retreat: The Politics of Academic Innovation* (Albuquerque: University of New Mexico Press, 1971). The Tufts experiment is treated at length in Richard Millburn, Gerald Grant, Blanche Geer and others, "Report on the College Within," mimeo, Tufts University, 1971.

14. We owe this analogy to Craig Eisendrath's and Thomas J. Cottle's discussion in *Out of Discontent: Visions of the Contemporary University* (Cambridge, Mass.: Schenkman, 1972), pp. 56–58.

15. University of California, Santa Cruz Catalogue (1973/74), pp. 20–21.

16. University of California, Santa Cruz Catalogue (1970/71), p. 41.

17. Jo Freeman, "The Tyranny of Structurelessness," *Berkeley Journal of Sociology*, 17 (1972–73), 151–64; see also the description of the Portland, Oregon, Learning Community, thinly disguised in David French, "After the Fall: What This Country Needs is a Good Counter 'Counter-Culture' Culture," *New York Times Magazine*, October 3, 1971, pp. 20–21 ff.

18. For accounts by various hands of the impact of student protest on an array of more or less prominent colleges and universities, see David Riesman and Verne Stadtman, eds., *Academic Transformation: Seventeen Institutions under Pressure* (New York: McGraw-Hill 1972); also, Seymour M. Lipset, *Rebellion in the University* (Boston: Little Brown, 1971).

19. A more comprehensive treatment of this period would need to describe the role of the People's Institute at Cooper Union, as well as many others. For a history of Commonwealth, see Raymond and Charlotte Koch, *Educational Commune: The Story of Commonwealth College* (New York: Schocken, 1972). Frank Adams (with Myles Horton) tells the story of Highlander Folk School in *Unearthing Seeds of Fire: The Idea of Highlander* (Winston-Salem, N.C.: John F. Blair, 1975).

20. For the early Antioch (as well as an admirable picture of the early Reed), see Burton Clark, *The Distinctive College: Antioch, Reed, and Swarthmore* (Chicago: Aldine, 1970); for a later portrait see Gerald Grant, "Let a Hundred Antiochs Bloom!" *Change*, 4, no. 7 (September 1972): 47–58.

21. *Antioch Record*, February 13, 1972, p. 2.

22. For his own account of these connections, see Birenbaum's autobiography, *Something for Everybody is Not Enough: An Educator's Search for His Education* (New York: Random House, 1971).

23. For a dramatic contrast with the more usual egalitarianism of American faculty, see Alexander Gerschenkron, "Getting Off the Bullock Cart: Thoughts on Educational Reform," *The American Scholar*, 45 (Spring 1976): 218–33, in which Gerschenkron describes (on p. 223) the shock of a great Swedish economist, Eli F. Heckscher, who gave a guest lecture at Williams College for which an undergraduate walked up to express his admiration. "It was a marvelous lecture, he said . . . Heckscher felt it was bordering on impertinence on the part of the student to presume he was capable of forming any judgment of the quality of a lecture given by a distinguished scholar."

24. Eva Brann, "What are the Beliefs and Teachings of St. John's College," p. 9.

25. Philip H. Phenix stipulates that "An organized field of inquiry, pursued by a particular group of men of knowledge, may be called a *scholarly discipline.*" *Realms of Meaning: A Philosophy of the Curriculum for Gen-*

eral Education (New York: McGraw-Hill, 1964), p. 312. He leaves out the notion of special methods. And it is true that there is a multiplicity of methods or distinctive angles of vision within traditionally defined disciplines as well as among them: The cognitive, clinical, and humanistic psychologists are worlds apart. One could find analogues *within* most disciplines for what Jurgen Habermas has labeled the empirical-analytic, historical-hermeneutic, and critical ways of knowing in *Knowledge and Human Interests* (Boston: Beacon Press, 1971), see especially the Appendix, "Knowledge and Human Interests: A General Perspective," pp. 301–17.

26. See Hugh G. Petrie's lucid essay, "Do You See What I See, The Epistemology of Interdisciplinary Inquiry," *Educational Researcher*, Journal of the American Educational Research Association, 5, no. 2 (February 1976): 9–15, in which he writes of a test devised for interdisciplinary perception. Martin Trow writes of the dangers of interdisciplinary dialogue in, "Higher Education and Moral Development," *AAUP Bulletin*, Spring 1976, p. 24.

27. John Dewey, *Experience and Education* (New York: MacMillan, 1936), p. 56, quoted in Kenneth D. Benne, "Authority in Education," *Harvard Educational Review*, 40, no. 3: 385–410, whose analysis of the authority of rule and authority of the expert helped us to clarify these distinctions. We are also indebted to our colleagues Manfred Stanley, Wendy Kohli, Marian Krizinofski, Thomas Ewens, and Emily Haynes, whose careful attention to an earlier draft of this chapter was invaluable.

28. Kresge College did seek in its early years that commitment to group cohesion that was characteristic of those utopian communities Kanter describes as requiring the "attachment of a person's entire fund of emotion and affectivity to the group." Rosabeth Moss Kanter, *Commitment and Community: Communes and Utopias in Sociological Perspective* (Cambridge, Mass.: Harvard University Press, 1972) p. 72.

29. Talcott Parsons and Gerald M. Platt with Neil J. Smelser, *The American University* (Cambridge; Mass.: Harvard University Press, 1973).

30. *Ibid.*, pp. 109–10.

31. *Ibid.*, p. 215. See also the discussion in Parsons, Platt, and Rita Kirshstein, "Faculty Teaching Goals, 1968–1973," *Social Problems*, December 1976.

32. Parsons and Platt, *American University*, p. 63.

Chapter 3

1. *Bulletin of St. John's College*, "Self-Evaluation Report," March 1964, p. 20.

2. Walter Lippmann, *New York Herald Tribune*, December 27, 1952.

3. From the Introduction to the *Portable Plato*, ed. Scott Buchanan (New York: Viking 1948).

4. Harris Wofford, ed., *Embers of the World: Conversations with Scott Buchanan* (Santa Barbara, Calif. Center for the Study of Democratic Institutions, 1970), pp. 32–33.

5. Mark Van Doren, *Autobiography* (New York: Greenwood, 1939), p. 160; and "Talk at 21st Anniversary of the New Program," St. John's College, May 31, 1958.

6. Interview, Annapolis, Md., February 1972.

7. Wofford, *Embers*, p. 157.

8. *Ibid.*, pp. 94–95.

9. *Ibid.*, pp. 32–44.

10. *Ibid.*, pp. 54–55.

11. *Ibid.*, pp. 58–59.

12. Scott Buchanan, "A Talk to Friends," May 31, 1958, St. John's College.

13. William A. Darkey, "Statement of Educational Policy," *The Collegian*, St. John's College, no. 121 (April 23, 1973): 9.

14. Amy Apfel Kass, *Radical Conservatives for Liberal Education*, Ph.D. dissertation, Johns Hopkins University, 1973, pp. 125–55.

15. Wofford, *Embers*, p. 88.

16. Scott Buchanan, 1937–38 *Catalogue* of St. John's College, p. 19.

17. Interview with John Kieffer, February 1973. Kieffer taught at both the old and the new St. John's and was at various times both president and dean at Annapolis. Kieffer quotes a colleague here; he was enthusiastic about the speech himself.

18. "An Interview with Jacques Maritain," *Commonweal*, February 3, 1939.

19. Milton S. Mayer, "Socrates Crosses the Delaware: St. John's College and the Great Books," *Harper's*, June 1939.

20. Mortimer Adler, "God and The Professors," *Daily Maroon*, University of Chicago, November 14, 1940.

21. Helen Merrill Lynd, "The Conflicting Education," *New Republic*, May 22, 1944, pp. 700–703.

22. Sidney Hook, "Ballyhoo at St. John's," *New Leader*, May 27, 1944. According to J. Winfree Smith, who was then a tutor and later a dean at St. John's: "Buchanan invited Sidney Hook to visit St. John's to find out what it was really like, but Hook declined to come. If he had come, he would have found no 'doctrinaire style'." Letter from Smith, July 1973.

23. John Dewey, "Challenge to Liberal Thought," *Fortune*, August 1944; and Alexander Meiklejohn, "A Reply to John Dewey," *Fortune*, January 1945.

24. Mark Van Doren, *Liberal Education* (New York: Holt, 1943), p. 153.

25. 1937–38 *Catalogue*, pp. 22–28.

26. Van Doren, *Liberal Education*, p. 148.

27. Eva Brann, "The Student's Problem," Lecture on the Liberal Arts, St. John's College, September 22, 1967. St. John's sends its applicants

copies of I. A. Richards's comment about the enormous critical apparatus that has grown up around every important author: "But somehow all this wealth of scholarly aid does not lift up our hearts as it should. It spreads attention out too thinly and daunts us with the thought that we would have to know everything before we could know anything," *How to Read a Page* (New York: Norton, 1942). Yet there are some works, say, Marx's *Critique of the Gotha Program*, which can hardly be understood apart from historical context.

28. Bulletin of St. John's College: *A Report on a Project of Self-Study*, 7, no. 2 (1955): 111–19.

29. 1937–38 *Catalogue*, p. 22. See also Laurence R. Veysey, *The Emergence of the American University* (Chicago: University of Chicago Press, 1965), Chap. 1, "Discipline and Piety," and also R. Storr and G. W. Pierson, *Yale College: An Educational History, 1871–1921* (New Haven: Yale University Press, 1952), pp. 69–79. Pierson notes that the Yale of 1875 would not have been at all strange to a medieval schoolman. "For what were the studies of the first two and one half years but the old liberal arts, whose trivium had been the Latin grammar, rhetoric, and logic, and whose quadrivium had been arithmetic, geometry, astronomy, and music? . . . It was dominated by what we today should call the school-and-tool subjects, to wit: mathematics and the languages, including practical English. These were studied in small divisions, by means of daily textbook assignments and remorseless recitations. Evidently, the main object was training in accurate observation, accurate memory, logical reasoning, and regular work—all that with a modicum of classical culture" (p. 71).

30. *Self-Evaluation Report*, St. John's College, 1955, p. 3.

31. Eva Brann, "The Student's Problem."

32. Kass, *Radical Conservatives*, p. 208. That Buchanan also expected others to take the moral revolution seriously was indicated by Richard McKeon, a member of the St. John's Board of Visitors, who recalled that Buchanan told the board "that if we were really serious about this new program and this college that we would retire from all else we were doing and settle in Annapolis and just pay attention to running the college." Tape-recorded interview with McKeon by John Kieffer, St. John's College, used with permission.

33. Wofford, *Embers*, p. 102.

34. *Ibid.*, p. 170.

35. Brann, "The Student's Problem."

36. Nancy M. Polk, letter to the *Collegian*, St. John's College, March 12, 1973, p. 15.

37. James Cass and Max Birnbaum, *Comparative Guide to American Colleges* (New York: Harper & Row, 1975).

38. Wofford, *Embers*, p. 33.

39. Alexander W. Astin, *College Dropouts: A National Profile*, Washington, D.C.: American Council in Education, February 1972.

40. Deborah Schifter, *Collegian*, March 5, 1973.

41. Interview with Jacob Klein, February 1973.

42. Buchanan, "The School of the People's Institute," *The Peoples Institute Announcements*, 1926, p. 9, quoted in *Kass*, Radical Conservatives, p. 15.

43. Interview with Jacob Klein, Annapolis, February 1973.

44. Jacob Klein, "The Dean's Statement of Educational Policy and Program, 1954," *Report on a Project of Self Study*, p. 134.

45. We have tried to make plain what is meant by the Socratic style in the St. John's context, but each time we have used the term we have been reminded of Samuel McCracken's gibe: "If all the people in the world who use the term 'Socratic method' were laid end to end, there would be a good deal less philosophical confusion among those left standing." See "Quackery in the Classroom," in *Radical School Reform*, ed. Cornelius Troost (Boston: Little, Brown, 1973), p. 22.

46. Eva Brann, Interview, Annapolis, November 1970.

47. Nabokov recalls his St. John's experiences in *Bagazh: Memoris of A Russian Cosmopolitan* (New York: Atheneum, 1975). For an interesting account of his later career in music, see "Days with Diaghilev," *American Scholar*, 44, no. 4 (Autumn 1975), adapted from the same volume.

48. 1970–71 *Catalogue* of St. John's College.

49. "Self-Evaluation Report," p. 4.

50. For a recent summary of such research, see Stephen B. Withey, *A Degree and What Else? Correlates and Consequences of a College Education*, a report prepared for the Carnegie Commission on Higher Education (New York: McGraw-Hill, 1971), particularly chap. 3, "The Impact of a College Experience," by Gerald Gurin.

51. Kass, *Radical Conservatives*, p. 229.

52. John S. Kieffer, "Commencement Address," St. John's College, June 1949.

53. Eva Brann, "The Student's Problem," p. 15.

Chapter 4

1. R. S. Edgar, "Interpersonal Communication: Thoughts about College Six," mimeographed (Kresge College, January 1970).

2. Michael Kahn, "The Return of the Repressed," in Elliot Aronson, ed., *Readings about the Social Animal* (San Francisco, Calif., W. H. Freeman, 1973), pp. 389–405.

3. "T-Grouping at Kresge," mimeographed, Fall 1970.

4. Letter from Gary Miles, September 1975.

5. See, for example, W. C. Schutz, *Joy* (New York: Grove Press, 1967). Calvin Tomkins discusses the reaction to Schutz and Fritz Perls in the early days at Esalen in "New Paradigms," *New Yorker*, January 5,

1976, pp. 30–56. For a discussion of the rubrics of the movement, see Laurence N. Solomon and Betty Berzon, eds., *New Perspectives on Encounter Groups* (San Francisco: Jossey-Bass, 1972), and Kurt W. Back, *Beyond Words* (Baltimore, Penguin, 1973).

6. Robert Edgar, "Intimacy in Community," memorandum (Kresge College, July 29, 1970).

7. "The Kresge Program: An Initial Design for an Educational Community," mimeographed, January 1971.

8. *Ibid.*

9. Robert Edgar, "The Kresge Curriculum: A Proposal," memorandum, July 20, 1971.

10. "A Survey of Kin Groups," Student Affairs Preceptor Committee (Kresge Archives, April 1972).

11. *Ibid.*

12. Robert Edgar, memorandum, October 25, 1971, in response to questions about goals and governance posed by consultant Dale Lake.

13. Richard Bandler, Dean Boyd, Claudia Carr, John Grinder, and Mary Lee Morris, "Building Community," mimeographed, January 1972.

14. Marcia Millman, Michael Kahn, and Ted Kroeber, "Memorandum: Re Kin Groups," to the Student Affairs Preceptor Group, March 9, 1972.

15. Quoted by William Trombley, *Los Angeles Times*, March 20, 1972.

16. Also quoted by Trombley, *Los Angeles Times*.

17. Len Armstrong, Kresge bursar, quoted in the *Kresge Hoo-Haa* (the student newsletter, named at various times *Kresge Hoo-Haa, Kresge Klein, Kresge Weekly Reader, Kresge Dreck, Kresge Clone, Palaset Periscope*), January 31, 1972.

18. *Kresge Weekly Reader*, May 5, 1972.

19. *Kresge Weekly Reader*, November 1, 1972.

20. *Kresge Weekly Reader*, April 24, 1972.

21. "Covering Statement on a Kresge College Program," mimeographed, January 1971, p. 2.

22. *Kresge Curriculum*, p. 2.

23. Memoranda, December 1 and December 20, 1971, Kresge College.

24. Michael Kahn, memorandum to Robert Edgar, January 17, 1972.

25. Michael Kahn, untitled, undated paper on the seminar, mimeographed.

26. "Kresge College: The Early Years (1970–74). An Appraisal for the Ford Foundation," mimeographed, June 1974, p. 7.

27. *Ibid.*

28. *Kresge Newsletter*, no. 43, undated, Fall 1972.

29. *Kresge Klone*, April 30, 1973.

30. *Kresge Klone*, April 14, 1973.

31. *Ibid.*

32. *Kresge Daily Dreck*, June 6, 1973.

33. *Kresge Klone*, April 23, 1973.

34. Report of the Community Affairs Meeting, December 5, 1973, *Kresge Klein*, January 15, 1974.

35. "Kresge College: The Early Years," p. 8.

36. *Ibid.*

37. Robert Edgar, memorandum to the Kresge faculty, January 21, 1974, "My Thoughts about a Kresge Curriculum," *Kresge Klein*, January 22, 1974.

38. Robert Edgar, memorandum to the Kresge faculty, January 16, 1974, "College Curriculum," *Kresge Klein*, January 22, 1974.

39. Donald Moine, *Kresge Klein*, October 2, 1973.

40. "Kresge College: The Early Years," p. 15.

41. Lorna Cutler, memorandum, *Kresge Klone*, February 4, 1974.

42. Frank Menagh, *ibid.*

43. Don McCormick, *ibid.*

44. Bob Solotar, *ibid.*

45. Robert Edgar, "Dear Friends," *Kresge Klein*, February 5, 1974.

46. Henry Hilgard, *Kresge Clone*, February 4, 1974.

47. *Ibid.*

48. *Ibid.*

49. Phiip Slater, "Report on Kresge," mimeographed, May 31, 1974, pp. 16, 29.

50. *The Key*, October 18, 1974; *City on a Hill Press*, October 17, 1974.

51. Gael A. Mathews, Minutes of the Kresge Advance, May 3–4, 1975, mimeographed.

52. *Ibid.*

53. For a review of the literature sympathetic to Kahn's view here, see David W. Johnson and Roger T. Johnson, "Instructional Goal Structure: Cooperative, Competitive, or Individualistic," *Review of Educational Research*, 44, no. 2 (Spring 1974): 213–40.

Chapter 5

1. Joseph Featherstone, "The Talent Corps: Career Ladders for Bottom Dogs," *New Republic*, September 13, 1969, 1–6.

2. "Final Report of the Women's Talent Corps New Careers Program: 1966–67," CHS, May 1968, p. 52. The college's annual reports are subsequently referred to by short title.

3. The Federal Comprehensive Employment and Training Act of 1973.

4. The data cited by the college in this area is from Arthur Pearl, "The Human Service Society: An Ecological Perspective," in *Public Service Employment*, ed. A. Gardner et al. (New York, Praeger, 1973), quoted in "Two-Year Professional Program Leading to the Degree of Master of Human Services," mimeographed, CHS, August 1974, I:iv.

5. Second Annual Report, April 1969, p. 41.

6. Third Annual Report, June 1970, p. 35. At this time major municipal workers' unions were also establishing career ladders that competed with those of CHS.

7. First Annual Report, May 1968, p. 27.

8. Second Annual Report, April 1969, p. 35.

9. Fourth Annual Report, 1970 program, 1972, p. 64.

10. For a delightful discussion of the importance of developing math skills that bring the student beyond mere calculation or computation, see Israel Scheffler, "Basic Mathematical Skills: Some Philosophical and Practical Remarks," *Teachers College Record*, 78, no. 2 (December 1976): 205–12.

11. Letter from the Student Council, June 30, 1972.

12. Letter from Preston Wilcox to the board of trustees, May 30, 1972.

13. Letters from Audrey Cohen to the faculty, August 14, 1970, December 9, 1971, and June 27, 1972.

14. For a detailed explanation of the curriculum, see "Legal Service Assistants, Report on Legal Training Phase of a Joint Demonstration Program, 1969–70," Columbia University Law School, Spring 1970.

15. Fourth Annual Report, 1970 Program, 1972, p. 41.

16. The results were reported by William P. Statsky in "Field Report on Sixteen Legal Service Assistants Now Working in Nine Community Law Offices in New York City," December 9, 1969, and "Supervision Report on Sixteen Legal Service Assistants Now Working in Ten Community Law Offices in New York City," March 31, 1970.

17. Nathan Glazer, "Conflicts in Schools for the Minor Professions," Harvard Graduate School of Education *Bulletin*, Spring 1974.

18. Letter from Audrey Cohen, September 26, 1976.

19. Laura P. Houston, "Black People and New Careers: Toward Humane Human Service," *Social Casework*, May 1970.

20. In the literature, "success" is usually translated as income and occupational status, which is not the same thing as competence, of course. Independent measures of competence are rare. The most comprehensive review of the relations between scores on cognitive tests (which are not exactly "grades"), level of schooling completed, and occupational success has been carried out by Christopher Jencks et al., in *Inequality: A Reassessment of the Effect of Family and Schooling in America* (New York: Basic Books, 1972). Jencks and his colleagues found that cognitive skill had little relationship to income, although cognitive test scores do correlate with educational attainment and educational attainment explains about one-fourth of the variance in occupational status. A few studies have attempted to relate professional competence to college grades. Correlations between schoolteachers' college grades and supervisors' ratings were low (between .2 and .3). Similarly, supervisors' ratings of medical interns were not correlated with either undergraduate grades or preclinical medical-school grades. See Jencks et al., pp. 185–99.

21. The often-criticized tendency of the established professions to place the interests of the profession ahead of those of particular clients is illustrated by an Australian study: D. S. Anderson, "A Study of Professional Socialization," Education Research Unit, Research School of the Social Sciences, Australian National University, 1973.

22. David C. McClelland, "Testing for Competence Rather Than for Intelligence;" *American Psychologist*, 28, no. 1 (January 1973): 1–14.

23. Charles Dailey, David McClelland et al., "Professional Competences of Human Service Workers," McBer and Company, January 1974.

24. "Two-Year Professional Program Leading to the Degree of Master of Human Services," mimeographed, August 1974, I:64.

25. "A Game of Change: The New Profession of the Human Services," mimeographed, June 1974, p. 1.

26. "Two-Year Professional Program," I:5.

27. Stephen Spurr, in *Academic Degree Structures: Innovative Approaches* (New York: McGraw-Hill, 1970), explores the miasma surrounding the definition of what a master's degree is.

28. For a careful review of polls comparing the factual knowledge of American high-school and college graduates over a 25-year period, which reveals that the smattering of knowledge is quite thin among the latter, see Herbert H. Hyman, Charles R. Wright, and John Shelton Reed, *The Enduring Effects of Education* (Chicago: University of Chicago Press, 1975).

29. "Lincoln Masters Program in Human Services," Lincoln University, Pennsylvania, mimeographed, August 1976, pp. 4–9.

30. See Burton R. Clark, *The Distinctive College: Antioch, Reed and Swarthmore* (Chicago: Aldine, 1970): There are striking parallels between CHS and Antioch.

Chapter 6

1. On the key role of faculty in initiating and supporting campus protest, see Alexander W. Astin, Helen S. Astin, Alan E. Bayer, and Ann S. Bisconti, *The Power of Protest* (San Francisco; Jossey-Bass, 1975), especially Chaps. 3, 4, and 5. This volume is based on a national survey begun by the American Council on Education in December 1969, and is augmented by a selective group of interviews and a study of the campus press during the years 1969–72, with some later follow-up.

2. Cf. Thomas J. Cottle, "Thank God for the Simple People," *Time's Children: Impressions of Youth* (Boston: Little Brown, 1971), Chap. 10.

3. For poll data illustrating how the working-class, while opposed to the war on pragmatic grounds and wanting it over with, was more strongly opposed to the activist students even when the latter demonstrated peaceably, see, e.g., Milton J. Rosenberg, Sidney Verba, and Philip E. Converse, *Vietnam and the Silent Majority: The Dove's Guide* (New York: Harper & Row, 1970).

4. See Michael Young, *The Rise of the Meritocracy, 1870 to 2033* (London and New York, Thames and Hudson, 1958, 1959); and discussion in David Riesman, "Notes on Meritocracy," *Daedalus*, 96, no. 3, (1967); 897–908.

5. Robert H. Somers, "The Mainsprings of Rebellion: A Survey of Berkeley Students in November 1964," in S. M. Lipset and Sheldon S. Wolin, eds., *The Berkeley Student Revolt: Facts and Interpretations* (New York: Doubleday, 1965), pp. 530–57. Somers notes that while students did not support protest out of pique with their teachers, this should not be interpreted as suggesting there were not many educational complaints. Somers also reports that a survey of 600 Berkeley demonstrators by Glenn Lyonns showed that 44 percent were dissatisfied with the educational process. Somers's sample of 285 was drawn randomly from the entire campus and showed no marked differences in satisfaction with quality of education between those who protested and those who did not. Somers found that about 17 percent were markedly dissatisfied with educational quality. Of course, on a campus of 27,000 this is a sizable number of students.

6. See "Harvard Students in the Midst of Crisis," *Sociology of Education*, 44 (Summer 1971): 245–69.

7. Nevitt Sanford's essay on graduate education is relevant here: "Graduate Education Then and Now," *American Psychologist*, 31 (November 1976): 756–64. Sanford indicates that Berkeley did not enter the race for national prestige or cease granting near-automatic tenure to all assistant professors until 1947.

8. William C. Perry, Jr., *Forms of Intellectual and Ethical Development in the College Years* (New York: Holt, Rinehart & Winston, 1970), has analyzed the shift in the nature of examination questions at Harvard from 1900 up to the present era. Perry shows how simplistic and often sheerly factual the questions of an earlier epoch were compared to the shifting and complex frames of reference now demanded of Harvard undergraduates.

9. The distinction between sponsored and contest mobility has been greatly illuminated by the work of Ralph H. Turner; see, for example, "Sponsored and Contest Mobility in the School System," *American Sociological Review*, 25 (1960): 855–56; see also "Mobility or Equality?," in Christopher Jencks and David Riesman, *The Academic Revolution* (New York, Doubleday, 1968), pp. 146–54.

10. Private communication with M. Elizabeth Jacka, executive vice-president of the National Merit Scholarship Corporation, March 29, 1974.

11. Although the SAT had been developed in 1926, it was not much used until Harvard, Princeton, and Yale broadened their meritocratic search in the late 1930s, and in 1937 it was augmented by three short achievement tests developed by the American Council on Education. Frank Bowles, *The Refounding of the College Board, 1948–1963* (New York: CEEB, 1967), and private communication with Sam A. McCandless of the College Entrance Examination Board, March 26, 1974.

12. Cf. David Ricks, "Tests and Scholarships: A Cautioning Tale," *Financial Aid News*, no. 3 (March 1961).

13. See the *Digest of Educational Statistics* (Washington: U.S. Office of Education, 1972), p. 14, and Seymour E. Harris, *A Statistical Portrait*

of Higher Education (New York: McGraw-Hill, 1972), pp. 351, 418. Though the proportion of graduates going on to college increased, what is particularly remarkable is the increase in the proportion finishing high school; about 17 percent of the age-grade graduated from high school in 1920, whereas by 1968, 75 percent graduated.

14. Cf. Howard S. Becker, Blanche Geer, and Everett C. Hughes, *Making the Grade: The Academic Side of College Life* (New York: John Wiley, 1968), based on a study of the undergraduate liberal-arts college of the University of Kansas. The study not only demonstrates that the University of Kansas had become a demanding institution but describes the cunning and cynical way in which some students were able to respond to those demands.

15. For a dour portrait of the pressures on faculty in private liberal-arts colleges, based on fieldwork in 1966–67, see Reese McGee, *Academic Janus: The Private College and Its Faculty* (San Francisco, Calif.: Jossey-Bass, 1971), especially chap. 3.

16. See Kenneth M. Wilson, *Increased Selectivity and Institutional Grading Standards* (Poughkeepsie, N.Y.: College Research Center, 1966), p. 6. Here Wilson compares successive classes to the 1958 norms. Thus, the average student in 1963 had a higher SAT math score than about 77 percent of her 1958 counterparts, higher CEEB achievement averages than about 75 percent of her 1958 counterparts, and higher secondary-school rank than about 60 percent of the 1958 class. There was no significant increase in freshman grades, however. Hollins, Mount Holyoke, Vassar, Wheaton (Mass.), and Sweet Briar Colleges participated in the study.

17. The highly stimulating studies of Matina S. Horner on "fear of success" among women present a less clear-cut picture of differentiation among the sexes, at least in high-status colleges, where the fear of success among men is also high, and where much depends on fields and context. See Horner, "Feminity and Successful Achievement: A Basic Inconsistency," in Judith Bardwick, Elizabeth Douvan, Matina S. Horner, and David Gutmann, *Feminine Personality and Conflict* (Belmont, Calif. Wadsworth Publishing Company, 1970), pp. 45–74. For another view see David Tresemer, *Fear of Success* (New York: Plenum, 1977). Paradoxically, even the options now open to women as a result of the women's-liberation movements and affirmative-action programs have sometimes served to paralyze them with a plethora of choices of potential careers, while delegitimating the former cushion of marriage and family on which they could once have fallen back.

18. Kenneth M. Wilson, *Characteristics of Freshmen Entering CRC-Member Colleges during the Period 1964–1970: A Summary of Survey Data* (Princeton: Educational Testing Service, 1971), pp. 897–908. It should be noted that women's test scores, notably including verbal SAT scores, have been dropping even more rapidly than the originally lower verbal scores of men. See the *Chronicle of Higher Education*, 12, no. 10

(May 3, 1976): 2; also, Galen Brewster, "Anxiety, Identity, and Declining Scores," *Independent School*, 36 (October 1976): 15–18, suggesting some of the reasons why women, faced (thanks to the women's movements), with greater options, have been more anxious even than hitherto about outdoing men and about the future implications of stellar, hence "unfair" and "undemocratic," verbal performance.

19. Cf. "Joreen" (Jo Freeman, since she is now prepared to abandon the pseudonym), "Trashing: The Dark Side of Sisterhood," *Ms.*, 4, no. 10 (April 1976): 49–51, 92–98; for more general discussion, see Jo Freeman, *The Politics of Women's Liberation* (New York: David McKay, 1975).

20. Cf. Kenneth S. Lynn, *The Dream of Success: A Study of the Modern American Imagination* (Boston: Little, Brown, 1955); also, Gordon H. Mills, "Jack London's Quest for Salvation," *American Quarterly* 7 (Spring 1955): 3–14; also, for a later era, "Lonely Successes," in David Riesman, Nathan Glazer, and Reuel Denney, *The Lonely Crowd* (New Haven: Yale University Press, 1950, 1961), pp. 155–56.

21. See Jesse R. Pitts, "The Hippies as Contrameritocracy," *Dissent* (July–August 1969); repr. (Spring 1974): 305–16. For a description of growing anti-meritocratic attitudes at Harvard College, see David Riesman, "Educational Reform at Harvard College: Meritocracy and its Adversaries," in Seymour Martin Lipset and David Riesman, *Education and Politics at Harvard*, two essays prepared for the Carnegie Commission (New York: McGraw-Hill, 1975), pp. 359–68. Since this essay was written, the behavior, as distinct from the attitudes, of Harvard College undergraduates has become more overtly competitive, with the notorious would-be pre-meds leading the way, often with a considerable burden of self-contempt for doing so. To be sure, upwardly mobile students, though they quickly learn the dogmas of anti-elitism, are less hesitant than others about recognizing that they sought entry into Harvard College for just such advantages.

22. Daniel Yankelovich, *The Changing Values on Campus: Political and Personal Attitudes of Today's College Students* (New York: Washington Square Press, 1972), p. 47.

23. On the lack of available candidates, cf. Humphrey Doermann, "Lack of Money: A Barrier to Higher Education," in *Barriers to Higher Education* (New York, College Entrance Examination Board: 1971), pp. 130–47.

24. A devastating account of this whole phenomenon is to be found in Thomas Sowell, *Black Education: Myths and Tragedies* (New York: David McKay, 1972), and especially Part II, "Black Students and White Colleges," pp. 129–216.

25. An illustration is provided by a comparison of attitudes toward affirmative action on behalf of minorities and women at Harvard College and at the University of California-Riverside in 1974. Although by this time themselves anxious about their own future prospects, Harvard College students (including those who define themselves politically as to the

right of their fellows) were by small majority willing to grant preferences to minorities in college admissions, while the majority of students, who even now identify with the left, are overwhelmingly prepared to do so. But at Riverside, a largely commuter university with older, often veteran students and with more precarious occupational futures, about three-quarters of the students insist that college admissions, graduate and professional school admissions, and hiring decisions should be made on only academic and personal qualifications; they certainly do not regard themselves as a sponsored elite, although in fact a number are the children of college graduates. See Marshall W. Meyer, "Student Perspectives at Harvard and UC Riverside, 1974–75," unpublished manuscript, University of California, Riverside, 1976.

26. Several years after St. Louis University recruited sizable numbers of black students from the inner city, Grant talked with white faculty members there who were dismayed because black students in their classes had accused them of being racist. The instructors thought of themselves as liberals concerned with the plight of these blacks, and as proof of their good intentions, several mentioned that they had given the black students higher grades than they would have given to comparable whites, even though these were often only Cs. Interviews with the black students revealed that most of them had no complaints about the grades they had received, but on the contrary were concerned about being patronized by such a policy, which they felt faculty adopted as an excuse for not really challenging them or teaching them. The students knew they had serious deficits but did not believe the faculty were sincere about trying to remedy them—hence the charge of racism.

27. For an account of the dilemmas faced by blacks in charge of black-studies programs, who are caught between divergent constituencies, see Thomas F. Slaughter, Jr., "The Status of Black Studies Programs in American Colleges and Universities," paper prepared for presentation at the American Sociological Association meetings, August 29, 1972; also, writings by Wilson Record, who has made a systematic study of the way white researchers have tended to be either driven out of black-studies programs or forced by internal and external pressures to become "blacker than thou." See e.g., Wilson Record, "White Sociologists and Black Students in Predominantly White Universities," *The Sociological Quarterly*, 15 (Spring 1974): 164–82; "Some Implications of the Black Studies Movement for Higher Education in the 1970's," *The Journal of Higher Education*, 44, no. 3 (March 1973): 191–216; "The Sociologist as Actor in the Research Drama," in Arthur B. Shostak, *The Eye of Sociology* (New York: Alfred Publishing Co., forthcoming). In a study based on findings from a survey of 115 colleges and universities by Talcott Parsons and Gerald Platt, R. Danforth Ross concludes that the institutionalization of new incrementally and hence academically legitimate programs (linguistics, computer sciences, statistics, biophysics—and, where more doubts might be raised, environmental studies) has depended mainly on the growth in size of the

institution, while the addition of programs in ethnic and urban studies tends to occur in selective colleges with a high proportion of nonwhite students, "indicating the importance of pressure from students in establishing these programs." See Ross, "The Institutionalization of Academic Innovations: Two Models," *Sociology of Education*, 49, no. 2 (April 1976): 146–55.

28. See Thomas Schelling, "On the Ecology of Micro-Motives," *Public Interest*, 25 (Fall 1971): 59–98.

29. Harold L. Hodgkinson, *Institutions in Transition* (New York: McGraw-Hill, 1971), pp. 26–33.

30. Samuel McCracken, "Quackery in the Classroom," in *Radical School Reform*, ed. Cornelius Troost (Boston: Little Brown, 1973).

31. See Samuel P. Huntington, "The Governability of Democracy: The American Case," in Samuel P. Huntington, Michel Crozier, and Joji Watanuki, eds., *The Governability of Democracies* (New York: New York University Press, 1975).

32. See Burton R. Clark, *The Open Door College: A Case Study* (New York: McGraw-Hill, 1960); also, Leland L. Medsker, *The Junior College: Progress and Prospects* (New York: McGraw-Hill, 1960). For discussion of the inequalities introduced in the contemporary altered situation, see Jerome Karabel, "Community Colleges and Social Stratification: Submerged Class Conflict in American Higher Education," in Jerome Karabel and A. H. Halsey, eds., *Power and Ideology in Education* (New York: Oxford University Press, 1977), pp. 215–34.

33. See Sidney Suslow, "A Report on an Interinstitutional Survey of Undergraduate Scholastic Grading, 1960's to 1970's," Office of Institutional Research, University of California, Berkeley, February 1976. Suslow queried the 50 leading research universities (those receiving the most federal funds). Usable replies were received from 23.

34. See the description by the chairman of the Sociology Department of the University of New Mexico of how he was himself censured for violating the supposed academic freedom of a teaching assistant by criticizing him and trying to prevent him from giving As to all students in his sections: Richard F. Tomasson, "Report of the Department of Sociology, 1971–1972," mimeographed, University of New Mexico, Albuquerque, 1973. Censure by a faculty committee was later reversed by the university president.

35. For a fictional account of some of the convolutions of and revulsions against such freedom, see Midge Decter, *Liberal Parents, Radical Children* (New York: Coward-McCann & Geoghan, 1975), espec. Chap. 4, "The Sexual Revolutionist," pp. 139–93.

36. See John DeLamater, "Intimacy in a Coeducational Community," in Albert A. Harrison, ed., *Explorations in Psychology* (Belmont, Calif.: Brooks/Coles, 1974), pp. 278–89. Even the incest taboo itself, with its enormous importance in protecting the young from sexual exploitation by adults and thereby the destruction of trust in adults, is today, along with

all other sexual customs, being questioned. Thus, from Sweden there comes a report that "a government committee has recommended that children be legally free to make their hetero- or homosexual debuts at 14, that all legal prohibitions of incest be lifted, and that the word 'homosexual' be dropped from the terminology of the law." This is a quotation from J. M. Cameron, "The Prison of Sexual Liberation," *New York Review of Books*, 23, no. 8 (May 13, 1976): 19.

37. See Oscar and Mary F. Handlin, *The American College and American Culture: Socialization as a Function of Higher Education* (New York: McGraw-Hill, 1970), espec. pp. 84–85.

Chapter 7

1. See "New College: D Minus Five Months," in W. Hugh Stickler, ed., *Experimental Colleges: Their Role in American Higher Education* (Tallahassee: Florida State University, 1964), pp. 49–56.

2. Cf. Peter Elbow, "The Pedagogy of the Bamboozled," *Soundings: An Interdisciplinary Journal* (Spring 1973), pp. 247–58, which deals with the faculty fear of being mentors for students and the ideological insistence in the culture on total autonomy and independence rather than on the necessary interdependence of any community of learners.

3. See "New College, Sarasota, Florida," in Paul L. Dressel, ed., *The New Colleges: Toward an Appraisal* (Iowa City: American College Testing Program, 1971), chap. 8, p. 179.

4. This letter is quoted with the writer's permission in Riesman's article, "New College," *Change*, 7 (May 1975):39.

5. See Oliver Fulton and Martin Trow, "Research Activities in American Higher Education, *Sociology of Education*, 47 (Winter 1974).

Chapter 8

1. See Karl A. Lamb et al., *Academic Quality at Santa Cruz: A Report of the Chancellor's Self-Study/Accreditation Commission*, December 1975, pp. 96–98.

2. For an account of the reasoning that led to the decision to build three new major university campuses in the early 1960s, including Santa Cruz, see Verne Stadtman's history, *The University of California, 1868–1968* (Berkeley: University of California Press, 1970).

3. Pat Berdge et al., *Solomon's House: A Self-Conscious History of Cowell College* (Felton, Calif.: Big Trees Press, 1970), pp. 18–19.

4. Byron Stookey, "Starting from Scratch: The University of California at Santa Cruz," *Harvard Educational Review* (Winter 1965).

5. Berdge et al., *Solomon's House*, p. 20.

6. Mark Messer, "Task Force on Undergraduate Instruction: Report and Retrospective Views of UCSC's Alumni 1967–1973," University of California at Santa Cruz, July 1974; hereafter referred to as the "Messer Survey."

7. Harold Hodgkinson, "San Diego and Santa Cruz: Some Comparisons," report to the University of California Regents, January 1972.

8. Messer Survey, pp. 22–23. No doubt the pedigrees of most Santa Cruz faculty compensated for the vagaries of pass/fail grading. It is reasonable to assume that letters of recommendation from Santa Cruz might have carried more weight than recommendations from a college where pass/fail grading was not coupled with the persuasive power and private networks of an elite faculty. Of those who went, 68 percent entered graduate schools within California, most of them in Northern California.

9. Richard E. Peterson, "Goals for California Higher Education: A Survey of 116 College Communities," prepared for the Joint Committee on the Master Plan for Higher Education of the California Legislature, Berkeley 1973.

10. Data in this section is drawn from the "Summary of Data on Entering Freshmen" for the years 1966–73, Cooperative Institutional Research Program of the American Council on Education, Washington, D.C.

11. Lamb et al., *Academic Quality at Santa Cruz*, p. 72.

12. Berdge et al., *Solomon's House*, p. 132.

13. Hodgkinson, "San Diego and Santa Cruz," shows that 50 percent of Santa Cruz faculty "feel that required courses are detrimental to student learning, compared with 21 percent of Berkeley faculty and 54 percent of Antioch faculty who share that view."

14. Robert F. Adams and Jacob B. Michaelson, "Assessing the Benefits of Collegiate Structure: The Case at Santa Cruz," mimeographed, Office of the Vice President for Planning and Analysis, University of California, February 1971, p. 42. Their argument is more applicable to beginners than to senior faculty with tenure. For the latter, the ability to teach general-education courses would add to their competence and even to their marketability. That is, if one is distinguished enough, being "more than a specialist" adds to one's reputation.

15. Messer Survey, pp. 38–39. The question read: "In terms of your overall experience as a student at UCSC, your college affiliation figures as . . . "

16. For anecdotal evidence, see J. T. Dewing, "The University of California at Santa Cruz, (B)," a case study prepared for the Institute of Educational Management at Harvard, mimeographed, Cambridge, Mass., 1971, p. 16.

17. Letter from a faculty member, August 24, 1975.

18. Carnegie Commission on Higher Education, *A Classification of Institutions of Higher Education* (Berkeley, Calif., 1973).

19. For a delightfully ironic—though somewhat overdrawn—account of these matters, see Lionel S. Lewis, *Scaling the Ivory Tower: Merit and*

Its Limits in Academic Careers (Baltimore: Johns Hopkins University Press, 1975), espec. chap. 2, and a review by Gerald Grant, *Contemporary Sociology*, forthcoming.

20. John Ellis, memorandum on restructuring the colleges, Stevenson College, November 1973.

21. Lamb et al., *Academic Quality at Santa Cruz*, pp. 199–211.

22. John Marcum, "The Santa Cruz Colleges: A Systemic Appraisal," January 24, 1974, mimeographed, Office of the Provost, Merrill College. For other documents relevant to this discussion, see Bruce D. Larkin, "Memorandum on the Concentration of Course Offerings by Colleges," Chancellor's Office file, January 14, 1974; "Suggested Guidelines for Discussion" of educational structures, Committee on Educational Policy, Office of the Academic Senate, February 4, 1974; and "The Need for Change and Three Alternatives at Santa Cruz," a report by the Wright Institute, prepared for the Task Force on Undergraduate Instruction at UCSC, October 14, 1974.

23. Lamb et al., *Academic Quality at Santa Cruz*, p. 137. In three instances, the college said the faculty members should be promoted, and they were, although the departments said not. In the other three, the college said promotions slated by the departments should be denied, and they were.

24. For an account of the reaggregation effort, see Anne Derry, "Program to Strengthen Colleges," *City on a Hill Press*, 10, no. 14 (January 30, 1975):1, 3, 12.

Chapter 9

---

1. Cf. Thomas Kuhn, *The Structure of Scientific Revolutions* (Chicago: University of Chicago Press, 1962).

2. Cf. Verne A. Stadtman, *The University of California, 1868–1968* (Berkeley: University of California Press, 1970); see also Neil J. Smelser and Gabriel Almond, eds., *Public Higher Education in California* (Berkeley and Los Angeles: University of California Press, 1974).

3. See "Undergraduate Enrollment Patterns of New Jersey Residents in Out-of-State Colleges," prepared by Kathleen Delehanty as *Research Report 76–5* for the New Jersey Department of Higher Education, June 1976, which breaks the "export trade" down. Close to 140,000 students attend, in four out of five cases, private colleges the majority of which are relatively unselective and located in neighboring states and Florida.

4. See Richard Carl Leone, *The Politics of Gubernatorial Leadership: Tax and Education Reform in New Jersey* (Ph.D. thesis, Woodrow Wilson School of Public and International Affairs, Princeton, 1969).

5. See George Potter, "A Call to Action," unpublished paper, Ramapo College, 1975, pp. 1–24, which borrows the title of the Report of the

Citizens Committee for Higher Education in New Jersey of 1966 and describes the initial planning of what began as the Northern State College. We have drawn on this account in the discussion of the site selection and start-up problems of Ramapo that follows.

6. See Laurie S. Potter and George T. Potter, "Designing and Operating a Barrier Free Campus," paper planned for presentation at the Society for College and University Planning, July 21–24, 1976. The campus was not the first in the country to take account of the needs of the handicapped—Southern Illinois University among others had pioneered in this respect a number of years earlier.

7. For an account of the Ramapo concentration within the School of Theoretical and Applied Science on "Science in Cultural Perspective," see Bernard Langer (whose field is History and Philosophy of Science) and Yole G. Sills (Sociology), "Science in Cultural Perspective," Ramapo College of New Jersey, rev. ms., November 1976—the document states the various courses and Senior Seminars, including Bioethics, Philosophies of Nature, Technological Mythologies, Science and Religion, etc., which are available to concentrators.

8. For a discussion of problems of the Freshmen program and other college-wide issues, see John Robert Cassidy, "Comments—Some Policy Directions for the New Academic Year," mimeographed, Memorandum for the Faculty Assembly and the Professional Staff Association, September 8, 1976.

9. *Ramapo College of New Jersey: The Self-Study Report*, prepared for accreditation purposes in August 1975, declares (pp. 8–9) that the minimum size for a school should be approximately 300 students (Intercultural Studies then had about 220); the account of the school in the *Report* indicates the wide range of its offerings, which of course appeal to students who are citizens in other schools as well, reflecting the commitment of the School of Intercultural Studies "to creating an intercultural dimension for the whole College" (pp. 35–42).

10. George W. Goethals and Dennis Klos, *Experiencing Youth: First Person Accounts*, 2d ed. (Boston: Little Brown, 1976).

11. For an account of the problem of tutorials in the light of the diverse emotional as well as cognitive needs of the student body, and of the extraordinary amount of time devoured by acting as advisor, monitor, and ombudsman for one's tutorial students, see Flavia Alaya: "In My Opinion: A Personal Comment on the Tutorial Experience," *Horizons*, January 24, 1977, p. 2.

12. Cf. Schumpeter, *Capitalism, Socialism, and Democracy* (New York: Harper & Bros., 1947); also Ernest Van den Haag, "Economics Is Not Enough—Notes on the Anticapitalist Spirit," *The Public Interest*, no. 45 (Fall 1976): 109–22.

13. Two reports to the faculty by the Professional Committee of the Faculty Assembly deal with the problem of the need for standards con-

cerning tenure and promotion. "Report on Personnel Policies," April 21, 1976; December 15, 1976.

14. An unpublished manuscript by Peter Elbow, Margaret Gribskov, and Bill Aldridge, professors of humanities at Evergreen State College, *One-to-One Faculty Development*, written in 1976 under a Danforth Foundation Grant for the Improvement of Teaching, deals directly with this subject. No institution we know of has wholly resolved such dilemmas, though Evergreen State College has made considerable progress in the teams of five faculty members which are set up to take one hundred students for an entire year and constitute a total academic program.

15. The general question of quality control is explored in Riesman, "The Scholar at the Border," *Columbia Forum*, 3 (Spring 1974).

16. See Ramapo College of New Jersey Catalogue, 1975–76, p. 109.

17. See *Horizons*, December 20, 1976, p. 1.

18. See *D.H.E. Data Briefs, no. 12* (September 1975), issued by the New Jersey Department of Higher Education Office of Research, under the heading "Minority Undergraduates in NJ Colleges have more than Doubled Since 1970," which gives figures for Ramapo and Stockton as well as for other colleges in the state.

19. Cf. Thomas F. Green, *Work: Leisure, and the American Schools* (New York: Random House, 1968). Green makes a distinction between one's job and one's work. Many faculty hope that Ramapo will continue to focus on the liberal arts for the sake of the entire life-cycle of their students, without reference to the paid work that they will actually find themselves doing (though they do not generally deprecate the latter).

20. See the excellent article by Allen Lacy, "Whatever Happened to Erewhon?," *The Chronicle of Higher Education*, December 1974, pp. 19–20. A charter member of the faculty at Kirkland College, Lacy came to Stockton as a member of its original faculty, and he is now professor of philosophy. For an account of demoralization among faculty at a new urban community college attended predominantly by white commuter students, see Howard B. London, "Pursuing Integrity: The Culture of a Working Class Community College," unpublished Ph.D. dissertation, Boston College, 1976.

21. The term "organized anarchy" comes from a book sponsored by the Carnegie Commission: Michael D. Cohen and James D. March, *The American College President* (New York: McGraw-Hill, 1973). For a discussion of faculty ambivalence concerning unions, as related to age, status, and liberal or conservative ideologies, see the discussion of the Carnegie Commission Survey of Student and Faculty Opinion, 1969, in Everett Carll Ladd, Jr., and Seymour Martin Lipset, *The Divided Academy: Professors and Politics* (New York: McGraw-Hill, 1975), pp. 243–98.

22. On "job-holders," see Riesman and Joseph Gusfield, "Faculty Culture and Academic Careers: Some Sources of Innovation in Higher Education," *Sociology of Education*, 37, no. 4 (Summer 1964).

23. See Stockton State College Bulletin, 1975–76, p. 32.

24. A story in the local paper is headed "Progressivism Eroding at Stockton State?"

25. For a profile of Stockton State College, see Harold L. Hodgkinson, *Campus Senate: Experiment in Democracy*, Center for Research and Development in Higher Education (Berkeley: University of California Press, 1974), pp. 89–99. The profile implies that Stockton is an "experimenting" institution, though President Bjork in responding to Hodgkinson's account, emphasizes that there is no "experiment" underway.

26. See statement before the New Jersey Assembly Education Committee, November 17, 1976, concerning the "Review of Academic Tenure in the Public Schools."

27. See Evaluation Team Report, as published in *Stockton Chronicle* insert, November 10, 1975, p. 1.

28. See Williard Waller, *The Sociology of Teaching* (New York: John Wiley, 1932); also Robert Dreeben, *On What Is Learned in School* (Boston: Addison-Wesley, 1968).

29. Cf. Richard Freeman, *The Overeducated American* (New York: Academic Press, 1976), for one of the most cogent analyses of this theme by an economist; see also Caroline Bird, *The Case Against College* (New York: David McKay, 1975), and Gerald Grant, "Universal BA?," *New Republic*, 166 (June 24, 1972): 13–16.

30. Stockton State College Bulletin, 1975–76, p. 48.

31. Cf. Peter Elbow, "Shall We Teach or Give Credit? A Model for Higher Education," *Soundings: An Interdisciplinary Journal*, 54 (Fall 1971): 237–52.

32. See the section on "Athletics and Recreation," in *Stockton State College: Annual Review and Planning*, Summer 1976.

33. *Ibid.*, p. 14. An attempt is being made also to introduce "students to the world of work early in a realistic fashion."

34. See *Campus Senate: Experiment in Democracy*, p. 82.

35. E. Alden Dunham, *The Colleges of the Forgotten Americans: A Profile of State Colleges and Regional Universities* (New York: McGraw-Hill, 1969).

36. See Robert H. Koenker, "Status of the Doctor of Arts Degree," mimeographed, Graduate School, Ball State University, Muncie, Indiana, February 28, 1976.

37. At a summer institute on college and university teaching, one of us was asked several years ago by some faculty members from CUNY what to do when one's students had combined aptitude scores that ranged from 600 to the very ceiling of 1600. We reponded that we ourselves would not know how to teach so wide a spread in one class, and hence would be inclined to subdivide it. The response was immediate: "This is tracking": hence, illegitimate even to consider. Our arguments to the contrary were clearly to no avail, and it became evident that faculty are not ordinarily invited to address such questions with inventiveness (yet awareness of "political" risks) in their graduate training.

Chapter 10

1. Hugh Hawkins, *Between Harvard and America: The Educational Leadership of Charles W. Eliot* (New York: Oxford University Press, 1972), pp. 91–113.

2. See Lionel Trilling, "The Uncertain Future of the Humanistic Educational Ideal," *American Scholar*, 44, no. 1 (Winter 1974–75): 57. See also Daniel Bell, "A Second Look at General Education," *Seminar Reports*, Columbia University, 1 (December 1973): 4–6, 7.

3. Ann Heiss, *An Inventory of Academic Innovation and Reform: A Technical Report Sponsored by the Carnegie Commission on Higher Education* (New York: McGraw-Hill, 1973), pp. 1–17.

4. Daniel L. Kegan, "Student Attrition at Hampshire College: Qualitative and Political Implications," mimeographed, September 1976. Kegan found that the number of students at Hampshire (60 percent) who felt "isolated from most of the people at their college" was half again as much as the rate at Amherst and the University of Massachusetts (40 percent).

5. See Kiyo Morimoto, Judith Gregory, and Penelope Butler, "On Trying to Understand the Frustrations of Students," Bureau of Study Counsel, Harvard University, 1972.

6. *Chronicle of Higher Education*, 12, no. 18 (July 12, 1976): 9.

7. Robert Blackburn et al., *Changing Practices in Undergraduate Education*, a report to the Carnegie Council, 1976, based on an examination of requirements as reported in catalogues of 271 colleges and universities. The departmental major did remain the bulwark of the curriculum, however.

8. Hawkins, *Between Harvard and America*, pp. 100–102.

9. John Agnew, "Institutional Goals Inventory: A Delphi Study," mimeographed, Evergreen State College, 1975.

10. L.B.R. Briggs, dean of Harvard College, in Hawkins, *Between Harvard and America*, p. 269.

11. *Ibid.*, p. 278.

12. See "The Student Sub-culture and the Examination System in Early 19th Century Oxbridge," in *The University in Society: Oxford and Cambridge from the 14th to the Early 19th Century*, ed. Lawrence Stone (Princeton, N.J.: Princeton University Press, 1974) 1: 296. Though competition and community are usually linked, this is not so at a college like Hampshire.

13. Listed in Jerry G. Gaff, ed., *The Cluster College* (San Francisco, Calif.: Jossey-Bass, 1970), pp. 17–18.

14. See, for example, Paul Heist and John Bilorusky, "A Special Breed of Student," in *The Cluster College*, and Robert C. Wilson et al., *College Professors and Their Impact on Students* (New York: Wiley, 1975), espec. chap. 16. There is a useful discussion of changes in student attitudes and values at St. Olaf, University of the Pacific, Reed, and Antioch in Burton S. Clark et al., *Students and Colleges: Interaction and Change*

(Berkeley, Calif.: Center for Research and Development in Higher Education, 1972). On Santa Cruz, see Mark Messer, "Task Force on Undergraduate Instruction," mimeographed, Santa Cruz, 1974.

15. For a sensitive discussion of the energy and intelligence required to create and sustain the kinds of programs we envision see Leo Marx, "Can We Create Together What We Can't Create Alone?" *Change*, 7, no. 6 (Summer 1975).

16. K. Patricia Cross discusses these "new students" in *Beyond the Open Door* (San Francisco, Calif.: Jossey-Bass, 1974), and in *Accent on Learning* (San Francisco, Calif.: Jossey-Bass, 1976).

17. For a perceptive account of the Alverno program, see Thomas Ewens, "Alverno College: A Case Study" (Syracuse, N.Y.: Educational Policy Research Center, 1976), and Alverno's own report, "Competence Based Learning at Alverno College" (Milwaukee, Wis.: Alverno College, 1974).

18. Alain Touraine, *The Academic System in American Society* (New York: McGraw-Hill, 1974), p. 22.

19. Daniel Bell, *The Reforming of General Education* (New York: Columbia University Press, 1966), p. 66.

20. For a different view see James Coleman, "The University and Society's New Demands upon It," in *Content and Context*, ed. Carl Kaysen (New York: McGraw-Hill, 1973), p. 395. Coleman suggests that the functions of the educational conglomerate can be partitioned into neat categories of undergraduate teaching, client-sponsored research, and basic research. We disagree.

21. Letter from a colleague, April 1976. For a more caustic view of the effects of unionization, see John W. Chapman, "Unionization and Tenure at Pittsburgh," *Newsletter of the International Council on the Future of the University*, 3, no. 3 (July 1976). Everett C. Ladd, Jr., and S. M. Lipset discuss the variable impact of campus unionism in *The Divided Academy: Professors and Politics* (New York: McGraw-Hill, 1975), espec. chap. 10. Joseph Garbarino and Bill Aussieker analyze the rise of unions and draw contrasts with patterns in Great Britain in *Faculty Bargaining: Change and Conflict* (New York: McGraw-Hill, 1975).

22. Cf. Rolf Meyersohn and Elihu Katz, "Notes on the Natural History of Fads," *American Journal of Sociology*, 62:594–601; reprinted in Eric Larabee and Rolf Meyersohn, *Mass Leisure* (Glencoe, Ill.: Free Press, 1958). The spread of styles and forms in American society, we are reminded, is not invariably from the top down.

Bibliography

In this volume we have not attempted any comprehensive survey of higher education. We have been selective in our choice of themes and of the institutions used to illustrate them. Our footnotes have been similarly selective. But we have drawn on a rich number of sources even when acknowledgment is not expressly footnoted in the text. In this bibliography we list those books and articles which have been influential in forming our thoughts and developing our factual understanding of higher education. Today the study of higher education includes many specialities: the student protest literature of the sixties and seventies, studies of student-teacher relationships and the impact on students of the college experience, economic analyses, stratification and mobility studies, and the literature dealing with "new students," adult learners, and nontraditional forms of on-campus and off-campus learning and teaching, to name only a few. A thorough exploration of any of these fields would yield a bibliography longer than this one. Still, it is hoped that even a limited bibliography may help others to study an arena which, once relatively neglected outside of departments of higher education in schools of education, has now attracted the interest of a variety of social scientists, of scholars in the humanities who are concerned with philosophical and conceptual problems, and of natural scientists and mathematicians who are concerned with pedagogy.

Abrams, Janet F., and Price, Charlton R. "The Learning Community, Portland, Oregon: A Report to the Carnegie Corporation of New York." December 1971.

"Abundance into Excellence." *Life*, October 5, 1959, p. 50.

Ackerman, James. "The Arts in Higher Education." In *Content and Context: Essays on College Education*, edited by Carl Kaysen. New York: McGraw-Hill, 1973.

419

Adamek, Raymond J., and Lewis, Jerry M. "Social Control, Violence, and Radicalization: The Kent State Case." Paper delivered at the American Sociological Association meeting, New Orleans, August 1972.

Adams, Frank, and Horton, Myles. *Unearthing Seeds of Fire: The Idea of Highlander*. Winston-Salem, N.C.: John F. Blair, 1975.

Adams, Robert F., and Michaelson, Jacob B. "Assessing the Benefits of Collegiate Structure: The Case at Santa Cruz." Mimeographed. Berkeley: Office of the Vice President for Planning and Analysis, University of California, February 1971.

Adelson, Joseph. "The Teacher as a Model." In *The American College: A Psychological and Social Interpretation of the Higher Learning*. New York: John Wiley, 1962.

Adler, Mortimer. "Can Catholic Education Be Criticized?" *Commonweal*, April 14, 1939, p. 682.

————. "God and the Professors." *Daily Maroon*, University of Chicago, November 14, 1940.

Agnew, John. "Institutional Goals Inventory: A Delphi Study." Mimeographed. Olympia, Wash.: Evergreen State College, 1975.

Aiken, Henry D., "Interdisciplinary and Transdisciplinary Studies in the Humanities: Problems and Possibilities," *Seminar Reports*, Columbia University, 1, no. 8 (May 15, 1974).

Alaya, Flavia. "In My Opinion: A Personal Comment on the Tutorial Experience." *Horizons*, Ramapo College of New Jersey, January 24, 1977, p. 2.

Altbach, Philip G., and Laufer, Robert S., eds. *Student Protest*, A Special Issue of the Annals of the American Academy of Political and Social Science, vol. 395 (May 1971).

Alverno College. "Competence Based Learning at Alverno College." Milwaukee: Alverno College, 1974.

American Council on Education. *A Fact Book on Higher Education*. Washington, D.C.: looseleaf, annual supplements.

————. "Summary of Data on Entering Freshmen, 1966–1973." Washington, D.C.: 1974.

Anderson, C. Arnold. "Inequalities in Schooling in the South." *American Journal of Sociology*, 60 (1955): 547–61.

————. "A Skeptical Note on the Relation of Vertical Mobility to Education." *American Journal of Sociology*, 66 (1961): 560–70.

————; Bowman, Mary Jean; and Tinto, Vincent. *Where Colleges are and Who Attends: Effects of Accessibility on College Attendance*. New York: McGraw-Hill, 1972.

Arendt, Hannah. *The Origins of Totalitarianism*. New York: Harcourt, Brace, 1951.

————. "Thinking and Moral Considerations: A Lecture." *Social Research*, 38, no. 3 (Autumn 1971).

Armbruster, Robert. "From the Boardroom: Young Trustees Speak." *Alma Mater*, 39 (May-June 1972): 3–9.

Ashby, Eric, and Anderson, Mary, *The Rise of the Student Estate in Britain*. Cambridge, Mass.: Harvard University Press, 1970.

Astin, Alexander. *College Dropouts: A National Profile*. Washington, D.C.: American Council on Education, February 1972.

————. "Productivity of Undergraduate Institutions." *Science*, 136 (April 13, 1962): 129–35.

————. "Undergraduate Achievement and Institutional 'Excellence.'" *Science*, 161 (1968): 661–68.

————. *Who Goes Where to College?* Chicago: Science Research Associates, 1965.

————; Astin, Helen S.; Bayer, Alan E.; and Bisconti, Ann S. *The Power of Protest*. San Francisco: Jossey-Bass, 1975.

————, and Holland, John L. "The Distribution of Wealth in Higher Education." *College and University*, Winter 1962, pp. 113–25.

————; Panos, Robert; and Creager, John. "National Norms for Entering College Freshmen—Fall 1966." *American Council on Education Research Reports*, 2, no. 1, Washington, D.C., 1967.

————; Panos, Robert; and Creager, John. "Supplementary Naitonal Norms for Freshmen Entering College in 1966." *American Council on Education Research Reports*, 2, no. 3, Washington, D.C., 1967.

Axelrod, Joseph. *Model Building for Undergraduate Colleges*. Berkeley, Calif.: Center for Research and Development in Higher Education, 1969.

————. *The University Teacher as Artist*. San Francisco: Jossey-Bass, 1973.

Back, Kurt W. *Beyond Words*. Baltimore: Penguin, 1973.

Baier, Kurt, and Rescher, Nicholas. *Values and the Future: The Impact of Technological Change on American Values*. New York: Free Press, 1969.

Bailey, Stephen K. *The Purposes of Education*. Phi Delta Kappa, Bloomington, Ind., 1976.

Baird, Leonard L. *The Graduates: A Report on the Characteristics and Plans of College Seniors*. Princeton: Educational Testing Service, 1973.

————. "The Practical Utility of Measures of College Environments." *Review of Educational Research*, 44, no. 3 (Summer 1974): 307–30.

Baltzell, E. Digby. "Bell Telephone's Experiment in Education." *Harper's Magazine*, March 1955, pp. 73–77.

Bandler, Richard; Boyd, Dean; Carr, Claudia; Grinder, John; and Morris, Mary Lee. "Building Community." Mimeographed. Kresge College, University of California at Santa Cruz, January 1972.

Bardwick, Judith; Douvan, Elizabeth; Horner, Matina S.; and Gutmann, David. *Feminine Personality and Conflict*. Belmont, Calif.: Wadsworth, 1970.

Barton, Allen H. *Studying the Effects of College Education: A Methodological Examination of "Changing Values in College."* New Haven: Hazen Foundation, 1959.

Barzun, Jacques. *The American University: How It Runs, Where It Is Going.* New York: Harper & Row, 1968.

Batchelder, Alan B. "Decline in the Relative Income of Negro Men." *Quarterly Journal of Economics,* 78 (November 1964): 525–48.

Bayer, Alan E. "College and University Faculty: A Statistical Description." Vol. 5, no. 5. Washington, D.C.: Office of Research, American Council on Education, 1970.

————, and Astin, Alexander W. "Campus Unrest, 1970–71: Was It Really All That Quiet?" *Education Record,* 52 (Fall 1971): 301–13.

————, and Astin, Alexander W. *Campus Disruption During 1968–69.* Washington, D. C.: American Council on Education Office of Research, August 1969.

Becker, Howard S., and Carper, James. "The Development of Identification with an Occupation." *American Journal of Sociology,* 61 (1956): 289–98.

————; Geer, Blanche; Hughes, Everett C.; and Strauss, Anselm. *Boys in White: Student Culture in Medical School.* Chicago: University of Chicago Press, 1961.

————; Geer, Blanche; and Hughes, Everett C. *Making the Grade: The Academic Side of College Life.* New York: John Wiley, 1968.

————, et al., eds. *Institutions and the Person: Essays in Honor of Everett C. Hughes.* Chicago: Aldine, 1968.

Beckerman, Bernard. "Arts Education for Undergraduates." *Seminar Reports,* Columbia University, 1, no. 8 (May 15, 1974): 1–3.

Bell, Daniel. *The Coming of Post-Industrial Society.* New York: Basic Books, 1973.

————. *The Reforming of General Education: The Columbia College Experience and Its National Setting.* New York: Columbia University Press, 1966.

————. "A Second Look at General Education," *Seminar Reports,* Columbia University, 1 (December 1973): 1–7.

Bellah, Robert N. "The New Religious Consciousness and the Secular University." *Daedalus,* 103 no. 4 (Fall 1974): 110–15.

Ben-David, Joseph, *American Higher Education: Directions Old and New.* New York: Mc-Graw-Hill, 1972.

————. *Centers of Learning: Britain, France, Germany, United States.* New York: McGraw-Hill, 1977.

————. "The Universities and the Growth of Science in Germany and the United States." *Minerva; a Review of Science, Learning, and Policy,* 7 (1968–69): 1–35.

————, and Collins, Randall. "Social Factors in the Origins of a New Science: The Case of Psychology." *American Sociological Review,* 31 (1966): 451–65.

Benne, Kenneth D. "Authority in Education." *Harvard Educational Review,* 40, no. 3, pp. 385–410.

Bennett, General D. V. "The United States Military Academy." *Phi Delta Kappan,* May 1967, pp. 448–49.

Berdge, Pat, et al. *Solomon's House: A Self-Conscious History of Cowell College*. Felton, Calif.: Big Trees Press, 1970.

Berelson, Bernard. *Graduate Education in the United States*. New York: McGraw-Hill, 1960.

Berger, Bennett. "On the Youthfulness of Youth Cultures." *Social Research*, 30 (1963): 319–42.

————. "Sociology and the Intellectuals; an Analysis of a Stereotype." *Antioch Review*, 17 (1957): 275–90. Reprinted in *Sociology: The Progress of a Decade*, edited by Seymour Martin Lipset and Neil J. Smelser. Englewood Cliffs, N.J.: Prentice-Hall, 1961.

Berger, Peter L., and Berger, Brigitte. "The Blueing of America." *New Republic*, 164 (April 3, 1971): 20–23.

Bergwerk, Ronald. "The Greening of Sarasota: A Study of Prehistoric New College." Independent Study project supervised by Marcello Truzzi. Sarasota, Fla.: New College, 1973.

Bernard, Jessie S. *Academic Women*. University Park: Pennsylvania State University Press, 1964.

Bird, Caroline. *The Case Against College*. New York: David McKay, 1975.

Birenbaum, William. *Something for Everybody Is Not Enough: An Educator's Search for His Education*. New York: Random House, 1971.

Bitton, Davis. "Anti-Intellectualism in Mormon History." *Dialogue: A Journal of Mormon Thought*, 1 (Autumn 1966): 111–34.

Bjork, Richard. "Review of Academic Tenure in the Public Schools: Statement before New Jersey Assembly Education Committee, November 17, 1976.

Blackburn, Robert T. *Tenure: Aspects of Job Security on the Changing Campus*. Atlanta: Southern Regional Education Board, 1972.

————; Armstrong, Ellen; Conrad, Clifton; Didham, James; and McKune, Thomas. *Changing Practices in Undergraduate Education*. New York: McGraw-Hill, 1976.

Blau, Peter M. "The Flow of Occupational Supply and Recruitment." *American Sociological Review*, 30 (August 1975): 475–90.

————. *The Organization of Academic Work*. New York: John Wiley, 1973.

————, and Duncan, Otis Dudley. *The American Occupational Structure*. New York: John Wiley, 1967.

Bogue, Donald J. *The Population of the United States*. Glencoe, Ill.: Free Press, 1957.

Boorstin, Daniel J. *The Americans: The National Experience*. New York: Random House, 1965.

Boruch, Robert F. "The Faculty Role in Campus Unrest." Washington, D.C.: American Council on Education Research Reports, 1969.

Boudon, Raymond. *Education, Opportunity and Social Inequality: Changing Prospects in Western Society*. New York: John Wiley, 1973.

Bowers, W. J. *Dishonesty and Its Control in College*. New York: Columbia University, Bureau of Applied Social Research, 1964.

Bowles, Frank. *The Refounding of the College Board, 1948–1963.* New York: College Entrance Examination Board, 1967.

Bowles, Samuel, and Gintis, Herbert. *Schooling in Capitalist America: Educational Reform and the Contradictions of Economic Life.* New York: Basic Books, 1976.

Bowman, Mary Jean. "The Land-Grant Colleges and Universities in Human Resource Development." *Journal of Economic History*, 22 (1962): 523–46.

Boyle, Marybelle. "The Measurement of Some Self-Concepts of Entering Students." Unpublished paper. Detroit: Wayne State University, 1965.

Bradbury, Malcolm. *The History Man.* Boston: Houghton-Mifflin, 1975.

Brann, Eva. "The Student's Problem." Lecture on the liberal arts. Annapolis, Md.: St. John's College, September 22, 1967.

———. "What Are the Beliefs and Teachings of St. John's College?" Annapolis, Md.: St. John's College *Collegian*, May 1975, p. 10.

Bresler, Jack B. "Teaching Effectiveness and Government Awards." *Science*, 160 (1968): 164–67.

Bressler, Marvin, and Westoff, Charles F. "Catholic Education, Economic Values, and Achievement." *American Journal of Sociology*, 69 (November 1963): 225–33.

Brewster, Galen. "Anxiety, Identity, and Declining Scores." *Independent School*, 36 (October 1976): 15–18.

Bronfenbrenner, Urie. "The Experimental Ecology of Education." *Teachers College Record*, 78, no. 2 (December 1976): 157–204.

Brotz, Howard. *The Black Jews of Harlem: Negro Nationalism and the Dilemmas of Negro Leadership.* New York: Free Press, 1964.

Brown, David G. *The Mobile Professors.* Washington, D.C.: American Council on Education, 1967.

Brown, Robert D. "Evaluation of Experimental Colleges: Some Questions That Need Asking." *Journal of Higher Education*, 43, no. 2 (February 1972): 133–41.

Buchanan, Scott, ed. *The Portable Plato.* New York: Viking, 1948.

———. "The School of the People's Institute." *The People's Institute Announcements*, 1926.

———. "A Talk to Friends." Annapolis, Md.: St. John's College, May 31, 1958.

Bullock, Henry Allen. *A History of Negro Education in the South from 1619 to the Present.* Cambridge, Mass.: Harvard University Press, 1967.

Bunzel, John H. "The Faculty Strike at San Francisco State College." *AAUP Bulletin*, 57 (Autumn 1971).

Burrage, Michael. "Democracy and the Mystery of the Crafts: Observations on Work Relationships in America and Britain." *Daedalus*, 101 (Fall 1972): 141–62.

Bushnell, John. "Student Culture at Vassar." In *The American College*, edited by Nevitt Sanford. New York: John Wiley, 1962.

Calhoun, Daniel H. *The American Civil Engineer: Origins and Conflict.* Cambridge, Mass.: M.I.T. Press, 1960.

California, University of. Center for the Study of Higher Education. *Omnibus Personality Inventory Research Manual.* Berkeley, Calif.: 1962.

California, University of, Santa Cruz. *Catalogue,* 1970/71–1976–77.

————. *So You're Thinking of Coming to Santa Cruz.* Santa Cruz: 1967.

————. "Suggested Guidelines for Discussion." Committee on Educational Policy, Office of the Academic Senate, February 4, 1974.

Cameron, J. M. "The Prison of Sexual Liberation." *New York Review of Books* 23, no. 8 (May 13, 1976): 19.

Caplow, Theodore, and McGee, Reece. *The Academic Marketplace.* New York: Basic Books, 1958.

Carlin, Jerome. *Lawyers on Their Own: A Study of Individual Practitioners in Chicago.* New Brunswick, N.J.: Rutgers University Press, 1962.

Carnegie Commission on Higher Education. *A Classification of Institutions of Higher Education.* Berkeley, Calif.: 1973.

————. *Quality and Equality: New Levels of Federal Responsibility for Higher Education.* New York: McGraw-Hill, 1968.

Carr-Saunders, A. M., and Wilson, P. A. *The Professions.* New York: Oxford University Press, 1933.

Cartter, Allan M. *An Assessment of Quality in Graduate Education.* A Study for the Commission on Plans and Objectives for Higher Education, American Council on Education. Washington, D.C.: American Council on Education, 1966.

————. "The Supply of and Demand for College Teachers." *Journal of Human Resources,* 1 (Summer 1966): 22–38.

————, ed. *American Universities and Colleges.* 9th ed. Washington, D.C.: American Council on Education, 1964.

————, and Farrell, R. "Higher Education in the Last Third of the Century." *Educational Record,* 46 (1965): 119–28.

Cass, James, and Birnbaum, Max. *Comparative Guide to American Colleges for Students, Parents, and Counselors.* Editions of 1968–69 through 1976–77. New York: Harper & Row, 1968–76.

Cassidy, John Robert. "Comments—Some Policy Directions for the New Academic Year." Mimeographed. Memorandum for the Faculty Assembly and the Professional Staff Association, Ramapo College. Mahwah, N.J.: September 8, 1976.

Cassidy, Sally W., et al. *Impact of a High-Demand College in a Large University on Working Class Youth.* Final report to the U.S. Office of Education for project no. 5–0818. Detroit: 1968.

Cayton, Horace R. *Long Old Road.* New York: Trident Press, 1965.

Chapman, John W. "Unionization and Tenure at Pittsburgh." *Newsletter of the International Council on the Future of the University,* 3 (July 1976).

Cheit, Earl F. *The New Depression in Higher Education: A Study of the Financial Conditions in 41 Colleges and Universities.* New York: McGraw-Hill, 1971.

―――. *The New Depression in Higher Education—Two Years Later.* Carnegie Commission, 1973.

Chickering, Arthur W. *Education and Identity.* San Francisco: Jossey-Bass, 1974.

Clark, Burton R. "The 'Cooling Out' Function in Higher Education." *American Journal of Sociology*, 65 (1960): 569–76.

―――. *The Distinctive College: Antioch, Reed, and Swarthmore.* Chicago: Aldine, 1970.

―――. *The Open Door College: A Case Study.* New York: McGraw-Hill, 1960.

―――, *Students and Colleges: Interaction and Change.* Berkeley: Center for Research and Development in Higher Education, 1972.

Clark, Harold F., and Sloan, Harold. *Classrooms in the Military.* New York: Teachers College, Columbia University, 1964.

Clark, Kenneth B., and Plotkin, Lawrence. *The Negro Student at Integrated Colleges.* New York: National Scholarship Service and Fund for Negro Students, 1963.

"A Clean Slate and a Free Hand: Michigan State University—Oakland." *Michigan State University Magazine*, 5 (November 1959): 9–24.

Cleary, T. Anne. "Test Bias: Validity of the Scholastic Aptitude Test for Negro and White Students in Integrated Colleges." Princeton: Educational Testing Service, 1966.

Clifford, Richard J., S.J., and Callahan, William B., S.J. "Catholic Higher Education: The Next Twenty Years." *America*, September 19, 1964, 288–91.

Cohen, Arthur M., and Brawer, Florence B., "The Experimental College Responds to Demands." Iowa City, Iowa: American College Testing Program, 1975.

Cohen, Audrey C., and Sunderland, Stephen. "College for Human Services: Performance-Based Undergraduate and Graduate Preparation for the Human Service Professional." Mimeographed. New York: College for Human Services, 1977.

Cohen, David. "Loss as a Theme in Social Policy." *Harvard Educational Review*, 46, no. 4 (November 1976): 558–59.

Cohen, Michael D., and March, James D. *The American College President.* New York: McGraw-Hill, 1973.

Coleman, James S. *The Adolescent Society: The Social Life of the Teenager and Its Impact on Education.* Glencoe, Ill.: Free Press, 1961.

―――, et al. *Equality of Educational Opportunity.* Washington, D.C.: U.S. Office of Education, 1966.

―――. *Youth: Transition to Adulthood, Report of the Panel on Youth to the President's Science Advisory Committee,* Chicago: University of Chicago Press, 1974.

College Entrance Examination Board. "Changing Patterns for Undergraduate Education." Conference report. New York: College Entrance Examination Board, 1972.

College for Human Services. "Final Report of the Women's Talent Corps New Careers Program: 1966–67." New York: College for Human Services, May 1968.

————. "A Game of Change: The New Profession of the Human Services." Mimeographed. New York: College for Human Services, 1974.

————. Second Annual Report. New York: College for Human Services, April 1969.

————. Third Annual Report. New York: College for Human Services, June 1970.

————. Fourth Annual Report. New York: College for Human Services, 1971.

————. "To Design a Faculty Model and a Field Agency Relationship for a Competence-Based Institute of Professional Education." Mimeographed. Proposal submitted to the Fund for the Improvement of Post-Secondary Education. New York: College for Human Services, January 1974.

————. *Two-Year Professional Program Leading to the Degree of Master of Human Services*. Mimeographed. New York: College for Human Services, August 1974.

Collins, Randall. "Some Comparative Principles of Educational Stratification." *Harvard Educational Review*, 47, no. 1 (February 1977): 1–27.

Columbia University Law School. "Legal Service Assistants, Report on Legal Training Phase of a Joint Demonstration Program, 1969–70." New York: Columbia University Law School, Spring 1970.

Commission on Educational Policy. *Critique of a College*. Swarthmore, Pa.: Swarthmore College, November 1967.

Commission on MIT Education. *Report of Colloquium on Knowledge and Values*. Cambridge, Mass.: Massachusetts Institute of Technology, May 27, 1971.

Conant, James B. *The Education of American Teachers*. New York: McGraw-Hill, 1963.

Cottle, Thomas J. "The Pains of Permanence." In *The Tenure Debate*, edited by Bardwell Smith. San Francisco: Jossey-Bass, 1972.

————. *Time's Children: Impressions of Youth*. Boston: Little Brown, 1971.

Coyne, John, and Hebert, Tom. *This Way Out: A Guide to Alernatives to Traditional College Education in the United States, Europe and the Third World*. New York: E. P. Dutton, 1972.

Cross, K. Patricia. *Accent on Learning*. San Francisco: Jossey-Bass, 1976.

————. *Beyond the Open Door*. San Francisco: Jossey Bass, 1974.

Cutler, Lorna; Menagh, Frank; McCormick, Don; and Solotar, Bob. Letters in *Kresge Klone*. University of California, Santa Cruz: Kresge College, February 4, 1974.

Dailey, Charles; McClelland, David C., et al. "Professional Competences of Human Service Workers." Cambridge, Mass.: McBer and Company, January 1974. Known as the McBer Report.

Danière, André. "Cost-Benefit Analysis of Federal Programs of Financial Aid to College Students." Mimeographed. Cambridge, Mass.: Harvard University, 1967.

―――. *Higher Education in the American Economy.* New York: Random House, 1964.

Darkey, William. Letter to Gerald Grant. July 3, 1973.

―――. "Statement of Educational Policy." Annapolis, Md.: St. John's College *Collegian*, April 23, 1973, p. 9.

Davis, James A. "The Campus as a Frog Pond: An Application of the Theory of Relative Deprivation to Career Decisions of College Men." *American Journal of Sociology*, 72 (1966): 17–31.

―――. *Great Aspirations: The Graduate School Plans of America's College Seniors.* Chicago: Aldine, 1964.

―――. "Higher Education: Selection and Opportunity." *School Review*, 71 (Autumn 1963): 249–65.

―――. *Undergraduate Career Decisions: Correlates of Occupational Choice.* Chicago: Aldine, 1965.

Davis, Junius. "What College Teachers Value in Students." *College Board Review*, Spring 1965, pp. 15–18.

Decter, Midge. *Liberal Parents, Radical Children.* New York: Coward-McCann & Geoghan, 1975.

DeLamater, John. "Intimacy in a Coeducational Community." In *Explorations in Psychology*, edited by Albert A. Harrison. Belmont, Calif.: Brooks/Coles, 1974.

Delehanty, Kathleen. "Undergraduate Enrollment Patterns of New Jersey Residents in Out-of-State Colleges." Prepared as *Research Report 76-5* for New Jersey Department of Higher Education, June 1976.

DeMott, Benjamin. "Letter to an Unhappy Alumnus." *Change*, 4 (Summer 1972): 24–29.

―――. "Seven Days in May." *Change*, 2 (September-October 1970): 55–68.

Denison, Edward F. *The Sources of Economic Growth in the United States and the Alternatives before Us.* New York: Committee for Economic Development, 1962.

Derry, Anne. "Program to Strengthen Colleges." University of California, Santa Cruz: *City on a Hill Press*, 10, no. 14 (January 30, 1975): 1.

Dewey, John. "Challenge to Liberal Thought." *Fortune*, August 1944.

―――. *Experience and Education.* New York: Macmillan, 1936.

Dickson, David. "Higher Education for One World or for Two?" Address at 1968 Annual Meeting of the Association of State Universities and Land-Grant Colleges.

Diesing, Paul. *Patterns of Discovery in the Social Sciences.* Chicago: Aldine-Atherton, 1971.

DiRenzo, Gordon J. "Personality Structures and Orientations toward Liturgical Change." Paper read at 1966 meeting of the American Catholic Sociological Society.

Doermann, Humphrey. "Baccalaureate Origins and Performance of Students in the Harvard Graduate School of Arts and Sciences." Unpublished paper, Harvard University, 1968.

———. "Lack of Money: A Barrier to Higher Education." In *Barriers to Higher Education.* New York: College Entrance Examination Board, 1971.

———. "The Market for College Education in the United States." Ph.D. dissertation, Harvard University, 1967.

Dohen, Dorothy. *Nationalism and American Catholicism.* New York: Sheed & Ward, 1967.

Donald, Cleveland, Jr. "Cornell: Confrontation in Black and White." In *Divided We Stand: Reflections on the Crisis at Cornell,* edited by Cushing Strout and David I. Grossvogel. Garden City, N.Y.: Doubleday, 1970.

Donovan, John D. *The Academic Man in the Catholic College.* New York: Sheed & Ward, 1964.

———. "The American Catholic Hierarchy: A Social Profile." *American Catholic Sociological Review,* 19 (June 1958): 98–113.

Dore, Ronald. *The Diploma Disease: Education, Qualification and Development.* London: Allen and Unwin, 1976.

Douglas, Jack D. "Urban Politics and Public Employee Unions." In *Public Employee Unions,* edited by Lawrence Chickering. San Francisco: Institute for Contemporary Studies, 1976.

Douglas, Mary, ed. *Rules and Meanings.* Baltimore: Penguin Books, 1973.

Drake, St. Clair. "The Social and Economic Status of the Negro in the United States." In *The Negro American,* edited by Talcott Parsons and Kenneth B. Clark. Boston: Houghton Mifflin, 1966.

Dreeben, Robert. *On What Is Learned in School.* Boston: Addison-Wesley, 1968.

———. "Reflections on Teacher Militancy and Unionization." *Sociology of Education,* 45 (Summer 1972): 326–37.

Dressel, Paul L., ed. *The New Colleges: Toward an Appraisal.* Iowa City: American College Testing Program, 1971.

Driver, Christopher. *The Exploding University.* London: Hodder Stoughton, 1971.

Duberman, Martin. *Black Mountain: An Exploration in Community.* New York: Dutton, 1972.

Duncan, Beverly. "Dropouts and the Unemployed." *Journal of Political Economy,* 73 (April 1956): 121–34.

Duncan, Otis Dudley. "The Trend of Occupational Mobility in the United States." *American Sociological Review,* 30 (August 1965): 491–98.

Dunham, E. Alden. *Colleges of the Forgotten Americans: A Profile of State Colleges and Regional Universities.* New York: McGraw-Hill, 1969.

Dunham, Raph E.; Wright, Patricia S.; and Chandler, Marjorie O. *Teaching Faculty in Universities and Four-Year Colleges, Spring 1963.* (OE–53022–63) Washington, D.C.: U.S. Department of Health, Education and Welfare, 1966.

Eckland, Bruce K. "Academic Ability, Higher Education, and Occupational Mobility." *American Sociological Review,* 30 (October 1965): 735–46.

———. "College Dropouts Who Came Back." *Harvard Educational Review,* 34 (Summer 1964): 402–20.

———. "Genetics and Sociology: A Reconsideration." *American Sociological Review,* 32 (April 1967): 172–93.

———. "Social Class and College Graduation: Some Misconceptions Corrected." *American Journal of Sociology,* 70 (1964): 36–50.

———. "A Source of Error in College Attrition Studies." *Sociology of Education,* 38 (1964): 60–72.

Edgar, Robert. "Dear Friends." University of California, Santa Cruz: *Kresge Klein,* February 5, 1974.

———. "Interpersonal Communication: Thoughts about College Six." Mimeographed. University of California, Santa Cruz, Kresge College, January 1970.

———. "Intimacy in Community." Mimeographed. Memo, University of California, Santa Cruz, Kresge College, July 29, 1970.

———. "The Kresge Curriculum: A Proposal." Mimeographed. Memo, University of California, Santa Cruz, Kresge College, July 20, 1971.

———. Memorandum in response to questions about goals and governance posed by consultant Dale Lake. University of California, Santa Cruz, Kresge College, October 25, 1971.

———. Memo to Faculty, January 16, 1974. Appearing as "College Curriculum" in *Kresge Klein,* January 22, 1974. University of California, Santa Cruz, Kresge College.

———. Memo to Faculty, January 21, 1974. Appearing as "My Thoughts about a Kresge Curriculum." University of California, Santa Cruz: *Kresge Klein,* January 22, 1974.

Eells, Walter Crosby. *Baccalaurate Degrees Conferred by American Colleges in the 17th and 18th Centuries.* Washington, D.C.: American Council on Education, 1958.

Eisendrath, Craig, and Cottle, Thomas J. *Out of Discontent: Visions of the Contemporary University.* Cambridge, Mass.: Schenkman, 1972.

Eisenstadt, S. N. *From Generation to Generation: Age Grades and the Social Structure.* Glencoe, Ill.: Free Press, 1956.

Elbow, Peter. "The Pedagogy of the Bamboozled." *Soundings: An Interdisciplinary Journal,* Summer 1973, pp. 247–58.

———. "Shall We Teach or Give Credit? A Model for Higher Education." *Soundings,* Fall 1971, pp. 237–52.

———; Gribskov, Margaret; and Aldridge, Bill. "One-to-One Faculty Development Draft." Olympia, Wash.: Evergreen State College, 1976.

Elliott, George P. "Revolution Instead—Notes on Passions and Politics." *Public Interest*, no. 20 (Summer 1970): 65–89.

Ellis, John Tracy. "American Catholics and the Intellectual Life." *Thought*, Fall 1955.

Ellis, Robert and Land, W. Clayton. "Social Mobility and Social Isolation: A Test of Sorokin's Dissociative Hypothesis." *American Sociological Review*, 32 (April 1967): 237–52.

Ellmann, Richard. "Oxford in the Seventies." *American Scholar*, 43, no. 4 (Autumn 1974): 567–75.

Elmendorf, John. *Transmitting Information about Experiments in Higher Education: New College as a Case Study*. New York: Academy for Educational Development, 1975.

Erikson, Erik H. "Inner and Outer Space: Reflections on Womanhood." In *The Woman in America*, edited by Robert J. Lifton. Boston: Houghton Mifflin, 1965.

Eurich, Alvin. "A Twenty-First Century Look at Higher Education." In *1963 Current Issues in Higher Education*. Proceedings of the 10th Annual National Conference on Higher Education. Washington, D.C.: Association for Higher Education, 1962.

Ewens, Thomas. "Alverno College: A Case Study." Syracuse: Educational Policy Research Center, 1976.

Farber, Leslie. *The Ways of the Will: Essays Toward a Psychology and Psychopathology of Will*. New York: Basic Books, 1966.

Fashing, Joseph and Deutsch, Steven E. *Academics in Retreat: The Politics of Academic Innovation*. Albuquerque: University of New Mexico Press, 1971.

Featherstone, Joseph. "Intellectual Realms." *New Republic*, June 28, 1975, 23–25.

———. "The Talent Corps: Career Ladders for Bottom Dogs." *New Republic*, September 13, 1969.

The Federal Government and Education. Washington, D.C.: House Committee on Education and Labor, 1963.

Federal Support for Academic Science and Other Educational Activities in Universities and Colleges, Fiscal Year, 1965. Washington, D.C.: National Science Foundation, 1965.

Fein, Rashi. "An Economic and Social Profile of the Negro American." In *The Negro American*, edited by Talcott Parsons and Kenneth B. Clark. Boston: Houghton Mifflin, 1966.

Feldman, Kenneth, and Newcomb, Theodore M. *The Impact of College on Students*. San Francisco: Jossey-Bass, 1969.

Feldman, Saul D. *Escape from the Doll's House: Women in Graduate and Professional School Education*. New York: McGraw-Hill, 1974.

Fenske, Robert H. "Who Selects Vocational-Technical Post-High School Education?" In *The Two-Year College and Its Students: An Empirial Report*. Iowa City: American College Program, 1969.

Fichter, Joseph, S. J. *Religion as an Occupation: A Study in the Sociology of the Professions.* Notre Dame, Ind.: University of Notre Dame Press, 1961.

Fine, Sidney A., and Wiley, Wretha W. *An Introduction to Functional Job Analysis.* Upjohn Institute, 1971.

Fishman, Joshua, and Pasanella, A. K. "College Admission-Selection Studies." *Review of Educational Research,* 30 (1960): 298–310.

Flacks, Richard, *Youth and Social Change.* Chicago: Markham Publishing Co., 1971.

Flanagan, John C., et al. *The American High School Student.* Pittsburgh: University of Pittsburgh Project TALENT Office, 1964.

————. *One Year Follow-Up Studies.* Pittsburgh: University of Pittsburgh Project TALENT Office, 1966.

Flax, Susan. " 'Everybody Has to Do His Own Thing': Life-Styles of College Youth." Unpublished paper by a participant-observer from Michigan State University, Merrill-Palmer Institute, June 1968.

Fleming, Donald H. *William H. Welch and the Rise of Modern Medicine.* Boston: Little, Brown, 1954.

Flexner, Abraham. *Universities: American, English, German.* New York: Oxford University Press, 1930.

Folger, John K. "Explaining Higher Educational Opportunity—Some Problems and Issues." Mimeographed. Paper prepared for Institute for Policy Studies' Congressional Seminar on Education and Public Welfare. Washington, D.C.: May 1966.

————. "Trends in Education in Relation to the Occupational Structure." *Sociology of Education,* 38 (Fall 1964): 19–33.

————, and Nam, Charles B. *The Education of the American Population.* Washington, D.C.: U.S. Bureau of the Census, 1967.

Foster, Julian. "Some Effects of Jesuit Education: A Case Study." In *The Shape of Catholic Higher Education,* edited by Robert Hassenger. Chicago: University of Chicago Press, 1967.

Franklin, H. Bruce. "The Real Issues of My Case." *Change,* 4 (June 1972): 31–39.

Freedman, Mervin. "The Passage Through College." *Journal of Social Issues,* 12 (1956): 13–28.

Freeman, Jo ["Joreen"]. *The Politics of Woman's Liberation.* New York: David McKay, 1975.

————. "Trashing: The Dark Side of Sisterhood." *Ms.,* 4 (April 1976): 49.

————. "The Tyranny of Structurelessness." *Berkeley Journal of Sociology,* 17 (1972–73): 151–64.

Freeman, Richard. *The Overeducated American.* New York: Academic Press, 1976.

————. *Black Elite: The New Market for Highly Educated Black Americans.* New York: McGraw-Hill, 1976.

French, David. "After the Fall: What This Country Needs Is a Good *Counter* 'Counter-Culture' Culture." *New York Times Magazine,* October 3, 1971, p. 20.

————, and French, Elena. *Working Communally: Patterns and Possibilities*, New York: Russell Sage Foundation, 1975.

Friedland, William H. "Making Sociology Relevant: A Teaching-Research Program for Undergraduates." *The American Sociologist*, 4 (1969): 104–10.

Friedman, Norman L. "Comprehensiveness and Higher Education: A Sociologist's View of Public Junior College Trends." *American Association of University Presidents Bulletin*, Winter 1966, pp. 417–23.

Fromm, Erich. "Sex and Character." In *Man for Himself: An Inquiry into the Psychology of Ethics*. New York: Rinehart, 1947.

Fulton, Oliver, and Trow, Martin. "Research Activity in American Higher Education." *Sociology of Education*, 47, no. 1 (Winter 1974): 69.

Gaff, Jerry G., ed. *The Cluster College*. San Francisco: Jossey-Bass, 1970.

————. *Innovations and Consequences: A Study of Raymond College, University of the Pacific*. U.S. Office of Education Research Project no. 6–1257. Berkeley, Calif.: 1967.

Gamson, Zelda F. "Social Control and Modification." Ph.D. dissertation, Harvard University, 1965.

————, and Levey, Richard H. "Structure and Emergence: Proceedings of an Institute on Innovation in Undergraduate Education." Ann Arbor, Mich.: Center for the Study of Higher Education, University of Michigan, 1976.

Garbarino, Joseph W., and Aussieker, Bill. *Faculty Bargaining: Change and Conflict*. New York: McGraw-Hill, 1975.

Gay, Peter, "History as an Interdisciplinary Discipline," *Seminar Reports*, Columbia University, I, no. 5 (March 27, 1974).

Gebhard, Paul H., et al. *Pregnancy, Birth, and Abortion*. New York: 1958.

Gerschenkron, Alexander. "Getting Off the Bullock Cart: Thoughts on Educational Reform." *The American Scholar*, 45 (Spring 1976): 218–33.

Glazer, Nathan. "Conflicts in Schools for the Minor Professions." Harvard Graduate School of Education *Bulletin*, Spring 1974.

————. *Remembering the Answers: Essays on the American Student Revolt*. New York: Basic Books, 1970.

————. " 'Student Power' in Berkeley." *Universities Quarterly*, 22 (1968): 404–24.

————. "Why a Faculty Cannot Afford a Franklin." *Change* 4 (June 1972): 40–44.

————, and Moynihan, Daniel Patrick. *Beyond the Melting Pot: The Negroes, Puerto Ricans, Jews, Italians, and Irish of New York City*. Cambridge, Mass.: M.I.T. Press, 1963.

Gleason, Philip. "American Catholic Higher Education: A Historical Perspective." In *The Shape of Catholic Higher Education*, edited by Robert Hassenger. Chicago: University of Chicago Press, 1967.

Glenny, Lyman A.; Shea, John R.; Ruyle, Janet H.; Freschi, Katheryn H. *Presidents Confront Reality: From Edifice Complex to University Without Walls*. San Francisco: Jossey-Bass, 1976.

Glock, Charles, and Stark, Rodney. "Is There an American Protestantism?" *Trans-Action*, 3 (November, December 1965): 8–13.

Goethals, George W., and Klos, Dennis. *Experiencing Youth: First Person Accounts*. 2d ed., Boston: Little, Brown, 1976.

Goffman, Erving. *Frame Analysis*. New York: Harper & Row, 1974.

––––––. "On Cooling the Mark Out: Some Aspects of Adaptation to Failure." *Psychiatry*, 15 (November 1952): 451–63.

Goldman, Ralph M. "San Francisco State: The Technology of Confrontation." In *Protest! Student Activism in America*, edited by Julian Foster and Durward Long. New York: William Morrow, 1970.

Goldner, Fred H., and Ritti, R. R. "Professionalization as Career Immobility." *American Journal of Sociology*, 72 (March 1967): 451–63.

Goode, Erich. "Social Class and Church Participation." *American Journal of Sociology*, 72 (July 1966), pp. 100–11.

Goodman, Paul. "The Present Moment in Education." *New York Review of Books*, 12 (April 10, 1969): 14–24.

Goodwin, Leonard. "The Academic World and the Business World: A Comparison of Occupational Goals." *Sociology of Education*, 42 (1969): 170–87.

Gordon, Margaret S., ed. *Higher Education and the Labor Market: A Volume of Essays*. New York: McGraw-Hill, 1974.

Grant, Gerald. "Black Mountain Lives." *Review of Education*, 1, no. 1 (February 1975): 141–45.

––––––. "Do Faculty That Groove Together Learn Together?" *Holy Cross Quarterly*, Spring 1972.

––––––. "The Generation Gap." *Saturday Review*, 50 (July 15, 1967): 65.

––––––. "The Last Academic Entrepreneur." *Change*, 1 (September 1969).

––––––. "Let a Hundred Antiochs Bloom!" *Change*, 4, No. 7 (September 1972): 47–58.

––––––. "On Equality of Educational Opportunity." *Harvard Educational Review*, 42, no. 1 (February 1972): 109–25.

––––––. "Post Industrial Society: Preference or Prophecy." *Teachers College Record*, 76 (Spring 1974): 151–55.

––––––. Review of "The American University." *Harvard Educational Review*, 44, no. 2 (May 1974): 314–18.

––––––. "Shaping Social Policy." *Teachers College Record*, 75, no. 1 (September 1973): 16–54.

––––––. "Universal BA?" *New Republic*, 166 (June 24, 1972): 13–16.

––––––, and Kohli, Wendy. "On the Contribution of Assessment to Learning." Syracuse, N.Y. Educational Policy Research Center, 1977.

––––––, and Riesman, David. "An Ecology of Academic Reform." *Daedalus*, 104 (1975): 166–91.

Gray, William H., Jr. "Pennsylvania College Enrollments." *American Teachers Association Bulletin*, December 1964.

Greeley, Andrew M. "Religion and Academic Career Plans." *American Journal of Sociology*, 72 (May 1967): 668–72.

————. *Religion and Career: A Study of College Graduates.* New York: Sheed & Ward, 1963.

————, and Rossi, Peter. *The Education of Catholic Americans.* Chicago: Aldine, 1966.

————; Van Cleve, William; and Carroll, Grace Ann. *The Changing Catholic College.* Chicago: Aldine, 1967.

Green, Thomas F. "Images of Education in *Kyklios Paideia.*" *Proceedings of the National Academy of Education,* 3 (1976): 109–49.

————. "Schools and Communities: A Look Forward." *Harvard Educational Review,* 39 no. 2 (Spring 1969): 221–52.

————. *Work, Leisure, and the American Schools.* New York: Random House, 1968.

Greenwood, Ernest. "Attributes of a Profession." In *Man, Work, and Society,* edited by Sigmund Nosow and William H. Form. New York: Basic Books, 1962.

Grossman, Edward; Kramer, Hilton; Novak, Michael; Ozick, Cynthia; Podhoretz, Norman; Richardson, Jack; and Trilling, Lionel. "Culture and the Present Moment: A Roundtable Discussion." *Commentary,* 58, no. 6 (December 1974): 31–50.

Grubb, W. Norton, and Lazerson, Marvin. "Rally 'Round the Workplace: Continuities and Fallacies in Career Education." *Harvard Educational Review,* 45, no. 4 (November 1975): 451–74.

Gusfield, Joseph R. *Symbolic Crusade.* Urbana: University of Illinois Press, 1964.

————, and Riesman, David. "Academic Standards and 'The Two Cultures' in the Context of a New State College." *School Review,* 74 (Spring 1966): 95–116.

Habermas, Jurgen. *Knowledge and Human Interests.* Boston: Beacon Press, 1971.

Hack, Sylvia. "A Statistical Report on the College for Human Services, 1967–72." New York: College for Human Services, June 1973.

Hagstrom, Warren O. "Departmental Prestige and Scientific Productivity." Paper presented at the American Sociological Association meetings, Boston, 1968.

————. *The Scientific Community.* New York: Basic Books, 1965.

Halsey, A. H. "British Universities." *European Journal of Sociology,* 3 (1962): 85–101.

————, and Trow, Martin. *The British Academics.* Cambridge, Mass.: Harvard University Press, 1971.

————. "A Study of the British Teachers." Mimeographed. University of California, Berkeley, August 1967.

Hammond, Phillip E. *The Campus Clergyman.* New York: Basic Books, 1966.

Hampshire College. "Report of the Long Range Curriculum Disappearing Task Force." Mimeographed. Amherst, Mass.: Hampshire College, June 1976.

Handlin, Oscar. *Fire-Bell in the Night: The Crisis in Civil Rights*. Boston: Little, Brown, 1964.

————, and Handlin, Mary F. *The American College and American Culture: Socialization as a Function of Higher Education*. New York: McGraw-Hill, 1970.

Hanfmann, Eugenia. Report on New College, Sarasota, Florida, 1970. Mimeographed. Waltham, Mass.: Brandeis University, 1971.

Hanoch, Giora. "Personal Earnings and Investment in Schooling." Ph.D. dissertation, University of Chicago, 1965.

Harris, Seymour E. *A Statistical Portrait of Higher Education*. New York: McGraw-Hill, 1972.

Harvard College. Office of Tests. "Testing and the Freshman Year: A Handbook for Harvard Advisers." Cambridge, Mass.: 1968.

Hassenger, Robert, ed. *The Shape of Catholic Higher Education*. Chicago: University of Chicago Press, 1967.

Hauser, Philip M. "Demographic Factors in the Integration of the Negro." In *The Negro American*, edited by Talcott Parsons and Kenneth B. Clark. Boston: Houghton Mifflin, 1966.

Havelock, Ronald G. *Planning for Innovation through Dissemination and Utilization of Knowledge*. Ann Arbor, Mich.: Institute for Social Research, University of Michigan, 1969.

Havemann, Ernest, and West, Patricia Salter. *They Went to College: The College Graduate in America Today*. New York: Harcourt Brace, 1952.

Hawkins, Hugh. *Between Harvard and America: The Educational Leadership of Charles W. Eliot*. New York: Oxford University Press, 1972.

Haywood, Mary. "Were There But World Enough and Time . . ." Undergraduate honors thesis, Harvard University, Department of Social Relations Library, 1960.

Heath, Roy. *The Reasonable Adventurer*. Pittsburgh: University of Pittsburgh Press, 1964.

Hefferlin, J B Lon, *The Dynamics of Academic Reform*. San Francisco: Jossey-Bass, 1969.

Heiss, Ann. *An Inventory of Academic Innovation and Reform: A Technical Report Sponsored by the Carnegie Commission on Higher Education*. New York: McGraw-Hill, 1973.

Henderson, Algo D., and Hall, Dorothy. *Antioch College: Its Design for Liberal Education*. New York: Harper & Row, 1946.

Herberg, Will. *Protestant, Catholic, Jew: An Essay in American Religious Sociology*. Garden City, N.Y.: Anchor Books, 1960.

Herrnstein, Richard. "IQ." *Atlantic Monthly,* 228 (September 1971): 43.

Hersey, John. *Letter to the Alumni*. New York: Knopf, 1970.

Hilberry, Conrad, and Keeton, Morris, eds., *Struggle and Promise: A Future for Private Colleges*. New York: McGraw-Hill, 1968.

Hildum, Donald C. Letter to the Editor, *Oakland Observer* (Oakland University, Rochester, Mich. November 15, 1968), p. 10.

Hirschman, Albert O. *Development Projects Observed*. Washington, D.C.: The Brookings Institution, 1967.

Hodge, Robert W.; Siegel, Paul M.; and Rossi, Peter. "Occupational Prestige in the United States, 1925–63." *American Journal of Sociology*, 70 (November 1964): 289–302.

Hodgkinson, Harold L. *Campus Senate: Experiment in Democracy*. Center for Research and Development in Higher Education (Berkeley: University of California Press, 1974).

————. *Institutions in Transition*. New York: McGraw-Hill, 1971.

————. "San Diego and Santa Cruz: Some Comparisons." Report to the University of California Regents, January 1972.

————; Hurst, Julie; and Levine, Howard. *Improving and Assessing Performance: Evaluation in Higher Education*. Berkeley, Calif.: Center for Research and Development in Higher Education, University of California, 1975.

Hofstadter, Richard. *Anti-Intellectualism in American Life*. New York: Knopf, 1963.

————, and Metzger, Walter P. *The Development of Academic Freedom in the United States*. New York: Columbia University Press, 1955.

Holmstrom, Engin. "Transfers from Junior to Senior Colleges." Washington, D.C.: American Council on Education, 1972.

Hook, Sidney. "Ballyhoo at St. John's." *New Leader*, May 27, 1944.

————; Kurtz, Paul; and Todorovich, Miro, eds. *The Idea of a Modern University*. Buffalo, N.Y.: Prometheus Books, 1974.

————. *The Philosophy of the Curriculum: The Need for General Education*. Buffalo, N.Y.: Prometheus Books, 1975.

Houston, Laura P. "Black People and New Careers: Toward Humane Human Service." *Social Casework*, May 1970.

Hoyt, Donald P. "The Relationship between College Grades and Adult Achievement." *American College Testing Program, Research Report no. 7*. Iowa City, 1965.

Hughes, Everett C. *Men and Their Work*. Glencoe, Ill.: Free Press, 1958.

————. "Stress and Strain in Professional Education." *Harvard Educational Review*, 29 (1959): 319–29.

Hughes, H. Stuart. *History as Art and as Science*. New York: Harper & Row, 1964.

Huntington, Samuel P. "The Governability of Democracy: The American Case." In *The Governability of Democracies*, edited by Samuel P. Huntington, Michel Crozier, and Joji Watanuke. New York: New York University Press, 1975.

————. "Power, Expertise, and the Military Profession." *Daedalus*, Fall 1963.

————. *The Soldier and the State*. Cambridge, Mass.: Harvard University Press, 1957.

Hyman, Herbert H. "The Value Systems of Different Classes." In *Class, Status, and Power: A Reader in Social Stratification*, edited by Reinhard Bendix and Seymour Martin Lipset. Glencoe, Ill.: Free Press, 1953.

————; Wright, Charles R.; and Reed, John Shelton. *The Enduring Effects of Education*. Chicago: University of Chicago Press, 1975.

Iffert, Robert. *Retention and Withdrawal of College Students.* Washington, D.C.: U.S. Department of Health, Education and Welfare, 1958.

Ingraham, Mark H. *The Mirror of Brass: The Compensation and Working Conditions of College and University Administrators.* Madison: University of Wisconsin Press, 1968.

Jackson, Elton F., and Crockett, Harry T., Jr. "Occupational Mobility in the United States: A Point Estimate and Trend Comparison." *American Sociological Review*, 29 (February 1964): 5–15.

Jackson, Philip W. *Life in Classrooms.* New York: Holt, Rinehart & Winston, 1968.

Jacob, Philip E. *Changing Values in College: An Exploratory Study of the Impact of College Teaching.* New York: Harper, 1957.

Jacobs, Paul, and Landau, Saul. *The New Radicals: A Report with Documents.* New York: Random House, 1966.

Jaffe, Adrian J., and Adams, Walter. "Trends in College Enrollment." *College Board Review*, Winter 1964–65.

Janowitz, Morris. *The Professional Soldier: A Social and Political Portrait.* Glencoe, Ill.: Free Press, 1960.

Jencks, Christopher. "A New Breed of B.A.s." *New Republic*, October 1, 1966.

———. "Private Schools for Black Children." *New York Times Magazine*, November 3, 1968, p. 30.

———. "Social Stratification and Mass Higher Education." *Harvard Educational Review*, Spring 1968.

———, et al. *Inequality: A Reassessment of the Effect of Family and Schooling in America.* New York: Basic Books, 1972.

———, and Riesman, David. *The Academic Revolution.* New York: Doubleday, 1968.

Jerome, Judson. *Culture out of Anarchy.* New York: Herder & Herder, 1970.

Johnson, Alvin S. *Pioneer's Progress.* New York: Viking, 1952.

Johnson, David W., and Johnson, Roger T. "Instructional Goal Structure: Cooperative, Competitive, or Individualistic." *Review of Educational Research*, 44, no. 2 (Spring 1974): 213–40.

Johnson, Tobe. "Black Studies: Their Origin, Present State, and Prospects." Proceedings of the Twenty-fifth Annual Meeting of the American Conference of Academic Deans, 1969.

Kahl, Joseph. "Educational and Occupational Aspirations of 'Common Man' Boys." *Harvard Educational Review*, 23 (Summer 1953): 186–203.

Kahn, Michael. "The Return of the Repressed." In *Readings about the Social Animal*, edited by Elliot Aronson. San Francisco: W. H. Freeman, 1973.

Kalberg, Stephen. "The Commitment to Career Reform: The Settlement Movement Leaders." *Social Service Review*, December 1975, p. 617.

Kanter, Rosabeth Moss. *Commitment and Community: Communes and Utopias in Sociological Perspective.* Cambridge, Mass.: Harvard University Press, 1972.

Karabel, Jerome. "Community Colleges and Social Stratification: Submerged Class Conflict in American Higher Education." In *Power and Ideology in Education*, edited by Jerome Karabel and A. H. Halsey. New York: Oxford University Press, 1977.

————. "Open Admissions: Toward Meritocracy or Equality?" *Change*, 4 (May 1972): 38–43.

Karel, Leonard. *Comparisons of Earned Degrees Awarded 1901–1962—with Projections to 2000*. Washington, D.C.: National Science Foundation, 1964.

Kass, Amy Apfel. *Radical Conservatives for Liberal Education*. Ph.D. dissertation, Johns Hopkins University, 1973.

Kateb, George. *Utopia and Its Enemies*. New York: Schocken Books, 1972.

Katz, Joseph. "Personality and Interpersonal Relations in the College Classroom." In *The American College*, edited by Nevitt Sanford. New York: John Wiley, 1962.

————, et al. *No Time for Youth: Growth and Constraint in College Students*. San Francisco: Jossey-Bass, 1968.

Kaysen, Carl, ed. *Content and Context*. New York: McGraw-Hill, 1973.

————. *The Higher Learning, the Universities, and the Public*. Princeton: Princeton University Press, 1969.

Kegan, Daniel L. "Student Attrition at Hampshire College: Qualitative and Political Implications." Mimeographed. Amherst, Mass.: Hampshire College, 1976.

Kelly, Frederick J., and Patterson, Betty A. *Residence and Migration of College Students*. Washington, D.C.: U.S. Office of Education, 1934.

Keniston, Kenneth. *The Uncommitted: Alienated Youth in American Society*. New York: Harcourt Brace, 1965.

————. *Young Radicals: Notes on Committed Youth*. New York: Harcourt, Brace, & World, 1968.

————. *Youth and Dissent: The Rise of a New Opposition*. New York: Harcourt, Brace, Jovanovich, 1971.

Kerr, Clark. "New Challenges to the College and University." *In Agenda for the Nation: Papers on Domestic and Foreign Policy Issues*, edited by Kermit Gordon. Washington, D.C.: The Brookings Institution, 1968.

————. *The Uses of the University*. Cambridge, Mass.: Harvard University Press, 1963.

Keyes, Ralph, et al. "The College That Students Helped Plan." *Change*, 1 (March-April 1969): 12–23.

Kieffer, John S. "Commencement Address." Annapolis, Md.: St. John's College, June 1949.

King, Larry. "The Buckle on the Bible Belt." *Harper's Magazine*, June 1966.

Klein, Jacob. "The Dean's Statement of Educational Policy and Program, 1954." In *Report on a Project of Self Study*. Annapolis, Md.: St. John's College, 1955.

Knapp, Robert H., and Greenbaum, J. J. *The Younger American Scholar: His Collegiate Origins.* Chicago: University of Chicago Press, 1953.

Knoell, Dorothy, and Medsker, Leland. "Factors Affecting Performance of Transfer Students from Two- to Four-Year Colleges." Mimeographed. Berkeley, Calif.: University of California Center for the Study of Higher Education, 1964.

Knott, Bob. "What Is Competence-Based Curriculum in the Liberal Arts?" *Journal of Higher Education,* 46 (January/February 1975).

Koch, Raymond, and Koch, Charlotte. *Educational Commune: The Story of Commonwealth College.* New York: Schocken, 1972.

Koch, Sigmund. "The Image of Man in Encounter Groups." *American Scholar.* 42, no. 4 (Autumn 1973): 636–52.

Koenker, Robert H. "Status of the Doctor of Arts Degree." Mimeographed report. Graduate School, Ball State University, Muncie, Ind., February 28, 1976.

Koerner, James D. *The Miseducation of American Teachers.* Boston: Houghton Mifflin, 1963.

Kohlberg, Lawrence, and Mayer, Rochelle. "Development as the Aim of Education." *Harvard Educational Review,* 42, no. 4 (November 1972): 449–96.

Kolko, Gabriel. *Wealth and Power in America: An Analysis of Social Class and Income Distribution.* New York: Praeger, 1962.

Komarovsky, Mirra. *Women in the Modern World: Their Education and Their Dilemmas.* Boston: Little, Brown, 1954.

Kossoff, Evelyn, "Evaluating College Professors by 'Scientific' Methods. *American Scholar,* vol. 41, no. 1 (Winter 1971–72): 93.

Kozol, Jonathan, "Politics, Rage and Motivation in the Free Schools." *Harvard Educational Review,* 42, no. 3 (August 1972): 414–22.

Kresge College. "Covering Statement on a Kresge College Program." Mimeographed. Santa Cruz, Calif.: January 1971.

———. "Kresge College: The Early Years (1970–74): An Appraisal for the Ford Foundation." Mimeographed. Santa Cruz, Calif.: June 1974.

Kresge Klone. April 14, 1973, April 23, 1973, April 30, 1973.

Kresge Newsletter. No. 43, undated, Fall 1972.

"The Kresge Program: An Initial Design for an Educational Community." Mimeographed documents growing out of the course, "Creating Kresge College." Santa Cruz, Calif.: January 1971.

Kresge Weekly Reader. April 24, 1972, May 5, 1972, November 1, 1972.

Kriegel, Leonard. "Playing It Black." *Change,* 1 (March-April 1969): 7–11.

———. "Surviving the Apocalypse: Teaching at City College." *Change,* 4 (Summer 1972): 54–62.

———. "Teaching the 'Pre-Baccs': Headstart for College." *Nation,* 206 (1968): 270–74.

Kristol, Irving. "The Negro Today Is Like the Immigrant Yesterday." *New York Times Magazine,* September 11, 1966.

The College Within." Mimeographed. Medford, Mass.: Tufts University, 1971.

Miller, Ann, ed. *A College in Dispersion: Women of Bryn Mawr, 1896–1975*. Boulder, Col.: Westview Press, 1976.

Miller, Herman P. "Annual and Lifetime Income in Relation to Education." *American Economic Review*, 50 (December 1960): 962–86.

————. *Income Distribution in the United States*. Washington, D.C.: U.S. Bureau of the Census, 1966.

Milman, Marcia; Kahn, Michael; and Kroeber, Ted. "Memorandum: Re Kin Groups." To Student Affairs Preceptor Group, Kresge College, University of California, Santa Cruz, March 9, 1972.

Mills, C. Wright. *The Power Elite*. New York: Oxford University Press, 1956.

Mills, Gordon Harrison. "Jack London's Quest for Salvation." *American Quarterly*, 7 (Spring 1955): 3–14.

Milton, Ohmer. *Alternatives to the Traditional*. San Francisco, Calif.: Jossey-Bass, 1972.

Mishan, Edward. "Some Heretical Thoughts on University Reform: The Economics of Changing the System." *Encounter*, 32 (1969): 3–15.

Moine, Donald. Article in *Kresge Klein*, October 2, 1973.

Monson, Charles H., Jr. "Teaching Assistants: The Forgotten Faculty." *Educational Record*, 50 (1969): 60–65.

Morimoto, Kiyo; Gregory, Judith; and Butler, Penelope. "On Trying to Understand the Frustrations of Students." Harvard University Bureau of Study Counsel, 1972.

Morison, Samuel Eliot. *Three Centuries of Harvard*. Cambridge, Mass.: Harvard University Press, 1936.

Morrison, Jack. *The Rise of the Arts on the American Campus*. New York: McGraw-Hill, 1973.

Moynihan, Daniel P. "Nirvana Now." In *Coping: Essays On the Practice of Government*, pp. 116–33. New York: Random House, 1973.

————. "'Peace'—Some Thoughts on the 1960's and 1970's." *Public Interest*, no. 32 (Summer 1973): pp. 3–12.

Mundy, Paul. "Some Convergences and the Identity Crisis in the American Catholic Sociological Society." *Sociological Analysis*, 26 (1966): 123–28.

Muscatine, Charles, et al. *Education at Berkeley*. University of California, Berkeley, Academic Senate, 1966.

Musgrove, Frank. *Ecstasy and Holiness: Counterculture and the Open Society*. Bloomington: Indiana University Press, 1974.

Nam, Charles B. "Some Comparisons of Office of Education and Census Bureau Statistics on Education." Paper read to the American Statistical Association, September 10, 1962.

Nash, George; Nash, Patricia; and Goldstein, Martin. "Financial Aid Policies and Practices at Accredited Four-Year Universities and Colleges." Columbia University, Bureau of Applied Social Research, 1967.

National Opinion Research Center. "Jobs and Occupations: A Popular Evaluation." In *Class, Status, and Power*, edited by Reinhard Bendix and Seymour Martin Lipset. Glencoe, Ill.: Free Press, 1953.

National Science Foundation. *The Duration of Formal Education for High Ability Youth*. NSF 61–36. Washington, D.C., 1961.

Nevins, Allan. *The State Universities and Democracy*. Urbana: University of Illinois Press, 1962.

New York, State University College at Old Westbury. Catalogue. Old Westbury, N.Y.: 1967.

Newcomb, Theodore M. "The Nature and Uses of Peer-Group Influence." Proceedings of Bowling Green State University Conference on Residential Colleges, October 1967.

———. *Personality and Social Change: Attitude Formation in a Student Community*. New York: Dryden, 1943.

———, et al. *Persistence and Change: Bennington College and Its Students after Twenty-five Years*. New York: John Wiley, 1967.

———, et al. "The University of Michigan's Residential College." In *The New Colleges: Toward an Appraisal*, edited by Paul L. Dressel. San Francisco: Jossey-Bass, 1971.

———, and Wilson, Everett K. *College Peer Groups: Problems and Prospects for Research*. Chicago: Aldine, 1966.

Nichols, Robert C. "College Preferences of Eleventh Grade Students." *NMSC Research Reports*, 2 (1966), National Merit Scholarship Corporation, Evanston, Ill.

Nisbet, Robert. *Degradation of the Academic Dogma: The University in America 1945–1970*. New York: Basic Books, 1971.

———. "Hutchins of Chicago." *Commentary*, 38 (1964): 52–55.

———. "Sociology and the Academy." In *Sociology and Contemporary Education*, edited by Charles H. Page. New York: Random House, 1964.

Novak, Michael. "Experiment at Old Westbury: Trying to Talk." *Commonweal*, 49 (1969): 560–63.

———. "Green Shoots of Counter Culture." In *Politics: Realism and Imagination*. New York: Herder & Herder, 1971.

O'Dea, Thomas F. *American Catholic Dilemma: An Inquiry into the Intellectual Life*. New York: Sheed & Ward, 1958.

Ogburn, William Fielding. "Technology and the Standard of Living in the United States." *American Journal of Sociology*, 60 (January 1955).

Ong, Walter J. "Agonistic Structures in Academia: Past and Present." *Daedalus*, 103, no. 4 (Fall 1974): 238.

Oregon State University: *Report to the President* by the Commission on University Goals. Corvallis, Ore.: University of Oregon, 1970.

Orlans, Harold, et al. *Private Accreditation and Public Eligibility*, 1 and 2, Washington, D.C.: The Brookings Institution, 1974.

Pace, Robert. *The Demise of Diversity? A Comparative Profile of Eight Types of Institutions*. New York: McGraw-Hill, 1974.

Panos, Robert, and Astin, Alexander. "Attrition among College Students." *American Council on Education Research Reports*, 2 (1967).

———. "They Went to College: A Descriptive Summary of the Class of 1965." *American Council on Education Research Reports*, 2 (1967).

Parker, Gail Thain. "While Alma Mater Burns." *Atlantic Monthly*, 238 (September 1976): 39–47.

Parsons, Talcott. "The Academic System: A Sociologist's View." *Public Interest*, 13 (1968): 173–97.

———, and Platt, Gerald M. "The American Academic Profession: A Pilot Study." Mimeographed. Cambridge, Mass.: Harvard University, March 1968.

———. "Considerations on the American Academic System." *Minerva; a Review of Science, Learning, and Policy*, 6 (1968): 497–523.

———; Platt, Gerald M.; and Kirshstein, Rita. "Faculty Teaching Goals, 1968–1973." *Social Problems*, December 1976.

———, and Platt, Gerald M., with Smelser, Neil J. *The American University*. Cambridge, Mass.: Harvard University Press, 1973.

———, and White, Winston. "The Link between Character and Society." In *Culture and Social Character*, edited by Seymour Martin Lipset and Leo Lowenthal. Glencoe, Ill.: Free Press, 1961.

Patterson, Franklin K., and Longsworth, Charles R. *The Making of a College: Plans for a New Departure in Higher Education*. Cambridge, Mass.: M.I.T. Press, 1966.

Patterson, Orlando. "Toward a Future That Has No Past—Reflections on the Fate of Blacks in the Americas." *Public Interest*, Spring 1972, pp. 25–62.

Pearl, Arthur. "The Human Service Society: An Ecological Perspective." In *Public Service Employment*, edited by A. Gardner et al. New York: Praeger 1973.

Peckham, Morse. *Humanistic Education for Business: An Essay in General Education*. Philadelphia: University of Pennsylvania Press, 1960.

Perry, William C., Jr. *Forms of Intellectual and Ethical Development in the College Years*. New York: Holt, Rinehart & Winston, 1970.

Peterson, Richard E. "Goals for California Higher Education: A Survey of 116 College Communities." Prepared for the Joint Committee on the Master Plan for Higher Education of the California Legislature. Berkeley: 1973.

———. *The Scope of Organized Student Protest in 1967–68*. Princeton: Educational Testing Service, 1968.

Petrie, Hugh G. "Do You See What I See? The Epistemology of Interdisciplinary Inquiry." *Educational Researcher* 5, no. 2 (February 1976): 9–15.

Phenix, Philip H. *Realms of Meaning: A Philosophy of the Curriculum for General Education*. New York: McGraw-Hill, 1964.

Pierson, George W. *Yale College: An Educational History, 1871–1921*. New Haven: Yale University Press, 1952.

Pitts, Jesse R. "The Hippies as Contrameritocracy." *Dissent*, July-August 1969, repr. Spring, 1974, pp. 305–16.

————. "Strike at Oakland University." *Change*, 3 (February 1972): 16–19.

Polk, Nancy M. Letter to *The Collegian*, March 12, 1973, p. 15. St. John's College, Annapolis, Md.

Posner, Judith. "The Stigma of Excellence: On Being Just Right." *Sociological Inquiry*, 46 (1976): 141–44.

Potter, George T. "A Call to Action." Unpublished paper, Ramapo College, Mahwah, N.J., 1975.

Potter, Laurie S., and Potter, George T. "Designing and Operating a Barrier Free Campus." Paper prepared for presentation at the Society for College and University Planning, July 21–24, 1976.

Potts, David B. " 'College Enthusiasm!' As a Public Response, 1800–1860." *Harvard Educational Review*, 47, no. 1 (February 1977): 28–42.

Power, Edward J. *A History of Catholic Higher Education in the United States*. Milwaukee: Bruce, 1958.

Price, Derek J. de Solla. *Science since Babylon*. New Haven: Yale University Press, 1961.

Rafflel, Stanley. "Some Effects of Columbia College on Its Students." Unpublished study, 1965.

Ramapo College of New Jersey. *Ramapo College of New Jersey: The Sef-Study Report*. August 1975.

Ramshaw, Warren C. "Religious Participation and the Fate of Religious Ideology on a Resident and Non-Resident College Campus: An Exploratory Study." Ph.D. dissertation, University of Illinois, 1966.

Raskin, Barbara. "Federal City College: Militancy in Microcosm." *Washington Monthly*, 1 (1969): 52–61.

————. "A Racial Split Hits New College." *Washington Post*, November 13, 1968, p. A–1.

Ravitch, Diane, "The Revisionists Revised: Studies in the Historiography of American Education." *Proceedings of the National Academy of Education*, 4 (1977): 11–84.

Record, Wilson. "The Sociologist as Actor in the Research Drama." In Arthur B. Shostak, *The Eye of Sociology*. New York: Alfred Publishing Company, forthcoming.

————. "Some Implications of the Black Studies Movement for Higher Education in the 1970's." *Journal of Higher Education*, 44, no. 3 (March 1973): 191–216.

————. "White Sociologists and Black Students in Predominantly White Universities." *Sociological Quarterly*, 15 (Spring 1974): 164–82.

Reiss, Ira. "Premarital Sexual Permissiveness among Negroes and Whites." *American Sociological Review*, 29 (October 1964): 688–98.

Reitzes, Dietrich. *Negroes in Medicine*. Cambridge, Mass.: Harvard University Press, 1958.

Reynolds, O. E. *Social and Economic Status of College Students*. Columbia University, Teachers College Contribution #272, 1927.

Ricks, David F. "Helpful and Harmful Intervention in Schizophrenic Development." Paper presented at the 7th annual meeting of the Department of Psychiatry, Harvard Medical School, 1965.

———. "Tests and Scholarships: A Cautioning Tale." *Financial Aid News*, no. 3 (March 1961).

Rieff, Philip, *Fellow Teachers*. New York: Harper & Row, 1972.

Riesman, David. "Alterations in Institutional Attitudes and Behavior." In *Emerging Patterns in American Higher Education*, edited by Logan Wilson. Washington, D.C.: American Council on Education, 1965.

———. "America Moves to the Right." *New York Times Magazine*, October 27, 1968, p. 34.

———. "The Collision Course of Higher Education." *Journal of College Student Personnel*, 10 (1969), 363–69.

———. Comment on "Universities and the Growth of Science in Germany and the United States." *Minerva; a Review of Science, Learning, and Policy*, 7 (1969): 751–55.

———. *Constraint and Variety in American Education*. Lincoln: University of Nebraska Press, 1956.

———. "The 'Jacob Report.' " *American Sociological Review*, 23 (1958): 732–39.

———. "The Local Press and Academic Freedom." *Political Research: Organization and Design*, 1 (January 1958): 3–8.

———. "New College." *Change*, 7 (May 1975).

———. "Notes on Meritocracy." *Daedalus* 96, no. 3 (1967): 897–908.

———. "Notes on New Universities, British and American." *Universities Quarterly*, 20 (1966): 128–46.

———. "Observations on Contemporary College Students—Especially Women." *Interchange*, 1 (1970): 52–63.

———. "Permissiveness and Sex Roles." *Journal of Marriage and Family Living*, 21 (August 1959): 211–17.

———. "Planning in Higher Education: Some Notes on Patterns and Problems." *Human Organization*, 18 (1958): 12–17.

———. Review of Richard Hofstadter's *Anti-Intellectualism in American Life*. *American Sociological Review*, 28 (1963): 1038–40.

———. Review of Theodore Newcomb et al. *Persistence and Change: Bennington College and Its Students after Twenty-five Years*. *American Journal of Sociology*, 73, no. 5 (March 1968): 628–30.

———. "The Scholar at the Border." *Columbia Forum*, 3 (Spring 1974).

———. "The Search for Alternative Models in Education." *American Scholar*, 38 (1969): 377–88.

———. "Some Continuities and Discontinuities in the Education of Women." In *Abundance for What? and Other Essays*. Garden City, N.Y.: Doubleday, Anchor, 1964.

———. "Some Informal Notes on American Churches and Sects." *Confluence*, 4 (July 1955): 151.

———. "Some Problems of a Course in 'Culture and Personality.' " *Journal of General Education*, 5 (1951): 122–36.

————. "Two Generations." In *The Woman in America*, edited by Robert J. Lifton. Boston: Houghton Mifflin, 1965.

————. "The Urban University." *Massachusetts Review*, 7 (1967): 476–86.

————, and Glazer, Nathan. "The Intellectuals and the Discontented Classes." *Partisan Review* (Winter 1955); reprinted with a further commentary in Daniel Bell, ed., *The Radical Right*. New York: Doubleday, 1963.

————; Glazer, Nathan; and Denney, Reuel. *The Lonely Crowd*. New Haven: Yale University Press, 1950, 1961.

————, and Grant, Gerald, "Evangelism, Egalitarianism, and Educational Reform." *Minerva; a Review of Science, Learning, and Policy*, 11, no. 3 (July 1973): 296–317.

————, and Gusfield, Joseph. "Faculty Culture and Academic Careers: Some Sources of Innovation in Higher Education." *Sociology of Education*, 37 (Summer 1964).

————; Gusfield, Joseph; and Gamson, Zelda. *Academic Values and Mass Education: The Early Years of Oakland and Monteith*. New York: McGraw-Hill paperback, 1975.

————, and Horton, Donald. "Notes on the Deprived Institution: Illustrations from a State Mental Hospital." *Sociological Quarterly*, Winter 1965, pp. 3–20.

————, and Stadtman, Verne, eds. *Academic Transformation: Seventeen Institutions under Pressure*. New York: McGraw-Hill, 1972.

Rivlin, Alice M. *The Role of the Federal Government in Financing Higher Education*. Washington, D.C.: The Brookings Institution, 1961.

Rodriguez, Richard. "Going Home Again: The New American Scholarship Boy." *American Scholar*, 44, no. 1 (Winter 1974–75): 15–28.

Rogoff, Natalie. "Local Social Structure and Educational Selection." In *Education, Economy, and Society*, edited by A. H. Halsey, Jean Floud, and C. Arnold Anderson. New York: Free Press, 1961.

Roper, Elmo. *Factors Affecting the Admission of High School Seniors to College*. Washington, D.C.: American Council on Education, 1949.

Rosenberg, Milton J.; Verba, Sidney; and Converse, Philip E. *Vietnam and the Silent Majority: The Dove's Guide*. New York: Harper & Row, 1970.

Ross, R. Danforth. "The Institutionalization of Academic Innovations: Two Models." *Sociology of Education* 49, no. 2 (April 1976): 146–55.

Rossi, Alice S. "Equality between the Sexes: An Immodest Proposal." In *The Woman in America*, edited by Robert J. Lifton. Boston: Houghton Mifflin, 1965.

Rothblatt, Sheldon. "The Student Sub-Culture and the Examination System in Early 19th Century Oxbridge." In Lawrence Stone, ed., *The University in Society: Oxford and Cambridge from the 14th to the Early 19th Century*. Princeton: Princeton University Press, 1974.

Rubin, Leonard. "Reactions to Negative Tenure Decisions." Paper given at American Sociological Association meetings, Montreal, August 1974.

Rudolph, Frederick. *The American College and University.* New York: Knopf, 1962.

————. *Curriculum: The American Undergraduate Course of Study Since the Founding of Harvard College.* Carnegie Council on Policy Studies in Higher Education, forthcoming.

Rudolph, Susanne, and Rudolph, Lloyd. "Rajput Adulthood: Reflections on the Amar Singh Diary." *Daedalus,* Spring 1976, pp. 145–67.

Ruml, Beardsley. *Memo to a College Trustee: A Report on Financial and Structural Problems of the Liberal College.* New York: McGraw-Hill, 1959.

St. John's College. *Bulletin of St. John's College: A Report on a Project of Self Study,* 7 (1955): 111–19.

————. *Bulletin of St. John's College.* "Self Evaluation Report," March 1964.

————. *Catalogue.* 1937–38.

Sanders, Edward, and Palmer, Hans. "The Financial Barrier to College Attendance in California." Mimeographed. Los Angeles: California State Scholarship Commission, 1965.

Sanford, Nevitt, ed. *The American College: A Psychological and Social Interpretation of the Higher Learning.* New York: John Wiley, 1962.

————. "Graduate Education Then and Now." *American Psychologist,* 31 (November 1976): 756–64.

————, ed. "Personality Development During the College Years." *Journal of Social Issues,* 12 (1956): 4.

Sarason, Seymour B. *The Creation of Settings and the Future Societies,* San Francisco: Jossey-Bass, 1972.

Scheffler, Israel. "Basic Mathematical Skills: Some Philosophical and Practical Remarks." *Teachers College Record,* 78, no. 2 (December 1976): 205–12.

Schelling, Thomas. "On the Ecology of Micro-Motives." *Public Interest,* 25 (Fall 1971): 59–98.

Schudson, Michael S. "Organizing the 'Meritocracy': A History of the College Entrance Examination Board." *Harvard Educational Review,* 42, no. 1 (1972): 34–69.

Schumpeter, Joseph. *Capitalism, Socialism, and Democracy.* New York: Harper, 1947.

Schutz, W. C. *Joy.* New York: Grove Press, 1967.

Schwartz, Mildred A. *The United States College-Educated Population: 1960.* Chicago: National Opinion Research Center, 1965.

Scott, John Finley. "The American College Sorority: Its Role in Class and Ethnic Endogamy." *American Sociological Review,* 39 (June 1965): 514–27.

Scott, Richard. "Black Student Life." Unpublished paper, 1968.

Seeman, Melvin. "The Intellectual and the Language of Minorities." *American Sociological Review,* 31 (April 1966): 159–68.

Sewell, William H. "Community of Residence and College Plans." *American Sociological Review,* 26 (February 1964): 24–37.

————, and Armer, Michael. "Neighborhood Context and College Plans." *American Sociological Review*, 31 (April 1966): 159–68.

Shaffer, Manfred. "The University of California at Santa Cruz (B)." Mimeographed. Case Study prepared for the Institute for Educational Management, Harvard University, Cambridge, Mass.; 1971.

Sharpe, Laura. "Five Years After the College Degree, Part I, Graduate and Professional Education." Mimeographed. Washington, D.C.: Bureau of Social Science Research, 1965.

————. *Two Years after the College Degree.* Washington, D.C.: National Science Foundation, 1963.

Shils. Edward. *The Intellectuals and the Powers and Other Essays.* Chicago: University of Chicago Press, 1972.

————. "Plenitude and Scarcity: The Anatomy of an International Cultural Crisis." *Encounter*, 32 (May 1969): 37–48.

————. *The Torment of Secrecy: The Background and Consequences of American Security Policies.* Glencoe, Ill.: Free Press, 1956.

Shotland, R. Lance. *University Communications Networks: The Small World Method.* New York: John Wiley, 1976.

Silber, John. "Campus Reform: From Within or Without." In *The Public Challenge and the Campus Response*, edited by Robert A. Altman and Carolyn M. Byerly. Berkeley: Center for Research and Development in Higher Education; Boulder, Colorado: Western Interstate Commission for Higher Education, 1971.

————. "The Need for Elite Education," *Harper's*, 254, no. 1525 (June 1977): p. 22–24.

Silver, Allan. "Who Cares for Columbia?" *New York Review of Books*, 12 (January 30, 1969): 15–24.

Simon, Herbert A. "The Job of a College President." *Educational Record*, 48 (1967): 68–78.

Simon, Kenneth A., and Grant, W. Vance. *Digest of Educational Statistics.* Washington, D.C.: U.S. Office of Education, 1965.

Slater, Philip. "Report on Kresge." Mimeographed. Kresge College, University of California, Santa Cruz, May 31, 1974.

Slaughter, Thomas F., Jr. "The Status of Black Studies Programs in American Colleges and Universities." Paper prepared for presentation at American Sociological Association meetings, New Orleans, August 29, 1972.

Smelser, Neil J., and Almond, Gabriel, eds. *Public Higher Education in California.* Berkeley and Los Angeles: University of California Press, 1974.

Snow, Charles P. *The Two Cultures: And a Second Look.* New York: New American Library, 1964.

Solomon, Lawrence, and Berzon, Betty, eds. *New Perspectives on Encounter Groups.* San Francisco: Jossey-Bass, 1972.

Solmon, Lewis C., and Taubman, Paul J., eds. *Does College Matter? Some Evidence on the Impacts of Higher Education.* New York: Academic Press, 1973.

Somers, Robert H. "The Mainsprings of Rebellion: A Survey of Berkeley Students in November 1974." In *The Berkeley Student Revolt: Facts and Interpretations*, edited by S. M. Lipset and Sheldon S. Wolin. New York: Doubleday, 1965.

Sowell, Thomas. *Black Education: Myths and Tragedies*. New York: David McKay, 1972.

Spady, William G. "Educational Mobility and Access: Growth and Paradoxes." *American Journal of Sociology*, 73 (1968): 273–86.

————. "Peer Integration and Academic Success: The Dropout Process among Chicago Freshmen." Ph.D. dissertation, University of Chicago, 1967.

Spaeth, Joe L. "The Allocation of College Graduates to Graduate and Professional Schools." *Sociology of Education*, 41 (1968): 342–49.

Spurr, Stephen H. *Academic Degree Structures: Innovative Approaches*. New York: McGraw-Hill, 1970.

Stadtman, Verne. *The University of California, 1868–1968*. Berkeley: University of California Press, 1970.

Stalling, William M., and Singho, Sue Shila. "Some Observations on the Relationships Between Research Productivity and Student Evaluations of Courses and Teaching." Paper presented at the American Educational Research Association meetings, Los Angeles, 1969; available from the Office of Instructional Resources, University of Illinois.

Stanford University. "The Study of Education at Stanford." Stanford, Calif., 1968.

Stanley, Julian C. Letter to the *Harvard Educational Review*, 37 (Summer 1967): 275–76.

————, and Porter, Andrew C. "Predicting College Grades of Negroes versus Whites." Mimeographed. Madison: University of Wisconsin, 1966.

Statera, Gianni. *Death of a Utopia: The Development and Decline of Student Movements in Europe*. New York: Oxford University Press, 1975.

Statsky, William P. "Field Report on Sixteen Legal Service Assistants Now Working in Nine Community Law Offices in New York City," December 9, 1969; and "Supervision Report on Sixteen Legal Service Assistants Now Working in Ten Community Law Offices in New York City," March 31, 1970. New York: College for Human Services.

Steiner, George. *Language and Silence: Essays in Language, Literature, and the Inhuman*. New York: Atheneum, 1970.

Stern, G. G. "Characteristics of the Intellectual Climate in College Environments." *Harvard Educational Review*, 33 (1963): 5–41.

————. *People in Context*. New York: John Wiley, 1970.

Stickler, W. Hugh, ed. *Experimental Colleges: Their Role in American Higher Education*. Tallahassee, Fla.: Florida State University, 1964.

Stinchcombe, Arthur. "Orientation to the Department of Sociology." Mimeographed address to sociology graduate students. University of California, Berkeley, October 1971.

Stockton State College. *Stockton State College: Annual Review and Planing.* Summer 1976.

———. Evaluation Team Report, insert in *Stockton Chronicle,* November 10, 1975.

Stookey, Byron. "Starting from Scratch: The University of California at Santa Cruz." *Harvard Educational Review,* Winter 1965.

Storr, Richard J. *The Beginnings of Graduate Education in America.* Chicago: University of Chicago Press, 1953.

———. *Harper's University: The Beginnings; A History of the University of Chicago.* Chicago: University of Chicago Press, 1966.

———, and Pierson, G. W. *Yale College: An Educational History, 1871–1921.* New Haven: Yale University Press, 1952.

Strout, Cushing. "A Personal Narrative of a Rude Awakening." In *Divided We Stand: Reflections on the Crisis at Cornell,* edited by Cushing Strout and David I. Grossvogel. New York: Doubleday, 1970.

"Student Admissions/Virginia State-controlled Institutions of Higher Education/Fall 1966." Richmond: State Council of Higher Education for Virginia, 1966.

Summary of Catholic Education. National Catholic Welfare Conference, annual.

Sunderland, Stephen. "Citizen Empowerment Manual." Mimeographed. College for Human Services, 1976.

———. "Evaluating the Citizen-Professional's Performance: The Constructive Action Paradigm." Mimeographed. College for Human Services, September 1976.

Suslow, Sidney. "A Report on an Interinstitutional Survey of Undergraduate Scholastic Grading, 1960's to 1970's." Office of Institutional Research, University of California, Berkeley, February 1976.

Taubman, Paul, and Wales, Terence. *Higher Education and Earnings: College as an Investment and a Screening Device.* New York: McGraw-Hill, 1974.

Tewksbury, Donald G. *The Founding of American Colleges and Universities before the Civil War: With Particular Reference to the Religious Influences Bearing upon the College Movement.* New York: Columbia University, Teachers College, 1932.

Thernstrom, Stephen A. *Poverty and Progress: Social Mobility in a 19th Century City.* Cambridge, Mass.: Harvard University Press, 1964.

Thomas, Hugh, ed. *The Establishment: A Symposium.* London: Blond, 1959.

Thomas, Russell. *The Search for Common Learning: General Education, 1800–1960.* New York: McGraw-Hill, 1962.

Thompson, Daniel C. "Problems of Faculty Morale." *Journal of Negro Education,* Winter 1960, pp. 37–46.

———. "Teachers in Negro Colleges." Ph.D. dissertation, Columbia University, 1955.

Thorne, Barrie. "Girls Who Say 'Yes' to Guys Who Say 'No': Women and the Draft Resistance Movement." Paper presented at the meetings of the American Sociological Association, New Orleans. 1972.

Tinto, Vincent. "Dropouts From Higher Education: A Theoretical Synthesis of Recent Research." *Review of Educational Research*, 45, no. 1 (Winter 1975): 89–126.

Tomasson, Richard F. "Report of the Department of Sociology, 1971–1972." Mimeographed. University of New Mexico, Albuquerque, 1973.

Tomkins, Calvin. "New Paradigms." *New Yorker*, January 5, 1976, pp. 30–56.

Touraine, Alain. *The Academic System in American Society*. New York: McGraw-Hill, 1974.

Trent, James W. *Catholics in College: Religious Commitment and the Intellectual Life*. Chicago: University of Chicago Press, 1967.

Tresemer, David. *Fear of Success*. New York: Plenum, 1977.

———. "Innovative Education in the Southwest: Notes on Visits to St. John's College, Sante Fe, and Prescott College, Arizona." Unpublished manuscript, Fall 1969.

Trilling, Lionel. "The Uncertain Future of the Humanistic Educational Ideal." *American Scholar*, 44 no. 1 (Winter 1974–75): 57.

Trombley, William. "College Plan for Negroes Passes Test—But 'Project 500' at Illinois U. Meets Obstacle." *Los Angeles Times*, December 19, 1968, Part 6, p. 4.

Trow, Martin. "Admissions and the Crisis in American Higher Education." In *Higher Education for Everybody?*, edited by W. Todd Furniss. Washington, D.C.: American Council on Education, 1970.

———. "The American Academic Department as a Context for Learning." *Studies in Higher Education*, 1 (1976): 11–22.

———. *Aspects of American Higher Education, 1969–1975*. Report for Carnegie Council for Policy Studies in Higher Education. New York: McGraw-Hill, 1976.

———. "The Campus as a Context for Learning: Notes on Education and Architecture." Address at Colloquim on Education and architecture, Sarah Lawrence College, Spring 1968.

———. "Conceptions of the University: The Case of Berkeley." *American Behavioral Scientist*, 11 (1968): 14–21.

———. "Higher Education and Moral Development." *AAUP Bulletin*, Spring 1976, p. 24.

———. "Notes on Undergraduate Teaching at Large State Universities." Unpublished paper, Berkeley, California, 1966.

———. "The Public and Private Lives of Higher Education." Paper read at the Second National Forum on New Planning and Management Practices in Post-Secondary Education, Education Commission of the States, Chicago, November 16, 1973; revised version in *Daedalus*, 104, no. 1 (Winter 1975): 113–27.

———. "Reflections on the Transition from Mass to Universal Higher Education." *Daedalus*, 99 (1970): 1–42.

————. "The Second Transformation of American Secondary Education." *International Journal of Comparative Sociology*, 2 (1961): 145–66.

————. "The Teaching Assistant." Unpublished paper, University of California, Berkeley, 1968.

————. "The Undergraduate Dilemma in Large State Universities." *Universities Quarterly*, 21 (December 1966): 17–43.

Tufts: The Total University in Changing Times. A Report to the President by the University Steering Committee. Medford, Mass.: Tufts University, 1973.

Turner, Ralph H. *The Social Context of Ambition: A Study of High School Seniors in Los Angeles.* San Francisco: Chandler, 1964.

————. "Sponsored and Contest Mobility in the School System." *American Sociological Review*, 25 (1960): 855–56.

Turner, Ralph H.; Michael, John A.; Sewell, William H.; and Armer, Michael. Exchange of views in *American Sociological Review*, 31 (October 1966): 698–712.

Tussman, Joseph. *Experiment at Berkeley.* New York: Oxford University Press, 1969.

Ulam, Adam. *The Fall of the American University.* New York: Library Press, 1972.

U.S. Department of Health, Education, and Welfare. *Reference Facts on Health, Education, and Welfare.* Washington, D.C.: U.S. Government Printing Office, 1966.

U.S. Office of Education. *Digest of Educational Statistics.* Washington, D.C.: 1972.

"U.S. Starts Arts Program in the Schools." *New York Times*, August 4, 1976, p. 35.

Uyeki, Eugene S. "The Service Teacher in Professional Education." *Human Organization*, 21 (1962): 51–55. Revised version of "Two Degrees of Marginality," a paper presented at the American Society for Engineering Education, 1960.

Van den Berghe, Pierre. *Academic Gamesmanship: How to Make a Ph.D. Pay.* London/New York/Toronto: Albelard/Schuman, 1970.

Van den Haag, Ernest. "Economics Is Not Eough—Notes on the Anticapitalist Spirit." *Public Interest*, no. 1945 (Fall 1976): 109–22.

Van Doren, Mark. *Autobiography.* Greenwood, N.Y.: 1939.

————. *Liberal Education.* New York: Holt, 1943.

————. "Talk at 21st Anniversary of the New Program." St. John's College, May 31, 1958.

Verdet, Paule. "Relationships among the Seniors." Unpublished paper, Monteith College, 1963.

Vermilye, Dyckman W., ed. *Individualizing the System: Current Issues in Higher Education.* San Francisco: Jossey-Bass, 1976.

Veysey, Laurence. *The Emergence of the American University.* Chicago: University of Chicago Press, 1965.

———. "The Humanities, 1860–1920." In *The Organization of Knowledge in American Society, 1860–1920*, edited by Alexandra M. Oleson. Forthcoming.

———. Review of *Black Mountain*, by Martin Duberman. *Harvard Educational Review*, 43, no. 2 (May 1973).

———. "Stability and Experiment in the American Undergraduate Curriculum." In *Content and Context*, edited by Carl Kaysen. New York: McGraw-Hill, 1973.

von Hoffman, Nicholas. *The Multiversity: A Personal Report on What Happens to Today's Students at American Universities*. New York: Holt, Rinehart & Winston, 1966.

Wakin, Edward. *The Catholic Campus*. New York: Macmillan, 1963.

Wallace, James C. *Chapel Hill Weekly*. Chapel Hill, N.C.: June 19, 1966.

Waller, Willard. *The Sociology of Teaching*. New York: John Wiley, 1932.

Wallerstein, Immanuel, and Starr, Paul. *The University Crisis Reader: The Liberal University under Attack*. New York: Random House, 1971.

Watson, James D. *The Double Helix*. New York: Atheneum, 1967.

Wax, Rosalie H. *Doing Fieldwork: Warnings and Advice*. Chicago: University of Chicago Press, 1971.

Wayne State University. *The Wayne State University Student*. Detroit: Wayne State University Division of Admissions and Records, Office of Divisional Studies, 1960.

Webb, Sam. "Measured Changes in College Grading Standards." *College Board Review*, 39 (1959), pp. 27–30.

Weber, Max. *From Max Weber: Essays in Sociology*. New York: Oxford University Press, 1946.

Weigel, Gustave. "American Catholic Intellectualism: A Theologian's Reflections." *Review of Politics*, 19 (July 1957).

Weinstein, Michael. "On Students Educating One Another." Ph.D. dissertation, Harvard University, 1967.

Weiss, Robert S.; Harwood, Edwin; and Riesman, David. "The World of Work." Pp. 602–37 in *Contemporary Social Problems*, edited by Robert K. Merton and Robert Nisbet. 4th ed. New York: Harcourt, Brace, Jovanovich, 1976.

West, Patricia Salter. "Social Mobility among College Graduates." In *Class, Status, and Power*, edited by Reinhard Bendix and Seymour Martin Lipset. Glencoe, Ill.: Free Press, 1953.

Wheelis, Allen. *The Quest for Identity*. New York: Norton, 1958.

"White, Negro Undergraduates at Colleges Enrolling 500 or More, as Compiled from Reports to U.S. Office for Civil Rights." *Chronicle of Higher Education*, April 22, 1968, pp. 3–4.

Whitla, Dean K., and Plinck, Dan C. "Perspectives on the Houses at Harvard and Radcliffe." Cambridge, Mass.: Office of Instructional Research and Evaluation, Harvard University, 1974.

Whitney, Rodger F. "The Berkeley Experimental College Program: A Core Curriculum Experiment and Its Impact on the Current General Education Reappraisal in Higher Education." Unpublished paper, Harvard Graduate School of Education, 1977.

Whyte, William F. "On Making the Social Sciences Relevant to Students." Unpublished paper, 1969.

————. *Street Corner Society*. Chicago: University of Chicago Press, 1943.

Wilcox, Preston. Letter to the Board of Trustees, College for Human Services, May 30, 1972.

Wilson, Alan. "Residential Segregation of Social Classes and Aspirations of High School Boys." *American Sociological Review*, 24 (December 1959): 836–45.

Wilson, James Q. "Liberalism versus Liberal Education." *Commentary*, 53 (June 1972): 50–54.

Wilson, Kenneth M. *Characteristics of Freshmen Entering CRC-Member Colleges During the Period 1964–1970: A Summary of Survey Data*. Princeton: Educational Testing Service, 1971.

————. "Increased Selectivity and Institutional Grading Standards." Research Memorandum. Poughkeepsie, N.Y.: College Research Center, 1966.

Wilson, Robert C., et al. *College Professors and Their Impact on Students*. New York: John Wiley, 1975.

Winter, David. "The Varieties and Causes of Harvard-Radcliffe Impact." Unpublished memorandum, Spring 1976.

Withey, Stephen B. *A Degree and What Else? Correlates and Consequences of a College Education*. New York: McGraw-Hill, 1971.

Wofford, Harris L., Jr. "Agent of Whom?" In *Colleges and Universities as Agents of Social Change*, edited by W. J. Minter and I. M. Thompson. Berkeley: Center for Research and Development in Higher Education, 1968.

————, ed. *Embers of the World: Conversations with Scott Buchanan*. Santa Barbara, Calif.: Center for the Study of Democratic Institutions, 1970.

Wolff, Robert Paul. *The Ideal of the University*. Boston: Beacon Press, 1969.

Wright, Erik. "A Psycho-Social Study of Student Leaves of Absence." Unpublished senior honors thesis. Committee on Social Studies, Harvard College, 1968.

Wright Institute. "The Need for Change and Three Alternatives at Santa Cruz." Report prepared for the Task Force on Undergraduate Instruction at University of California, Santa Cruz, October 14, 1974.

Wright, Stephen; Mays, Benjamin; Gloster, Hugh; and Dent, Albert. "The American Negro College, Four Responses." *Harvard Educational Review*, 37 (Summer 1967): pp. 451–64.

Yankelovich, Daniel. *The Changing Values on Campus: Political and Personal Attitudes of Today's College Students*. New York: Washington Square Press, 1972.

Young, Michael. *The Rise of the Meritocracy, 1870 to 2033*. London and New York: Thames and Hudson, 1958, 1959.

Zaretsky, Irving I., Leone, Mark P., eds. *Religious Movements in Contemporary America*. Princeton: Princeton University Press, 1974.

Zelan, Joseph. "Religious Apostasy, Higher Education, and Occupational Choice." *Sociology of Education*, 41 (1968): 370–79.

———. "Undergraduates in Sociology." In *Teachers and Students*, edited by Martin Trow, New York: McGraw-Hill, 1975.

Zuckerman, Harriet, and Merton, Robert K. "Age, Ageing and Age Structure in Science." In Matilda White Riley, et al., eds., *A Theory of Age Stratification*, vol. 3 of *Ageing and Society*. New York: Russell Sage, 1972.

Name Index

Subject Index